IMMIGRATION LAW

IMMIGRATION LAW

Kevin Browne, LLB, Solicitor

CLP

Published by

College of Law Publishing,
Braboeuf Manor, Portsmouth Road, St Catherines, Guildford GU3 1HA

British Library Cataloguing-in-Publication Data

A catalogue record for this book is available from the British Library.

ISBN 978 1 908604 36 1

Typeset by Style Photosetting Ltd, Mayfield, East Sussex

Printed in Great Britain by Ashford Colour Press Ltd, Gosport, Hampshire

Preface

This book is intended to provide an introduction to immigration law and practice. I hope that it will be of use to students studying in this area, as well as practitioners who are new to the various topics covered or who wish to update their knowledge.

After a short, practical introduction in **Chapter 1** (which includes a list of useful websites at **1.2.8**), the book deals with British nationality and the right of abode in the United Kingdom in **Chapter 2**. This is followed by a detailed analysis of immigration controls in **Chapter 3**. The unique immigration status of EEA nationals and their family members is considered in **Chapter 4**, along with how a family member of a British citizen who has engaged Treaty rights might use EU rather than domestic law to enter the UK. The next four chapters then address the key immigration categories of entry to the UK. Asylum seekers and refugees are considered in **Chapter 9**. Enforcement of immigration law, the appeals system and judicial review are dealt with in the last three chapters. In each chapter I have tried to present the information in a logical, structured order with practical examples. I would welcome comments from readers which can be sent via CLP (clponline.co.uk).

Immigration law and practice constantly change. At least one major piece of legislation is introduced each year and, as at November 2011, there had already been six statements of changes to the Immigration Rules in 2011. In this edition, I have extensively rewritten Chapters 6 (on Tier 4: Students), 7 (on Employment, Business and Investment) and 10 (on Deportation and Administrative Removal). Details of a new visitor category, the prospective entrepreneur, appear at **5.12**. Judicial review proceedings now have their own Chapter (12) with a specimen letter before claim (at **12.5**), and the judicial review pre-action protocol can be found at **Appendix 17**. I have included new worked examples in many of the chapters and there are several new Appendices, including details of spent convictions under the Rehabilitation of Offenders Act 1974 and a flow diagram on the Tier 1 Entrepreneur category.

New cases in this edition (v *Secretary of State for the Home Department* unless stated otherwise) include: *R (Syed)* (2011) (immigration rules); *R (Thamby)* (2011) (naturalisation); *AA (Nigeria)* (2010) (false statements); *R (Fu)* (2010) (specified forms procedure); *MD (Jamaica)* (2010) (long residence rule); *JS v Secretary of State for Work and Pensions* (2011) and *FMB (Uganda)* (2010) (EEA worker); *Kamau (Kenya)* (2010) (EEA self-sufficient person); *Amos* (2011) and *PM* (2011) (EEA spouse and civil partner); *C* (2010) and *Okafor* (2011) (EEA right of residence); *OB (Morocco)* (2010) (UK national and EEA rights); *VP (Italy)* (2010) (removal of EEA national); *R (Quila)* (2011) (age limits for spouse and civil partner); *French v Entry Clearance Officer Kingston* (2011) (maintenance requirement); *RT (Zimbabwe)* (2010), *TM (Zimbabwe)* (2010), *R (MN (Tanzania))* (2011), *RU (Bangladesh)* (2011), *BA (Demonstrators in Britain – risk on return) Iran CG* (2011) and *AP (Trinidad & Tobago)* (2011) (asylum and refugees); *SG (Zimbabwe)* (2011), *MJ (Angola)* (2010), *H (Tanzania)* (2011), *E-A (Article 8 – best interests of child) Nigeria* (2011), *Odawey v Entry Clearance Officer* (2011), *R (Kotecha)* (2011) and *Zambrano v Office national de l'emploi (ONEm)* (2011) (deportation and administrative removal); *R (Adebisi)* (2011), *R (Cart) v The Upper Tribunal* (2011), *PR (Sri Lanka)* (2011) and *R (MD (Gambia))* (2011) (appeals).

I would like to thank David Stott, Sue Hall and the team at CLP for all their hard work on this title.

I would also like to thank my wife, children, colleagues and past students for their help and inspiration.

This edition is dedicated to Alistair, Mary, Chris, Tom, Phil, Harry and Rene. All much missed.

Kevin Browne
The College of Law,
London

Contents

Table of Cases

O

P

R

S

T

U

V

W

Z

Table of Statutes

Page numbers in bold refer to text of legislation in the Appendices

Table of Secondary Legislation

Page numbers in bold refer to text of legislation in the Appendices

EU secondary legislation

Table of Abbreviations

AIA 1996	Asylum and Immigration Act 1996
AIAA 1993	Asylum and Immigration Appeals Act 1993
AIT	Asylum and Immigration Appeal Tribunal
AI(TC)A 2004	Asylum and Immigration (Treatment of Claimants, etc) Act 2004
BACIFHE	British Accreditation Council for Independent Further and Higher Education
BNA 1981	British Nationality Act 1981
BOCs	British overseas citizens
BOTCs	British overseas territories citizens
CEE	Central and Eastern European
CLS	Community Legal Service
CPR 1998	Civil Procedure Rules 1998
CUKC	citizen of the UK and colonies
DfES	Department for Education and Skills
DfWP	Department for Work and Pensions
ECHR	European Convention on Human Rights
ECtHR	European Court of Human Rights
ECJ	European Court of Justice
EEA	European Economic Area
EU	European Union
GP	general medical practitioner
HMRC	HM Revenue and Customs
HND	Higher National Diploma
HRA 1998	Human Rights Act 1998
IA 1971	Immigration Act 1971
IA 1988	Immigration Act 1988
IAA 1999	Immigration and Asylum Act 1999
IAC	Immigration and Asylum Chamber
IANA 2006	Immigration, Asylum and Nationality Act 2006
I(EEA) Regs 2006	Immigration (European Economic Area) Regulations 2006
ILPA	Immigration Law Practitioners Association
LAG	Legal Action Group
LSC	Legal Services Commission
NHS	National Health Service
NIAA 2002	Nationality, Immigration and Asylum Act 2002
NICs	National Insurance contributions
NINo	National Insurance number
NVQ	National Vocational Qualification
PAQ	Political Asylum Questionnaire
SAL	Standard Acknowledgement Letter
SIAC	Special Immigration Appeals Commission
SSAA 1992	Social Security Administration Act 1992
SSCBA 1992	Social Security Contributions and Benefits Act 1992
SS(I&A)CA Regs 2000	Social Security (Immigration and Asylum) Consequential Amendments Regulations 2000
UKBA	UK Borders Agency
UNHCR	United Nations High Commissioner for Refugees

Chapter 1
Introduction

1.1 Public law and practical problems

This book aims to provide an introduction to immigration and nationality law and practice.

This is a public law subject, dealing with relations between the State and the individual, concerned fundamentally with the exercise of discretion by officials. It is easy to understand the practical problems which arise in this area of the law, as it concerns the individual's ability to live, work and enjoy family life in the country of his or her choice. In practice, it involves a great deal of client contact, argument with officials, advocacy in tribunals and familiarity with a wide range of legal sources. It therefore calls upon the full range of legal skills.

1.2 Sources of immigration law and general principles

1.2.1 Legislation

The main piece of legislation dealing with immigration law is the Immigration Act 1971 (IA 1971). This replaced existing immigration controls and introduced the concept of the right of abode in the United Kingdom (UK). The starting point for any immigration practitioner is the following general principles set out in s 1:

> (1) All those who are in this Act expressed to have the right of abode in the United Kingdom shall be free to live in, and to come and go into and from, the United Kingdom without let or hindrance except such as may be required under and in accordance with this Act to enable their right to be established or as may be otherwise lawfully imposed on any person.
>
> (2) Those not having that right may live, work and settle in the United Kingdom by permission and subject to such regulation and control of their entry into, stay in and departure from the United Kingdom as is imposed by this Act …

As to s 1(1) and the right of abode in the UK, see **1.4.1**.

Section 1(2) establishes what are known as immigration controls: see **1.4.2**.

The IA 1971 has been amended by numerous subsequent Acts, almost on an annual basis.

British nationality law is dealt with mainly in the British Nationality Act 1981 (as amended). This Act came into force on 1 January 1983 and Pt 1 sets out the provisions which determine whether or not a person is a British citizen. The date is significant, as different tests apply to determine British citizenship depending on whether or not the individual was born before 1983 (ie up to and including 31 December 1982) or after 1982 (ie from and including 1 January 1983). Note that British citizenship is also affected by whether or not the person was born in the UK. Full details are to be found in **Chapter 2**.

A British citizen has the right of abode in the UK. Therefore a British citizen is not subject to immigration controls. So a preliminary question for an immigration practitioner to answer when seeing a new client is whether or not the client is a British citizen.

1.2.2 The Immigration Rules

Whilst the IA 1971 (as amended) is the framework of immigration law, it does not contain any detail. This is because ss 1(4) and 3(2) permit rules to be laid down and amended by the Secretary of State as to the practice to be followed in the administration of the Act for regulating the entry into and stay in the UK of persons not having the right of abode. These are the Immigration Rules. A copy can be found in **Appendix 1**. Quickly skim through the contents to get some idea of their wide coverage.

The Immigration Rules structure the discretion given by the IA 1971 to grant leave to enter, to vary leave, or to make a deportation order. They bind immigration officers, but not the Home Secretary who, in the exercise of his discretion, may, in appropriate circumstances, depart from the Rules he has laid down, for instance granting leave to remain in the UK when the Rules would require refusal. They are, therefore, not rules of law in the strict sense (*R v Secretary of State for the Home Department, ex p Hosenball* [1977] 3 All ER 452; *Odelolar v Secretary of State for the Home Department* [2008] EWCA Civ 308). But as the Rules are laid before and approved by Parliament, published Government policy guidance cannot add requirements that are not in the Rules themselves: see *Secretary of State for the Home Department v Pankina* [2010] EWCA Civ 719.

Nevertheless, a lawyer can base his advice on the Rules because they are normally followed by the immigration authorities, and because failure to apply them may give grounds for appeal or judicial review (see **Chapters 11** and **12**).

The current Rules are cited as the Statement of Changes in Immigration Rules 1994 (HC 395). As the Rules are not delegated legislation, they are cited as a House of Commons Paper and not as a statutory instrument. Later amendments to the Rules are cited similarly.

1.2.3 Home Office practices

Since the Home Office has considerable discretion not governed by the Rules, it is inevitable that informal practices evolve in order to ensure that comparable cases are treated in like ways. An example is the concession for visitors who wish to enter or remain to care for a sick relative (see **5.12**). These practices are not generally binding, although under the administrative law doctrine of legitimate expectation, a decision which disregards them may be quashed as unreasonable (*R v Secretary of State for the Home Department, ex p Asif Mahmood Khan* [1984] 1 WLR 1337).

The Home Office has made public some of the internal instructions to staff on the handling of immigration cases. These are available via the Internet (see **1.2.8**).

1.2.4 Case law

Immigration cases have in recent years formed the largest single category of applications to the High Court for judicial review. In addition, cases may reach the higher courts by way of appeal. These cases may be reported in the standard series of law reports, but may also be found in the specialist *Immigration and Nationality Law Reports* (INLR), published six times a year by Jordans, and the *Immigration Appeal Reports* (Imm LR), published quarterly by The Stationery Office.

1.2.5 EU law

Nationals of EU and EEA Member States (see the list in **Appendix 2**) have special rights under EU law (eg under Article 45 TFEU (freedom of movement of workers)). These rights are set out in detail in EU Regulations and Directives. The rights often have direct effect and so override conflicting provisions of UK immigration law. The UK Government will try to ensure that legislation and the Immigration Rules give effect to EU law, but be aware that UK provisions may be open to challenge.

In addition, there is a considerable body of case law of the European Court of Justice (ECJ) on the meaning and effect of Treaty provisions and legislation. This is binding on UK courts. Directives, Regulations, EU judgments etc can be found on the European Union on-line website at www.europa.eu.

Probably the most significant Directive is Directive 2004/38/EC of the European Parliament and Council. A copy appears at **Appendix 3**. This sets out the terms and limits of the right of free movement. It has been implemented into domestic law by the Immigration (European Economic Area) Regulations 2006 (I(EEA) Regs 2006) (see **Chapter 4** and **Appendix 4**).

It is important to note that a family member of a British citizen may sometimes be able to use EU law rather than domestic UK immigration law to enter the UK. The most common example is where a British citizen goes to work in another EEA country, thereby exercising and engaging EU Treaty rights. The British citizen marries or enters into a civil partnership with a non-EEA national. The couple then wants to travel to the UK to live together. The British citizen has a right of abode in the UK and so is not subject to immigration controls (see **1.2.1** and **Chapter 2**). His or her spouse or civil partner may be able to seek entry to the UK under EU law rather than domestic law (see **4.4.12** and **8.3** respectively).

1.2.6 The European Convention on Human Rights and the Human Rights Act 1998

The Human Rights Act 1998 (HRA 1998) interprets, rather than incorporates, the European Convention on Human Rights (ECHR). Although the legislation requires UK courts to apply Acts of Parliament even if they are incompatible with the Convention, it contains a number of measures which will enable practitioners to rely on the Convention in immigration cases. In outline these are as follows.

Section 3 requires UK courts to try to interpret an Act of Parliament in a way which is compatible with listed Convention rights, whether or not the Act is ambiguous.

Section 4 enables the courts to make a declaration that an Act is incompatible with Convention rights. The court must still apply the Act in the case before it, but s 10 enables the Government to introduce fast-track delegated legislation to alter the law.

Section 6 is probably the most far-reaching provision. It states that it is unlawful for public authorities (such as the Home Office) to act in a way which infringes Convention rights, unless required to do so by Act of Parliament. So, when exercising a discretion, the Home Secretary must take Convention rights into account and, if statute permits it, he must avoid decisions which infringe them. As the Immigration Rules themselves are made in the exercise of a discretion, both the Rules and decisions made under them are open to challenge if they infringe Convention rights. So, in applying the Rules and exercising his powers, the Secretary of State must respect Convention rights, whether or not the Rules explicitly refer to them: see *R (Syed) v Secretary of State for the Home Department* [2011] EWCA Civ 1059.

So immigration lawyers need a good working knowledge of human rights. The main Convention rights that might be relevant are set out in **Appendix 5**. Detailed references to human rights cases and principles can be found in the **Chapters 9, 10** and **11**.

1.2.7 Practitioner texts

The practitioner in immigration law relies heavily on a limited number of secondary sources. These include:

(a) *Macdonald's Immigration Law and Practice* (Butterworths): the leading practitioner text;

(b) *Butterworths Immigration Law Service*: in the form of a loose-leaf encyclopaedia, particularly useful as a source for Home Office practices;

(c) *Tolley's Immigration and Nationality Law and Practice*: a quarterly journal;

(d) *Immigration, Nationality and Refugee Law Handbook* (Joint Council for the Welfare of Immigrants): an invaluable practical guide (*JCWI Handbook*);

(e) Fransman, *British Nationality Law* (Butterworths);

(f) Webb and Grant, *Immigration and Asylum Emergency Procedures* (Legal Action Group).

1.2.8 Websites

There are many useful websites, most of which have links to other, related sites. You might start with the following:

Home Office, UK Border Agency: www.ukba.homeoffice.gov.uk
International Group: www.ukvisas.gov.uk
European Union on-line: www.europa.eu
Immigration and Asylum (Chamber) Tribunal: www.justice.gov.uk
European Court of Human Rights: www.echr.coe.int
Ministry of Justice: www.justice.gov.uk
The Supreme Court: www.supremecourt.gov.uk
Joint Council for the Welfare of Immigrants: www.jcwi.org.uk
Refugee Council: www.refugeecouncil.org.uk
UNHCR UN Refugee Agency: www.unhcr.org
Electronic Immigration Network: www.ein.org.uk

1.3 Institutions

1.3.1 The Home Office

Under the IA 1971, the Home Secretary has overall responsibility for the administration of immigration control. The Act designates him as the person who makes the Immigration Rules, appoints immigration officers, and takes specific decisions such as the decision to deport. The law generally recognises that, in practice, he acts through his civil servants (*Carltona Ltd v Commissioner of Works* [1943] 2 All ER 560). However, there is a division of functions under s 4 of the IA 1971. The immigration service is specifically made responsible for granting leave to enter the UK, whilst the Home Office in general deals with the subsequent variation of leave.

1.3.2 The immigration service

The immigration service consists of immigration officers, chief immigration officers and inspectors appointed by the Home Secretary. As explained in **1.3.1**, they are responsible for control on entry to the UK. They operate from the various ports of entry (including airports). Division of functions between the immigration service and the Home Office in general is not always clear-cut, as the Home Secretary may validly delegate some functions (eg the decision to deport overstayers) to the immigration service (*Oladehinde v Secretary of State for the Home Department; Alexander v Secretary of State for the Home Department* [1990] 3 WLR 797).

1.3.3 The UK Border Agency

The UK Border Agency (UKBA) is a shadow agency of the Home Office. It is responsible for managing border controls, as well as enforcing immigration and customs regulations. It considers applications for permission to enter or stay in the UK, citizenship and asylum.

1.3.4 The Identity and Passport Service

This is an executive agency of the Home Office. It issues UK passports.

1.3.5 International Group

The International Group is part of the UKBA. It operates visa offices, manned by entry clearance officers, in 250 locations throughout the world. The largest handles 300,000 applications a year; the smallest fewer than 10.

1.3.6 The First-tier Tribunal (Immigration and Asylum Chamber)

Many, but not all, of the decisions made by an official in an immigration context are appealable to the First-tier Tribunal (Immigration and Asylum Chamber). Any further appeal on a point of law is to the Upper Tribunal and the Court of Appeal. See further **Chapter 11**.

1.4 Immigration controls

1.4.1 Right of abode in the UK

As we have seen, a British citizen has a right of abode in the UK. So, if a British citizen leaves the UK, he is free to return at any point in time and enter the UK via an airport or a port. Subject to producing evidence of that right of abode, usually by way of a British passport, he is not subject to immigration controls. This applies equally to a British citizen born abroad who travels to the UK for the first time.

Note that certain Commonwealth citizens also have a right of abode in the UK (see **2.3**). Also, EEA nationals are not subject to domestic UK immigration laws when entering the UK under EU law (see **Chapter 4**).

1.4.2 Entry clearance, leave to enter and leave to remain in the UK

Immigration controls are dealt with in detail in **Chapter 3**. However, it is important to grasp the following points at this stage. As a general rule, immigration controls may exist at three particular points in time, namely:

(a) before a person travels to the UK. This is known as entry clearance and most persons, apart from some people who wish to enter for less than six months, must obtain it;

(b) on arrival in the UK at the port of entry. This is known as leave to enter the UK. All people who are subject to immigration controls must obtain permission to enter the UK when first arriving;

(c) after arrival, if an extension of the initial limited time granted for the stay is required.

1.4.3 Visa nationals

A 'visa national' is a person who always needs entry clearance in advance of travelling to the UK for whatever purpose. The entry clearance document he needs to obtain from the British High Commission or embassy in his own country before travelling is a visa, and this will state the purpose of the entry to the UK, for example as a visitor or student, etc. Most visas appear as a stamp in the person's passport. A list of countries whose nationals must obtain visas appears in Appendix 1 to the Immigration Rules (see **Appendix 1** to this book).

Upon arriving at a UK port of entry, a visa national usually requires leave to enter the UK, that is, he must convince the immigration officer that entry is pursuant to the terms of his visa. If leave is given, a stamp to that effect is put in his passport.

Example

Kim is Chinese. He is a visa national. He wishes to come to the UK for a holiday. If he is to be given leave to enter the UK, he must, as a general rule:

(a) obtain a visa in China before travelling; and

(b) on arrival in the UK, convince the immigration officer that he is entering as a genuine visitor.

1.4.4 Non-visa nationals

A non-visa national is a person who is not on the visa list. He does not require entry clearance in advance of travelling to the UK for short-term purposes, ie a stay of up to six months in the UK, such as a visitor (see **Chapter 5**). However, he will require it for long-term purposes (ie a stay of more than six months), for example as an employee or a businessman, or if he wishes to stay permanently in the UK. The entry clearance document he needs to obtain from the British High Commission or embassy in his own country before travelling is an entry certificate. This will state the purpose of the entry to the UK, for example 'settlement as spouse', and usually appears as a stamp in the person's passport.

Upon arriving at a UK port of entry, a non-visa national will require leave to enter the UK, ie he must convince the immigration officer that entry is pursuant to the Immigration Rules.

Example

Bob is an American. He is a non-visa national. He wishes to come to the UK for a holiday (ie for up to six months). He does not have to obtain an entry certificate in America before travelling but, on arrival, he must convince the immigration officer that he is entering as a genuine visitor, if he is to be given leave to enter. But if Bob wanted to enter and stay for more than six months, he would need to obtain an entry certificate before travelling to the UK.

1.4.5 Settled status

A person with 'settled status' (also known as unconditional leave, permanent stay, permanent residence, indefinite leave and settlement) does not have the right of abode in the UK and so, in theory, can be deported (see **Chapter 10**). This is a person who is legally in the UK without any conditions or restrictions being placed on his residence. Hence, it is not limited in time. If a person with settled status leaves the UK, he will be subject to immigration control on return, ie he will need leave to enter the UK on the basis that he is returning to reside again (see **3.8.3**).

1.4.6 Summary: who does what?

- Entry clearance officer – visas and entry certificates;
- Immigration officer – leave to enter the UK;
- Home Office – extension of stay in UK, including switching of category.

Chapter 2
British Nationality and Right of Abode

2.1 Introduction

The law relating to nationality or citizenship forms the background to immigration law because a person's right to live in the country of his choice often depends on his nationality. This is true in UK law, in that a British citizen has a right to live in the UK.

There are two categories of people who have a statutory 'right of abode in the UK': all British citizens (see **2.2**) and certain Commonwealth citizens (see **2.3**). A person with the right of abode can freely enter the UK (ie he is not subject to immigration controls (see **1.4** and **Chapter 3**)). Moreover, he cannot be excluded from the UK (ie he cannot be removed or deported (see **Chapter 11**)). Nationals of the EEA do not have the right of abode, although they have a right of entry to and residence in the UK under EU law (see **Chapter 4**).

2.2 British citizenship

British nationality law has changed considerably over the last century. For an historical analysis, see **2.4**. The British Nationality Act 1981 (BNA 1981) was implemented on 1 January 1983, thereby creating the nationality of British citizenship. The starting points for determining whether a person is a British citizen or not is to ask two questions:

(a) was he born before 1983 or after 1982; and

(b) was he born in the UK or elsewhere?

There is a summary of the key requirements at **Appendix 6**.

2.2.1 People born in the UK before 1983

A person is a British citizen if, before 1983, he was born in the UK.

2.2.2 People born outside the UK before 1983

A person is a British citizen if, before 1983, he was born outside the UK and:

(a) his father was born in the UK; or

(b) his father was registered or naturalised (see **2.2.6.1** and **2.2.7**) as a British citizen in the UK before the child's birth (if a father becomes British after the child's birth, this does not retrospectively make the child British); and

(c) his parents were married, or subsequently marry in a country where that marriage operates to legitimise the child.

So, before 1983, a father could pass on his British citizenship acquired in the UK only to his legitimate child. An illegitimate child could not 'inherit' British citizenship through his father.

Examples

1. Joshua was born in 1962 in the UK. He is therefore a British citizen (see **2.2.1**). In 1980 he married Grace (who is not a British citizen). In 1981 their daughter, Sophie, was born outside the UK. Sophie is a British citizen as her father was born in the UK and married to her mother at the time of Sophie's birth.
2. Harry was born in 1961 in the UK. He is therefore a British citizen (see **2.2.1**). In 1979 he started a relationship with Lynda (who is not a British citizen). In 1981 their son, Michael, was born outside the UK. In 1982 Harry and Lynda married in a country where their marriage operated to legitimise Michael who thereby became a British citizen.
3. James was born in 1960 in the UK. He is therefore a British citizen (see **2.2.1**). In 1978 he started a relationship with Lilly (who is not a British citizen). In 1981 their daughter, Katie, was born outside the UK. James and Lilly never marry. Katie is not a British citizen on these facts.

Before 1983, a mother could not pass on her British citizenship acquired by her birth, registration or naturalisation in the UK to any child born outside the UK. However, in those circumstances, the Home Office allowed for the child to be registered as British, and this is now possible pursuant to BNA 1981, s 4C (see **2.2.6**).

Example

Ruby was born in 1959 in the UK. She is therefore a British citizen (see **2.2.1**). In 1980 she married Gary (who is not a British citizen). In 1982 their son, Simon, was born outside the UK. Although Ruby is a British citizen at the time of her son's birth, she cannot pass that citizenship on to him. However, she could have applied to register him as a British citizen whilst he was a child, or he may do so as an adult: see **2.2.6**.

2.2.3 People born in the UK after 1982

A person is a British citizen if, after 1982, he was born in the UK and at the time of his birth either of his parents was:

(a) a British citizen; or

(b) settled in the UK. (As to settled status, see **1.4.5** and **3.8**. Note that for these purposes a Commonwealth citizen with the right of abode (see **2.3**) is treated as 'settled'.)

Note that until the Nationality, Immigration and Asylum Act 2002 (NIAA 2002) came into force on 1 July 2006, a 'parent' in this context did not include a father of a child who was not married to the child's mother. However, the BNA 1981, as amended by the NIAA 2002, provides at s 50(9A) that from 1 July 2006 a child's father is:

(a) the husband, at the time of the child's birth, of the woman who gives birth to the child (and remember that if the parents subsequently marry that may operate to legitimise the child);

(b) where a person is treated as the father of the child under s 28 of the Human Fertilisation and Embryology Act 1990, that person; or

(c) where neither paragraph (a) nor (b) applies, any person who is proven to be the father by the production of either a birth certificate identifying him as such that is issued by the competent registration authority within 12 months of the birth of the child to which it relates, or such other evidence (eg a DNA test report or court order) as may satisfy the Secretary of State on this point.

This means that subject to satisfying (c) above, an illegitimate person born in the UK on or after 1 July 2006 is a British citizen if his father was either a British citizen or settled at that time. What if an illegitimate person can meet these requirements but he was born in the UK before July 2006? In these circumstances the person may apply to register as a British citizen which the Home Office may grant at its discretion. Note that in addition to the usual requirements, if the applicant is a child the consent of all parties with parental responsibility must be given.

Examples

1. Evie was born in 1965 in the UK. She is therefore a British citizen (see **2.2.1**). In 1990 she gave birth to her daughter, Charlotte, in the UK. Charlotte is a British citizen as her mother was a British citizen at the time of Charlotte's birth.
2. Chloe was born outside the UK in 1967 as a visa national. In 1970 she entered the UK with her family for the purposes of settlement. She had indefinite leave to remain in the UK when she gave birth to her son, Lewis, in 1987 in the UK. Lewis is a British citizen as his mother was settled in the UK at the time of his birth.
3. John was born in 1970 in the UK. He is therefore a British citizen (see **2.2.1**). In 1995 he married Helen (who is not a British citizen). In 1997 their daughter, Sally, was born in the UK. Sally is a British citizen as her father was a British citizen and married to her mother at the time of Sally's birth.
4. Oliver was born outside the UK in 1980 as a visa national. In 1992 he entered the UK with his family for the purposes of settlement. He had indefinite leave to remain in the UK when his girlfriend, Jessica, gave birth to his son, Alfie, in 2008 in the UK. Jessica had limited leave to remain in the UK at that point in time. Alfie is a British citizen if Oliver and Jessica subsequently marry in a country where their marriage operates to legitimise him; or if Oliver is named as his father on his birth certificate that was issued within one year his birth; or if the Secretary of State accepts other evidence that Oliver is his father.
5. What if, in Example 4, Alfie had been born before 1 July 2006? In those circumstances Alfie could be registered as a British citizen at the discretion of the Secretary of State. See further **2.2.6**.

2.2.4 People born outside the UK after 1982

A person is a British citizen if, after 1982, he is born outside the UK, and:

(a) his father or mother was a British citizen otherwise than by descent by birth in the UK (see **2.2.5**) ; or

(b) his father or mother was registered or naturalised (see **2.2.6.1** and **2.2.7**) as a British citizen in the UK before the child's birth (if either parent becomes British after the child's birth, this does not retrospectively make the child British).

As noted at **2.2.3**, until the NIAA 2002 came into force on 1 July 2006, a 'parent' in this context did not include a father of a child who was not married to the child's mother.

This means that subject to satisfying condition (c) of s 50(9A) of the BNA 1981 (**2.2.3**), an illegitimate person born outside the UK on or after 1 July 2006 is a British citizen if his father was a British citizen otherwise than by descent (see **2.2.5**), or registered or naturalised as a British citizen before the child's birth.

Examples

1. Amelia was born in 1970 in the UK. She is therefore a British citizen otherwise than by descent (see **2.2.5.1**). In 1990 she gave birth to her son, Charles, outside the UK. Charles is a British citizen (by descent: see **2.2.5.2**) as his mother was a British citizen otherwise than by descent at the time of Charles' birth.

2. Benjamin was born in 1972 in the UK. He is therefore a British citizen otherwise than by descent (see **2.2.5.1**). In 1997 he married Adela, a visa national. In 1999 their daughter, Ramona, was born outside the UK. Ramona is a British citizen (by descent: **2.2.5.2**) as her father was a British citizen otherwise than by descent and married to her mother at the time of Ramona's birth.

3. Ethan was born in the UK in 1980. He is therefore a British citizen otherwise than by descent (see **2.2.5.1**). In 2007 his girlfriend, Alice, gave birth to his son, Zach, outside the UK. Alice is a visa national. Zach is a British citizen by descent (see **2.2.5**.2) if Ethan and Alice subsequently marry in a country where their marriage operates to legitimise him; or if Ethan is named as his father on his birth certificate that was issued within one year his birth; or if the Secretary of State accepts other evidence that Ethan is his father.

2.2.5 British citizenship: what about subsequent generations?

2.2.5.1 British citizen otherwise than by descent

A person who acquires British citizenship by birth in the UK (see **2.2.1** and **2.2.3**), or by registration or naturalisation in the UK (see **2.2.6.1** and **2.2.7**) is classified as a *British citizen otherwise than by descent.* This means he can automatically pass on British citizenship to a child born outside the UK in the circumstances described at **2.2.2** and **2.2.4** above.

2.2.5.2 British citizen by descent

Where a person is born outside the UK (see **2.2.2** and **2.2.4**) and acquires British citizenship only because one or both of his parents is a British citizen, he is classified as a *British citizen by descent.* This means that he cannot automatically pass on British citizenship to any child who is also born abroad. However, some second-generation children can be registered abroad at the British consulate as British citizens (by descent) if:

(a) one of the parents is a British citizen by descent; and

(b) the British parent has a parent who is or was British otherwise than by descent; and

(c) the British parent had at some time before the child's birth lived in the UK for a continuous period of three years, not being absent for more than 270 days in that period.

What if (a) and (b) are met but not (c)? It will be possible to register the child in the UK as a British citizen if during his childhood his father and mother come and live in the UK with him for a continuous period of three years and are not absent during that time for more than 270 days. Note that the requirement is that both parents live in the UK unless one of them is dead or the couple have divorced. Further note that such a child is treated as a British citizen otherwise than by descent.

Example

James was born in Germany in 1970. His father, Larry, was born in London, England in 1940. Larry had married James's mother in 1965. In 1990, James married Steffi, a German national. In 1999, their son, Thomas was born in Germany.

Larry was born before 1983 in the UK and is therefore a British citizen otherwise than by descent. His son, James, was born outside the UK before 1983 and is therefore British by descent. Thomas can only be registered as a British citizen if James has lived in the UK at some time for a continuous period of three years before Thomas's birth.

What if James has not lived in the UK for the requisite period before Thomas's birth? If James, Steffi and Thomas all come to live in the UK whilst Thomas is still a child and do so for a continuous period of three years, Thomas will have a right to register as a British citizen and will, in fact, be treated as a British citizen otherwise than by descent.

Can a British citizen by descent apply for naturalisation as a British citizen (see **2.2.7**) in order that his children born abroad automatically become British citizens? No, held the Court of Appeal in the case of *R v Secretary of State for the Home Department, ex p Azad Ullah* [2001] INLR 74.

2.2.6 Registration as a British citizen

2.2.6.1 Child born in the UK after 1982

A child can apply to register as a British citizen, pursuant to s 1(3) and (4) of the BNA 1981, if he was born in the UK after 1982 and, after his birth:

(a) one of his parents becomes settled in the UK (see **3.8**); or

(b) he remains in the UK for the first 10 years of his life and is not absent for more than 90 days each year during that period. By s 1(7), a longer period of absence may be acceptable.

In addition the applicant will have to satisfy the Secretary of State that he is of good character.

Such a person is a British citizen otherwise than by descent (see **2.2.5**).

2.2.6.2 Child born outside the UK before 1983

As we saw at **2.2.2**, a British mother could not before 1983 transmit her British citizenship acquired in the UK to her child born outside the UK. However, by concession, the Home Office did allow such a child to be registered as British provided the application was made before the child reached 18. What if no such registration occurred, given that the concession, by its very nature, expired at the end of 2000? Section 4C of the BNA 1981 now gives a right to such a person born before 1 January 1983 to apply to register as a British citizen. Such a person is a British citizen by descent (see **2.2.5**). An applicant under s 4C has to satisfy the Secretary of State that he is of good character before being registered.

2.2.7 Naturalisation

If a foreign national living in the UK has settled status (see **1.4.5** and **3.8**), he may wish to apply to become a British citizen by a process known as naturalisation. Under s 6 of the BNA 1981, the Home Secretary has a discretion to grant a certificate of naturalisation to any person who is not a British citizen. The grant of British citizenship under s 6 is not a fundamental human right: *R v Secretary of State for the Home Department, ex p Al Fayed* [2001] Imm AR 134 and *R (AHK) v Secretary of State for the Home Department* [2009] EWCA Civ 287. As Blake J stated at first instance in *AHK* (in a judgment entitled *MH v Secretary of State for the Home Department* [2008] EWHC 2525, at [41]): 'In general terms ... no claimant [under s 6] has a right to British citizenship, but only a right to have an application fairly considered under the statutory scheme.'

The requirements are slightly different, depending on whether or not the applicant is married to or in a civil partnership with a British citizen at the time the application is made. Broadly, those requirements are as follows.

2.2.7.1 If the applicant is married to, or in a civil partnership with, a British citizen

The applicant:

(a) must be settled (see **3.8**) at the time of the application;

(b) must have been living in the UK legally for three years continuously;

(c) must have been physically present in the UK on the date three years before the application. The start of the qualifying period of three years is the day after the corresponding application date. So, for example, if the application date is 5 January 2012, the three-year qualifying period starts on 6 January 2009;

(d) must not have been absent for more than 270 days in total, and not more than 90 days in the year immediately before the application. The Home Office has indicated that it will normally disregard 30 days over this limit provided all the other requirements are met. If the absences are greater than that, see the Home Office guidance, 'Naturalisation Booklet – The Requirements' on the UKBA website (see **1.2.8**);

(e) must have sufficient knowledge of the English language and sufficient knowledge about life in the UK. How can an applicant demonstrate this? The answer is to be found in the British Nationality (General) Regulations 2003 (SI 2003/548, as amended), reg 5A. Broadly, the requirements are that the applicant either:

   (i) passes a formal test known as the 'Life in the UK Test'; or

   (ii) has already satisfied the Secretary of State that he has sufficient knowledge of language and life in the UK when granted indefinite leave to remain (see **3.8.7**); or

   (iii) attends a course at an accredited college where the course materials include 'Citizenship Materials for English for Speakers of Other Languages (ESOL) Learners', can demonstrate relevant progress on that course and is awarded an ESOL qualification in speaking and listening. In order to demonstrate relevant progress on the course, the applicant's ability is assessed before the course starts and he must achieve at least one grade higher by the end of the course, eg if the applicant is assessed as being below Entry 1, he must attain his qualification at Entry 1, 2 or 3.

What is the 'Life in the UK Test'? The test has to be taken on a computer and consists of 24 questions, such as: where is the Prime Minister's official home in London, and is it true or false that UK citizens can vote in an election at the age of 18? It is based on the Government handbook, 'Life in the United Kingdom: A Journey to Citizenship'. It can only be taken at an official testing centre. Note that in Wales and Scotland the test can be taken in Welsh or Scottish Gaelic, as appropriate. Full details are on the website, www.lifeintheuktest.gov.uk.

If an applicant already has sufficient knowledge of English (Welsh or Scottish Gaelic) then, as we have seen, passing the Life in the UK Test will satisfy both requirements. If an applicant is unsure of his language ability, he can obtain an initial assessment from any further education college or learndirect centre (www.learndirect.co.uk).

In what circumstances will the Home Office waive these requirements? If the applicant is aged over 65; suffers from a long-term illness or disability which severely restricts his ability to attend ESOL classes or to prepare for the test; is deaf, mute or suffers from any speech impediment which limits his ability to converse in the relevant language; or suffers from a mental impairment and is thereby unable to speak or learn the relevant language. UKBA guidance is that if an applicant claims to have a physical disability or a mental impairment, he must provide original and current medical evidence from a medical practitioner. This must state the condition and explain why it is unreasonable to expect the applicant to take the Life in the UK test or attend an ESOL course; and

(f) must show good character. This requirement is not defined in the BNA 1981. In *R (Thamby) v Secretary of State for the Home Department* [2011] EWHC 1763 Parker J stated, at [41]:

> It is a term capable of carrying a range of meanings, and requires an exercise in evaluation to apply it. It is established that this means that the proper approach of the courts to considering the standard of good character adopted by the Secretary of State and the application of the concept in a particular case is to ask whether the standard and its application were such as could reasonably be adopted in the circumstances: *ex p Al Fayed* [2001] Imm AR 134, [41] (Nourse LJ), [93] (Kennedy LJ) and [97] (Rix LJ). It is open to the Secretary of State, so long as she acts rationally, to adopt a high standard of good character, and one higher than other reasonable decision-makers might have adopted: *ex p Al Fayed* at [41] (Nourse LJ).

The application form requires all previous convictions, save those that are spent, to be revealed. UKBA policy is that the Secretary of State will normally accept that an applicant is of good character where enquiries of other government departments and agencies are clear; there are no unspent convictions (see **Appendix 8**); there is no information on file to cast serious doubts on the applicant's character; and there is written confirmation from HM Revenue and Customs that the applicant's business affairs are in order.

2.2.7.2 If the applicant is neither married to, nor in a civil partnership with, a British citizen

The applicant:

(a) must have been settled (see **3.8**) for at least one year before the application;

(b) must have been living in the UK legally for five years continuously;

(c) must have been physically present in the UK on the date five years before the application;

(d) must not have been absent for more than 450 days in total, and not more than 90 days in the year immediately before the application (see **2.2.7.1(d)** for Home Office policy where this is exceeded);

(e) must have sufficient knowledge of the English language and sufficient knowledge about life in the UK (see **2.2.7.1(e)**);

(f) must show good character (see **2.2.7.1(f)**); and

(g) must show an intention to live in the UK. Government policy is that this requirement is usually met if the applicant's stated intention is to have his home or, if more than one, his principal home in the UK. Factors affecting this will include whether a home here (owned or rented) has already been established and the reason for any past or intended absences.

2.2.7.3 EEA nationals

Certain EEA nationals are treated as settled for the purposes of naturalisation. See **3.8.9**.

2.2.8 Formalities for registration and naturalisation

These are governed by the BNA 1981 and the British Nationality (General) Regulations 2003 (SI 2003/548). In particular, applicants of full age are required to make an oath of allegiance and pledge. The latter states that the person will respect the rights and freedoms of the UK and will uphold its democratic values, observe its laws, and fulfil the duties and obligations of citizenship.

2.2.9 Deprivation of citizenship obtained by registration or naturalisation

This is governed by s 40 of the BNA 1981 and the British Nationality (General) Regulations 2003 (SI 2003/548). The Secretary of State may by order deprive a person of his British citizenship status if he is satisfied that it would be conducive to the public good. The UKBA guidance is that this can be done in cases involving national security, terrorism, serious organised crime, war crimes and unacceptable behaviour such as preaching *jihad*.

The Secretary of State may also by order deprive a person of his British citizenship status where it was obtained by registration or naturalisation, if he is satisfied that such was obtained by means of fraud, false representation or concealment of a material fact.

The Secretary of State may not make either of the above orders if it would make a person stateless: see *Al-Jedda v Secretary of State for the Home Department* [2010] EWCA Civ 212. The Court held that the burden is on the appellant to show on the balance of probabilities that he will become stateless.

Before making a deprivation order the Secretary of State must give the person concerned written notice specifying that a decision has been made to make the order and the reasons for it. The notice must also advise the person of his right to appeal (see **Chapter 11**).

2.3 Commonwealth citizens with right of abode

There are two categories of Commonwealth citizens who have the right of abode in the UK, ie the right to enter the UK without being subject to immigration controls (see **1.4** and **Chapter 3**). There is a list of Commonwealth countries in **Appendix 9**.

2.3.1 Parental link

The first category concerns those Commonwealth citizens with a 'parental link' to the UK. The requirements are that:

(a) the person was a Commonwealth citizen on 31 December 1982, and continues to be such; and

(b) either parent was born in the UK. 'Parent' in this context includes the mother, but not the father, of an illegitimate child.

Example

Bill was born in New Zealand in 1979. His mother, Ada, was born in London, England. His father was a citizen of New Zealand. Assuming that Bill is a citizen of New Zealand under that country's nationality laws and so remained, Bill was a Commonwealth citizen on 31 December 1982. Bill cannot be a British citizen by descent as his father was not British and, before 1983, mothers could not pass on their citizenship (see **2.2.2**). However, as a Commonwealth citizen, he has the right of abode in the UK by virtue of his mother's birth in the UK. Query if Ada registered him as British in these circumstances before he reached 18 or, if she failed to do so, whether he can now apply (see **2.2.6.2**).

2.3.2 Acquired by marriage

The second category concerns those Commonwealth citizen women who acquired the right of abode by marriage. The requirements are that:

(a) the woman was a Commonwealth citizen on 31 December 1982 and continues to be such; and

(b) on or before 31 December 1982, she married a man who at the time of the marriage was either:

   (i) born, registered or naturalised in the UK, or

   (ii) was a Commonwealth citizen with a right of abode through a parental link (see **2.3.1**).

Note that any subsequent divorce or the death of the husband does not affect her status.

Examples

1. Anna was a citizen of Barbados on 31 December 1982 and continues to be such. In 1980 she married Frank. He had been born in the UK in 1960. Anna acquired the right of abode in the UK by marrying Frank.

2. Barbara was a citizen of Fiji on 31 December 1982 and continues to be such. In 1975 she married Luke. He had been born in Fiji in 1955 and was a Fijian national. His mother had been born in the UK. Provided Barbara can produce evidence that Luke was a Commonwealth citizen with the right of abode by his parental link (see **2.3.1**), she acquired the right of abode by marrying him. There is no requirement that Luke must have obtained his own certificate evidencing his right of abode.

2.3.3 Certificate of entitlement

A Commonwealth citizen with the right of abode will travel under his or her own country's passport. Before travelling to the UK for the first time, he or she should apply to the British High Commission for a certificate showing that right of abode.

To get the certificate in the first category, the applicant will need to produce:

(a) evidence of being a Commonwealth citizen on 31 December 1982 and that he remains a Commonwealth citizen;

(b) his own full birth certificate naming the appropriate parent;

(c) the appropriate parent's full UK birth certificate; and

(d) if claiming through the father, the parent's marriage certificate or evidence of relationship.

A check should always be made to see if the applicant can claim British citizenship (see **2.2.2**).

To get the certificate in the second category, the applicant will need to produce:

(a) evidence of being a Commonwealth citizen on 31 December 1982 and that she remains a Commonwealth citizen;

(b) her marriage certificate; and

(c) evidence that her husband was either British by birth, registration or naturalisation in the UK (eg his UK birth, registration or naturalisation certificate), or a Commonwealth citizen with his own right of abode (as above).

2.3.4 Excluded Commonwealth nationals

It is important to note that, as Cameroon, Mozambique, Namibia, Pakistan and South Africa were not members of the Commonwealth on 31 December 1982, nationals of those countries cannot take advantage of the above provisions.

2.3.5 Deprivation of right of abode

Section 2A of the IA 1971 gives the Secretary of State power to remove this right of abode if it is conducive to the public good to remove or exclude the Commonwealth citizen from the UK. There is a similar power for deprivation of British citizenship (see **2.2.9**).

There is a right of appeal to the IAC or, if issues of national security arise, to the Special Immigration Appeals Commission (see **Chapter 11**).

2.3.6 Flow diagram: summary

We have seen that before 1983 some Commonwealth citizens acquired the right of abode in the UK. The requirements are summarised in the flow diagram at **Appendix 10**.

2.4 Historical background

One of the difficulties in understanding the law in this area is that a person's citizenship may change over time. Someone born in the UK in 1940 would have had the status of 'British subject' at common law. Under the British Nationality Act 1948, he would have become a citizen of the UK and colonies (CUKC). Under the BNA 1981, he would become a British citizen. The problem is that his current citizenship status is defined in the legislation in terms of his earlier status. Thus, it is necessary to know a little of the history of citizenship law – in particular, three major developments, illustrated in the diagram below.

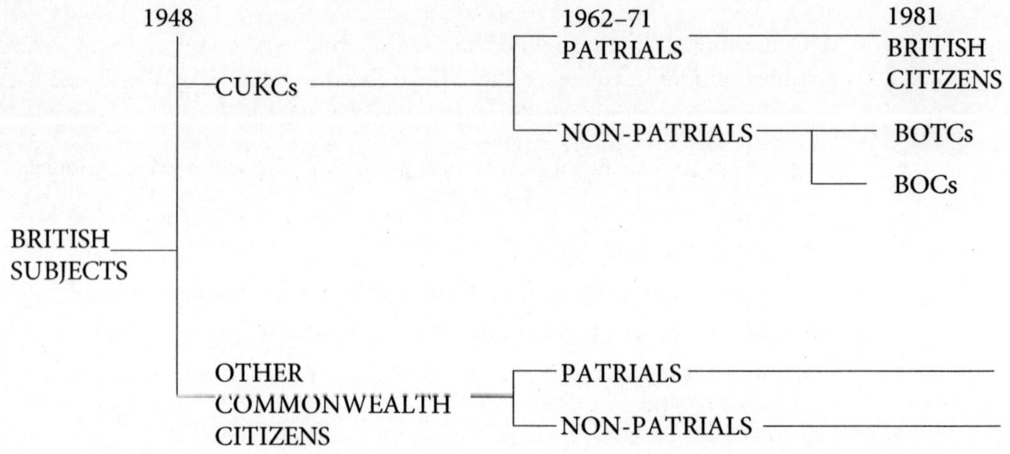

The terms used in the diagram have the broad meanings set out in **2.4.1** to **2.4.7** below.

2.4.1 British subjects

Before 1948, anyone who owed allegiance to the Crown, regardless of the Crown territory in which he was born.

2.4.2 CUKCs

After 1948, anyone connected with the UK or a Crown colony (such as Hong Kong).

2.4.3 Commonwealth citizens

After 1948, anyone having citizenship of an independent Commonwealth country, according to the law of that country. Independent Commonwealth countries included the former Dominions (eg Canada, Australia, New Zealand) and also former colonies (eg Jamaica) when they gained independence. On independence, existing citizens who were CUKCs might lose that status by becoming citizens of the newly independent Commonwealth country. The current list of countries whose citizens are Commonwealth citizens is given in **Appendix 9**. In addition, anyone who has British citizenship, British overseas territories citizenship or British overseas citizenship (see **2.4.5** to **2.4.7** below) is also a Commonwealth citizen.

2.4.4 Patrials

Anyone who under the IA 1971 had the right of abode in the UK. Until 1962, Commonwealth citizens and CUKCs could enter the UK freely. From that year, controls were introduced which were finally enacted in the 1971 Act. The controls extended to both CUKCs and Commonwealth citizens, but CUKCs and Commonwealth citizens who had a close connection with the UK were recognised as 'patrials', having the right of abode.

2.4.5 British citizens

Anyone who at 1 January 1983 was a CUKC with right of abode in the UK, and anyone who acquired British citizenship after that date (eg by birth in the UK, see **2.2.1**). British citizenship and the following categories of citizenship were created by BNA 1981.

2.4.6 British overseas territories citizens (BOTCs)

Anyone who at 1 January 1983 was a non-patrial CUKC, with a close connection with a colony, together with those later becoming BOTCs (eg by birth in the colony). The list of British overseas territories is given in **Appendix 11** to this book. By the Overseas Territories Act 2002, all BOTCs were granted British citizenship.

2.4.7 British overseas citizens (BOCs)

Anyone who at 1 January 1983 was a non-patrial CUKC, but without a close connection with a colony. This category included CUKCs living in a colony which gained independence, who did not acquire citizenship of the newly independent country (eg those of Asian origin in former colonies in East Africa).

This list is not exhaustive. There are other minor categories such as British protected persons, British nationals (overseas) and British subjects under the 1981 Act.

The following other major categories of citizens were unaffected by these changes in UK law.

2.4.8 Irish citizens

Citizens of the Republic of Ireland. They were not Commonwealth citizens under the British Nationality Act 1948. They are not subject to immigration controls (see **3.9**, Common Travel Area), but may be liable to deportation (see **Chapter 10**).

2.4.9 Aliens

Broadly, anyone who does not fall into the above categories. Immigration controls were introduced for aliens in 1905. They do not have the right of abode. However, UK law does permit dual nationality, so that someone who lacks the right of abode as an alien, may nevertheless have it if he can also claim British citizenship.

Chapter 3
Immigration Status

3.1 Immigration controls

As we saw at **1.4**, a person with the right of abode in the UK (British citizens: see **2.2** and certain Commonwealth citizens: see **2.3**) can enter without being subject to any immigration controls. All that person has to do is produce documentary evidence of that right of abode, usually a British passport or a Commonwealth country passport with a certificate of the right of abode.

Nationals of the EEA may enter the UK under EU law (see **Chapter 4**) rather than domestic UK law.

Everyone else is subject to immigration controls. Full details are given at **3.4**.

3.2 Immigration Rules

3.2.1 An overview

You will find it useful to take a brief look at the contents of the Immigration Rules. You will see that they start with a brief introduction, and importantly there are some useful definitions of key terms in para 6. The Rules are then divided into 13 parts, each part dealing with a discrete topic. So, for example, Part 1 sets out the general provisions regarding leave to enter or remain in the UK.

3.2.2 Structure

Parts 2 to 8 of the Rules set out the various different categories of entry to the UK. Why is the structure of the Rules for some categories different from others? This is because some categories require entry clearance, whilst a few do not for non-visa nationals. Also, some categories can lead to settlement, whilst others cannot.

Let us briefly consider two examples. Look at Part 2 and the category of general visitor at para 41. You should already appreciate that only a non-visa national can enter as a general visitor without obtaining entry clearance (see **1.4.2**). So why does the paragraph state that it deals with 'The requirements to be met by a person seeking leave to enter the United Kingdom as a general visitor'? For the answer we need to go back to para 26, which provides that 'An application for entry clearance will be considered in accordance with the provisions in these Rules governing the grant or refusal of leave to enter.' So, a visa national general visitor must satisfy the entry clearance officer that he meets the requirements of para 41 in order to get his visa before travelling to the UK. Then, on arrival at a UK airport or port, he may have to satisfy the immigration officer that he meets the requirements of para 41 in order to get leave to enter the UK. Any such leave will be granted pursuant to para 42, and so will be for a period not exceeding six months and subject to a condition prohibiting employment (see **3.3.1**). As a general visitor cannot subsequently apply for settlement, that is the basic structure of the provisions dealing with a visitor.

Now contrast that with a category that may lead to settlement. Look at para 281. This sets out the requirements for both entry clearance and leave to enter as a spouse or civil partner of a person settled in the UK. So the spouse or civil partner applies for a visa (if a visa national) or an entry certificate (if a non-visa national) before travelling to the UK. On arrival he or she may have to satisfy the immigration officer that he or she meets the requirements of para 281. If successful, limited leave will usually be granted for 27 months: see para 282. After 24 months settled status may be applied for under para 287.

In 2008 the Government introduced a points system for entry to work in the UK (see Part 6A, dealt with in **Chapter 7**). It took that opportunity to re-structure the paragraphs dealing with those categories, which now clearly state which requirements are for entry clearance etc.

3.2.3 Legal status of the requirements

After entering the UK an entrant does not commit a criminal offence by no longer meeting any particular requirement. For example, a student may no longer be following any course of study at all (see *OO v Secretary of State for the Home Department* [2008] EWCA Civ 747). However, if that comes to the attention of the Home Office, it may end the leave by what is known as curtailment (see **3.7**). If an application is made to extend or vary the leave (see **3.6**) it is likely to be refused.

3.3 Conditions of limited leave

By s 3(1) of the IA 1971, a person granted limited leave to enter or remain in the UK may be subject to all or any of the following conditions:

(a) a condition restricting his employment or occupation in the UK;

(b) a condition requiring him to maintain and accommodate himself, and any dependants of his, without recourse to public funds;

(c) a condition requiring him to register with the police;

(d) a condition requiring him to report to an immigration officer or the Secretary of State; and

(e) a condition about residence.

3.3.1 Restricting employment or occupation

The category of entry will determine the nature of this condition, and the answer can be found by looking at the relevant paragraph under which leave is granted. So, as we saw at **3.2.2**, a general visitor's limited leave is subject to a condition prohibiting employment. That is because a general visitor should not work at all. A student can work only within prescribed guidelines (see para 95 and **6.6.4**). An entrepreneur is not permitted to take employment, other than working for the business or businesses which he has established, joined or taken over (see para 245M and **7.4**).

Note that para 6 defines 'employment' as including paid and unpaid employment, paid and unpaid work placements undertaken as part of a course or period of study, self-employment and engaging in business or any professional activity.

3.3.2 Not to have recourse to public funds

3.3.2.1 What are public funds?

All entrants with limited leave are subject to a condition not to have recourse to public funds. This is because all entrants are supposed to be self-sufficient and able to maintain and accommodate themselves and any dependants. So what count as public funds? All that follow:

(a) housing of homeless persons under Pts VI or VII of the Housing Act 1996 and under Pt II of the Housing Act 1985;

(b) the non-means tested welfare benefits of attendance allowance, carer's allowance, child benefit and disability living allowance;

(c) the means-tested benefits of income support, income-related employment and support allowance, income-based jobseeker's allowance, council tax benefit and housing benefit, State pension credit, child tax credit and working tax credit; and

(d) a Social Fund payment.

The following do not count as public funds:

(a) the National Insurance-based welfare benefits of contribution-based jobseeker's allowance, contributory employment and support allowance, State pension and bereavement benefits;

(b) National Health Service treatment and education for a child at a local authority maintained school.

3.3.2.2 Additional public funds

Very often entry to the UK is for the purposes of family re-union (see **Chapter 8**), for example a child joining a parent who is already settled in the UK. The person settled in the UK is often known as the 'sponsor'. If a sponsor already receives public funds, will entry clearance be refused? Paragraph 6A makes an important qualification to this condition. It states that

> For the purpose of these Rules, a person (P) is not to be regarded as having (or potentially having) recourse to public funds merely because P is (or will be) reliant in whole or in part on public funds provided to P's sponsor unless, as a result of P's presence in the United Kingdom, the sponsor is (or would be) entitled to increased or additional public funds (save where such entitlement to increased or additional public funds is by virtue of P and the sponsor's joint entitlement to benefits under the regulations referred to in paragraph 6B).

So, for example, if P seeks entry clearance to live permanently with his sponsor (S) in the UK, the application will not necessarily fail if S already receives one or more of the public funds. It will fail, however, if S becomes entitled either to an increase in the amount of his existing public funds, or to another public fund because of P's joining S in the UK.

Paragraph 6B provides as follows:

> Subject to paragraph 6C, a person (P) shall not be regarded as having recourse to public funds if P is entitled to benefits specified under section 115 of the Immigration and Asylum Act 1999 by virtue of regulations made under subsections (3) and (4) of that section or section 42 of the Tax Credits Act 2002.

Normally a person with limited leave to enter or remain in the UK is excluded from claiming mainstream welfare benefits (including those on the public funds list) by s 115 of the IAA 1999. However, a claim might be made by such a person if he meets the exceptions in subsections (3) and (4). Also, if the person has a partner who is entitled to apply for child and/or working tax credits, uniquely the application can be made jointly, and both count when the tax credits are calculated under the 2002 Act.

Paragraph 6C provides as follows:

> A person (P) making an application from outside the United Kingdom will be regarded as having recourse to public funds where P relies upon the future entitlement to any public funds that would be payable to P or to P's sponsor as a result of P's presence in the United Kingdom (including those benefits to which P or the sponsor would be entitled as a result of P's presence in the United Kingdom under the regulations referred to in to paragraph 6B).

What is the effect of paragraph 6C? First, note that it only concerns an application by P for entry clearance. That application will be refused if P shows that he will be adequately maintained in the UK only by relying upon his or his sponsor's future entitlement to any public funds, including tax credits or those payable to him under the IAA 1999, s 115(3) and (4).

This form of sponsorship should not be confused with the more formal and detailed sponsorship of students and workers, etc under Part 6A of the Immigration Rules (see **Chapters 6** and **7**).

For further details on this topic, see Chapter 10 of ***Welfare Benefits***.

3.3.3 Registration with the police

Adult nationals of certain countries are listed in Appendix 2 to the Immigration Rules (see **Appendix 1** to this book) as they are required to register with the police within seven days of arriving in the UK (see Part 10 of the Rules). To register they need to produce their passports and pay a registration fee. If they are staying in the Metropolitan Police area in London, they should register at the Overseas Visitors Records Office, Brandon House, 180 Borough High Street, London, SE1 1LH. Otherwise they should contact their local police station for the address and opening hours of the nearest police registration office.

3.3.4 Reporting to an immigration officer or Secretary of State

This condition and the next (**3.3.5**) were introduced by s 16 of the UK Borders Act 2007. The Government's view was that without these powers it was difficult for the UKBA to maintain contact with foreign nationals during the currency of their limited leave, and to enforce their removal should that leave be curtailed (see **3.7**). The Government stated that it would use these conditions against foreign national criminals, who cannot currently be removed due to the ECHR, and to certain children about whom there are particular concerns or who have been placed on discretionary leave (see **9.10**) with a view to their removal when they reach 18.

3.3.5 Residence

See **3.3.4** above.

3.3.6 Consequences of breach of a condition

Although it is an offence under s 24(1)(b) of the IA 1971 for a person with limited leave knowingly to breach a condition of leave, it is unusual for the Home Office to prosecute. Government policy is that if the breach is sufficiently serious, the person should be removed from the UK (see **10.2**).

3.4 Entry clearance

3.4.1 The general rule

The entry clearance procedure is, in effect, a form of pre-entry control, in which a UK official known as a visa or entry clearance officer acts as an immigration officer, applying the Immigration Rules, but usually in the country in which the entrant is living before travel to the UK.

The form of clearance depends on the nationality of the entrant. The Immigration Rules specify countries whose nationals (known as 'visa nationals') require entry clearance in the form of a visa (usually stamped on the passport). A list of these countries is given in Appendix 1 to the Immigration Rules (**Appendix 1** to this book). In the case of some 'non-visa nationals', entry clearance is required for a stay of more than six months (see **2.1**). In this case, the entry clearance is shown by a different stamp, known as an entry certificate (see para 25 of the Immigration Rules).

An applicant for entry clearance as a visitor must apply to a particular designated post. However, any other type of application must be made to the appropriate designated post in the country or territory where the applicant is living. Applicants from certain countries can apply on-line at www.visa4uk.fco.gov.uk, although it should be noted that the website currently only supports applications made in English. Once they have submitted their on-line applications they are given an appointment to produce their original passports and supporting documents, and pay the appropriate fees if they have not already done so on-line. At that appointment the applicant's biographic and biometric data are collected (see **3.4.3**). These are then transmitted to the UK for checks.

Forms and guidance notes for making an application in writing can be found at www.ukvisas.gov.uk/en/howtoapply/vafs.

3.4.2 Leave under the Immigration and Asylum Act 1999

The IAA 1999 provides for greater flexibility in the way permission to enter the UK and to remain may be granted. Instead of leave to enter always having to be given in writing at a port of entry, the IAA 1999 allows for additional ways of giving leave to enter to be specified, eg that a visa or other entry clearance is to be treated as leave to enter. This means that holders of visas, for example, will be able to pass through the port control with only a quick check on identity and on the rightful ownership of the travel document and entry clearance, unless there is a need to examine for, among other matters, change of circumstances.

Most entry clearance now takes effect as leave to enter as well. This means that there are two significant dates to look out for on a visa or entry certificate, namely, the *effective date* and the *expiry date*. In most cases, the effective date will be the date on which the entry clearance is issued. However, some people may not intend or be able to travel to the UK immediately following their application, and in these circumstances an entry clearance officer will usually exercise his discretion to defer the effective date for up to three months after entry clearance has been authorised. So, in order to avoid the cost of making an unnecessary application for an extension of stay, an applicant should always confirm his date of travel.

For applicants in categories that require a qualifying period to be met before applying for settlement, or who have a limit imposed on their total length of stay in that category, their leave to enter will normally begin on the date they arrive in the UK within the three-month limit. This ensures that the maximum leave to which they are entitled is given.

The expiry date on a visa or entry certificate reflects the date on which the entry clearance and leave to enter are no longer effective. After this date the entry clearance will not be valid for travel to the UK, neither will it confer leave to enter.

3.4.3 Biometric information

All applicants are now routinely required to provide 10-digit fingerscans and a digital photograph when applying for UK entry clearance. The applicant attends a pre-arranged appointment. Fingerprints are taken on a glass screen scan. A digital photograph is taken. The biometric data are stored on a central government database in the UK and checked against UK government records.

3.4.4 Financial undertakings

Often entry clearance is sought for the purposes of immediate or ultimate settlement (eg child joining parent in UK, or grandparent joining grandchild in UK or spouse joining partner in UK, etc). The person based in the UK is usually known as 'the sponsor'. See the definition in Immigration Rules, para 6. This does not necessarily mean that that person has signed a written agreement with the DfWP to be financially responsible for the entrant. As para 35 of the Immigration Rules states, 'A sponsor of a person ... may be asked to give an undertaking in writing to be responsible for that person's maintenance and accommodation'. Only if such a written undertaking is given can the DfWP seek to recover any benefits paid. Guidance from the UKBA is that written undertakings should only be required in exceptional circumstances or for certain categories such as parents, grandparents and other dependent relatives under para 317 of the Immigration Rules (see **8.10**). As to what constitutes a written undertaking, see *Ahmed v Secretary of State for Work and Pensions* [2005] EWCA Civ 535.

The UKBA uses Sponsorship Undertaking Form SU07. It can be found on the UKBA website (see **1.2.8**).

3.4.5 Refusal of entry clearance

3.4.5.1 Mandatory grounds

The general grounds for refusal of entry clearance (and leave to enter) are set out in para 320 of the Immigration Rules. Some of these are described as mandatory grounds, although in such cases an entry clearance officer should always consider any human rights grounds (in particular the right to family life under Article 8 ECHR) which would justify issuing the entry clearance.

Mandatory grounds for refusal are given in para 320(1) to (7). These include that entry clearance must be refused in the following circumstances:

(a) Where entry clearance is being sought for a purpose not covered by the Rules.

(b) Where the applicant is currently the subject of a deportation order (see **10.1**).

(c) Where the applicant has failed to produce a valid national passport or other document satisfactorily establishing his identity.

(d) Where the Secretary of State has personally directed that the exclusion of a person from the UK is conducive to the public good.

(e) Where the Medical Inspector has confirmed that, for medical reasons, it is undesirable to admit a person seeking entry clearance to the UK and an entry clearance officer is satisfied that there are no strong, compassionate reasons justifying admission.

(f) Where false representations have been made or false documents have been submitted (whether or not material to the application, and whether or not to the applicant's knowledge), or material facts have not been disclosed, in relation to the application. The UKBA guidance is that a false representation is made when an applicant or third party lies or makes a false statement in an application, either orally or in writing. To refuse the application, an entry clearance officer must be satisfied to a high standard that a false representation has been made.

    The UKBA gives the following two examples of false representations:

    (i) A visa applicant states that he is a project manager for a company, earning a significant salary. It is discovered that he is in fact the cleaner for the company on a low salary.

    (ii) An applicant applies for entry clearance on the basis of his marriage to a British citizen, and states in his application form that he has never been married before. But a marriage certificate is received from another wife, which is verified, showing that he is already married.

Does a false statement mean one made dishonestly? Yes: see *AA (Nigeria) v Secretary of State for the Home Department* [2010] EWCA Civ 773. This is because 'a false representation stated in all innocence may be simply a matter of mistake, or an error short of dishonesty' (per Rix LJ at [68]).

What is a false document? The UKBA guidance is that this includes a genuine document which has been altered or tampered with; a counterfeit document (one that is completely false); a genuine document that is being used by an impostor; a genuine document which has been fraudulently obtained or issued; and a genuine document which contains a falsified or counterfeit visa or endorsement.

What about material facts that have not been disclosed? Here the entry clearance officer will need to show that the withheld information would have been relevant to his decision. Note that an ECO cannot refuse an applicant on this ground if he has not indicated to the applicant the kind of information that is relevant to the application. The UKBA gives the following example. The wife of a man in the UK who has limited leave to remain as a highly skilled worker (see **7.3**), applies to join her husband as his dependant, but does not mention that the marriage has broken down. The husband has sent a letter stating that the marriage no longer subsists.

(g) Where the applicant has previously breached the UK's immigration laws. That breach must be the result of overstaying; breaching a condition attached to leave; being an illegal entrant; or using deception in an application for entry clearance, leave to enter or remain (whether successful or not). All of these are dealt with in **Chapter 10**.

Are there any exceptions to this? Yes, but these result in time limits being imposed on the applicant applying again. This is because the limited circumstances in which the ground does not apply are: if the applicant overstayed for 28 days or less and left the UK voluntarily, not at the expense (directly or indirectly) of the Secretary of State; if he used deception in an application for entry clearance more than 10 years ago; if he left the UK voluntarily, not at the expense (directly or indirectly) of the Secretary of State, more than 12 months ago; if he left the UK voluntarily, at the expense (directly or indirectly) of the Secretary of State, more than five years ago; or if he was removed or deported from the UK more than 10 years ago.

The significance of refusal under this ground is that applications will not be considered for the following periods from the date the applicant left the UK:

(i) 1 year if he left the UK voluntarily and not at public expense; or

(ii) 5 years if he left the UK voluntarily at public expense (eg received an assisted voluntary return); or

(iii) 10 years if he was removed or deported from the UK.

If an applicant has previously been refused entry clearance because a false document was used or a false representation was made, the applicant may claim that he was unaware that the document or representation was false. Unless the applicant can prove this, he must be automatically refused entry clearance under this ground for 10 years from the date the deception was used.

Note that where more than one breach of the UK's immigration laws has occurred, only the breach which leads to the longest period of absence from the UK is relevant. The UKBA gives the following example. An applicant left the UK voluntarily at her own expense in January 2008 and applied for entry clearance using false documents in February 2008. Any subsequent entry clearance application must be automatically refused for 10 years, until February 2018. This is the longer refusal period where deception has been used in an entry clearance application. The shorter refusal period of one year for leaving the UK voluntarily is not applicable.

It is important to note that this ground for refusal does not apply in the following circumstances:

(i) where the applicant is applying as a spouse, civil partner, or unmarried or same-sex partner; a fiancé(e) or proposed civil partner; a parent, grandparent or other dependent relative; a person exercising rights of access to a child; a spouse, civil partner, unmarried or same-sex partner of a refugee or person with humanitarian protection; or

(ii) where the individual was under the age of 18 at the time of his most recent breach of the UK's immigration laws.

3.4.5.2 Discretionary grounds

The general grounds on which entry clearance (and leave to enter) should normally be refused are set out in para 320(8) to (20) of the Immigration Rules, and these include the following:

(a) Failure to supply any information, documents, copy documents or medical report that has been formally requested.

(b) Where the applicant has previously contrived in a significant way to frustrate the intentions of the Immigration Rules. This is where an applicant has previously been an illegal entrant, overstayed, breached a condition attached to his leave or used deception in a previous application, and there are aggravating circumstances. The UKBA guidance is that aggravating factors include offences such as absconding; not complying with reporting restrictions; using an assumed identity or multiple identities to obtain State benefits; a sham marriage; harbouring an immigration offender and facilitating people smuggling. All cases must be considered on their merits, taking into account family life in the UK and the level of responsibility for the breach in the case of children.

There is, of course, an overlap here with the mandatory ground for refusal highlighted at (g) in **3.4.5.1**. The UKBA guidance is that where an applicant falls to be refused under the mandatory ground, an entry clearance officer must also consider whether it is also appropriate to refuse the applicant on this discretionary ground. If an applicant is exempt from the mandatory ground refusal, an entry clearance officer must consider whether a refusal under this discretionary ground is appropriate.

(c) Refusal by a sponsor to give, if requested to do so, an undertaking in writing (see **3.4.2**) to be responsible for that person's maintenance and accommodation for the period of any leave granted.

(d) Refusal to undergo a medical examination when required to do so.

(e) Save where the entry clearance officer is satisfied that admission would be justified for strong compassionate reasons, conviction in any country, including the UK, an offence which, if committed in the UK, is punishable with imprisonment for a term of 12 months or any greater punishment, or which, if committed outside the UK, would be so punishable if the conduct constituting the offence had occurred in the UK. Spent convictions under the Rehabilitation of Offenders Act should be ignored for these purposes.

(f) Where, from information available, it seems right to refuse the application on the ground that exclusion from the UK is conducive to the public good; if, for example, in the light of the character, conduct or associations of the person seeking leave to enter, it is undesirable to grant the application. The UKBA gives the following examples: where a person's admission could adversely affect the conduct of foreign policy; where there is reliable evidence that a person has been involved in criminal activities, even though he has not been convicted; where the person's admission would be contrary to internationally agreed travel restrictions; where the person's admission might lead to infringement of UK law; where the person's admission might lead to an offence being committed by someone else; and where a person's activities are such that his presence in the UK is likely to cause a public order concern. What is involved is an evaluation of risk to the public. The question the entry clearance officer must answer is whether or not there a substantial risk of disorder: see *CB (United States of America) v Entry Clearance Officer (Los Angeles)* [2008] EWCA Civ 1539.

3.5 Leave to enter

3.5.1 The general rule

Leave to enter is dealt with in paras 7–11 of the Immigration Rules. Everyone must, on arrival in the UK, produce a passport or other document establishing his nationality and identity. On examination by an immigration officer, the entrant must furnish such information as may be required to enable the officer to decide whether he requires leave to enter, whether leave should be given, and the terms of leave. It is para 2(1) of Sch 2 to the IA 1971 which gives an immigration officer the power to examine any person who arrives in the UK and sets out the purpose for which such an examination is conducted, namely to determine whether:

(a) he is or is not a British citizen; and, if not,

(b) if he may or may not enter the UK without leave; and, if not,

(c) if he has been given leave which is still in force, or should be given leave and for what period or on what conditions (if any), or should be refused leave.

If it is concluded that a person is a British citizen, the immigration officer takes no further action. If he is not a British citizen, however, he will be examined to determine whether or not he requires permission to enter the UK. This permission is called leave to enter. If a person qualifies for leave to enter then the immigration officer will go on to decide the length of the leave and any conditions, such as permission to work, which will apply. Finally, if a person does not qualify for leave to enter then the immigration officer may refuse leave to enter.

These controls do not, however, apply to persons arriving from another part of the Common Travel Area (see **3.9**).

3.5.2 Documentary evidence

Documentary evidence to be produced to an immigration officer may include:

(a) a UK passport: required to be produced by a British citizen as evidence of his right of abode;

(b) a certificate of entitlement issued by the UK Government: evidence of right of abode which may be produced as an alternative to (a) above (by a Commonwealth citizen who has the right of abode, see **2.3**);

(c) entry clearance in the form of a visa or entry certificate;

(d) a non-UK passport or identity card: identity cards can be used as a substitute for a passport by EEA nationals.

3.5.3 Grant of limited leave

The immigration officer grants leave by written notice, usually in the form of a stamp on the entrant's passport. The stamp gives the date and port of entry, the time limit of the leave, and any conditions imposed, but does not indicate the Rule under which leave has been granted.

However, if a person's entry clearance also takes effect as leave to enter the UK (see **3.4.2**), an immigration officer may still question that person to establish that he is the rightful holder of the document, that the document does take effect as limited leave, that the passport is genuine and that there are no circumstances under which the entry clearance should be cancelled (see **3.5.4**).

3.5.4 Refusal of limited leave

An immigration officer may refuse leave to enter the UK on exactly the same grounds that an entry clearance officer may refuse entry clearance (see **3.4.5**).

Paragraph 321 of the Immigration Rules provides three instances where a person seeking leave to enter the UK who holds an entry clearance which was duly issued to him and is still current may be refused leave to enter. These are where an immigration officer is satisfied of any of the following:

(a) False representations were made or false documents were submitted (whether or not material to the application, and whether or not to the holder's knowledge), or material facts were not disclosed, in relation to the application for entry clearance.

(b) A change of circumstances since it was issued has removed the basis of the holder's claim to admission, except where the change of circumstances amounts solely to the person becoming over age for entry in one of the categories contained in paras 296 to 316 of the Rules since the issue of the entry clearance.

(c) Refusal is justified on grounds of restricted return ability; on medical grounds; on grounds of criminal record; because the person seeking leave to enter is the subject of a deportation order; or because exclusion would be conducive to the public good.

Paragraph 321A sets out the grounds on which a person's leave to enter which is in force on his arrival in, or whilst he is outside, the UK may be cancelled by an immigration officer. These include that:

(a) There has been such a change in the circumstances of that person's case since the leave was given, that it should be cancelled.

(b) False representations were made or false documents were submitted (whether or not material to the application, and whether or not to the holder's knowledge), or material facts were not disclosed, in relation to the application for leave.

(c) For medical reasons it is undesirable to admit the person.

(d) The Secretary of State has personally directed that exclusion is conducive to the public good.

After admission, any extension of the time limit, or variation of conditions, is dealt with by an application to the Home Office (see **3.6**).

3.5.5 Temporary admission

If a decision on whether to grant leave cannot be reached quickly, the immigration officer will usually issue a notice of temporary admission (in Form IS96). This tells the entrant that he is liable to detention, but may physically enter the UK without having leave to enter. He may be directed to reside at a particular place, and is asked to report back to an immigration officer at a specified time. He may not take employment.

As an alternative to temporary admission, the entrant can be detained, but may apply to an Immigration Judge for bail if he remains detained seven days after his arrival in the UK.

3.5.6 Entry without a passport

By s 2(1) of the Asylum and Immigration (Treatment of Claimants, etc) Act 2004 (AI (TC)A 2004), a person commits an offence if, when seeking leave either to enter or remain in the UK or asylum, he does not have with him a passport (or similar immigration document) which is in force and satisfactorily establishes his identity and nationality or citizenship. By s 2(4) various defences may be raised, such as proving a reasonable excuse for not being in possession of the required document. The defendant has the legal burden of proving the defence on the balance of probabilities: see *R v Navabi and Embaye* [2005] EWCA Crim 2865.

However, note that by s 2(7) the fact that a document was deliberately destroyed or disposed of is not such a reasonable excuse unless it is shown that the destruction or disposal was for a reasonable cause, or that it was beyond the control of the person charged with the offence. So what is a 'reasonable cause'? By s 2(7)(b) this does not include the purpose of (i) delaying the handling or resolution of a claim or application or the taking of a decision, (ii) increasing the chances of success of a claim or application, or (iii) complying with instructions or advice given by a person who offers advice about, or facilitates, immigration into the UK, unless in the circumstances of the case it is unreasonable to expect non-compliance with the instructions or advice.

3.6 Leave to remain in the UK: extension or variation of existing leave

3.6.1 Application made to Home Office

The general framework is laid down by s 3(3) of the IA 1971, which provides that limited leave may be varied, whether by restricting, enlarging, or removing the time limit, or by adding, varying, or removing conditions. If the time limit is removed, the leave becomes indefinite and any conditions cease to have effect. Indefinite leave cannot be varied.

Application for variation is made to the Home Office. Immigration officers have no powers to deal with variations. Application should be made before expiry of the time limit on leave, because overstaying is a criminal offence, and may result in refusal of the application to extend leave.

If the application is granted, an appropriate entry is made in the applicant's passport and that is returned with a covering letter. Any refusal (see **3.6.5**) is notified to the applicant by letter, stating the reasons for the refusal and setting out any rights of appeal (see **Chapter 11**).

3.6.2 Effect of application on existing leave

By s 3C of the IA 1971, when a person applies for variation of his leave before that leave expires, but it then expires before a decision is taken, the leave is automatically extended to the point at which the appropriate period for appealing a refusal expires (see **Chapter 11**). This will protect the immigration status of that person and prevent him from becoming an overstayer. All conditions attached to the leave will still apply. So if a person who entered the UK as a fiancé(e) subsequently applies to stay as a spouse following the marriage, until the variation is granted by the Home Office, the applicant cannot lawfully work (see **8.7**). A person will not be able to submit further applications during the leave as extended under this section, although he would be able to vary his original application: this is to ensure that all issues raised are covered by one decision and consequently one appeal (see further **Chapter 11**).

An applicant who wishes to extend his stay in the UK in his existing category or to switch to a new category must have 'effective' or 'valid' limited leave. For example, under para 284(i) of the Immigration Rules, an extension of stay as a spouse (see **8.3.3**) requires that the applicant *has* limited leave to remain in the UK. So, if the Home Office finds that the original leave was obtained by deception, it may determine that the applicant is an illegal entrant (see **10.2.2**) and as such without effective or valid limited leave. In those circumstances the applicant may be subject to administrative removal (see **10.2**).

3.6.3 Switching categories

In many cases, an entrant will apply to vary his leave by switching from one category of entry to another. For example, someone who has entered as a student may wish to remain as the spouse of someone living in the UK. In every case, it will be necessary to check the detailed provisions of the Rules relating to the new category.

On the other hand, if a person with limited leave marries someone settled in the UK, para 284 does not prevent him (unless he is a visitor) obtaining an extension as a spouse solely on the ground that he failed to obtain entry clearance in that capacity – even though a spouse or fiancé(e) would usually have to obtain entry clearance before coming to the UK.

Is there any danger in applying to switch categories? The danger is that the Home Office may refuse the application and curtail the existing leave (see **3.7**).

3.6.4 Procedure for variation

3.6.4.1 Specified forms

Paragraphs 34 and 34A to 34J of the Immigration Rules lay down the procedure that must be followed for most applications to the Home Office (apart from EEA matters: see **3.6.4.3**). First, certain applications must be made on the form specified by the Home Office. To date, the following are specified forms:

FLR(M): application for an extension of stay in UK as the spouse, civil partner or unmarried partner of a person present and settled here.

FLR(O): application for extension of stay in UK if applying in certain categories, such as visitor, person with UK ancestry and any other purpose or reason not covered by other application forms.

SET(DV): application for indefinite leave to remain in UK as a victim of domestic violence.

SET(M): application for indefinite leave to remain in UK as the spouse, civil partner or unmarried partner of a person who is present and settled here.

SET(O): application for indefinite leave to remain in UK on completion of five years of continuous leave to remain in UK in categories such as Tier 1 entrepreneur or investor migrant and person with UK ancestry. The form is also used to apply for indefinite leave to remain in one of the following categories: long residence in UK, bereaved partner and any other purpose or reason not covered by other application forms.

SET(F): application for indefinite leave to remain in UK as a family member (other than husband or wife or unmarried partner) of a person present and settled in UK, ie a child under 18 of a parent, parents or relative present and settled in UK and the parent, grandparent or other dependent relative of a person present and settled in UK.

BUS: application for an extension of stay or for indefinite leave to remain in UK as a sole representative.

Tier 1 (entrepreneur): application to switch or extend stay as an entrepreneur.

Tier 1 (investor): application to switch or extend stay as an investor.

Tier 1 (dependant): application for extension of stay as dependant of person granted leave to remain under points-based system.

Tier 4 (general): application to switch or extend stay as a student.

3.6.4.2 Following the specified forms procedure

It is absolutely vital that an applicant follows the specified form procedure or his application will be invalid. An invalid application is returned to the applicant and treated as if it was never made. Of course, if a valid application is not made in time, the applicant becomes an overstayer liable to removal from the UK (see **3.6.5** and **Chapter 11**).

What will make an application invalid? Any of the following:

(a) failing to use the specified form;

(b) failing to pay the specified fee, or paying it in a manner not specified in the form and/or guidance notes;

(c) failing to complete in full those parts of the specified form marked as mandatory. Every question in these parts of the form must be answered and all the information required given;

(d) failing to provide biographical or biometric information as required;

(e) failing to provide any photographs or documents specified as mandatory (see, for example, *R (Fu) v Secretary of State for the Home Department* [2010] EWHC 2922);

(f) failing to sign the form as required;

(g) failing to deliver the form in the manner stated on it.

As the requirements for an application to be valid are part of the Immigration Rules there is an element of discretion, but the UKBA guidance is that this is limited to exceptional circumstances, such as where an applicant is unable to sign the form or to provide photographs because of a serious illness or accident.

It is vital that the Home Office receives the specified form before the applicant's current leave expires. If possible, therefore, it should be delivered by hand to the public enquiry office and a receipt obtained. If it is posted, the application is treated as made on the day it was posted by reference to the postmark.

If an application is rejected but then re-submitted, and fully complies with the requirements of para 34A, the date of application is the date that it is re-submitted.

Note that if parts of a specified form which are not designated as mandatory are incomplete, a Home Office caseworker may attempt to obtain the missing information from the applicant, or consider the application on the basis of the information provided, but the application will be valid.

3.6.4.3 EEA forms

Note that the following four forms all relate to EEA nationals (see **Chapter 4**) and are not forms specified under para 34.

EEA1: application for a registration certificate by an EEA national.

EEA2: application for a residence card by a non-EEA family member of an EEA national.

EEA3: application for permanent residence by an EEA national.

EEA4: application for permanent residence by a non-EEA family member of an EEA national.

3.6.5 Refusal by Home Office

In addition to the grounds for refusal of extension of stay for the various immigration categories set out in Parts 2 to 8 of the Immigration Rules, para 322 provides a list of grounds similar to those used by entry clearance officers and immigration officers to refuse entry clearance (see **3.4.4** and **3.5.4**).

3.7 Curtailment of existing leave to enter or remain

If a person enters the UK in one category and before his limited leave expires he applies to switch to another category, there is a danger not only that the application might be refused but also that the existing leave might be curtailed (or the applicant removed from the UK).

> **Example**
>
> Bob enters the UK as a student with 12 months' limited leave. After three months he applies to remain in the UK as the spouse of a British citizen. The suspicion may well be that he never intended to leave the UK because he always intended to marry. Not only might his leave be curtailed, but alternatively he may be removed from the UK as an illegal entrant (see **Chapter 10**).

The power to curtail a person's leave is contained in s 3(3)(a) of the IA 1971. It may be used when a person has failed to comply with certain requirements of the Immigration Rules or has lost the justification for his presence here, eg an employee's job ends. It is only available when a person has limited leave. Guidance from the UKBA is that curtailment should not normally be used unless the person has at least six months' leave outstanding.

Paragraph 323 of the Immigration Rules allows curtailment, for example, if:

(a) false representations have been made or material facts not disclosed in order to obtain leave to enter or a previous variation of leave;

(b) the person has failed to comply with any conditions attached to his leave;

(c) the person has failed to maintain and accommodate himself and any dependants without recourse to public funds;

(d) the person ceases to meet the requirements of the Rules under which that leave was granted.

As curtailment is a matter of Home Office discretion it is not automatic. The burden of proof rests with the Secretary of State. Very often a person will be removed rather than his leave curtailed, eg where a person has failed to disclose relevant facts or has made false representations in order to obtain leave, consideration may be given to curtailing any subsisting leave, but it is more usual to proceed directly to administrative removal (see **Chapter 10**) or, in the case of leave to enter, removal for illegal entry (also **Chapter 10**). Equally, although leave may be curtailed where a person fails to observe the conditions of his leave to enter or remain, normally the Home Office proceeds direct to administrative removal for breach of conditions (see **Chapter 10**). Curtailment therefore is only normally considered where the person's actions are not so serious as to merit enforcement action, but where it would be inappropriate to let him remain for the duration of his leave.

Note that by s 3D of the IA 1971, a person's leave is deemed to continue if he makes an appeal whilst in the UK against curtailment (see **Chapter 11**).

3.8 Settlement

3.8.1 What is it?

A person is settled according to the definition in s 33(2A) of the IA 1971 if he is ordinarily resident in the UK without being subject under the immigration laws to any restriction on the period for which he may remain. The status will be acquired by a person given unlimited leave who satisfies the 'ordinary residence' test (see **3.8.2**). A person who has been given indefinite leave to remain in the UK would not be 'settled' in the UK under the IA 1971, if he has emigrated to another country and is no longer ordinarily resident in the UK.

A person who is settled in the UK has, subject to the Immigration Rules, the right to continue to live in the UK. Unlike a person with right of abode, he may be deported (see **Chapter 10**).

3.8.2 Ordinary residence

This is a condition of settled status. It has a quite distinct meaning. Case law from various fields suggests that a person can be 'ordinarily resident' without having the right, or the intention, to reside here permanently. All that is necessary is that a person resides in a place with a 'settled purpose' (eg to undertake a course of education). It is possible to have ordinary residence in more than one place at the same time. A person may be ordinarily resident in the UK even though temporarily absent (eg on holiday). Generally, however, for purposes other than exemption from deportation, a person cannot be so resident at a time when he is in breach of immigration laws (eg overstaying) (see the IA 1971, s 33(2)).

Examples

(1) Erasmus has been in the UK for the last eight years, periodically renewing his leave to remain.

He is 'ordinarily resident' in the UK, but not 'settled' as he is subject to limited leave.

(2) Farooq was given indefinite leave to remain in the UK 10 years ago, but emigrated six years ago. He is now here for a holiday, having been admitted as a visitor.

He is not 'ordinarily resident'. Neither is he 'settled' as his indefinite leave to remain was not renewed on his return to the UK.

(3) As (2), but Farooq has been admitted as a student, with 12 months' leave.

He is 'ordinarily resident', but not 'settled'.

3.8.3 Returning resident rule

If a person with settled status leaves the UK and returns within two years, his leave will continue, leave to enter has to be given again and his settled status in effect confirmed. This is usually automatic under para 18 of the Rules, dealing with 'returning residents', provided that the entrant satisfies the immigration officer that he had indefinite leave to enter or remain in the UK when he last left, that he has not been away for longer than two years, and that he now seeks admission for the purpose of settlement. If a person is returning periodically only for a limited period simply to show residence in the UK within two years of each departure, then eventually he or she is likely to be denied the benefit of para 18 of the Immigration Rules.

What if a person with settled status does not return to the UK within two years of last leaving it? See para 19 of the Immigration Rules.

3.8.4 Who is treated as settled under the Immigration Rules?

Note that the Immigration Rules use the term 'settled' to cover British citizens and Commonwealth citizens who have the right of abode, as well as those people who have indefinite leave. So the Rules applying to 'the spouse of a person settled in the UK' will apply also to the spouse of a British citizen or a Commonwealth citizen with the right of abode (see **8.3**).

3.8.5 Entry clearance

Only certain family members of a person already settled in the UK may apply for entry clearance for the purposes of settlement in the UK with that relative. These are dealt with in **Chapter 8,** but for now note that they include, under Part 8 of the Immigration Rules:

(a) a spouse or civil partner where the couple have already lived together for four years outside the UK (para 281(i)(b)(i));

(b) an unmarried or a same-sex partner where the couple have already lived together for four years outside the UK (para 295A(i)(b)(i));

(c) a child of a parent, parents or a relative present and settled or being admitted for settlement in the UK (para 297);

(d) a parent, grandparent or other dependent relative of a person present and settled in the UK (para 317).

3.8.6 Switching where permitted

Some categories of entrants with limited leave are by their very nature temporary and so cannot lead to settlement, eg visitors (see **Chapter 5**) and students (see **Chapter 6**). However, most other categories may lead to settlement, and the answer is always found by studying the appropriate Immigration Rules. For example, a Tier 1 (Entrepreneur) Migrant can apply for settlement under para 245DF. See further **Chapters 7** and **8**.

3.8.7 Knowledge of language and life in the UK

Any adult, aged between 16 and 65, who has entered the UK with limited leave and subsequently applies for settlement, must satisfy the language and life in the UK tests that also apply to applicants for naturalisation (see **2.2.7**).

3.8.8 The long-residence rules

Even where the requirements of the Immigration Rules for a switch to settled status are not met, it may be possible to obtain indefinite leave by virtue of long residence in the UK. Pursuant to Immigration Rules, para 276B, it is Home Office practice to consider this in cases where the applicant has been continuously resident in the UK for 10 years. The residence must have been lawful and continuous. In addition, where the applicant has been in the UK continuously for 14 years or more, indefinite leave may be granted even though the residence has been unlawful for the whole or part of the period. As to the meaning of continuous residence, see *TT (Long residence – 'continuous residence' – interpretation) British Overseas Citizen* [2008] UKAIT 00038.

Will a claimant lose the benefit of the 10-year rule if at any point he became an overstayer? Yes, para 276A(b) has an exhaustive definition of lawful residence: see *MD (Jamaica) v Secretary of State for the Home Department* [2010] EWCA Civ 213. However, UKBA guidance is that if an applicant has a single short gap in lawful residence through making one single previous application out of time by a few days (not usually more than 10 calendar days late unless there are extenuating reasons for this such as a postal strike, hospitalisation or an administrative error by the Home Office), caseworkers may exercise discretion to grant indefinite leave to remain provided the application meets all the other requirements. An application by a claimant with more than one gap in his lawful residence is normally refused as he would not have shown the necessary commitment to ensuring he has maintained lawful leave throughout his time in the UK.

How is the 10- or 14-year period calculated? Continuity of residence is not broken by a small number of short absences abroad of up to six months at any one time during the relevant period. Short absences cannot be said to disrupt or sever ties with the UK. These absences should normally be ignored, unless the trips are frequent. In such cases, the reasons for the frequent trips are requested by the UKBA, which will be concerned that the applicant may have a business abroad or might be maintaining family ties abroad. In some cases, a lengthier absence may still not sever the ties to the UK. In each case the strength of the ties to the UK, the reason for, and effect of, the absence are taken into account. However, continuity of residence is considered by the UKBA as being broken if:

(a) the applicant has been removed or deported (see **Chapter 10**) or has left the UK having been refused leave to enter or remain here; or

(b) the applicant has left the UK and, on doing so, evidenced a clear intention not to return; or

(c) he has left the UK in circumstances in which he could have had no reasonable expectation at the time of leaving that he would lawfully be able to return; or

(d) he has been convicted of an offence and was sentenced to a period of imprisonment or was directed to be detained in an institution other than a prison (including, in particular, a hospital or an institution for young offenders), provided that the sentence in question was not a suspended sentence; or

(e) he has spent a total of more than 18 months absent from the UK during the period in question.

What factors does the Home Office consider? The public interest is the key concern, namely that there are no reasons why it would be undesirable for the applicant to be given indefinite leave to remain on the ground of long residence, taking into account the applicant's age; strength of connections in the UK; his personal history, including character, conduct, associations and employment record; his domestic circumstances; any previous criminal record and the nature of any offence of which he has been convicted; any compassionate circumstances and any representations received on his behalf.

Indefinite leave to remain is normally granted in the absence of any strong countervailing factors. These include deliberate and blatant attempts to evade or circumvent the control, for example by using forged documents (or a false identity: see *ZH (Bangladesh) v Secretary of State for the Home Department* [2009] EWCA Civ 8); absconding and contracting a marriage of convenience. Criminal offences which are spent under the Rehabilitation of Offenders Act 1974 and behaviour which happened five years or more ago are not normally sufficient to outweigh positive ties with the UK. If the continuous residence is in excess of 14 years, indefinite leave is invariably granted unless the countervailing factors are exceptionally serious.

Example

Vijay, a citizen of India, has studied in the UK since he was sent to an English public school at the age of 13. He is now 23, has obtained a degree at an English university, and is enrolled on a postgraduate vocational course. His parents are now dead and he would like to remain in the UK rather than return to India.

Apart from occasional visits home he has been resident in the UK with leave as a student, periodically renewed. When he was 21 he failed to apply for an extension of stay in time (he was late by 3 weeks as he forgot), but the Home Office allowed him to remain to continue his studies. It is now more than 10 years since he first arrived in the UK. On his next application for an extension, will he be given indefinite leave?

As Vijay was an overstayer for a period (exceeding 10 calendar days without good reason) he has not had 10 years' continuous lawful residence in the UK, and is therefore ineligible under the 10-year provision. He must wait nearly 4 years to qualify under the 14-year provision. (He must be able to obtain extensions, or somehow remain without deliberately evading immigration control.)

3.8.9 EEA nationals

Nationals of the EEA do not need leave to enter or remain while exercising rights in EU law (see **Chapter 4**). Does this mean that while in the UK they have no restriction on the period for which they can remain and are therefore 'settled' under UK immigration law? The answer is, 'No'. However, by reg 15(1) of the I(EEA) Regs 2006 (see **4.4.9** and **Appendix 4**), EEA nationals acquire the right to reside in the UK permanently where, as a general rule, they have resided in the UK in accordance with the Regulations for a continuous period of five years. In limited circumstances, the right to reside in the UK permanently may be acquired more quickly, eg under reg 15(1) by a worker or self-employed person who has ceased activity as defined in reg 5. People falling within reg 15(1) are treated as settled for the purposes of applying for naturalisation (see **2.2.7**).

3.8.10 Criminality requirement for settlement

In April 2011 the Government introduced a requirement that any person applying for settlement under the Immigration Rules must show that he does not have any unspent convictions as defined by the Rehabilitation of Offenders Act 1974. The basic details are in **Appendix 8**.

3.9 The Common Travel Area

The Common Travel Area consists of the UK, Ireland, the Channel Islands and the Isle of Man. The basic principle, set out in s 1(3) of the IA 1971, is that persons arriving on local journeys to the UK from elsewhere in the Common Travel Area are not subject to immigration control, and no leave to enter is required. Control operates only on initial entry to the Area from outside. This is subject to some exceptions, for example under the Immigration (Control on Entry through the Republic of Ireland) Order 1972 (SI 1972/1610). This subjects some persons to immigration control (such as visa nationals without a visa for entry to the UK). If such persons enter the UK, for example, from Ireland, they are illegal entrants, even though they have never been examined by the immigration service. The 1972 Order also imposes conditions in other cases (eg where a person who is not Irish, and does not have the right of abode in the UK, travels to the UK from outside the Area, via the Republic). Usually such persons will have deemed leave to enter for three months, with a prohibition on employment and business for non-EEA nationals. As the person will not have passed through immigration control, there will be no indication of these conditions on his passport.

Chapter 4
EEA Nationals

4.1 Who are EEA nationals?

'EEA nationals' are nationals of the Member States of the European Union together with Iceland, Liechtenstein and Norway (which are parties to the European Economic Area Agreement). See **Appendix 2** to this book for the full list of relevant countries.

Note that by an Agreement on the Free Movement of Persons made between the EC (now EU) and the Swiss Confederation (Cm 4904), Swiss nationals and their family members were from 1 June 2002 given broadly similar rights of entry to and residence in the UK as are enjoyed by EEA nationals. See the Immigration (Swiss Free Movement of Persons) (No 3) Regulations 2002 (SI 2002/1241).

Nationals of Cyprus, the Czech Republic, Estonia, Hungary, Latvia, Lithuania, Malta, Poland, Slovakia and Slovenia became members of the EU on 1 May 2004 (the so-called 'Accession States').

4.2 What is their immigration status?

Nationals of the EEA have a hybrid status. They do not have the right of abode possessed by British citizens but, unlike other aliens, they do not require leave to enter or remain while exercising rights in EU law (s 7(1) of the IA 1988). Paragraph **4.3** outlines their rights in EU law. These have been implemented in UK law by the I(EEA) Regs 2006, considered in detail in the rest of this chapter.

4.3 Rights under EU law

Article 20 TFEU states that:

> 1. Citizenship of the Union is hereby established. Every person holding the nationality of a Member State shall be a citizen of the Union. Citizenship of the Union shall be additional to and not replace national citizenship.
> 2. Citizens of the Union shall enjoy the rights and be subject to the duties provided for in the Treaties.

Article 21(1) TFEU provides that:

> Every citizen of the Union shall have the right to move and reside freely within the territory of the Member States, subject to the limitations and conditions laid down in the Treaties and by the measures adopted to give them effect.

It can be seen that Article 21 TFEU provides for a right of residence and movement of EEA nationals throughout the EU. Directive 2004/38/EC of the European Parliament and Council of 29 April 2004 sets out the terms and limits of this right of movement. It is a consolidation and modernisation of existing EU secondary legislation in this area. It has been implemented into domestic law by the I(EEA) Regs 2006 (see **4.4**). This book will look at the detail of the 2006 Regs. There is a chart at **4.5** which sets out where the 2006 Regs implement the 2004 Directive. A copy of the Directive is set out in **Appendix 3**.

More detailed treatment of this topic is to be found in Part III of ***Legal Foundations***. The following is a summary of the main principles.

4.3.1 Free movement of workers

Article 45 TFEU requires free movement for workers within the Union. Article 45(3) TFEU provides that this entails the right to:

(a) accept offers of employment;

(b) move freely within the EU for this purpose;

(c) stay in a Member State for employment;

(d) remain after employment, subject to conditions.

4.3.2 Self-employed activities and establishment of businesses

Article 49 TFEU requires abolition of restrictions on the freedom of establishment of EU nationals. This freedom includes the right to pursue activities as self-employed persons, and to set up and manage undertakings such as companies or firms.

4.3.3 Provision of services

Article 56 TFEU requires abolition of the restrictions on freedom to provide services within the Community in respect of nationals of Member States who are established in a State of the Community other than that of the person for whom the services are intended.

Article 57 TFEU states that the provider of a service (including industrial, commercial, craft, and professional activities) may temporarily pursue his activity in a State where the service is provided. Permanent provision of the service would involve 'establishment'.

Freedom of movement extends not only to the providers, but also to the recipients of services. In Joined Cases 286/82 and 26/83 *Luisi (Graziana) and Carbone (Giuseppe) v Ministero del Tesoro* [1984] ECR 377, the ECJ held that this covered tourists, and those who travel for medical treatment, education or business.

Does the EEA national have to travel to another EEA country and provide services there? 'No', held the ECJ in Case C-384/93 *Alpine Investments BV v Minister van Financiën* (1995) – an offer to provide services over the telephone to potential recipients established in other Member States is sufficient. On a proper construction, Article 56 applies to services which a provider supplies, without moving from the Member State in which he is established, to recipients established in other Member States.

4.3.4 When the 2004 Directive applies

The 2004 Directive applies only to EEA nationals exercising Treaty rights. So a non-EEA national cannot directly benefit from it.

An EEA national will exercise his Treaty rights by, for example, moving to another EEA country and living there. This is the combined effect of Articles 20 and 21 TFEU (see **4.3**). The EEA national might take employment pursuant to Article 45 TFEU (see **4.3.1**), or run a business under Article 49 (see **4.3.2**). His right of entry to and residence in the host EEA country will be governed by the 2004 Directive as implemented into the domestic law of the host EEA country; as we saw at **4.3**, in the UK that means the 2006 Regs.

Examples

(1) Abdus is a citizen of Pakistan. He is a single man. He travelled from Pakistan and entered Spain, an EEA country, pursuant to domestic Spanish immigration laws. Abdus is not an EEA national. He cannot exercise Treaty rights.

(2) Marie is a French national living in Paris. She is single and an EEA national. She has a right of entry to and residence in the other EEA countries. She travels to Madrid, Spain (an EEA country) and starts working there. She is thereby exercising her Treaty rights.

(3) Boris is a German national living in Berlin. He travels to Jamaica and works there for several years. He marries Alisha, a Jamaican national. The couple decide that they want to live together in Germany. As Jamaica is not an EEA country, Boris has not exercised his Treaty rights. Alisha will have to comply with domestic German law to enter and live with Boris there.

(4) Marie, from example (2) above, meets Abdus from example (1) in Spain. They fall in love and marry. The couple subsequently decide to live together in France. As Marie is an EEA national who has exercised her Treaty rights, Abdus, as her spouse, can benefit indirectly. Rather than applying under domestic French immigration laws to enter France with Marie, he can choose to rely on EU law and enter as the spouse of an EEA national. See further **4.4.6** and **4.4.7**.

4.4 The Immigration (European Economic Area) Regulations 2006

The I(EEA) Regs 2006 enact EU law rights of free movement in UK law. A copy may be found at **Appendix 4** to this book. The immigration adviser can refer directly to the I(EEA) Regs 2006 but should be aware that, in the event that they fail to give effect to EU law, EU law will prevail. In addition, EU case law may affect the interpretation of the Regulations.

All references in the rest of this chapter are to the I(EEA) Regs 2006 unless otherwise stated.

4.4.1 Right of admission for EEA nationals (reg 11(1))

An EEA national must be admitted to the UK if he produces on arrival a valid national identity card or passport issued by an EEA State.

4.4.2 Right of admission for family members of EEA nationals (reg 11(2))

A person who is not an EEA national must be admitted to the UK if he is a family member of an EEA national and he produces on arrival a valid passport or an EEA family permit (see **4.4.7**), a residence card (see **4.4.8**) or a permanent residence card (see **4.4.10**).

The family member may be travelling with the EEA national to the UK, or joining the EEA national who is already in the UK. If the family member is travelling independently of the EEA national and not joining him in the UK then the Immigration Rules apply.

4.4.3 Initial right of residence for three months (reg 13)

An EEA national and his family member(s) are entitled to reside in the UK for a period not exceeding three months. The only condition is that the EEA national and any family member must not become an unreasonable burden on the social assistance system of the UK (see further **4.4.5.4**).

4.4.4 Residence beyond three months (reg 14)

An EEA national is entitled to reside in the UK for a period exceeding three months if he is a qualified person. Indeed, he has the right to reside in the UK for as long as he remains a qualified person. His family member(s) have the same right.

It is important to appreciate that the family member's right to reside is dependent upon the EEA national having a right to reside. The problem that arises if the EEA national dies or leaves the UK, etc is considered at **4.4.11**.

4.4.5 Who is a qualified person? (reg 6)

A qualified person is an EEA national who is in the UK in any of the following categories:

(a) a jobseeker;

(b) a worker;

(c) a self-employed person;

(d) a self-sufficient person; or

(e) a student.

4.4.5.1 Jobseeker

A 'jobseeker', as defined in reg 6(4), is an EEA national who enters the UK in order to look for employment. He must be able to provide evidence that he is seeking employment and that he has a genuine chance of securing employment.

There is no set limit on the amount of time an EEA national can spend looking for employment, although six months is often used as a rule of thumb. This is because in the case of *R v IAT, ex p Antonissen* [1991] 2 CMLR 373, the ECJ stated that

> . . . it is not contrary to the provisions of Community law governing the free movement of workers for the legislation of a Member State to provide that a national of another Member State who entered the first State in order to seek employment may be required to leave the territory of that State (subject to appeal) if he has not found employment there after six months, unless the person concerned provides evidence that he is continuing to seek employment and that he has genuine chances of being engaged.

4.4.5.2 Worker

Regulation 4(1)(a) defines a worker by a simple cross-reference to Article 45 TFEU (see **4.3.1**), namely an employee.

So what constitutes employment? Does it include part-time employment? Yes, held the ECJ in *Levin v Secretary of State for Justice* [1982] ECR 1035, although it will not include activities on such a small scale as to be regarded as purely marginal and ancillary. Work means to pursue an economic activity.

Note that by reg 6(2), an EEA national who has worked in the UK but is currently not working may in certain limited circumstances still be classified as a worker, eg if he is temporarily unable to work due to illness or accident. So a woman who ceases work because she is pregnant does not retain the status of a worker since pregnancy is not an illness: see *JS v Secretary of State for Work and Pensions* [2011] EWCA Civ 806. An employed woman will, of course, still remain a worker whilst on maternity leave.

Also note the definition of a worker who has ceased activity in reg 5(2)–(5). This includes, for example, an EEA national who has resided in the UK for more than three years and worked for at least 12 months before ceasing work when reaching retirement age, and also an EEA national who has resided in the UK for at least two years prior to termination of his work or self-employment due to a permanent disability. The definition is important, as such a person may acquire permanent residence in the UK (see **4.4.9**).

What is the difference between a worker who is 'temporarily' unable to work due to illness or accident (reg 6(2)(a)) and a worker with a 'permanent' incapacity to work (reg 5(3))? '[I]f a person's inability or incapacity is not permanent, then it should be regarded as temporary', per Blake J in *FMB (Uganda) v Secretary of State for the Home Department* [2010] UKUT 447 at para 23.

4.4.5.3 Self-employed person

Regulation 4(1)(b) defines a self-employed person by a simple cross-reference to Article 49 TFEU (see **4.3.2**).

Note that by reg 6(3), an EEA national who is temporarily unable to work due to illness or accident retains the stautus of a self-employed person.

Also note the definition of a self-employed person who has ceased activity in reg 5(2)–(5). This includes, for example, an EEA national who has had to stop work due to a permanent incapacity, and either he resided in the UK for more than two years before that incapacity or the incapacity results in him becoming entitled to a pension payable in whole or part by a UK institution. The definition is important, as such a person may acquire permanent residence in the UK (see **4.4.9**).

4.4.5.4 Self-sufficient person

A 'self-sufficient person', as defined in reg 4(1)(c), is an EEA national who has (i) sufficient resources not to become a burden on the social assistance system of the UK during his period of residence; and (ii) comprehensive sickness insurance cover in the UK. Guidance from the UKBA is that, for example, a retired person would be self-sufficient if he could demonstrate that he was in receipt of a pension and/or had sufficient funds or income from investments not to become a burden on the UK's social assistance system. Can resources supplied by another person be taken into account? Yes: see *Commission v Belgium* [2006] ECR I-2647.

Is a set amount of money required to demonstrate self-sufficiency? Directive 2004/58 EC, Article 8(4) prohibits this. However, reg 4(4) provides that a person's resources are regarded as sufficient if they exceed the maximum level of resources which a UK national and his family members may possess if he is to become eligible for social assistance under the UK benefit system.

If an EEA national claims a UK 'minimum subsistence benefit' like income support or income-based jobseeker's allowance, at what point might he become an unreasonable burden on the UK's welfare benefits system? The UK Government should carry out a proportionality test, and recital 16 of the 2004 Directive suggests that the following questions need to be posed and answered:

(1) Duration
- For how long is the benefit being granted?
- Outlook: is it likely that the EEA citizen will get out of the safety net soon?
- How long has the residence lasted in the UK?

(2) Personal situation
- What is the level of connection of the EEA citizen and his family members with the society of the UK?
- Are there any considerations pertaining to age, state of health, family and economic situation that need to be taken into account?

(3) Amount
- Total amount of aid granted?
- Does the EEA citizen have a history of relying heavily on social assistance?
- Does the EEA citizen have a history of contributing to the financing of social assistance in the UK?

Only receipt of social assistance benefits can be considered relevant to determining whether the person concerned is a burden on the UK's social assistance system. As long as the beneficiaries of the right of residence do not become an unreasonable burden on the social assistance system of the UK, they cannot be expelled for this reason.

Is the requirement that the EEA national has comprehensive sickness insurance cover in the UK strictly enforced? Yes. It is not a mere formality but an integral part of the concept of self-sufficiency under the Regulations: see *Kamau (Kenya) v Secretary of State for the Home Department* [2010] EWCA Civ 1302.

4.4.5.5 Student

A 'student', according to reg 4(1)(d), is an EEA national who:

(a) is enrolled at a private or public establishment, included on the Department for Education and Skills' Register of Education and Training Providers or financed from public funds, for the principal purpose of following a course of study, including vocational training;

(b) has comprehensive sickness insurance cover in the UK; and

(c) assures the Secretary of State, by means of a declaration, or by such equivalent means as the person may choose, that he has sufficient resources not to become a burden on the social assistance system of the UK during his period of residence.

4.4.6 Who is a family member of an EEA national?

Under reg 7, as a general rule, the following are family members of an EEA national:

(a) his spouse or his civil partner;

(b) direct descendants (children, grandchildren, etc) of him, his spouse or his civil partner who are—

  (i) under 21, or

  (ii) dependants of him, his spouse or his civil partner;

(c) dependent direct relatives in his ascending line (parents, grandparents, etc) or that of his spouse or his civil partner.

4.4.6.1 Spouse or civil partner

A spouse or civil partner ((a) in **4.4.6** above) will not cease to be a family member in the event of marital breakdown or separation as long as the EEA national continues to exercise Treaty rights in the same Member State: see *Diatta v Land Berlin* [1985] ECR 567 and *Amos v Secretary of State for the Home Department* [2011] EWCA Civ 552. The right of residence will continue until any divorce is finalised by decree absolute, or until a civil partnership is dissolved. See further **4.4.11**.

4.4.6.2 Marriage or civil partnership of convenience

Note that by reg 2, a 'spouse' does not include a party to a marriage of convenience; and a 'civil partner' does not include a party to a civil partnership of convenience.

The 'convenience' referred to involves the non-EEA national seeking to obtain a right of residence in the UK under EU law by marriage to, or entering into a civil partnership with, an EEA national. That might occur whilst the parties are outside the UK, and so the non-EEA national seeks to enter under an EEA family permit (see **4.4.7**), or whilst they are in the UK. The objective is to avoid UK domestic immigration law. Typically, but not always, it takes place after the non-EEA national has been refused entry clearance or leave to remain in the UK.

Article 35 of the 2004 Directive (see **Appendix 3**) allows the UK Government to refuse, terminate or withdraw any rights conferred on the non-EEA national in these circumstances, provided that is a proportionate response, taking into account Article 8 of the ECHR (see **Appendix 5**), and subject to the safeguards in Articles 30 and 31 of the Directive. Further details may be found in Pt 4 of the I(EEA) Regs 2006 (see **Appendix 4**).

What factors might suggest a marriage or civil partnership of convenience? In *TC (Kenya) v Secretary of State for the Home Department* [2008] EWCA Civ 543, the Court of Appeal indicated that these may include the fact that the marriage occurs after the non-EEA national has been refused leave to remain under domestic law; that the application for a residence certificate or card (see **4.4.8**) is made quickly after the marriage or civil partnership ceremony; a lack of financial support between the parties; a considerable difference in age or background between the parties; no common language; the limited time that the parties to the relationship spend together; lack of cohabitation; the length of time which any party spends abroad without any compensating cohabitation whilst in the UK; the fact that the couple never go away together on holiday; one party being vague about the other's movements; the lack of credibility or reliability of a party as a witness; and limited (or no) supporting evidence from family and friends about the relationship between the parties.

The UKBA has published its policy in this area. Factors taken into account by an ECO when considering an application for a family permit include:

(a) *Evidence of previous relationship*. In all cases, in order to refuse on the basis of a marriage of convenience, an ECO must be satisfied that there is little or no evidence of a relationship between the applicant and the EEA national. An applicant might provide email exchanges, letters, joint bank accounts, photographs, etc to show evidence of their relationship.

There are a number of other factors which may cause an ECO to suspect that the applicant is party to a marriage of convenience. The following may raise doubts as to the credibility of a relationship:

(b) *The applicant has an adverse immigration history*. The applicant may have had previous entry clearance applications refused or had otherwise attempted to gain entry or leave to remain in the UK, eg a failed asylum application.

(c) *Intention to live together in the UK*. The applicant and the EEA national should generally intend to live together in the UK. This should be evidenced by a clear commitment from both parties that they will do so following the outcome of the application.

(d) *Claims of previous marriage*. The applicant may have previously claimed to be married to someone else. In such cases they should produce documentary evidence of that marriage being dissolved.

(e) *Reason to question the plausibility of the marriage*. For example, factors may include considerable differences in age and background or where the applicant and EEA national have no common language.

(f) *A sum of money has been handed over in order for the marriage to be contracted*. This would not include money given in the form of a dowry in the cases of nationals of countries where the provision of a dowry is common practice.

To summarise: first, the UK Government will need to demonstrate that the marriage or civil partnership is one of convenience, secondly, before deciding to refuse an EEA family permit or withdraw any residence card and expel the non-EEA national, the issues of proportionality and Article 8 ECHR must be addressed.

4.4.6.3 Direct descendants

The direct descendants ((b) in **4.4.6** above) of the EEA national, his spouse or civil partner also count. So this will include children, grandchildren, great-grandchildren etc who are either under 21 years of age or dependent on the EEA national, his spouse or civil partner. As to dependency, see **4.4.6.7**.

'Children' include step-children, and adopted children provided that the adoption is recognised by the UK.

4.4.6.4 Dependent direct relatives in ascending line

The parents, grandparents, etc of the EEA national and his spouse or civil partner count. As to dependency, see **4.4.6.7**.

4.4.6.5 Family members of a student after three months

Whilst the list of those who constitute family members in **4.4.6** above is the general rule, there is a major exception. Once a student has been residing in the UK for a period of three months, his family members are limited to (i) his spouse or his civil partner, and (ii) his dependent children or those of his civil partner.

4.4.6.6 Other (extended) family members

What about direct descendants (children, etc) aged 21 or over, or direct relatives in the ascending line (parents, etc) who cannot show dependency? What about other relatives, such as brothers and sisters, uncles and aunts, cousins, etc? These may fall within reg 8, which deals with 'extended family members'. These are any of the following:

(a) a person who is a relative of an EEA national, his spouse or his civil partner and –
   (i) who is residing in a country other than the United Kingdom with the EEA national and who is either dependent upon the EEA national or a member of his household,
   (ii) who satisfied the condition in para (i) and is accompanying the EEA national to the UK or wishes to join him here, or
   (iii) who satisfied the condition in para (i), has joined the EEA national in the UK and continues to be either dependent upon him or a member of his household;

(b) a person who is a relative of an EEA national, or his spouse or his civil partner and, on serious health grounds, who strictly requires the personal care of the EEA national, his spouse or his civil partner;

(c) a person who is a relative of an EEA national and who would meet the requirements in the Immigration Rules (other than those relating to entry clearance) for indefinite leave to enter or remain in the UK as a dependent relative of the EEA national were the EEA national a person present and settled in the UK (see **8.10**);

(d) a person who is the partner of an EEA national (other than a civil partner) and who can prove to the decision maker that he is in a durable relationship akin to marriage or a civil partnership with the EEA national. The UKBA advises that the test it imposes is similar to that in Immigration Rules, para 295A (see **8.8**). Note that the fiancé(e) or proposed civil partner of an EEA national is not his or her family member under EU law. Such a person would have to apply under the Immigration Rules, para 290 (see **8.7.3**).

In category (a), when is someone a member of the EEA national's household? The UKBA guidance is that the family member should normally have lived with the EEA national under the same roof for at least six months.

In category (a), evidence is required of recent dependency or recent household membership. Historic but lapsed dependency or membership is irrelevant to the Directive policy of removing obstacles to the Union citizen's freedom of movement and residence rights: see *Bigia v Entry Clearance Officer* [2009] EWCA Civ 79 and *SM (India) v Entry Clearance Officer* [2009] EWCA Civ 1426.

What are the requirements in order to meet category (b) above? The Tribunal in *TR (reg 8(3) EEA Regs 2006) Sri Lanka* [2008] UKAIT 00004 held that the 'serious health grounds' need to be significantly beyond ordinary ill-health and require detailed medical evidence in support. Personal care must be provided on a day-to-day basis and relate either or both to the physical and mental tasks and needs required for a person to function. 'Strictly' is a restrictive or limiting requirement and imports a need for complete compliance or exact performance, and reinforces the need for personal care to be provided on a day to day basis.

For further UKBA guidance on extended family members, see **4.4.6.8** below.

4.4.6.7 Meaning of dependency

Some of the above categories have a test of dependency on the EEA national. Guidance from the UKBA is that the dependency may be one of choice rather than necessity, but the definition of 'dependency' includes only financial dependency and not emotional dependency. Financial dependency might be shown by the family member being unemployed.

According to the case of *Lebon* [1987] ECR 2811, the status of 'dependent' family member is the result of a situation characterised by the fact that material support for that family member is provided by the EEA national, or by his spouse or partner. In order to determine whether a family member is dependent, it must be assessed in the individual case whether, having regard to his financial and social conditions, he needs material support to meet his essential needs in his country of origin or the country from which he came at the time when he applied to join the EEA national (ie not in the host Member State where the EEA national resides).

In the case of *Jia* [2007] ECR I-0001, when addressing the concept of dependency, the Court did not refer to any level of standard of living for determining the need for financial support by the EEA national. The 2004 Directive does not lay down any requirement as to the minimum duration of the dependency, or the amount of material support provided, as long as the dependency is genuine and structural in character.

In *Bigia v Entry Clearance Officer* [2009] EWCA Civ 79, the Court stated that the dependency test was met where the EEA national provided his adult daughter with rent-free accommodation and sent her money on a regular basis for 'bills, daily expenses and clothes'. She had no other source of income. The Court concluded that without that support she would be unable to meet her essential needs.

4.4.6.8 The UKBA guidance on extended family members

Guidance from the UKBA is that Directive 2004/38 refers in Article 3 only to facilitating the entry and residence of extended family members. When deciding whether to issue a residence card, the UKBA must assess whether refusal would deter the EEA national from exercising his EC Treaty rights, or would create an effective obstacle to the exercise of those rights. An example is given that it might be appropriate to issue a residence card where the family member was very elderly or incapacitated. In assessing such a case the UKBA states that it would be important to consider whether there were relatives to care for the person in the home country.

In considering cases under reg 8, the UKBA normally refuses those who have, for example, their own family unit (unless there are sufficient compassionate circumstances), or who lived as part of the EEA national's household many years ago.

4.4.7 Does a family member need a travel document? (reg 12)

To be admitted to the UK, a family member should apply to an entry clearance officer for a travel document known as an EEA family permit before travelling to the UK. It is required only where the family member is not an EEA national. In order to obtain the permit the family member will have to produce documentation demonstrating the relationship with the EEA national (eg marriage certificate, etc).

4.4.8 How can an EEA national or family member confirm his right of residence?

Under regs 16 and 17, an EEA national or a non-EEA family member entitled to residence can apply to the Secretary of State for a residence certificate or residence card respectively. A residence certificate or card is normally valid for five years.

A family member may find it useful to obtain a residence card, particularly when applying for employment, as it confirms his entitlement to take employment in the UK. Also, if he leaves the UK, it will prove his right of re-entry (otherwise he will need to obtain an EEA family permit: see **4.4.7**).

4.4.9 Permanent right of residence in UK (reg 15)

The following persons can acquire the right to reside in the UK permanently:

(a) an EEA national who has resided in the UK in accordance with the 2006 Regulations for a continuous period of five years;

(b) a family member of an EEA national (who is not himself an EEA national) who has resided in the UK with the EEA national in accordance with the 2006 Regs for a continuous period of five years;

(c) a worker or self-employed person who has ceased activity;

(d) the family member of a worker or self-employed person who has ceased activity;

(e) a person who was the family member of a worker or self-employed person where –

  (i) the worker or self-employed person has died,

  (ii) the family member resided with him immediately before his death, and

  (iii) the worker or self-employed person had resided continuously in the UK for at least the two years immediately before his death, or the death was the result of an accident at work or an occupational disease;

(f) a person who –

  (i) has resided in the UK in accordance with the 2006 Regulations for a continuous period of five years; and

  (ii) was, at the end of that period, a family member who has retained the right of residence.

So as to (a) this would include an EEA national who works in the UK for two years and then is unable to work for the next three years due to illness – this person would initially be a worker as defined in reg 6(1)(b) and would remain a worker when subsequently temporarily unable to work due to illness under reg 6(2)(a). The Home Office may well require medical evidence that there was a genuine inability to work during those three years. These are the facts of *FMB (Uganda) v Secretary of State for the Home Department* [2010] UKUT 447.

Note that as to (b) above (and subject to reg 10: see **4.4.11**), the family member must have held that status for five years. So an extended family member who was in a durable relationship with an EEA national but whose relationship breaks down before he fulfils the five-year requirement is excluded: see *CS (Brazil) v Secretary of State for the Home Department* [2009] EWCA Civ 480.

In (b) above, does the 'residing with' requirement relate just to presence in the UK or does it require living in a common family home? In *PM v Secretary of State for the Home Department* [2011] UKUT 246, the Tribunal held the former. So, in respect of a spouse, (b) is met where the couple entered a genuine marriage; both parties have resided in the UK for five years since the marriage; the EEA national's spouse has resided as the family member of a qualified person or otherwise in accordance with the Regulations and the marriage has not been dissolved. Obviously, if the parties have separated there may be an issue as to whether the marriage is one of convenience (see **4.4.6.2**). But that did not apply in the case as there was genuine matrimonial cohabitation for some time, a child had been born to the couple and there were continuing social relations by the parties to the marriage in the context of contact with the child.

Note that as to (c) above (a worker or self-employed person who has ceased activity) this category of person is defined by reg 5. So, for example, it includes a worker or self-employed person who has to stop work as a result of a permanent incapacity (see **4.4.5.2**) and who had resided in the UK continuously for more than two years prior to his work ending.

Some of the above categories are based on a period of continuous residence in the UK. What about any periods of absence? Regulation 3 provides that continuity of residence is not affected by:

(a) periods of absence from the UK which do not exceed six months in total in any year;

(b) periods of absence from the UK on military service; or

(c) any one absence from the UK not exceeding 12 months for an important reason, such as pregnancy and childbirth, serious illness, study or vocational training, or an overseas posting.

Is any period of continuous residence in the UK broken if the person is imprisoned? Yes, see *C v Secretary of State for the Home Department* [2010] EWCA Civ 1406, as 'the worker is not legally resident in the host state as an EEA worker during the period of imprisonment and that any period, which includes that period of imprisonment, cannot be part of the necessary "continuous" period for the purpose of calculating the five years continuous legal residence necessary to acquire the right permanently to reside here' (per Longmore LJ at [47]).

Can the right of permanent residence be lost once acquired? Yes, but only through absence from the UK for a period exceeding two consecutive years.

4.4.10 How can an EEA national or family member confirm his permanent residence?

Under reg 18, an EEA national or non-EEA family member entitled to permanent residence can apply to the Secretary of State for a document certifying permanent residence or a permanent residence card respectively.

A document certifying permanent residence does not have an expiry date. A permanent residence card is valid for 10 years and is renewable.

4.4.11 What is the status of a family member who has not acquired permanent residence on the death or departure from the UK of the qualified person, or the termination of marriage or civil partnership?

Until a family member acquires his own right of permanent residence he is in a vulnerable position: What if the qualified person dies or leaves the UK? If his right of residence is dependent on marriage to, or on a civil partnership with, a qualified person, what is his immigration status when that relationship formally ends?

The answer is to be found in reg 10, which allows certain family members to retain the right of residence. This includes, for example, a person who:

(a) is a family member of a qualified person when the qualified person dies;

(b) resided in the UK in accordance with the 2006 Regs for at least the year immediately before the death of the qualified person; and

(c) if he had been an EEA national himself, would qualify as a worker, a self-employed person or a self-sufficient person as defined by reg 6, or who is the family member of a person who was a worker, a self-employed person or a self-sufficient person as defined by reg 6.

A non-EEA ex-spouse or ex-civil partner may be able to rely on reg 10(5)(d)(i) where:

(a) His or her divorce [or termination of civil partnership is] from the EEA national.

(b) He or she was residing in the UK in accordance with the Regulations at the date of the divorce [or termination of civil partnership]. He or she will have been so residing if regulation 14 applied, ie if the EEA national spouse [or civil partner] was a 'qualified person', ie, for present purposes, a worker or self-employed person (as to which see the definitions in regulations 2 and 6).

(c) He or she is a worker or self-employed person, and therefore satisfies paragraph (6).

(d) 3 years' marriage, including at least one year's residence in the UK.

(per Stanley Burnton LJ at [30] in *Amos v Secretary of State for the Home Department* [2011] EWCA Civ 552).

How might the applicant show (b) above? Payslips, bank statements, accounts, letters from employers or customers may help. On appeal to the tribunal (see **Chapter 11**) the applicant may be able to apply for a witness summons requiring his or her ex-spouse or ex-civil partner to attend and give evidence. Additionally, or alternatively, a direction can be sought requiring the Secretary of State to provide any information necessary for the determination of the appeal.

What must an applicant show to meet (d) above? That prior to starting proceedings for divorce or the termination of the civil partnership, the marriage or civil partnership had lasted for at least three years and the parties had resided in the UK for at least one year during that time. Note, however, that reg 10(5)(d) does include alternative qualifying tests.

The UKBA guidance is that it will normally revoke, or refuse to issue or renew, a residence card where a family member's marriage to, or civil partnership with, a qualified person terminates, or there is evidence that the EEA national has left the UK, unless the family member has retained the right of residence under reg 10.

The burden is on the applicant to show that the conditions under which the right of residence is said to be retained are met: *Okafor v Secretary of State for the Home Department* [2011] EWCA Civ 499.

Can a family member who retains the right of residence ever acquire permanent residence? Yes, after five years' continuous residence in the UK, provided that has been in accordance with the 2006 Regs (see **4.4.9**).

4.4.12 British citizens who exercise Treaty rights and then return to the UK (reg 9)

If a British citizen travels to another EEA country to work or otherwise exercise Treaty rights, he is entitled to be accompanied by, or later joined by, his family members. Equally, if a British citizen travels to the UK from an EEA country after exercising Treaty rights there as a worker or self-employed person, his family may accompany him. So, for example, the Indian spouse of a British citizen who has worked in another EEA country may take advantage of Article 44 TFEU, acquiring rights of residence in the UK itself beyond those given by UK immigration law – see *R v Immigration Appeal Tribunal and Surinder Singh, ex p Secretary of State for the Home Department* [1992] 3 CMLR 358. The facts of the case were as follows.

Mr Singh, an Indian national, married a British citizen in the UK in 1982. At no time did the authorities allege that the marriage was a sham. It appears that Mr Singh was lawfully in the UK, but his immigration status is not clear from the case report. In 1983 Mr and Mrs Singh went to Germany, where they were both employed for two years. At the end of 1985 the couple returned to the UK to open a business. The ECJ held that the provisions of the Council Regulations and Directives on freedom of movement within the Community for employed and self-employed persons provide that Member States must grant the spouse and children of such a person rights of residence equivalent to those granted to the person himself. A national of a Member State might be deterred from leaving his country of origin in order to pursue an activity as an employed or self-employed person as envisaged by the Treaty in the territory of another Member State if, on returning to the Member State of which he is a national in order to pursue an activity there as an employed or self-employed person, the conditions of his entry and residence were not at least equivalent to those which he would enjoy under the Treaty or secondary law in the territory of another Member State. He would in particular be deterred from so doing if his spouse and children were not also permitted to enter and reside in the territory of his Member State of origin under conditions at least equivalent to those granted them by Community law in the territory of another Member State.

Regulation 9 is said to give effect to the *Surinder Singh* judgment.

4.4.12.1 Regulation 9(2)(a)

Where a UK national is residing in an EEA State as a worker or self-employed person, or was so residing before returning to the UK, he is entitled to be accompanied by his family members (spouse, civil partner, partner in a durable relationship, child under 21, etc: see **4.4.6**).

The UKBA advises that the UK national must either have been employed in an EEA State other than on a transient or casual basis, or have established himself there as a self-employed person. As a rule of thumb it is said that the UK national should have carried out such an activity for at least six months. It might be less if he was required to return to the UK earlier for a good reason, eg health grounds.

Does reg 9(2)(a) require that the UK national must be residing in an EEA State as a worker or self-employed person immediately before returning to the UK? No, held the Upper Tribunal in *OB (Morocco) v Secretary of State for the Home Department* [2010] UKUT 420. In the case the UK national married a national of Morocco in August 2006 whilst both were in the Republic of Ireland. The couple stayed there until July 2008. During that time the UK national worked from November 2006 to April 2007. In July 2008 the UK national returned to Northern Ireland, UK (where she had previously lived) to live and work there permanently. Her husband joined her and in September 2008 he applied for a residence card as the spouse of a UK national who had exercised Treaty rights. This application was refused. The Tribunal stated that the link between the UK national's right under EU law to reside and work in the Republic of Ireland and her right to return to the UK accompanied by her family members had not been broken. Further, in general, a period of interruption of employment for maternity and child rearing purposes, temporary illness or involuntary unemployment would also not break such a link.

Does it make any difference if the British citizen deliberately went to another EEA country and worked there in order that he might use EU rather than domestic law to bring a family member back to the UK? No, held the ECJ in *Secretary of State for the Home Department v Akrich* [2003] 3 CMLR 26, provided the British citizen was properly a worker and, in the case of a spouse or civil partner, the relationship is genuine and not one of convenience. As to the latter, see **4.4.6.2**.

4.4.12.2 Regulation 9(2)(b)

If the family member of the UK national is his or her spouse or civil partner, there are additional requirements. Either:

(a) the couple are living together in the EEA State before the UK national returns to the UK; or

(b) the couple entered into the marriage or civil partnership and were living together in the EEA State before the UK national returned to the UK.

4.4.12.3 Rights of family members

UKBA guidance is that because EEA nationals have an initial three-month right of residence in the UK (see **4.4.3**), there is no requirement for the British citizen to be the equivalent of a qualified person on arrival back in the UK. However, the first two questions on the application form for an EEA family permit are: what is the main purpose of your visit to the UK, and how long do you intend to stay in the UK? Detailed disclosure is then required of the couple's financial situation, as well as details of where they intend to live in the UK, etc. If an ECO takes the view that after three months in the UK the British citizen will not then be the equivalent of a qualified person (see **4.4.4**), it is possible that the application may be refused. However, note that UKBA guidance is that where the ECO has strong grounds to doubt that the EEA (or thereby British) national is, or will be, a qualified person, he should first interview the couple.

Additionally, a family permit might be refused on public policy, public health or public security grounds (see **4.4.14**) or, where the non-EEA national is the spouse or civil partner of the British national, that the relationship is one of convenience (see **4.4.6.2**).

On entering the UK the family member will be entitled to a residence card (see **4.4.8**) and, in due course, permanent residence (see **4.4.9**) under the same conditions as any family member of an EEA national.

If the family member of the UK national is his spouse or civil partner, he has the choice of entry under EU law or domestic law (see **8.3**). If he chooses EU law and is successful, he will be issued with a family permit and a residence card. He may qualify for permanent residence after five years. Compare this to domestic law, where settled status can be acquired after two years (see **8.3.6**).

Is it discrimination under EU law that the spouse of an EEA national has to wait five years (rather than two years as applies under UK domestic law – see **8.3.6**) to potentially gain settled status? The ECJ answered that question in the negative when considering the point in the case of *Kaba v Secretary of State for the Home Department* (Case C-356/98) [2000] All ER (EC) 537. The ECJ held that there was no discrimination contrary to Community law.

4.4.13 Summary of key terms

'Qualified person'	An EEA national who is exercising Treaty rights as a jobseeker; worker; self-employed person; a self-sufficient person or student.
'EEA family permit'	A form of entry clearance issued to a non-EEA national who is the family member of an EEA national.
'Registration certificate'	This is issued to an EEA national who is exercising Treaty rights (reg 16).
'Residence card'	This is issued to a non-EEA national who is the family member of a qualified person (reg 17).
'A document certifying permanent residence'	This is issued to an EEA national who has been residing in the UK for at least five years exercising Treaty rights (reg 18).
'A permanent residence card'	This is issued to a non-EEA national who is the family member of a qualified person, when he has resided for at least five years with a qualified person, who, during those five years has exercised Treaty rights (reg 18).

4.4.14 Excluding and removing an EEA national from the UK

Regulation 19 of the I(EEA) Regs 2006 provides for the exclusion and removal of an EEA national or his family member who has ceased to qualify, or whose removal is justified on the grounds of public policy pursuant to reg 21. Note that protection from removal is enhanced if the person has a permanent right of residence after five years ('serious grounds of public policy or public security' are required under reg 21(3))) and further enhanced after continuous residence of 10 years ('imperative grounds of public security' are required under reg 21(4))). As to the meaning of these terms, see *VP (Italy) v Secretary of State for the Home Department* [2010] EWCA Civ 806. Further, note that in *HR (Portugal) v Secretary of State for the Home Department* [2009] EWCA Civ 371 it was held that both these qualifying periods must consist of lawful residence and so do not include time spent in prison.

For a person to be excluded or removed on public policy grounds under reg 21, he must present a serious threat to the fundamental interests of society by his personal conduct. Guidance from the UKBA provides that previous criminal convictions are not in themselves sufficient grounds, unless the offence(s) are particularly serious (eg rape, murder, drug smuggling) and it is likely that the person will reoffend. A person charged with minor customs offences is not refused admission on that basis alone, whereas a person who is the leader of an extreme political party might present such a threat. Facilitation of illegal entry may, in itself, be sufficient grounds to refuse admission to EEA nationals. National security can also fall under this heading.

Public security under reg 21 does not necessarily equate with national security. Public security may also be a matter of personal security within society. Certain medical conditions (eg drug addiction or profound mental disturbance) may pose a threat to public policy or public security. These conditions might provide reasons for exclusion on public policy or public security grounds, but not on public health grounds.

As to public health, only a disease that has epidemic potential as defined by the World Health Organisation, or a disease to which s 38 of the Public Health (Control of Disease) Act 1984 applies (detention in hospital of a person with a notifiable disease), will constitute a ground for a decision to exclude or remove. However, if the person concerned is in the UK, any disease occurring after the initial three-month period does not count.

The UKBA guidance is that once it is established that the threat posed by a person is sufficient in principle to justify his deportation on grounds of public policy or security under EU law, there will be a presumption that the public interest requires deportation. Regulation 21(5)(a) of the I(EEA) Regs 2006 requires such a decision to deport to comply with the principle of proportionality. Regulation 21(6) lists the type of considerations that must be taken into account, such as age; state of health; family and economic situation; length of residence in the UK; social and cultural integration into the UK and the person's links with his country of origin. The proportionality test under EU law requires that any interference with a person's free movement rights must be both appropriate in the circumstances of the case and go no further than is necessary to achieve the public policy or public security need; and the consideration of proportionality encompasses human rights considerations.

4.5 Chart cross-referencing key aspects of 2006 Regulations and 2004 Directive

Coverage	2006 Regulations	2004 Directive
Definitions	reg 2 'EEA national'	Art 2 'Union citizen'
	reg 7 'family member' reg 8 'extended family member'	Art 2 Art 3(2)
Right of entry	reg 11	Art 5
Initial right of residence up to 3 months	reg 13	Art 6
Right of residence for more than 3 months	reg 14	Art 7
Issue of residence cards	reg 17	Art 10
Retention of right of residence by family members on death or departure of qualified person	reg 10	Art 12
Retention of right of residence by family members on formal ending of marriage or registered civil partnership with qualified person	reg 10	Art 13
Right of permanent residence	reg 15	Arts 16, 17 and 18
A document certifying permanent residence	reg 18	Art 19
A permanent residence card	reg 18	Art 20
Continuity of residence	reg 3	Art 21
Protection against expulsion	reg 21	Art 28
Public health	reg 21	Art 29

Chapter 5
Visitors

5.1 Introduction – who is a visitor?

A person may want to enter the UK temporarily as a visitor for many different reasons – for a holiday, to visit family or friends, to conduct some sort of business, to have private medical treatment, get married or enter into a civil partnership, etc. Part 2 of the Immigration Rules deals with these different routes into the UK for a visitor, and we shall look at the key categories in this chapter.

5.1.1 Entry clearance

Except in the case of visa nationals (see **1.4.3**), no entry clearance is required for a visit to the UK of up to six months. So it is possible for non-visa nationals (see **1.4.4**) to arrive in the UK and seek leave to enter. It may, however, reduce any potential problems for those who are not simply tourists, if entry clearance is obtained in advance.

5.1.2 Leave to enter and conditions

Most kinds of visitors under Part 2 will be given leave to enter the UK for a period not exceeding six months, subject to a condition prohibiting employment (see **3.3.1**). Like all limited leave entrants, all visitors will also be subject to the condition not to have recourse to public funds (also see **3.3.2**).

5.1.3 Frequency of visits

Is there any restriction on the number of visits a person may make to the UK? Is there any requirement that a specified period of time must elapse between successive visits? The answer to both these questions is 'No'. The UKBA's guidance is that a person who has made a series of visits to the UK with only brief intervals between them would not, in the absence of any other relevant factors, be refused entry as a visitor. However, an immigration officer will consider the stated purpose of a visit in light of the length of time that has elapsed since previous visits. As a rule of thumb, a visitor should not normally spend more than six out of any 12 months in the UK.

Note that the UKBA accepts that, occasionally, a business visitor (see **5.6**) may be required to stay for a period of weeks or even months in the UK, for example where machinery is being installed or faults are being diagnosed and corrected. An immigration officer should be satisfied, however, that a person's presence in the UK on business for more than six out of any 12 months does not mean that he is basing himself here and holding down a specific post which constitutes employment, and which would therefore require the individual to seek entry under the points-based system (see **Chapter 7**).

5.2 General visitor

For the purposes of paras 41 to 46 of the Immigration Rules, a general visitor includes a person living and working outside the UK who wishes to enter or remain in the UK as a tourist.

5.2.1 Requirements

The requirements to be met by a person seeking leave to enter the UK as a general visitor are set out in para 41, namely, that he:

(a) is genuinely seeking entry as a general visitor for a limited period as stated by him not exceeding six months, or not exceeding 12 months in the case of a person seeking entry to accompany an academic visitor (see **5.6.2**), provided in the latter case that the visitor accompanying the academic visitor has entry clearance (para 41(i)); and

(b) intends to leave the United Kingdom at the end of the period of the visit as stated by him (para 41(ii)); and

(c) does not intend to take employment in the United Kingdom (para 41(iii)); and

(d) does not intend to produce goods or provide services within the United Kingdom, including the selling of goods or services direct to members of the public (para 41(iv)); and

(e) does not intend to undertake a course of study (para 41(v)); and

(f) will maintain and accommodate himself and any dependants adequately out of resources available to him without recourse to public funds or taking employment; or will, with any dependants, be maintained and accommodated adequately by relatives or friends (para 41(vi)); and

(g) can meet the cost of the return or onward journey (para 41(vii)); and

(h) is not a child under the age of 18 (see **5.3**) (para 41(viii)); and

(i) does not intend to do any of the activities provided for in paras 46G(iii), 46M(iii) or 46S(iii) (see **5.6**) (para 41(ix)); and

(j) does not, during his visit, intend to marry or form a civil partnership, or to give notice of marriage or civil partnership (see **5.7**) (para 41(x)); and

(k) does not intend to receive private medical treatment during his visit (see **5.8**) (para 41(xi)); and

(l) is not in transit to a country outside the Common Travel Area (see **5.11**) (para 41(xii)).

5.2.1.1 UKBA policy

What should have struck you when reading the requirements in para 41 for a general visitor, is that most concern the applicant's intention. So he must *genuinely* be seeking entry as a general visitor and *intend* to leave the UK at the end of his visit, and he must *not intend* to take employment, etc whilst in the UK. It is therefore not surprising that the UKBA's policy focuses as follows on the credibility of a passenger seeking entry to the UK:

> The fact that a passenger claiming to be a visitor may be able to produce a return ticket (and other supporting evidence) does not guarantee that he intends to abide by his conditions of stay or that his intention to leave at the end of his visit is genuine. All documents produced by a passenger should be assessed in conjunction with any other evidence, however circumstantial, which may be relevant to the case.
>
> If there are any doubts as to a passenger's intentions, it is essential to obtain and record not only his statements as to his intentions but also full details of his background.

> A visitor's proposed purpose in coming to the United Kingdom must bear some reasonable relationship to his financial means and his family, social and economic background. Previous immigration history and evidence of a pattern of family migration, both here and abroad, are also matters to be taken into account.
>
> If a passenger or his sponsor is shown to have attempted to deceive the immigration officer or some other person in some material respect or where there are material discrepancies between what the passenger and his sponsor say, when the sponsor can reasonably have been expected to know the facts, these are again grounds for doubting the passenger's credibility and not therefore being satisfied as to his intentions.

Example

Ada, aged 22, is a non-visa national. She arrives in the UK without an entry certificate. She informs the immigration officer that she is visiting her sister in the UK for six months. When questioned, she discloses that:

(a) she recently lost her job;

(b) she will be looking after her sister's children whilst she is in the UK because her sister and brother-in-law have just got jobs;

(c) her sister will not pay her but will provide her with food and accommodation;

(d) she has only a few pounds in cash on her;

(e) her sister bought her a one-way ticket to the UK.

The immigration officer may decide that she does not meet the requirements of para 41, as follows:

(a) Ada is not genuinely seeking entry as a general visitor for six months; rather, her purpose is to enter the UK to be a childminder for her sister and brother-in-law indefinitely.

(b) Ada does not intend to leave the UK after six months, especially as she has no return ticket and no apparent means of saving enough money to buy one whilst in the UK.

(c) Ada intends to take unpaid employment.

(d) Ada has no evidence to support her claim that she will be maintained and accommodated adequately by her sister.

(e) Ada has no evidence that she can meet the cost of her return journey after six months.

Note that in addition, the immigration officer will have consulted the UKBA guidance on a general visitor acting as a temporary childminder for a relative. This will give an additional reason for refusing the application, as the childminding arrangement appears to have come about simply to enable Ada's sister and brother-in-law to take gainful employment.

5.2.2 Leave to enter

By para 42, a person seeking leave to enter to the UK as a general visitor may be admitted for a period not exceeding six months (or not exceeding 12 months in the case of a person accompanying an academic visitor – see **5.6.2**), subject to a condition prohibiting employment (see **3.3.1**). Like all limited leave entrants, he will also be subject to the condition not to have recourse to public funds (also see **3.3.2**).

5.2.3 Multi-entry visa

Visit visas are normally valid for six months, 12 months, two years, five years and 10 years. A visa is valid for unlimited journeys within its period of validity. However, a person with a visit visa may remain in the UK for a maximum of only six months on any one visit, or until the visa expires if less than six months.

5.2.4 Written statements and undertakings

As we have seen at **5.2.1**, a general visitor must demonstrate that he intends to enter the UK for the purpose of a visit, say with family or friends, or simply as a tourist, and that he will leave the UK. The UKBA guidance is that in exceptional circumstances, where the application would normally be refused but the person is given the benefit of the doubt, it may ask the applicant to sign a written statement of his declared intentions. If a person then acted in contradiction to such a written statement by applying in the UK for leave to remain, the Home Office would normally refuse that leave under para 322(7) of the Immigration Rules (see further **3.6.5**).

Applications for leave to enter as a general visitor are often supported by a family member or a friend in the UK. Such a person may offer to sponsor the proposed visitor formally, ie enter into a written undertaking to be responsible for the visitor's maintenance and accommodation during the visitor's stay (see **3.3.2**).

5.2.5 Leave to enter as visitor under Approved Destination Status Agreement with China

This Agreement allows groups of Chinese tourists to enter the UK. A very limited number of designated tour operators have been accredited and trained by the British Embassy in China, and these may submit visa applications to the British Embassy for each member of the proposed tour group. The details are to be found in para 56G.

5.3 Child visitor

A child is a person under the age of 18. A child might be travelling to the UK alone or with an adult. Usually the purpose of the visit is to see family, but it may be for some short-term educational reasons.

5.3.1 Requirements

By para 46A, the requirements to be met by a person seeking leave to enter the UK as a child visitor are that he:

(a) is genuinely seeking entry as a child visitor for a limited period as stated by him not exceeding six months (or not exceeding 12 months to accompany an academic visitor – see **5.6.2**, provided the child visitor has entry clearance) (para 46A(i)); and

(b) meets the requirements of para 41(ii)–(iv), (vi)–(vii) and (x)–(xii) (see **5.2.1**) (para 46A(ii)); and

(c) is under the age of 18 (para 46A(iii)); and

(d) can demonstrate that suitable arrangements have been made for his travel to, and reception and care in, the United Kingdom (see **5.3.1.1**) (para 46A(iv)); and

(e) has a parent or guardian in his home country or country of habitual residence who is responsible for his care (see **5.3.1.2**) (para 46A(v)); and

(f) if a visa national (see **5.3.1.3**) –

  (i) holds a valid United Kingdom entry clearance for entry as an accompanied child visitor, and is travelling in the company of the adult identified on his entry clearance who is on the same occasion being admitted to the United Kingdom, or

  (ii) holds a valid United Kingdom entry clearance for entry as an unaccompanied child visitor (para 46A(vi)); and

(g) if he has been accepted for a course of study (see **5.3.1.4**), this is to be provided by an institution which is –

(i) the holder of a Sponsor Licence for Tier 4 of the Points Based System, or

(ii) accredited by a UKBA approved accreditation body, or

(iii) an independent fee-paying school registered with the Department for Children, Schools and Families and which is outside the maintained sector (para 46A(vii)); and

(h) if he is undertaking an exchange or educational visit only, this is to be provided by a school in the maintained sector, a non-maintained special school, an independent non fee-paying or an independent fee-paying school (as described in guidance published by the UKBA).

Some of these requirements are explored further below.

5.3.1.1 Suitable travel, reception and care arrangements in UK

The UKBA's guidance is that where there are no other factors which give cause for concern, this requirement may simply involve the inclusion of the child in the travel and accommodation arrangements of the parent(s), relative(s) or friend(s) accompanying him, or a letter from a relative or friend at the UK address, inviting the child to visit.

What evidence will an ECO require for entry clearance purposes? He will need the name, address and landline telephone number of the parent or carer in the child's home country, the host in the UK and the person accompanying the child. Where these details are missing or unclear, or other factors raise concerns about the child's welfare, further enquiries will be undertaken to confirm the identity and residence of the host and that the child is expected in the UK. The application will be refused if the ECO remains concerned about the child's welfare in the UK.

Where an immigration officer considering leave to enter has concerns about the child's welfare, the UKBA's policy is that both the social service departments in the host's area and those local to the port of entry should be contacted so that enquiries can be made to ascertain the host's suitability.

5.3.1.2 Parent or guardian responsible for child's care in home country or country of habitual residence

In the majority of cases where an application is being made for entry clearance abroad, the parent or guardian will be the person making the application on behalf of the child, and this requirement should be met. Otherwise, provided there are no other factors which give cause for concern, a letter from the parent or guardian confirming his relationship to the child and consenting to the child's application is normally sufficient.

What if the child's parents are divorced? Written consent must be given by the parent who has residence or legal custody, or sole responsibility of the child.

5.3.1.3 A child who is a visa national

Where a child is travelling in the company of an adult, he must hold a visa which identifies the adult with whom he seeks to enter the UK. The identification is by way of the adult's passport number, initial and surname, which is included on the child's visa document.

Where a child is travelling unaccompanied, his visa will state this.

5.3.1.4 Accepted for a course of study

A child visitor may be given entry clearance to study in the UK for up to six months, provided the institution he intends to attend is either the holder of a Sponsor Licence for Tier 4 of the Points Based System, or is accredited by a UKBA approved accreditation body, or is an independent fee-paying school registered with the Department for Children, Schools and Families (for further details, see **Chapter 6**).

5.3.2 Leave to enter

By para 46B, a person seeking leave to enter the UK as a child visitor may be admitted for a period not exceeding six months, or not exceeding 12 months in the case of a child visitor accompanying an academic visitor (see **5.6.2**) subject to a condition prohibiting employment (see **3.3.1**). Like all limited leave entrants, a child visitor will also be subject to the condition not to have recourse to public funds (also see **3.3.2**).

5.4 Parent of a child at school in UK

This category allows entry to the UK of the parent of a child under 12 who is at school in the UK. Paragraph 56A sets out the following requirements:

(a) the parent meets the requirements set out in para 41(ii)–(xii) (see **5.2.1**) (para 56A(i)); and

(b) the child is a Tier 4 (Child) Student attending an independent fee-paying day school (see **Chapter 6**) (para 56A(ii)); and

(c) the child is under 12 years of age (para 56A(iii)); and

(d) the parent can provide satisfactory evidence of adequate and reliable funds for maintaining a second home in the UK (para 56A(iv)); and

(e) the parent is not seeking to make the UK his main home (para 56A (v)); and

(f) the parent was not last admitted to the UK under the Approved Destination Status Agreement with China (see **5.2.4**) (para 56A(vi)).

5.4.1 UKBA policy

The UKBA's policy is that this category allows for a parent to stay with a young child at school in the UK, provided that the child is under 12, attending a private day school, the parent of the child is not working, there is evidence of adequate and reliable funds for maintaining a second home in the UK, and there is no reason to believe that the family is seeking to make its principal home in the UK.

As to the maintenance requirements for child students accompanied by parents with whom they are living, see **Chapter 6**.

5.4.2 Entry clearance and leave to enter

By para 56B, a person seeking leave to enter or remain in the UK as the parent of a child at school, may be admitted or allowed to remain for a period not exceeding 12 months, subject to a condition prohibiting employment (see **3.3.1**). Like all limited leave entrants, the parent will also be subject to the condition not to have recourse to public funds (also see **3.3.2**).

Entry clearance is mandatory for visa nationals and for all those seeking entry for up to the maximum of 12 months.

Leave to enter may be granted for six months, or for the maximum of 12 months if the parent has entry clearance in this category.

5.5 Student visitor

This category allows a person to enter the UK either:

(a) as a visitor, but also to undertake a short period of study which must be completed within that person's six months' limited leave; or

(b) as a student to study on a course of six months' duration or less, provided he does not intend to take part-time employment, or undertake a paid or unpaid work placement as part of that course. Only a Tier 4 (Adult) Student (see **Chapter 6**) may work part-time or take up a work placement.

5.5.1 Requirements

Paragraph 56K sets out the following requirements, namely, that the student visitor:

(a) is genuinely seeking entry as a student visitor for a limited period as stated by him, not exceeding six months (para 56K(i)); and

(b) has been accepted on a course of study which is to be provided by an institution which is:

  (i) the holder of a sponsor licence for Tier 4 of the points-based system (see **Chapter 6**), or

  (ii) accredited by a UKBA approved accreditation body, or

  (iii) an overseas Higher Education Institution offering only part of its programmes in the UK, holding its own national accreditation and offering programmes that are of a level equivalent to a UK degree (para 56K(ii)); and

(c) intends to leave the UK at the end of his visit as stated by him (para 56K(iii)); and

(d) does not intend to take employment in the UK (para 56K(iv)); and

(e) does not intend to engage in business, to produce goods or provide services within the UK, including the selling of goods or services direct to members of the public (para 56K(v)); and

(f) does not intend to study at a maintained school (para 56K(vi)); and

(g) will maintain and accommodate himself and any dependants adequately out of resources available to him without recourse to public funds or taking employment; or will, with any dependants, be maintained and accommodated adequately by relatives or friends (para 56K(vii)); and

(h) can meet the cost of the return or onward journey (para 56K(viii)); and

(i) is not a child under the age of 18 (see **5.3**) (para 56K(ix)); and

(j) meets the requirements set out in para 41(ix)–(xii) (see **5.2.1**) (para 56K(x)).

5.5.2 Entry clearance and leave to enter

By para 56L, a person seeking leave to enter to the UK as a student visitor may be admitted for a period not exceeding six months, subject to a condition prohibiting employment (see **3.3.1**). Like all limited leave entrants, the student visitor will also be subject to the condition not to have recourse to public funds (also see **3.3.2**).

Only a visa national must obtain entry clearance before travelling to the UK in this category.

5.5.3 Prospective student

Note that if an applicant has not yet been accepted on a course of study, he might first enter the UK as a prospective student under paras 82 to 87 of the Immigration Rules.

5.5.4 English language course concession

From January 2011 the Government announced a concession for an applicant seeking entry as a student visitor to undertake a course in English language only. This can be longer than six months but no more than 11 months. The applicant must still meet all the other requirements of the student visitor category.

For the purposes of this concession the student must be learning English as a foreign language. Mixed courses with only a portion of time spent learning English do not qualify.

Non-visa nationals must obtain prior entry clearance if they wish to undertake an English language course that is for longer than six months.

5.6 Business visitor

Who is a business visitor? Surprisingly, Part 2 of the Immigration Rules creates a wide category, as we will see below. However, any business visitor must satisfy three key tests, namely, that:

(a) he is based abroad and has no intention of transferring his base to the UK, even temporarily;

(b) he will not receive his salary from a UK source; and

(c) he will not be involved in selling goods or services direct to members of the public.

5.6.1 Requirements

Paragraph 46G sets out the requirements for business visitor, namely, that he:

(a) is genuinely seeking entry as a business visitor for a limited period as stated by him –
   (i) not exceeding six months, or
   (ii) not exceeding 12 months if seeking entry as an academic visitor (see **5.6.2**) (para 46G(i));

(b) meets the requirements of para 41(ii)–(viii) and (x)–(xii) (see **5.2.1**) (para 46G(ii));

(c) intends to do one or more of the following during his visit –
   (i) to carry out a 'permissible activity' as defined in para 6 (see **5.6.3**),
   (ii) to take part in a location shoot as a member of a film crew (see **5.6.4**),
   (iii) to represent overseas news media, including as a journalist, correspondent, producer or cameraman, provided he is employed or paid by an overseas company and is gathering information for an overseas publication,
   (iv) to act as an academic visitor, but only if he has been working as an academic in an institution of higher education overseas, or in the field of his academic expertise immediately prior to seeking entry,
   (vi) to be a secondee to a UK company which is directly contracted with the visitor's overseas company, with which it has no corporate relationship, to provide goods or services, provided the secondee remains employed and paid by the overseas company throughout the secondee's visit (see **5.6.6**),
   (vii) to undertake some preaching or pastoral work as a religious worker (see **5.6.7**), provided his base is abroad and he is not taking up an office, post or appointment,
   (viii) to act as an adviser, consultant, trainer or troubleshooter (see **5.6.8**) to the UK branch of the same group of companies as the visitor's overseas company, provided the visitor remains employed and paid by the overseas company and does not undertake work, paid or unpaid with the UK company's clients,
   (xi) specific, one-off training on techniques and work practices used in the UK (see **5.6.9**), where:
      (1) the training is to be delivered by the UK branch of the same group of companies to which the individual's employer belongs; or
      (2) the training is to be provided by a UK company contracted to provide goods or services to the overseas company; or
      (3) a UK company is contracted to provide training facilities only, to an overseas company (para 46G(iii)).

5.6.2 Academic visitor

An 'academic visitor' is defined in para 6 as a person who is from an overseas academic institution, or who is highly qualified within his own field of expertise, seeking leave to enter the UK to carry out research and associated activities for his own purposes.

The UKBA's guidance is that an academic visitor must either be a person on sabbatical leave from an overseas academic institution who wishes to make use of his leave to carry out research in the UK (research for a book, for example), or an academic (including a doctor) taking part in a formal exchange arrangement with a UK counterpart, or an eminent senior doctor or dentist coming to the UK to take part in research, teaching or clinical practice.

Note that academic visitors must not receive funding for their work from any UK source, although the UKBA states that payments of expenses or honoraria to cover their needs whilst in the UK may be disregarded, as may payments on an exchange basis. The applicant must not intend to take up employment or engage in any work other than the academic activity for which he is being admitted, and he must not be filling a normal post or a genuine vacancy.

An academic visitor is not permitted to switch into employment under the points-based system (see **Chapter 7**).

Note that a doctor applying to enter the UK to take the Professional and Linguistic Assessment Board (PLAB) Test, or wishing to undertake a clinical attachment, and a dentist wanting to undertake dental observer post, must meet the requirements of paras 75A and 75G respectively.

5.6.3 'Permissible activity'

What activities may a business person carry out during his six months' limited leave? The UKBA's guidance is that permissible activities may cover any of the following:

(a) attending meetings, including interviews that have been arranged before coming to the UK, or conferences;

(b) attending trade fairs, provided this is restricted to promotional work and does not involve direct selling;

(c) arranging deals, or negotiating or signing trade agreements or contracts, undertaking fact-finding missions;

(d) conducting site visits;

(e) delivering goods and passengers from abroad, eg lorry drivers and coach drivers, provided they are genuinely working an international route;

(f) tour group couriers who are contracted to a firm outside the UK, who are seeking entry to accompany a tour group and who intend to leave with that tour group;

(g) speaking at a conference where this is not run as a commercial concern (organisers not making a profit) and where the conference is a 'one off';

(h) representing computer software companies by coming to install, debug or enhance their products. Representatives of such companies may also be admitted as business visitors in order to be briefed as to the requirements of a UK customer; but if they are to provide a service involving the use of their expertise to make a detailed assessment of a potential customer's requirements, this should be regarded as consultancy work for which entry under the points-based system (see **Chapter 7**) would be required;

(i) representing foreign manufacturers by coming to service or repair the company's products within their initial period of guarantee;

(j) representing foreign machine manufacturers by coming to erect and install machinery too heavy to be delivered in one piece, as part of the contract of purchase and supply;

(k) interpreting or translating for visiting business persons, provided the interpreter/translator is employed by the overseas company and is coming solely to provide this service for the visiting company member;

(l) monteurs (eg mechanics or servicepeople) coming for up to six months to erect, dismantle, install, service, repair or advise on the development of foreign-made machinery;

(m) board-level directors attending board meetings in the UK, provided they are not employed by a UK company, although they may be paid a fee for attending the meeting.

Note that the UKBA accepts that it is reasonable to expect those coming to the UK as business visitors in order to attend meetings, etc, to want to make use of their laptops/Blackberrys whilst here. Provided this is solely to enable such visitors to keep up to date with their own workload abroad, or to liaise with contacts in the UK, the UKBA does not consider this to be 'work' for the purposes of the Immigration Rules.

5.6.4 Taking part in a location shoot as a member of a film crew

A film crew includes actors, producers, directors and technicians for these purposes. The purpose of entry must be to take part in location shoots only here in the UK, and the film crew must be employed or paid by an overseas company.

5.6.5 Visiting professor

Paragraph 6 defines a 'visiting professor' as a person who is seeking leave to enter the UK as an academic professor to accompany students who are studying here on Study Abroad Programmes.

5.6.6 Secondee

This provision relates specifically and only to the situation where a UK company is to provide goods or services to an overseas company on a direct contractual basis (not vice versa), and where there is no corporate relationship between the two companies, ie they are not part of the same group of companies. The individual must be seconded in a supernumerary capacity for the purpose of assisting the UK company to deliver the contract, for example to clarify his company's specifications. The secondee must remain employed and paid by the overseas company throughout his visit.

Where a person is employed by an overseas company and is being seconded to a UK company which is related to the overseas employer, he must apply under Tier 2 of the points-based system as an intra-company transfer migrant (see **7.9**).

5.6.7 Religious worker

A religious worker, visiting the UK for a particular event, such as a conference, may also undertake some preaching or pastoral work during the course of his visit, provided he is based abroad and does not intend to take up an office, post or appointment in the UK.

A person coming to the UK to fill a vacancy or work temporarily as a religious worker should apply under Tiers 2 and 5 respectively of the points-based system (see **Chapter 7**).

5.6.8 Adviser, consultant, trainer or troubleshooter

The provision relates only to a person who is employed by an overseas company and who is coming to provide advice, consultancy, training or troubleshooting services to its UK branch. The applicant cannot conduct work, paid or unpaid, for or on behalf of the UK branch, including, but not limited to, providing services for the UK branch to other companies, working in a supernumerary capacity (eg internship, project-managing, or by way of short-term temporary cover for the UK branch), or having direct involvement in producing goods for the UK company's clients. The applicant must remain employed and paid by the overseas company throughout the visit, and typically his visit would be of a one-off short-term nature.

Where a person is employed by an overseas company and is being transferred to fill a skilled post in a UK entity that is related to the overseas company, he must apply under Tier 2 of the points-based system as an intra-company transfer migrant (see **7.9**).

5.6.9 One-off training on techniques and work practices

This provision allows a person to enter the UK for specific, one-off training in techniques and work practices used in the UK. The training might typically be classroom-based and/or involve familiarisation or observation. The UKBA's guidance is that the provision applies in the following circumstances:

(a) Where the visitor is an employee from the same group of companies overseas as the UK company and the training is to be provided in-house. For example, where an overseas branch sends an employee to find out about the UK branch's marketing systems.

(b) Where the training relates to a product or service that has been sold by a UK company under contract to the overseas company and the latter is to receive training on its use. In this instance the two companies do not need to be related corporately. For example, training on how to use a piece of computer software that has been purchased.

(c) Where a company has contracted to provide training facilities only, and no tuition, to an overseas company, the trainees and the trainers from the overseas company will be business visitors. For example, provision of a classroom or piece of equipment.

(d) Where the visitor is an employee from the same group of companies overseas as the UK company, and is participating in a corporate training exercise provided to the UK company by an outside provider.

A person seeking to enter the UK for training other than in the above circumstances – most commonly for English language training – must qualify to do either as a Tier 4 Student (see **Chapter 6**), or as a student visitor (see **5.5**).

5.6.10 Leave to enter

By para 46H, a person seeking leave to enter to the UK as a business visitor may be admitted for a period not exceeding six months, subject to a condition prohibiting employment (see **3.3.1**). Like all limited leave entrants, the business visitor will be subject to the condition not to have recourse to public funds (also see **3.3.2**).

An academic visitor (see **5.6.2**) without entry clearance may be admitted for a period not exceeding six months, but with entry clearance may be admitted for up to 12 months.

5.6.11 Multi-entry visa

Business visit visas are normally valid for six months, 12 months, two years, five years and 10 years. The visa will be valid for unlimited journeys during its period of validity.

5.7 Marriage and civil partnership visit

If a person wishes to enter the UK to marry or to enter into a civil partnership, this route may be used, provided, of course, that the couple do not intend to stay in the UK after the marriage or civil partnership ceremony.

If the couple wish to remain in the UK permanently, the applicant should apply as a fiancé(e) or proposed civil partner (see **8.7**).

5.7.1 Requirements

Paragraph 56D sets out the requirements, namely, that the person seeking leave to enter the UK as a visitor for marriage or civil partnership must:

(a) meet the requirements set out in para 41(i)–(ix) and (xi)–(xii) (see **5.2.1**) (para 56D(i));

(b) show that he intends to give notice of the marriage or civil partnership, or marry or form a civil partnership, in the United Kingdom within the period for which entry is sought (para 56D(ii));

(c) produce satisfactory evidence, if required to do so, of the arrangements for giving notice of marriage or civil partnership, or for his wedding or civil partnership to take place, in the United Kingdom during the period for which entry is sought (para 56D(iii)); and

(d) hold a valid United Kingdom entry clearance for entry in this capacity (para 56D(iv)).

5.7.2 Entry clearance and leave to enter

Entry clearance is mandatory for all applicants.

By para 56E, a person seeking leave to enter the UK as a visitor for marriage or civil partnership may be admitted for a period not exceeding six months, subject to a condition prohibiting employment (see **3.3.1**). Like all limited leave entrants, the visitor in this category will be subject to the condition not to have recourse to public funds (also see **3.3.2**).

5.8 Private medical treatment visit

This provision allows a person who is genuinely seeking entry for the purpose of receiving private medical treatment in the UK to do so. The ECO and immigration officer must be satisfied that he does not intend to seek free treatment under the National Health Service (NHS); that he des not represent a danger to public health; that the treatment is of finite duration; and that he has sufficient funds available to pay for the cost of treatment and all other expenses until the treatment ends.

Although any initial leave is for a maximum of six months, the UKBA's guidance is that where a bona fide passenger returns to the UK to continue private medical treatment after a previous stay here for the same purpose, no account will be taken of the normal six-month time limit for visitors.

5.8.1 Requirements

Paragraph 51 sets out the requirements to be met by a person seeking leave to enter the UK as a visitor for private medical treatment, namely, that he:

(a) meets the requirements set out in para 41(iii)–(vii), (ix)–(x) and (xii) for entry as a general visitor (see **5.2.1**) (para 51(i));

(b) in the case of a person suffering from a communicable disease, has satisfied the medical inspector that there is no danger to public health (see **5.8.1.1**) (para 51(ii)); and

(c) can show, if required to do so, that any proposed course of treatment is of finite duration (see **5.8.1.2**) (para 51(iii));

(d) intends to leave the United Kingdom at the end of his treatment (para 51(iv));

(e) can produce satisfactory evidence (see **5.8.1.3**), if required to do so, of –

 (i) the medical condition requiring consultation or treatment, and

 (ii) satisfactory arrangements for the necessary consultation or treatment at his own expense,

 (iii) the estimated costs of such consultation or treatment,

 (iv) the likely duration of his visit, and

 (v) sufficient funds available to him in the United Kingdom to meet the estimated costs and his undertaking to do so (para 51(v)).

5.8.1.1 No danger to public health

A person suffering from a communicable disease may be given leave to enter if he satisfies the port medical inspector that there is no danger to public health. However, an applicant who otherwise meets all the requirements of para 51 may still be refused entry under para 320(7) if the port medical inspector confirms that his admission is undesirable for medical reasons (see **3.4.5.1**).

5.8.1.2 Proposed course of treatment is of finite duration

The UKBA's guidance is that a commonsense view should be taken of the meaning of 'finite'. A long period of treatment, although not precisely defined, may be acceptable, provided that there is a clear need for the patient to be in the UK to receive that treatment and he has sufficient funds. It is reasonable to scrutinise carefully the likely duration and success of, for example, fertility treatment which could have been going on for some years without success. It would be acceptable (with the applicant's consent) to approach the consultant direct to ask about the likelihood of eventual success of the treatment.

5.8.1.3 Evidence

What evidence is required? The UKBA's guidance is as follows:

> A letter from a registered medical practitioner who holds an NHS consultant post or who appears in the Specialist Register of the General Medical Council, providing full details of the nature of the illness; the proposed treatment; the frequency of the consultations (whether weekly, monthly etc); the likely duration of the treatment; details of the cost of the treatment and confirmation that all expenses are being met and, where treatment amounts to private visits to a consultant for what appears to be a relatively minor ailment, details of the progress being made. An original letter on headed notepaper giving a private practice or hospital address and describing the signatory as a consultant is normally taken as sufficient evidence of that status.
>
> Evidence of the applicant's ability to pay for the treatment and to support and accommodate himself and any dependants without working or recourse to public funds needs to be provided. Where the applicant is, or appears to be, sponsored, fresh confirmation of the sponsor's willingness and financial ability to meet the likely costs is obtained. The applicant will if he is dependent upon funds from abroad, be asked to prove that the funds are transferable as certain countries operate strict exchange controls.

5.8.2 Leave to enter

By para 52, a person seeking leave to enter the UK as a visitor for private medical treatment may be admitted for a period not exceeding six months, subject to a condition prohibiting employment (see **3.3.1**). Like all limited leave entrants, the visitor in this category will be subject to the condition not to have recourse to public funds (also see **3.3.2**).

5.8.3 Extension of limited leave

Given that a person's treatment may take longer than six months, a visitor in this category may apply to the Home Office to extend his limited leave. The requirements for an extension of stay as a visitor to undergo or continue private medical treatment are set out in para 54, and are that the applicant:

(a) meets the requirements set out in para 41(iii)–(vii), (ix)–(x) and (xii) (see **5.2.1**), and para 51(ii)–(v) (see **5.8.1**) (para 54(i));

(b) has produced evidence from a registered medical practitioner who holds an NHS consultant post, or who appears in the Specialist Register of the General Medical Council, of satisfactory arrangements for private medical consultation or treatment and its likely duration; and, where treatment has already begun, evidence as to its progress (para 54(ii)); and

(c) can show that he has met, out of the resources available to him, any costs and expenses incurred in relation to his treatment in the United Kingdom (para 54(iii)); and

(d) has sufficient funds available to him in the United Kingdom to meet the likely costs of his treatment and intends to meet those costs (para 54(iv)); and

(e) was not last admitted to the United Kingdom under the Approved Destination Status Agreement with China (see **5.2.5**) (para 54(v)).

5.9 Sports visitor

This provision is intended for sportspersons coming to the UK usually for a one-off event, or a series of linked events. Sportspersons coming to base themselves in the UK permanently or temporarily to work should apply under Tier 2 or Tier 5 respectively of the points-based system (see **Chapter 7**).

5.9.1 Who is a sportsperson?

The UKBA's guidance is that the following people may qualify for entry as a sportsperson:

(a) amateurs and professionals coming to the UK to take part either as individuals or as a team in a specific event or tournament, such as Wimbledon, or a series of events;

(b) members of the technical or support staff of amateurs or professionals, who are attending for the same event. Examples of such staff include team managers, personal coaches, doctors, physiotherapists, dieticians, bodyguards and press officers. Also polo grooms, provided they are not intending to base themselves at the stables for the season;

(c) officials, including those officials coming on a voluntary basis, attending the same event as the sportsperson. Examples include linespersons and umpires;

(d) amateurs and professionals coming for a specific one-off charity sporting event or exhibition match, either as individuals or as members of an overseas team, provided the organisers are not making a profit and the sportsperson is not receiving a fee. An example would be the London Marathon;

(e) those seeking entry for personal appearances and promotions such as book signings, television interviews, negotiating contracts or to discuss sponsorship deals;

(f) sportspeople seeking entry for 'trials', provided that the trial is not in front of an audience, either paying or non-paying;

(g) those coming for training for short periods (whether as an individual or as part of team), provided that they are not basing themselves in the UK, are not being paid by a UK sporting body or joining a UK team, and that any matches they are involved in are of the friendly or exhibition type.

What is the difference between an amateur and professional sportsperson? Paragraph 6 defines an amateur as a person who engages in a sport or creative activity solely for personal enjoyment and who is not seeking to derive a living from the activity. So, by contrast, a professional is a person paid a salary for participation in sport, such as someone contracted to play for a sport or club.

5.9.2 Requirements

By para 46M, the requirements to be met by a person seeking leave to enter the UK as a sports visitor are that he:

(a) is genuinely seeking entry as a sports visitor for a limited period as stated by him, not exceeding six months (para 46M(i)); and

(b) meets the requirements of para 41(ii)–(viii) and (x)–(xii) (see **5.2.1**) (para 46M(ii)); and

(c) intends to do one or more of the following during his visit (see **5.9.3**):

  (i) to take part in a particular sporting event as defined in guidance published by the UKBA, tournament or series of events,

  (ii) to take part in a specific one-off charity sporting event, provided no payment is received other than for travelling and other expenses,

  (iii) to join, as an amateur, a wholly or predominantly amateur team, provided no payment is received other than for board and lodging and reasonable expenses,

(iv) to serve as a member of the technical or personal staff, or as an official, attending the same event as a visiting sportsperson coming for one or more of the purposes listed in (i), (ii) or (iii) (para 46M(iii)).

5.9.3 What are permissible activities for a sports visitor?

The question is largely answered in **5.9.1** above. But what about participation in competitions that do not fall within the definition of 'sports', such as a chess tournament? The UKBA's guidance is that this may qualify, provided the applicant does not receive any fee or sponsorship for his participation, although he may receive cash prizes, board, lodging and living expenses.

What counts as a series of events? This is defined by para 6 as two or more linked events, such as a tour or rounds of a competition, which do not add up to a league or a season, eg football teams coming to the UK to participate in pre-season friendly matches against English clubs in competitions. This also includes those coming for a series of events that, although not part of the same competition, are being held in the UK at the same time. For example, the AEGON Tennis Championship is held immediately before Wimbledon, and the UKBA would not expect players to return home and seek fresh entry clearance.

5.9.4 Leave to enter

By para 46N, a person seeking leave to enter the UK as a sports visitor may be admitted for a period not exceeding six months, subject to a condition prohibiting employment (see **3.3.1**). Like all limited leave entrants, the sports visitor will be subject to the condition not to have recourse to public funds (also see **3.3.2**).

5.10 Entertainer visitor

This provision is intended for entertainers and their entourages, who wish to come to the UK (usually) for a one-off event or a series of events. Entertainers who wish to base themselves in the UK permanently or temporarily to work should apply under Tier 2 or Tier 5 respectively of the points-based system (see **Chapter** 7).

5.10.1 Requirements

By para 46S, the requirements to be met by a person seeking leave to enter the UK as an entertainer visitor are that he:

(a) is genuinely seeking entry as an entertainer visitor for a limited period as stated by him, not exceeding six months (para 46S(i)); and

(b) meets the requirements of para 41(ii)–(viii) and (x)–(xii) (see **5.2.1**) (para 46S(ii));

(c) intends to do one or more of the following during his visit (see **5.10.2**) –

(i) to take part as a professional entertainer in one or more music competitions, and/or

(ii) to fulfil one or more specific engagements as either an individual amateur entertainer or as an amateur group, and/or

(iii) to take part, as an amateur or professional entertainer, in a cultural event (or one or more of such events) that appears in the list of events to which this provision applies that is published in guidance issued by the UKBA, and/or

(iv) serve as a member of the technical or personal staff, or of the production team, of an entertainer coming for one or more of the purposes listed in (i), (ii), or (iii) (para 46S(iii)).

5.10.2 Who is an entertainer visitor and what activities can he carry out?

The UKBA's guidance is that an entertainer visitor includes the following:

(a) professional entertainers coming to take part in music competitions;

(b) internationally famous people coming to the UK to take part in broadcasts or public appearances, provided they are not performing or not being paid;

(c) those undertaking an audition, provided this is not performed in front of an audience (either paying or non-paying);

(d) amateur entertainers seeking entry as an individual performer for a specific engagement;

(e) amateur entertainers seeking entry as part of a group, such as a choir or youth orchestra coming for a specific engagement. This can include conductors, choreographers, stage managers and other non-performing staff supporting the group;

(f) professional entertainers taking part in a charity concert or show where the organisers are not making a profit and no fee is to be paid to the entertainer;

(g) members of the technical or support staff of amateurs or professionals who are attending the same event, such as make-up artists, personal bodyguards and press officers;

(h) officials attending the same event as the entertainer, such as choreographers and stage managers.

The definitions of 'amateur' and 'professional' are the same as for a sports visitor – see **5.9.1**.

5.10.3 Leave to enter

By para 46T, a person seeking leave to enter the UK as an entertainer visitor may be admitted for a period not exceeding six months, subject to a condition prohibiting employment (see **3.3.1**). Like all limited leave entrants, the entertainer visitor will be subject to the condition not to have recourse to public funds (also see **3.3.2**).

5.11 Visitor in transit to country outside the Common Travel Area

Who is a visitor in transit? This refers to any passenger whose sole purpose is to pass through the UK within 48 hours and who either:

(a) arrives at one port or airport and needs to transfer to another port or airport to continue his journey; or

(b) wishes to spend the time between his arrival and embarkation outside the transit area (ie pass through immigration controls at the port or airport).

As to the Common Travel Area, see **3.9**.

5.11.1 Requirements

Paragraph 47 sets out the requirements to be met by a person (not being a member of the crew of a ship, aircraft, hovercraft, hydrofoil or train) seeking leave to enter the UK as a visitor in transit to another country. He must:

(a) be in transit to a country outside the Common Travel Area (para 47(i)); and

(b) have both the means and the intention of proceeding at once to another country (para 47(ii)); and

(c) be assured of entry there (para 47(iii)); and

(d) intend and be able to leave the United Kingdom within 48 hours (para 47(iv)).

5.11.2 Leave to enter

A person seeking leave to enter the UK as a visitor in transit may be admitted for a period not exceeding 48 hours with a prohibition on employment.

5.12 Prospective entrepreneur

The prospective entrepreneur category allows an individual entrepreneur to come to the UK to secure funding to set up a business here.

5.12.1 Who is a prospective entrepreneur?

At the time of applying for entry clearance, the applicant must be in discussions with a UKBA-designated funding body to secure funding in order to join, set up or take over, and be actively involved in the running of, a business in the UK.

Which funding bodies are designated? These are:

(a) registered venture capitalist firms regulated by the Financial Services Authority;

(b) UK entrepreneurial seed funding competitions which are listed as endorsed on the UK Trade & Investment website; and

(c) one or more UK government departments.

What is a venture capitalist firm? It is a company that draws on private equity funds to invest in new businesses with high growth potential and in exchange takes a stake in the business (which it subsequently hopes to sell at a profit). A registered firm is one regulated by the Financial Services Authority.

What UK entrepreneurial seed funding competitions are listed as endorsed on the UK Trade & Investment website? At the time of writing these are Springboard and Seedcamp (at www.ukti.gov.uk/uktihome/item/128990.html).

5.12.2 Requirements

By para 56O the requirements to be met by a person seeking leave to enter the UK in this category are as follows:

(a) The applicant must provide an original, signed letter on headed paper supporting the application from one or more of the UKBA-designated funding bodies (see **5.12.1**).

(b) That letter must be dated no earlier than three months before the date of the application. It must be signed by an authorised official and contain the information set out in para 56O(b). This includes, by sub-para (iv), a commitment by the individual(s) and/or organisation(s) supporting the applicant to decide within six months of the applicant entering the UK whether or not to provide a minimum of £50,000 funding for the proposed business. Note that if more than one individual and/or organisation is supporting the applicant, each amount proposed may be less than £50,000 provided that the total amount is at least £50,000.

(c) The applicant's primary intention in applying must be to secure funding in order to join, set up or take over, and be actively involved in the running of, a business in the UK.

(d) The applicant must intend to carry out one (or more) of the UKBA-permitted activities listed in guidance. Currently these activities are: attending meetings (which may be arranged when in the UK, including interviews arranged before coming to the UK, or conferences); attending trade fairs (provided this is restricted to promotional work and does not involve selling directly to members of the public); arranging deals, or negotiating or signing trade agreements or contracts; conducting site visits; speaking at a one-off conference (which is not organised as a commercial concern and is a 'one-off'); undertaking fact-finding missions; purchasing, checking details of, or examining goods; and recruiting staff for the proposed business activity which is the object of the application.

(e) The applicant must intend to leave the UK at the end of the period of the visit as stated by him, unless he makes a successful application for leave to remain as a Tier 1 (Entrepreneur) Migrant (see **7.4**) before the end of the period of the visit.

(f) The applicant must maintain and accommodate himself and any dependants adequately out of resources available to him without recourse to public funds or taking employment; or will, with any dependants, be maintained and accommodated adequately by relatives or friends.

(g) The applicant must not intend during his visit to:
   (i) take employment in the UK;
   (ii) produce goods or provide services within the UK, including the selling of goods or services direct to members of the public;
   (iii) undertake a course of study;
   (iv) marry or form a civil partnership, or to give notice of marriage or civil partnership; or
   (v) receive private medical treatment.

(h) The applicant must not be under the age of 18.

(i) The applicant must not be in transit to a country outside the Common Travel Area.

(j) The applicant must hold a valid UK entry clearance for entry in this capacity.

Note that, as to requirement (g), a prospective entrepreneur is also not allowed to undertake activities permitted under the business (see **5.6**), sports (see **5.9**) or entertainer (see **5.10**) categories, apart from those set out in requirements (c) and (d).

5.12.3 Leave to enter

By para 56P, a person seeking leave to enter to the UK in this category may be admitted for a period not exceeding six months, subject to a condition prohibiting employment (see **3.3.1**). Like all limited leave entrants, he will also be subject to the condition not to have recourse to public funds (see **3.3.2**).

5.12.4 Switching to Tier 1 (Entrepreneur) Migrant

If, after entering the UK, the applicant secures funding then he may be able to apply to switch to the Tier 1 (Entrepreneur) Migrant category (see **7.4**). Otherwise he must leave the UK at the end of his limited leave.

5.12.5 Alternative entry as a business visitor

If an applicant is unable to satisfy the requirements for this category, he might consider entering the UK as a business visitor instead (see **5.6**). Note, however, that a business visitor is not allowed to switch into the Tier 1 Entrepreneur category whilst in the UK.

5.13 Visitors as carers

There is no provision in the Immigration Rules for leave to enter or remain to be granted solely to allow a person to care for a friend or relative in the UK. Applications for leave to enter as a carer may thus be refused on the ground that there is no provision for this in the Rules. However, where an applicant wishes to care for a friend or relative for a short period, the application may be considered under the requirements of the rules relating to visitors. Applications from persons already in the UK in a temporary capacity seeking leave to remain to care for a sick relative or friend who is suffering from a terminal illness, such as cancer or AIDS, or who is mentally or physically disabled, are dealt with outside the Immigration Rules under the Secretary of State's discretion. If leave to remain is granted, it is made clear to the applicant that it is only in a temporary capacity and that, once alternative arrangements have been made or if the patient should die, the 'carer' is expected to return home. An extension of stay on this basis will not lead to settlement.

Where the application is to care for a sick or disabled relative, leave for three months is usually granted. Where it is decided to grant leave for three months exceptionally, outside the Rules, the applicant is informed that leave has been granted on the strict understanding that, during this period, arrangements must be made for the future care of the patient by a person who does not require leave to remain outside the Immigration Rules. However, applications for leave to remain in order to care for a sick or disabled friend are normally refused save in an emergency (eg the patient has suddenly fallen ill and there is insufficient time to arrange permanent care, or there is nobody else in the UK to whom the patient can turn). In those circumstances, leave to remain may be granted for a period of three months. An extension of further leave will not be given unless there are wholly exceptional circumstances.

When the UKBA is considering whether a period of leave should be granted, it takes into account the following:

(a) the type of illness/condition (this should be supported by a doctor's letter); and

(b) the type of care required; and

(c) the care which is available (eg from the social services or other relatives/friends); and

(d) the long-term prognosis.

In cases where there are sufficient exceptional compassionate circumstances to continue the exercise of discretion, leave to remain may be granted for up to 12 months.

5.14 Switching to another category

Visitors are not normally permitted to remain under another category. However, the Rules do permit applications to remain as a close relative of someone settled in the UK (see **8.9** and **8.10**), or as the spouse of someone who has limited leave (see **8.6**). Also, a prospective entrepreneur (**5.12**) may be able switch to a Tier 1 (Entrepreneur) Migrant (see **7.4**). Note in particular that a visitor is prohibited from switching his category to that of a spouse under para 284(i) of the Immigration Rules.

Chapter 6
Students

6.1 Who is a student?

6.1.1 Tier 4 of the points-based system

Part 6A of the Immigration Rules deals with the points-based system of entry to the UK. Students come within Tier 4. The other tiers deal with working and conducting business in the UK (see **Chapter 7**).

There are two main types of student categories in Tier 4. First, an adult student, known in the Immigration Rules as a Tier 4 (General) Student. Here an adult is any person coming to the UK for post-16 education. We shall focus on this category in this chapter, as it attracts a large number of applicants. Secondly, a child student or a Tier 4 (Child) Student. This category covers children aged between 4 and 17 who wish to enter the UK for their education. Note that a child aged between 4 and 15 may be educated only at an independent fee-paying school. The details of this second category, which has a limited number of applicants, are beyond the scope of this book.

The following special considerations apply to a student aged 16 or 17:

(a) If he wants to study a course at National Qualification Framework (NQF) level 3 or above, he can apply as an adult or a child student, but if the course is longer than two years the UKBA recommends that the application is made as an adult student. If he is proposing to study a course below NQF level 3, he must apply as a child student. Note that the NQF sets out the levels against which a qualification may be recognised in England, Wales and Northern Ireland. Broadly, the levels are as follows: 1 (GCSE at grades D–G), 2 (GCSE at grades A*–C), 3 (A Level), 4 (Certificate of Higher Education), 5 (HND, HNC), 6 (Bachelor's degree), 7 (Master's degree) and 8 (Doctorate). Full details can be found at www.qcda.gov.uk.

(b) If he wants to study for an English language qualification at the Common European Framework of Reference for Languages (CEFRL) level A2 or above, he must apply as an adult student. Note that the CEFRL provides a basis for the mutual recognition of language qualifications in the EEA.

For further details of the courses that may be studied, see **6.3.2.4**.

All students can enter to study at a UKBA-approved education provider only (see **6.2**). This is otherwise known as sponsorship.

6.1.2 Entry clearance

All Tier 4 students must apply for entry clearance. As part of the visa or entry certificate application they must produce certain documentation (see **6.3.2**) from the UKBA approved educational institution at which they will be studying in the UK.

6.2 Sponsorship: approved education provider

6.2.1 Obtaining a licence from the UKBA

All education providers that want to provide courses for international students need a licence from the UKBA (known as 'highly trusted sponsor' status). One key step is for the provider to obtain a satisfactory review or inspection by one of the publicly recognised inspection bodies approved for Tier 4 purposes (namely Ofsted and its equivalents in the devolved administrations, the Quality Assurance Agency and the Department for Education-approved inspectorates for independent schools). In addition, a provider must be able to show that it has allocated a number of key roles to its staff using the UKBA online sponsorship management system; it can comply with its sponsorship duties; and it has the appropriate human resource systems in place to be able to monitor its students' attendance.

For ease of reference, throughout the rest of this chapter we shall refer to an approved education provider as the 'sponsor'.

6.2.2 Sponsorship duties

The key duties of a sponsor are to keep copies of all students' passports, to keep up-to-date contact details for students, and to tell the UKBA if a student has any unauthorised absences, fails to enrol on his course or stops his studies.

6.2.3 Tier 4 register

Once a sponsor has a licence, it is added to the Tier 4 register with details of its name and location. The register can be found on the UKBA's website (see **1.2.8**).

6.3 Tier 4 (General) Student

6.3.1 Requirements

Paragraph 245ZV provides that to qualify for entry clearance as a Tier 4 (General) Student, an applicant must meet the following requirements:

(a) The application must not fall for refusal under the general grounds for refusal (see **3.5.4**).

(b) The applicant must have a minimum of 30 points under paras 113 to 119 of Appendix A ('Sponsorship' – see **6.3.2**).

(c) The applicant must have a minimum of 10 points under paras 10 to 13 of Appendix C ('Maintenance' – see **6.3.3**).

An applicant therefore needs to score 40 points to qualify. Although the wording of para 245ZV(b) and (c) suggests that a range of points may be available to collect to meet the minimum required, the tests in Appendix A and Appendix C in fact only have 30 and 10 points available each, so either the applicant scores the necessary number of points by meeting the tests or he does not.

Note also that an applicant must, if required to do so by an entry clearance officer or an immigration officer, on examination or interview, be able to demonstrate, without the assistance of an interpreter, English language proficiency of the required standard (see **6.3.2.1**).

6.3.2 Sponsorship points

A Tier 4 (General) Student is awarded 30 points only if he has obtained from a sponsor a confirmation of acceptance for studies.

6.3.2.1 The Confirmation of Acceptance for Studies

Once a sponsor has been granted a licence, the sponsor can access the UKBA's IT sponsorship management system. This can be used to create and assign a Confirmation of Acceptance for Studies (CAS). This is therefore not an actual certificate or paper document. It is a virtual document similar to a database record. Each CAS has a unique reference number and contains information about the course of study for which it has been issued and the student's personal details.

An application for entry clearance or leave to remain must be made no more than three months before the start date of the course of study as stated on the CAS. A CAS expires if it is not used to apply for entry clearance or leave within six months of being issued. In addition a CAS can only be used once.

Before allocating a CAS, the sponsor must ensure that the student is competent in English language at a set minimum level. This is met if the student is a national of a UKBA-recognised majority English-speaking country (see the list at **7.4.3.2**) or has successfully completed an academic qualification, at least equivalent to a UK Bachelor's degree, which was taught in a UKBA-recognised majority English-speaking country (see the list at **7.4.3.3**). Otherwise, the student must have passed an approved English language test that is still within its validity date. Normally a student must demonstrate knowledge of English equivalent to level B2 of the Council of Europe's Common European Framework for Language Learning, or above. Details are on the Council's website at www.coe.int/T/DG4/Linguistic/CADRE_EN.asp. A list of UKBA-approved test providers and their contact details are on the UKBA's website.

6.3.2.2 Supporting documents

In order to be awarded points, the applicant must also supply any documentary evidence, such as qualification certificates and references, that he used to obtain the offer of the place on the course from the sponsor.

Note that students who are nationals of Argentina, Australia, Brunei, Canada, Chile, Croatia, Hong Kong, Japan, New Zealand, Singapore, South Korea, Taiwan, Trinidad and Tobago, and the United States of America who apply for entry clearance in their country of nationality or for leave to remain in the UK are treated by the UKBA as 'low risk', and so generally do not have to produce any supporting documents (see also **6.3.3.2**) unless required by the UKBA to do so. Evidence of the student's nationality will be his passport. A 'low risk' student has to confirm that he meets the points requirements on his visa or entry clearance application form and that he has the required documentary evidence. Entry clearance officers do spot checks and sometimes require such a student to send the documents.

6.3.2.3 Re-sitting examinations or repeating course module

If an applicant is re-sitting examinations or repeating a module of a course, he must not previously have re-sat the same examination or repeated the same module more than once. If this requirement is not met, no points will be awarded.

If a student's leave will expire before he is able to re-sit an exam, he will not get an extension as a Tier 4 student unless he scores the required points. It is therefore not possible for a student to remain in the UK just to re-sit an exam. Such a student is expected to leave the UK and revise for the re-sit in his own country (or at least outside the UK). The student should then seek entry to take the re-sit exam as a student visitor (see *RS (Pakistan) v Secretary of State for the Home Department* [2011] EWCA Civ 434 and **5.5**).

6.3.2.4 Academic requirements and approved qualifications

Points are awarded only if the course in respect of which the confirmation is issued satisfies each of the following requirements:

(a) The course must meet the UKBA's minimum academic requirements and must lead to an approved qualification. The minimum academic requirement is that the course must be a full-time course of study, as either:
   (i) a full-time course of study that leads to a UK-recognised bachelor degree, postgraduate degree, postgraduate diploma or postgraduate certificate;
   (ii) an overseas course of degree level study that is recognised as being equivalent to a UK Higher Education course and is being provided by an overseas Higher Education Institution; or
   (iii) a full-time course of study involving a minimum of 15 hours per week organised daytime study and, except in the case of a pre-sessional course, lead to a qualification below bachelor degree level.

   The following are approved qualifications:
   (i) level 3 or the same as or above on the NQF (see **6.1.1**);
   (ii) short-term study abroad programmes in the UK as part of a qualification at an overseas higher education institution, as long as the qualification is confirmed as the same as a UK degree level by the National Academic Recognition Information Centre for the United Kingdom (UK NARIC) (see **7.3.2.1**).
   (iii) an English language course at level B2 or above of the CEFRL (see **6.1.1**).

(b) Other than when the applicant is actually on a work placement (see **6.6.2**), all study that forms part of the course must take place on the premises of the sponsor.

6.3.3 Maintenance points

6.3.3.1 How much maintenance?

To score the required 10 points, the level of maintenance funds that the applicant will have to show that he has available depends on two factors: how long the course is, and where the course is being studied.

If the applicant has already paid to his sponsor some of his course fees and/or accommodation fees where that university or college accommodation is arranged by the sponsor, that amount can be deducted from the total required provided that is confirmed in the CAS or the student can produce an original paper receipt issued by his sponsor.

If the applicant is receiving all or any of his funding from an official financial sponsorship or government sponsor, see **6.3.3.3**.

Table 6.1 below sets out the details regarding maintenance funds.

Table 6.1 Amount of maintenance funds dependent on length of course and location

Length of course	Location	Amount of maintenance funds needed
Nine months or less	Inner London	Course fees and £800 to cover living costs for each calendar month (or any part of a month) of the course

Length of course	Location	Amount of maintenance funds needed
Nine months or less	Outer London or anywhere else in the UK	Course fees and £600 to cover living costs for each calendar month (or any part of a month) of the course
More than nine months	Inner London	First year's fees and £7,200 to cover living costs for nine months in the UK
More than nine months	Outer London or anywhere else in the UK	First year's fees and £5,400 to cover living costs for nine months in the UK

When is a Tier 4 (General) Student considered to be studying in Inner London? The answer is if more than 50% of his study time is spent in any of the following London boroughs: Camden, City of London, Hackney, Hammersmith and Fulham, Haringey, Islington, Kensington and Chelsea, Lambeth, Lewisham, Newham, Southwark, Tower Hamlets, Wandsworth and Westminster.

6.3.3.2 Supporting documents

The money to be used for the applicant's maintenance must be in the form of cash. Shares, bonds, pension funds and similar savings accounts are not acceptable.

The applicant will need to produce documentary evidence to show that the minimum level of maintenance funds has been available to him for a consecutive period of at least 28 days ending no more than one month before the date of the application. Provided it covers that period, any of the following documents in the name of the applicant is acceptable:

(a) personal bank or building society statements;

(b) a building society pass book;

(c) a letter from the applicant's bank confirming that the funds are available;

(d) a letter from a financial institution regulated either by the Financial Services Authority or, in the case of overseas accounts, the home regulator (official regulatory body for the country the institution is in and where the money is held) confirming that the funds are available;

(e) a letter from a financial institution regulated either by the Financial Services Authority or, in the case of overseas accounts, the home regulator (official regulatory body for the country the institution is in and where the money is held) confirming that the funds are available as a loan.

What if a student is relying on money held by a parent or legal guardian? In addition to providing the above evidence of available funds, the applicant will have to produce:

(a) evidence of the relationship, eg the student's birth certificate showing the names of his parent(s), or the student's certificate of adoption showing the names of his parent(s) or legal guardian, or a court document naming his legal guardian. The original document or a notarised copy must be produced;

(b) a letter from his parent(s) or legal guardian confirming the relationship and consenting to the student using their funds to study in the UK.

Remember that if the student is 'low risk' (see **6.3.2.2**) he will only have to produce documentation if required.

6.3.3.3 Official financial sponsorship

An applicant might receive financial help from the UK Government, his home government, the British Council or any international organisation, company or university.

Details must either be set out in the CAS, or a letter is required from any official financial sponsor confirming the length of the sponsorship, that it will cover all of the applicant's fees and living costs, or the amount available. The applicant must produce evidence to meet any shortfall.

6.3.3.4 Family members

If an applicant is bringing any family members (spouse, civil partner, unmarried or same-sex partner and children under 18) with him, he will have to demonstrate that additional maintenance funds are available (see **6.8**).

6.4 Leave to enter the UK

If granted entry clearance, how long will a Tier 4 (General) Student get as limited leave in the UK? The answer depends on the nature and length of the course, as set out in **Table 6.2** below.

Table 6.2 Amount of limited leave

Length of course	Amount of limited leave granted
Less than six months	The full length of the course plus one month after the end of the course
At least six months but less than 12 months	The full length of the course plus two months after the end of the course
12 months or more	The full length of the course plus four months after the end of the course
Postgraduate doctor or dentist	The full length of the course (up to a maximum of three years) plus one month after the end of the course

Note that if a Tier 4 (General) Student has an official financial sponsor (see **6.3.3.3**) who pays all his fees and living expenses but limits the time the student may study in the UK, the permission to stay is limited to the same length of time plus the usual post-course period specified in **Table 6.2**.

Note also that a Tier 4 (General) Student is not allowed to spend more than three years when he is an adult in the UK studying at below UK Bachelor's degree level.

6.5 Extending limited leave

After finishing one course, a Tier 4 (General) Student may wish to take another course. In these circumstances the student will need to meet the same requirements as he did to secure entry clearance (see **6.3.1** above). The only difference will be as to the level of maintenance required if the student has within the last four months completed a course of at least six months' duration. In such a case, the figures in **Table 6.3** below will apply.

Table 6.3 Amount of maintenance funds required for extending limited leave

Length of course	Location	Amount of maintenance funds needed
Two months or less	Inner London	Course fees and £800 to cover living costs for each calendar month of the course up to a maximum of two months

Length of course	Location	Amount of maintenance funds needed
Two months or less	Outer London or anywhere else in the UK	Course fees and £600 to cover living costs for each calendar month of the course up to a maximum of two months
More than two months	Inner London	First year's fees and £1,600 to cover two months of living costs in the UK
More than two months	Outer London or anywhere else in the UK	First year's fees and £1,200 to cover two months of living costs in the UK

6.6 What can a Tier 4 (General) Student do in addition to studying?

6.6.1 Students' union sabbatical officer

A students' union sabbatical post is a full-time, salaried, elected executive union position. A Tier 4 (General) Student may take up this post for a maximum of two years, either during his course of study or in the academic year immediately after he graduates. The post must be at the institution which is the student's sponsor.

6.6.2 Work placement

A course of study for a Tier 4 (General) Student may include a work placement, but it must not exceed 50% of the length of the course in the UK unless the student is doing a course where there is a statutory requirement for it to contain a specific period of work placement.

For example, if a course is two years long, the first year of the course might involve full-time study, and the last year might involve a work placement.

In addition, the work placement must form an assessed part of the course.

A sponsor remains responsible for the student throughout the term of his work placement, and must continue to comply with all the sponsor duties throughout this time.

6.6.3 Extra studies

Tier 4 (General) Students are allowed to undertake supplementary courses, for example evening classes. These do not need to relate to the course of study for which the student was granted entry clearance or leave. No permission is needed and the student does not have to inform his sponsor.

6.6.4 Employment

A Tier 4 (General) Student following a course with a sponsor which is a UK higher education institution, or on a short-term study abroad degree programme at an overseas higher education institution, or at a publicly-funded further education college, may work whilst in the UK. This is in addition to any work placement (see **6.6.2**) he is doing as part of his course. However, the student must not fill a full-time, permanent vacancy (other than on a recognised Foundation Programme).

Students may work full time during vacations but only part time for a prescribed maximum number of hours during term time. What are the limits?

(a) Students following a course at NQF 6 (Bachelor's degree level) or above with a sponsor which is a UK higher education institution, or undertaking a short-term study abroad degree programme at an overseas higher education institution, can work for no more than 20 hours per week in term time.

(b) Students following a course at NQF 3, 4 or 5 (below degree level) with a sponsor which is a UK higher education institution can work for no more than 10 hours per week in term time.

(c) Students following a course at any level with a sponsor which is a publicly-funded further education college can work for no more than 10 hours per week in term time.

The following categories of employment are not permitted at any time:

(a) self-employment;

(b) employment as a doctor in training (other than on a recognised Foundation Programme);

(c) employment as a professional sportsperson (including a sports coach); and

(d) employment as an entertainer.

6.7 Conditions attached to leave

A Tier 4 (General) Student's limited leave is subject to the following conditions:

(a) no recourse to public funds (see **3.3.2**);

(b) registration with the police, if this is required (see **3.3.3**);

(c) no employment except:

   (i) (as detailed at **6.6.4**),

   (ii) employment as part of a course-related work placement which forms an assessed part of the applicant's course and provided that any period that the applicant spends on that placement does not exceed half of the total length of the course undertaken in the UK except where it is a UK statutory requirement that the placement should exceed half the total length of the course (see **6.6.2**),

   (iii) employment as a Student Union Sabbatical Officer, for up to two years, provided the post is elective and is at the institution which is the applicant's sponsor (see **6.6.1**);

(d) no study except:

   (i) study at the institution that the UKBA records as the migrant's sponsor;

   (ii) supplementary study (see **6.6.3**).

Note the effect of condition (d)(i) is to tie the student's leave to his sponsor. So a student cannot lawfully change courses and study with a different sponsor without obtaining a CAS from the new sponsor and further leave to remain from the Home Office.

6.8 Family members of a Tier 4 (General) Student

6.8.1 Entry clearance and leave to remain and permission to work

Can all Tier 4 (General) Students bring their family members to the UK? No. So who can? Only either (a) students sponsored by a higher education institution on a course at NQF level 7 or above that lasts 12 months or more, or (b) Government-sponsored students following a course that is longer than six months.

Who are family members? If subject to immigration controls, the spouse, civil partner, unmarried or same-sex partner ('the Partner') and children under 18 will require entry clearance in order to enter the UK as the family member. If relevant, they should subsequently apply for an extension at the same time as the Tier 4 (General) Student.

Note that such a family member is able to work in the UK.

6.8.2 Partner

6.8.2.1 Requirements

The requirements are set out in para 319C, as follows:

(a) The applicant must not fall for refusal under the general grounds for refusal (see **3.5.4**) and, if applying for leave to remain, must not be an illegal entrant (see **10.2.2**).

(b) The applicant must be the spouse or civil partner, unmarried or same-sex partner of a person who:

  (i) has valid leave to enter or remain as a Tier 4 (General) Student; or

  (ii) is, at the same time, being granted entry clearance or leave to remain as a Tier 4 (General) Student.

(c) An applicant who is the unmarried or same-sex partner of a Tier 4 (General) Student must also meet the following requirements:

  (i) any previous marriage or civil partnership or similar relationship by the applicant or the Tier 4 (General) Student with another person must have permanently broken down;

  (ii) the applicant and the Tier 4 (General) Student must not be so closely related that they would be prohibited from marrying each other in the UK; and

  (iii) the applicant and the Tier 4 (General) Student must have been living together in a relationship similar to marriage or civil partnership for a period of at least two years (see further **8.8**).

(d) The marriage or civil partnership, or relationship similar to marriage or civil partnership, must be subsisting at the time the application is made. See further **8.3.3.5**.

(e) The applicant and the Tier 4 (General) Student must intend to live with the other as their spouse or civil partner, unmarried or same-sex partner throughout the applicant's stay in the UK. See further **8.3.3.5**.

(f) The applicant must not intend to stay in the UK beyond any period of leave granted to the Tier 4 (General) Student.

(g) There must be a sufficient level of funds available to the applicant, as set out in Appendix E.

6.8.2.2 Maintenance funds

As to (g) in **6.8.2.1** above, the same requirements for available maintenance funds apply to a Partner as to an applicant (see **6.3.3**). Appendix E of the Immigration Rules (see **Appendix 1**) sets out the following requirements:

(a) If the Tier 4 Migrant is studying in Inner London, there must be £533 in funds for each month for which the applicant would, if successful, be granted leave, up to a maximum of £4,797.

(b) If the Tier 4 Migrant is not studying in Inner London, there must be £400 in funds for each month for which the applicant would, if successful, be granted leave, up to a maximum of £3,600.

> **Example**
>
> Anne applies for entry clearance as a Tier 4 (General) Student. She has a CAS issued by an Inner London-based sponsor. She has a place on a 24-month Master's degree course. She does not have an official financial sponsor. She has not yet paid anything towards her course fees or the accommodation arranged by her sponsor. Her civil partner, Brenda, will be travelling with her. In addition to meeting the requirements of para 319C(a)–(f) above, what maintenance funds under (g) do they need to have available? Anne needs the amount of her first year's fees and £7,200 to cover living costs for nine months in the UK (see **6.3.3.1**). As she will get 28 months' leave (see **6.4**), there must be the maximum additional amount available for Brenda of £4,797.

6.8.2.3 Leave and conditions

If the application is successful, the Partner is granted entry clearance and leave to remain for a period which expires on the same day as the leave granted to the Tier 4 (General) Student. That leave will be subject to conditions not to have recourse to public funds and registration with the police, if this is required (see **3.3.2** and **3.3.3** respectively).

6.8.3 Child

6.8.3.1 Requirements

The requirements are set out in para 319H, as follows:

(a) The applicant must not fall for refusal under the general grounds for refusal (see **3.5.4**) and, if applying for leave to remain, must not be an illegal entrant (see **10.2.2**).

(b) The applicant must be the child of a parent who:

  (i) has valid leave to enter or remain as a Tier 4 (General) Student; or

  (ii) is, at the same time, being granted entry clearance or leave to remain as a Tier 4 (General) Student.

(c) The applicant must be under the age of 18 on the date the application is made, or if over 18 and applying for leave to remain, must have, or have last been granted, leave as the child of a Tier 4 (General) Student.

(d) The applicant must not be married or in a civil partnership, must not have formed an independent family unit, and must not be leading an independent life. See further **8.9.4.6**.

(e) The applicant must not intend to stay in the UK beyond any period of leave granted to the Tier 4 (General) Student parent.

(f) Both of the applicant's parents must either be lawfully present in the UK, or being granted entry clearance or leave to remain at the same time as the applicant, unless:

  (i) the Tier 4 (General) Student is the applicant's sole surviving parent; or

  (ii) the Tier 4 (General) Student parent has and has had sole responsibility for the applicant's upbringing (see **8.9.4.3**); or

  (iii) there are serious or compelling family or other considerations which would make it desirable not to refuse the application and suitable arrangements have been made in the UK for the applicant's care (see **8.9.4.4**).

(g) There must be a sufficient level of funds available to the applicant, as set out in Appendix E.

It is important to note the effect of (c) above in respect of a child now aged 18 or over. That child will still qualify for an extension of leave in this category, provided he had previously obtained such leave when under 18.

6.8.3.2 Maintenance funds

As to (g) in **6.8.3.1** above, the additional available maintenance funds are exactly the same as for any Partner (**6.8.2.2**).

> **Example**
>
> Lewis applies for entry clearance as a Tier 4 (General) Student. He has a CAS issued by an Outer London-based sponsor. He has a place on a 12-month Master's degree course. He does not have an official financial sponsor. He has not yet paid his course fees. He is not using accommodation arranged by his sponsor. His wife, Alice, and six-year-old son, John, will be travelling with him. In addition to meeting the requirements of paras 319C and 319F(a)–(f) respectively, what maintenance funds under (g) do they need to have available? Lewis needs the amount of his course fees and £5,400 to cover living costs for nine months in the UK (see **6.3.3.1**). As he will get 16 months' leave (see **6.4**), there must be the maximum additional amount available for his wife, Alice, of £3,600 and also the maximum additional amount available for his son, John, of £3,600.

6.8.3.3 Leave and conditions

If the application is successful, the child is granted entry clearance and leave to remain for a period which expires on the same day as the leave granted to his Tier 4 (General) Student parent. This will be subject to conditions of no recourse to public funds and registration with the police, if this is required (see **3.3.2** and **3.3.3** respectively).

6.9 Postgraduate doctors and dentists

A doctor or dentist who graduates from a UK education institution will be allowed to remain in the UK do a recognised Foundation Programme as a postgraduate in the Tier 4 (General) Student category, as long as he meets all the usual requirements for the category and the following additional requirements:

(a) The applicant must have successfully completed a recognised UK degree in medicine or dentistry from an approved education provider who has a Tier 4 licence to bring in students, or from a UK publicly-funded institution of further or higher education, or from an institution on the Department for Innovation, Universities and Skills list of recognised bodies or listed bodies list, which keeps satisfactory records of enrolment and attendance. These lists may be viewed on the Department's website at www.dcsf.gov.uk.

(b) The applicant must have been given permission to stay in the UK as a student under the rules in place before 31 March 2009 or as a Tier 4 (General) Student. This permission must have covered his final academic year and at least one other academic year of his studies leading to his degree.

If successful, the applicant will get a maximum period of three years' permission to stay in this category.

6.10 Who can switch to become a Tier 4 (General) Student?

The following migrants already in the UK may switch from their current category and apply for leave to remain as a Tier 4 (General) Student, namely a:

(a) Tier 2 General Worker (see **7.9**);

(b) Tier 2 Intra-Company Transfer Worker (see **7.9**);

(c) Tier 2 Minister of Religion (see **7.10**);

(d) Tier 4 Child Student (see **6.1.1**);

(e) Prospective Student (see **5.5.3**).

6.11 Tier 4 (General) Student switching to another category

A Tier 4 (General) Student may be able to switch categories whilst in the UK. The most usual routes would be into the category of a Tier 1 (Entrepreneur) Migrant (see **7.4**), Tier 1 (Investor) Migrant (see **7.5**), Tier 2 Migrant (see **7.7**), the spouse or civil partner of a person settled in the UK (see **8.3**), or the same-sex partner of a person settled in the UK (see **8.8**).

Note that if a Tier 4 (General) Student switches to a category that may lead to settlement, the time spent in the student category cannot count towards the time needed to qualify for settlement.

6.12 Summary of points and evidence required for a Tier 4 (General) Student

Points	How obtained	Evidence required
30	Sponsorship – studying a course that meets the UKBA's minimum academic requirements and leads to an approved qualification with a licensed education provider (see **6.3.2**).	Confirmation of acceptance for studies from the sponsor with supporting documents (see **6.3.2**).
10	Maintenance – having enough cash available to pay course fees and monthly living costs (see **6.3.3**).	Bank statement or letter confirming level of cash funds (see **6.3.3.2**). It must be shown that the applicant has held the money for at least 28 days ending no more than one month before the date of the application.

6.13 Summary of different types of student categories

Category	Key details
Child visitor (see **5.3**)	Aged 17 or less and coming to UK to do a course of study for up to six months.
Tier 4 (Child) Student	Aged between 4 and 17. If aged between 4 and 15 must be entering UK to be educated at an independent fee-paying school.
Student visitor (see **5.5**)	Aged 18 or over, coming to UK to do a course for up to six months and not working whilst in UK.
Prospective student (see **5.5.3**)	Enters UK to consider which course to study, or planning to start a course of study within six months.
Tier 4 (General) Student	Adult student coming to UK for post-16 education.

Chapter 7
Employment, Business and Investment

7.1 Introduction

7.1.1 Who can work, conduct business or invest in the UK?

In this chapter we shall consider entry to the UK for the specific purpose of working, conducting business or investing.

Nationals of the EEA can work, conduct business and invest in the UK exercising EU Treaty rights (see **Chapter 4**). If a UK business wants to employ an EEA national, it will not have to use any of the domestic law routes of entry dealt with in this chapter.

A general visitor (see **5.1.2**) is prohibited from working. A student (see **6.6.4**) is restricted as to what work he may do. But the following people can freely carry out any of these activities:

(a) anyone admitted for settlement (see **Chapter 8**);

(b) anyone given limited leave with a view to settlement, eg spouses, civil partners and those in a non-marital relationship (see **Chapter 8**);

(c) refugees and those granted humanitarian protection (see **Chapter 9**);

(d) anyone admitted, without prohibition on employment, as the dependant of someone with limited leave in the UK, eg the spouse or civil partner of a Tier 1 or Tier 2 Migrant (see **7.6** and **7.8.9**).

7.1.2 Overview of the categories covered in this chapter

A person seeking to enter the UK may fall into one of the following categories:

(a) A person with officially recognised 'exceptional talent' in the field of science, humanities, engineering or the arts, an entrepreneur (business person) and an investor. These are known as *Tier 1 Migrants*. They form part of a points-based system detailed in paras 245AA to 245DF.

In the Immigration Rules, these Tier 1 Migrants are normally given limited leave initially for three years. This may be extended for two years, followed by an application for settlement. Note that in certain circumstances an entrepreneur or investor may be able to apply for settlement earlier.

See further **7.2**.

(b) A skilled (general) worker, minister of religion or sports person. These applicants are known as *Tier 2 Migrants* and form part of the points system detailed in the Immigration Rules, paras 245G to 245HF. Each person must have a UK-based sponsor who is licensed by the UKBA. Limited leave is initially for three years. This may be extended for two years, followed by an application for settlement. See further **7.8**.

(c) Temporary work in the creative and sporting sector, charity and religious workers, government authorised exchange workers, workers under an international agreement and workers under a youth mobility scheme. These are known as *Tier 5 Migrants* and form part of the points system detailed in the Immigration Rules, paras 245ZI to 245ZS. Each category has its own sponsorship arrangements. As this tier provides for temporary work only, leave is usually limited to one or two years and cannot lead to settlement. See further **7.12**.

(d) A sole representative of an overseas firm who will establish a wholly-owned subsidiary or branch in the UK. This is a long-standing category and it is not part of the points system. The requirements are set out in para 144 of the Immigration Rules. A person who meets the requirements is given three years' limited leave. That may be extended for two years, followed by an application for settlement. See further **7.13**.

(e) A Commonwealth citizen with a UK-born grandparent. This is a long-standing category reflecting the UK's historical links with the Commonwealth. It is not part of the points system. The requirements are set out in para 186 of the Immigration Rules. A person who meets the requirements may enter the UK to look for, or take up, work. Five years' limited leave is given, after which an application for settlement can be made. See further **7.14**.

Note that at the time of writing the Government has indicated that it does not intend to implement Tier 3 for low-skilled workers for the foreseeable future.

7.2 Overview of Tier 1

7.2.1 A profile of each category

7.2.1.1 Exceptional talent

This category allows a person who is internationally recognised as a world leader or potential world-leading talent in the field of science, humanities, engineering or the arts to work in the UK provided he has the official endorsement of a UKBA-specified Designated Competent Body (DCB).

7.2.1.2 Entrepreneur

This category might otherwise be called the 'business person' route into the UK. The individual (or team of two entrepreneurs) must be investing in the UK. How? By either setting up a new business, or joining or taking over an existing business. Note that the minimum investment in a business is either £200,000 from any source or £50,000 from a UKBA-approved source such as a registered and regulated venture capital firm.

7.2.1.3 Investor

This category is for an individual who is able to make substantial financial investment of at least £1,000,000 in the UK.

7.2.2 Common features: entry clearance

7.2.2.1 Points system

An entrepreneur is required to score 95 points from three different areas, namely attributes (a minimum of 75 points), English language (10 points) and maintenance (10 points).

A person with exceptional talent and an investor are required to score 75 points for attributes. These categories are not subject to the English language and maintenance requirements in order to obtain entry clearance. However, a person with exceptional talent will need to meet the English language requirement when applying for an extension of leave (see **7.3.3**).

7.2.2.2 Attributes

Briefly, the specific attributes are as follows:

(a) Person with exceptional talent – the applicant must have the official endorsement of a UKBA-specified DCB.

(b) Entrepreneur – the applicant must have access to at least £200,000 that is in a regulated financial institution, being disposable in the UK to invest in business; or £50,000 in a UKBA-approved source such as a registered and regulated venture capital firm.

(c) Investor – the applicant must have access to either £1 million that is in a regulated financial institution and disposable in the UK; or personal assets exceeding £2,000,000 and at least a £1 million loan from a regulated financial institution.

Full details are set out below, where each category is considered further.

7.2.2.3 English language test for entrepreneur

An entrepreneur must have a minimum level of English language. This requires scoring 10 points for either passing a UKBA-prescribed English language test, or being a national of a UKBA-desginated majority English-speaking country or having a UKBA-recognised degree that was taught in English. Further details are given at **7.4.3**.

7.2.2.4 Available maintenance funds test for entrepreneur

An entrepreneur must be able to demonstrate that he can support himself in the UK. This requires scoring 10 points for available maintenance funds of £2,800 or more. Further details are set out at **7.4.4**.

7.2.2.5 Self-assessment

A Tier 1 applicant can assess the likely number of points he will score by using the UKBA on-line points-based calculator. This is at www.ukba.homeoffice.gov.uk/pointscalculator.

7.2.2.6 Forms and guidance notes

Applicants can find application forms and guidance notes on the UKBA's website.

7.2.2.7 Not liable to refusal on general grounds

An applicant will fail if his application is liable to be refused under the general grounds in Part 9 of the Immigration Rules (see **3.4.5**).

7.2.3 Common features: extension of leave

Just before the initial limited leave of a Tier 1 Migrant expires, an application should be made to extend it. Basically the applicant will have to demonstrate that the original requirements have been met, eg an exceptional talent migrant must show that he is economically active in his expert field and still endorsed by his DCB; an entrepreneur must show that the full amount of cash has been invested in business in the UK; and an investor must show that he has invested at least £750,000 within three months.

An applicant will fail if his application for an extension is liable to be refused under the general grounds in Part 9 of the Immigration Rules (see **3.4.5**) or he is an illegal entrant (see **10.2.2**).

See further **7.3.3**, **7.4.5** and **7.5.3**.

7.2.4 Common features: limited leave conditions

In each category it will be a condition of a person's limited leave that he does not have recourse to public funds (see **3.3.2**).

A person must also register with the police if this is necessary under the Immigration Rules, para 326 (see **3.3.3**).

Additionally, it is a condition of an entrepreneur's limited leave that he does not take employment other than working for the business or businesses that he has established, joined or taken over, nor as a professional sportsperson (including as a sports coach).

Also, it is a condition of the limited leave of a person with exceptional talent that he does not take employment as a doctor or dentist in training, or as a professional sportsperson (including as a sports coach).

7.2.5 Common features: settlement

As a general rule, once a Tier 1 Migrant has spent a continuous period of five years in the UK in that category, an application can be made for settlement.

Note that an entrepreneur can apply to settle more quickly if he creates 10 jobs or turns over £5 million in a three-year period. See further **7.4.6**.

Note also that an investor is able to settle here faster if he invests larger sums of money. Those who invest at least £5 million can apply to settle after three years, whilst those investing £10 million or more can apply to settle after two years. See further **7.5.4**.

7.2.6 Common features: family members

Who are the family members of a Tier 1 applicant? The answer is his spouse, civil partner, unmarried or same-sex partner, and children under 18.

Does a family member have to obtain entry clearance? Yes. The requirements are in the Immigration Rules, paras 319A–319K. See further **7.6**.

7.2.7 Common features: verification of documentation

Each application form lists the various specified documents (see **3.6.4.1**) that are needed. Where a UKBA officer has a reasonable doubt that a specified document is genuine, it is normal practice to verify the document with an independent person or government agency.

There are three possible outcomes of a document verification check:

(a) If the document is confirmed as genuine, the application will proceed unaffected.

(b) If the document is confirmed as false, the application will be refused, whether or not the document is essential to the application.

(c) If the verification check is inconclusive then that document will be ignored as evidence for scoring points.

7.2.8 Switching to a Tier 1 category

Switching of categories by way of an application to the Home Office is possible, as shown in **Table 7.1** below.

Table 7.1 Switching to a Tier 1 category

To	From
Entrepreneur	Investor, Tier 2 Migrant (see **7.8**), Tier 4 Migrant (see **Chapter 6**).
Investor	Entrepreneur, Tier 2 Migrant (see **7.8**), Tier 4 Migrant (see **Chapter 6**).

7.3 Tier 1: (Exceptional Talent) Migrant

7.3.1 Overview

An applicant must be internationally recognised in his field as a world leading talent and be endorsed by a UKBA-specified DCB.

7.3.2 The attributes

An applicant must score 75 points for the specific attribute of having been issued with the endorsement of a UKBA-specified DCB. Each DCB's criteria for the endorsement of an applicant is on the UKBA's website.

What DCBs have been specified by the UKBA? Currently, just four, namely: the Arts Council for arts and culture applications; The British Academy for humanities and social science applications; The Royal Society for natural sciences and medical science research applications; and The Royal Academy of Engineering for engineering applications.

So what steps must an applicant take? The applicant must request a Tier 1 (Exceptional Talent) Unique Reference Number (URN) from the UKBA. This request must state the appropriate DCB to endorse the applicant. As there is a limit of places on this route (see **7.3.5**), the UKBA will only provide the applicant with a URN if there is a place available within the limit for his selected DCB. The applicant can then make an application to the UKBA, together with the URN and supporting documentation as required by the DCB's endorsement criteria. Note that the application must be submitted to the UKBA Visa Services and not to the DCB. The UKBA sends the relevant documentation to the applicant's chosen DCB, which will advise the UKBA whether the applicant meets its endorsement criteria. If so, the UKBA will then consider the application, taking into account whether the DCB has endorsed the applicant, make its decision and notify the applicant of the result.

7.3.3 Post-entry: extension

Just before the initial three years' limited leave of a person with exceptional talent expires, an application should be made to extend it under the Immigration Rules, para 245BD.

An applicant will fail if his application is liable to be refused under the general grounds in Part 9 of the Immigration Rules (see **3.4.5**) or he is an illegal entrant (see **10.2.2**).

The applicant must be economically active in his expert field as previously endorsed by a DCB, in employment or self-employment or both; and the DCB must not have withdrawn its endorsement.

The applicant must now satisfy the English language test (the details are at **7.4.3**).

7.3.4 Post-entry: settlement

Once a person with exceptional talent has spent a continuous period of five years in the UK in that category, an application can be made for settlement under the Immigration Rules, para 245BF. The applicant will have to show that he:

(a) does not have one or more unspent convictions within the meaning of the Rehabilitation of Offenders Act 1974 (see **Appendix 8**), does not fall for refusal under the general grounds for refusal (see **3.4.5**) and is not an illegal entrant (see **10.2.2**);

(b) has spent a continuous period of five years lawfully in the UK as a Tier 1 (Exceptional Talent) Migrant;

(c) is economically active in his expert field as previously endorsed by a DCB, in employment or self-employment or both, and the DCB has not withdrawn its endorsement; and

(d) has sufficient knowledge of the English language (see **7.4.3**) and sufficient knowledge about life in the UK (see **3.8.7**).

If an applicant has any family members (spouse, civil partner, unmarried or same-sex partner and children under 18) living with him, they may be able to apply for settlement at the same time (see **7.6**).

7.3.5 Tier 1 (Exceptional Talent) Migrant annual limit

At the time of writing, the Government has stated that for the period ending 5 April 2012 the maximum number of endorsements in this category will be 1,000 divided as follows:

(a) The Arts Council has 300 places;

(b) The British Academy has 200 places;

(c) The Royal Society has 300 places; and

(d) The Royal Academy of Engineering has 200 places.

7.4 Tier 1: Entrepreneur

7.4.1 Overview

This category might otherwise be called the 'business person' route into the UK.

The applicant (or a team of two entrepreneurs) must either be setting up a new business, joining or taking over an existing business by investing in it.

How much is required? A minimum of £200,000 from any source or £50,000 from a UKBA-approved source such as a registered and regulated venture capital firm.

In addition, the applicant must be able to speak English and have enough money to support himself and any dependants.

See the flow diagram summary at **Appendix 12**.

The investment must be in one or more UK businesses. UKBA guidance is that a business is only considered to be in the UK if:

(a) it is trading within the UK economy;

(b) it has a registered office in the UK, except where the applicant is registered with HM Revenue and Customs (HMRC) as self-employed and does not have a business office;

(c) it has a UK bank account; and

(d) it is subject to UK taxation.

Multinational companies that are registered as UK companies with either a registered office or head office in the UK are acceptable.

Where two entrepreneurs apply as a team, each must separately pass the English language and maintenance tests.

7.4.2 The entrepreneur attributes

An applicant must score 75 points for specific attributes regarding the level of his investment, where the money is held and the fact that it is disposable in the UK.

The details are set out in Table 4 of Appendix A to the Immigration Rules (see **Appendix 1** to this book).

7.4.2.1 Points

The points required for specific attributes are shown in **Table 7.2** below.

Table 7.2 Entrepreneur – specific attributes points

Investment	Points
The applicant has access to not less than £200,000; or The applicant has access to not less than £50,000 from: (a) one or more registered venture capitalist firms regulated by the Financial Services Authority; and/or (b) one or more UK entrepreneurial seed funding competitions listed as endorsed on the UK Trade & Investment website; and/or (c) one or more UK government departments, and made available by the department(s) for the specific purpose of establishing or expanding a UK business.	25
The money is held in one or more regulated financial institutions	25
The money is disposable in the UK	25

It can be seen that to score the required 75 points the applicant must meet all three requirements. We shall now look at each in more detail.

7.4.2.2 The applicant has access to the prescribed investment

First, let us consider the £200,000 route.

An applicant must demonstrate that he has at least £200,000 of his own money available to make a fresh investment into business in the UK. The UKBA guidance is that the applicant may include money made available by one or more other people ('a third party or parties'). This includes another investor or corporate body, as well as an applicant's spouse, civil partner, unmarried or same-sex partner. In those circumstances the applicant must also provide a declaration from each third party that the money is available to the applicant, together with confirmation from a legal representative that the declaration document is valid (see **7.4.2.5**).

Secondly, what about the £50,000 alternative route?

An applicant must demonstrate that he has access to at least £50,000 to invest in business. Those funds can be made up of any combination of the three prescribed sources. But an applicant cannot use any of his own funds to meet this requirement.

What is a venture capitalist firm? It is a company that draws on private equity funds to invest in new businesses with high growth potential, and in exchange it takes a stake in the business (which it subsequently hopes to sell at a profit). A registered firm is one regulated by the Financial Services Authority (FSA).

What UK entrepreneurial seed funding competitions are listed as endorsed on the UK Trade & Investment website? At the time of writing these are Springboard and Seedcamp (at www.ukti.gov.uk/uktihome/item/128990.html).

Where a UK government department is providing all or some of the funds specifically for the purpose of setting up or expanding a business in the UK, the funding package can be considered for the award of points here.

7.4.2.3 The money is held in one or more regulated financial institutions

The financial institution or institutions that provide confirmation that the money is available to the applicant must be regulated by the home regulator, ie an official financial regulatory body in the country where the financial institution operates and the funds are located. This body must be appropriate to the type of financial transaction. For example, where a financial institution does business in the UK, the appropriate regulator is the FSA.

7.4.2.4 The money is disposable in the UK

If the money is held in the UK then it must be with an institution that is regulated by the FSA. Where the money is held outside the UK, all of the amount required to qualify must be freely transferable to the UK and able to be converted to pounds sterling.

If the money is held overseas but in an institution that has a presence in the UK and is regulated by the FSA, the UKBA requires no further evidence that the money can be transferred into the UK. In all other cases that evidence is needed by way of a document from the bank or financial institution.

Funds in a foreign currency are converted into pounds sterling using an official exchange rate currency converter recognised by the UKBA at www.oanda.com. This is done on the date on which the application is made.

7.4.2.5 Specified documents

To satisfy each of the three requirements and thereby score 25 points for each, the applicant must produce an original letter, on official headed paper, from each financial institution holding the applicant's funds, confirming that the stated amount of money is available and disposable in the UK.

Each letter must have been produced within the three months immediately before the date of the application. Each letter must also confirm that the institution is regulated by the appropriate body. Details of the amount of money being provided by any third party must also be given.

If the applicant is relying on third-party funding, he must supply a declaration from every third party that they have made the money available for the applicant to invest in a business in the UK, and a letter from a legal representative confirming the validity of signatures on each third-party declaration provided.

7.4.2.6 Team of two entrepreneurs

The required investment funds can be shared by an entrepreneurial team of two people. Each member of the team may apply to come to the UK in this category using the same investment funds.

Where two applicants apply using funds from a third party, each provider of funds must confirm that both applicants have equal access to, and are able to dispose of, the money in the UK.

7.4.3 English language

An applicant must score 10 points for English language. There are three different ways in which an applicant might achieve this, as set out in Appendix B to the Immigration Rules (see **Appendix 1** to this book). In summary these are that the applicant:

(a) has passed a UKBA-approved English language test;

(b) is a national of a UKBA-designated majority English-speaking country; or

(c) holds a degree accepted by the UKBA as taught in English that is equivalent to a UK Bachelor's degree or above.

7.4.3.1 English language UKBA-approved test

An applicant must demonstrate knowledge of English equivalent to level C1 of the Council of Europe's Common European Framework for Language Learning, or above. Details are on the Council's website at www.coe.int/T/DG4/Linguistic/CADRE_EN.asp. A list of UKBA-approved test providers and their contact details are on the UKBA's website.

The original test result certificate must be submitted with the application. It must show the applicant's name, the qualification obtained and the date of the award.

7.4.3.2 National of a UKBA-designated majority English-speaking country

Nationals of UKBA-designated majority English-speaking countries automatically meet the English language requirement. To prove their nationality they must produce a current valid original passport or travel document.

Nationals of the following countries are designated for these purposes by UKBA:

Antigua and Barbuda
Australia
The Bahamas
Barbados
Belize
Canada
Dominica
Grenada
Guyana
Jamaica
New Zealand
St Kitts and Nevis
St Lucia
St Vincent and the Grenadines
Trinidad and Tobago
United States of America

7.4.3.3 Degree accepted by the UKBA as taught in English

An applicant meets the English language requirement if he can produce an academic qualification (not a professional or vocational qualification) from an educational establishment in a UKBA-prescribed country listed below. These are deemed by the National Academic Recognition Information Centre for the United Kingdom (UK NARIC) to meet or exceed the recognised standard of at least a Bachelor's degree in the UK.

Academic qualifications from the following countries count:

Antigua and Barbuda
Australia
The Bahamas
Barbados
Belize
Dominica
Grenada
Guyana
Ireland
Jamaica
New Zealand
St Kitts and Nevis
St Lucia

St Vincent and the Grenadines
Trinidad and Tobago
United Kingdom
United States of America

What if an applicant's relevant qualification was taught in English but not in one of the above countries? Points will be awarded if the qualification is equivalent to at least a UK Bachelor's degree and the degree was taught to a competent standard of English equivalent to level C1 on the Council of Europe's Common European Framework of Reference for Languages. In these circumstances an applicant should use the UKBA's points-based calculator on its website (see **7.2.2.5**).

7.4.4 Available maintenance funds

Applicants must be able to support themselves for the entire duration of their stay in the UK without needing public funds (see **3.3.2**). An applicant must score 10 points for having available sufficient maintenance funds. As to what constitute 'sufficient' funds, the requirement is set out in Appendix C to the Immigration Rules (see **Appendix 1** to this book).

An applicant must have at least £2,800 of personal savings. The applicant must demonstrate that he has held at least that amount for a consecutive 90-day period of time, ending no earlier than one calendar month before the date of his application. So access to a bank overdraft facility in excess of that amount will not satisfy this requirement: see *R (Adeyemi-Doro) v Secretary of State for the Home Department* [2011] EWCA Civ 849.

Points will be awarded only if the UKBA receives the specified documentary evidence of the applicant's personal savings. So an applicant must produce personal bank or building society statements, or building society passbooks covering the 90-day period. These should clearly show the applicant's name; the account number; the date; the financial institution's name and logo; transactions covering the 90-day period; and a balance that does not fall below £2,800. Alternatively, a letter confirming these details from the applicant's bank or a financial institution regulated by the FSA may be acceptable.

If an applicant is bringing any family members (spouse, civil partner, unmarried or same-sex partner and children under 18) with him, he will have to demonstrate that additional maintenance funds are available. See **7.6**.

An applicant may not use any moneys included in his investment as evidence of maintenance funds.

7.4.5 Post-entry: extension

Just before the initial three years' limited leave of an entrepreneur expires, an application should be made to extend it under para 245DD of the Immigration Rules.

An applicant will fail if his application is liable to be refused under the general grounds in Part 9 of the Immigration Rules (see **3.5.4**) or he is an illegal entrant (see **10.2.2**).

Basically, the applicant has to demonstrate that the original requirements have been met, ie the entrepreneur must show that the full amount of £200,000 or £50,000 (as appropriate) in cash has been invested in business in the UK and the applicant must again score at least 75 points. See **7.4.5.1**.

As the applicant will have satisfied the English language test when applying for entry clearance, that requirement does not apply again.

The applicant will have to demonstrate that he has maintained and will continue to maintain himself (and any dependants). See **7.4.5.6**.

7.4.5.1 Attributes for an extension

An applicant must score 75 points for specific attributes in relation to the investment steps he has taken since entering the UK.

The details are set out in Table 5 of Appendix A to the Immigration Rules (see **Appendix 1** to this book), as shown in **Table 7.3** below.

Table 7.3 Entrepreneur – attributes points for an extension

Investment and business activity	Points
The applicant has invested, or had invested on his behalf, not less than £200,000 or £50,000 (as appropriate) in cash directly into one or more businesses in the UK.	20
The applicant has: (a) registered with HMRC as self-employed; (b) registered a new business in which he is a director; or (c) registered as a director of an existing business. Where the applicant's last grant of entry clearance, leave to enter or leave to remain was as a Tier 1 (Entrepreneur) Migrant, this condition must have been met within six months of his entry to the UK (if he was granted entry clearance in this category and there is evidence to establish his date of arrival to the UK), or, in any other case, the date of the grant of leave to remain.	20
On a date no earlier than three months prior to the date of application, the applicant has: (a) registered with HMRC as self-employed; (b) registered a new business in which he is a director; or (c) registered as a director of an existing business.	15
The applicant has: (a) established a new business or businesses that has or have created the equivalent of at least two new full-time jobs for persons settled in the UK; or (b) taken over or joined an existing business or businesses, and his services or investment have resulted in a net increase in the employment provided by the business or businesses for persons settled in the UK by creating the equivalent of at least two new full-time jobs. Where the applicant's last grant of entry clearance or leave to enter or remain was as a Tier 1 (Entrepreneur) Migrant, the jobs must have existed for at least 12 months of the period for which the previous leave was granted.	20

It can be seen that to score the required 75 points the applicant must meet all four requirements. We shall now look at each in more detail.

7.4.5.2 Invested at least £200,000 or £50,000 (as appropriate) cash in UK business

The applicant must show that the full amount of £200,000 or £50,000 (as appropriate) in cash has already been invested in business in the UK. If the entrepreneur is no longer involved in a business, evidence of the investment must still be produced.

What property, if any, purchased by the applicant counts as an investment? The UKBA guidance is that only commercial premises count, and it does not include the value of any residential accommodation, nor property development or property management. If the applicant has bought property which includes residential accommodation for himself and his family, the value of that part is excluded.

If the applicant has made the investment in the form of a director's loan, does that count? The UKBA guidance is that this counts only if it is unsecured and ranks after any third-party creditors of the company. The original legal agreement between the applicant and the company must be provided.

What other documentary evidence is required? If the business is a registered company that is required to produce audited accounts, these must be provided. Businesses that are not required to produce audited accounts must provide their unaudited management accounts, together with a certificate of confirmation from an UK regulated accountant. Audited accounts, or management accounts accompanied by an accountant's certificate, must show how much the applicant has invested in the business.

For each business that an applicant relies on to claim points, documents from a prescribed list must be produced in order to prove that it is a UK business. That UKBA list is set out at **Appendix 13**. Note that one piece of evidence from rows 1, 2 and 3 in the list has to be provided for each business or company.

7.4.5.3 Registration requirements

Self-employed applicants must provide either their original welcome letter from HMRC, or any Small Earnings Exemption Certificate from HMRC.

A director of a new or existing company must provide his Current Appointment Report from Companies House.

The UKBA guidance is that each document must be dated no more than six months after the date of entry clearance.

7.4.5.4 Engaged in a business activity

Although an applicant does not have to be engaged in the same business in which he was working when he first entered the UK, he must still be either a self-employed business person or a director of a company at the time the extension application is made. A self-employed person might prove this by producing evidence of payment of Class 2 National Insurance Contributions. A director should produce his Current Appointment Report from Companies House. The report must show that the applicant is a director of the business, and that it is actively trading and not struck off, dissolved or in liquidation.

7.4.5.5 Created at least the equivalent of two new full-time jobs

What is the purpose of this requirement? The UKBA states that the creation of employment for settled workers shows the applicant's contribution to the UK economy. However, the jobs do not have to exist at the time of the application. The requirement is that during the entrepreneur's three years' limited leave he must have created jobs that existed for at least 12 months of that period.

A self-employed applicant must employ the settled workers directly. If the applicant is a director of a business, he must show that his business has created the new posts for settled workers.

What is a full-time job? The UKBA considers a 30-hour working week to be full-time. But can part-time work form part of the total number of hours of employment created? Yes. Does the employment created need to be in a single period? No, it can be made up of shorter periods. Does it need to be for any particular number of workers? No, a single person may be employed for this time, or several people. But in all cases the employment must comply with UK regulations.

The UKBA gives the following useful examples:

(a) The working hours of two part-time workers can be combined to add up to 30 hours a week or more and form the equivalent of one full-time post.

(b) A worker who is employed for part of a year and then leaves the job can be replaced by another worker so that the employment as a whole adds up to at least 12 months. However, if there is a gap between one worker leaving a post and another worker starting employment, the period when the post is not filled will not be counted in the 12-month period. Only periods during which a worker is employed in a post will qualify for the award of points.

(c) If a single worker is employed for 24 months, this employment will qualify for the award of points. The employment can also be made up of a six-month period for one worker and an 18-month period for another.

(d) If four workers are employed for 26 weeks (six months) each, their hours of employment may be added together for the award of points.

What documents need to be produced? These include copies of the documents kept by the employer as evidence that the employee is a settled worker; documents registering the employee with HMRC; Form P11 (a report to HMRC recording the earnings of each separate employee); and payslips.

How does an applicant who has taken over or joined an existing UK business show that he has created new posts that result in a net increase? The applicant must produce a duplicate Form P35 (this is an annual return made to HMRC listing the names of employees of the business) and an original accountant's letter verifying that the new posts have been created.

7.4.5.6 Available maintenance funds

The level of funds required on an extension application is £800. The same documentation (see **7.4.4**) is required, evidencing that the applicant has held at least that amount for a consecutive 90-day period of time, ending no earlier than one calendar month before the date of his application.

If an applicant has any family members (spouse, civil partner, unmarried or same-sex partner and children under 18) living with him, he will have to demonstrate that additional maintenance funds are available. See **7.6**.

7.4.6 Post-entry: settlement

Once an entrepreneur has spent a continuous period of five years in the UK in that category (or three years in the circumstances set out in **Table 7.4** below), an application can be made for settlement under the Immigration Rules, para 245DF. The applicant will have to show that he:

(a) does not have one or more unspent convictions within the meaning of the Rehabilitation of Offenders Act 1974 (see **Appendix 8**), does not fall for refusal under the general grounds for refusal (see **3.5.4**) and is not an illegal entrant (see **10.2.2**);

(b) scores 75 points for specific attributes (see **7.4.6.1**); and

(c) has sufficient knowledge of the English language and sufficient knowledge about life in the UK (see **3.8.7**).

If an applicant has any family members (spouse, civil partner, unmarried or same-sex partner and children under 18) living with him, they may be able to apply for settlement at the same time (see **7.6**).

UKBA guidance is that the partner of an entrepreneur can apply for settlement at the same time as the entrepreneur provided they have lived together in the UK for at least two years before applying for settlement. An entrepreneur's child can apply for settlement at the same time as the entrepreneur, as long as the child meets the requirements of the Immigration Rules.

7.4.6.1 Specific attributes for settlement

An applicant must score 75 points for specific attributes in relation to the investment steps he has taken since entering the UK. The details are set out in Table 6 of Appendix A to the Immigration Rules (see **Appendix 1** to this book), as shown in **Table 7.4** below.

Table 7.4 Entrepreneur – attributes points for indefinite leave to remain

Investment and business activity	Points
On a date no earlier than three months prior to the date of application, the applicant has: (a) registered with HMRC as self-employed; (b) registered a new business in which he is a director; or (c) registered as a director of an existing business.	20
The applicant has: (a) established a new business or businesses that has or have created the equivalent of at least two new full-time jobs for persons settled in the UK; or (b) taken over or joined an existing business or businesses, and his services or investment have resulted in a net increase in the employment provided by the business or businesses for persons settled in the UK by creating the equivalent of at least two new full-time jobs. Where the applicant's last grant of entry clearance or leave to enter or remain was as a Tier 1 (Entrepreneur) Migrant, the jobs must have existed for at least 12 months of the period for which the previous leave was granted.	20
The applicant has spent the specified continuous period lawfully in the UK in this category, with absences from the UK of no more than 180 days in any 12 calendar months during that period. The specified continuous period is: (a) three years if the number of new full-time jobs referred to above is at least 10; (b) three years if the applicant has: (i) established a new UK business that has had an income from business activity of at least £5 million during a three-year period in which the applicant has had leave as a Tier 1 (Entrepreneur) Migrant; (ii) taken over or invested in an existing UK business and his services or investment have resulted in a net increase in income from business activity to that business of £5 million during a three-year period in which the applicant has had leave as a Tier 1 (Entrepreneur) Migrant, when compared to the immediately preceding three-year period; or (c) five years in all other cases.	35

It can be seen that to score the required 75 points the applicant must meet all three requirements. The first 40 points are the same as for an extension (see **7.4.5.3** and **7.4.5.4**). Securing the remaining 35 points will determine when the application can be made.

7.5 Tier 1: Investor

7.5.1 Overview

This category is for an individual who is able to make a substantial financial investment of at least £1 million in the UK.

An applicant does not have to meet any English language requirement because he is investing in the UK and can choose whether or not he wants to work. In addition, given the level of investment, he does not have to demonstrate that he has enough money to support himself (and any dependants).

7.5.2 The investor attributes

An applicant must score 75 points for either having access to £1 million that is in a regulated financial institution and disposable in the UK, or having personal assets exceeding £2 million and at least a £1 million loan from a regulated financial institution. These attributes are set out in Table 7 of Appendix A to the Immigration Rules (see **Appendix 1** to this book) as follows:

> The applicant:
>
> (a) has money of his own held in a regulated financial institution and disposable in the UK amounting to not less than £1 million; or
>
> (b) (i) owns personal assets which, taking into account any liabilities to which they are subject, have a value exceeding £2 million; and
>
> (ii) has money under his control held in a regulated financial institution and disposable in the UK amounting to not less than £1 million which has been loaned to him by a financial institution regulated by the Financial Services Authority.

7.5.2.1 The £1 million route

The applicant must show that he can make an investment of at least £1 million in the UK. The money may already be in the UK or held overseas at the time of application. If it is not in pounds sterling, the applicant must convert its value into that using the Oanda website (see **7.4.2.4**) on the date on which the application is made.

Can an applicant rely on money that he owns jointly with his spouse, civil partner, unmarried or same-sex partner? Yes. The UKBA guidance is that he may also rely on money that is owned solely by that person. However, the applicant must have an unrestricted right to transfer and dispose of that money, and the applicant must have permission from his spouse, civil partner or unmarried or same-sex partner to have control of the money in the UK. The applicant and/or his spouse, civil partner, unmarried or same-sex partner must be the beneficial owner of the funds. They must not be holding the investments on behalf of anyone else.

An applicant must produce the following documents to earn 75 points by this route:

(a) A portfolio report or breakdown of investments in a letter produced by a financial institution regulated by the FSA covering the three consecutive months in the period immediately before the application.

If the money has already been invested in the UK in the last 12 months or is held abroad, but in either case the applicant has such a report, he may use it as evidence that the money is available. Alternatively, the applicant may supply a breakdown of his investments in a letter from an authorised financial institution.

Only investments made in the UK within the 12 months immediately before the date of the application are eligible for the award of points. What investments count? Those in government bonds, share capital or loan capital in active and trading companies registered in the UK.

(b) Where the applicant manages his own investments or has a portfolio manager who does not operate in the UK, he must produce documentary evidence of his holdings. This may include certified copies of bonds, share certificates and audited accounts. All documents must cover the three consecutive months in the period immediately before the application.

(c) If the funds are in a bank account, the applicant must provide personal bank statements from a bank that is regulated by the official regulatory body for the country in which the institution operates and the funds are located. These must show the amount of money available in the name of the applicant and/or his spouse, civil partner, unmarried or same-sex partner. Consecutive bank statements covering the three months immediately before the date of application are required. Alternatively a letter from that bank may be acceptable.

What if the money has not been held in a portfolio or bank account for at least three months prior to the application? Then the applicant will have to provide evidence of the source of the money. The UKBA guidance is that it will consider the sources of funds set out in **Table 7.5** below if the specified supporting evidence is produced.

Table 7.5 Investor – sources of funds

Source of funds	Supporting evidence required
Gift	The original irrevocable memorandum of gift and a letter from a legal adviser confirming that it is valid and binding according to the laws of the country in which it was made.
Deeds of sale	The original deeds of sale of assets (such as property or business) and a letter from a legal adviser confirming that the sale was genuine and that the money is available to the applicant.
Evidence from a business	Business accounts and a letter from a legal adviser confirming that the applicant can lawfully extract the money from the business.
Will	A notarised copy of the will and a letter from a legal adviser confirming the validity of the will.
Divorce settlement	A notarised copy of the terms of the divorce settlement and a letter from a legal adviser confirming that the document is valid.
Award of winnings	A letter from the organisation issuing the financial award or winnings and a letter from a legal adviser confirming the money has been transferred.

In all other cases the applicant will need to produce original documentation as evidence of the source of the money, together with independent supporting evidence. For example, if the money was received as a result of court action, the UKBA requires original documents in the form of a letter of confirmation of the court proceedings and a suitable letter from the applicant's solicitor.

(d) Applicants who have funds that are not held in the UK, or who have a portfolio of investments that are not in the UK, must provide a letter from their bank or financial institution confirming that the money can be transferred into the UK.

If an applicant relies on money held jointly or solely by his spouse, civil partner, unmarried or same-sex partner, he must provide evidence that:

(i) establishes that relationship; and

(ii) confirms that his partner gives permission for the applicant to control the money in the UK.

This should include for (i) the original certificate of marriage or civil partnership, or evidence that demonstrates a two-year relationship similar in nature to marriage or civil partnership (as to the latter see **8.8**), and for (ii) a declaration from the partner that he will permit all joint or personal money used to claim points for the application to be under the control of the applicant in the UK, along with a letter from a legal adviser confirming that the declaration is valid.

7.5.2.2 The £2 million route

If an applicant intends to borrow money from an authorised financial institution regulated by the FSA to make an investment in the UK, his level of personal net worth must be at least £2 million. Applicants may borrow all of their £1 million investment funds. Can assets held by the applicant's spouse, civil partner, unmarried or same-sex partner, either jointly or in the partner's own name, be taken into account when assessing the applicant's net worth? Yes. But applicants cannot mix personal funds and borrowed funds in order to meet the total £1 million investment required for the award of 75 points.

The applicant will need to produce a letter from an authorised financial institution in the UK which confirms the following:

(a) that not less than £1 million is available for the applicant to borrow;

(b) the money is available on the date that the letter is issued;

(c) the institution is regulated by the FSA;

(d) the applicant's personal net worth is at least £2 million; and

(e) that the institution will confirm the content of the letter to the UKBA if required to do so.

How should the authorised financial institution calculate the applicant's personal net worth? The UKBA guidance is that it should add up the applicant's assets and deduct from that his liabilities. Assets can include personal cash, investments and property belonging to the applicant and/or his spouse, civil partner, unmarried or same-sex partner. Liabilities may include mortgages and loans.

7.5.3 Post-entry: extension

Just before the initial three years' limited leave of an investor expires, an application should be made to extend it under para 245ED of the Immigration Rules.

An applicant will fail if his application is liable to be refused under the general grounds in Part 9 of the Immigration Rules (see **3.5.4**) or he is an illegal entrant (see **10.2.2**).

Basically, the applicant has to demonstrate that the original requirements have been met, ie the investor has made the required investment, and the applicant must again score at least 75 points. The attributes are set out in Table 8 of Appendix A to the Immigration Rules (see **Appendix 1** to this book), as shown in **Table 7.6** below.

Table 7.6 Investor – attributes for extension

Assets and investment	Points
The applicant: (a) has money of his own under his control in the UK amounting to not less than £1 million; or (b) (i) owns personal assets which, taking into account any liabilities to which they are subject, have a value of not less than £2 million; and (ii) has money under his control held in a regulated financial institution and disposable in the UK amounting to not less than £1 million which has been loaned to him by a financial institution regulated by the FSA.	30

Assets and investment	Points
The applicant has invested not less than £750,000 of his capital in the UK by way of UK government bonds, share capital or loan capital in active and trading UK registered companies other than those principally engaged in property investment.	30
The investment referred to above was made within three months of obtaining entry clearance, leave to enter or leave to remain as a Tier 1 (Investor) Migrant, and the investment has been maintained for the whole of the remaining period of that leave.	15

It can be seen that to score the required 75 points the applicant must meet all three requirements. We shall now look at each in more detail.

7.5.3.1 £1 million in the UK

The first requirement has two alternatives that reflect the same original attributes (see **7.5.2.1** and **7.5.2.2**). An applicant will be awarded 30 points if he can show that he has £1 million or more in the UK. This should consist of money invested here and any further money necessary to bring the total funds to at least £1 million. This is a requirement for all applicants who used their own money, or joint money, or who borrowed their investment money for the initial application. See further **7.5.3.3**.

7.5.3.2 Invested at least £750,000 in a specified manner

The UKBA's stated policy is that the money must have been invested in ways that help to stimulate growth in the UK as directly as possible. To be awarded 30 points the applicant must have invested not less than £750,000 of his capital in the UK by way of UK government bonds, share capital or loan capital in active and trading companies that are registered in the UK.

7.5.3.3 Investment made within three months and maintained

An applicant must show that he invested at least the required £750,000 within three months of entry clearance.

The UKBA will accept investments made in the required form in the previous 12 months. Moreover, the applicant must show that his investment was kept at no less than £750,000 during his limited leave.

Can an applicant change investments within those permitted? Yes.

What if the value of any investment in stocks or shareholdings is reduced by fluctuations in share prices? If this occurs the applicant must correct it by the next reporting period, so that the overall value of the investments is maintained at no less than £750,000.

To be awarded 15 points an applicant will have to produce a portfolio of investments totalling at least £750,000, duly certified as correct by a financial institution that is regulated by the FSA.

In addition, if the investments amount to between £750,000 and £1 million, the applicant must provide evidence of the balance of the funds (such as documents confirming the purchase of assets, like property, in the UK; or a letter from a financial institution that holds the money on deposit).

7.5.4 Post-entry: settlement

Once an investor has spent a continuous period of five years in the UK in that category (or a shorter period of two or three years in the circumstances set out in **Table 7.11** below), an application can be made for settlement under para 245EF of the Immigration Rules.

The applicant will have to show that he:

(a) does not have one or more unspent convictions within the meaning of the Rehabilitation of Offenders Act 1974 (see **Appendix 8**), does not fall for refusal under the general grounds for refusal (see **3.5.4**) and is not an illegal entrant (see **10.2.2**);

(b) scores 75 points for specific attributes; and

(c) has sufficient knowledge of the English language and sufficient knowledge about life in the UK (see **3.8.7**).

If an applicant has any family members (spouse, civil partner, unmarried or same-sex partner and children under 18) living with him, they may be able to apply for settlement at the same time (see **7.6**).

UKBA guidance is that the partner of an investor can apply for settlement at the same time as the investor, provided they have lived together in the UK for at least two years before applying for settlement.

An investor's child can apply for settlement at the same time as the investor, as long as the child meets the requirements of the Immigration Rules.

7.5.4.1 Specific attributes for settlement

An applicant must score 75 points for specific attributes in relation to the investment steps he has taken since entering the UK. The details are set out in Table 9 of Appendix A to the Immigration Rules (see **Appendix 1** to this book), as shown in **Table 7.7** below.

Table 7.7 Investor – attributes points for indefinite leave to remain

Assets and investment	**Points**
The applicant: (a) (i) has money of his own under his control in the UK amounting to not less than £10 million; or (ii) (1) owns personal assets which, taking into account any liabilities to which they are subject, have a value of not less than £20 million; and (2) has money under his control and disposable in the UK amounting to not less than £10 million which has been loaned to him by a UK regulated financial institution; or (b) (i) has money of his own under his control in the UK amounting to not less than £5 million; or (ii) (1) owns personal assets which, taking into account any liabilities to which they are subject, have a value of not less than £10 million; and (2) has money under his control and disposable in the UK amounting to not less than £5 million which has been loaned to him by a UK regulated financial institution;	20

Assets and investment	Points
or (c) (i) has money of his own under his control in the UK amounting to not less than £1 million; or (ii) (1) owns personal assets which, taking into account any liabilities to which they are subject, have a value of not less than £2 million; and (2) has money under his control and disposable in the UK amounting to not less than £1 million which has been loaned to him by a UK regulated financial institution.	
The applicant has invested not less than 75% of the specified invested amount of his capital in the UK by way of UK government bonds, share capital or loan capital in active and trading UK registered companies, and has invested the remaining balance of the specified invested amount in the UK by the purchase of assets or by maintaining the money on deposit in a UK regulated financial institution. The specified invested amount is: (a) £10 million if the applicant scores points from (a)(i) or (ii) in the box above; (b) £5 million if the applicant scores points from (b)(i) or (ii) in the box above; or (c) £1 million if the applicant scores points from (c)(i) or (ii) in the box above.	20
The applicant has spent the specified continuous period lawfully in the UK, with absences from the UK of no more than 180 days in any 12 calendar months during that period. The specified continuous period must have been spent with leave as a Tier 1 (Investor) Migrant and/or as an Investor, of which the most recent period must have been spent with leave as a Tier 1 (Investor) Migrant. The specified continuous period is: (a) two years if the applicant scores points from (a)(i) or (ii) in the first box above; (b) three years if the applicant scores points from (b)(i) or (ii) in the first box above; or (c) five years if the applicant scores points from (c)(i) or (ii) in the first box above.	20
The applicant has maintained the full specified invested amount referred to in the relevant part of the second box above throughout the relevant specified continuous period referred to in the third box above, other than in the first three months of that period and, in relation to time spent with leave as a Tier 1 (Investor) Migrant, has provided specified documents to show that this requirement has been met. When calculating the specified continuous period, the first day of that period will be taken to be the day three months before the full specified amount is invested.	15

7.6 Family members of a Tier 1 Migrant

7.6.1 Entry clearance and leave to remain

If subject to immigration controls, the spouse, civil partner, unmarried or same-sex partner ('the Partner') and children under 18 of a Tier 1 Migrant will require entry clearance in order to enter the UK, and should usually subsequently apply for an extension at the same time as the Tier 1 Migrant. The requirements are set out in the Immigration Rules, paras 319A–319K.

7.6.1.1 Partner

The requirements are set out in para 319C as follows:

(a) The applicant must not fall for refusal under the general grounds for refusal (see **3.5.4**), and if applying for leave to remain must not be an illegal entrant (see **10.2.2**).

(b) The applicant must be the spouse or civil partner, unmarried or same-sex partner of a person who:

  (i) has valid leave to enter or remain as a Tier 1 Migrant; or

  (ii) is, at the same time, being granted entry clearance or leave to remain as a Tier 1 Migrant.

(c) An applicant who is the unmarried or same-sex partner of a Tier 1 Migrant must also meet the following requirements:

  (i) any previous marriage or civil partnership, or similar relationship by the applicant or the Tier 1 Migrant with another person must have permanently broken down;

  (ii) the applicant and the Tier 1 Migrant must not be so closely related that they would be prohibited from marrying each other in the UK; and

  (iii) the applicant and the Tier 1 Migrant must have been living together in a relationship similar to marriage or civil partnership for a period of at least two years (see further **8.8**).

(d) The marriage or civil partnership, or relationship similar to marriage or civil partnership, must be subsisting at the time the application is made. See further **8.3.3.5**.

(e) The applicant and the Tier 1 Migrant must intend to live with the other as his spouse or civil partner, unmarried or same-sex partner throughout the applicant's stay in the UK. See further **8.3.3.5**.

(f) The applicant must not intend to stay in the UK beyond any period of leave granted to the Tier 1 Migrant.

(g) If the applicant's partner is a Tier 1 Entrepreneur Migrant, there must be a sufficient level of funds available to the applicant, as set out in Appendix E.

As to (g) above, the same requirements for available maintenance funds for an applicant (see **7.4.4**) apply to a partner. Appendix E of the Immigration Rules (see **Appendix 1** to this book) sets out the following requirements:

(a) Where the Tier 1 Entrepreneur Migrant to whom the application is connected is outside the UK, or has been in the UK for a period of less than 12 months, there must be £1,600 in funds.

(b) Where the Tier 1 Entrepreneur Migrant to whom the application is connected has been in the UK for a period of 12 months or more, there must be £533 in funds.

(c) Where the applicant is applying as the partner of a Tier 1 Entrepreneur Migrant, the relevant amount of funds must be available to either the applicant or the Tier 1 Entrepreneur Migrant.

(d) Where the Tier 1 Entrepreneur Migrant is applying for entry clearance or leave to remain at the same time as the applicant, the amount of funds available to the applicant must be in addition to the level of funds required separately of the Tier 1 Entrepreneur Migrant.

> **Examples**
>
> Adam applies for entry clearance as a Tier 1 Entrepreneur Migrant. His civil partner, Brian, will be travelling with him. In addition to meeting the requirements of para 319C(a)–(f) above, what maintenance funds do they need to have available? Adam needs £2,800 for himself (see **7.4.4**). As he is applying from outside the UK there must be an additional £1,600 available for Brian.
>
> Janet has been in the UK for the last two years as a Tier 1 Entrepreneur. She recently married David, a foreign national. He is outside the UK and is applying for entry clearance to join Janet in the UK. In addition to meeting the requirements of para 319C(a)–(f) above, there must be £533 in maintenance funds available for David.

If the application is successful, the Partner is granted entry clearance and leave to remain for a period which expires on the same day as the leave granted to the Tier 1 Migrant. That leave will be subject to conditions not to have recourse to public funds and registration with the police, if this is required (see **3.3.2** and **3.3.3** respectively). The Partner will be free to work in the UK, but not as a doctor in training.

7.6.1.2 Child

The requirements are set out in para 319H as follows:

(a) The applicant must not fall for refusal under the general grounds for refusal (see **3.5.4**), and if applying for leave to remain must not be an illegal entrant (see **10.2.2**).

(b) The applicant must be the child of a parent who:

  (i) has valid leave to enter or remain as a Tier 1 Migrant; or

  (ii) is, at the same time, being granted entry clearance or leave to remain as a Tier 1 Migrant.

(c) The applicant must be under the age of 18 on the date the application is made, or if over 18 and applying for leave to remain, must have, or have last been granted, leave as the child of a Tier 1 Migrant.

(d) The applicant must not be married or in a civil partnership, must not have formed an independent family unit, and must not be leading an independent life. See further **8.9.4.6**.

(e) The applicant must not intend to stay in the UK beyond any period of leave granted to the Tier 1 Migrant parent.

(f) Both of the applicant's parents must either be lawfully present in the UK, or being granted entry clearance or leave to remain at the same time as the applicant, unless:

  (i) the Tier 1 Migrant is the applicant's sole surviving parent;

  (ii) the Tier 1 Migrant parent has and has had sole responsibility for the applicant's upbringing (see **8.9.4.3**); or

  (iii) there are serious or compelling family or other considerations which would make it desirable not to refuse the application and suitable arrangements have been made in the UK for the applicant's care (see **8.9.4.4**).

(g) If the applicant's parent is a Tier 1 Entrepreneur Migrant, there must be a sufficient level of funds available to the applicant, as set out in Appendix E.

(h) An applicant who is applying for leave to remain must have, or have last been granted leave as the child of a parent who had leave under any category of the Immigration Rules.

It is important to note the effect of (c) above in respect of a child now aged 18 or over. That child will still qualify for an extension of leave in this category, provided he had previously obtained such leave when under 18.

As to (g) above, the same requirements for available maintenance funds for an applicant (see **7.4.4**) apply to a child. For details of (g) and Appendix E, see **7.6.1.1**. In addition, note that the required funds must be available either to the child, or to the parent who is the Tier 1 Entrepreneur Migrant or to the child's other parent. In the case of the other parent, he or she must either be lawfully present in the UK, or being granted entry clearance or leave to enter or remain, at the same time.

Examples

Mona applies for entry clearance as a Tier 1 Entrepreneur Migrant. Her daughter, Janice, will be travelling with her. Janice's father is dead. In addition to meeting the requirements of para 319H(a)–(f) above, what maintenance funds need to be available? Mona needs £2,800 for herself (see **7.4.4**). As she is applying from outside the UK there must be an additional £1,600 available for Janice.

Clive has been in the UK for the last three years. He applies to switch to a Tier 1 Entrepreneur worker. Clive's wife and six-month-old baby live with him. What maintenance funds do they need to have available? Clive needs £800 for himself (see **7.4.4**). As Clive has been in the UK for longer than 12 months, he needs £533 for his wife and £533 for his child.

If the application is successful, the child is granted entry clearance and leave to remain for a period which expires on the same day as the leave granted to his Tier 1 Migrant parent. This will be subject to conditions of no recourse to public funds and registration with the police, if this is required (see **3.3.2** and **3.3.3** respectively).

7.6.2 Settlement by a partner

Once a Tier 1 Migrant is in a position to apply for settlement, the applicant's partner may apply for settlement at the same time, provided the couple have lived together for at least two years. All the requirements are set out in the Immigration Rules, para 319E, as follows:

(a) The applicant must not fall for refusal under the general grounds for refusal (see **3.5.4**) and must not be an illegal entrant (see **10.2.2**).

(b) The applicant must be the spouse or civil partner, unmarried or same-sex partner of a person who is, at the same time, being granted indefinite leave to remain as a Tier 1 Migrant.

(c) The applicant must have, or have last been granted, leave as the partner of the Tier 1 Migrant who is being granted indefinite leave to remain.

(d) The applicant and the Tier 1 Migrant must have been living together in the UK in marriage or civil partnership, or in a relationship similar to marriage or civil partnership, for a period of at least two years.

(e) The marriage or civil partnership, or relationship similar to marriage or civil partnership, must be subsisting at the time the application is made.

(f) The applicant and the Tier 1 Migrant must intend to live permanently with the other as spouse or civil partner, unmarried or same-sex partner. See further **8.3.3.5**.

(g) The applicant must have sufficient knowledge of the English language and sufficient knowledge about life in the UK (see **3.8.7**).

(h) The applicant must not have one or more unspent convictions within the meaning of the Rehabilitation of Offenders Act 1974 (see **Appendix 8**).

7.6.3 Settlement by a child

Once a Tier 1 Migrant is in a position to apply for settlement, the applicant's children may apply for settlement at the same time, provided the following requirements in the Immigration Rules, para 319J are met:

(a) The applicant must not fall for refusal under the general grounds for refusal (see **3.5.4**) and must not be an illegal entrant (see **10.2.2**).

(b) The applicant must be the child of a parent who is, at the same time, being granted indefinite leave to remain as a Tier 1 Migrant.

(c) The applicant must have, or have last been granted, leave as the child of the Tier 1 Migrant who is being granted indefinite leave to remain.

(d) The applicant must not be married or in a civil partnership, must not have formed an independent family unit, and must not be leading an independent life.

(e) Both of an applicant's parents must either be lawfully present in the UK, or being granted entry clearance, limited leave to remain, or indefinite leave to remain at the same time as the applicant, unless:

  (i) the Tier 1 Migrant is the applicant's sole surviving parent;

  (ii) the Tier 1 Migrant parent has and has had sole responsibility (see **8.9.4.3**) for the applicant's upbringing; or

  (iii) there are serious or compelling family or other considerations which would make it desirable not to refuse the application, and suitable arrangements have been made for the applicant's care (see **8.9.4.4**).

(f) The applicant must have sufficient knowledge of the English language and sufficient knowledge about life in the UK (see **3.8.7**), unless the applicant is under the age of 18 at the time the application is made.

(g) The applicant must not have one or more unspent convictions within the meaning of the Rehabilitation of Offenders Act 1974 (see **Appendix 8**).

7.7 Summary of Tier 1: at a glance

Table 7.8 Summary of Tier 1

Requirements	Exceptional Talent	Entrepreneur	Investor
English language for entry clearance	X	✓	X
English language for extension	✓	✓	X
English language and Life in UK test for settlement	✓	✓	✓
Maintenance for entry clearance	X	✓	X
Maintenance for extension	X	✓	X
Annual limit	✓	X	X

7.8 Overview of Tier 2

7.8.1 A profile of each category

7.8.1.1 Tier 2 (General) Migrant and Tier 2 (Intra-company Transfer) Migrant

A Tier 2 (General) Migrant must already have accepted a job offer from a UK-based employer which holds an appropriate licence from the UKBA. However, note that migration here is only for the purpose of filling gaps in the UK labour force that cannot be filled by the resident workforce. So there are tests that have to be met to demonstrate that. How skilled? The job skill level must be at graduate level or above.

The Tier 2 Intra-company Transfer category is for existing employees of multi-national companies who are being transferred from outside the EEA by their overseas employer to a training position or skilled job in a related UK entity. The transfer must be for training purposes, or to fill a specific vacancy at graduate level or above that cannot be filled by a

British or EEA worker. The transferring employee must have at least six months' experience of working directly for the overseas entity before the transfer.

The applicant must be paid at or above the appropriate rate for the job in accordance with published UKBA codes of practice (see **7.9.1**).

7.8.1.2 Minister of religion

This category is for a religious worker within a recognised religion and anyone who ministers, whether regularly or occasionally, and/or performs pastoral duties.

Note that Tier 5 (see **7.12**) will cover ministers of religion entering the UK on a temporary basis as religious workers in a non-pastoral role, whose duties include performing religious rites.

7.8.1.3 Sports person

This category is for an elite sports person or a coach who wishes to be based in the UK. The person must be internationally established at the highest level, and his employment should make a significant contribution to the development of the particular sport at the highest level in the UK.

7.8.2 Common features: entry clearance

7.8.2.1 Sponsorship

A Tier 2 Migrant cannot apply for entry clearance without a certificate of sponsorship issued by a UK-based sponsor which has been licensed by the UKBA (see **7.8.3**). Note that a certificate of sponsorship does not guarantee that entry clearance will be given.

7.8.2.2 The points system

Each Tier 2 Migrant is required to score 70 points from three different areas, namely attributes (50 points), English language (10 points) and maintenance (10 points).

Note, however, that an intra-company transfer migrant who does not wish to remain in the UK beyond three years only has to score 60 points from two different areas, namely attributes (50 points) and maintenance (10 points).

7.8.2.3 Attributes

For each category an applicant must score 50 points for specific attributes. Briefly, these are as follows:

(a) General migrant – attributes are based on sponsorship and annual salary.

(b) Minister of religion and sports person – the only attribute concerns sponsorship.

Full details are set out below, where each category is considered in detail.

7.8.2.4 English language

A Tier 2 Migrant must have a minimum level of competence in the English language. This requires scoring 10 points for either:

(a) passing a prescribed English language test at the required minimum level (as set out in **Table 7.9** below); or

Table 7.9 English language test requirements

Entry Clearance Applicant	Council of Europe's Common European Framework for Language Learning Level
Tier 2 (General)	B1
Tier 2 (Minister)	B2
Tier 2 (Intra-company Transfer)	A1
Tier 2 (Sports Person)	A1

(b) being a national of a UKBA-designated majority English-speaking country (see the list at **7.4.3.2**); or

(c) having obtained a UKBA-recognised academic qualification (not a professional or vocational qualification) which is deemed by UK NARIC to meet or exceed the recognised standard of a Bachelor's degree in the UK (see **7.4.3.3**).

Note that an intra-company transfer migrant needs to demonstrate the required English language skills only if he wishes to stay in the UK beyond three years.

7.8.2.5 Available maintenance funds

A Tier 2 Migrant must be able to demonstrate that he can support himself in the UK. This requires scoring 10 points for available maintenance funds of at least £800 of personal savings. These must have been held for a consecutive 90-day period of time, ending no earlier than one calendar month before the date of the application. Alternatively, if the Tier 2 Migrant has an A-rated sponsor (see **7.8.3**), that sponsor may provide a written undertaking that, should it become necessary, it will maintain and accommodate the migrant until the end of the first month of his employment. The undertaking may be limited, provided the limit is at least £800.

If any family members (see **7.8.9**) of the Tier 2 Migrant are travelling with him, each must have available savings of at least £533, which must have been held for a consecutive 90-day period of time, ending no earlier than one calendar month before the date of the application. Alternatively, if the Tier 2 Migrant has an A-rated sponsor (see **7.8.3**), that sponsor may provide a written undertaking that, should it become necessary, it will maintain and accommodate the dependant until the end of the first month of the migrant's employment. The undertaking may be limited, provided the limit is at least £533 per dependant.

The details are otherwise the same as for Tier 1 (see **7.3.4**).

7.8.2.6 Forms and guidance notes

Applicants may find detailed guidance and application forms on the UKBA's website (see **1.2.8**).

7.8.2.7 Not liable to refusal on general grounds

An applicant will fail if his application is liable to be refused under the general grounds in Part 9 of the Immigration Rules (see **3.5.4**).

7.8.2.8 Length of initial limited leave

All Tier 2 Migrants, apart from an intra-company transfer migrant in the Short Term Staff, Graduate Trainee or Skills Transfer sub-categories, are granted leave up to three years with the possibility of extending for a further two years and then applying for settlement.

A Tier 2 Intra-company Transfer Migrant in the Short Term Staff, Graduate Trainee or Skills Transfer sub-categories will be granted leave no longer than 12 months. Then he must leave the UK and he will not be able to reapply for further leave under an Intra-Company Transfer category (other than in the Long Term Staff sub-category) until 12 months after his last leave as an intra-company transfer migrant expired.

7.8.3 Common features: sponsorship

7.8.3.1 An appropriate sponsor

Each Tier 2 Migrant must be sponsored as shown in **Table 7.10** below.

Note that if the sponsor is a limited company, the applicant must not own more than 10% of the sponsor's shares unless he is applying as an intra-company transfer migrant.

Table 7.10 Tier 2 Migrant – appropriate sponsors

Tier 2 category	UK-based sponsor
General migrant	A genuine organisation or sole trader operating legally in the UK.
Intra-company transfer migrant	An UK entity with a direct link by common ownership or control with the overseas entity where the migrant is currently working. For definitions of common ownership or control see **Appendix 14**.
Minister of religion	A genuine religious institution, which is a registered, excepted or exempt UK charity according to the relevant charity legislation in force in its part of the UK, or is an ecclesiastical corporation (either corporation sole or body corporate) established for charitable purposes.
Sports person	A genuine club, or equivalent, which has a recognised governing body. A list of approved bodies is expected to be published by the UKBA in due course.

7.8.3.2 How to become a sponsor

Sponsorship applies to Tiers 2, 4 (see **Chapter 6**) and 5 (see **7.12**). Full details are beyond the scope of this book and the UKBA-published guidance on its website (see **1.2.8**) should be consulted.

In outline, a prospective sponsor must apply for a licence for each Tier that it requires and indicate the number of certificates of sponsorship it intends to issue. The application must be made online, and the applicant must pay a prescribed fee and submit certain specified documents. Once licensed, a sponsor can issue certificates of sponsorship up to a set number. A licence lasts for four years, unless it is withdrawn or surrendered before then.

A licensed sponsor is rated A or B according to the UKBA's assessment of any risk posed. A sponsor that is B-rated must comply with a time-limited action plan, which will set out the steps it needs to take in order to gain or regain an A-rating. If the sponsor does not comply with this action plan, it is likely to lose its licence altogether.

7.8.3.3 Duties of a sponsor

A licensed sponsor must comply with certain duties, including reporting the following situations to the UKBA:

(a) the migrant does not turn up for his first day at work;

(b) the migrant is absent from work for more than 10 working days without permission;

(c) the migrant's contract of employment ends, including if he resigns or is dismissed;

(d) the name and address of any known new employer;

(e) any significant changes in the migrant's circumstances, for example change of job or salary;

(f) any suspicions that the migrant is breaching the conditions of his leave;

(g) any significant changes in the sponsor's circumstances, for example if it stops trading or becomes insolvent, or substantially changes the nature of its business, or is involved in a merger or is taken over.

A sponsor must also keep proper records of the migrants it sponsors, including contact details and the migrant's identity card details.

7.8.3.4 Certificates of sponsorship

A licensed sponsor will provide its proposed Tier 2 Migrant with a certificate of sponsorship. But this is not an actual certificate or a paper document. It is a unique reference number that the sponsor issues to the migrant, along with details of the sponsorship. This information needs to be produced to the entry clearance officer with the entry clearance application. The certificate acts as confirmation from the sponsor that it wishes to bring the migrant to the UK and that to the best of its knowledge the applicant meets the requirements for the issue of the certificate of sponsorship. The certificate does not guarantee that entry clearance will be given. The entry clearance officer will check the application against the requirements of the Immigration Rules, including whether the applicant has enough points.

7.8.3.5 Job or sponsorship ends

What happens if a migrant's employment ends before his limited leave has expired? Or if, during his limited leave, his sponsor does not renew its licence or has it withdrawn? In these circumstances the Home Office usually curtails (see **3.7**) the person's leave to 60 days, unless only six months or less is remaining. During that time the person could apply for leave to remain in another category or as a Tier 2 Migrant with another sponsor if he finds one.

7.8.4 Common features: extension

Just before the initial three years' limited leave of a Tier 2 Migrant expires, an application should be made to extend it. Basically, the applicant will have to demonstrate that the original requirements have been met. Note that the migrant must be issued with a further certificate of sponsorship (see **7.8.3.3**) for his continued employment before making the application.

An applicant will fail if his application for an extension is liable to be refused under the general grounds in Part 9 of the Immigration Rules (see **3.5.4**) or he is an illegal entrant (see **10.2.2**).

7.8.5 Common features: change of employment

What if a Tier 2 Migrant changes his employment, either within the same organisation or with a new organisation? He will need to apply for an extension of leave, and this will involve passing the relevant attributes test.

In these circumstances the migrant will automatically receive points for English language ability because he will have shown this for the initial application, although this may not apply to an intra-company transfer migrant (see **7.8.2.4**).

The migrant will also not have to give fresh evidence of maintenance.

7.8.6 Common features: supplementary employment

Can a Tier 2 Migrant work in addition to that for which he was granted leave? Yes, but any supplementary work must be:

(a) in the same profession and at the same professional level as the main employment;

(b) no more than 20 hours a week; and

(c) outside of the applicant's normal working hours for which his certificate of sponsorship was issued.

In addition, a migrant may do voluntary work in any sector, provided he is not paid and does not receive any other payment for his work except reasonable expenses.

7.8.7 Common features: limited leave conditions

In each category it will be a condition of a person's limited leave that he does not have recourse to public funds (see **3.3.2**).

A person must also register with the police if this is required by the Immigration Rules, para 326 (see **3.3.3**).

Additionally, it is a condition that the Tier 2 Migrant cannot take up employment except for his sponsor in the employment stated in his certificate, supplementary employment (see **7.8.6**) and voluntary work (see **7.8.6**).

7.8.8 Common features: settlement

Once a Tier 2 Migrant has spent a continuous period of five years in the UK in that category (but including any time as a Tier 1 Entrepreneur or Investor), an application can be made for settlement.

7.8.9 Common features: family members

Who are the family members of a Tier 2 applicant? The answer is the spouse, civil partner, unmarried or same-sex partner, and children under 18.

A family member will have to obtain entry clearance and a subsequent extension. He or she may be able to apply for settlement at the same time as the Tier 2 Migrant. The provisions are the same as for a Tier 1 Migrant family member: see **7.6**.

7.8.10 Switching

Switching to a Tier 2 Migrant category (apart from intra-company transfer) is by way of an application to the Home Office. The applicant must be lawfully in the UK already as either a Tier 1 Migrant (see **7.2**), another Tier 2 Migrant, a Tier 4 Migrant (see **Chapter 6**) or a Tier 5 (Temporary Worker) Migrant (see **7.12**).

7.9 Tier 2: General migrant and intra-company transfer worker

7.9.1 Overview

A general migrant must already have accepted a job offer from a UK-based licensed employer that fills a recognised gap in the UK labour force.

An intra-company transfer worker is an employee of multi-national company who is being transferred by an overseas employer to a skilled job in a related UK entity. There are four sub-categories of intra-company transfer workers:

(a) Established Staff – the applicant is an established employee of a multi-national company who is being transferred to a skilled job that could not be carried out by a new recruit from the resident workforce.

(b) Short Term Staff – the applicant is an established employee of a multi-national company and is being transferred to a skilled job in the UK for 12 months or less that could not be carried out by a new recruit from the resident workforce.

(c) Graduate Trainee – the applicant is a recent graduate of a multi-national company who is being transferred to the UK branch of the same organisation as part of a structured graduate training programme, which clearly defines progression towards a managerial or specialist role.

(d) Skills Transfer – the applicant is an overseas employee of a multi-national company who is being transferred to the UK branch of the same organisation in a graduate occupation to learn the skills and knowledge he will need to perform his job overseas, or to impart his specialist skills to the UK workforce.

What is a job at graduate level or above? If a sponsor has any doubts, the UKBA website reproduces the standard occupational classification codes produced by the Office for National Statistics. This contains nine major groups consisting of managers and senior officials, professional occupations, associate professional and technical occupations, administrative and secretarial occupations, skilled trades occupations, personal service occupations, sales and customer service occupations, process, plant and machine operatives, and elementary occupations. Having identified the appropriate group, the sponsor should check the relevant occupational code of practice which is also on the UKBA website.

7.9.2 The attributes

Table 7.11 General migrant – attributes points

Certificate of Sponsorship	Points
Shortage occupation	30
Job offer passes Resident Labour Market Test	30
Job offer with annual salary of £150,000 or more	30

Appropriate salary	Points
Appropriate annual salary of £20,000 or more	20

To score the required 50 points, the general migrant applicant has to be entitled to a certificate of sponsorship for one of the three possible reasons and also have an appropriate salary.

We shall look at each of these in more detail at **7.9.3.1–7.9.3.4.**

Table 7.12 Intra-company transfer worker – attributes points

	Points
Certificate of Sponsorship	30
Appropriate annual salary	20

It can be seen that to score the required 50 points the intra-company applicant will have to be entitled to a certificate of sponsorship and also have an appropriate salary.

We shall look at each of these in more detail at **7.9.3.5–7.9.3.6.**

7.9.3 Attributes: what the requirements mean

7.9.3.1 General migrant: shortage occupations list

For many years the UK has had a shortage of workers in certain occupations – that is to say, there are not enough resident workers to fill available jobs in particular sectors of the UK's economy. Historically this has included various healthcare and teaching jobs, as well as veterinary surgeons.

The UKBA has published a list of shortage occupations on its website (see **1.2.8**), and this is reproduced at **Appendix 15**.

If an applicant is to be awarded 30 points here, the job must, at the time the Certificate of Sponsorship was assigned to him, have appeared on the list published by UKBA and his contracted working hours must be for at least 30 hours a week.

7.9.3.2 General migrant: resident labour market test

The UKBA recognises that it may be necessary for a sponsor to recruit a migrant from outside the UK to fill a particular vacancy that cannot be filled by a settled worker and that is not on the list of shortage occupation list (see **7.9.3.1**). However, this will be possible only if the sponsor can show that no suitably qualified settled worker is available to fill that vacancy.

How does a sponsor satisfy this test? The vacancy must usually be advertised as follows:

(a) As a general rule the job must be advertised in Jobcentre Plus. Details can be found on its website at www.jobcentreplus.gov.uk.

(b) The sponsor must also advertise the vacancy in accordance with a code of practice specific to the type of sector or job. The codes of practice can be found on the UKBA's website (see **1.2.8**).

(c) The vacancy must be advertised to settled workers for a minimum of 28 calendar days from the date the advertisement first appears.

(d) The sponsor must use the medium of advertising set out in the relevant code of practice, often a professional journal or the employment section of a national UK newspaper. The advertisement must include the job title; the main duties and responsibilities of the job; the location of the job; an indication of the salary package or salary range or terms on offer; the skills, qualifications and experience required; and the closing date for applications.

Can a sponsor use other recruitment methods? Yes, if allowed by the appropriate code of practice. These may include Internet advertising, as well as the use of a recruitment agency or head-hunters.

If the recruitment process produces no suitable resident workers, the sponsor can recruit from abroad, but any certificate of sponsorship must be issued within six months of the advertisement being placed. Why? Because that will ensure that the results of the advertising reflect the current availability of the skills the sponsor requires.

7.9.3.3 General migrant: job offer with annual salary of £150,000 or more

In order for the applicant to be awarded 30 points here, the applicant's Certificate of Sponsorship must show that his gross annual salary, including such allowances as are acceptable for this purpose (see **7.9.3.4**), to be paid by his sponsor is £150,000 or more.

7.9.3.4 General migrant: appropriate annual salary of £20,000 or more

In order for the applicant to be awarded 20 points here, the applicant's Certificate of Sponsorship must show that his gross annual salary, including such allowances as are acceptable, to be paid by his sponsor is £20,000 or more.

So what counts? The UKBA considers the basic gross pay (before tax) plus any allowances, such as London weighting which would also be paid to a settled worker in similar circumstances, provided these allowances are part of the applicant's guaranteed salary package.

What is not taken into account? The UKBA will not consider other benefits, such as bonus or incentive pay, travel and subsistence (including travel to and from the applicant's home country).

Points are only awarded for up to a maximum of 48 hours a week, even if the applicant will be working more than this. For example, if the applicant will earn £10 per hour, working 60 hours per week, the salary taken into account is £24,960 (£10 x 48 x 52).

7.9.3.5 Intra-company transfer: certificate of sponsorship

Table 7.13 Intra-company transfer worker – 30 points for Certificate of Sponsorship

Certificate of Sponsorship for long term or short term staff The applicant has been employed by his sponsoring organisation for at least 12 months immediately before the date of the application either outside the UK; and/or in the UK if the applicant has or was last granted leave to work for his sponsoring organisation in the category of Tier 2 (Intra-Company Transfer: Short Term Staff) or Tier 2 (Intra-Company Transfer: Established Staff).
Certificate of Sponsorship for graduate trainee The applicant has been employed outside the UK by his sponsoring organisation as part of a graduate training programme for at least three months immediately before the date of the application.
Certificate of Sponsorship for skills transfer The applicant has been employed outside the UK by his sponsoring organisation immediately before the date of his application. The sole purpose of the transfer to the UK branch of the multi-national company must be for the applicant to learn the skills and knowledge needed to perform his role overseas or to transfer skills and knowledge to the sponsor's UK workforce. The applicant's appointment must be additional to his sponsor's UK staffing requirements; if it were not for the need for skills transfer, the role in the UK would not exist.

7.9.3.6 Intra-company transfer: appropriate salary

Table 7.14 Intra-company transfer worker – 20 points for appropriate annual salary

Long Term Staff	at least £40,000
Short Term Staff, Graduate Trainee or Skills Transfer	at least £24,000

These annual salary figures are the minimum. It is the gross salary that is taken into account and calculated as for a general migrant (**7.9.3.4**). The actual rate of pay must meet the rate set out in the appropriate UKBA code of practice.

7.9.4 Tier 2 (General) Migrant annual limit

From April 2011, the Government introduced an annual limit on the number of certificates of sponsorship that can be issued for Tier 2 (General) Migrants. For the period 6 April 2011 to 5 April 2012, the limit is 20,700 certificates. Note that this does not apply to an applicant filling a vacancy with an annual salary of £150,000 or more.

For full details, see the UKBA's website.

7.10 Tier 2: Minister of religion

7.10.1 Overview

This category is for a religious worker within a recognised religion and anyone who ministers, whether regularly or occasionally, and/or performs pastoral duties. The UKBA guidance is that pastoral duties include leading worship regularly and on special occasions; providing religious education for children and adults by preaching or teaching; officiating at marriages, funerals and other special services; offering counselling and welfare support to members of the congregation; recruiting, training and co-ordinating the work of any local volunteers and lay preachers.

This category is also for a migrant coming to work in the UK as a missionary, a member of a religious order such as a monastic community of monks or nuns, or a similar religious community which involves permanent commitment.

As to English language, see **7.8.2.4**.

7.10.2 Attributes: sponsorship

The minister must score 50 points by way of sponsorship. This requires the following:

(a) The minister must be qualified to do the job in question. For example, he must be an ordained minister of religion where ordination is prescribed by a religious faith as the sole means of entering the ministry.

(b) The minister must intend to be based in the UK for the duration of his limited leave.

(c) The minister must intend to depart from the UK when his leave expires.

7.10.3 Resident labour market test

What about the resident labour market test (see **7.9.3.2**)? The sponsor must confirm that the minister will not be displacing or denying an employment opportunity to a suitably qualified member of the resident UK labour force. Either the sponsor must have undertaken an appropriate resident labour market test for the role, or, if that is inappropriate, the migrant must be additional to the sponsor's normal staffing requirements. The minister must not be taking a position that would otherwise need to be filled by a resident UK worker.

7.10.4 Maintenance

As to maintenance, note that the sponsor must provide an undertaking to support the minister through funds and/or accommodation that are sufficient for the minister to maintain himself throughout the duration of the certificate of sponsorship.

7.11 Tier 2: Sports person

7.11.1 Overview

This category is for elite sports people and coaches who are internationally established at the highest level, whose employment will make a significant contribution to the development of their sport at the highest level in the UK, and who intend to base themselves in the UK.

7.11.2 Attributes: sponsorship

The sports person must score 50 points by way of sponsorship. This requires the following:

(a) The sports person must be qualified to do the job in question.

(b) The sports person must intend to be based in the UK for the duration of his limited leave.

(c) The sports person must intend to depart from the UK when his leave expires.

All migrants in this category must have the approval of the appropriate governing body for their sport. This is officially known as an endorsement. This endorsement will confirm that the sports person meets the code of practice as agreed between the UKBA and the sporting body, and also confirms that:

(a) the migrant is internationally established at the highest level;

(b) the migrant will make a significant contribution to the development of his sport at the highest level in the UK; and

(c) it is appropriate to fill the post with a migrant who is not settled in the UK. The endorsement therefore replaces the resident labour market test for this category.

As to English language and maintenance, see **7.8.2.4** and **7.8.2.5** respectively.

7.12 Tier 5: Temporary migrants

This tier covers temporary sponsored workers (and their family members) who can remain in the UK for no longer than 12 months (creative and sporting workers and charity workers) or 24 months (religious workers, Government authorised exchange workers, international agreement workers and workers under a youth mobility scheme), or up to a maximum of 72 months (Government authorised exchange workers). We shall consider each type of worker briefly in turn. Details of sponsorship are given at **7.8.3**.

Note that a Tier 5 Migrant cannot switch into any other immigration category. However, during his limited leave he can do additional work, provided that it is for no longer than 20 hours per week, it is outside his normal working hours, and it is in the same sector and at the same level as the work for which his certificate of sponsorship was issued.

Applicants can find detailed guidance and application forms on the UKBA website (see **1.2.8**).

7.12.1 Creative and sporting worker

7.12.1.1 A profile

This category is for creative artists (performers and entertainers) and sports people who wish to work in the UK for up to 12 months. Entertainers may be individuals, or part of a large touring entourage working in areas such as dance and theatre. Sports people should be internationally established at the highest level in their sport, and/or their employment in the UK should make a significant contribution to the development and operation of that particular sport in this country. A sports coach must be suitably qualified.

7.12.1.2 Sponsorship

In order to gain a licence as a sponsor of creative workers and their entourage, the prospective sponsor must be operating, or intend to operate, in the creative sector. Examples include a national body, event organiser, producer, venue, agent or other similar organisation.

In order to gain a licence as a sponsor of sports people, the prospective sponsor must be a sporting body, sports club, events organiser or other organiser operating, or intending to operate, in the sporting sector.

7.12.1.3 Resident labour market test

A sponsor of creative artists operating in dance, theatre, film and television must follow the codes of practice for taking into account the needs of the resident labour market in these areas. Otherwise the sponsor must conduct a resident labour market test, unless the migrant falls into one of the following categories that are deemed to be making an additional contribution to the UK creative sector and therefore are not a threat to the resident labour force:

(a) The migrant is required for continuity in the creative sector. Here the migrant must have worked for a period of one month or more on the same production outside the EEA prior to coming to the UK.

(b) The migrant is internationally famous in his field.

(c) The migrant is established at the highest level in his profession within the creative sector, ie he has performed at the highest level and has established a reputation in his profession. This category also includes groups of people.

(d) The migrant is engaged by a unit company within the creative sector. A unit company is a large group of entertainers who have regularly performed together in their own country and overseas as part of an established production before entering the UK. The UKBA guidance is that pop and music groups are not classed as unit companies.

If a Tier 5 sports person does not have the endorsement of his governing body (see **7.11.2**), the resident labour market test must be carried out.

7.12.1.4 The points system

The migrant must score 40 points, as shown in **Table 7.15** below.

Table 7.15 Tier 5 creative and sporting worker – the points system

Criteria	Requirements	Points
Sponsorship	The migrant is seeking entry to the UK to work or perform in the UK in the relevant sector,	30
	The migrant is not intending to establish himself in business in the UK, His employment must not threaten the resident labour force, *and* The migrant must comply with the conditions of leave and will depart when his limited leave ends.	
Maintenance	£800 and £533 for each dependant *or* the certificate of sponsorship is issued by an A-rated sponsor and the sponsor certifies that the migrant will not claim benefits while in the UK. However, the sponsor cannot certify maintenance for any dependants.	10

7.12.2 Charity worker

7.12.2.1 A profile

This category is for a charity worker undertaking voluntary activity and not paid employment. The migrant should intend to carry out fieldwork directly related to the purpose of the sponsoring organisation.

As the migrant is not taking paid employment, the resident labour market test does not apply.

7.12.2.2 Sponsorship

In order to gain a licence as a sponsor of voluntary workers, the employer must be a registered, excepted or exempt UK charity according to the relevant legislation in force in its part of the UK.

7.12.2.3 The points system

The migrant must score 40 points, as shown in **Table 7.16** below.

Table 7.16 Tier 5 charity worker – the points system

Criteria	Requirements	Points
Sponsorship	The migrant must intend to do voluntary work directly relating to the sponsor's purpose. The migrant must not be paid or otherwise remunerated for his work. The migrant must not take up a permanent position. The migrant must comply with the conditions of leave and depart when his limited leave ends.	30

Criteria	Requirements	Points
Maintenance	£800 and £533 for each dependant *or* the certificate of sponsorship is issued by an A-rated sponsor and the sponsor certifies that the migrant will not claim benefits while in the UK. However, the sponsor cannot certify maintenance for any dependants.	10

7.12.3 Religious worker

7.12.3.1 A profile

This category is for either:

(a) a religious worker; or

(b) a visiting religious worker who is employed overseas in the same capacity as that for which he is seeking to come to the UK, although the exact detail of his duties in the UK may differ. This employment should be ongoing, and the time spent in the UK should be consistent with a break from the worker's employment.

In either case the worker may perform religious rites, such as tending to deities or reading scripture aloud to the congregation, but cannot carry out any of the pastoral duties of a Tier 2 minister (see **7.10**).

7.12.3.2 Sponsorship

In order to gain a licence as a sponsor, the employer must be a genuine religious institution, which is a registered, excepted or exempt UK charity according to the relevant charity legislation in force in its part of the UK, or an ecclesiastical corporation (either corporation sole or body corporate) established for charitable purposes.

7.12.3.3 Resident labour market test

When issuing a certificate of sponsorship, the sponsor thereby certifies that the migrant will not be displacing or denying an employment opportunity to a suitably qualified member of the resident labour force.

7.12.3.4 The points system

The migrant must score 40 points, as shown in **Table 7.17** below.

Table 7.17 Tier 5 religious worker – the points system

Criteria	Requirements	Points
Sponsorship	The migrant must be qualified to do the job in question. The migrant must not intend to take employment for the sponsor except as a visiting religious worker or a religious worker. The migrant must not claim benefits while in the UK. The migrant must be filling a genuine vacancy that cannot be filled with a suitable qualified member of the resident labour force. *and* The migrant must comply with the conditions of leave and depart when his limited leave ends.	30

Criteria	Requirements	Points
Maintenance	£800 and £533 for each dependant *or* the certificate of sponsorship is issued by an A-rated sponsor and the sponsor certifies that the migrant will not claim benefits while in the UK. However, the sponsor cannot certify maintenance for any dependants.	10

7.12.4 Government authorised exchange worker

7.12.4.1 A profile

This category is for migrants coming to the UK through approved schemes that aim to share knowledge, experience and best practice. It is for work experience. It cannot be used to fill a job vacancy.

7.12.4.2 Sponsorship

Sponsorship for this category is rather novel. Government policy is that in order to prevent potential abuse of this category and the formation of small individual schemes, employers and organisations cannot sponsor migrants. Instead, there will be an overarching body to administer the exchange scheme. This overarching body will be the sponsor and will need to apply for a licence. The scheme and the body must have the support of a UK government department. The body will issue certificates of sponsorship to migrants who meet the requirements of the scheme.

Example

The Law Society is an overarching body that can authorise eligible firms to issue certificates of sponsorship to prospective short-term migrants under internship and secondment programmes.

7.12.4.3 The points system

The migrant must score 40 points, as shown in **Table 7.18** below.

Table 7.18 Tier 5 government authorised exchange worker – the points system

Criteria	Requirements	Points
Sponsorship	The migrant must be taking part in a work experience scheme, The migrant must not be filling a genuine vacancy, The migrant's work must be in addition to the normal staffing needs, The migrant must be undertaking skilled work at S/NVQ level 3 or above, *and* The migrant's work must conform with relevant UK and European legislation.	30
Maintenance	£800 and £533 for each dependant *or* the certificate of sponsorship is issued by an A-rated sponsor and the sponsor certifies that the migrant will not claim benefits while in the UK. However, the sponsor cannot certify maintenance for any dependants.	10

7.12.5 International agreement worker

This category is for migrants who are coming to the UK under contract to provide a service that is covered under international law, including the General Agreement on Trade in Services; similar agreements between the UK and another country; employees of overseas governments and international organisations; and private servants in diplomatic households.

This is a specialised category the details of which are beyond the scope of this book.

7.12.6 Worker under a youth mobility scheme

7.12.6.1 A profile

This is a novel category, as the sponsors under the youth mobility scheme are the national governments of the UKBA approved participating countries – currently Australia, Canada, Japan, Monaco and New Zealand. Places on the scheme for each of those countries are capped each year by the UK Government. Once the limit is reached, no further applications will be considered that year.

So how young does a national of an approved participating country have to be? The answer is between the ages of 18 and 30 inclusive when his entry clearance is granted.

Anything else? Yes, two matters.

First, an applicant must not previously have been in the UK in this category (or its predecessor, which was known as the 'working holidaymaker scheme').

Secondly, an applicant must not have dependent children, ie children under 18 who either are living with the applicant or for whom he is financially responsible.

What about a spouse or partner? The UKBA guidance is that there is nothing to prevent an applicant who is married or has a partner from participating in the scheme, whether his spouse or partner accompanies him or not. However, spouses and partners of participants under the scheme cannot enter as dependants. They may accompany a participant, or join him in the UK, provided that they qualify and obtain an entry clearance in their own right either under the scheme or in another category.

A young foreign national who has entered the UK in this category may, during his two years' limited leave, do whatever work he likes, except for setting up his own business, professional sport, or working as a doctor in training. An employer is therefore free to employ a youth mobility participant on that basis.

A person can be granted leave in this category only once.

7.12.6.2 The points system

The migrant must score 50 points in three areas, as shown in **Table 7.19** below.

Table 7.19 Tier 5 worker under a youth mobility scheme – the points system

Criteria	Requirements	Points
Sponsorship	Citizen of an approved participating country (currently Australia, Canada, Japan, Monaco and New Zealand) and that country's quota of places has not been exhausted, or a British Overseas Citizen, British Overseas Territories Citizen or British National (Overseas) Citizen (see **2.4**).	30
Age	The applicant must be between 18 and 30 years of age inclusive at the date that his entry clearance becomes valid for use, and under the age of 31 on the date his application was made.	10

Maintenance	The applicant must be able to support himself from the point at which he enters the UK until he begins earning. An applicant will need to demonstrate sufficient funds for the first two months following arrival in the UK in the amount of £1,600 which is held in his personal bank account on the date his application was made.	10

7.13 Sole representative of an overseas firm

7.13.1 A profile

If an overseas firm has no branch, subsidiary or representative in the UK, it may wish to send one of its senior employees to the UK to establish a wholly-owned subsidiary or branch in the UK. This is a long-standing category and it is not part of the points system. The requirements are set out in the Immigration Rules, para 144, as follows.

7.13.2 Paragraph 144(i) requirement

The first requirement to be met by a person seeking leave to enter the UK as a sole representative is that the applicant has been recruited and taken on as an employee outside the UK as a representative of a firm which has its headquarters and principal place of business outside the UK and which has no branch, subsidiary or other representative in the UK.

The overseas firm must be a genuine commercial enterprise. This is judged in the round, taking into account the length of time that the company has been established, its turnover, profitability, the number of employees, etc. It must be the intention that the business remains centred abroad. This does not mean, however, that an otherwise sound application is refused because of evidence of an intention to make the branch in the UK flourish so vigorously that it might, at some time in the longer term, overshadow the overseas parent company. Companies which have been trading for less than 12 months are required to justify the need to establish an overseas branch here.

The overseas parent company must be sending the sole representative to the UK in order that he establishes a commercial presence for the company here in the form either of a registered branch or of a wholly-owned subsidiary. A 'branch' is a part of a company which is organised so as to conduct business on behalf of the company. This means that a person is able to deal directly with the branch in the UK, instead of the company overseas. The company setting up a branch in the UK must apply to register with Companies House within one month of having opened the branch. A wholly-owned subsidiary is a separate corporate body and is not subject to these registration requirements, being treated in the same way as any other company incorporated in the UK.

Finally note that the branch of the overseas business which is to be established in the UK must be concerned with the same type of business activity as the overseas firm.

7.13.3 Paragraph 144(ii) requirement

The second requirement is that the applicant must seek entry to the UK as a senior employee with full authority to take operational decisions on behalf of the overseas firm for the purpose of representing it in the UK by establishing and operating a registered branch or wholly-owned subsidiary of that overseas firm.

The sole representative must have been recruited outside the UK and joined the parent company abroad. The UKBA guidance is that 'he is likely to be someone who has been employed by the parent company for some time and holds a senior position there'. If the sole representative is not an existing employee, or has been employed for a short time only, then he must be able to demonstrate a good track record in the same or in a closely related field, in order to show that the reasons for his appointment are compelling. Sole representatives must, in the first instance, be employed by the overseas firm direct (although they may later be employed by the UK subsidiary). Agents who are hired to market the company's product in the UK are normally self-employed and provide their services for a fee. Such people cannot therefore qualify as sole representatives. Neither can sales representatives or others, such as buyers, who fulfil a single function only. However, senior sales staff who have other responsibilities, such as marketing and distribution, are not debarred from qualifying as sole representatives.

The applicant is required to provide a document detailing the terms and conditions of his employment. The importance of the position should be reflected in the salary and other benefits. The UKBA expects a sole representative to be vested with the authority to take the majority of decisions locally, but accepts that it is unreasonable to expect him to take unilateral decisions on all matters.

7.13.4 Paragraph 144(iii) requirement

The applicant must intend to be employed full time as a representative of that overseas firm.

Sole representatives are expected to base themselves in the UK and to spend a minimum of nine months of the year here. However, applications may be approved from those who intend to spend less time in the UK, provided that the additional absences are essential to the running of the UK business, for example, if the UK office is to be the centre of European operations. Applicants who intend to spend less than four months of the year in the UK are unlikely to satisfy the UKBA that they are making genuine efforts to establish a commercial presence in the UK. Such persons should be advised to apply instead as business visitors (see **5.2**).

7.13.5 Paragraph 144(iv) requirement

The applicant must not be a majority shareholder in the overseas firm.

Majority shareholders in the parent company are not eligible for entry as sole representatives. When the sole representative is a major shareholder in the parent company, the UKBA guidance provides that care must be taken to establish that the arrangement is not one devised simply to circumvent the more rigorous requirements of the business rules. As a rule of thumb, shareholdings in excess of 30% should attract detailed scrutiny. If it is evident that the applicant, as well as being a major shareholder, is also the driving force behind the parent company such that his presence in the UK is likely to mean that the centre of operations has shifted to this country, the application should be refused. The factors to be weighed in deciding this include:

(a) the size of the applicant's shareholding;

(b) his position within the firm;

(c) the number of senior employees who will remain abroad; and

(d) the extent to which the company's success seems linked to the applicant's specific talents and performance.

7.13.6 Paragraph 144(v) requirement

The applicant must not intend to take other employment.

Sole representatives are required to work full time as such, but this is not linked to a set number of hours per week. The main consideration is that the parent firm should be paying a 'full-time' salary sufficient for the sole representative to support and accommodate himself and any dependants without taking other work or resorting to public funds.

7.13.7 Paragraph 144(vi) requirement

The applicant must be able to demonstrate English language skills at a basic user standard. How can he do this?

(a) he is the national of a UKBA-designated English-speaking country (see the list at **7.4.3.2**);

(b) he has a UKBA-recognised qualification from a prescribed country (see the details at **7.4.3.3**);

(c) he has a recognised qualification that was taught or researched in English to a prescribed minimum standard; or

(d) he passes a prescribed English language test.

7.13.8 Paragraph 144(vii) requirement

The applicant must be able to maintain and accommodate himself and any dependants adequately without recourse to public funds.

Sole representatives may be offered a remuneration package consisting of a basic salary and commission. This is acceptable to the UKBA as long as the salary element is sufficient to support the applicant and his family without recourse to public funds. As this category is not part of the points system, no set amount is prescribed for maintenance. Full details may be found at **8.3.3.6** and **8.3.3.7**.

7.13.9 Paragraph 144(viii) requirement

The applicant must hold a valid UK entry clearance for entry in this capacity.

Entry clearance is mandatory for a person who wishes to enter the UK in this category.

It is not possible to switch into this category.

7.13.10 Supporting documentation for entry clearance

The UKBA requires the following documents to support the application:

(a) a full description of the company's activities with details of the company's assets and accounts, including full details of the company share distribution for the previous year;

(b) confirmation that the overseas company will establish a wholly-owned subsidiary or register a branch in the UK;

(c) the applicant's job description, salary and contract of employment;

(d) confirmation that the applicant is fully familiar with the company's activities and that he has full powers to negotiate and take operational decisions without reference to the parent company;

(e) a notarised statement from the company that the applicant will be its sole representative and that it has no other branch, subsidiary, or representative in the UK;

(f) a notarised statement confirming that the company's operations will remain centred overseas;

(g) a notarised statement that the applicant will not engage in business of his own, neither will he represent any other company's interest.

7.13.11 Extension

Leave is initially given for three years. Towards the end of that time an application may be made to the Home Office for a two-year extension of stay under the Immigration Rules, para 147.

This requires that the sole representative:

(a) entered the UK with a valid UK entry clearance as a sole representative of an overseas firm;

(b) can show that the overseas firm still has its headquarters and principal place of business outside the UK;

(c) is employed full time as a representative of that overseas firm and has established and is in charge of its registered branch or wholly-owned subsidiary;

(d) is still required for the employment in question, as certified by his employer; and

(e) meets the requirements of para 144(v)–(vii) (see **7.13.6–7.13.8**).

The application should be supported by the following evidence:

(a) a letter from the parent company stating that it wishes to continue to employ the applicant as previously;

(b) evidence in the form of accounts of the business generated (this form can be flexible according to the nature of the company's business);

(c) evidence of the salary paid to the applicant in the first two years of operation and the terms on which the salary will be paid in future;

(d) evidence that he has established and is in charge of a registered branch or wholly-owned subsidiary of the overseas parent company.

7.13.12 Settlement

When a sole representative has remained in the UK for five years in this capacity, he may be eligible to apply for settlement under the Immigration Rules, para 150.

This requires that the sole representative:

(a) has spent a continuous period of five years in the UK in this capacity;

(b) has met the requirements of para 147 (see **7.13.11**) throughout the five-year period;

(c) is still required for the employment in question, as certified by his employer;

(d) has sufficient knowledge of the English language and sufficient knowledge about life in the UK (see **3.8.7**); and

(e) does not have one or more unspent convictions within the meaning of the Rehabilitation of Offenders Act 1974 (see **Appendix 8**).

7.13.13 Family members of a sole representative

The spouse, civil partner, same-sex or unmarried partner and children under 18 of an applicant will need to apply for entry clearance (see paras 194 and 197 respectively). They may also subsequently apply for settlement (see paras 196D and 198 respectively). See further **Chapter 8**.

7.14 Commonwealth citizen with UK ancestry

7.14.1 A profile

A Commonwealth citizen (see the list at **Appendix 9**), aged 17 or over, who can show that one of his grandparents was born in the UK (and Islands) and who intends to take or seek employment in the UK and support himself without needing public funds, may be granted entry clearance in this category. Entry clearance is compulsory and limited leave is given of five years. Thereafter an application can be made for settlement.

In this category an applicant does not need to meet the requirements of the points system under any of the tiers. The requirements to be met are set out in the Immigration Rules, para 186, as follows.

7.14.2 A Commonwealth citizen

The applicant must satisfy the entry clearance officer that he is a citizen of a Commonwealth country.

7.14.3 Aged 17 or over

The applicant must satisfy the entry clearance officer that he is or will be at least 17 years of age when entering the UK.

7.14.4 Proof of ancestry

The applicant must be able to provide proof that one of his grandparents was born in the UK and Islands, and that any such grandparent is the applicant's blood grandparent or grandparent by reason of an adoption recognised by the laws of the UK relating to adoption.

As regards proof of birth in the UK and Islands, the applicant must be able to demonstrate that the grandparent on whom the claim is based was born in:

(a) the UK;

(b) Channel Islands;

(c) the Isle of Man; or

(d) if the grandparent was born before 31 March 1922, what is now the Republic of Ireland.

The UKBA guidance is that birth on a British registered ship or aircraft also counts.

The applicant may be related to that grandparent in one of two ways. First, by blood. So a qualifying connection can be made through a legitimate or an illegitimate line. Secondly, by adoption. An applicant who has been adopted, or whose parents were, can qualify if:

(a) he has been adopted by someone who has a UK-born parent; or

(b) one of his parents was adopted by a person born in the UK; or

(c) his natural grandparents were born in the UK.

No claim can be made through step-parents.

What sort of proof of the relationship is required by an entry clearance officer? The applicant should produce his own full birth certificate; where appropriate the marriage certificates of his parents and appropriate grandparents (or, if unmarried, evidence of the relationship if the claim is made through the paternal line); if applicable the legal adoption papers of the applicant or his parents; and the full birth certificates of the parent and grandparent through whose ancestry he is making the application.

Example

Charles is a Commonwealth citizen, aged 20. His mother, Florence, was not born in the UK. His grandmother, Rose, on his maternal side (ie Florence's mother) was born in the UK. What documents should Charles produce to prove this ancestral link? A minimum of three documents are required to confirm the following details:

(a) his birth certificate naming Florence as his mother;

(b) Florence's birth certificate naming Rose as her mother; and

(c) Rose's UK birth certificate showing she was born in the UK.

7.14.5 Able to work and intends to take or seek employment in the UK

Entry clearance is for the purpose of work in the UK, not to study or visit. The applicant must satisfy the entry clearance officer that he has arranged employment in the UK already, or that he genuinely intends to seek employment and has a realistic prospect of securing it. The UKBA guidance is that the entry clearance officer will consider such factors as the applicant's age and health, eg any medical problems that may prevent the applicant from taking employment.

7.14.6 No recourse to public funds

The applicant must be able to maintain and accommodate himself and any dependants adequately without recourse to public funds (see **3.3.2**).

As this category is not part of the points system, no set amount is prescribed for maintenance. Full details can be found at **8.3.3.6** and **8.3.3.7**.

7.14.7 Holds a valid UK entry clearance for entry in this capacity

Entry clearance is mandatory for a person who wishes to enter the UK in this category.

It is not possible to switch into this category.

7.14.8 Settlement

Near to the end of the person's five years' limited leave he should apply for settlement. The requirements are set out in para 192, as follows:

(a) the applicant meets the requirements of para 186(i)–(v) (see **7.14.2–7.14.7**);

(b) the applicant has spent a continuous period of five years in the UK in this capacity;

(c) the applicant has sufficient knowledge of the English language and sufficient knowledge about life in the UK (see **3.8.7**); and

(d) does not have one or more unspent convictions within the meaning of the Rehabilitation of Offenders Act 1974 (see **Appendix 8**).

Although (a) above requires the applicant to have resided continuously in the UK in this category for five years, there is no requirement that any employment taken must be continuous. The UKBA guidance is that if the applicant is in employment at the time of the application then all that is required is a letter from his current employers confirming the employment will continue. If, however, the applicant is not employed then he will need to produce evidence of his employment record throughout the five years and evidence of the attempts made to find employment. If it is clear that the applicant has not been in employment for any length of time over the five years he will be asked to provide reasons as to why he has failed to obtain employment. Unless there is a very good reason for this, the application will be refused. The Home Office will also make enquiries as to how the applicant has been supporting himself without a regular income.

7.14.9 Family members

The spouse, civil partner, same-sex or unmarried partner and children under 18 of an applicant will need to apply for entry clearance (see paras 194 and 197). They may also subsequently apply for settlement (see paras 196D and 198). See further **Chapter 8**.

7.15 Illegal working in the UK

7.15.1 Employer's duties

The law on preventing illegal migrant working in the UK has evolved over time. An employer's legal responsibilities may therefore vary according to when he recruited his existing staff. There is a very useful summary of the previous legal requirements on the UKBA's website (see **1.2.8**). The current law may be found in ss 15 to 26 of the IANA 2006 which applies to staff recruited from 1 March 2008. This makes an employer liable to payment of a civil financial penalty of up to £10,000 if he employs a person aged 16 or over who is subject to immigration control and who has no permission to work in the UK, or who works in breach of his conditions of stay in the UK (see **3.3.1**).

Note that it is essential that any appeal against a civil penalty is made promptly as the court has no discretion to extend the time limits laid down in the IANA 2006: see *Massan v Secretary of State for the Home Department* [2011] EWCA Civ 686.

7.15.2 Civil penalty

How can an employer avoid civil liability? This is answered by the Immigration (Restrictions on Employment) Order 2007 (SI 2007/3290, as amended). The employer must obtain from the prospective employee certain original documents that need to be checked in accordance with art 6, for example, if the document contains a date of birth, the employer must be satisfied that this is consistent with the appearance of the prospective employee. The employer must keep a copy of any document for a period of not less than two years after the employment comes to an end. So what documents count? The employer can choose from documents in the Schedule. This consists of two lists: list A, which includes a British or EEA national's passport; and list B, which includes a biometric immigration document issued by the UKBA to the holder which indicates that the person named in it can stay in the UK and is allowed to do the work in question. List A documents only have to be checked once by the employer. However, list B documents must be checked at least once every 12 months.

7.15.3 Criminal offence

An employer commits a criminal offence if he knowingly employs a person aged 16 or over who is subject to immigration control and who has no permission to work in the UK, or who works in breach of his conditions of stay in the UK. What sentence might the employer face? An unlimited fine and/or a maximum two-year prison sentence can be imposed.

Chapter 8
Family Reunion

8.1 Introduction

The Immigration Rules, Part 8, relating to family, marriage and civil partnerships, deals with a range of possibilities. A person may seek entry to the UK as the spouse or civil partner of someone who has the right of abode, or of someone who is settled, or entering for settlement, or of someone with limited leave (eg as a Tier 1 Entrepreneur). A fiancé(e) or proposed civil partner may seek entry in order to marry or enter into a civil partnership. A person who has entered the UK with limited leave may wish to settle here on marriage to, or having entered into a civil partnership with, a British citizen, or to someone who is already settled. This chapter covers some of the many permutations.

8.2 Exempt groups

The rules in Part 8 do not apply to those who do not need leave, or who are seeking entry under another Part of the Rules. For example:

(a) persons who already have the right of abode (see **2.1** and **2.2**);

(b) persons with settled status re-entering as returning residents (see **3.8.3**);

(c) EEA citizens and family members entering by virtue of EC law (see **Chapter 4**);

(d) persons who are entering in another category under the Rules (eg visitors, etc).

Example 1

Ben is a citizen of Canada. He was born there in 1972. Ben's father is Canadian but his mother was born in the UK and she is British.

Ben is a Commonwealth citizen with right of abode, and can enter the UK without the need to comply with the spouse or civil partner rules (he needs a 'certificate of entitlement'). See **2.3**. A check should be made to see if he is registered as a British citizen. See **2.2.6.2**.

Example 2

Vlad is a citizen of Russia who is married to Maria, a citizen of Austria.

As an EEA national, Maria can enter the UK, and Vlad may enter as her spouse, without the need to comply with the spouse rules. See **Chapter 4**.

> **Example 3**
>
> Carla is a citizen of The Philippines. She married Denis, a British citizen, whilst he was on holiday there, but has not yet agreed to join him in the UK. She has applied for a visa to enter the UK as a general visitor, to see whether she would wish to live in the UK.
>
> In principle, Carla could obtain a general visitor visa, but would need to satisfy the entry clearance officer that she did intend to leave the UK at the end of her visit (see **5.11**).

8.3 Spouses or civil partners of persons who are settled

8.3.1 Introduction

A couple may well marry or enter into a civil partnership outside the UK but wish to live together permanently in the UK. If only one of them is a British citizen (see **2.2**) or a Commonwealth citizen with the right of abode in the UK (see **2.3**), or has indefinite leave to remain in the UK (see **1.4.5** and **3.8**), the other member of the couple will usually need entry clearance as a spouse or civil partner before travelling to the UK. The requirements are set out in para 281 of the Immigration Rules. An alternative route into the UK may be open to a foreign national who is the family member of an EEA national (see **4.4.6**) or a British citizen who has exercised EU Treaty rights (see **4.4.12**).

In outline, domestic law works like this. The British citizen, Commonwealth citizen with the right of abode in the UK, or the person with indefinite leave to remain in the UK, is known as the sponsor. There are *two different* routes into the UK:

(a) If the couple married or entered into a civil partnership at least four years ago and since then have lived together outside the UK. In these circumstances, entry clearance will normally be given to the applicant for settlement in the UK. See **8.3.3.2**.

(b) If the couple married or entered into a civil partnership less than four years ago. Typically, a couple apply shortly after marrying or entering into a civil partnership. In these circumstances, leave to enter the UK for 27 months is given – see **8.3.3.1**. Then, after two years in the UK, provided the couple are still together, an application for settlement can be made.

An applicant given limited leave for 27 months will be subject to a condition not to have recourse to public funds (see **3.3.2**) and, if appropriate, registration with the police (see **3.3.3**). However, the applicant will be free to work in the UK.

8.3.2 Minimum age

Paragraph 277 of the Immigration Rules provides that both the applicant and the sponsor must be at least 18 years of age on the day they arrive in the UK. In cases where the applicant is within a couple of months of his eighteenth birthday and the sponsor is aged 18 or over, an entry clearance officer may be persuaded to issue entry clearance that is valid from when the applicant has reached his eighteenth birthday.

In November 2008, the age was increased to 21 by the Home Office as part of its policy to address the issue of forced marriages. However, in *R (Quila) v Secretary of State for the Home Department* [2010] EWCA Civ 1482, the Court of Appeal rejected that and held that insofar as one spouse is a British citizen, the rule is unlawful. The Supreme Court heard the Government's appeal in June 2011 and handed down its judgment in October 2011 ([2011] UKSC 45). By a majority (4 to 1) the Court dismissed the appeal. As a result the Government amended para 277 in November 2011 and reset the minimum age at 18.

8.3.3 Paragraph 281 requirements

8.3.3.1 The applicant is married to or the civil partner of a person present and settled in the United Kingdom or who is on the same occasion being admitted for settlement

Under para 281(i)(a), the marriage or civil partnership must be valid.

The UKBA guidance is that the type of marriage must be recognised in the country in which it took place, it must satisfy the legal requirements of that country, and there must not be anything in the law of either party's country of domicile that restricted their freedom to enter into the marriage.

The UKBA has a list of countries where it recognises a civil partnership as valid.

What is meant by the sponsor being 'present and settled' in the UK? Paragraph 6 states that this means the sponsor is settled in the UK and, at the time that the application under the Rule is made, is physically present here, or is coming here with or to join the applicant and intends to make the UK his home with the applicant if the application is successful. As noted at **8.3.1**, the sponsor will be either a British citizen, or a Commonwealth citizen with the right of abode in the UK, or have indefinite leave to remain in the UK. The sponsor will normally be with his partner, often helping him or her make the entry clearance application, with the intention of travelling together to the UK to make the UK their home. But in other cases the sponsor might be travelling to the UK later to join his partner. Otherwise the sponsor must be in the UK.

8.3.3.2 The applicant is married to or the civil partner of a person who has a right of abode in the United Kingdom or indefinite leave to enter or remain in the United Kingdom and is on the same occasion seeking admission to the United Kingdom for the purposes of settlement and the parties were married or formed a civil partnership at least 4 years ago, since which time they have been living together outside the United Kingdom

This requirement under para 281(i)(b)(i) is an *alternative* to that in para 281(i)(a) above.

To meet this requirement, the applicant and sponsor must have been validly married or in a valid civil partnership for at least four years, and during that time they must have been living together outside the UK. In addition, they must now be travelling together with the intention of making the UK their home. See also **8.3.3.3**.

8.3.3.3 The applicant has sufficient knowledge about English language and life in the UK (unless he is aged 65 or over at the time he makes his application) and no unspent convictions

These requirements under para 281(i)(b)(ii) and (iii) *only* apply to an applicant under para 281(i)(b)(i) (see **8.3.3.2**), ie where the couple have already been married or in a civil partnership for at least four years. The test details are at **3.8.7**. If an applicant meets these requirements and all of those that follow below, he will be granted entry clearance for the purpose of immediate settlement in the UK. However, if the applicant does not meet the knowledge requirement but does meet all the others, he will be granted the usual 27 months' limited leave. Leave is refused if the applicant has an unspent conviction (see **Appendix 8**).

Examples

1. Andrew is a British citizen. He entered into a civil partnership five years ago with Zach, a visa national. They have lived together ever since outside the UK. Zach can apply under para 281(i)(b)(i) (see **8.3.3.2**), and if he passes the Life in the UK test and has no unspent convictions and meets all the other requirements that follow below, he should be granted entry clearance to settle in the UK.

2. Alexander has indefinite leave to remain in the UK. Last month he married Olivia, a visa national. Olivia cannot apply under para 281(i)(b)(i) as the couple have not been married for at least four years. So she should apply under para 281(i)(a) (see **8.3.3.1**). She will not have to pass the English language and Life in the UK test at this stage – she will have to do this when she later applies for settlement. Provided she meets all the other requirements that follow below, she should be granted a spouse visa and the usual 27 months' limited leave when entering the UK. She will have to demonstrate that she has no unspent convictions when later applying for settlement (see **8.3.6**).

8.3.3.4 The parties to the marriage or civil partnership have met

The UKBA guidance, following case law, is that 'met' in para 281(ii), requires the parties to have made the acquaintance of one another. This need not have been in the context of marriage or a civil partnership. So if the parties had been childhood friends, that might be acceptable. Simply coming face to face, followed by telephone or written contact, will not suffice, as 'met' implies a face-to-face meeting which results in the making of mutual acquaintance. Therefore a relationship developed over the Internet would potentially satisfy this requirement only if it included a personal face-to-face meeting between the couple concerned.

8.3.3.5 Each of the parties intends to live permanently with the other as his or her spouse or civil partner and the marriage or civil partnership is subsisting

Paragraph 6 of the Immigration Rules defines 'intention to live permanently with the other' as 'an intention to live together, evidenced by a clear commitment from both parties that they will live together permanently in the UK immediately following the outcome of the application in question or as soon as circumstances permit thereafter'.

Example

Anne is a British citizen. She enters into a civil partnership with Jamila, a citizen of Nigeria, in order to enable Jamila to settle in the UK without having to apply for refugee status. Anne has no intention of continuing the relationship with Jamila once she has obtained settlement.

The Home Office may contest an application by Jamila on the grounds that the parties do not intend to live permanently with each other.

The requirement is clearly not met by a marriage or civil partnership of convenience: see **4.4.6.2**. So an entry clearance officer's suspicions might be raised if the parties have not known each other for more than a few weeks or months before marrying or entering into a civil partnership; the marriage or civil partnership occurs shortly after the applicant was refused an entry certificate in another category; the application is made quickly after the marriage or civil partnership ceremony; there is a lack of financial support between the parties; there is a considerable difference in age or background between the couple; there is no common language; the time that the parties to the relationship spend together is limited; there is lack of cohabitation; one party is vague about the other's movements; there is lack of credibility or reliability of a party as a witness; and there is limited or no supporting evidence from family and friends about the relationship between the parties.

Where both partners are clearly committed to stay together irrespective of whether they live in the UK or not, the intention to live together will be shown. But what if one party says that he will live with his partner only in a particular country, or will not live with his partner in a particular country?

Example

Sumeina is a British citizen. Her father arranged her marriage to Khalid, a citizen of Pakistan, by correspondence with his father, on the basis that the couple were first cousins, between whom marriage is customary. Sumeina travelled to Pakistan to marry Khalid, and then returned to the UK. He later applied for a visa to enter the UK as her spouse. He has admitted that he lacks the means to support her in Pakistan, and she has made it clear that she is not prepared to emigrate to Pakistan.

The Home Office may argue that both parties lack the intent to live permanently with each other, as their intent is conditional on Khalid gaining entry to the UK, and that the marriage is not yet 'subsisting'.

However, it may be perfectly reasonable for Sumeina as a British citizen to insist on continuing to live in the UK (see *R v Immigration Appeal Tribunal, ex p Wali* [1989] Imm AR 86). The fact that material considerations outweigh emotional ones at this stage need not mean that the marriage is a sham, particularly in the context of an arranged marriage.

If a couple live separately after the marriage or civil partnership, that might be said to show a lack of intent to live together. Very often, a couple will seek to rebut that by producing details of letters sent and telephone calls made during this period to illustrate their 'intervening devotion'. In the case of *Amarjit Kaur* (1999) INLP 110, the immigration judge had found the appellant's 'overriding wish was to marry someone from abroad. The letters and phone calls were evidence, not of intervening devotion, but merely of intervening contact'. No further evidence of letters or phone calls was produced to the Tribunal, and although the sponsor had visited his wife in India, the appeal was dismissed. The immigration judge had taken a dim view of the fact that the sponsor was a divorcée 20 years older than the appellant, who had turned down Indian-based suitors in order to marry him. The Tribunal did not demur from that.

The question whether parties intend to live together is basically one of fact and decisions will depend on the credibility of evidence, and in particular whether the parties to the marriage have contradicted themselves.

8.3.3.6 There will be adequate accommodation for the parties and any dependants without recourse to public funds in accommodation which they own or occupy exclusively

First, have another look at **3.3.2**, which deals with public funds.

Secondly, what accommodation owned or occupied exclusively by the couple and any dependants will be adequate?

The couple will have to provide evidence if property is either owned or rented by them. This may be in the form of a letter from their mortgagee if bought with the aid of a mortgage, a copy of the property deeds and, in the case of rented accommodation, a rent book and lease agreement. Where the accommodation is rented from a local authority or housing association, correspondence from the landlord is normally regarded as genuine and sufficient. The UKBA suggests that greater care needs to be taken where there is a private tenancy. If there are any aspects of the case which raise substantial doubts, it might seek corroborative evidence of residence.

Can a third party provide accommodation for the couple? Yes, provided that that is a firm arrangement. In *AB (Third-party provision of accommodation)* [2008] UKAIT 00018, the sponsor wife was living in premises provided by a relative. She contributed to the household bills but did not pay any rent. The relative was happy for this arrangement to continue if she was joined by her husband. The Tribunal indicated that the mere mention of a relative or friend who was prepared to accommodate the parties was probably not enough, but a real and stable arrangement for accommodation provided by another might be. In this case the offer of accommodation was a real and stable one. It was credible and practical, and satisfied the requirement. In these circumstances it obviously helps if the third party supplies a statement setting out the accommodation arrangements.

If the accommodation is not 'owned', in the sense that the sponsor is not the head of the household but is, for instance, a son or daughter of the family, the Rules require there to be adequate accommodation which the couple and any dependants will occupy themselves for their exclusive use. What does this mean in practice? In *KJ ('Own or occupy exclusively') Jamaica* [2008] UKAIT 00006, the Tribunal said that:

> it is clear that it cannot mean either 'alone' nor 'with a legal right to exclude all others' ... it ought not to be enough for an applicant to say that he will be accommodated by a series of friends allowing him to sleep on sofas, or that he has enough money to put up his dependants in hotels from time to time, or that he or they will find space in hostels. What appears to be required is that there is somewhere that the person or people in question can properly, albeit without any legal accuracy, describe as their own home. They may not own it; and they may share it; but it is adequate for them, it is in a defined place, and it is properly regarded as where they live, with the implications of stability that that phrase implies. (*per* Mr C M G Ockelton, Deputy President, at para 9)

The UKBA guidance is that where accommodation is shared with other family members, it may be adequate if the couple has use of a separate bedroom, provided that that does not cause overcrowding as defined in the Housing Act (HA) 1985.

The HA 1985, s 324 contains two tests to determine whether or not a house or flat is overcrowded. If by coming to live in the property the applicant will cause it to be overcrowded under either test, the application will fail. The relevant law is as follows:

324 Definition of overcrowding

A dwelling is overcrowded for the purposes of this Part when the number of persons sleeping in the dwelling is such as to contravene—

(a) the standard specified in section 325 (the room standard), or

(b) the standard specified in section 326 (the space standard).

325 The room standard

(1) The room standard is contravened when the number of persons sleeping in a dwelling and the number of rooms available as sleeping accommodation is such that two persons of opposite sexes who are not living together as husband and wife must sleep in the same room.

(2) For this purpose—

(a) children under the age of ten shall be left out of account, and

(b) a room is available as sleeping accommodation if it is of a type normally used in the locality either as a bedroom or as a living room.

326 The space standard

(1) The space standard is contravened when the number of persons sleeping in a dwelling is in excess of the permitted number, having regard to the number and floor area of the rooms of the dwelling available as sleeping accommodation.

(2) For this purpose—

(a) no account shall be taken of a child under the age of one and a child aged one or over but under ten shall be reckoned as one-half of a unit, and

(b) a room is available as sleeping accommodation if it is of a type normally used in the locality either as a living room or as a bedroom.

(3) The permitted number of persons in relation to a dwelling is the number specified in the following Table but no account shall be taken for the purposes of the Table of a room having a floor area of less than 50 square feet.

Table

Number of rooms	Number of persons
1	2
2	3
3	5
4	7.5
5	10
6 or more	2 persons for each room

As you will have noted, the first test is called 'the room standard'. It means that a property is overcrowded if two people aged 10 years old or more of the opposite sex, other than a husband and wife or civil partners, have to sleep in the same room. The second test is 'the space standard'. Basically, it is whether or not the number of people sleeping in the property exceeds that permitted by the Act. The table sets out the limits.

Example

Ian, a widower, lives in a house with three rooms that can be used for sleeping. Living with him is his son, Lionel, aged 12, and his daughter, Diane, aged 13. Ian's mother, Mary, also lives with them. Ian recently travelled to Moscow and married Vika, a Russian national. Will the house be overcrowded if she is allowed to join Ian in the UK?

First, apply the room standard and answer the question: Who will sleep in each room? Ian and Vika, as husband and wife, can share one room. Lionel, aged 12, and Diane, aged 13, as two persons of 10 years old or more of the opposite sex, cannot share. So they must be in separate rooms. The house will not be overcrowded, therefore, if Diane shares with Mary (two persons of 10 years old or more of the same sex) and Lionel has a room of his own.

Secondly, apply the space standard. The permitted number of persons for a property with three rooms is five and there will be five people in the household if Vika joins them, ie Ian (an adult counts as one); Vika (an adult counts as one); Lionel (aged 12, so 10 years old or more which counts as one); Diane (aged 12, so 10 years old or more which counts as one) and Mary (an adult counts as one). A check should be made that each room is at least 50 square feet.

Also note that these guidelines on overcrowding are used by the UKBA and Tribunals when considering other categories of entrants, for example children joining parents (see **8.9.4.7**).

8.3.3.7 The parties will be able to maintain themselves and any dependants adequately without recourse to public funds

The requirement under para 281(v) concerns the parties' maintenance. First, have a look back at **3.3.2**, which deals with public funds.

Unlike the points-based system (see **Chapters 6** and 7) there is no minimum prescribed sum of money for maintenance. However, there is an accepted minimum standard, namely income support levels. In *AM (Ethiopia) v Entry Clearance Officer* [2008] EWCA Civ 1082 the Court of Appeal stated that the requirement that maintenance is 'adequate' cannot properly be ignored. The use of that word imposes an objective standard. It is not sufficient that maintenance is available at a standard which the parties and their family are prepared to tolerate. The Court observed that there is a good reason for using the levels of income support as a test. The reason is that income support is the level of income provided by the UK Government to those who have no other source of income. It follows that a family who do not have as much as they would have on income support are not adequately maintained. The decision was approved in *French v Entry Clearance Officer Kingston* [2011] EWCA Civ 35.

Note that the income support level in 2011/12 was £105.95 a week for a couple. What if the couple have dependants? The weekly income support level in 2011/12 for an adult was £67.50 and for a child it was £62.33.

Can a couple make up a shortfall in their weekly income by using savings? In *Begum v Secretary of State for the Home Department* [2011] UKUT 246, the couple's income came to £256.34 per week as against a total requirement of £381.50 per week at the level of income support for their family unit. There was, therefore, a shortfall of £125.16 per week. They had £20,000 in savings. As the Tribunal observed, £20,000 divided by £125.16 comes to 159. So there would be 159 weeks during which the maintenance shortfall could be made good by the savings. As the applicant would be given limited leave for 27 months, that equated to approximately 117 weeks. So the savings were adequate to account for the maintenance shortfall for the maximum period of limited leave with a £5,356.28 surplus. The Tribunal held that as the couple were able to meet the requirements of adequate maintenance for the period of the initial visa, and there was no reason at that stage to believe that they would not be able to meet the maintenance requirements in the longer term, then entry clearance should have been granted.

Can a sponsor who receives disability living allowance count that as part of the family's income for maintenance purposes? Yes, held a majority of the Court of Appeal in *MK (Somalia v Entry Clearance Officer)* [2007] EWCA Civ 1521. Disability living allowance is a non-means-tested benefit and can be spent by the sponsor in any way he sees fit. It would appear that this principle applies to any other similar non-means-tested benefits.

Can a couple meet this requirement with financial assistance from a third party? Potentially yes, held the Supreme Court in *Ahmed Mahad (previously referred to as AM) (Ethopia) v Entry Clearance Officer* [2009] UKSC 16. As Lord Brown explained at para 19:

> First, whilst I accept that generally speaking unenforceable third party promises are likely to be more precarious and less easily verifiable than a sponsor's own legal entitlements, that will not invariably be so. And it would surely be somewhat anomalous if ECOs could accept promises of continuing accommodation and/or employment and yet not promises of continuing payments, however regularly they can be shown to have been made in the past and however wealthy the third party can be seen to be. Are rich and devoted uncles (or, indeed, large supportive immigrant communities such as often assist those seeking entry) really to be ignored in this way? A second consideration, never to be lost sight of, is that it is always for the Applicant to satisfy the ECO that any third party support relied upon is indeed assured. If he fails to do so, his application will fail. That this may be difficult was recognised by Collins J himself in *Arman Ali* (p 103):
>
>> 'I do not doubt that it will be rare for Applicants to be able to satisfy an entry clearance officer, the Secretary of State or an adjudicator that long-term maintenance by a third party will be provided so that there will be no recourse to public funds. But whether or not such long-term support will be provided is a question of fact to be determined on the evidence.'

UKBA guidance is that the ECO will need to verify and assess an offer of third-party support in order to determine whether an applicant satisfies this requirement. The ECO will usually request evidence of the third party's assets, such as original bank statements.

What pointers may be found in the UKBA guidance? To be satisfied that the couple will be able to maintain themselves and any dependants adequately without recourse to public funds, the UKBA will need to see evidence of:

(a) sufficient independent means; or
(b) employment for one or both of the parties; or
(c) sufficient prospects of employment for one or both the parties.

When conducting an interview, the following areas of questioning in relation to maintenance may be put by the authorities:

(a) the applicant's present employment;
(b) the applicant's educational achievement;

(c) other skills or qualifications the applicant may have acquired that would assist in getting established in the UK;

(d) similar information about the sponsor;

(e) what plans the applicant may have for obtaining employment in the UK;

(f) what arrangements have been or could be made to obtain employment by the applicant, sponsor or friend or relatives in the UK;

(g) what other support is available to the couple from friends or relatives in the UK.

Lastly, it should be noted that the parties will always greatly assist their case if they produce a schedule of income and outgoings, of assets and liabilities. This is especially true at any appeal hearing.

8.3.3.8 The applicant has sufficient knowledge of English language

Unless the applicant is a national of a UKBA-recognised majority English-speaking country (see the list at **7.3.3.2**) or has a UKBA-recognised qualification taught in English (see **7.3.3.3**), he must pass a prescribed test conducted by an UKBA-approved provider to demonstrate that he is able to understand and use familiar everyday expressions and very basic phrases, to introduce himself and others, and to ask and answer questions about very basic personal details (level A1 of the Council of Europe's Common European Framework of Reference).

8.3.4 Key questions on the entry clearance application form

Entry certificate application forms can be found on the International Group's website (see **1.2.8**). As you would expect, questions on the settlement form (VAF4) reflect the requirements of para 281 and include the following:

(a) When did you first meet your sponsor?

(b) Where did you first meet?

(c) When did your relationship begin?

(d) How often do you meet?

(e) When did you last see your sponsor?

(f) Have you kept in touch since your last meeting?

(g) When and where did you marry/enter into a civil partnership?

(h) Do you intend to live with your sponsor permanently?

(i) Who supports you financially and what is your relationship to them?

(j) Is your sponsor responsible for anyone else's financial support?

(k) Where do you and your sponsor plan to live in the UK?

(l) Does your sponsor own this property?

(m) If no, on what basis does your sponsor occupy this property, ie rented, owned by a parent etc

(n) How many bedrooms are there in the property?

(o) How many other rooms are there in the property (*not* including kitchens, bathrooms, toilets)?

(p) Does anyone, other than your sponsor, live in the property?

(q) What is your present work or job or occupation?

(r) What is your total monthly income from all sources of employment or occupation after tax?

(s) Do you receive income from any other sources, including friends or family?

(t) Do you have any savings, property or other income, for example, from stocks and shares?

(u) Do you intend to work in the UK?

(v) What is your sponsor's National Insurance number?

(w) What is your sponsor's present work or job or occupation?

(x) Do they have any other source of income from a second job or occupation?

(y) What is your sponsor's total monthly income from all sources of work or employment after tax?

(z) Does your sponsor receive income from any other sources, including friends or family?

(aa) Does your sponsor have any savings, property or other income, for example, from stocks and shares?

(bb) Does your sponsor receive any money from public funds?

(cc) How much of your sponsor's total monthly income is given to their family members and other dependants?

(dd) How much does your sponsor spend each month on living costs?

8.3.5 Grant of leave to enter

If a person is granted leave to enter as the spouse or civil partner of someone settled in the UK, the leave will be for an initial period of 27 months, often called the 'probationary period'. After 24 months, indefinite leave may be granted (see below).

Why is the initial leave for 27 months? This is because entry clearance issued to a spouse or civil partner usually takes effect as his leave to enter (see **3.4.2**) and so commences on the date the entry clearance is issued. Provided the person delays travelling to the UK only for up to three months he will still be able to complete the two year probationary period in the UK. Otherwise he will have to apply and pay for a short extension in order to make up the full two years in the UK.

The spouse or civil partner may obtain employment within the initial probationary period.

You will recall that there is a second type of applicant, namely a spouse or civil partner falling under para 281(i)(b) of the Immigration Rules (see **8.3.3.2** and **8.3.3.3**). As the couple have already been married or in a civil partnership for at least four years, the applicant may be granted indefinite leave to enter the UK and so will have no probationary period to serve, provided he meets the English language and 'life in the UK' tests.

8.3.6 Grant of settled status

8.3.6.1 Para 287 requirements

Shortly before the probationary period expires, an application should be made, under para 287 of the Immigration Rules and on the prescribed form (see **3.6.4.1**), for indefinite leave to remain. The key is for the applicant to demonstrate that the couple have lived together for two years. So the Home Office requires the applicant to provide 20 letters or other documents addressed to the couple jointly or in both their names. If they do not have enough items in joint names, an applicant may also provide items addressed to each of the couple individually, if they show the same address for both of them. The dates of the letters or documents should spread over the whole two years. They should be from at least five different sources. What if the couple lived with relatives or friends for some or all of the two-year period? Then they should provide a letter from those people confirming this.

The UKBA guidance is that detailed enquiries are normally made only where doubts exist as to whether the relationship is genuine and subsisting, for example:

(a) where there is an allegation or other information suggesting that the marriage or civil partnership may not be genuine or the couple are not living together;

(b) where an applicant switched into marriage or civil partnership whilst here as a student or has an outstanding asylum application and whose record was less than satisfactory.

On completion of the probationary period, applicants are required to provide full details of how they have maintained and accommodated themselves when completing the prescribed application form to apply for settlement. Paragraph 287(a)(iv) and (v) require that the couple should be able to maintain and accommodate themselves and any dependants without recourse to (additional) public funds. However, if a person has, through no fault of his or her own, had to have strictly temporary assistance from public funds, UKBA guidance is that he should not be refused on this basis.

8.3.6.2 What if the sponsor dies?

What if the marriage or civil partnership ends during the probationary period due to the death of the sponsor? An application for settlement can still be made pursuant to para 287(b).

8.3.6.3 What if the sponsor has deserted the applicant?

What if the marriage or civil partnership has ended during the probationary period because of the sponsor's desertion? The normal expectation is that the spouse or civil partner should return to his home country. Sympathetic consideration may be given to such applications, but will be granted only where there are exceptional compassionate circumstances over and above the desertion of the spouse. Consideration is given to such factors as the applicant's circumstances in the UK and his home country; and the presence of children from the relationship, especially if the children have the right of abode in the UK. An application made in these circumstances is normally refused.

8.3.6.4 Presence in UK during probationary period

Must the applicant have been present in the UK throughout the probationary period? There is no specific requirement in the Immigration Rules that the entire probationary period must be spent in the UK. For example, where an applicant has spent a limited period outside of the UK in connection with his employment, this should not count against him. However, if he has spent the majority of the period overseas, there may be reason to doubt that all the requirements of the Rules have been met. Each case must be judged on its merits, taking into account reasons for travel, length of absences, and whether the applicant and sponsor travelled and lived together during the time spent outside the UK. These factors will need to be considered against the requirements of the Rules.

8.3.6.5 Convictions

When applying for settlement, the applicant must not have one or more unspent convictions within the meaning of the Rehabilitation of Offenders Act 1974 (see **Appendix 8**).

8.3.7 Switching

8.3.7.1 Applying to switch categories

If a person with limited leave marries or enters into a civil partnership with a person who is settled here, he or she may seek an extension of stay under para 284 unless he or she is a visitor. This imposes similar conditions to para 281, but in addition, the Home Office must be satisfied that the applicant is not remaining in breach of the immigration laws, or liable to be deported. There is no requirement in this case to obtain entry clearance as a spouse or civil partner, since obviously the parties may have become acquainted only after the non-settled party entered. However, evidence of 'queue-jumping' (ie entering without revealing the intention to marry or enter into a civil partnership, thus bypassing the requirement to obtain entry clearance as a fiancé(e) or proposed civil partner), may be used to establish that the applicant does not have effective limited leave (see **3.6.2** and **10.2.2**).

8.3.7.2 Limited leave

If an extension is granted to remain as the spouse or civil partner of someone settled in the UK, the initial period of leave will be 24 months.

8.3.7.3 EEA national

If an EEA national marries or enters into a civil partnership with a British citizen or a settled person, he can apply under the Immigration Rules for leave to remain. Why might an EEA national take this step? The most common reason is to obtain permanent residence within two years rather than five years (see **4.4.9** and **8.3.6**) in order to apply for British citizenship (by naturalisation: compare **2.2.7.1** and **2.2.7.2**) at an earlier stage.

8.4 Marriage or civil partnership breakdown

A person who marries or enters into a civil partnership with someone settled in the UK is in a vulnerable position until he or she obtains settled status. If there are problems in the marriage or civil partnership during the initial probationary period of leave, the non-settled spouse or civil partner may be faced with the threat of removal if the marriage or civil partnership breaks down. Settled status will not be granted unless the marriage or civil partnership is subsisting. Once the initial period of leave expires, the non-settled spouse or civil partner will become an overstayer, liable to removal (see **Chapter 10**). This is not inevitable, as the Home Office should consider compassionate circumstances, for example where children would be left behind in the UK (see **10.2.4**). In addition, by para 289A of the Immigration Rules, the Home Office may grant settled status where the applicant is a victim of domestic violence (see *AI v Secretary of State for the Home Department* [2007] EWCA Civ 386 and *AN (Pakistan) v Secretary of State for the Home Department* [2010] EWCA Civ 757).

Once settled status has been granted, breakdown of a relationship cannot affect immigration status.

It is possible for a divorced or separated parent who lacks settled status to apply to enter the UK for up to 12 months, to exercise rights of contact (access) to a child resident in the UK (para 246) and thereafter to seek indefinite leave to remain (para 248D).

8.5 Polygamous marriages or civil partnerships

See para 278 of the Rules and the practitioners' texts referred to at **1.2.7**. The details of this topic are outside the scope of this book.

8.6 Spouses or civil partners of persons with limited leave

There are separate provisions applying to spouses and civil partners of persons in each category of limited leave, other than those such as visitors, where the spouse or civil partner would be expected to obtain leave in his or her own right.

The relevant provisions may be found as shown in **Table 8.1** below.

Table 8.1 Provisions applying to spouses or civil partners of persons with limited leave

Spouse or civil partner of	See	Immigration Rules, paras
Student	Chapter 6	76–78
Sole representative	7.13	194–196F
Person with UK ancestry	7.14	194–196F
Family members of Tier 1 Migrant	7.2	319A–319K
Family members of Tier 2 Migrant	7.8.9	319A–319K

8.7 Fiancé(e)s or proposed civil partners of persons who are settled

8.7.1 Minimum ages

Note that by para 289AA of the Immigration Rules, both the applicant and the party in the UK must be at least 18 years of age, but see further **8.3.2**.

8.7.2 Paragraph 290 requirements

Paragraph 290 applies conditions similar to those in para 281 (see **8.3.3**) to persons seeking admission in order to marry or enter into a civil partnership with a person present and settled in the UK. However, two main points should be considered.

(a) The fiancé(e) or proposed civil partner will be prohibited from taking employment until granted 24 months' leave following the marriage or civil partnership (see **8.3.5**).

(b) It is unreasonable to require a fiancé(e) or proposed civil partner overseas to be as clear as a spouse or civil partner may be about the couple's future accommodation.

8.7.2.1 Maintenance

The maintenance test in most cases is based on the sponsor's income and/or employment and the applicant's employment prospects. There will also be cases where a friend or relative in the UK may offer assistance until the marriage or civil partnership takes place and the applicant is free to take employment. An applicant may have a specific job waiting for him, although where he is relying on this job offer to meet the maintenance requirement of the Rules, the UKBA will take care to ensure that the job offer is genuine and will be held open for him until such time as he is free to take employment.

8.7.2.2 Accommodation

Accommodation for the couple will often be prospective rather than available on arrival. The test used by the UKBA is whether there is a reasonable prospect that adequate accommodation will be available after the marriage or civil partnership has taken place. This requirement will, of course, have to be satisfied on application for leave to remain on the basis of the marriage or civil partnership (see above). In the period before the marriage or civil partnership takes place, temporary accommodation provided by relatives or friends is acceptable.

Example

Ghulam has obtained entry clearance in order to marry someone settled in the UK. When will he be able to take a job, and when will he himself obtain settled status?

Ghulam will not be able to take a job until he has obtained an extension to remain in the UK as a spouse, after his marriage. This will give him leave to remain for a further 24 months. He will not be given settled status until he has remained in the UK as a spouse for 24 months (para 287).

8.7.3 EEA national

Can the fiancé(e) or proposed civil partner of an EEA national who is exercising Treaty rights in the UK make use of para 290? Yes, since para 290A of the Immigration Rules provides that an EEA national who has been issued with a registration certificate valid for five years is regarded as present and settled in the UK even if that EEA national has not been granted permanent residence.

8.7.4 Switching

Can a person in the UK already switch to this status? There is no provision in the Immigration Rules for a person admitted in another temporary capacity to be granted leave to remain as a fiancé(e) or proposed civil partner, and such applications are normally refused. However, where the UKBA is satisfied that there are exceptional compassionate circumstances, such as the serious terminal illness of one of the parties to the relationship, further leave to remain may be granted exceptionally outside the Rules. The maintenance and accommodation requirements must be met if an extension is granted exceptionally. Whether a case can be considered to have exceptional compassionate circumstances is assessed according to the individual circumstances of the case. However, the inconvenience or the expense of having to travel home to obtain a visa is not sufficient reason to grant outside the Rules.

8.8 Non-marital relationships

8.8.1 Paragraph 295A requirements

Paragraph 295A of the Immigration Rules deals with partners in stable relationships, whether a heterosexual or homosexual relationship. Note that by para 295AA of the Immigration Rules, both the partner seeking entry to the UK and the partner in the UK must be at least 18 years of age, but see further **8.3.2**.

In effect, such partners will be treated as spouses or civil partners for the purpose of applications to enter or remain for settlement. The special additional conditions are that:

(a) any previous marriage, civil partnership or similar relationship of either party must have broken down permanently;

(b) the parties have been living together in a relationship akin to marriage or civil partnership which has subsisted for two years or more; and

(c) the relationship is subsisting and the couple intend to live together permanently.

Each of the parties is required to provide information regarding any previous marital, civil partnership or similar relationship they have had. They are asked to specify how long ago the previous relationship was terminated, by divorce, dissolution or separation.

8.8.2 Living together in relationship akin to marriage or civil partnership

According to UKBA guidance, 'living together', should be applied fairly tightly, in that the UKBA expects a couple to show evidence of cohabitation for the preceding two-year period. Short breaks apart would be acceptable for good reasons, such as work commitments, or looking after a relative which takes one partner away for a period of up to six months where it was not possible for the other partner to accompany and it can be seen that the relationship continued throughout that period by visits, letters, etc. 'Akin to marriage or a civil partnership' is said to be a relationship that is similar in its nature to a marriage or a civil partnership, which would include both common-law and same-sex relationships. In order to demonstrate a two-year relationship, evidence of cohabitation is needed. In order to show a relationship akin to marriage or a civil partnership, the UKBA looks for evidence of a committed relationship. The following type of evidence is useful in this respect:

(a) joint commitments (such as joint bank accounts, investments, rent agreements, mortgage, death benefit, etc);

(b) if there are children of the relationship, a record of their birth entry;

(c) correspondence which links them to the same address;

(d) any official records of their address (eg doctor's records, DfWP record, National Insurance record, etc);

(e) any other evidence that adequately demonstrates their commitment to each other.

It is not necessary to provide all of the above, but UKBA caseworkers are instructed to look for conclusive evidence of the relationship.

8.8.3 Leave and settlement

A successful applicant will be given leave to enter or remain for an initial period of 27 or 24 months respectively. He may then apply for indefinite leave after completing a period of 24 months as an unmarried partner, provided the relationship is still subsisting etc (see para 295G).

Note that like spouses and civil partners (see **8.3.6**), if the couple are living outside the UK and have already been in a relationship akin to marriage or civil partnership for at least four years, the applicant may be granted indefinite leave to enter the UK and so will have no probationary period to serve, provided the English language and 'life in the UK' tests are met.

8.8.4 Examples

Example 1

David is a British citizen. He has worked abroad for some years and for the past two years has been living abroad with John, who is a US citizen. David now wishes to return to the UK and John wishes to return with him. If John is admitted he intends to live with David permanently.

John is within para 295A and should be given entry clearance and 27 months' leave to enter.

Example 2

May is a British citizen who lives in the UK. At university she met June who was a US citizen admitted to the UK with limited leave as a student. They have lived together in a committed relationship for more than two years, June overstaying her leave to remain with May. She wishes to apply for an extension of leave as May's partner.

June is not within para 295D. As with spouses, it is a requirement that the applicant has effective limited leave and should not have remained in breach of immigration law.

Example 3

Edward is a British citizen. He is married to Deirdre who is also a British citizen. They have children. For the last five years, Edward has been working abroad, and for the past three years he has been living with Rashida who is a citizen of India. On visits home, he stayed with his wife and family. He now wishes to return to the UK and set up home with Rashida, if she can be admitted for settlement. Deirdre has said that she will divorce him if this happens.

Rashida is within para 295A in that she and Edward have lived together for at least two years. However, an entry clearance officer may refuse Rashida a visa if he is not satisfied that Edward's relationship with Deirdre has broken down permanently.

Example 4

Anna is a British citizen. At university she met Bill who is a US citizen. They have been living together for two years in the UK, Bill having obtained extensions to his limited leave as a student. They do not wish to marry, but intend to have children and live together permanently. Bill now wishes to apply to remain in the UK as Anna's partner.

Bill is within para 295D and may apply.

8.9 Children

8.9.1 Who is a child?

A child is a person under the age of 18.

8.9.2 Exempt groups

A child will usually need to apply for entry clearance under Part 8 of the Immigration Rules to join a parent or relative in the UK for the purposes of settlement. Alternatively, a child's parent may have limited leave to remain in the UK and the child may wish to apply under an associated Immigration Rule to join that parent during the rest of his leave. However, those Rules will not apply to the following:

(a) children who have the right of abode (see **Chapter 2**);

(b) children who have rights of residence, as the family members of EEA nationals (see **Chapter 4**);

(c) children who are entering in their own right under other provisions of the Rules (eg as visitors or students etc).

Example 1

Eva is a German citizen, aged 17. Her father, also German, is working in the UK. She is entitled to enter the UK in her own right (I(EEA) Regs 2006, reg 11). Whether she has any right of residence beyond three months (reg 14) depends on establishing a qualifying status under reg 6. In the alternative she can enter and reside as the family member of her father who is an EEA national. The Immigration Rules do not apply.

Example 2

Abdul is a citizen of Saudi Arabia, aged 17. His father has 12 months' leave to enter as a Tier 5 charity worker. Abdul has obtained a place at a college in the UK.

He should apply for leave to enter the UK as a Tier 4 student, rather than as the child of a person with limited leave, so that his period of leave will not have to depend on that of his father.

8.9.3 Who is a parent?

The term 'parent', for the purposes of the Immigration Rules, is defined in para 6 and includes:

(a) the step-father of a child whose father is dead, and the reference to 'step-father' includes a relationship arising through civil partnership;

(b) the step-mother of a child whose mother is dead, and the reference to 'step-mother' includes a relationship arising through civil partnership;

(c) the father, as well as the mother, of an illegitimate child (where he is proved to be the father);

(d) an adoptive parent (provided that the child was legally adopted in a country whose adoption orders are recognised by the UK – see **8.9.6**).

8.9.4 Children entering to settle in the UK

Normally a child will be seeking entry clearance to join one or both parents who are already settled in the UK. Exceptionally he might be joining a relative who is here and settled. The requirements are set out in para 297.

8.9.4.1 Overview of requirements

The starting point is to identify the parent, parents or relative the child is seeking to join in the UK, as listed in para 297(i)(a)–(f). Unless one of those categories is established, the application will fail at this first hurdle.

Then proceed to consider the remaining requirements in para 297(ii)–(v). The main points concern the child's maintenance and accommodation in the UK.

As you would expect, there is a requirement to obtain entry clearance (see para 297(vi)).

8.9.4.2 Parent, parents or relative

There are four straightforward categories of entry for a child. These are listed in para 297(i) as follows:

(a) both parents are present and settled in the UK; or

(b) both parents are being admitted on the same occasion with the child for settlement; or

(c) one parent is present and settled in the UK and the other parent is being admitted on the same occasion with the child for settlement; or

(d) one parent is present and settled in the UK or being admitted on the same occasion with the child for settlement and the other parent is dead.

As can be seen, (a)–(c) involve both parents, and in (d) one parent is dead.

The remaining categories impose additional tests. This is because one parent is alive but will *not* be involved in the family reunion. This is likely where the parents have never lived together, or have separated or divorced. On what basis will the child be allowed to join the one parent who is present and settled in the UK? This is provided for in para 297(i), as follows:

(e) one parent is present and settled in the UK or being admitted on the same occasion with the child for settlement and has had sole responsibility for the child's upbringing; or

(f) one parent or a relative is present and settled in the UK or being admitted on the same occasion with the child for settlement, and there are serious and compelling family or other considerations which make exclusion of the child undesirable and suitable arrangements have been made for the child's care.

The sole responsibility test in (e) is discussed at **8.9.4.3**. The serious and compelling reasons test in (f) is examined at **8.9.4.4**.

You will have noted that the only way a child can join a relative other than a parent in the UK is under category (f).

8.9.4.3 Sole responsibility

According to UKBA guidance, the phrase 'sole responsibility' is intended to reflect a situation where parental responsibility for a child, to all intents and purposes, rests chiefly with one parent. Such a situation is in contrast to the ordinary family unit where responsibility for a child's upbringing is shared between the two parents (although not necessarily equally).

In *Suzara Ramos v Immigration Appeal Tribunal* [1989] Imm AR 148, the Court of Appeal (per Dillon LJ) held that:

> . . . the words 'sole responsibility' have to carry some form of qualification in that the rule envisages that a parent who is settled in the United Kingdom will or may have had the sole responsibility for the child's upbringing in another country. Obviously there are matters of day-to-day decision in the upbringing of a child which are bound to be decided on the spot by whoever is looking after the child in the absence of the parent settled here, such as getting the child to school safely and on time, or putting the child to bed, or seeing what it has for breakfast, or that it cleans its teeth, or has enough clothing, and so forth. . . . The question must be a broad question.
>
> Direction and control of upbringing are . . . factors which are part of the total pattern of facts on which the adjudicator had to make his decision. Another matter was of course the extent of contact that the mother had had with the child since the mother went to the United Kingdom . . .

A parent claiming to have had 'sole responsibility' for a child must satisfactorily demonstrate that he has, for a period of time, been the chief person exercising parental responsibility. For such an assertion to be accepted by the UKBA, it must be shown that he has had, and still has, the ultimate responsibility for the major decisions relating to the child's upbringing, and provides the child with the majority of the financial and emotional support he requires. It must also be shown that he has had and continues to have care and control of the child. In the case of *Nmaju v Entry Clearance Officer* (2000) *The Times*, 6 September, the Court of Appeal held that this requirement could be satisfied even where the parent in question had exercised sole responsibility only for a short period of time (namely about two and a half months on the facts). The court said that the question posed by the rules was: had the parent settled in the UK sole responsibility for the upbringing of the child? In this case the Tribunal had found that the mother had had sole responsibility for the upbringing of the appellants. Having concluded that, the Tribunal was not at liberty under the rules to find that the appellants did not qualify for entry merely because that sole responsibility had not been assumed for a period of in excess of much over two months.

In *Nmaju* the Court of Appeal indicated that:

> While legal responsibility under the appropriate legal system will be a relevant consideration, it will not be a conclusive one. One must also look at what has actually been done in relation to the child's upbringing by whom and whether it has been done under the direction of the parent settled here (per Schiemann LJ).

In *Cenir v Entry Clearance Officer* [2003] EWCA Civ 572 Buxton LJ stated that the following was a useful rule of thumb:

> . . . all the important decisions in the child's life, questions concerning health and place of abode, schooling and probably going as far as serious questions of behaviour, mode of dress and the like must be under the oversight of the parent claiming sole responsibility or delegated to someone obliged to consult and act upon her instructions. To have responsibility means to be answerable.

8.9.4.4 Serious and compelling reasons

Guidance from the UKBA states that:

> . . . the objective of this provision is to allow a child to join a parent or relative in this country only where that child could not be adequately cared for by his parents or relatives in his own country. It has never been the intention of the Rules that a child should be admitted here due to the wish of or for the benefit of other relatives in this country. This approach is entirely consistent with the internationally accepted principle that a child should first and foremost be cared for by his natural parent(s) or, if this is not possible, by his natural relatives in the country in which he lives. Only if the parent(s) or relative(s) in his own country cannot care for him should consideration be given to him joining relatives in another country. It is also consistent with the provisions of the European Convention on Human Rights, and the resolution on the harmonization of family reunification agreed by EU Ministers in June 1993.

The degree to which these considerations should be taken into account, and whether they should solely relate to the child or include those of the sponsor, is determined by two factors, namely:

(a) whether the sponsor is a parent or other relative of the child; and
(b) whether or not the sponsor is settled here.

If the sponsor is not a parent but another relative (eg an aunt or grandparent), the factors which are to be considered relate only to the child and the circumstances in which he lives or lived prior to travelling to the UK. These circumstances should be exceptional in comparison with the ordinary circumstances of other children in his home country. It is not, for instance, sufficient to show he would be better off here by being able to attend a State school. The circumstances relating to the sponsors here (eg the fact that they are elderly or infirm and need caring for) are not taken into account.

If the sponsor in the UK is one of the child's parents, consideration needs to be given as to whether or not he or she is settled here or being admitted for settlement. If he or she is not, then the relevant circumstances relate solely to the child (as detailed above). But, if the child's sponsor is one of his parents and he or she is settled here (or being admitted for settlement), the considerations to be taken into account may relate either to the child and his circumstances in the country in which he lives or lived prior to travelling here, or to the parent who is settled here or being admitted for settlement. The circumstances surrounding the child must be exceptional in relation to those of other children living in that country, but in this case, circumstances relating to the parent here, both of an emotional and of a physical nature, may be taken into account. Such circumstances may include illness or infirmity which requires assistance.

Example

Marlene is the mother of Dora, who is aged 14. Both are citizens of Barbados. Marlene is divorced from Dora's father, who never contacts his daughter. When Dora was eight, Marlene came to the UK and left Dora in the care of her grandmother, who supports her granddaughter financially. She is now settled in the UK. She wishes to know whether Dora can now join her in the UK.

Marlene cannot establish her sole responsibility for Dora, as she has not provided financial support for her from the UK. She must instead show that there are serious and compelling considerations which make Dora's exclusion undesirable (eg because Dora's grandmother is seriously ill, and incapable of looking after her). If this requirement is not met, Dora cannot be admitted for settlement in the UK.

8.9.4.5 Age

By para 297(ii) the child must be under the age of 18. The UKBA guidance is that it is irrelevant if the child turns 18 after the application has been lodged.

8.9.4.6 Dependent life-style

By para 297(iii) the child must not be leading an independent life, must be unmarried and not a civil partner, and must not have formed an independent family unit. The UKBA guidance is that this means the child is:

(a) unmarried and not in a civil partnership, and has not at any previous time been married or in a civil partnership;

(b) not currently in, or has not previously formed, a relationship with another person (such as a common-law or homosexual relationship) which could be said to be the equivalent of being married, except for name and legal recognition;

(c) still living with his parent(s) and any brothers and sisters who are living with their parent(s), except where he is at boarding school as part of his full-time education;

(d) not employed full-time or for a significant number of hours per week, although a 'Saturday' job or a temporary job during his school holidays is irrelevant; and

(e) wholly or mainly dependent upon his parent(s) (or relative other than parents, if appropriate) for both his financial and emotional support.

8.9.4.7 Accommodation

By para 297(iv) the child must be accommodated adequately by the parent, parents or relative the child is seeking to join, without recourse to public funds in accommodation which the parent, parents or relative the child is seeking to join, own or occupy exclusively. The equivalent provision is discussed for spouses and civil partners at **8.3.3.6**.

An example is the case of *Loresco* (1999) INLP 18. Three teenage children (one girl and two boys) sought to join their mother in the UK. Was the sponsor's two-bedroomed flat (with a living room that was also available as sleeping accommodation) too small for her, her husband, their 1-year-old child and the three teenagers? The Tribunal said 'Yes'. Three rooms were available to sleep in. There was one room for the sponsor and her husband, one room for the girl over 10, and the third room for the two boys over 10. So the room standard was met. However, under the space standard, with only three available rooms, the permitted number of persons was five, but now the child aged 1 counted as half a person, and so that meant the total complement of the household would be five and a half persons. Despite the appellants' solicitors' argument that the flat would only be 'technically' overcrowded, the Tribunal insisted that it would be statutorily overcrowded.

8.9.4.8 Maintenance

By para 297(v) the child must be maintained adequately by the parent, parents, or relative the child is seeking to join, without recourse to public funds. As to public funds, see **3.3.2.**

Does para 297(v) exclude any financial support the sponsor receives from a third party? No, held the Supreme Court in *Ahmed Mahad (previously referred to as AM) (Ethopia) v Entry Clearance Officer* [2009] UKSC 16 (but see the discussion at **8.3.3.7**).

A schedule of the sponsor's capital, current income and outgoings, and a schedule of how this will change after the child enters the UK, may be useful in persuading the entry clearance officer on this point.

8.9.4.9 Convictions

The applicant must not have one or more unspent convictions within the meaning of the Rehabilitation of Offenders Act 1974 (see **Appendix 8**).

8.9.5 Children of persons with limited leave

There are separate provisions applying to children of a parent (or parents) in each category of limited leave, other than those such as visitors, where the child is required to obtain leave in his or her own right.

The relevant provisions may be found as shown in **Table 8.2** below.

Table 8.2 Provisions applying to children of parents with limited leave

Child of	See Textbook	Immigration Rules, paras
Tier 4 General Student	Chapter 6	319F–319K
Sole representative	7.13.13	197–199
Person with UK ancestry	7.14.9	197–199
Family members of Tier 1 Migrant	7.7.3	319F–319K
Family members of Tier 2 Migrant	7.8.9	319F–319K
Parent who enters as a spouse or civil partner	8.3	301

If a spouse or civil partner enters the UK pursuant to para 281 (see **8.3**), or switches into this category under para 284 (see **8.3.7**), then any child should apply under para 301.

8.9.6 Adopted children

Adopted children are dealt with in paras 309A–316F of the Immigration Rules. The details are beyond the scope of this book.

8.10 Parents, grandparents and other relatives

8.10.1 Introduction

There may be many reasons why a foreign national parent or grandparent may wish permanently to join his adult child or grandchild who is settled in the UK. Equally, an adult son, daughter, sister, brother, uncle or aunt may wish to live permanently with his or her appropriate relative who is settled in the UK. These people will usually need to apply for entry clearance under Part 8 of the Immigration Rules, and to meet the requirements of para 317.

8.10.2 Exempt groups

A parent, grandparent or other relative does not have to meet the requirements in Part 8 if:

(a) he has a right of abode in the UK and so is not subject to immigration controls (see **1.4**, **2.2** and **2.3**); or

(b) he has settled status and is re-entering as a returning resident (see **3.8.3**); or

(c) he can enter the UK under EU law instead, as the family member of an EEA national (see **4.4.6**) or a British citizen who has exercised EU Treaty rights (see **4.4.12**).

Example

Bashir is a British citizen. He went to live and work in Paris, France for six months. While there he was joined by his mother, Amina. She is financially dependent on him and therefore his family member under EU law. He wishes to know whether she can return with him to live in the UK.

He may seek to rely on Surinder Singh and reg 9 of the I(EEA) Regs 2006 (see **4.4.12**) to show that he has the right to bring his mother with him on his return to the UK. If Bashir had not worked in another EU country, Amina would have to satisfy the requirements of the Rules for entry as a parent.

8.10.3 Overview of paragraph 317 requirements

The starting point is to identify a qualifying relationship between the applicant and sponsor, as listed in para 317(i)(a)–(f). Unless one of those categories is established, the application will fail at this first hurdle. So, for example, the relationship of mother-in-law and daughter-in-law is not within that list: see *KP (Para 317: mothers-in-law) India* [2006] UKAIT 00093.

Then proceed to consider the remaining requirements in paras 317(ii)–(vii). The main points concern the applicant's financial dependency, maintenance and accommodation in the UK.

As you would expect, there is a requirement to obtain entry clearance (see para 317(vi)).

8.10.4 Qualifying relative

The applicant must be related to a person present and settled in the UK in one of the following ways listed in para 317(i):

(a) A parent or grandparent who is divorced, widowed, single or separated, aged 65 years or over.

(b) Parents or grandparents who are travelling to the UK together, where at least one of them is 65 years of age or older.

(c) A parent or grandparent, aged 65 or over, who has entered into a second relationship of marriage or civil partnership. However, he cannot look to his spouse, civil partner or any children of that second relationship for financial support. Moreover, the sponsor must be able and willing to maintain him, along with any spouse, or civil partner, and any child of that second relationship who is also entering the UK as a dependant. This category is difficult to fulfil and quite rare.

(d) A parent or grandparent, under the age of 65, who is living alone, outside the UK, in the most exceptional compassionate circumstances.

As to the 'living alone outside the UK' test, see **8.10.5**.

As to the 'most exceptional compassionate circumstances' test, see **8.10.6**.

(e) Parents or grandparents, travelling together, who are both under the age of 65 and living in the most exceptional compassionate circumstances.

As to the 'most exceptional compassionate circumstances' test, see **8.10.6**.

(f) This final category is for 'other relatives' but these are limited to the adult son, daughter, sister, brother, uncle or aunt who wishes to join his or her appropriate relative who is settled in the UK. It must be shown that the other relative is living alone outside the UK (see **8.10.5**) in the most exceptional compassionate circumstances (see **8.10.6**).

8.10.5 Living alone outside the UK

Does living alone mean that there must be no one else in the applicant's home? No, but it depends on what support any other occupier gives to the applicant. In *Hosan Jan v Entry Clearance Officer* [2002] UKIAT 05330, the Tribunal took the view that an applicant could be regarded as living alone, although physically there was another person in the same household, if that other person was not either willing or able to give the applicant any necessary support.

In *EK v Secretary of State* [2006] EWCA Civ 926, the applicant was living with her father's two sisters. The Court observed that 'they were not treating her unkindly or harshly. She was paying them rent which was being provided by her father in England, and although the accommodation was overcrowded, even in the absence of her mother it could not be said that she was living alone' (*per* Brooke LJ).

In *KC v Secretary of State for the Home Department* [2007] EWCA Civ 327, the applicant was living with her two daughters, aged 15 and 17. She was held not to be living alone as they provided her with companionship and support. At the Court of Appeal the advocate for the Secretary of State submitted that the test is whether the applicant lives in a household as opposed to living alone. A degree of support is to be expected in the context of 'household', and the children here were of an age to supply a degree of support which prevented the applicant from satisfying the test. The applicant was not 'without others who could provide meaningful support'. It was accepted that the presence in the household of an 18-month-old baby would not necessarily defeat a claim to be living alone. The Court refused the appeal but was reluctant to give further guidance.

> The most I would be prepared to say, following the concession made on behalf of the Secretary of State, is that it cannot have been intended that the company of a baby child prevents a claimant from establishing that she is living alone. There may possibly be other common sense exceptions. Secondly, it may be – I put it no higher – the notion of the presence of a person able to offer a degree of support was the reason for including the expression. (*per* Pill LJ at [24])
>
> The requirement that there be the most exceptional compassionate circumstances sets the barrier very high and if satisfied might on its own be thought to provide sufficient reason for allowing a person to enter this country on humanitarian grounds. However, to that there has been added, presumably for some purpose, the requirement that the applicant be living alone. The difficulty lies in discerning that purpose with a view to giving the rule its proper meaning. Does it refer to a person living on his or her own with no-one else sharing the same dwelling (a construction for which the Secretary of State has not contended on this appeal); or does it mean a person living without anyone to provide human company or a reasonable degree of psychological and physical support, as might be the case, for example, of a woman living on her own with a very young child?
>
> In the present case the adjudicator found that that the appellant would be living with her two adolescent children and in the absence of evidence to the contrary he was in my view entitled to assume, having regard to their ages, that they could be expected to provide her with companionship and support. Accordingly, he decided that she would not be 'living alone'. (*per* Moore-Bick LJ at [31] and [32])

8.10.6 Most exceptional compassionate circumstances

This test applies to categories (d), (e) and (f) (see **8.10.4**). The UKBA guidance is that each application must be considered on its own merits, and so it is not possible to list every circumstance which may arise. However, illness, incapacity, isolation and poverty are compassionate circumstances which should be considered. Those circumstances will have to be such that the applicant cannot function without the help and support of friends or relatives, and that no such help or support is available to him in the country where he is living.

Illness or incapacity of the applicant should, where available, be supported by medical evidence.

Evidence of isolation might be given by the applicant or sponsor. This might be physical isolation because the applicant lives in a sparsely populated area; or mental isolation, in the sense that although the applicant might live in a village or town, he does not play any role in the local community, perhaps being treated as an outcast by that local community.

The UKBA guidance stresses that this is an additional requirement. So an applicant must demonstrate that he is wholly or mainly finacially dependent on his UK sponsor and has no other close relatives to turn to for financial support, and that his circumstances are exceptional in relation to other applicants in the same position.

8.10.7 Financial dependence

The applicant must demonstrate that he is financially dependent on the appropriate relative who is present and settled in the UK. Evidence should be obtained of money sent to the applicant by the sponsor and of any other support the sponsor may provide. The UKBA guidance is that the evidence should normally be in the form of international money orders, or a letter from the bank confirming when and how much money has been transferred. Other support may be a house provided by the sponsor, or rent from land or property owned by the sponsor. This should be compared with any other financial support available to the applicant from other sources, including any money given to him by other relatives not in the UK and any income received from land, property or a pension. Consideration should then be given as to whether or not the payments from the sponsor are essential to help the applicant achieve a reasonable life style. The question is whether or not the support from the sponsor makes up all or most of the finances the applicant has to live off. A schedule of the applicant's income and outgoings will often assist in answering this question.

Is it possible to have more than one sponsor? Yes, provided the sponsors live together in the UK and the applicant is coming to live with them, eg a parent applying to join two daughters living together in the UK who have jointly funded the applicant's life abroad and propose continuing to do so in the UK: see *Ahmed Mahad (previously referred to as AM) (Ethopia) v Entry Clearance Officer* [2009] UKSC 16 at para 32.

Can all or some of the funds sent by the sponsor come from a third party? Potentially yes, held the Supreme Court in *Ahmed Mahad v Entry Clearance Officer* (see the discussion at **8.3.3.7**).

8.10.8 Accommodation

By para 317(iv), it is a requirement that the applicant can, and will, be accommodated adequately, together with any dependants, without recourse to public funds, in accommodation which the sponsor owns or occupies exclusively.

The equivalent provision for spouses and civil partners is discussed at **8.3.3.6**.

8.10.9 Maintenance

By para 317(iva), it is a requirement that the applicant can, and will, be maintained adequately, together with any dependants, without recourse to public funds.

It is important to appreciate that just because the sponsor has so far provided all or most of the applicant's financial support, that does not necessarily mean that he can provide adequate maintenance when the applicant is here. Why? Well, the cost of living in the UK is likely to be much higher than in the applicant's own country. The entry clearance officer will have to be satisfied on these points. So producing a schedule of the sponsor's income and likely outgoings when the applicant is living in the UK will usually help.

The equivalent provision for spouses and civil partners is discussed at **8.3.3.7**.

8.10.10 No other close relative

By para 317(v), it is a requirement that the applicant has no other close relatives in his own country to whom he could turn for financial support.

Who is a close relative? The UKBA guidance is that close relations may include sons, daughters, brothers, sisters, grandchildren, uncles, aunts, and possibly nephews, nieces or in-laws. However, this will vary with the local culture. For example, in the sub-continent married women may be unable to provide support. Alternatively, if there are a number of close relatives, there is no reason why there cannot be a collective ability to support the applicant.

The UKBA also states that the application of a couple who have no other close relatives should not be refused solely on the grounds that they have each other to turn to.

The test is whether there is a close relative in the applicant's own country who, while not necessarily as able and willing to maintain the applicant as the sponsor in the UK, has both the ability and the willingness to provide a home and/or financial support so as to make it reasonable to expect the applicant to depend on that relative rather than on the sponsor.

An entry clearance officer must be satisfied that support from the other relative is a permanent commitment, rather than aid in an emergency.

An entry clearance officer must also take account of the distance between the relatives, particularly in those countries where travelling even short journeys can be difficult. The age and health of the applicant, and whether the relatives' other commitments may affect their ability to make regular visits, should be taken into account.

8.10.11 Convictions

The applicant must not have one or more unspent convictions within the meaning of the Rehabilitation of Offenders Act 1974 (see **Appendix 8**).

8.10.12 Examples

Example 1

Sayana is a widow aged 72, and a citizen of Bangladesh. Her only son, Abdul, is settled in the UK, and she wishes to join him. He has been sending her money for many years, and could support her in the UK. The evidence presented to the entry clearance officer shows that she is living in her son's home in Bangladesh, and has brothers living in the same area who are fairly well off and would look after her if necessary. Does she meet the requirements of para 317?

She does not need to meet the 'exceptional compassionate circumstances' test, as she is a widow aged 72. She is financially dependent on her son. However, the Home Office may argue that she has close relatives in Bangladesh, to whom she could turn if necessary for financial support. Sayana cannot argue in reply that her brothers could not give the emotional support which her only son could provide, as para 317(v) makes financial support the crucial issue. She arguably does not meet the requirements of para 317.

Example 2

Agnes is a US citizen, aged 60. She is a divorcée. Her son, Bruce, is settled in the UK. Agnes is fairly wealthy, but is suffering from terminal cancer and wishes to spend her last years with her son in the UK. She has no close relatives in the USA. Does she meet the requirements of the Rules?

As a divorcée under 65, she would have to meet the 'exceptional compassionate circumstances' test, and in the circumstances might well do so. However, she does not appear to be financially dependent on her son at all. She does not meet the requirements of the Rules, and would have to seek leave outside them.

Chapter 9
Asylum-seekers and Refugees

9.1 Overview

People may flee their own countries for many different reasons – social, economic, political, religious, etc. On arrival in the UK or subsequently, they may state that they do not wish to return to their country of nationality or habitual residence.

An asylum-seeker is a person who flees because of a fear of persecution in his own country and who, as a consequence, is seeking the protection of the UK Government. Such protection is granted if that person is given the immigration status of a refugee. Otherwise, on human rights grounds, he may be granted what is known as humanitarian protection or discretionary leave (see **9.10**).

9.2 Law and procedure

9.2.1 Relevant law

Set out below is a list of the key legal provisions referred to in this chapter:

(a) The United Nations' 1951 Convention and 1967 Protocol Relating to the Status of Refugees (generally known as 'the Geneva Convention').

(b) UNHCR *Handbook on Procedures and Criteria for Determining Refugee Status.*

(c) Parts 11 and 11B of the Immigration Rules.

(d) The Refugee or Person in Need of International Protection (Qualification) Regulations 2006 (SI 2006/2525) ('Qualification Regulations 2006'). A copy is reproduced at **Appendix 16.**

(e) UK and ECHR case law.

(f) The UKBA asylum policy instructions and process guidance.

9.2.2 Procedure

Asylum claims are dealt with by the UKBA. This chapter offers only an outline of the procedure involved. Those who wish to have a detailed understanding should consult the UKBA's guidance, issued to its asylum staff and published on its website (see **1.2.8**).

Anyone in the UK can make an asylum claim, whatever his immigration status. He may be someone who has arrived without a visa or with forged documents, or someone who has obtained limited leave to enter for a different reason (eg as a visitor), an overstayer, or even an illegal entrant. The claim can be made on entry or after entry to the UK.

The Home Office 'New Asylum Model' (NAM) aims to make a decision on an asylum claim within one month of the claim being made. To act so quickly, the Home Office official responsible for the case, known as 'the case owner', conducts the claim from start to finish to a strict timetable. The case owner should also work closely with the claimant's representative.

On the day a claim is made, the claimant has a screening interview to establish his identity and nationality. At this point fingerprints and photographs are also taken. A few basic questions about the claim are asked. The claim is then transferred to a NAM centre at Glasgow, Cardiff, Leeds, Liverpool, Solihull, Central London or West London. The claimant meets the case owner within three working days. By the tenth working day, the representative should submit the claimant's statement and any supporting evidence. In the following days, the case owner and representative discuss the case to work out what parts of the claim are accepted and what further evidence is needed. On the fifteenth working day, the claimant has an interview. On the UKBA website you will find a protocol and guidance notes for asylum staff conducting an interview, as well as a code of conduct for any interpreter used at an interview. Following any further discussion between the case owner and the representative, the case owner's decision, whether to grant or refuse asylum, is given by the twentieth working day.

9.3 What is an asylum claim?

9.3.1 The Geneva Convention

The Immigration Rules, para 327 defines an applicant for asylum as a person who makes a request to be recognised as a refugee under the Geneva Convention on the basis that it would be contrary to the UK's obligations under that Convention for him to be removed from or required to leave the UK, or otherwise makes a request for international protection.

To be granted asylum, or the status of a refugee, a claimant must meet the following requirements as set out in Article 1A of the Geneva Convention:

> . . . owing to well-founded fear of being persecuted for reasons of race, religion, nationality, membership of a particular social group or political opinion, is outside the country of his nationality and is unable or, owing to such fear, is unwilling to avail himself of the protection of that country; or who, not having a nationality and being outside the country of his former habitual residence . . . is unable, or owing to such fear, is unwilling to return to it.

By para 334 of the Immigration Rules, an asylum applicant will be granted asylum in the UK if the Secretary of State is satisfied that:

(a) he is in the UK or has arrived at a port of entry in the UK;

(b) he is a refugee falling within Article 1A (see **9.4**) and not excluded (see **9.5.1**);

(c) there are no reasonable grounds for regarding him as a danger to the security of the UK (see **9.5.2**);

(d) he does not, having been convicted by a final judgment of a particularly serious crime, constitute danger to the community of the UK (see **9.5.2**); and

(e) refusing his application would result in him being required to go (whether immediately or after the time limited by any existing leave to enter or remain) in breach of the Geneva Convention, to a country in which his life or freedom would threatened on account of his race, religion, nationality, political opinion or membership of a particular social group.

9.3.2 Sources of persecution

Before we look in detail at each requirement of Article 1A, and in particular at what may amount to persecution, we will consider the possible source of that fear. It might be the government or State itself. Legislation may discriminate against or persecute a certain group, for example, laws may discriminate against women or homosexuals. Or the persecution might come from State bodies, like the police or the army, acting on government orders. Additionally, there may be persecution if the State fails to take steps to protect its citizens from officials who abuse their authority. This might include, for example, a policeman who rapes a woman for his own sexual gratification.

A person may also fear being persecuted by people who have nothing to do with the government. These are known as non-State actors (see further **9.4.1.5**). Common examples concern political or religious intolerance, such as where one section of society does not respect the political or religious beliefs of another. Here we need to remember that part of the Geneva Convention test is that the claimant is unwilling to avail himself of the protection of his country. The question is whether or not the State has a system of criminal law which makes attacks by non-State actors punishable *and* if the State is prepared to take reasonable steps to enforce that law.

9.4 Meeting the requirements of the Geneva Convention

9.4.1 Well-founded fear of persecution

9.4.1.1 Subjective and objective tests

The claimant must be in fear of persecution, but his claim can be rejected if there is no real risk or reasonable likelihood of persecution (*R v Secretary of State for the Home Department, ex p Sivakumaran and conjoined appeals (UN High Commissioner for Refugees Intervening)* [1988] 1 All ER 193). The main issue will be the credibility of the claimant's testimony (see also **9.6.2**) that he has a genuine fear (the subjective test), but the Home Office may rely on evidence of conditions in the country from which he is fleeing to show that there is insufficient basis for the fear (the objective test). The Home Office Country of Origin Information Service has produced assessments of certain countries that produce a significant number of asylum claims. These are used for background purposes by caseworkers (see further **9.7**).

In some cases applicants may be able to provide some documentary evidence to support their claims, such as newspaper or Internet articles, passports or identity cards, political party membership cards, arrest warrants, photographs and medical reports. Organisations such as Amnesty International and the Refugee Legal Centre may be able to provide helpful evidence. As to medical evidence of torture, an applicant may be able to obtain a report from the charity Medical Foundation for the Care of Victims of Torture (see www.torturecare.org.uk). This organisation provides medical and social care, practical assistance and therapy to survivors of torture. If the applicant is already seeing a doctor or consultant, he may be able to provide a report.

When obtaining medical evidence of a claimant's injuries or scarring, it is important that the expert assesses how they were caused: see *SA (Somalia)* [2006] EWCA Civ 1302 and *RT (medical reports, cause of scarring) Sri Lanka* [2008] UKAIT 00009. Where the expert makes findings that there is a degree of consistency between the injuries or scarring and the claimant's allegations as to how they were caused by his persecutors, the expert should also include any other possible causes (whether many, few or unusually few), and gauge how likely they are, bearing in mind what is known about the individual's life history and experiences. Where possible an expert should be instructed to consider the degree of consistency on the following scale:

(1) *Not consistent*: the injury or scarring could not have been caused as alleged.

(2) *Consistent with*: the injury or scarring could have been caused as alleged, but it is non-specific and there are many other possible causes.

(3) *Highly consistent*: the injury or scarring could have been caused as alleged, and there are few other possible causes.

(4) *Typical of*: this is an appearance that is usually found with this type of injury or scarring, but there are other possible causes.

(5) *Diagnostic of*: this appearance could not have been caused in any way other than that alleged.

9.4.1.2 Benefit of the doubt

Obviously, the applicant may find it difficult to provide evidence of events in his home country and many statements may be unsupported. According to the UNHCR *Handbook*, statements should not necessarily be rejected for that reason: 'If the applicant's account appears credible, he should, unless there are good reasons to the contrary, be given the benefit of the doubt' (para 196). Unsupported statements need not, however, be accepted if they are inconsistent with the general account put forward by the applicant (para 197).

9.4.1.3 Acts of persecution

'Persecution' is not defined in the Geneva Convention on refugees. The UNHCR *Handbook* suggests that while it will often involve a threat to life or liberty, it could extend to other threats. Discrimination against a particular group does not of itself amount to persecution; but it may do so if serious, for example if it stops someone practising his religion, or earning a livelihood. 'Persecution' does not mean 'punishment'. A person who fears punishment for commission of a common-law crime will not normally be regarded as a refugee, unless, for example, the law under which he is to be punished is seriously discriminatory.

Further examples of persecution are listed in reg 5(2) of the Qualification Regulations 2006. These include an act of physical or mental violence, including an act of sexual violence; a legal, administrative, police, or judicial measure which in itself is discriminatory, or which is implemented in a discriminatory manner; and prosecution or punishment which is disproportionate or discriminatory.

In *R (Sivakumar) v Secretary of State for the Home Department* [2003] 2 All ER 1097, the House of Lords held that it is the severity of the treatment inflicted on the applicant that has a logical bearing on the issues. Excessive or arbitrary punishment can amount to persecution.

Regulation 5(1) of the Qualification Regulations 2006 provides that an act of persecution must be sufficiently serious by its nature or repetition as to constitute a severe violation of a basic human right, in particular a right from which derogation cannot be made under Article 15 of the ECHR. The basic human rights from which derogation cannot be made under the ECHR include Article 2 (right to life – save that derogation is permitted in respect of deaths resulting from lawful acts of war); Article 3 (prohibition of torture, inhuman or degrading treatment or punishment); Article 4(1) (prohibition of slavery) and Article 7 (no punishment without law). Alternatively, persecution may arise from an accumulation of various measures, including a violation of a human right which is sufficiently severe as to affect an individual in this manner.

A person does not have to be singled out for adverse treatment in order to be said to be persecuted (see *R v Secretary of State for the Home Department, ex p Jeyakumaran (Selladurai)* [1994] Imm AR 45). Discrimination may amount to persecution – this accords with the Tribunal decision of *Padhu* (12318), concerning the inability to work and deprivation of State benefits due to ethnic origin. What if the persecution feared comes from non-State actors? In the case of *Gashi and Nikshiqi v Secretary of State for the Home Department (United Nations High Commissioner for Refugees Intervening)* [1997] INLR 96, the Tribunal held that persecution includes the failure of a State to protect:

(a) those rights which are non-derogative even in times of compelling national emergency (the right to life; prohibition against torture and cruel, inhumane or degrading treatment);

(b) those rights which are derogative during an officially recognised life-threatening public emergency (freedom from arbitrary arrest and detention; fair trial);

(c) some aspects of those rights which require States to take steps to the maximum of their available resources to realise rights progressively in a non-discriminatory manner (the right to earn a livelihood; the right to a basic education; the right to food, housing and medical care).

9.4.1.4 Current fear and past acts of persecution

Whilst there must be a current fear of persecution for a Convention reason upon return (see *Adan v Secretary of State for the Home Department* [1999] 1 AC 293), persecution suffered in the past is relevant to whether a person has a current, well-founded fear of persecution. This is recognised by para 339K of the Immigration Rules. It provides that the fact that a person has already been subject to persecution, or to direct threats of such persecution, will be regarded as a serious indication of the person's well-founded fear of persecution, unless there are good reasons to consider that such persecution will not be repeated. Equally, whilst a past history of no persecution is not determinative of future risks, unless circumstances in an asylum-seeker's return country have deteriorated or some other special factor is present, it is inevitable that an asylum-seeker will have difficulty in showing future risk in the absence of any finding of past persecution: see *Becerikil v Secretary of State for the Home Department* [2006] EWCA Civ 693.

9.4.1.5 Persecution by non-State actors

The applicable law as to persecution by non-State actors is the House of Lords' decision in *Horvath v Secretary of State for the Home Department* [2001] 1 AC 489. This established that persecution implied a failure by the State to make protection available against the ill-treatment or violence which had been suffered at the hands of the persecutors. In such a case, the failure of the State to provide protection was an essential element, and accordingly the person claiming refugee status had to show that the feared persecution consisted of acts of violence against which the State was unable or unwilling to provide protection. Such a conclusion was consistent with the principle of surrogacy which underpinned the Convention, namely that the protection afforded by the Convention was activated only upon the failure of protection by the home State. Moreover, the application of that principle rested upon the assumption that the home State was not expected to achieve complete protection against random and isolated attacks.

Accordingly, in determining whether the protection afforded by the applicant's home country was sufficient for the purposes of the Convention, the court had to apply a practical standard which took proper account of the duty owed by a State to all its nationals, rather than a standard which eliminated all risk. Thus, the sufficiency of State protection was to be measured not by the existence of a real risk of an abuse of human rights but by the availability of a system for the protection of the citizen and a reasonable willingness to operate that system. This is now reflected in reg 4 of the Qualification Regulations 2006.

9.4.1.6 Attacks on applicant's family members

Can an attack upon an applicant's spouse or close family member amount to persecution of the applicant for the purposes of an asylum claim, even though there was no direct threat to the applicant himself? 'Yes', said the Court of Appeal in *Frantisek Katrinak v Secretary of State for the Home Department* [2001] INLR 499. As Schiemann LJ said:

> If I return with my wife to a country where there is a reasonable degree of likelihood that she will be subjected to further grave physical abuse for racial reasons, that puts me in a situation where there is a reasonable degree of risk that I will be persecuted. It is possible to persecute a husband

> or a member of a family by what you do to other members of his immediate family. The essential task for the decision taker in these sort of circumstances is to consider what is reasonably likely to happen to the wife and whether that is reasonably likely to affect the husband in such a way as to amount to persecution of him.

9.4.1.7 Should the applicant have to change his behaviour to avoid persecution if returned?

Is a claimant required to take reasonable measures if returned home to avoid persecution? For example, where an applicant claims to have been persecuted as a homosexual, is it relevant to take into account whether it would be reasonable to expect him to behave 'discreetly' if returned? No, held the Supreme Court in *HJ (Iran) v Secretary of State or the Home Department* [2010] UKSC 31. In considering such a claim, the Home Office must address the following issues.

(a) Is it satisfied on the evidence that the applicant is gay, or that he would be treated as gay by potential persecutors in his country of nationality?

(b) Is it satisfied on the available evidence that gay people who lived openly would be liable to persecution in the applicant's country of nationality?

(c) What will the applicant do if returned to that country?

(d) If he would in fact live openly and thereby be exposed to a real risk of persecution, then he has a well-founded fear of persecution – even if he could avoid the risk by living 'discreetly'.

(e) If, on the other hand, the applicant would in fact live discreetly and so avoid persecution, the question to be answered is why he would do so.

(f) If the conclusion is that the applicant would choose to live discreetly simply because that was how he himself would wish to live, or because of social pressures, eg not wanting to distress his parents or embarrass his friends, then his application should be rejected.

(g) If, on the other hand, the material reason for the applicant living discreetly on his return would be a fear of the persecution which would follow if he were to live openly as a gay man, then, other things being equal, his application should be accepted. Such a person has a well-founded fear of persecution. To reject his application on the ground that he could avoid the persecution by living discreetly would be to defeat the very right which the Convention exists to protect – his right to live freely and openly as a gay man without fear of persecution.

So, equally, as 'a general proposition a person found to have genuine political beliefs cannot be refused refugee status merely because they have declined to hide those beliefs, or to act "discreetly", in order to avoid persecution': per Carnwath LJ in *RT (Zimbabwe) v Secretary of State for the Home Department* [2010] EWCA Civ 1285 at [25].

9.4.1.8 Examples

Example 1

Bela has fled from his own country which is engaged in civil war. His farm has been destroyed in a battle, and he has no other means of earning his living.

The Home Office may argue that Bela is a displaced person rather than a refugee, unless he can show, for example, that he is likely to suffer persecution because he is identified with one of the sides in the civil war.

Example 2

Chaka has left his country because high taxes and an economic crisis have caused his business to fail.

The Home Office may argue that he is an economic migrant rather than a refugee, unless he can show, for example, that the tax measures were directed at a particular ethnic group of which he is a member, designed to destroy their economic position.

9.4.2 'For reasons of race, religion, nationality, membership of a particular social group or political opinion'

9.4.2.1 Race

The concept of race includes, for example, colour, descent, or membership of a particular ethnic group. The fact that a claimant belongs to a certain racial group is not normally enough to prove a claim.

9.4.2.2 Religion

As to the meaning of the word 'religion' see *Omoruyi v Secretary of State for the Home Department* [2001] INLR 33. In the case the applicant was a Nigerian Christian persecuted by a group described variously as 'a secret cult ... associated with idol worshipping to the extent of drinking blood', 'a mafia organisation involving criminal acts', and a 'devil cult' carrying out 'rituals', namely 'the sacrificing of animals to a graven image'. The court held that the persecution was not for a Convention reason (ie it was not related to the applicant's beliefs but to the fact that he had failed to comply with certain demands made by the cult) and therefore his application for asylum failed.

Note that reg 6(1)(b) of the Qualification Regulations 2006 provides that the concept of religion includes, for example, the holding of theistic, non-theistic and atheistic beliefs; the participation in, or abstention from, formal worship in private or in public, either alone or in community with others; other religious acts or expressions of view, or forms of personal or communal conduct based on or mandated by any religious belief.

9.4.2.3 Nationality

The term 'nationality' includes citizenship, or the lack of it, as well as membership of a group determined by such matters as its cultural, ethnic, or linguistic identity. Persecution for reasons of nationality may consist of adverse actions and measures against a national, ethnic or linguistic minority, and in certain circumstances the fact of belonging to such a minority may in itself give rise to a well-founded fear of persecution.

9.4.2.4 Membership of a particular social group

Over recent years, the courts have given much consideration as to what is meant by the expression 'particular social group'. In the joint cases of *Islam (Shahana) v Secretary of State for the Home Department; R v Immigration Appeal Tribunal and Secretary of State for the Home Department, ex p Syeda Shah* [1999] INLR 144, the House of Lords had to decide if two Pakistani women, who had fled Pakistan after false allegations of adultery and violence by their husbands, were part of such a group. The House held that a 'particular social group' consists of a group of persons who share a common, immutable characteristic that either is beyond the power of an individual to change, or is so fundamental to the individual's identity or conscience that he ought not to be required to change it. Thus, as gender is an immutable characteristic that is beyond the power of the individual to change, and as discrimination against women is prevalent in Pakistan, in violation of fundamental rights and freedoms, women in Pakistan constitute a particular social group.

In the *Islam* and *Shah* appeals, Lord Hoffmann asked:

> What is the reason for the persecution which the appellants fear? Here it is important to notice that it is made up of two elements. First, there is the threat of violence to Mrs Islam by her husband and his political friends and to Mrs Shah by her husband. This is a personal affair,

> directed against them as individuals. Secondly, there is the inability or unwillingness of the State to do anything to protect them. There is nothing personal about this. The evidence was that the State would not assist them because they were women. It denied them a protection against violence which it would have given to men. These two elements have to be combined to constitute persecution within the meaning of the Convention.

See also *RG (Ethiopia) v Secretary of State for the Home Department* [2006] EWCA Civ 339, where it was held that women and girls in Ethiopia constitute a particular social group. The Court found institutionalised discrimination, since the penal law in Ethiopia legitimises the marriage of abducted and raped girls to their violators, which marriage then exempts the latter from punishment. This, and the evidence of a lack of protection of women against sexual abuse and serious discrimination, shows a degree of complicity by the State in the treatment of women in Ethiopia, sufficient to conclude that women constitute a particular social group.

Regulation 6(1)(d) of the Qualification Regulations 2006, as interpreted in *K v Secretary of State for the Home Department; Fornah v Secretary of State for the Home Department* [2006] UKHL 45, [2007] 1 All ER 671, provides two useful guidelines defining a particular social group. First, where members of that group share an innate characteristic, or a common background that cannot be changed, or share a characteristic or belief that is so fundamental to identity or conscience that a person should not be forced to renounce it. Secondly, where the group has a distinct identity in the relevant country, because it is perceived as being different by the surrounding society.

9.4.2.5 Political opinion

To show persecution on grounds of political opinion, it is not enough for the claimant to establish that he holds opinions which his government opposes. He must show that they will not tolerate his opinions, and that they are aware that he holds them. Where the claimant has committed criminal offences in the course of political opposition, he cannot base a claim to refugee status on fear of his country's normal punishment for that offence.

Example

Enrico is a member of a minority linguistic group, and of the political party which represents it. The party is campaigning for language rights, for example in regional schools, and its political activities are permitted. His national government will not concede these rights and pursues discriminatory policies. Enrico has fled the country after setting fire to a school which refused to use the minority language.

The Home Office may argue that Enrico does not fear persecution on grounds of his political opinions, but rather punishment for an ordinary criminal offence. However, he may be able to show that his punishment would be excessive or arbitrary, which would amount to persecution. The discriminatory measures in themselves may not be sufficiently serious to amount to persecution on grounds of nationality.

In what circumstances may a person who objects to carrying out compulsory military service be granted asylum? In *Sepet v Secretary of State for the Home Department* [2003] 3 All ER 304, the House of Lords held that refugee status should be accorded to a person who refuses to undertake compulsory military service on the grounds that such service would or might require him to commit atrocities or gross human rights abuses, or participate in a conflict condemned by the international community, or where refusal to serve would earn grossly excessive or disproportionate punishment.

Even if a claimant does not hold political views which his government opposes, it may well be that the government believes that he does. So a person to whom a political opinion is imputed may qualify for refugee status: see *Sivakumar v Secretary of State for the Home Department* [2002] INLR 310. Imputed political opinion may include those who are perceived to be members or supporters of an opposition party, as well as anyone who is unable to demonstrate support for, or loyalty to, the government regime or ruling political party: see *TM (Zimbabwe) v Secretary of State for the Home Department* [2010] EWCA Civ 916.

> **Example**
>
> Alexander has fled from his own country because his brother has been imprisoned for political activities.
>
> The Home Office may argue that Alexander's fear is not well founded, unless he can show that persecution is for an imputed political opinion or extends to the social group associated with the political activity.

9.4.3 'Is outside the country of his nationality'

No one can claim to be a refugee until he has left the country of which he is a citizen. This means that a claimant cannot normally obtain a visa from a UK entry clearance officer in his country, clearing him to enter the UK as a refugee. He must (somehow) find his way to the UK and make the claim on arrival. This may be difficult, as airlines are fined for carrying people without correct travel documents (Immigration (Carriers' Liability) Act 1987).

9.4.3.1 The internal flight alternative or internal relocation

The claimant must be outside his country owing to fear of persecution there. What if the persecution is to be feared in only part of the country? Paragraph 339O of the Immigration Rules provides that the Secretary of State will not grant asylum if in part of the country of origin a person would not have a well-founded fear of being persecuted, and the person can reasonably be expected to stay in that part of the country. So if someone would be safe only if he lived in a remote village, separated from his family, his flight from the country can still be said to be based on a fear of persecution there (see *R v Immigration Appeal Tribunal, ex p Jonah* [1985] Imm AR 7).

The House of Lords, in *Januzi v Secretary of State for the Home Department* [2006] UKHL 5, gave further guidance on this issue. Lord Hope of Craighead said (para 47):

> The question where the issue of internal relocation is raised can, then, be defined quite simply. As Linden JA put it in *Thirunavukkarasu v Canada (Minister of Employment and Immigration)* (1993) 109 DLR (4th) 682, 687, it is whether it would be unduly harsh to expect a claimant who is being persecuted for a Convention reason in one part of his country to move to a less hostile part before seeking refugee status abroad. The words 'unduly harsh' set the standard that must be met for this to be regarded as unreasonable. If the claimant can live a relatively normal life there judged by the standards that prevail in his country of nationality generally, and if he can reach the less hostile part without undue hardship or undue difficulty, it will not be unreasonable to expect him to move there.

9.4.3.2 Safe third country exception (AI(TC)A 2004, Sch 3)

There will be no breach of obligation if the UK returns the refugee to a 'safe country' which itself has an obligation to grant him asylum, and which could be expected to fulfil the requirements of the Geneva Convention on refugees. The general principle operated by governments is that a refugee should seek asylum in the first 'safe country' he reaches.

Under EC Council Regulation 343/2003 ('the Regulation') or the Dublin Convention, the UK may return an asylum seeker to the EU Member State which has responsibility for the asylum claim under the terms of the Geneva Convention on refugees (eg because that State granted him a visa, or he first entered that State as an illegal entrant). The Home Office will not remove the asylum seeker until the State receiving him has accepted its responsibility under the Regulation or the Dublin Convention. Once that has happened, the Home Office will assume that the receiving State will itself consider the claim and grant refugee status if the claim is well founded.

In these cases, it is possible for someone who meets the Geneva Convention on refugees' definition of 'refugee' to claim asylum in the UK, but for his claim, on examination by the Home Office, to fall outside the statutory definition of an asylum claim in the UK. Because return is to a 'safe country', the Home Office may refuse these claims 'without substantive consideration', that is without looking at other aspects of the claimant's case, such as whether he fears persecution in his home country (Immigration Rules, para 345).

Schedule 3 to the AI(TC)A 2004 (which replaced earlier similar provisions) is intended to deal with the fact that many Regulation or Dublin Convention cases were, in the Government's opinion, subject to unnecessary and lengthy delay as a result of judicial review applications which challenged the safety of the transfer. The Schedule sets out in Parts 2 to 5 a graduated approach to the 'safety' of third countries for the purposes of the Geneva Convention on refugees and the ECHR. Broadly, these are as follows.

Part 2 of Sch 3 deals with countries that are deemed safe for Geneva Convention purposes and for claims that onward removal from the State would breach the ECHR. All human rights claims against removal will be certified by the Secretary of State as clearly unfounded unless he is satisfied that they are not. The countries listed at para 2 of Part 2 are those which are subject to or have agreed to be bound by the Dublin Convention, currently the members of the EU (see **Appendix 2** to this book) together with Norway, Switzerland and Iceland. In *Nasser v Secretary of State for the Home Department* [2009] UKHL 23, the claimant challenged the legality of the Part 2, para 2 list. The Supreme Court held that whilst the statute creates an irrebuttable presumption that the claimant may be removed from the UK to a country listed at para 2 of Part 2, the presumption does not preclude an inquiry into whether the claimant's ECHR, Article 3 rights would be infringed for the different purpose of deciding whether the provision is incompatible with his Convention rights. In this case the Secretary of State accepted that that if removal to the country would infringe those rights then the conclusive presumption would be incompatible.

Paragraph 4 of Part 2 disapplies s 77 of the NIAA 2002 (which prevents removal while an asylum claim is pending) where the Secretary of State certifies that a person is to be removed to a listed State and he is not a national or citizen of that State. Paragraph 5 of Part 2 prevents a person being removed from bringing an appeal within the UK on the basis that the country is not safe for Geneva Convention on refugees' purposes or ECHR purposes in terms of onward removal. Paragraph 5 provides that where a human rights claim made on another basis is certified as clearly unfounded, a person being removed is similarly prevented from bringing an appeal within the UK. Lastly, para 5 provides that any human rights claim against removal (other than on the basis of onward removal) will be certified by the Secretary of State as clearly unfounded unless he is satisfied that it is not.

9.4.3.3 *Sur place* claims

Can a claimant have a well-founded fear of being persecuted or a real risk of suffering serious harm based on events which take place after he leaves his country of origin and/or activities which he engages in since leaving his country of origin? Yes, this provision can be found in the Immigration Rules, para 339P. It will apply, in particular, where it is established that the activities relied upon constitute the expression and continuation of convictions or orientations held in the country of origin by the claimant. The most common example is a claimant who carries on political activities in the UK.

In assessing a *sur place* claim, the key question is whether the claimant's activities create a real risk of persecution in his home country. The claim fails if the activities are not likely come to the attention of the authorities of that country or the authorities are likely to ignore them: see *TM (Zimbabwe) v Secretary of State for the Home Department* [2010] EWCA Civ 916.

How should a *sur place* claim be assessed? In *BA (Demonstrators in Britain – risk on return) Iran CG* [2011] UKUT 36 the Tribunal identified the following factors.

(i) Nature of sur place *activity*

- Theme of demonstrations – what do the demonstrators want (eg reform of the regime through to its violent overthrow); how will they be characterised by the regime?
- Role in demonstrations and political profile – can the person be described as a leader; mobiliser (eg addressing the crowd); organiser (eg leading the chanting); or simply a member of the crowd; if the latter is he active or passive (eg does he carry a banner); what is his motive, and is this relevant to the profile he will have in the eyes of the regime?
- Extent of participation – has the person attended one or two demonstrations, or is he a regular participant?
- Publicity attracted – has a demonstration attracted media coverage in the United Kingdom or the home country; nature of that publicity (quality of images; outlets where stories appear etc)?

(ii) Identification risk

- Surveillance of demonstrators – assuming the regime aims to identify demonstrators against it, how does it do so: through filming them, having agents who mingle in the crowd, reviewing images/recordings of demonstrations etc?
- Regime's capacity to identify individuals – does the regime have advanced technology (eg for facial recognition); does it allocate human resources to fit names to faces in the crowd?

(iii) Factors triggering inquiry/action on return

- Profile – is the person known as a committed opponent or someone with a significant political profile; does he fall within a category which the regime regards as especially objectionable?
- Immigration history – how did the person leave the country (illegally; type of visa); where has the person been when abroad; is the timing and method of return more likely to lead to inquiry and/or being detained for more than a short period and ill-treated (overstayer; forced return)?

(iv) Consequences of identification

- Is there differentiation between demonstrators depending on the level of their political profile adverse to the regime?

(v) Identification risk on return

- Matching identification to person – if a person is identified, is that information systematically stored and used; are border posts geared to the task?

9.4.4 'And is unable, or, owing to such fear, is unwilling to avail himself of the protection of that country'

A claimant would be unable to avail himself of his country's protection if, for example, it refused entry to him, or refused to issue him with a passport. A claimant who fears persecution will normally be unwilling to accept his government's protection, and it is inconsistent with his claim to refugee status if, for example, he wishes to retain his national passport.

9.5 Exclusion from refugee status

Even if an applicant meets the tests under the Geneva Convention, the UK Government will in certain circumstances refuse to grant him refugee status (**9.5.1**) or forcibly remove him

(**9.5.2**). However, in either circumstance it must still go on to consider if it is appropriate to award the applicant humanitarian protection or discretionary leave (see **9.10**).

9.5.1 Exclusion under Article 1F

Article 1F of the Geneva Convention excludes the following claimants from asylum because they are considered not to be deserving of international protection. This is because there are serious reasons for considering that they:

(a) have committed a crime against peace, a war crime or a crime against humanity; or

(b) have committed a serious non-political crime outside the country of refuge prior to admission into that country; or

(c) are guilty of acts contrary to the purposes and principles of the United Nations.

The UKBA has set up a War Crimes Team to focus on modern-day war crimes. The team assists in the identification of people who may have committed or been complicit in war crimes, and supports action taken against them.

There is an evidential burden on the Secretary of State to establish serious reasons for considering that a claimant has committed an act under Article 1F (see *Gurung (Exclusion – Risk – Maoist) Nepal* [2002] UKIAT 04870 and *JS (Sri Lanka) v Secretary of State for the Home Department* [2009] EWCA Civ 364). However, it does not have to be shown to the criminal standard of proof, ie beyond reasonable doubt (see *Al-Sirri v Secretary of State for the Home Department* [2009] EWCA Civ 222).

So when does Article 1F apply?

> I would hold an accused disqualified under Article 1F if there are serious reasons for considering him voluntarily to have contributed in a significant way to the organisation's ability to pursue its purpose of committing war crimes, aware that his assistance will in fact further that purpose. (per Lord Brown in *R (on the application of JS) (Sri Lanka) v Secretary of State for the Home Department* [2010] UKSC 15 at para 38)

What is a 'crime against humanity' for the purposes of Article 1F(a)? It is an act of torture or killing as part of a widespread or systematic attack directed at any civilian population (*MH (Syria) v Secretary of State for the Home Department* [2009] EWCA Civ 226).

Note that reg 7(2) of the Qualification Regulations 2006 interprets the meaning of Article 1F(b) as follows:

> The reference to 'serious non-political crime' includes a particularly cruel action, even if it is committed with an allegedly political objective. The reference to the crime being committed outside the country of refuge prior to his admission as a refugee shall mean the time up to and including the day on which a residence permit [signifying the grant of refugee status] is issued.

Also note that s 54 of the IANA 2006 interprets the meaning of Article 1F(c). It provides that acts of committing, preparing or instigating terrorism, or encouraging or inducing others to do so, are included within the meaning of what constitutes 'acts contrary to the purposes and principles of the United Nations'.

The application of Article 1F(c) will be straightforward in the case of an active member of an organisation that promotes its objects only by acts of terrorism. There will almost certainly be serious reasons for considering that he has been guilty of acts contrary to the purposes and principles of the United Nations. However, what if the organisation pursues its political ends in part by acts of terrorism and in part by military action directed against the armed forces of the government? A person may join such an organisation because he agrees with its political objectives, and may be willing to participate in its military actions, but he may not agree with and may not be willing to participate in its terrorist activities. The higher up in the organisation a person is, the more likely will be the inference that he agrees with and promotes all of its activities, including its terrorism.

Example

Danilow fled from his country after being imprisoned for distributing political leaflets. In order to finance his escape he commits an armed robbery.

Whether the armed robbery amounts to a serious non-political crime depends on whether it has been committed for political motives, or for personal reasons or gain, and whether the act was proportionate to the alleged objective. The Home Office may well argue that Danilow's criminal character outweighs his character as a bona fide refugee (see *T v Secretary of State for the Home Department* (1996) *The Times*, 23 May).

9.5.2 Enforced removal under Article 33(2)

Article 33(2) of the Geneva Convention allows the UK Government to remove a person who is otherwise a refugee where there are reasonable grounds for regarding him as a danger to the security of the UK, or who, having been convicted by a final judgment of a particularly serious crime, constitutes a danger to the community of the UK.

The UKBA guidance is that for a person to be a danger to the security of the UK, the actions or anticipated actions of that person need not create a direct threat to the UK's system of government or its people. The interests of national security could be threatened indirectly by activities directed against other States. Thus the definition of a threat to national security is very wide: for example, depending on the specific facts of the case, if someone is believed or known to be a terrorist then, due to the nature of international terrorism, and regardless of the immediate threat of his particular terrorist group, it may be reasonable to regard the person as a threat to the UK's national security.

What is a particularly serious crime such that the person constitutes a danger to the community of the UK? By s 72 of the NIAA 2002, there is a general presumption of this where the person was sentenced to a period of imprisonment of at least two years. Note, however, that in *EN (Serbia) v Secretary of State for the Home Department* [2009] EWCA Civ 630, the Court of Appeal held that the presumption is rebuttable and that the Nationality, Immigration and Asylum Act 2002 (Specification of Particularly Serious Crimes) Order 2004 (SI 2004/1910), which specifies a large number of offences as offences to which s 72 applies, irrespective of the sentence imposed, is ultra vires and unlawful.

The Court in *EN (Serbia)* stressed that the second ground for enforced removal under Article 33(2) requires two conditions to be met: first, that the refugee has been convicted by a final judgment of a particularly serious crime; and, secondly, that he constitutes a danger to the community. The presumption that each of these conditions is met is rebuttable. So, for example, if the refugee can demonstrate that he is not a danger to the community, Article 33(2) cannot apply. Note, however, that the Court indicated (at [45] and [46]) that where a person is convicted of a particularly serious crime, and there is a real risk of its repetition or the recurrence of a similar offence, he is likely to constitute a danger to the community. The Court also gave the example of a person convicted of a particularly serious offence of violence who the Government can establish is a significant drug dealer as being one where removal under Article 33(2) is likely.

9.6 Consideration of cases

9.6.1 The UKBA checklist

The UKBA asylum owners use the following checklist when assessing a claim:

(a) What is the applicant's basis of claim?

(b) Which of the applicant's claims about past events can be accepted?

Are the applicant's claims as to his past experiences consistent with objective country of origin information (see **9.7**) relating to the relevant period, including generally known facts?

Are the applicant's claims consistent with other evidence submitted, eg the evidence of other witnesses, family members or documents specifically referring to the applicant?

Are any of the applicant's claims about his past experiences not able to be corroborated by reference to country of origin information or other evidence? If so, can the benefit of the doubt be given to any of these claims? If not, why not?

After due consideration of the principle of the benefit of the doubt, which of the applicant's material claims can be accepted, and which can be rejected?

(c) Taking into account the applicant's statements and behaviour, does the applicant have a subjective fear of persecution?

(d) Objectively, are there reasonable grounds for believing that the harm feared might in fact occur in the applicant's country of origin?

Who are the actors of persecution? Do the authorities of the home country conduct the persecution, or support persecution committed by others?

How far is the State or organisations controlling the State (including international organisations) able to provide protection from persecution caused by others? What laws are in place and are they enforced effectively?

Has the applicant sought the protection of the authorities? If so, what was the outcome? If not, why not?

Considering the objective country of origin information, the past experiences of the applicant and the attitude of the State authorities, is there a reasonable likelihood that the applicant would experience harm if returned?

(e) Can the applicant return to a part of the country in which he would not be subject to the harm feared (see **9.4.3.1**)?

(f) Is the harm feared a form of persecution (see **9.4.1.3**)?

Is the harm of sufficient gravity to constitute persecution, or is it something less serious?

Does the cumulative effect of lesser prejudicial actions or threats amount to persecution?

If the applicant has a fear of prosecution or punishment for an offence, is the punishment discriminatory or disproportionate? Does this give rise to a fear of persecution?

If the fear of prosecution is due to draft evasion or desertion, special considerations may apply.

(g) If the harm feared is serious enough to constitute persecution, would it be inflicted for one or more of the reasons set out in the Refugee Convention, ie race, religion, nationality, membership of a particular social group or political opinion? See further **9.4.2**.

(h) In the light of (a)–(g) above, does the applicant satisfy all the criteria of the 1951 Convention?

(i) Should the applicant be excluded from international protection by operation of the exclusion clauses of the Convention? See further **9.5**.

(j) If an applicant fails to qualify for asylum, decision makers should consider whether to grant humanitarian protection or discretionary leave (see **9.10**).

9.6.2 Adverse inferences

9.6.2.1 Claimant's duties

The Immigration Rules (paras 339I–339N) list some factors which are taken into account. These start by imposing a duty on the claimant to submit to the Secretary of State, as soon as possible, all material factors needed to substantiate the asylum claim. These material factors include the claimant's statement of the reasons for making an asylum claim; all documentation at the claimant's disposal regarding his age, background, identity, nationality(ies), country(ies) and place(s) of previous residence, previous asylum applications, and travel routes; and identity and travel documents.

It is further the duty of the claimant to substantiate the claim. Paragraph 339L of the Immigration Rules provides that where aspects of the claimant's statements are not supported by documentary or other evidence, those aspects will not need confirmation when *all* of the following conditions are met:

(a) the claimant has made a genuine effort to substantiate his asylum claim;

(b) all material factors at the claimant's disposal have been submitted, and a satisfactory explanation regarding any lack of other relevant material has been given;

(c) the claimant's statements are found to be coherent and plausible, and do not run counter to available specific and general information relevant to his case;

(d) the claimant has made an asylum claim at the earliest possible time, unless he can demonstrate good reason for not having done so; and

(e) the general credibility of the claimant has been established.

Paragraph 339M of the Immigration Rules provides that the Secretary of State may consider that a person has not substantiated his asylum claim if he fails, without reasonable explanation, to make a prompt and full disclosure of material facts, either orally or in writing, or otherwise to assist the Secretary of State in establishing the facts of the case. This includes, for example, a failure to attend an interview, failure to report to a designated place to be fingerprinted, failure to complete an asylum questionnaire or failure to comply with a requirement to report to an immigration officer for examination.

9.6.2.2 Statutory adverse inferences

Section 8(1) of the AI(TC)A 2004 includes similar guidelines for assessing the credibility of the claimant. The key provisions are as follows:

> (1) In determining whether to believe a statement made by or on behalf of a person who makes an asylum claim or a human rights claim, a deciding authority shall take account, as damaging the claimant's credibility, of any behaviour to which this section applies.
>
> (2) This section applies to any behaviour by the claimant that the deciding authority thinks—
>
> (a) is designed or likely to conceal information,
>
> (b) is designed or likely to mislead, or
>
> (c) is designed or likely to obstruct or delay the handling or resolution of the claim or the taking of a decision in relation to the claimant.
>
> (3) Without prejudice to the generality of subsection (2) the following kinds of behaviour shall be treated as designed or likely to conceal information or to mislead—
>
> (a) failure without reasonable explanation to produce a passport on request to an immigration officer or to the Secretary of State,
>
> (b) the production of a document which is not a valid passport as if it were,
>
> (c) the destruction, alteration or disposal, in each case without reasonable explanation, of a passport,
>
> (d) the destruction, alteration or disposal, in each case without reasonable explanation, of a ticket or other document connected with travel, and

(e) failure without reasonable explanation to answer a question asked by a deciding authority.

(4) This section also applies to failure by the claimant to take advantage of a reasonable opportunity to make an asylum claim or human rights claim while in a safe country.

(5) This section also applies to failure by the claimant to make an asylum claim or human rights claim before being notified of an immigration decision, unless the claim relies wholly on matters arising after the notification.

(6) This section also applies to failure by the claimant to make an asylum claim or human rights claim before being arrested under an immigration provision, unless—

(a) he had no reasonable opportunity to make the claim before the arrest, or

(b) the claim relies wholly on matters arising after the arrest.

9.6.2.3 How adverse?

What is the effect of s 8(1)? In *JT (Cameroon) v Secretary of State for the Home Department* [2008] EWCA Civ 878, the Court of Appeal held that the section lays down a framework of factors that may potentially damage a claimant's credibility. However, it is for the decision maker to decide the extent to which that person's credibility is damaged, if at all, and what weight should be given to any adverse finding of credibility. In this case the claimant had used false papers to enter the UK and false identities whilst in the UK. The Home Office refused the claimant asylum and the AIT determined that under s 8 the claimant's conduct had seriously damaged his credibility.

9.6.2.4 Reasonable explanation

What is a reasonable explanation for the purposes of s 8(3)(a) and (c)–(e)? The UKBA guidance is that this may include exceptional situations where the applicant could not easily have disobeyed the instructions of an agent who facilitates immigration into the UK; cases where an adult is severely traumatised, or where cultural norms may make it difficult for a person to answer questions at interview or to disobey instructions, including instructions about documents; situations where a person can show that a document was destroyed or disposed of as a direct result of force, threats or intimidation, eg where an individual was forced at knifepoint to give a document to someone else; or where the document has been lost or stolen and the individual can substantiate such a claim, usually with a police report of the loss or theft.

What is a safe country for the purposes of s 8(4)? It is any country listed in Part 2 of Sch 3 to the AI(TC)A 2004 (see **9.4.3.2**). What is a reasonable opportunity to claim asylum in such a country? The UKBA's guidance is that the claimant could have approached the authorities at the border or internally, as long as there is no reason to think that the claim would not have been received. For example, it might be thought that someone who spent several weeks in France before coming to the UK must have had a reasonable opportunity to claim asylum there; but this would not be reasonable if the applicant was imprisoned by traffickers throughout that time.

As to what is an immigration decision for the purposes of s 8(5), see **11.2**.

As to s 8(6), the UKBA guidance is that an applicant's credibility must be treated as damaged if the claim is made after the applicant's arrest under an immigration provision unless there was no reasonable opportunity to make the claim before the arrest, or the claimant relies wholly on matters arising after the arrest. An applicant has had a reasonable opportunity to claim asylum before being arrested if he could have approached the authorities at any time after his arrival in the UK. Each case should be considered on its merits. So, for example, someone who is apprehended by the police soon after getting out of a back of a lorry is less likely to have been able to make a claim before arrest than someone who passed through immigration control when arriving in the UK.

9.7 Country of origin information

The Country of Origin Information Service (COI Service) produces key documents that are used by the UKBA asylum staff as part of assessing a claim. These include Country of Origin Information Reports, Country of Origin Bulletins and Country of Origin Key Documents.

The Reports provide a brief summary of the general, political and human rights situations in particular countries, and describe common types of claim. As at August 2008, over 40 countries have Reports, from Afghanistan to Zimbabwe.

The Bulletins are issued on an ad hoc basis and aim to provide clear guidance on how to deal with particular country-specific issues arising in asylum and human rights applications.

The Key Documents provide an indexed list of reports, papers and articles produced by a wide range of recognised external information sources, mainly on human rights issues. They does not contain any UKBA opinion or policy.

Full details and the documents can be found at www.homeoffice.gov.uk/rds/country_reports.html.

9.8 Refugee status

9.8.1 Five years' limited leave

A refugee is normally granted five years' leave to remain in the UK. Pursuant to para 339Q(i) of the Immigration Rules, the Secretary of State issues what is known as a UK Residence Permit valid for five years. During this time the refugee is free to work and claim all mainstream welfare benefits.

9.8.2 Settlement

After holding limited leave for five years, a refugee may apply for settlement.

9.8.3 Review of status

A refugee's status is liable to a review which may lead to that status being withdrawn, cancelled or revoked. Such a step does not in itself affect the person's leave but, in practice, it will normally result in curtailment of any limited leave (see **3.7**) or revocation of any indefinite leave, and in action being taken to remove the person from the UK (see **Chapter 10**).

9.8.3.1 Withdrawal of refugee status

Paragraph 339A of the Immigration Rules gives the Secretary of State power to withdraw refugee status from a person where:

(a) he has voluntarily re-availed himself of the protection of the country of nationality;

(b) having lost his nationality, he has voluntarily re-acquired it; or

(c) he has acquired a new nationality, and enjoys the protection of the country of his new nationality;

(d) he has voluntarily re-established himself in the country which he left or outside which he remained owing to a fear of persecution;

(e) he can no longer, because the circumstances in connection with which he has been recognised as a refugee have ceased to exist, continue to refuse to avail himself of the protection of the country of nationality;

(f) being a stateless person with no nationality, he is able, because the circumstances in connection with which he has been recognised a refugee have ceased to exist, to return to the country of former habitual residence.

Note that (a)–(d) are voluntary steps taken by the refugee. In respect of (e) and (f) the Secretary of State must issue a Ministerial Statement announcing that significant and non-temporary changes have occurred in a particular country such that nationals can be expected to return, or that there are exceptional circumstances for that.

9.8.3.2 Cancellation of refugee status

Paragraph 339A of the Immigration Rules gives the Secretary of State power to cancel a person's refugee status where:

(a) he should have been or is excluded from being a refugee in accordance with reg 7 of the Qualification Regulations 2006 (see **9.5.1**);

(b) his misrepresentation or omission of facts, including the use of false documents, was decisive for the grant of asylum;

(c) there are reasonable grounds for regarding him as a danger to the security of the UK (see **9.5.2**);

(d) having been convicted by a final judgment of a particularly serious crime he constitutes danger to the community of the UK (see **9.5.2**).

9.8.3.3 Revocation of refugee status

The UKBA guidance is that revocation of refugee status may be appropriate where a refugee's conduct is so serious that it warrants withdrawal of that status. Where there are serious reasons for considering that a person has committed a crime or act that falls within the scope of Article 1F(a) or (c) (see **9.5.1**), subsequent to the grant of asylum, it will be appropriate to revoke a person's refugee status.

9.9 Human rights issues

A person may claim that he should be allowed to remain in the UK as his removal would be a breach of his human rights and that he cannot reasonably be expected to return voluntarily.

9.9.1 Domestic and foreign cases

The House of Lords in *R (Ullah) v Special Adjudicator; Do v Secretary of State for the Home Department* [2004] UKHL 26 distinguished between what it called domestic and foreign cases. A domestic case is where an applicant alleges that the UK has acted in a way which infringes the applicant's enjoyment of a Convention right within the UK. The most common example is where a person claims that his removal would separate him from his family in the UK and so breach Article 8 ECHR.

A foreign case is where a person claims that requiring him to leave the UK will lead to a violation of his Convention rights in the country of return, ie the alleged violation of the Convention right will occur outside the UK. For example, an applicant may allege that on return he will suffer death contrary to Article 2; inhuman or degrading treatment in breach of Article 3; unlawful detention breaching Article 5; an unfair trial contrary to Article 6; or restrictions on his freedom of religion or expression in breach of Articles 9 and 10. Article 8 claims may arise in respect of a claimant's private life. For example, a person may claim that he would be unable to be openly homosexual in the receiving State because of societal prejudice and/or legislation banning homosexuality, and that his removal from the UK would therefore lead to a breach of his right to respect for private life in the receiving country.

9.9.2 Article 2 ECHR

The UKBA guidance is that it will not normally seek to return a person to a country where there are substantial grounds for believing that there is a real risk he would be unlawfully killed either by the State, or through the State being unable or unwilling to protect him. In *R (Ullah) v Special Adjudicator; Do v Secretary of State for the Home Department* (**9.9.1** above) the House of Lords cited the decision of the ECtHR in *Dehwari v Netherlands* (2000) 29 EHRR CD 74, where the Court doubted whether a real risk was enough to resist removal under Article 2 and suggested that the loss of life must be shown to be a 'near-certainty'.

9.9.3 Article 3 ECHR

A person will not be removed from the UK to a country where there are substantial reasons for believing that he faces a real risk of serious harm or other treatment contrary to Article 3. This includes torture, as well as treatment or punishment that is degrading because it arouses in the victim feelings of fear, anguish or inferiority capable of humiliating and debasing him, and possibly breaking his physical and moral resistance. Severe discrimination based on race, sex or other grounds is also capable of constituting degrading treatment.

Ever since the ECtHR held in *D v United Kingdom* (1997) 24 EHRR 423 that the expulsion of an AIDS sufferer to St Kitts would breach Article 3 of the ECHR, the Strasbourg court has sought to distinguish that case. In the case of *D*, the court extended the reach of Article 3. The court noted that Contracting States have the right, as a matter of well-established international law and subject to their treaty obligations including the ECHR, to control the entry, residence and expulsion of aliens. The court applied Article 3 in what it described as the 'very exceptional circumstances' of that case, namely that the applicant was in the final stage of a terminal illness, AIDS, and had no prospect of medical care or family support on expulsion to St Kitts. In *N(FC) v Secretary of State for the Home Department* [2005] UKHL 31, [2005] 2 WLR 1124, the House of Lords was not persuaded to extend Article 3 any further. The House held that it must be shown that the applicant's medical condition has reached such a critical state that there are compelling humanitarian grounds for not removing him or her to a place which lacks the medical and social services which he or she would need to prevent acute suffering. This approach was confirmed when the case was appealed to the ECtHR: see *N v UK* [2008] LTL 28 May (App No 00026565/05).

It can be seen that the case of *D v United Kingdom* establishes that Article 3 may be engaged where the harm will not result from inhuman and degrading treatment by the receiving authority. For example, in *Bensaid v United Kingdom* [2001] ECHR 82, the applicant suffered from long-term schizophrenia. He claimed that his condition would seriously deteriorate if he were returned to his home country because of difficulties in obtaining suitable medication there. The Court stated at para 37: 'Deterioration in his already existing mental illness could involve relapse into hallucinations and psychotic delusions involving self-harm and harm to others, as well as restrictions in social functioning (such as withdrawal and lack of motivation). The Court considers that the suffering associated with such a relapse could, in principle, fall within the scope of Article 3.' However, the Court went on to find that Article 3 would not be violated in this case as there were no exceptional circumstances.

9.9.4 Other Convention Articles

When considering a foreign case involving an article other than Articles 2 and 3 ECHR, the UKBA guidance is that case owners should assess the likelihood of the alleged treatment or conduct occurring on return and whether that would be a breach of the ECHR; then they should consider whether any breach would be sufficiently serious that it would amount to a flagrant violation of the relevant Convention right.

Article 8 arguments are common but rarely accepted. This is because in most cases the demands of immigration control are likely to make removal proportionate, and so compatible with Article 8 as a consequence: see *AG (Eritrea) v Secretary of State for the Home Department* [2007] EWCA Civ 801, *Huang v Secretary of State for the Home Department* [2007] UKHL 11 and the commentary at **10.5.3**.

9.10 Humanitarian protection and discretionary leave

9.10.1 Humanitarian protection

9.10.1.1 Overlap with asylum claim

The great majority of claims for humanitarian protection are likely to arise in the context of asylum claims. However, where an individual claims that although he is in need of international protection he is not seeking asylum, and the reasons given clearly do not engage the UK Government's obligations under the Refugee Convention (ie the fear of persecution is clearly not for one of the five Convention reasons: see **9.4.2**), then it is accepted as a stand-alone claim for humanitarian protection.

9.10.1.2 Paragraph 339C requirements

A person will be granted humanitarian protection in the UK if the Secretary of State is satisfied that the following requirements of para 339C of the Immigration Rules are met:

(a) he is in the UK or has arrived at a port of entry in the UK; and

(b) he does not qualify as a refugee (see **9.1**); and

(c) substantial grounds have been shown for believing that the person concerned, if he returned to the country of return, would face a real risk of suffering serious harm and is unable, or, owing to such a risk, unwilling to avail himself of the protection of that country; and

(d) he is not excluded from a grant of humanitarian protection. Exclusion is on the same grounds as that for asylum: see **9.5**.

For the purposes of (c) above, serious harm is defined as:

(a) the death penalty or execution;

(b) unlawful killing;

(c) torture, or inhuman or degrading treatment or punishment of a person in the country of return; or

(d) serious and individual threat to a civilian's life or person by reason of indiscriminate violence in situations of international or internal armed conflict.

In considering whether there are substantial grounds for believing that a person would face a real risk of suffering serious harm (para 339C(iii)), the standard of proof applied is that of a reasonable degree of likelihood or a real risk.

9.10.1.3 Grant of humanitarian protection

A person granted humanitarian protection is normally granted five years' leave to remain in the UK. Pursuant to para 339Q(i) of the Immigration Rules, the Secretary of State issues what is known as a UK Residence Permit, valid for five years. After holding limited leave for five years an application can be made for settlement. Life a refugee, this status is liable to a review, which may lead to its being withdrawn, cancelled or revoked (see **9.8.3**).

9.10.2 Discretionary leave

9.10.2.1 Overlap with asylum claim

The great majority of claims for discretionary leave are likely to arise in the context of asylum claims. However, a stand-alone human rights claim may also result in a grant of discretionary leave if the qualifying criteria are met.

9.10.2.2 Qualifying criteria for discretionary leave

Article 3 ECHR

In exceptional cases a person's medical condition, or severe humanitarian conditions in the country of return, can make his removal contrary to Article 3 ECHR. The UKBA guidance is that the fact that the applicant is suffering from a distressing medical condition involving, say, a limited life expectancy or affecting his mental health, may not, in itself, be sufficient. However, there may be some extreme, albeit rare, cases where a person would face such poor conditions if returned, like absence of water, food or basic shelter, that removal could be a breach of the UK's Article 3 obligations.

Article 8 ECHR

If the removal of an individual would involve a breach of Article 8 of the ECHR on the basis of family life established in the UK, that individual should normally be granted discretionary leave.

This category applies to both asylum and non-asylum cases. In non-asylum cases it is most likely to arise in the context of a marriage or civil partnership application where, although the requirements of the Immigration Rules are not met, eg because the correct entry clearance is not held, there are genuine Article 8 reasons which would make return inappropriate.

9.10.2.3 Grant of discretionary leave

Where an applicant would have established that he was a refugee under the Geneva Convention (see **9.1**) or eligible for humanitarian protection (see **9.10.1**) but for the fact that he was excluded from that protection (see **9.8.3** and **9.10.1.3**), he is normally granted discretionary leave for six months which is then reviewed. For an example, see *R (C) v Secretary of State for the Home Department* [2008] LTL, 25 September.

A grant of discretionary leave is otherwise usually made for three years initially. It may then be extended. All applicants need to complete at least six years in total, or at least 10 years in excluded cases, before being eligible to apply for settlement.

Life a refugee and those granted humanitarian protection, this status is liable to a review, which may lead to its being withdrawn, cancelled or revoked (see **9.10.1.3**).

9.10.3 Asylum claims

All asylum claims are treated by the UKBA as containing an implied claim for humanitarian protection on the ground that the applicant will face a real risk of serious harm in the country of return, and/or a claim for discretionary leave on the basis that requiring the applicant to leave the UK will otherwise breach the UK's obligations under Article 3 because of the ill-treatment the applicant alleges he will suffer on return. In other words, all asylum claims should be treated as an implied Article 3 foreign case (see **9.9.1**); and if the asylum claim is refused, consideration should be given to whether return would breach the UK's obligations under Article 3, first by reference to the requirements for humanitarian protection and then by reference to any residual Article 3 issues that may entitle the applicant to discretionary leave.

9.11 Claims certified as being unfounded

Section 94 of the NIAA 2002 allows the Secretary of State to certify that certain asylum or human rights claims are unfounded. The result is that there is no right of appeal in the UK. Further details are given at **11.15**.

9.12 Danger of unsuccessful claims

In many cases, an entrant may feel that he has nothing to lose in making an asylum claim. However, his adviser should consider whether he has any other basis for remaining in the UK which might be prejudiced by an unsuccessful claim. If an applicant already has limited leave, the Home Office may, having refused asylum, proceed to consider whether he still meets the requirements of the Rules under which he was admitted to the UK. If he does not, his existing leave can be curtailed (see **3.7**) and he may then be removed from the UK.

> **Example**
>
> Manuel was admitted to the UK as a student with 12 months' leave. Three months later he claims asylum. The Home Office refuses the claim. The Home Office may argue that he no longer meets the requirements of para 57 of the Immigration Rules (see **6.2**), for example because he does not intend to leave the UK at the end of his studies. His leave can be curtailed (see **3.7**) so that he is required to leave his course before it ends.

9.13 Asylum appeals

Any right of appeal is dependent on the outcome of the application.

By s 83 of the NIAA 2002, where an asylum claim is rejected by the Secretary of State but the applicant is granted leave to enter or remain in the UK for a period exceeding one year, an appeal can be made to the First-tier Tribunal (Immigration and Asylum Chamber) against the rejection of the asylum claim. So a person granted humanitarian protection (see **9.10.1**) and discretionary leave (see **9.10.2**) for at least 12 months may use this provision.

A person refused asylum outright will have no right of appeal unless an immigration decision is made at the same time that can be appealed under s 82 of the NIAA 2002 – normally this will be a direction that the person is to be removed from the UK (see **11.2**).

9.14 Making a 'fresh' asylum (or human rights) claim

What can a claimant do if his asylum (or human rights) claim has been refused by the Home Office and all his appeal rights (see **Chapter 11**) have been exhausted?

Successive UK Governments have taken the view that many failed asylum seekers attempt to prolong their stay in the UK by making more than one claim. This has led to two key powers being given to the Secretary of State. First, the ability to certify an asylum (or human rights) claim as clearly unfounded, with the result that no appeal can be made in the UK (see s 94 of the NIAA 2002 at **11.15**). Secondly, another possible bar to an appeal lies in s 96 of the NIAA 2002. This enables the Secretary of State (or an immigration officer) to issue a certificate preventing an appeal when a second asylum (or human rights) claim relies on a matter that should have been raised in an appeal against the first claim (see **11.5**).

Now let us answer the question we posed above. Further submissions in support of an asylum claim can be made to the Home Office. If these are accepted, asylum will be granted. But what if they are rejected? Is there any right of appeal in the UK? Only if the further submissions amount to a 'fresh claim' for the purposes of para 353 of the Immigration Rules. When will the submissions amount to a fresh claim? Only if they are 'significantly different from the material that has previously been considered' because:

(a) the content has not already been considered; and

(b) taken together with the previously considered material, the claim has a realistic prospect of success, notwithstanding its rejection.

If the Secretary of State concludes that a fresh claim has not been made, this can be challenged by way of judicial review on the traditional *Wednesbury* ground of irrationality: see *R (MN (Tanzania)) v Secretary of State for the Home Department* [2011] EWCA Civ 193. This will involve the tribunal answering two questions:

> First, has the Secretary of State asked himself the correct question? The question is not whether the Secretary of State himself thinks that the new claim is a good one or should succeed, but whether there is a realistic prospect of an [immigration judge], applying the rule of anxious scrutiny, thinking that the applicant will be exposed to a real risk of persecution on return ... The Secretary of State of course can, and no doubt logically should, treat his own view of the merits as a starting-point for that enquiry; but it is only a starting-point in the consideration of a question that is distinctly different from the exercise of the Secretary of State making up his own mind. Second, in addressing that question, both in respect of the evaluation of the facts and in respect of the legal conclusions to be drawn from those facts, has the Secretary of State satisfied the requirement of anxious scrutiny? If the court cannot be satisfied that the answer to both of those questions is in the affirmative it will have to grant an application for review of the Secretary of State's decision. (per Buxton LJ in *WM (DRC) v Secretary of State for the Home Department* [2006] EWCA Civ 1495)

See also **Chapter 12**.

9.15 Asylum checklist

Consider the following questions when advising an asylum claimant. If a claim is refused, check any appeal rights (see **9.13**).

(a) Can the applicant return to a part of the country in which he would not be subject to the harm feared (see **9.4.3.1**)?

(b) Does the safe third country exception apply (see **9.4.3.2**)?

(c) Is the harm feared a form of persecution (see **9.4.1.3**)?

(d) What ECHR Articles are engaged (see **9.9**)?

(e) Is that fear of persecution well founded? Taking into account the applicant's statements and behaviour, does the applicant have a subjective fear of persecution (see **9.4.1**)?

(f) What evidence is available or should be obtained?

(g) Are any adverse inferences to be drawn (see **9.6.2**)?

(h) Is that fear of persecution well founded? Objectively, are there reasonable grounds for believing that the harm feared might in fact occur in the applicant's country of origin (see **9.4.1**)?

(i) Check any relevant Country of Origin Information Reports, Country of Origin Bulletins and Country of Origin Key Documents (see **9.7**).

(j) If the harm feared is serious enough to constitute persecution, would it be inflicted for one or more of the reasons set out in the Refugee Convention, ie race, religion, nationality, membership of a particular social group or political opinion (see **9.4.2**)?

(k) Does the applicant satisfy all the criteria of the 1951 Convention?

(l) Should the applicant be excluded from international protection by operation of the exclusion clauses of the Convention (see **9.5**)?

(m) If an applicant fails to qualify for asylum, should he be granted humanitarian protection or discretionary leave (see **9.10**)?

Chapter 10
Deportation and Administrative Removal

10.1 Deportation

10.1.1 General

Under s 5 of the IA 1971, the Secretary of State has a discretionary power to make a deportation order. This requires a person to leave the UK and prohibits him from lawfully re-entering while the order is in force. It also invalidates any existing leave to enter or remain.

British citizens and others with the right of abode in the UK (see **2.2** and **2.3**) cannot be deported. Some Commonwealth and Irish citizens are exempt from deportation (see **10.1.5**). Anyone else, including a person who is settled in the UK (see **3.8** and the example of *Samaroo and Sezek v Secretary of State for the Home Department* [2001] UKHRR 1150), is liable to deportation.

10.1.2 Grounds for deportation and its effects

10.1.2.1 Grounds

The Secretary of State may order that a person is to be deported but only on the alternative grounds specified in s 3(5)(b) and (6) of the IA 1971. These are as follows:

(a) that the Secretary of State considers his deportation to be 'conducive to the public good' (see **10.1.2.2**);

(b) a person is a member of the family of a deportee (see **10.1.2.4** and **10.1.4**);

(c) a court has recommended deportation, in the case of a person aged 17 or over, convicted of an offence punishable with imprisonment (see **10.1.2.3**).

As to the steps the Secretary of State should take to establish any ground, see *DA (Colombia) v Secretary of State for the Home Department* [2009] EWCA Civ 682.

10.1.2.2 Conducive to the public good

The Secretary of State has traditionally determined that deportation is beneficial for the public where a person has been convicted of either one serious crime or a series of lesser offences. The former category has been largely superseded by the fact that foreign nationals sentenced to a period of imprisonment of at least 12 months are invariably 'automatically' deported (see **10.1.2.3**). But an offender who repeatedly commits minor offences or a person who commits a single offence involving, for example, the use of false identity documents for which he receives a custodial sentence of less than 12 months, may be deported at the Secretary of State's discretion.

10.1.2.3 Automatic deportation of foreign criminals

By s 32 of the UK Borders Act 2007, the Secretary of State must, subject to limited exceptions in s 33, make a deportation order in respect of a foreign adult criminal. This is a person who is not a British citizen (see **2.2**) or a Commonwealth citizen with the right of abode (see **2.3**) or exempt (see **10.1.5**) and who has been convicted in the UK of an offence where he was sentenced to a period of imprisonment of at least 12 months. Such a person has no right of appeal against an order automatically to deport him. However, he may appeal against the decision that he falls within this provision (see **11.2**).

The main exception to automatic deportation can be found in s 33(2), namely that removal of the foreign criminal in pursuance of the deportation order would breach either his ECHR rights and/or the UK's obligations under the Refugee Convention. Moreover, a person may appeal on the ground that his removal from the UK would breach his ECHR rights and/or the UK's obligations under the Refugee Convention (see, for example, *RU (Bangladesh) v Secretary of State for the Home Department* [2011] EWCA Civ 651, *AP (Trinidad & Tobago) v Secretary of State for the Home Department* [2011] EWCA Civ 551, **Chapter 9** and **11.3**).

A person liable to automatic deportation might seek to oppose it by claiming asylum in the UK. However, even if the asylum claim is accepted, the person may still be removed if he had been sentenced to a term of imprisonment of at least two years (see **9.5.2**).

What if the foreign criminal is an EEA citizen? He is an exception to the rule on automatic deportation if removal would breach rights he is exercising under the European Union Treaties. He may be removed only on grounds of public policy, public security or public health in accordance with reg 19(3)(b) of the I(EEA) Regs 2006 (see **4.4.14**).

What is the effect of s 32 on a criminal court's power to recommend deportation? The Court of Appeal in *R v Kluxen* [2010] EWCA Crim 1081 held that:

(a) in cases to which the 2007 Act applies, it is no longer necessary or appropriate to recommend the deportation of the offender concerned; and

(b) in cases to which the 2007 Act does not apply (eg the foreign criminal does not receive any single custodial sentence of 12 months or more, or receives a non-custodial sentence), it will rarely be appropriate to recommend the deportation of the offender concerned. Those cases remain within the discretion of the Secretary of State (see **10.1.2.2**).

10.1.2.4 Who are the family members of a deportee?

By s 5(4) of the IA 1971, the family members liable to be deported with the deportee are his spouse or civil partner and his or her children under 18. For these purposes an adopted child, whether legally adopted or not, may be treated as the child of the adopter and, if legally adopted, must be regarded as the child only of the adopter. Also an illegitimate child (unless adopted) is regarded as the child of the mother.

See further **10.1.4**.

10.1.2.5 Effect

What are the effects of a deportation order? A person may not legally enter the UK whilst an order is in force (see **10.1.8** as to revoking an order). By para 320(2) of the Immigration Rules, entry clearance and leave to enter will be refused to such a person.

10.1.3 Presumption of deportation

Where a person is not liable to automatic deportation, whether or not he is deported is a matter for the Secretary of State's discretion (see **10.1.2.2**). However, the Immigration Rules, para 364 makes it clear that where a person is liable to deportation then the presumption is that the public interest requires it. Paragraph 364 goes on to state that the Secretary of State must consider all relevant factors when considering whether the presumption is outweighed in any particular case. However, it will only be in exceptional circumstances that the public interest in deportation will be outweighed in a case where it would not be contrary to the ECHR or Refugee Convention to deport a person.

10.1.4 Deportation of family members

This can be a controversial ground for deportation, as someone who is deported as the family member of the deportee may have committed no breach of immigration law or indeed any other laws. Remember, however, that it cannot be used to deport anyone who has the right of abode in the UK (see **2.2** and **2.3**) or is exempt (see **10.1.5**).

Where a spouse or civil partner is being deported, his spouse or civil partner and the children under 18 of either of them can also be deported as family members. However, no family deportation can be made once eight weeks have elapsed since the other family member was deported (see IA 1971, s 5).

The UKBA guidance is that the Secretary of State will not normally decide to deport the spouse or civil partner of a deportee where:

(a) he or she has qualified for settlement in his or her own right; or
(b) he or she has been living apart from the deportee.

The Secretary of State will not normally decide to deport the child of a deportee where:

(a) he and his parent are living apart from the deportee; or
(b) he has spent some time in the UK and is nearing the age of 18;
(c) he has left home and established himself on an independent basis; or
(d) he married or formed a civil partnership before deportation came into prospect.

In considering whether to require a spouse, civil partner or child to leave with the deportee, the Secretary of State will take account of all relevant factors, including:

(a) the ability of the spouse or civil partner to maintain him- or herself and any children in the UK, or to be maintained by relatives or friends without recourse to public funds, not merely for a short period but for the foreseeable future; and
(b) in the case of a child of school age, the effect of removal on his education; and
(c) the practicality of any plans for a child's care and maintenance in this country if one or both of his parents were deported; and
(d) any representations made on behalf of the spouse, civil partner or child.

As to human rights and possible EU law arguments, see **10.5** and **10.6**.

Note that Government policies on marriage and co-habitation known as DP 3/96 and DP 2/93 were withdrawn in April 2008.

10.1.5 Exemption from deportation

The main exemptions from deportation are dealt with in s 7(1)(b) and (c) of the IA 1971. They apply only to Commonwealth or Irish citizens who had that citizenship at 1 January 1973 and were then ordinarily resident in the UK. Such persons are exempt from deportation on any ground if they have been ordinarily resident in the UK and Islands for five years before the date of the Secretary of State's decision to deport.

The term 'ordinary residence' is considered in **3.8.2**. However, s 7(2) provides that, for the purpose of this exemption, if a person has at any time acquired ordinary residence in the UK, he does not lose it by remaining in breach of immigration laws. This means that a person who has overstayed, or broken conditions of entry, may nevertheless qualify for exemption.

10.1.6 Procedure

The general procedure is described in paras 381, 382 and 384 of the Immigration Rules. Initially, the Home Office takes a decision to deport. Notice of this is then normally given to the deportee. He may then exercise his rights of appeal. If he fails to appeal, or loses his appeal, the Secretary of State may then sign the deportation order. Under Sch 3 to the IA 1971, the deportee may then be removed to the country of which he is a national, or to another country which is likely to receive him. He may also be detained following the decision to deport.

Rights of appeal against deportation are dealt with in **Chapter 11**.

10.1.7 Voluntary departure

What if a person is subject to enforcement action but a deportation order has not yet been signed? As an order cannot be made against a person who is not in the UK, it is open to the person to leave the UK voluntarily. Enforcement action will cease if it is known that a person has embarked. The advantage is that the person is not subsequently debarred from re-entering the UK (although he must, of course, satisfy the requirements of the Immigration Rules for which he is seeking entry in the normal way).

10.1.8 Revoking a deportation order

By para 390 of the Immigration Rules, an application can be made for revocation of a deportation order, and this will be considered in the light of all the circumstances, including the following:

(a) the grounds on which the order was made;

(b) any representations made in support of revocation;

(c) the interests of the community, including the maintenance of an effective immigration control; and

(d) the interests of the applicant, including any compassionate circumstances.

Note that by para 391, if an applicant was deported following conviction for a criminal offence then revocation will not occur until:

(a) in the case of a conviction which is capable of being spent under the Rehabilitation of Offenders Act 1974 (see **Appendix 8**), the conviction is spent within the meaning of that Act; but if the conviction is spent in less than 10 years then at least 10 years must have elapsed since the making of the deportation order; or

(b) in the case of a conviction not capable of being spent under that Act, at any time, unless refusal to revoke the deportation order would be contrary to the ECHR or the Geneva Convention.

In other cases, revocation of the order will not normally be authorised unless the situation has materially altered, either by a change of circumstances since the order was made, or by fresh information coming to light which was not before the appellate authorities or the Secretary of State. The passage of time since the person was deported may also in itself amount to a change of circumstances justifying revocation of the order.

Revocation of a deportation order does not entitle the person concerned to re-enter the UK. It only renders him eligible to apply for admission under the Immigration Rules.

10.2 Administrative removal

10.2.1 Grounds for removal

Removal from the UK is often described as 'administrative removal', as that is what it is in reality, namely an administrative step. Under s 10 of the IAA 1999, the following people may be administratively removed from the UK:

(a) anyone who has failed to observe the conditions attached to his leave;

(b) overstayers;

(c) anyone who has obtained leave to remain by deception, or who sought to obtain such leave by deception;

(d) the family members of such people.

The most common grounds for administrative removal are that a person has remained beyond the period specified in his limited leave, or has broken a condition attached to it. For example, a person's leave to enter or remain will often either prohibit or restrict his freedom to take employment, and the person is liable to administrative removal procedures if he is found to be working without authority. The UKBA guidance is that there must be firm and recent (within six months) evidence of working in breach. The immigration officer will look for at least an admission by the offender under caution of working in breach; or a statement by the employer; or pay slips or the offender's details on the payroll; or visual observation, by the immigration officer, of the applicant working.

As explained in **3.6.2**, a person who wishes to extend his stay should apply for a variation before his leave expires. He commits a criminal offence under s 24(1)(b) of the IA 1971 if he knowingly overstays or fails to observe a condition of the leave. Note that it is not usual practice for a prosecution to occur. Removal does not require a knowing breach and so normally the person is removed and not prosecuted.

In addition, illegal entrants (see **10.2.2**) may be removed from the UK in the same way.

10.2.2 Definition of illegal entrant

An illegal entrant is a person who unlawfully enters or seeks to enter in breach of a deportation order or of the immigration laws. This includes a person who has so entered.

Typically a person might enter the UK without leave clandestinely, eg concealed in a vehicle such as a lorry. Or he might present a forged or false British or EEA passport to an immigration officer.

A person who, contrary to the IA 1971, knowingly enters the UK in breach of a deportation order or without leave commits a criminal offence under s 24(1)(a). However, it is possible to be an illegal entrant without having committed any criminal offence, for instance, where a person obtains leave by producing false documents, without knowing them to be false (*R v Immigration Officer, ex p Chan* [1992] 1 WLR 541).

A person will be an illegal entrant if he obtains leave to enter by deception, although mere non-disclosure of material facts will not amount to deception, as the entrant has no positive duty to reveal facts if a relevant question is not asked. It is for the Home Office to prove the deception (*R v Secretary of State for the Home Department, ex p Khawaja* [1984] AC 74).

10.2.3 Relevant factors

Before deciding to remove an individual, para 395C of the Immigration Rules requires the Secretary of State to have regard to the following factors:

(a) *Age*

Current UKBA policy is that there is no upper age limit to removal. Previous policy was that, as a general rule, the Home Office did not enforce the departure of those aged 65 or over. But currently age is just one of several factors taken into account. The onus is on the applicant to show that there are extenuating circumstances, such as particularly poor health or close dependency on family members in the UK, coupled with a lack of family and care facilities in the country of origin. See further at (g) below.

(b) *Length of residence in the United Kingdom*

If a person does not meet the long residence rules of the Immigration Rules (see **3.8.7**), the UKBA guidance is that in general the longer a person has lived in the UK, the stronger his ties with the UK will be.

(c) *Strength of connections with the United Kingdom*

Connections such as business or lawful employment will be considered. If a person has spent his formative years (ie from birth to 10 years of age) in the UK then consideration must be given as to whether he has adapted to life in the UK and/or whether he can adapt to life outside the UK. Family ties, including marriage or civil partnership and relationships akin to marriage or a civil partnership, are also relevant. If the Home Office accepts that such a relationship is genuine and subsisting, and with a person lawfully resident in the UK, then Article 8 ECHR (see **10.5.5**) will be a key consideration. In addition, the Home Office is required to take into account the impact of removal of a person on his spouse, civil partner and children living with or in regular contact with him. Indeed, the best interests of any children are a primary consideration (see **10.5.5**).

(d) *Personal history*

This includes the person's character, conduct and employment record. In considering character and conduct, the UKBA takes into account any known criminal activity, especially any evidence of absconding, a history of deception or reasonable suspicion that deception has been used to avoid enforcement action. It is relevant to consider whether a person has maintained contact with the Home Office as required and has been actively pressing for resolution of their immigration status. Likewise, a person's lawful employment history and how he has supported himself and/or his family during his stay in the UK will also form part of the consideration. Equally, working when not entitled to do so and by having obtained a national insurance number by deception will count against the person: see *R (Daley-Murdock) v Secretary of State for the Home Department* [2010] EWHC 1488. Conversely, is a person's good character relevant, eg beneficial activities in the community in the UK? Yes, as part of an argument under Article 8 ECHR (see **10.5.5**).

(e) *Domestic circumstances*

The UKBA guidance is that this includes aspects such as the person's housing (eg tenancy as well as ownership), whether he or his children are in education, or whether anyone in the UK relies on the person for physical, financial or emotional support. All of these may increase the strength of ties between a person and the UK, but are weighed against any adverse evidence.

(f) *Previous criminal record and the nature of any offence of which the person has been convicted*

A previous unspent conviction (see **Appendix 8**) will be considered irrespective of the section of the Act under which enforcement action is being pursued. However, the seriousness of the offence is balanced against any mitigating factors.

(g) *Compassionate circumstances*

Any compelling or compassionate circumstances will be considered, with the gravity of the circumstances being given due weight. Examples of compassionate circumstances given by the UKBA include: ill health, medical treatment, the inability of the person to look after himself and reliance upon persons resident in the UK. In *SG (Zimbabwe) v Secretary of State for the Home Department* [2011] EWCA Civ 71 the Court indicated that compassionate circumstances falling short of ECHR, Article 3 should be taken into account, if, in the context of all the other relevant factors, it would be unduly harsh for removal to occur. As to ill health and ECHR arguments, see **9.9.3** and **10.5.2**.

(h) *Any representations received on the person's behalf*
This is self-explanatory.

10.2.4 Removal of family members

A spouse, civil partner or child of a person liable to administrative removal, who has no right of abode of his or her own in the UK and who is not settled, may also be removed. This is just as controversial as deporting the same family members of a deportee (see **10.1.4**). But there is a different starting point. Remember, deportation may be automatic (see **10.1.2.3**) or otherwise there is a presumption of deportation (see **10.1.3**). Administrative removal is never automatic nor is there any presumption of removal. So, the factors relevant to whether or not a person will be removed (see **10.2.3**) apply equally and additionally to his family members. Moreover, the same considerations apply as to family members of a deportee (see **10.1.4**).

As UKBA guidance recognises, the presence in the UK of dependent children aged under 18 must be taken into account when deciding whether removal of a parent is the appropriate action to take. In all cases involving the children of a family, the following must be established:

(a) the children's ages;

(b) ties with the natural parent; how often the children see their natural parent; whether any maintenance is paid towards the children's upkeep;

(c) whether the children could easily adapt to a life abroad; whether such a move would cause hardship or put their health at risk;

(d) whether the children have a right of abode in the UK and the nationality of the children.

The above factors are balanced against the parents' immigration history and any criminal record.

As to human rights and possible EU law arguments, see **10.5** and **10.6** respectively.

Note that Government policies on marriage, cohabitation and children under 7, known as DP 3/96, DP 2/93 and DP5/96, have all been withdrawn.

10.2.5 Procedure

If the Home Office decides not to remove the person, he is normally granted indefinite to leave to remain.

If, after consideration of all the relevant facts, the UKBA decides that administrative removal is the correct course of action, a notice of liability to administrative removal is served. The immigration officer normally serves the notice in person. It still remains open to the person who is subject to enforcement action to leave the UK voluntarily. Otherwise the immigration officer will set removal directions. The costs of complying with removal directions (so far as reasonably incurred) are met by the Secretary of State. Directions for removal of a person given under s 10 of the 1999 Act invalidate any leave to enter or remain in the UK.

There is no right of appeal in the UK against a decision that a person is to be removed from the UK by way of directions under s 10, save on asylum or human rights grounds (see **11.3**).

10.2.6 Effect of administrative removal

Unlike someone who has been deported, a person who is subject to administrative removal does not need to have the decision to remove him rescinded before he may return to the UK (provided that he otherwise qualifies for admission under the Immigration Rules).

10.3 Detention of a person being deported or removed

The power to detain a person who is subject to deportation action is set out in para 2 of Sch 3 to the IA 1971 and s 36 of the UK Borders Act 2007. This includes those whose deportation has been recommended by a court pending the making of a deportation order, those who have been served with a notice of intention to deport pending the making of a deportation order, those who are being considered for automatic deportation or pending the making of a deportation order as required by the automatic deportation provisions, and those who are the subject of a deportation order pending removal.

The power to detain an illegal entrant or a person liable to administrative removal (or someone suspected to be such a person) is found in para 16(2) of Sch 2 to the IA 1971.

Details are beyond the scope of this book.

10.4 Government policy: deportation and administrative removal

It is important to remember that deportation may be automatic (see **10.1.2.3**) or otherwise there is a presumption of deportation (see **10.1.3**). But administrative removal is never automatic nor is there a presumption of administrative removal. Why the difference? It is because different Government policies are pursued by the use of deportation and administrative removal as methods to expel a person from the UK.

10.4.1 Deportation

In *OH (Serbia)* [2009] INLR 109 (approved by the Court of Appeal in *RU (Bangladesh) v Secretary of State for the Home Department* [2011] EWCA Civ 651) the court identified three important features of the public interest in deportation, namely:

(a) the risk of re-offending by the person concerned;

(b) the need to deter foreign nationals from committing serious crimes by leading them to understand that, whatever the other circumstances, one consequence for them may well be their deportation; and

(c) the role of deportation as an expression of society's revulsion at serious crimes and in building public confidence in the criminal justice system's treatment of foreign citizens who have committed serious crimes.

As to (a), the risk of re-offending is normally addressed in the report prepared for sentencing and commented on by the trial judge when giving reasons for the sentence imposed.

10.4.2 Administrative removal

In *UE (Nigeria) v Secretary of State for the Home Department* [2010] EWCA Civ 975 the Court identified that the main element of public interest in administrative removal is the need for the Government to maintain a firm policy of immigration control.

10.4.3 Practical consequences of difference

As we have just seen, deportation and administrative removal involve different Government policies. In deportation cases it is the prevention of crime, deterrence and public confidence (see **10.4.1**). In administrative removal cases it is the maintenance of effective immigration control (see **10.4.2**). The difference in aims is important because that explains why the factors in favour of expulsion are capable of carrying greater weight in a deportation case than in a case of administrative removal. This led Richards LJ in *JO (Uganda) v Secretary of State for the Home Department* [2010] EWCA Civ 10 to observe at [29] that:

> The maintenance of effective immigration control is an important matter, but the protection of society against serious crime is even more important and can properly be given correspondingly greater weight in the balancing exercise. Thus I think it perfectly possible in principle for a given set of considerations of family life and/or private life to be sufficiently weighty to render expulsion disproportionate in an ordinary removal case, yet insufficient to render expulsion disproportionate in a deportation case because of the additional weight to be given to the criminal offending on which the deportation decision was based.

10.5 Human rights: deportation and administrative removal

Human rights challenges to deportation do not call for a materially different approach from that required in administrative removal cases. The issues arise under the same legal framework and involve the same essential questions. So, for example, with a qualified right such as to a private or family life under Article 8 ECHR, the key question is whether, if expulsion would interfere with a right protected by Article 8(1), such interference is proportionate in accordance with Article 8(2) to the legitimate aim (ie Government policy) pursued. The outcome might be different but only because of the difference in Government policy objectives between deportation and administrative removal (see **10.4.3**).

10.5.1 Articles 2 and 3 ECHR

A person will not be removed from the UK to a country where there are substantial reasons for believing that he faces a real risk of:

(a) being unlawfully killed either by the State, or through the State being unable or unwilling to protect him contrary to Article 2 ECHR; or

(b) suffering serious harm or other treatment contrary to Article 3 ECHR. This includes torture, as well as treatment or punishment that is degrading because it arouses in the victim feelings of fear, anguish or inferiority capable of humiliating and debasing him, and possibly breaking his physical and moral resistance. Severe discrimination based on race, sex or other grounds is also capable of constituting degrading treatment.

UKBA guidance is that Article 3 may also be engaged where the person has an illness that has reached such a critical stage (ie he is dying) that it would be inhuman treatment to deprive him of the care he is currently receiving and send him home to an early death, unless there is care available there to enable him to meet that fate with dignity.

In *Bensaid v United Kingdom* [2001] ECHR 82 the applicant suffered from long-term schizophrenia. He claimed that his condition would seriously deteriorate if he were returned to his home country because of difficulties in obtaining suitable medication there. The Court stated at para 37:

> Deterioration in his already existing mental illness could involve relapse into hallucinations and psychotic delusions involving self-harm and harm to others, as well as restrictions in social functioning (such as withdrawal and lack of motivation). The Court considers that the suffering associated with such a relapse could, in principle, fall within the scope of Article 3.

However, it should be noted that the Court in *Bensaid* went on to find that Article 3 would not be violated in the case as there were no exceptional circumstances.

See further **9.9.2** and **9.9.3**.

10.5.2 Articles 5 and 6 ECHR

In resisting removal on the ground that his Article 5 ECHR right will be threatened in the country to which he is sent, a person must establish that there are substantial grounds for believing that, if removed, he will face a real risk of a flagrant breach of that Article. In this context, a flagrant breach is a breach the consequences of which are so severe that they override the right of a State to expel an alien from its territory. In describing such a breach of Article 5 in *R (Ullah) v Special Adjudicator* [2004] UKHL 26, Lord Steyn (at [43]) gave by way of example the case of intended expulsion to a country in which the rule of law is flagrantly flouted, *habeas corpus* is unavailable and there is a real risk that the individual may face arbitrary detention for many years.

Before the removal of a person will be capable of violating Article 6, there must be substantial grounds for believing that there is a real risk:

(a) that there will be a fundamental breach of the principles of a fair trial guaranteed by Article 6 ('What is required is that the deficiency or deficiencies in the trial process should be such as fundamentally to destroy the fairness of the prospective trial', per Lord Phillips in *RB (Algeria) v Secretary of State for the Home Department* [2009] UKHL 10 at [136]); and

(b) that this failure will lead to a miscarriage of justice that itself constitutes a flagrant violation of the victim's fundamental rights. This was the situation in *RB (Algeria)* where the appellant had already been tried in his absence and sentenced to life imprisonment. There were substantial grounds for believing that he would not be able to obtain a retrial and would be imprisoned to serve the sentence imposed in his absence.

Article 6 ECHR might also be engaged where the person has an outstanding civil claim in the UK for private law damages, eg a personal injury claim, or is a prospective party to such a civil claim which he is actively pursuing. The UKBA guidance is that it may be relevant if the person:

(a) does not have access to communication facilities in the country of return;
(b) needs to undertake a medical examination;
(c) will not have access to funding to pursue his civil action;
(d) will not be able to have access to interpreters;
(e) wants to represent himself in court;
(f) is required to give evidence in court; and
(g) needs direct personal contact in order to instruct his UK legal representatives.

Other factors may include the complexity of the case; access to telephone and conferencing facilities in the country to which the individual is to be returned; the reliability of postal, e-mail and fax facilities in that country; and whether or not liability has been admitted.

10.5.3 Article 8 ECHR

10.5.3.1 Private and family life in the UK

For the purposes of Article 8 ECHR what is a person's private life in the UK? The answer is found by establishing the strength of his ties to the UK which he has established here in terms of friends, education, work and leisure activities. Can a person's contribution to society whilst in the UK, such as voluntary work for a charity, be taken into account as a factor in the balancing exercise necessary to decide whether his removal from the UK will breach this right? The Court of Appeal answered this question in the affirmative in *UE (Uganda) v Secretary of State for the Home Department* [2010] EWCA Civ 975. The Court held that a person's contributions to the community in which he lived would reduce the need to maintain effective immigration control for administrative removal purposes, but it is unlikely to make much difference in a deportation case. However, the greater the person's contribution, the more weight the factor might be given, especially if the person is an essential worker in a company engaged in a successful export business, or a social worker upon whom a local community depend, or a scientific research worker engaged on research of public importance.

Article 8 ECHR may also be engaged where the person claims that to remove him from the UK will separate him from his family here and would therefore constitute a breach of his right to respect for family life in the UK. Who might form part of a family? Partners in a lawful and genuine marriage or civil partnership, or a relationship akin to such, will normally constitute family life. The UKBA guidance is that a relationship between unmarried and same-sex partners of sufficient substance or stability will qualify even if the couple do not meet the usual two years' cohabitation requirement in the Immigration Rules, para 295A (see **8.8**). In any event such relationships would fall under a person's private life. A new or casual relationship will not suffice.

In the case of natural parents and their minor children, there is a general presumption of family life. Further, the relationship between an adoptive parent and an adopted person is in principle the same. The UKBA accepts that family life may exist between a child and his natural parent even if at the time of birth the relationship between the two parents has ended and even if the child does not live with his parent. However, the fact that a parent has only infrequent contact with his child may be relevant to the question of whether removal would disproportionately interfere with their family life.

Relationships of grandparents and grandchildren, uncles and aunts, nephews and nieces, may fall within the scope of family life, depending upon the strength of the emotional ties. It is rare, however, for relationships between adult siblings or adult children and their parents to count (*Odawey v Entry Clearance Officer* [2011] EWCA Civ 840) unless there are special elements of dependency beyond normal emotional ties (for example, the support of an elder brother for his very sick younger brother in *R (Ahmadi) v Secretary of State for the Home Department* [2005] EWCA Civ 1721).

10.5.3.2 Five questions need to be answered

Question 1

Does the person have a private and/or family life in the UK?

See **10.5.3.1** above.

Question 2

If a private and/or family life exists, will removal interfere with that?

As to family life, the answer depends to some extent on whose family life is being considered – only that of the person being removed, or that of all members of his family unit? The House of Lords, in *Beoku-Betts v Secretary of State for the Home Department* [2008] UKHL 39, held that the effect of removal on all members of the person's family unit should be taken into account. Together these members enjoy a single family life, and whether or not the removal would interfere with it has to be looked at by reference to the family unit as a whole and the impact of removal upon each member.

In *Huang v Secretary of State for the Home Department* [2007] UKHL 11, the House of Lords held that the removal of the person must prejudice his family life in a manner sufficiently serious to amount to a breach of Article 8 ECHR. However, as Sedley LJ indicated in *AG (Eritrea) v Secretary of State for the Home Department* [2007] EWCA Civ 801 at [28], the threshold of engagement is not a specifically high one. So, for example, in *A (Afghanistan) v Secretary of State for the Home Department* [2009] EWCA Civ 825, the Court held that the interference with family life which would result from not allowing a husband and his heavily pregnant wife in a genuine and subsisting marriage to cohabit, engaged the operation of Article 8.

Question 3

If there is interference with a private and/or family life, is it in accordance with the law?

The answer will be yes, provided the decision is in accordance with the relevant statutory provisions and the published policies of the UKBA.

Question 4

Is the interference in pursuit of one or more of the permissible aims set out under Article 8(2)? This will include the maintenance of effective immigration controls by administrative removal and public safety, the prevention of crime and disorder, and national security by deportation.

The answer will be yes, provided the decision is in accordance with the stated Government policy (see **10.4**).

Question 5

Is the interference proportionate to the permissible aim or aims?

This is normally the key question and often a difficult one to answer as the assessment of proportionality is a balancing exercise between the individual's private interests and the Government's permissible aims (see **10.4**).

What weight should be given to the best interests of children who are affected by the decision to remove one or both of their parents from the UK? The Supreme Court addressed this question in *H (Tanzania) v Secretary of State for the Home Department* [2011] UKSC 4. The Court held that the best interests of the child must be a primary consideration. A decision-maker must identify what the best interests of the child requires and then assess whether the strength of any other consideration, or the cumulative effect of other considerations, outweighs the consideration of the best interests of the child. That involves asking whether it is reasonable to expect the child to live in another country. Relevant to this will be the level of the child's integration in the UK and the length of absence from the other country; where and with whom the child is to live and the arrangements for looking after the child in the other country; and the strength of the child's relationships with parents or other family members which will be severed if the child has to move away.

In *E-A (Article 8 – best interests of child) Nigeria* [2011] UKUT 00315, the Upper Tribunal (IAC) held that:

> (i) The correct starting point in considering the welfare and best interests of a young child would be that it is in the best interests of a child to live with and be brought up by his or her parents, subject to any very strong contra-indication. Where it is in the best interests of a child to live with and be brought up by his or her parents, then the child's removal with his parents does not involve any separation of family life.
>
> (ii) Absent other factors, the reason why a period of substantial residence as a child may become a weighty consideration in the balance of competing considerations is that in the course of such time roots are put down, personal identities are developed, friendships are formed and links are made with the community outside the family unit. The degree to which these elements of private life are forged and therefore the weight to be given to the passage of time will depend upon the facts in each case.
>
> (iii) During a child's very early years, he or she will be primarily focused on self and the caring parents or guardian. Long residence once the child is likely to have formed ties outside the family is likely to have greater impact on his or her well being.

In what circumstances is it proportionate to remove a parent where the effect will be that a child who is a British citizen will also have to leave? The Supreme Court also addressed this question in *H (Tanzania) v Secretary of State for the Home Department* (see above). The Court stated that whilst nationality is not a 'trump card', it is of particular importance in assessing the best interests of any child. The intrinsic importance of British citizenship should not be played down. As a British citizen, a child has rights which he will not be able to exercise if he moves to another country. He will lose the advantages of growing up and being educated in his own country, his own culture and his own language.

The test is not whether it is 'impossible or exceptionally difficult' for a family member to go with the removed person but rather whether the family member 'could not reasonably be expected' to follow the removed person: see *KB (Trinidad and Tobago) v Secretary of State for the Home Department* [2010] EWCA Civ 11.

The UKBA guidance is that in considering the proportionality of removal under Article 8, it may be appropriate to give particular weight to the following compassionate circumstances:

(a) age – where a person is under 18, unaccompanied (or has family here with indefinite leave), and no adequate reception and accommodation arrangements exist in the country of origin;

(b) length of residence in the UK – where a person has been residing in the UK for 25 years or more (excluding time spent in custody);

(c) strength of connections to the UK – where a person has been in the UK for the majority of his formative years (birth to 10 years of age) and has been resident here since;

(d) lack of links to country of origin – where a person has no family in his country of origin, does not speak the language and has not lived in that country for a significant period.

As to (c), where a person has lawfully spent all or the major part of his childhood and youth in the UK, very serious reasons are required to justify deportation or administrative removal. This is all the more so in a deportation case where the person committed the offences underlying the deportation decision as a juvenile (*MJ (Angola) v Secretary of State for the Home Department* [2010] EWCA Civ 557 and *Maslov v Austria* [2009] INLR 47, ECtHR (Grand Chamber)).

As to deportation, the UKBA guidance is that the more serious the nature of the offence, the sentence given, or the previous criminal history of the person concerned, the less likely it is that other relevant factors will outweigh automatic deportation or otherwise the presumption of deportation. As Richards LJ indicated in *JO (Uganda) v Secretary of State for the Home Department* [2010] EWCA Civ 10 at para 27:

> ... even if the difficulties do make it unreasonable to expect family members to join the applicant in the country to which he is to be deported, that will not necessarily be a decisive feature in the overall assessment of proportionality. It is plainly an important consideration but it may not be determinative, since it is possible in a case of sufficiently serious offending that the factors in favour of deportation will be strong enough to render deportation proportionate even if does have the effect of severing established family relationships.

10.5.3.3 Removal to require entry clearance

In *Chikwamba v Secretary of State for the Home Department* [2008] UKHL 40, the House of Lords had to answer this question: when determining an appeal under ss 82 and 84 of the NIAA 2002 (see **Chapter 11**) against the Secretary of State's refusal of leave to remain on the ground that to remove the appellant would interfere disproportionately with his Article 8 right to respect for his family life, when, if ever, is it appropriate to dismiss the appeal on the basis that the appellant should be required to leave the country and seek leave to enter from an entry clearance officer abroad? The answer was 'comparatively rarely, certainly in family cases involving children, should an Article 8 appeal be dismissed on the basis that it would be proportionate and more appropriate for the appellant to apply for leave from abroad' (per Lord Brown of Eaton-under-Heywood, at [44]). For an example of an exceptional case justifying removal for an application to be made, see *R (Kotecha) v Secretary of State for the Home Department* [2011] EWHC 2070.

10.6 Interference with EU Treaty rights by deportation or administrative removal

10.6.1 Spouse or civil partner

What if a British citizen is exercising EU Treaty rights but his non-EEA family member is threatened with deportation or removal from the UK? In *Carpenter v Secretary of State for the Home Department* [2003] 2 WLR 267, Mrs C was a national of The Philippines. She was given leave to enter the UK as a visitor in September 1994 for six months. She overstayed that leave and failed to apply for any extension of her stay. In May 1996 she married Mr C, a British citizen. Mr C ran a business selling advertising space in medical and scientific journals, and offering various administrative and publishing services to the editors of those journals. A significant proportion of the business was conducted with advertisers established in other Member States of the EU. Mr C travelled to other Member States for the purpose of his business.

In July 1996 Mrs C applied to the Secretary of State for leave to remain in the UK as the spouse of a British citizen. Her application was refused, and the Secretary of State also decided to make an order removing her to The Philippines. Mrs C argued that since her husband's business required him to travel around in other Member States, providing and receiving services, he could do so more easily as she was looking after his children from his first marriage. Therefore, her removal would restrict her husband's right to provide and receive services. It was accepted that Mrs C's marriage was genuine and that she played an important part in the upbringing of her stepchildren. It was also accepted that her husband was a provider of services for the purposes of EU law.

Mrs C accepted that she had no right of her own to reside in any Member State but claimed that her rights derived from those enjoyed by Mr C to provide services and to travel within the EU. Her removal would require Mr C either to go to live with her in The Philippines or separate the members of the family unit if he remained in the UK. The ECJ agreed that the separation of Mr and Mrs C would be detrimental to their family life and, therefore, to the conditions under which Mr C exercised his fundamental EU Treaty rights. Those rights could not be fully effective if Mr C were to be deterred from exercising them by obstacles raised by the UK Government to the residence of his spouse.

The ECJ then went on to link the interference with Mr C's EU rights with the interference with his Article 8 ECHR rights. The decision to remove Mrs C did not strike a fair balance between the competing interests, on the one hand, of Mr C to respect for his family life and, on the other hand, the UK Government's removal policy. Although Mrs C had infringed UK immigration laws, her conduct since her arrival in the UK had not been the subject of any other complaint. The Court held that to remove Mrs C constituted an infringement which was not proportionate to the objective pursued of maintaining immigration control.

10.6.2 Children

What if a child is a British citizen and the parent being removed or deported is not an EEA national? Can the child's EEA rights assist the parent if the child will otherwise be leaving the UK with that parent? In *Zambrano v Office national de l'emploi (ONEm)* (Case C-34/09) [2011] 2 CMLR 46 the applicant and his wife were both Columbian nationals who had sought and been refused refugee status in Belgium. However, the couple were allowed to stay in Belgium temporarily and had two children who acquired Belgian nationality under national law.

The Court held that Article 20 TFEU (see **4.3**) confers the status of citizen of the European Union on every person holding the nationality of a Member State. Since the children of the applicant possessed Belgian nationality under Belgian law they undeniably enjoyed that status. Further, Article 20 TFEU precludes national measures which have the effect of depriving citizens of the European Union of the genuine enjoyment of the substance of the rights conferred by virtue of their status as citizens of the European Union. A refusal to grant a right of residence to a third country national with dependent minor children in the Member State where those children were nationals and resided had such an effect. Such a refusal would lead to a situation where those children, citizens of the European Union, would have to leave the territory of the European Union in order to accompany their parents. In these circumstances, the children as citizens of the European Union would, as a result, be unable to exercise the substance of the rights conferred on them by virtue of their status as citizens of the European Union.

Chapter 11
Immigration Appeals

11.1 Appeals: the general rule

The NIAA 2002 sets out a revised system of appeals, including a system for a 'one stop' comprehensive appeal following refusal of leave to enter or remain. It replaces all rights of appeal established in earlier legislation. The Act establishes the principle that there is one right of appeal against any of the listed 'immigration decisions' (see **11.2**). Where multiple decisions would result in multiple rights of appeal, these are subsumed into one appeal. All appealable grounds can and should be raised in an appeal (see **11.5**). Most, but not all, appeal rights can be exercised by the appellant in the UK (see **11.4**). Exceptions and limitations restrict rights of appeal in certain circumstances (see **11.8** onwards).

11.2 Decisions against which there is a right of appeal

By s 82(2) an appeal can be made against an 'immigration decision', namely:

(a) refusal of leave to enter the UK;

(b) refusal of entry clearance;

(c) refusal of a certificate of entitlement of the right of abode [see **2.3.3**];

(d) refusal to vary a person's leave to enter or remain in the UK if the result of the refusal is that the person has no leave to enter or remain;

(e) variation of a person's leave to enter or remain in the UK if when the variation takes effect the person has no leave to enter or remain;

(f) revocation of indefinite leave to enter or remain in the UK;

(g) a decision that a person is to be removed from the UK by way of directions under s 10 of the IAA 1999 [see **10.2.5**];

(h) a decision that an illegal entrant is to be removed from the UK by way of directions under Sch 2 to the IA 1971 [see **10.2.2**];

(ha) a decision that a person whose leave has been statutorily extended [see **3.6.2** and **3.7**] is to be removed from the UK;

(i) a decision to remove a family member of a person refused leave to enter the UK or who is an illegal entrant;

(ia) a decision to remove a seaman or aircraft crew;

(ib) a decision to deprive a Commonwealth citizen of right of abode [see **2.3.5**];

(j) a decision to make a deportation order [see **10.1**]; and

(k) refusal to revoke a deportation order [see **10.1.8**].

As to (h) above, the appeal is limited to challenging the decision to remove and not the directions made to carry that out: see *MS (Palestinian Territories) v Secretary of State for the Home Department* [2010] UKSC 25.

As to (j) above, a foreign criminal may not appeal against an order to deport him automatically (see **10.1.2.3**). However, he may appeal against the decision that he falls within that provision and additionally, or alternatively, on the ground that removal from the UK would be incompatible with his ECHR rights (see **11.3**).

These rights of appeal are subject to exceptions and limitations (see **11.8** onwards).

11.3 Grounds of appeal

By s 84, an appeal against an immigration decision (see **11.2**) must be brought on one or more of the following grounds:

(a) that the decision is not in accordance with Immigration Rules (eg a person argues that he meets a particular Rule);

(b) that the decision is unlawful discrimination by public authorities;

(c) that the decision is unlawful under s 6 of the Human Rights Act 1998 as being incompatible with the appellant's ECHR rights;

(d) that the appellant is an EEA national or a member of the family of an EEA national and the decision breaches the appellant's rights under the EU Treaties in respect of entry to or residence in the UK;

(e) that the decision is otherwise not in accordance with the law (eg a person claims the benefit of a Government policy that is not contained in the Rules);

(f) that the person taking the decision should have exercised differently a discretion conferred by Immigration Rules (eg a person refused by an exercise of discretion under the Immigration Rules, para 320: see **3.4.5**);

(g) that removal of the appellant from the UK in consequence of the immigration decision would breach the UK's obligations under the Geneva Convention on refugees, or would be unlawful under s 6 of the Human Rights Act 1998 as being incompatible with the appellant's Convention rights.

Any number of grounds can be set out but such will constitute one appeal (see **11.5**).

11.4 Appeal rights exercisable in the UK

By s 92, an appeal right is not exercisable whilst the appellant is in the UK unless:

(a) the appeal is against an immigration decision of the kind specified in s 82(2)(c), (d), (e), (f), (ha) and (j) (see **11.2**);

(b) the appeal is against refusal of leave to enter where at the time of the refusal the appellant is in the UK and on his arrival he had entry clearance;

(c) the appeal is against an immigration decision and the appellant has made an asylum claim, or a human rights claim, while in the UK, or is an EEA national or a member of the family of an EEA national and makes a claim to the Secretary of State that the decision breaches the appellant's rights under the Community Treaties in respect of entry to or residence in the UK.

All other appeal rights can be exercised only from abroad.

Note that by s 113, a 'human rights claim' is defined as a claim made by a person to the Secretary of State at a place designated by the Secretary of State that to remove the person from or require him to leave the UK would be unlawful under s 6 of the Human Rights Act 1998. An 'asylum claim' means a claim made by a person to the Secretary of State at a place designated by the Secretary of State that to remove the person from or require him to leave the UK would breach the UK's obligations under the Geneva Convention on refugees.

11.5 The 'one stop' process

11.5.1 Notice of appealable decision

The Immigration (Notices) Regulations 2003 (SI 2003/658) provide that a decision-maker (eg entry clearance officer, immigration officer, Secretary of State) must give written notice to a person of any immigration decision taken in respect of him which is appealable. The notice must include or be accompanied by a statement of the reasons for the decision to which it relates and, if it relates to an immigration decision specified in s 82(2)(a), (g), (h), (ha), (i), (ia) or (j) of the 2002 Act, state the country or territory to which it is proposed to remove the person.

The notice must also include, or be accompanied by, a statement which advises the person of his right of appeal and the statutory provision on which his right of appeal is based; whether or not such an appeal may be brought while in the UK; the grounds on which such an appeal may be brought; and the facilities available for advice and assistance in connection with such an appeal. It must also be accompanied by a notice which indicates the time limit for bringing the appeal (see **11.6.3**), the address to which it should be sent or may be taken by hand and a fax number for service by fax. Where the exercise of the appeal right is restricted by an exception or limitation (see **11.8** onwards), the notice must also include or be accompanied by a statement which refers to the provision limiting or restricting the right of appeal.

Further, by s 120, if a person has made an application to enter or remain in the UK, or an immigration decision (see **11.2**) has been taken or may be taken in respect of him, then the Secretary of State or an immigration officer may by notice in writing require him to state:

(a) his reasons for wishing to enter or remain in the UK;
(b) any grounds on which he should be permitted to enter or remain in the UK; and
(c) any grounds on which he should not be removed from or required to leave the UK.

11.5.2 Consequences of failing to disclose all grounds of appeal

What if a s 120 notice is not answered? Any attempt to raise such grounds later on may lead to certification under s 96, with the effect that there can be no appeal against the decision, or that those grounds cannot be raised in connection with a further appeal.

Before the Secretary of State can lawfully decide to certify, four steps must be taken:

(Step 1) The Secretary of State must be satisfied that the person was notified of a right of appeal under s 82 against another immigration decision (s 96(1)), or that the person received a notice under s 120 by virtue of an application other than that to which the new decision relates or by virtue of a decision other than the new decision (s 96(2)).

(Step 2) The Secretary of State must conclude that the claim or application to which the new decision relates relies on a matter that could have been raised in an appeal against the old decision (s 96(1)(b)), or that the new decision relates to an application or claim which relies on a matter that should have been but has not been raised in a statement made in response to that notice (s 96(2)(b)).

(Step 3) The Secretary of State must form the opinion that there is no satisfactory reason for that matter not having been raised in an appeal against the old decision (s 96(1)(c)), or that there is no satisfactory reason for that matter not having been raised in a statement made in response to that notice (s 96(2)(c)).

(Step 4) The Secretary of State must consider whether, having regard to all relevant factors, he should exercise his discretion to certify, and must conclude that it is appropriate to exercise the discretion in favour of certification.

11.5.3 Other certificates under s 96

Certificates can be issued under s 96 otherwise than in relation to s 120 notices (see **11.5.2**).

Note that no appeal can be brought on any ground against an otherwise appealable decision if the Secretary of State or immigration officer certifies that the person was notified of a right of appeal against another decision (whether or not any appeal was lodged or completed) *and* that in his opinion the person made the claim or application in order to delay removal, or the removal of a family member, *and* that in his opinion the person had no other legitimate purpose for making the claim or application. If an appeal has already been brought, the appeal may not be continued if a certificate is issued.

Further s 96 prevents an appeal being brought if the Secretary of State or immigration officer certifies that a new decision relates to a ground which was raised on an earlier appeal or could have been raised at an appeal had the applicant chosen to exercise a right of appeal. If an appeal has already been brought, the appeal may not be continued if a certificate is issued.

Finally, where a further appeal right does arise, the Secretary of State or immigration officer may certify that certain grounds of appeal were already considered in an earlier appeal. The appellant is not then allowed to rely on those grounds.

The certificate may be challenged by way of an application for judicial review: see *R (Adebisi) v Secretary of State for the Home Department* [2011] LTL, 5 May; *R (J) v Secretary of State for the Home Department* [2009] EWHC 705 and **Chapter 12**.

11.6 The appeals system

11.6.1 The First-tier Tribunal (Immigration and Asylum Chamber) (IAC)

A right of appeal lies to the IAC, under s 82 of the NIAA 2002, against an immigration decision (see **11.2**); in certain circumstances, against a decision to reject an asylum claim (see **9.1**); and, under s 40A of the BNA 1981, against a decision to make an order depriving a person of a British citizenship status (see **2.2.9**).

The title of the legally qualified member of the IAC is an Immigration Judge. All IAC appeals are heard in various appeal centres across the UK.

An appeal to the IAC may only be started by giving notice of appeal on a prescribed form in accordance with the Asylum and Immigration Tribunal (Procedure) Rules 2005 (SI 2005/230, as amended). Practitioners must also be familiar with the IAC Practice Directions. Normally there is an initial case management review hearing. This will determine the issues in dispute and the evidence necessary to deal with them. Directions are usually given as to the filing of evidence, etc.

At the appeal hearing the Immigration Judge determines whether or not to uphold the original decision. If it is upheld, appeal lies on a point of law to the Upper Tribunal (Asylum and Immigration Chamber). Permission to appeal is required from the IAC or, failing that, the Upper Tribunal. If both the IAC and Upper Tribunal refuse permission to appeal, that decision can be judicially reviewed but limited to the grounds that either:

(a) the proposed appeal would raise some important point of principle or practice; or
(b) there is some other compelling reason for the court to hear the appeal: see *R (Cart) v The Upper Tribunal* [2011] UKSC 28.

As to ground (b), note that in *PR (Sri Lanka) v Secretary of State for the Home Department* [2011] EWCA Civ 988, the Court of Appeal (per Carnwath LJ at [35]) stated that 'compelling means *legally* compelling, rather than compelling, perhaps, from a political or emotional point of view, although such considerations may exceptionally add weight to the legal arguments.' See also **Chapter 12**.

Appeal on a point of law from the Upper Tribunal lies to the Court of Appeal. It is necessary to obtain that court's permission first.

11.6.2 Appeals to the Court of Appeal

The Court of Appeal has the power to give any decision which might have been given by the IAC. It can also remit the matter for rehearing and determination by the IAC, and then may offer the IAC its opinion and make directions with which the IAC must comply.

11.6.3 The appeals timetable

11.6.3.1 Appealing to the IAC

An appellant appealing in the UK to the IAC must give notice of appeal within five working days of receiving the decision if he is in detention. Otherwise the time limit is 10 working days. However, if the appeal is being made from outside the UK, he must give notice of appeal within 28 calendar days after receiving notice of the decision.

11.6.3.2 Asking the IAC for permission to appeal to the Upper Tribunal

An application for permission to appeal to the Upper Tribunal must be made to the IAC within five working days of receiving the IAC's decision if the appellant is in the UK, but 28 days if he is outside the UK.

11.6.3.3 Asking the Upper Tribunal for its permission to appeal

What are the time limits if the IAC refuses permission? If the appellant is in the UK, the period is seven working days after the date on which notice of the First-tier Tribunal's refusal of permission was sent or five working days if that notice was sent electronically or delivered personally. Where the appellant is outside the UK, the respective periods are 56 and 28 days.

11.6.3.4 Seeking permission of the Court of Appeal

An application for leave to appeal to the Court of Appeal must be made within 12 days of receipt of the Upper Tribunal's determination.

11.6.3.5 Appeals timetable if appellant is detained

Appeals are expedited or 'fast tracked' if the appellant is in detention. For details see the AIT (Fast Track Procedure) Rules 2005 (SI 2005/560, as amended).

11.7 Pending and abandoned appeals

Section 104 sets out when an appeal is pending and when it ends: it clarifies that an appeal ceases to be pending when it is 'abandoned'. An appeal may be treated as abandoned because the appellant leaves the UK, is granted leave to enter or remain, or a deportation order is made against him. However, an appeal continues to be pending so long as a further appeal may be brought and until such further appeal is finally determined.

As a general rule, while an appeal is pending, the leave to which the appeal relates and any conditions subject to which it was granted continue to have effect. Hence, the person has a right to remain in the UK whilst pursuing the appeal. But what does 'the leave to which the appeal relates' mean? It is referring to the leave that the appellant had when he made the application that has been refused. It does not mean the leave for which the appellant applied.

By s 77, while a person's claim for asylum is pending he may not be removed from or required to leave the UK in accordance with a provision of the Immigration Acts.

However, this does not prevent the giving of a direction for the claimant's removal from the UK, the making of a deportation order in respect of the claimant, or the taking of any other interim or preparatory action.

By s 78, while a person's appeal under s 82 is pending he may not be removed from or required to leave the UK in accordance with a provision of the Immigration Acts. However, this does not prevent the giving of a direction for the appellant's removal from the UK, the making of a deportation order in respect of the appellant (subject to s 79: see below), or the taking of any other interim or preparatory action.

Section 78 only applies to an appeal brought while the appellant is in the UK in accordance with s 92 (see **11.4**).

By s 79 a deportation order may not be made in respect of a person while an appeal under s 82 against the decision to make the order could be brought (ignoring any possibility of an appeal out of time with permission), or is pending.

Note that s 99 provides that where a certificate is issued under s 96 (see **11.5.2**) or ss 97 or 98 (see **11.12** and **11.13**) in respect of a pending appeal, then that appeal lapses.

11.8 Ineligible appeals

Section 88 applies to an immigration decision of the kind referred to in s 82(2)(a), (b), (d) or (e). These are detailed at **11.2**. A person may not appeal under s 82 against such an immigration decision which is taken on the grounds that he or a person of whom he is a dependant:

(a) does not satisfy a requirement as to age, nationality or citizenship specified in immigration rules;

(b) does not have an immigration document of a particular kind (or any immigration document);

(ba) has failed to supply a medical report or a medical certificate in accordance with a requirement of immigration rules;

(c) is seeking to be in the UK for a period greater than that permitted in his case by immigration rules; or

(d) is seeking to enter or remain in the UK for a purpose other than one for which entry or remaining is permitted in accordance with immigration rules.

For the purposes of (b) above, an 'immigration document' means either entry clearance, a passport, a work permit or other immigration employment document, or a document which relates to a national of a country other than the UK and which is designed to serve the same purpose as a passport.

An appeal may nevertheless be brought on asylum, human rights or race discrimination grounds.

11.9 Refusal of entry clearance

Section 88A provides that a person may not appeal under s 82 against refusal of an application for entry clearance unless the application was made for the purpose of:

(a) visiting a person of a class or description prescribed by regulations for the purpose of this subsection, or

(b) entering as the dependant of a person in circumstances prescribed by regulations for the purpose of this subsection.

As at the time of writing, no such regulations had been made.

Note that when this provision was brought into force by the Immigration, Asylum and Nationality Act 2006 (Commencement No 8 and Transitional and Saving Provisions) Order 2008 (SI 2008/310), it was stated that it would have effect only so far as it relates to applications of a kind identified in the Immigration Rules as requiring to be considered under a 'points based system'. To date only Part 6A of the Rules is points based (see **Chapters 6** and **7**).

11.10 Refusal of leave to enter

By s 89, a person may not appeal under s 82 against refusal of leave to enter the UK unless on his arrival in the UK he had entry clearance and the purpose of entry specified in the entry clearance was the same as that specified in his application for leave to enter. However, an appeal may still be brought on asylum, human rights or race discrimination grounds.

11.11 National security and similar matters

Section 97 provides that an appeal under s 82 cannot be made or continued where the Secretary of State certifies that a decision was taken to exclude or remove a person from the UK:

(a) in the interests of national security;

(b) in the interests of the relationship between the UK and another country; or

(c) otherwise in the public interest.

However, under the Special Immigration Appeals Commission Act 1997 an appeal can be made to the Special Immigration Appeals Commission (SIAC). This body was set up specifically to deal with appeals where national security and other sensitive matters are a consideration. The proceedings of the SIAC are governed by the Special Immigration Appeals Commission (Procedure) Rules 2003 (SI 2003/1034).

11.12 Deportation order made on national security grounds

Section 97 (see **11.11**) does not apply where the Secretary of State certifies that the decision to make a deportation order (see **10.1**) in respect of a person was taken on the grounds that his removal from the UK would be in the interests of national security. In those circumstances s 97A applies instead, and an appeal can be made only from outside the UK. If the appellant makes a human rights claim the appeal can be brought in country, unless the Secretary of State certifies that removal would not breach the ECHR. Provision is made for an in-country appeal against such a certificate to the SIAC.

11.13 'Public good' exclusion

Section 98 provides that an appeal cannot be made or continued against a refusal of leave to enter or refusal of entry clearance if the Secretary of State has certified that the person's exclusion from the UK is conducive to the public good, or directed that the person be refused on that ground. However, this does not prevent the person appealing on human rights or race discrimination grounds, or from appealing refusal of leave to enter on asylum grounds.

11.14 EEA nationals

The I(EEA) Regs 2006 give rights of appeal which have been prescribed under EU law for EEA nationals, members of their family and certain non-EEA nationals who are members of a UK national's family (see **4.4**). There are also additional categories of persons who are entitled to similar rights under agreements to which the UK is a party or by which it is bound. The rights of appeal cover decisions relating to admission, residence and the issue or withdrawal of relevant documentation. Appeals against decisions will be heard by the IAC or, where appropriate, by the SIAC. A copy of the Regulations may be found at **Appendix 4** to this book.

11.15 Unfounded human rights or asylum claims

By s 94(1A), a person may not bring an appeal whilst in the UK against an immigration decision of a kind specified in s 82(2)(c), (d), (e) or (ha) (see **11.2**) in reliance on s 92 (see **11.4**) if the appellant has also made a human rights and/or asylum claim and the Secretary of State certifies that the human rights and/or asylum claim is or are clearly unfounded.

By s 94(2), a person may not bring a human rights and/or asylum appeal whilst in the UK if the Secretary of State certifies that either claim is or both claims are clearly unfounded.

Note that if the Secretary of State is satisfied that an asylum claimant or human rights claimant is entitled to reside in a State listed in s 94(4), he *must* certify the claim unless he is satisfied that it is not clearly unfounded. The s 94(4) States considered to be generally safe in the context of asylum and human rights claims are:

(a) the Republic of Albania;
(b) Bosnia-Hertzegovina;
(c) Jamaica;
(d) Macedonia;
(e) the Republic of Moldova;
(f) India;
(g) Bolivia;
(h) Brazil;
(i) Ecuador;
(j) South Africa;
(k) Ukraine;
(l) Mongolia;
(m) Ghana (in respect of men);
(n) Nigeria (in respect of men);
(o) Gambia (in respect of men);
(p) Kenya (in respect of men);
(q) Liberia (in respect of men);
(r) Malawi (in respect of men);
(s) Mali (in respect of men);
(t) Mauritius;
(u) Montenegro;
(v) Peru;
(w) Serbia;
(x) Sierra Leone (in respect of men);
(y) Kosovo;
(z) South Korea

The UKBA gives the following as examples of clearly unfounded claims:

(a) A claim which raises nothing that could be construed as amounting to an expression of a fear of mistreatment upon return. For example, a person says he is seeking asylum but gives as his reason that he is fleeing poverty or unemployment.

(b) The claimant expresses a fear of mistreatment, but from the objective evidence it is not arguable that the mistreatment, even if it occurred, would amount to persecution or treatment contrary to Article 3 ECHR.

(c) The claimant expresses a fear of persecution or Article 3 treatment by non-State actors but the State provides a sufficiency of protection against such actions.

Further, a person may not bring an appeal if the Secretary of State certifies that it is proposed to remove the person to a country of which he is not a national or citizen, and there is no reason to believe that the person's rights under the ECHR will be breached in that country. In determining whether a person in relation to whom such a certificate has been issued may be removed from the UK, the country specified in the certificate is to be regarded as a place where a person's life and liberty is not threatened by reason of his race, religion, nationality, membership of a particular social group, or political opinion, and a place from which a person will not be sent to another country otherwise than in accordance with the Geneva Convention on refugees.

UKBA guidance is that claims should be assessed at their highest and are only certified when they are bound to fail (following *R (Yogathas) v Secretary of State for the Home Department* [2002] UKHL 36).

A certificate may be challenged by way of judicial review.

> It follows that a challenge to the Secretary of State's conclusion that a claim is clearly unfounded is a rationality challenge. There is no way that a court can consider whether her conclusion was rational other than by asking itself the same question that she has considered. If the court concludes that a claim has a realistic prospect of success when the Secretary of State has reached a contrary view, the court will necessarily conclude that the Secretary of State's view was irrational. (per Lord Phillips in *ZT (Kosovo) v Secretary of State for the Home Department* [2009] UKHL 6 at para 23)

How should the Secretary of State set about making the decision? His Lordship explained at para 22 that five steps need to be taken, namely that the Secretary of State should:

> (i) consider the factual substance and detail of the claim,
>
> (ii) consider how it stands with the known background data,
>
> (iii) consider whether in the round it is capable of belief,
>
> (iv) if not, consider whether some part of it is capable of belief,
>
> (v) consider whether, if eventually believed in whole or in part, it is capable of coming within the Convention.
>
> If the answers are such that the claim cannot on any legitimate view succeed, then the claim is clearly unfounded; if not, not.

Where a certificate is issued concerning a national of a country listed in s 94(4), the first challenge may be as to whether the country in question has been properly listed. To succeed, the claimant will have to demonstrate that the evidence clearly establishes that there is a serious risk of persecution in that country that affects a significant number of people: see *R (MD (Gambia)) v Secretary of State for the Home Department* [2011] EWCA Civ 121. It follows that if the listing is lawful, the next question is whether the Secretary of State was obliged to certify the claim on the basis that it was clearly unfounded.

See further **Chapter 12**.

11.16 Persons excluded from asylum

Where the UKBA decides that a claimant is excluded from asylum (see **9.5**), the Secretary of State will issue a certificate to that effect. As a result, any appeal made to the IAC or SIAC must start by considering the statements made in the Secretary of State's certificate. By s 55(4) of the IANA 2006, if the Tribunal or Commission agrees with those statements, it must dismiss such part of the appeal as amounts to an asylum claim before considering any other aspect of the case.

11.17 European Common List of Safe Countries of Origin

Section 94A allows the Secretary of State by order to prescribe a list of States to be known as the European Common List of Safe Countries of Origin. This is pursuant to EC Council Directive 2005/85, which provides that the Council shall adopt a minimum common list of third countries which shall be regarded by Member States as safe third countries of origin. At the time of writing no order had been made.

If a national of a State which is listed in the European Common List of Safe Countries of Origin, or a Stateless person who was formerly habitually resident in such a State, makes an asylum claim or a human rights claim (or both), the Secretary of State will certify such under s 94 as unfounded unless he is satisfied that there are serious grounds for considering that the State in question is not safe given the particular circumstances of the claimant.

11.18 Deprivation of citizenship orders

By s 40A of the BNA 1981, a person given notice of a decision to make an order depriving him of his British citizenship (see **2.2.9**) has a right of appeal to the IAC. Where, however, the Secretary of State has certified that the decision to deprive was based wholly or partly in reliance on information which he believes should not be made public, the appeal at first instance will instead be heard by the SIAC.

11.19 Administrative review

11.19.1 Refusal of entry clearance under points-based system

In **Chapters 6** and **7** we looked at the points-based system for entry to the UK by students, employees, business people and investors. If an applicant for entry clearance is refused, any appeal is limited to grounds (b) and (c) at **11.3** above. Additionally, or alternatively, the applicant can seek administrative review (AR) of any refusal he believes was made in error, including any refusal under the general grounds (see **3.4.5.2**).

11.19.2 What is administrative review?

Administrative review is a non-statutory scheme and the policy is contained solely in the UKBA's guidance notes. It is free of charge. The request for a review must be made to an Entry Clearance Manager (ECM) on the AR Request Notice sent with the entry clearance refusal notice. It must be returned within 28 days, and only in exceptional circumstances will a late application be accepted.

Only one request can be made unless the ECM upholds a refusal on different grounds. The applicant may then request an AR of the new refusal grounds.

Administrative review is normally completed within 28 days. The applicant is notified of the outcome by letter.

11.19.3 The administrative review process

The ECM will consider the areas the applicant has asked to be reviewed and check that points were correctly assessed, documents were properly scrutinised and verification checks appropriately carried out.

11.19.4 Conclusion of the administrative review process

An ECM may recommend that the reason for refusal should be overturned, and issue entry clearance where he finds that the ECO:

(a) failed properly to consider evidence submitted with the original application;

(b) failed correctly to apply the Immigration Rules; or

(c) made a mistake in processing the application.

11.20 Grounds of appeal to IAC

11.20.1 Asylum appeals

When appealing the refusal of the Secretary of State to grant asylum, the appellant should consider completing, as appropriate, boxes 1 to 7 of Section 3D of the Appeal Form IAFT-1. The form is available on the Ministry of Justice website (see **1.2.8**). The boxes read as follows:

1. If you disagree with the Home Office's interpretation of the situation in your country, please explain why in this box, and give reasons to support your point of view.
2. If the Home Office has suggested that you could live safely in another part of the country of origin, and you disagree, please explain why in this box.
3. If the Home Office has stated that your claim is not credible, and you disagree, please explain why in this box.
4. If the Home Office has stated that you do not qualify as a refugee on grounds of race, religion, nationality, membership of a particular social group or political opinion (under the criteria of the 1951 Geneva Convention), and you disagree, please explain why in this box.
5. If the Home Office has stated that specific articles of the European Convention on Human Rights (ECHR) do not apply to your case, and you disagree, please explain why in this box.
6. If the Home Office has stated that you do not qualify as a person who is eligible for humanitarian protection (under the Refugee or Person in Need of International Protection Regulations 2006), and you disagree, please explain why in this box.
7. If there is anything else that you disagree with in the Home Office letter, please explain why in this box.

11.20.2 Non-asylum appeals

When appealing an immigration decision that does not concern asylum, the appellant should complete box 8 of Section 3D of the Appeal Form IAFT-1. This reads as follows:

8. If your appeal relates to a non-asylum decision with which you disagree, you must give your reasons below and refer to the paragraphs of the refusal letter (you may continue on a separate sheet if necessary).

11.20.3 Appeal against decision of an Entry Clearance Officer

Where an appellant is able to appeal from abroad against the refusal of entry clearance, he should use Appeal Form IAFT-2.

11.21 Examples of grounds of appeal

11.21.1 Appeal against deportation or removal order

11.21.1.1 Error in law: Article 8 ECHR

Decision	Grounds of appeal
Family life not established	Family life engaged

Case law example

Kugathas v Secretary of State for the Home Department [2003] EWCA Civ 31 per Sedley LJ at [14]:

> Generally, the protection of family life under Article 8 involves cohabiting dependants, such as parents and their dependant minor children. Whether it extends to other relationships depends on the circumstances of the particular case. Relationships between adults, a mother and her 33 year old son in the present case, would not necessarily acquire the protection of Article 8 of the Convention without evidence of further elements of dependency, involving more than the normal emotional ties.

Decision	Grounds of appeal
Deportation or removal is proportionate in the terms of Article 8(2)	Deportation or removal is disproportionate in the terms of Article 8(2)

Case law example

AC (Turkey) v Secretary of State for the Home Department [2009] EWCA Civ 327 per Laws LJ at [14]:

> Clearly the Secretary of State has a particular responsibility to make judgments as to what Judge LJ called 'broad issues of social cohesion and public confidence' within the system of immigration control. The Secretary of State's judgment on those matters must broadly be respected by the [IAC], at least so far as the policy itself is concerned. As Wall LJ stated in *OP (Jamaica) v Secretary of State for the Home Department* [2008] EWCA Civ 440 (paragraph 24), the Secretary of State's assessment of those matters has 'to be taken as a given unless it is palpably wrong'. But then the [IAC] must exercise its own judgment as to whether, in view of that axiom or given, the decision to remove or deport is disproportionate in the terms of Article 8(2) of the Convention. That decision is to be arrived at on the merits and is entirely in the hands of the Tribunal.

11.21.1.2 Error in law: EEA national

Decision	Grounds of appeal
Removal of EEA national justified on public policy grounds	Wrong test applied – by I(EEA) Regs 2006, reg 21(3), as the EEA national had a permanent right of residence, he could only be removed if there were 'serious' grounds of public policy.
Removal of EEA national justified on public security grounds	Wrong test applied – by I(EEA) Regs 2006, reg 21(4), as the EEA national had resided in UK for a continuous period of at least 10 years, he could only be removed if there were 'imperative' grounds of public security.

Case law example

LG (Italy) v Secretary of State for the Home Department [2008] EWCA Civ 190 per Carnwath LJ at [32]:

> The words 'imperative grounds of public security' at the third level are clearly intended to embody a test which is both more stringent and narrower in scope than 'serious grounds of public policy or public security' at the second level… level three requires, not simply a serious matter of public policy, but an actual risk to public security, so compelling that it justifies the exceptional course of removing someone who (in the language of the Preamble to the Directive) has become 'integrated' by 'many years' residence in the host state.

Chapter 12
Judicial Review Proceedings

12.1 What is judicial review?

> Judicial review involves a challenge to the legal validity of the decision. It does not allow the court of review to examine the evidence with a view to forming its own view about the substantial merits of the case. It may be that the tribunal whose decision is being challenged has done something which it had no lawful authority to do. It may have abused or misused the authority which it had. It may have departed from the procedures which either by statute or at common law as matter of fairness it ought to have observed. As regards the decision itself it may be found to be perverse, or irrational, or grossly disproportionate to what was required. Or the decision may be found to be erroneous in respect of a legal deficiency, as for example, through the absence of evidence, or of sufficient evidence, to support it, or through account being taken of irrelevant matter, or through a failure for any reason to take account of a relevant matter, or through some misconstruction of the terms of the statutory provision which the decision-maker is required to apply. But while the evidence may have to be explored in order to see if the decision is vitiated by such legal deficiencies it is perfectly clear that in a case of review, as distinct from an ordinary appeal, the court may not set about forming its own preferred view of the evidence. (per Lord Clyde in *Reid v Secretary of State for Scotland* [1998] UKHL 43)

12.1.1 Use of judicial review in immigration cases

As we saw at **11.2**, the NIAA 2002 sets out those immigration decisions against which there is a right of appeal. But what about those decisions where there is no right of appeal? Or where all appeal rights have been exhausted? This is where judicial review proceedings may be an appropriate step for the client to take.

Judicial review will be refused if an alternative remedy is more appropriate, such as where an applicant has failed to use a right of appeal, unless he can show that the circumstances are exceptional: see *R v Secretary of State for the Home Department, ex p Swati* [1986] 1 All ER 717. It is not enough to show that the right of appeal is a less convenient remedy, for instance because it must be conducted from abroad: see *Soon Ok Ryoo v Secretary of State for the Home Department* [1992] Imm AR 59. However, if it would be practically impossible to conduct the appeal from abroad, permission may be given: see *R v Chief Immigration Officer, Gatwick Airport, ex p Kharrazi* [1980] 1 WLR 1396 and *R v Secretary of State for the Home Department and Immigration Officer, Waterloo International Station, ex p Canbolat* [1997] INLR 198.

The vast majority of judicial review proceedings concern aspects of asylum and human rights claims, eg when the Secretary of State does not accept that a fresh claim was made (**9.14**), or certifies a claim as no longer appealable (**11.5.2** and **11.5.3**) or unfounded (**11.15**); deportation and removal cases (particularly human rights-based challenges: **Chapter 10**); as well as cases where the Secretary of State refuses to register or naturalise a person as a British citizen (**Chapter 2**).

12.1.2 Grounds for judicial review

The most common grounds for judicial review are set out in the extract from *Reid* at **12.1**.

The usual starting point is to consider if the decision-maker made an error of law, eg did the Secretary of State ask himself the right question? Otherwise, in many cases the client will be arguing that the decision made was irrational or unreasonable. The test for this was originally laid down by Lord Greene MR in the landmark Court of Appeal case of *Associated Provincial Picture Houses Ltd v Wednesbury Corporation* [1948] 1 KB 223, namely, having regard to relevant considerations only, did the decision-maker come to a conclusion that was so unreasonable that no reasonable authority could ever have come to it? Note that here consideration needs to be given as to whether the Secretary of State took into account factors that were irrelevant and/or omitted to take relevant matters into account. Equally, it should be asked whether the Secretary of State gave undue weight to one or more factors over other relevant factors.

Subsequently, the test of irrationality has been refined. In *CCSU v Minister for Civil Service* [1984] 3 All ER 935, Lord Diplock stated that, to be irrational, a decision needs to be so outrageous in its defiance of logic, or of accepted moral standards, that no sensible person could have arrived at it. In the later case of *R v Ministry of Defence, ex p Smith* [1996] 1 All ER 257, the Court of Appeal found that, to establish irrationality, the decision or policy should be beyond the range of reasonable responses open to the decision-maker.

When making a decision, the Secretary of State or a court must take all relevant considerations into account. This is often known as the 'anxious scrutiny' requirement. In *WM (DRC) v Secretary of State for the Home Department* [2006] EWCA Civ 1495, Buxton LJ stated, at [7], that in an asylum case, for example, 'the consideration of all the decision-makers, the Secretary of State, the [immigration judge] and the court, must be informed by the anxious scrutiny of the material that is axiomatic in decisions that if made incorrectly may lead to the Applicant's exposure to persecution.' As Carnwath LJ later explained in *R (YH) v Secretary of State for the Home Department* [2010] EWCA Civ 116, at [24], the requirement has 'by usage acquired special significance as underlining the very special human context in which such cases are brought, and the need for decisions to show by their reasoning that every factor which might tell in favour of an Applicant has been properly taken into account'.

12.1.3 Remedies

The most common remedy sought in an immigration case is for the decision to be quashed, ie declared void. The court may, in addition, remit the case to the Secretary of State for the Home Department, or relevant tribunal, with a direction to reconsider it according to the findings of the court. See further **12.3.6**.

12.2 Making a claim: pre-action steps

Before an application is made to the court, the Pre-Action Protocol for Judicial Review should be consulted (there is a copy at **Appendix 17**). The Protocol sets out a code of best practice and contains the steps which parties should normally follow before starting court proceedings. The Protocol will not be appropriate where judicial review is required of a tribunal decision or in urgent cases, for example when directions have been set, or are in force, for the client's removal from the UK.

When following the Protocol, a claimant must always have in mind the fact that any application for judicial review must be filed promptly, and in any event, not later than three months after the grounds to make the claim first arose.

12.2.1 Letter before claim

Where the Protocol applies, the claimant should send a letter before claim to the defendant. This will be the Secretary of State for the Home Department. The relevant address is the UKBA's Judicial Review Unit at St Anne's House, 20–26 Wellesley Road, Croydon CR9 2RL. The letter should clearly, succinctly and accurately identify the issues in dispute and seek to establish whether litigation can be avoided. Normally, the suggested standard format for the letter outlined at Annex A should be used, but in addition you should include, where known and appropriate, the client's Home Office, Port, Tribunal and National Asylum Support Service reference numbers. Otherwise, ensure the client's full name, nationality and date of birth are set out.

There is a specimen letter before claim at **12.5**.

12.2.2 Home Office response

UKBA guidance is that if the caseworker decides the representations in the letter before claim have merit then he should try to rectify the problem without the need for court proceedings. If the representations are without merit, the letter of response should fully explain the reasons for that decision and answer any queries the claimant has made. If the caseworker decides that some of the claim has merit but other points do not, the response should comprehensively set out the reasons for this decision, with a full explanation of what is agreed and what steps will be taken to rectify this, and why the other points are not accepted.

12.3 Court proceedings

Judicial review proceedings must be started in the High Court (see the Senior Courts Act 1981, s 31). Claims are dealt with by the Administrative Court (save a challenge to the Secretary of State's refusal to treat submissions as a fresh asylum or human rights claim (**9.14**) as these reviews are normally transferred to the Upper Tribunal under the Senior Courts Act 1981, s 31A).

The judicial review procedure is governed by Part 54 of the Civil Procedure Rules 1998 (SI 1998/3132) (CPR 1998). By r 54.1(2)(a), a 'claim for judicial review' is defined as 'a claim to review the lawfulness of an enactment; or a decision, action or failure to act in relation to the exercise of a public function'.

12.3.1 The two stages of an application

The judicial review procedure has the unusual feature of two separate stages. First, the claimant must start the proceedings by filing a CPR 1998, Part 8 claim form and obtain the court's permission to proceed with it. If permission is granted then, secondly, after the parties have filed various documents, a full judicial review hearing takes place.

12.3.2 The need for a prompt application

An application for permission to apply for judicial review must be made promptly, and in any event within three months from the date when grounds for the application first arose. The time limit cannot be extended by agreement between the parties. The court may extend the period if there is good reason for the delay, but delay may still result in refusal of a remedy at the final hearing (*R (Lichfield Securities Ltd) v Lichfield District Council* (2001) *The Times*, 30 March).

12.3.3 Applying for permission

The claim form and other documents prescribed by CPR 1998, Practice Direction 54A (such as a detailed statement of the grounds for bringing the claim, a statement of the facts relied on, any written evidence relied on and a copy of any order sought to have quashed) must be filed and served on the defendant and any interested party. Where the review is sought of a tribunal decision, the Secretary of State will be an interested party. Rule 6.10 of the CPR 1998 provides that service on a government department must be effected on the solicitor acting for that department, which in the case of the UKBA is the Treasury Solicitor. The address for the Treasury Solicitor can be found in the Annex to Part 66 of the CPR 1998.

The defendant and any interested party have 21 days to acknowledge service of the claim form. Where a party filing an acknowledgment intends to contest the claim, a summary of the grounds on which it will be contested must be included.

12.3.4 Permission hearing

Normally the court determines whether or not to grant permission to proceed without an oral hearing. Permission is granted if the claimant can show on the materials filed a case which is 'arguable' and so requires a full investigation of the substantive merits (see *R v Inland Revenue Commissioners, ex p National Federation of Self-Employed and Small Businesses Ltd* [1982] AC 617).

If permission to proceed is refused or granted subject to conditions and/or on certain grounds only, the claimant can within seven days request an oral hearing for that decision to be reconsidered.

12.3.5 Next steps if permission granted

If permission to proceed is granted, the court will normally give case management directions as to how the parties are to prepare for the final hearing. This normally includes the the filing and service of a detailed response by the defendant and any interested parties, along with their written evidence. The claimant will prepare the trial bundle and each party should file a skeleton argument.

12.3.6 The hearing

The hearing usually takes place before a single judge nominated to hear cases in the Administrative Court. The parties' advocates make their respective submissions on the evidence filed. Only in exceptional cases will any witnesses be called and cross-examined.

What if the key factual evidence submitted to the court is disputed? The court's approach to this issue was summarised by Silber J in *R (McVey) v Secretary of State for Health* [2010] EWHC 437 as follows (at [35]):

> (i) The basic rule is that where there is a dispute on evidence in a judicial review application, then in the absence of cross-examination, the facts in the defendants' evidence must be assumed to be correct;
>
> (ii) An exception to this rule arises where the documents show that the defendants' evidence cannot be correct; and that
>
> (iii) The proper course for a claimant who wishes to challenge the correctness of an important aspect of the defendant's evidence relating to a factual matter on which the judge will have to make a critical factual finding is to apply to cross-examine the maker of the witness statement on which the defendant relies.

What are the court's powers when making a quashing order? The court will usually remit the matter to the decision-maker, direct it to reconsider the case and reach a decision in accordance with the judgment of the court.

When can the court substitute its own decision? Only if that decision was made by a court or tribunal, the decision is quashed on the ground that there was an error of law, and without that error there would have been only one decision which the court or tribunal could have reached.

12.4 Appeals from judicial review decisions

What if permission to proceed is refused at an oral hearing or on reconsideration? The claimant can apply within seven days to the Court of Appeal for permission to appeal that decision. Note that the Court of Appeal is not limited to granting permission to appeal but may grant permission for the judicial review. What if the Court of Appeal refuses permission to appeal? That is the end of the matter. Only if permission to appeal is granted but permission to proceed with the judicial review claim is refused can an appeal be made to the Supreme Court.

What if a party does not agree with the outcome of a judicial review? Permission to appeal can be sought from the court or the Court of Appeal. Any further appeal will be to the Supreme Court.

12.5 Specimen letter before claim

To
The Secretary of State for the Home Department,
Judicial Review Unit, UKBA,
St Anne's House, 20–26 Wellesley Road,
Croydon, CR9 2RL.

The claimant
Christopher Katongo

Reference details
Home Office reference number [ ].

The details of the matter being challenged
The decision made by the Secretary of State under Section 94 of the Nationality Immigration and Asylum Act 2002 (NIAA 2002) to certify as clearly unfounded the claimant's claim that his removal from the UK would be a disproportionate interference with his right to a family and private life under Article 8 of the European Convention on Human Rights (ECHR).

The issue

1. *Date of decision*: [ ]

2. *Relevant law*

A case which is clearly unfounded is one which has no real prospect of success if an appeal was made to the First Tier Tribunal, Immigration and Asylum Chamber.

The Secretary of State was required to give the claim anxious scrutiny. In determining whether the test was met, the Secretary of State had to consider, amongst other matters, the factual substance and detail of the claim; how it stands with the known background data; whether in the round it is capable of belief; if not, whether some part of it is capable of belief; and whether if eventually believed, in whole or in part, it is capable of coming within the ECHR. Only if the answers are such that the claim cannot on any legitimate view succeed is the claim clearly unfounded (*ZT (Kosovo) v Secretary of State for the Home Department* [2009] UKHL 6).

The Secretary of State had to approach the matter by addressing the questions set out by Lord Bingham in paragraph 17 of *R (Razgar) v Secretary of State for the Home Department* [2004] 2 AC 368, as further explained by the subsequent case of *R (Huang) v Secretary of State for the Home Department* [2007] UKHL 11, namely:

(a) Will the proposed removal be an interference by a public authority with the exercise of the applicant's rights to respect for his private or, as the case may be, family life?

(b) If so, will such interference have consequences of such gravity as potentially to engage the operation of Article 8?

(c) If so, is such interference in accordance with law?

(d) If so, is such interference necessary in a democratic society in a number of legitimate interests including, on the established case law, the maintenance of effective immigration control?

(e) If so, is such interference proportionate to the legitimate public ends sought to be achieved?

As to proportionality, the Supreme Court (then the House of Lords) in *Huang* stated at paragraph 20 that the ultimate question for the appellate authority is whether the refusal of leave to enter or remain, in circumstances where the life of the family cannot reasonably be expected to be enjoyed elsewhere, taking full account of all considerations weighing in favour of the refusal, prejudices the family life of the applicant in a manner that is sufficiently serious to amount to a breach of the fundamental right protected by Article 8.

3. Relevant facts

The claimant is a national of Zambia, aged 22. He was born in Zambia and lived there until he was 15. When he was 5 years old, his mother died. Shortly afterwards his father was diagnosed with a terminal illness. The claimant was an only child. He was cared for, together with his father, by his paternal grandmother. His father died when he was 10. The claimant's grandmother died when he was 15. It was at this point that the claimant was invited by his aunt, Mrs Francis, to visit her and her family in Huddersfield, England. Mrs Francis is a British citizen and the claimant's only living relative.

The claimant entered the UK as a minor. His passport was stamped with a 6 month visitor's visa but he stayed on in the UK when that period expired. His case, supported by Mrs Francis, is that Mrs Francis decided the claimant should stay with her family in the UK permanently but she overlooked applying for the appropriate permissions for the claimant from the immigration authorities.

The claimant had no formal education in Zambia. Mrs Francis describes him as very slow in his learning. She says that he is not capable of looking after himself as an adult. The claimant is dependent on her both financially and emotionally. This is supported by a doctor's report. The report also confirms that the claimant has suffered from time to time with depression and that he has mentioned on several occasions that he was thinking of committing suicide because he is very lonely and, in particular, because he misses his father.

4. Why the decision is wrong

The claimant has established a family life in the UK. He entered as a child and has been here for approximately 7 years. During that time he has been staying with and has been both financially and emotionally dependent on his aunt, Mrs Francis. The Secretary of State failed to give sufficient weight to the significant relationship that the claimant has with, and his dependency on, Mrs Francis. He is dependent upon her for his day to day health and wellbeing. He has no other relatives alive to support him.

To remove the claimant from the UK is a disproportionate interference with that established family life. The Secretary of State's conclusion that the claimant entered the UK by deception is erroneous. It is the claimant's case that when he arrived in the UK he told the Immigration Officer that he was coming to stay with his aunt in Huddersfield and his visa was stamped. It is Mrs Francis' evidence that she had given the claimant a letter to hand to the immigration authorities confirming this. It was only after the claimant had lived with the family in Huddersfield for several months that it was decided the claimant should remain here permanently with them. This is not a case where the claimant chose to enter or remain in the UK unlawfully. Nor is it a case where the claimant has developed a private and family life in flagrant disregard of orders requiring him to leave the UK.

The claimant is a depressed young man who is suffering from the loss of all of his immediate family members. He was brought up in a family environment and this has continued for the last 7 years in the UK. To separate him from Mrs Francis' family unit, will, as the medical report states, significantly contribute to his state of alienation and depression.

In all these circumstances the Secretary of State's conclusion that the claimant would be able to establish and maintain a family life in his own right on his return to Zambia is irrational.

The claimant has a realistic prospect of persuading an appeal tribunal that to remove him from the UK would be a disproportionate interference with the family life that he has established here.

The details of the action that the defendant is expected to take
The Secretary of State is asked to review the decision and revoke the certificate.

The details of the legal advisers dealing with this claim and the claimant's address for reply and service of court documents
The details of the claimant's legal advisers and his address for service are as follows:

XYZ Lawyers LLP
1 The Avenue
Nowhere
Mythshire
MY11 1AB
Tel: 012345678
Ref: 123/ABC/CK

The details of any interested parties
n/a

Information sought and documents that are considered relevant and necessary
If the Secretary of State intends to rely on additional information and/or documents, please ensure that full details and copies are enclosed with the reply to this letter.

Proposed reply date
Please ensure that a reply is given within 14 days.

APPENDICES

Appendix 1

Immigration Rules 1994 (HC 395)

Includes all statements of changes up to and including HC 1622, 7 November 2011

	Paragraph number
Introduction	
Implementation and transitional provisions	4
Application	5
Interpretation	6
Public funds clarification	6A–6C
Part 1: General provisions regarding leave to enter or remain in the United Kingdom	
Leave to enter the United Kingdom	7–9
Exercise of the power to refuse leave to enter the United Kingdom	10
Suspension of leave to enter or remain in the United Kingdom	10A
Cancellation of leave to enter or remain in the United Kingdom	10B
Requirement for persons arriving in the United Kingdom or seeking entry through the Channel Tunnel to produce evidence of identity and nationality	11
Requirement for a person not requiring leave to enter the United Kingdom to prove that he has the right of abode	12–14
Common Travel Area	15
Admission for certain British passport holders	16–17
Persons outside the United Kingdom	17A–17B
Returning residents	18–20
Non-lapsing leave	20A
Holders of restricted travel documents and passports	21–23
Leave to enter granted on arrival in the United Kingdom	23A–23B
Entry clearance	24–30C
Variation of leave to enter or remain in the United Kingdom	31–33A
Knowledge of language and life in the United Kingdom	33B–33F
Specified forms and procedures for applications or claims in connection with immigration	34–34D
Variation of applications or claims for leave to remain	34E–34F
Determination of the date of an application or claim (or variation of an application or claim) in connection with immigration	34G–34I
Withdrawn applications or claims for leave to remain in the United Kingdom	34J
Undertakings	35
Medical	36–39
Students	39A
Part 2: Persons seeking to enter or remain in the United Kingdom for visits	
Visitors	40–46X
Visitors in transit	47–50
Visitors seeking to enter or remain for private medical treatment	51–56

	Paragraph number
Parent of a child at school	56A–56C
Visitors seeking to enter for the purposes of marriage or to enter into a civil partnership	56D–56F
Visitors seeking leave to enter under the Approved Destinations Status (ADS) agreement with China	56G–56J
Student visitors	56K–56Q
Part 3: Persons seeking to enter or remain in the United Kingdom for studies	
Students	57–62
Student nurses	63–69
Resits of examinations	69A–69F
Writing up a thesis	69G–69L
Overseas qualified nurses and midwives	69M–69R
Postgraduate doctors and dentists	70–75M
Spouses or civil partners of students or prospective students granted leave under this part of the Rules	76–78
Children of students or prospective students granted leave under this part of the Rules	79–81
Prospective students	82–87
Student union sabbatical officers	87A–87F
Part 4: Persons seeking to enter or remain in the United Kingdom in an 'au pair' placement, as a working holidaymaker or for training or work experience	
Au pair placements	88–94
Working holidaymakers	95–100
Children of working holidaymakers	101–103
Seasonal agricultural workers	104–109
Teachers and language assistants coming to the United Kingdom under approved exchange schemes	110–115
Home Office approved training or work experience	116–121
Spouses of persons with limited leave to enter or remain under paragraphs 110–121	122–124
Children of persons with limited leave to enter or remain under paragraphs 110–121	125–127
Part 5: Persons seeking to enter or remain in the United Kingdom for employment	
Work permit employment	128–135
Highly skilled migrants	135A–135HA
Sectors-Based Scheme	135I–135N
International Graduates Scheme	135O–135T
Representatives of overseas newspapers, news agencies and broadcasting organisations	136–143
Fresh Talent: Working in Scotland scheme	143A–143F
Representatives of Overseas Business	144–151
Private servants in diplomatic households	152–159
Domestic workers in private households	159A–159H
Overseas government employees	160–169

	Paragraph number
Ministers of religion, missionaries and members of religious orders	170–177A
Visiting religious workers and religious workers in non-pastoral roles	177B–177G
Airport based operational ground staff of overseas-owned airlines	178–185
Persons with United Kingdom ancestry	186–193
Spouses or civil partners of persons who have or have had leave to enter or remain under paragraphs 128–193 (but not paragraphs 135I–135K)	194–196F
Children of persons with limited leave to enter or remain under paragraphs 128–193 (but not paragraphs 135I–135K)	197–199
Multiple entry work permit employment	199A–199C
Part 6: Persons seeking to enter or remain in the United Kingdom as a businessman, self-employed person, investor, writer, composer or artist	
Persons intending to establish themselves in business	200–210
Innovators	210A–210H
Persons intending to establish themselves in business under the provisions of EC Association Agreements	222–223A
Investors	224–231
Writers, composers and artists	232–239
Spouses or civil partners of persons who have or have had limited leave to enter or remain under paragraphs 200–239	240–242F
Children of persons with limited leave to enter or remain under paragraphs 200–239	243–245
Part 6A: Points-Based System	
Tier 1 (Exceptional Talent) Migrants	245A–245BF
Tier 1 (General) Migrants	245C–245CE
Tier 1 (Entrepreneur) Migrants	245D–245DF
Tier 1 (Investor) Migrants	245E–245EF
Tier 1 (Post-Study Work) Migrants	245F–245FE
Tier 2 (Intra Company Transfer) Migrants	245G–Z45GF
Tier 2 (General) Migrants, Tier 2 (Minister of Religion) Migrants and Tier 2 (Sportsperson) Migrants	245H–245HF
Tier 5 (Youth Mobility Scheme) Temporary Migrants	245ZI–245ZL
Tier 5 (Temporary Worker) Migrants	245ZM–245ZS
Tier 4 (General) Student	245ZT–245ZY
Tier 4 (Child) Student	245ZZ–245ZZD
Part 7: Other Categories	
Persons exercising rights of access to a child resident in the United Kingdom	246–248F
EEA nationals and their families	255–262
Retired persons of independent means	263–270
Spouses or civil partners of persons who have or have had limited leave to enter or remain in the United Kingdom as retired persons of independent means	271–273F
Children of persons with limited leave to enter or remain in the United Kingdom as retired persons of independent means	274–276
Long residence	276A–276D
HM Forces	276E–276Q

	Paragraph number
Spouses, civil partners, unmarried or same-sex partners of persons settled or seeking settlement in the United Kingdom in accordance with paragraphs 276E to 276Q (HM Forces rules) or of members of HM Forces who are exempt from immigration control under section 8(4)(a) of the Immigration Act 1971 and have at least 5 years' continuous service	276R–276W
Children of a parent, parents or a relative settled or seeking settlement in the United Kingdom under paragraphs 276E to 276Q (HM Forces rules) or of members of HM Forces who are exempt from immigration control under section 8(4)(a) of the Immigration Act 1971 and have at least 5 years' continuous service	276X–267AC
Spouses, civil partners, unmarried or same-sex partners of armed forces members who are exempt from immigration control under section 8(4) of the Immigration Act 1971	276AD–276AF
Children of armed forces members who are exempt from immigration control under Section 8(4) of the Immigration Act 1971	276AG–276AI
Part 8: Family members	
Spouses and civil partners	277–289
Victims of domestic violence	289A–289C
Fiance(e)s and proposed civil partners	289AA–295
Unmarried and same-sex partners	295AA–295O
Children	296–316F
Parents, grandparents and other dependent relatives	317–319
Family members of relevant points-based system migrants	319A–319K
Other family members of persons with limited leave to enter or remain in the United Kingdom as a refugee or beneficiary of humanitarian protection	319L–319U
Parents, grandparents and other dependent relatives of persons with limited leave to enter or remain in the United Kingdom as a refugee or beneficiary of humanitarian protection	319V–319Y
Part 9 – General grounds for the refusal of entry clearance, leave to enter, leave to remain, variation of leave to enter or remain and curtailment of leave in the United Kingdom	
Refusal of entry clearance or leave to enter the United Kingdom	320
Refusal of leave to enter in relation to a person in possession of an entry clearance	321
Refusal of variation of leave to enter or remain or curtailment of leave	322–323B
Crew members	324
Part 10: Registration with the police	325–326
Part 11: Asylum	326A–352G
Part 11A: Temporary Protection	354–356B
Part 11B: Asylum	357–361
Part 12: Procedure and Rights of appeal	353–352A
Part 13: Deportation	362–395F
Appendix 1: Visa requirements for the United Kingdom	
Appendix 2: Countries or territories whose nationals or citizens are relevant foreign nationals for the purposes of Part 10 of these Rules	
Appendix 3: List of Countries participating in the Working Holidaymaker Scheme	
Appendix 4: DELETED	

	Paragraph number
Appendix 5: DELETED	
Appendix 6: Disciplines for which an Academic Technology Approval Scheme certificate from the Counter-Proliferation Department of the Foreign and Commonwealth Office is required for the purposes of Tier 4 of the Points Based System	
Appendix A: Attributes	
Appendix B: English language	
Appendix C: Maintenance (funds)	
Appendix D: Immigration rules for leave to remain as a Highly Skilled Migrant as at 28 February 2008 [not reproduced]	
Appendix E: Maintenance (funds) for the family of Relevant Points Based Systems Migrants	
Appendix F: Immigration rules relating to Highly Skilled Migrants, the International Graduates Scheme, the Fresh Talent: Working in Scotland Scheme, Businesspersons, Innovators, Investors and Writers, Composers and Artists as at 29 June 2008 [not reproduced]	
Appendix G – Countries participating in the Tier 5 Youth Mobility Scheme	
Appendix H – Countries whose nationals are subject to different documentary requirements under Tier 4 of the Points Based System	

Introduction

1. The Home Secretary has made changes in the Rules laid down by him as to the practice to be followed in the administration of the Immigration Acts for regulating entry into and the stay of persons in the United Kingdom and contained in the statement laid before Parliament on 23 March 1990 (HC 251) (as amended). This statement contains the Rules as changed and replaces the provisions of HC 251 (as amended).
2. Immigration Officers, Entry Clearance Officers and all staff of the Home Office Immigration and Nationality Directorate will carry out their duties without regard to the race, colour or religion of persons seeking to enter or remain in the United Kingdom and in compliance with the provisions of the Human Rights Act 1998.
3. In these Rules words importing the masculine gender include the feminine unless the contrary intention appears.

Implementation and transitional provisions

4. These Rules come into effect on 1 October 1994 and will apply to all decisions taken on or after that date save that any application made before 1 October 1994 for entry clearance, leave to enter or remain or variation of leave to enter or remain other than an application for leave by a person seeking asylum shall be decided under the provisions of HC 251, as amended, as if these Rules had not been made.

Application

5. Save where expressly indicated, these Rules do not apply to those persons who are entitled to enter or remain in the United Kingdom by virtue of the provisions of the 2006 EEA Regulations. But any person who is not entitled to rely on the provisions of those Regulations is covered by these Rules.

Interpretation

6. In these Rules the following interpretations apply:

'the Immigration Acts' mean the Immigration Act 1971 and the Immigration Act 1988.

'the 1993 Act' is the Asylum and Immigration Appeals Act 1993.

'the 1996 Act' is the Asylum and Immigration Act 1996

'the 2006 EEA Regulations' means the Immigration (European Economic Area) Regulations 2006

'adoption' unless the contrary intention appears, includes a de facto adoption in accordance with the requirements of paragraph 309A of these Rules, and 'adopted' and 'adoptive parent' should be construed accordingly.

'Approved Destination Status Agreement with China' means the Memorandum of Understanding on visa and related issues concerning tourist groups from the People's Republic of China to the United Kingdom as a approved destination, signed on 21 January 2005.

'a bona fide private education institution' is a private education institution which:

(a) maintains satisfactory records of enrolment and attendance of students, and supplies these to the Border and Immigration Agency when requested;

(b) provides courses which involve a minimum of 15 hours organised daytime study per week;

(c) ensures a suitably qualified tutor is present during the hours of study to offer teaching and instruction to the students;

(d) offers courses leading to qualifications recognised by the appropriate accreditation bodies;

(e) employs suitably qualified staff to provide teaching, guidance and support to the students;

(f) provides adequate accommodation, facilities, staffing levels and equipment to support the numbers of students enrolled at the institution; and

(g) if it offers tuition support to external students at degree level, ensures that such students are registered with the UK degree awarding body.

'civil partner' means a civil partnership which exists under or by virtue of the Civil Partnership Act 2004 (and any reference to a civil partner is to be read accordingly);

'degree level study' means a course which leads to a recognised United Kingdom degree at bachelor's level or above, or an equivalent qualification at level 6 or above of the revised National Qualifications Framework, or levels 9 or above of the Scottish Credit and Qualifications Framework.

Under Part 8 of these Rules, **'post-graduate level study'** means a course at level 7 or above of the revised National Qualifications Framework or Qualifications and Credit Framework, or level 11 or above of the Scottish Credit and Qualifications Framework, which leads to a recognised United Kingdom postgraduate degree at Master's level or above, or an equivalent qualification at the same level.

'foundation degree' means a programme of study which leads to a qualification awarded by an English higher education institution with degree awarding powers which is at a minimum of level 5 on the revised National Qualifications Framework, or awarded on a directly equivalent basis in the devolved administrations.

A **'UK recognised body'** is an institution that has been granted degree awarding powers by either a Royal Charter, an Act of Parliament or the Privy Council.

For the purposes of these Rules we will consider the Foundation Programme Office and the Yorkshire and Humber Strategic Health Authority as equivalent to UK Recognised Bodies.

A **'UK listed body'** is an institution that is not a UK recognised body but which provides full courses that lead to the award of a degree by a UK recognised body.

'EEA national' has the meaning given in regulation 2(1) of the 2006 EEA Regulations.

'an external student' is a student studying for a degree from a UK degree awarding body without any requirement to attend the UK degree awarding body's premises or a UK Listed Body's premises for lectures and tutorials.

'United Kingdom passport' bears the meaning it has in the Immigration Act 1971.

'a UK Bachelors degree' means

(a) A programme of study or research which leads to the award, by or on behalf of a university, college or other body which is authorised by Royal Charter or by or under an Act of Parliament to grant degrees, of a qualification designated by the awarding institution to be of Bachelors degree level; or

(b) A programme of study or research, which leads to a recognised award for the purposes of section 214(2)(c) of the Education Reform Act 1988, of a qualification designated by the awarding institution to be of Bachelors degree level.

'Immigration Officer' includes a Customs Officer acting as an Immigration Officer.

'Multiple Entry work permit employment' is work permit employment where the person concerned does not intend to spend a continuous period in the United Kingdom in work permit employment.

'public funds' means

(a) housing under Part VI or VII of the Housing Act 1996 and under Part II of the Housing Act 1985, Part I or II of the Housing (Scotland) Act 1987, Part II of the Housing (Northern Ireland) Order 1981 or Part II of the Housing (Northern Ireland) Order 1988;

(b) attendance allowance, severe disablement allowance, carer's allowance and disability living allowance under Part III of the Social Security Contribution and Benefits Act 1992;, income support, council tax benefit and housing benefit under Part VII of that Act; a social fund payment under Part VIII of that Act; child benefit under Part IX of that Act; income based jobseeker's allowance under the Jobseekers Act 1995, income related allowance under Part 1 of the Welfare Reform Act 2007 (employment and support allowance) state pension credit under the State Pension Credit Act 2002; or child tax credit and working tax credit under Part 1 of the Tax Credits Act 2002.

(c) attendance allowance, severe disablement allowance, carer's allowance and disability living allowance under Part III of the Social Security Contribution and Benefits (Northern Ireland) Act 1992; income support, council tax benefit and, housing benefit under Part VII of that Act; a social fund payment under Part VIII of that Act; child benefit under Part IX of that Act; income based jobseeker's allowance under the Jobseekers (Northern Ireland) Order 1995 or income related allowance under Part 1 of the Welfare Reform Act (Northern Ireland) 2007.

'settled in the United Kingdom' means that the person concerned:

(a) is free from any restriction on the period for which he may remain save that a person entitled to an exemption under Section 8 of the Immigration Act 1971 (otherwise than as a member of the home forces) is not to be regarded as settled in the United Kingdom except in so far as Section 8(5A) so provides; and

(b) is either:

(i) ordinarily resident in the United Kingdom without having entered or remained in breach of the immigration laws; or

(ii) despite having entered or remained in breach of the immigration laws, has subsequently entered lawfully or has been granted leave to remain and is ordinarily resident.

'**a parent**' includes

(a) the stepfather of a child whose father is dead and the reference to stepfather includes a relationship arising through civil partnership;

(b) the stepmother of a child whose mother is dead and the reference to stepmother includes a relationship arising through civil partnership and;

(c) the father as well as the mother of an illegitimate child where he is proved to be the father;

(d) an adoptive parent, where a child was adopted in accordance with a decision taken by the competent administrative authority or court in a country whose adoption orders are recognised by the United Kingdom or where a child is the subject of a de facto adoption in accordance with the requirements of paragraph 309A of these Rules (except that an adopted child or a child who is the subject of a de facto adoption may not make an application for leave to enter or remain in order to accompany, join or remain with an adoptive parent under paragraphs 297–303);

(e) in the case of a child born in the United Kingdom who is not a British citizen, a person to whom there has been a genuine transfer of parental responsibility on the ground of the original parent(s)' inability to care for the child.

'**intention to live permanently with the other**' means an intention to live together, evidenced by a clear commitment from both parties that they will live together permanently in the United Kingdom immediately following the outcome of the application in question or as soon as circumstances permit thereafter, and 'intends to live permanently with the other' shall be construed accordingly.

'**present and settled**' means that the person concerned is settled in the United Kingdom, and, at the time that an application under these Rules is made, is physically present here or is coming here with or to join the applicant and intends to make the United Kingdom their home with the applicant if their application is successful.

'**sponsor**' means the person in relation to whom an applicant is seeking leave to enter or remain as their spouse, fiance, civil partner, proposed civil partner, unmarried partner, same-sex partner or dependent relative, as the case may be, under paragraphs 277 to 295O or 317 to 319.

'**visa nationals**' are the persons specified in Appendix 1 to these Rules who need a visa for the United Kingdom.

'**non-visa nationals**' are persons who are not specified in Appendix 1 to these Rules.

'**specified national**' is a person specified in Appendix 3 to these Rules who seeks leave to enter the United Kingdom for a period of more than 6 months.

'**employment**' unless the contrary intention appears, includes paid and unpaid employment, paid and unpaid work placements undertaken as part of a course or period of study, self employment and engaging in business or any professional activity.

'**the Human Rights Convention**' means the Convention for the Protection of Human Rights and Fundamental Freedoms, agreed by the Council of Europe at Rome on 4th November 1950 as it has effect for the time being in relation to the United Kingdom.

'**immigration employment document**' means a work permit or any other document which relates to employment and is issued for the purpose of these Rules or in connection with leave to enter or remain in the United Kingdom.

'**Employment as a Doctor in Training**' means employment in a medical post or training programme which has been approved by the Postgraduate Medical Education and Training Board, or employment in a postgraduate training programme in dentistry.

'**these Rules**' means these immigration rules (HC 395) made under section 3(2) of the Immigration Act 1971.

'**Tier 1 (General) Migrant**' means a migrant who is granted leave under paragraphs 245A to 245D of these Rules.

A **'refugee'** is a refugee as defined in regulation 2 of The Refugee or Person in Need of International Protection (Qualification) Regulation 2006.

In part 6A of these Rules, 'relevant grant allocation period' means a specified period of time, which will be published by the Secretary of State on the UK Border Agency website, during which applications for entry clearance or leave to enter in respect of a particular route may be granted subject to the grant allocation for that period;

In part 6A of these Rules, 'grant allocation' means a limit, details of which will be published by the Secretary of State on the UK Border Agency website, on the number of grants of entry clearance or leave to enter which may be granted in respect of a particular route during the relevant grant allocation period;

Under Part 6A of these Rules, **'Highly Skilled Migrant'** means a migrant granted leave under paragraphs 135A to 135G of the Rules in force before 30th June 2008.

Under Part 6A of these Rules, **'Highly Skilled Migrant Programme Approval Letter'** means a letter issued by the Home Office confirming that the applicant meets the criteria specified by the Secretary of State for entry to or stay in the UK under the Highly Skilled Migrant Programme.

Under Part 6A of these Rules, **'Innovator'** means a migrant granted leave under paragraphs 210A to 210F of the Rules in force before 30th June 2008.

Under Part 6A of these Rules, **'Lawfully'** means with valid leave.

Under Part 6A of these Rules, **'Participant in the Fresh Talent Working in Scotland Scheme'** means a migrant granted leave under paragraphs 143A to 143F of the Rules in force before 30th June 2008.

Under Part 6A of these Rules, **'Participant in the International Graduates Scheme'** means a migrant granted leave under paragraphs 135O to 135T of the Rules in force before 30th June 2008.

Under Part 6A of these Rules, **'Postgraduate Doctor or Dentist'** means a migrant who is granted leave under paragraphs 70 to 75 of these Rules.

Under Part 6A of these Rules, **'Self-Employed'** means an applicant is registered as self-employed with HM Revenue & Customs, or is employed by a company of which the applicant is a controlling shareholder.

Under Part 6A of these Rules, **'Student'** means a migrant who is granted leave under paragraphs 57 to 62 of these Rules.

Under Part 6A of these Rules, **'Student Nurse'** means a migrant who is granted leave under paragraphs 63 to 69 of these Rules.

Under Part 6A of these Rules, **'Student Re-Sitting an Examination'** means a migrant who is granted leave under paragraphs 69A to 69F of these Rules.

Under Part 6A of these Rules, **'Student Writing-Up a Thesis'** means a migrant who is granted leave under paragraphs 69G to 69L of these Rules.

Under Part 6A of these Rules, **'Work Permit Holder'** means a migrant who is granted leave under paragraphs 128 to 133 of these Rules.

Under Part 6A of these Rules, **'Prospective Student'** means a migrant who is granted leave under paragraphs 82 to 87 of these rules.

Under Part 6A of these Rules, an **'A-rated Sponsor'** is a Sponsor which is recorded as being 'A-rated' on the register of licensed Sponsors maintained by the United Kingdom Border Agency.

Under Part 6A and Appendix A of these Rules, a **'B-Rated Sponsor'** is a sponsor which is recorded as being 'B-Rated' on the register of licensed sponsors maintained by the United Kingdom Border Agency.

Under Part 6A of these Rules, **'Highly Trusted Sponsor'** means a sponsor which is recorded as being 'Highly Trusted' on the register of licensed sponsors maintained by the United Kingdom Border Agency.

Under Part 6A of these Rules, **'Certificate of Sponsorship'** means an authorisation issued by the Secretary of State to a Sponsor in respect of one or more applications, or potential applications, for entry clearance, leave to enter or remain as a Tier 2 migrant or a Tier 5 migrant in accordance with these Rules.

Under Part 6A and Appendix A of these Rules, **'Confirmation of Acceptance for Studies'** means a unique reference number electronically issued by a sponsor via the Sponsor Management System to an applicant for entry clearance, leave to enter or remain as a Tier 4 Migrant in accordance with these Rules.

Under Part 6A of these Rules, **'Certificate of Sponsorship Checking Service'** means a computerised interface with the Points Based System computer database which allows a United Kingdom Border Agency caseworker or entry clearance officer assessing a migrant's application for entry clearance, leave to enter or leave to remain to access and review details of the migrant's Certificate of Sponsorship, including details of the migrant's Sponsor, together with details of the job and other details associated with the circumstances in which the Certificate of Sponsorship was issued.

Under Part 6A and Appendix A of these Rules, **'length of the period of engagement'** is the period beginning with the employment start date as recorded on the Certificate of Sponsorship Checking service entry which relates to the Certificate of Sponsorship reference number for which the migrant was awarded points under Appendix A and ending on the employment end date as recorded in the same entry.

Under Part 6A and Appendix A of these Rules, **'working for the same employer'** includes working for the business or concern in respect of which employment the earlier grant of leave was granted where that business or concern has, since that date, merged with, or been taken over by, another entity.

Under Part 6A and Appendix A of these Rules, **'Designated Competent Body'** means an organisation which has been approved by the UK Border Agency to endorse applicants as a Tier 1 (Exceptional Talent) Migrant.

Under Part 6A and Appendix A of these Rules, **'Tier 1 (Exceptional Talent) Unique Reference Number'** means a unique reference number issued for the purposes of managing the Tier 1 (Exceptional Talent) Limit and provided by the UK Border Agency to an applicant prior to making his application as a Tier 1 (Exceptional Talent) Migrant.

For the purpose of para 320(7B) of these Rules 'Removal Decision' means (a) a decision to remove in accordance with section 10 of the Immigration and Asylum Act 1999; (b) a decision to remove an illegal entrant by way of directions under paragraphs 8 to 10 of Schedule 2 to the Immigration Act 1971 or (c) a decision to remove in accordance with section 47 of the Immigration, Asylum and Nationality Act 2006. Pending appeal has the same meaning as in section 104 of the nationality, immigration and asylum act 2002.

Under Part 6A of these Rules, **'Confirmation of Acceptance for Studies Checking Service'** means a computerised interface with the Points Based System computer database which allows a United Kingdom Border Agency caseworker or entry clearance officer assessing a migrant's application for entry clearance, leave to enter or leave to remain as a Tier 4 migrant under these Rules to access and review details of the migrant's Confirmation of Acceptance for Studies, including details of the migrant's Sponsor, together with details of the course of study and other details associated with the circumstances in which the Confirmation of Acceptance for Studies was issued.

Under Part 6A of these Rules, '**Established Entertainer**' means an applicant who is applying for leave to remain as a Tier 2 (General) Migrant or a Tier 2 (Intra-Company Transfer) Migrant in respect of whom the following conditions are satisfied:

(a) the Certificate of Sponsorship Checking Service entry to which the applicant's Certificate of Sponsorship reference number relates, records that the applicant is being sponsored in an occupation which is defined in the United Kingdom Border Agency's Transitional Guidance as being a job in the entertainment sector,

(b) the applicant has, or has previously had, entry clearance, leave to enter or leave to remain in the UK as a Work Permit Holder, and the work permit that led to that grant was issued in the sports and entertainment category to enable him to work in the occupation in which he is, at the date of the application for leave to remain, currently being sponsored,

(c) the applicant's last grant of leave was:

  (i) as a Work Permit Holder in the sports and entertainment category, provided the work permit on the basis of which that leave was granted was issued in the sports and entertainment category to enable him to work either in the occupation in which he is, at the date of the current application for leave to remain, currently being sponsored, or in another occupation which is defined in the UK Border Agency's Transitional Guidance as being a job in the entertainment sector, or

  (ii) leave to remain as a Tier 2 (General) Migrant or a Tier 2 (Intra-Company Transfer) Migrant, provided (in either case):

    (1) he previously had leave as a Work Permit Holder in the sports and entertainment category to work as described in (i) above,

    (2) he has not been granted entry clearance in this or any other route since his last grant of leave as a Work Permit Holder, and

(3) his last grant of leave was made to enable him to work either in the occupation in which he is, at the date of the current application for leave to remain, currently being sponsored or in another occupation which is defined in the UK Border Agency's Transitional Guidance as being a job in the entertainment sector,

(d) the Certificate of Sponsorship Checking Service entry to which the applicant's Certificate of Sponsorship reference number relates records:

(i) that the applicant will be paid a salary for the job that is at or above the appropriate entertainments industry rate, as listed in the United Kingdom Border Agency's Transitional Guidance; and

(ii) that before agreeing to employ the applicant, the Sponsor consulted with such bodies as the United Kingdom Border Agency's Transitional Guidance indicates that it should consult with before employing someone in this capacity, and

(e) the applicant has not spent a period of 5 years or more in the UK, beginning with the last grant of entry clearance, as a Qualifying Work Permit Holder, Tier 2 (General) Migrant or Tier 2 (Intra-Company Transfer) Migrant, or in any combination of these.

Under Part 6A of these Rules, '**Qualifying Work Permit Holder**' means a Work Permit Holder who was issued a work permit in the business and commercial or sports and entertainment work permit categories.

Under Part 6A of these Rules, '**Senior Care Worker**' means an applicant who is applying for leave to remain as a Tier 2 (General) Migrant or a Tier 2 (Intra-Company Transfer) Migrant in respect of whom the following conditions are satisfied:

(a) the Certificate of Sponsorship Checking Service entry to which the applicant's Certificate of Sponsorship reference number relates, records that the applicant is being sponsored in an occupation which is defined in the codes of practice for Tier 2 sponsors published by the UK Border Agency as being a Senior Care Worker role,

(b) the applicant's last grant of leave was:

(i) as a Qualifying Work Permit Holder, or

(ii) leave to remain as a Tier 2 (General) Migrant or a Tier 2 (Intra-Company Transfer) Migrant, provided (in either case):

(1) he previously had leave as a Qualifying Work Permit Holder, and

(2) he has not been granted entry clearance in this or any other route since his last grant of leave as a Qualifying Work Permit Holder.

(c) the work permit or Certificate of Sponsorship that led to the last grant of leave was issued to enable the applicant to work as a senior care worker, and

(d) the applicant has not spent a period of 5 years or more in the UK, beginning with the last grant of entry clearance, as a Qualifying Work Permit Holder, Tier 2 (General) Migrant or Tier 2 (Intra-Company Transfer) Migrant, or in any combination of these.

Under Part 6A of these Rules, '**Sponsor**' means the person or Government that the Certificate of Sponsorship Checking Service or Confirmation of Acceptance for Studies Checking Service records as being the Sponsor for a migrant.

Under Part 6A of these Rules, a reference to a '**sponsor licence**' means a licence granted by the Secretary of State to a person who, by virtue of such a grant, is licensed as a Sponsor under Tiers 2, 4 or 5 of the Points Based System.

Under Part 6A of these Rules, '**supplementary employment**' means other employment in the same profession and at the same professional level as that which the migrant is being sponsored to do provided that:

(a) the migrant remains working for the Sponsor in the employment that the Certificate of Sponsorship Checking Service records that the migrant is being sponsored to do,

(b) the other employment does not exceed 20 hours per week and takes place outside of the hours when the migrant is contracted to work for the Sponsor in the employment the migrant is being sponsored to do.

Under part 6A and Appendix A of these Rules, '**overseas higher education institution**' means an institution which holds overseas accreditation confirmed by UK NARIC as offering degree programmes which are equivalent to UK degree level qualifications, and which teach no more than half of a degree programme in the UK as a study abroad programme.

'Business person' means a migrant granted leave under paragraphs 200 to 208 of the Rules in force before 30th June 2008.

'Investor' means a migrant granted leave under paragraphs 224 to 229 of the Rules in force before 30th June 2008.

'Self-employed Lawyer' means a migrant granted entry clearance, or leave to enter or remain, outside the Rules under the concession for Self-employed lawyers that formerly appeared in Chapter 6, Section 1 Annex D of the Immigration Directorate instructions.

'Tier 1 (General) Migrant' means a migrant who is granted leave under paragraphs 245B to 245F of these Rules.

'Tier 1 (Entrepreneur) Migrant' means a migrant who is granted leave under paragraphs 245H to 245N of these Rules.

'Tier 1 (Investor) Migrant' means a migrant who is granted leave under paragraphs 245O to 245U of these Rules.

'Tier 1 (Post-Study Work) Migrant' means a migrant who is granted leave under paragraphs 245V to 245ZA of these Rules.

'Tier 1 Migrant' means a migrant who is granted leave as Tier 1 (General) Migrant, a Tier 1 (Entrepreneur) Migrant, a Tier 1 (Investor) Migrant or a Tier 1 (Post-Study Work) Migrant.

'Points Based System Migrant' means a migrant applying for or granted leave as a Tier 1 Migrant, a Tier 2 Migrant, a Tier 4 Migrant or a Tier 5 Migrant.

'Tier 2 (General) Migrant' means a migrant granted leave under paragraphs 245ZB to 245ZH of these Rules and who obtains points under paragraphs 59 to 84 of Appendix A but who does not obtain points under the intra-company transfer provisions in Table 10 of that Appendix.

'Tier 2 (Intra-Company Transfer) Migrant' means a migrant granted leave under paragraphs 245ZB to 245ZH of these Rules and who obtains points under paragraphs 59 to 84 of Appendix A including points under the intra-company transfer provisions of that Appendix.

'Tier 2 (Minister of Religion) Migrant' means a migrant granted leave under paragraphs 245ZB to 245ZH of these Rules and who obtains points under paragraphs 85 to 92 of Appendix A.

'Tier 2 (Sportsperson) Migrant' means a migrant granted leave under paragraphs 245ZB to 245ZH of these Rules and who obtains points under paragraphs 93 to 100 of Appendix A.

'Tier 2 Migrant' means a migrant granted leave under paragraphs 245ZB to 245ZH of these Rules.

'Tier 4 (General) Student' means a migrant granted leave under paragraphs 245ZT to 245ZY of these Rules.

'Tier 4 (Child) Student' means a migrant granted leave under paragraphs 245ZZ to 245ZZD of these Rules.

'Tier 4 Migrant' means a Tier 4 (General) Student or a Tier 4 (Child) Student.

'Tier 5 (Youth Mobility) Temporary Migrant' means a migrant granted leave under paragraphs 245ZI to 245ZL of these Rules.

'Tier 5 (Temporary Worker) Migrant' means a migrant granted leave under paragraphs 245ZM to 245ZS of these Rules.

'Tier 5 Migrant' means a migrant who is either a Tier 5 (Temporary Worker) Migrant or a Tier 5 (Youth Mobility) Temporary Migrant.

'Tier 2 Interim Limit' means: the number of Certificates of Sponsorship available to be assigned by the Secretary of State to Sponsors under the Tier 2 (General) Migrant route between 21 December 2010 and 5 April 2011.

'Exceptional Consideration Process' means: the process for assigning additional Certificates of Sponsorship to Sponsors under the Tier 2 Interim Limit as set out in the Addendum to the 'Policy Guidance for Tier 2 and Tier 5 Sponsors'.

'Jewish Agency Employee' means a migrant granted leave outside of these Rules under the concession that formerly appeared in Chapter 17 Section 5 Part 2 of the Immigration Directorate Instructions.

'Member of the Operational Ground Staff of an Overseas-owned Airline' means a migrant granted leave under paragraphs 178 to 185 of the Rules in force before 27 November 2008.

'Minister of Religion, Missionary or Member of a Religious Order' means a migrant granted leave under paragraphs 170 to 177A of the Rules in force before 27 November 2008.

'Overseas Qualified Nurse or Midwife' means a migrant granted leave under paragraphs 69M to 69R of the Rules in force before 27 November 2008.

'Participant in the Science and Engineering Graduates Scheme' means a migrant granted leave under paragraphs 135O to 135T of the Rules in force before 1 May 2007.

'Representative of an Overseas Newspaper, News Agency or Broadcasting Organisation' means a migrant granted leave under paragraphs 136 to 143 of the Rules in force before 27 November 2008.

'**Student Union Sabbatical Officer**' means a migrant granted leave under paragraphs 87A to 87F of the Rules in force before 27 November 2008.

'**Working Holidaymaker**' means a migrant granted leave under paragraphs 95 to 97 of the Rules in force before 27 November 2008.

A '**Business Visitor**' is a person granted leave to enter or remain in the UK under paragraphs 46G–46L, 75A–F or 75G–M of these Rules.

An '**Academic Visitor**' is a person who is from an overseas academic institution or who is highly qualified within his own field of expertise seeking leave to enter the UK to carry out research and associated activities for his own purposes.

A '**Visiting Professor**' is a person who is seeking leave to enter the UK as an academic professor to accompany students who are studying here on Study Abroad Programmes.

A '**Sports Visitor**' is a person granted leave to enter or remain in the UK under paragraphs 46M–46R of these Rules.

An '**Amateur**' is a person who engages in a sport or creative activity solely for personal enjoyment and who is not seeking to derive a living from the activity.

A '**Series of events**' is two or more linked events, such as a tour, or rounds of a competition, which do not add up to a league or a season.

An '**Entertainer Visitor**' is a person granted leave to enter or remain in the UK under paragraphs 46S–46X of these Rules.

A '**Special Visitor**' is a person granted leave for a short-term visit in the following circumstances:

(a) A person granted leave to enter or remain in the UK as a visitor for private medical treatment under paragraphs 51–56 of these Rules

(b) A person granted leave to enter or remain in the UK for the purpose of marriage or to enter into civil partnership under paragraphs 56D–56F of these Rules

(c) A person granted leave to enter or remain in the UK as a Parent of a child at school under paragraphs 56A–56C of these Rules

(d) A person granted leave to enter or remain in the UK as a Child Visitor under paragraphs 46A–46F of these Rules

(e) A person granted leave to enter or remain in the UK as a Student Visitor under paragraphs 56K–56M of these Rules

(f) A person granted leave to enter or remain in the UK as a Prospective Student under paragraphs 82–87 of these Rules

(g) A person granted leave to enter the UK as a Visitor in transit under paragraphs 47–50 of these Rules, or

(h) A person granted entry clearance, leave to enter or leave to remain in the UK as a Prospective Entrepreneur under paragraphs 56n–56Q of these Rules.

A '**Permissible Activity**' means a business activity of a type listed in United Kingdom Border Agency guidance specifying the activities that a business person may undertake during a short-term business visit to the UK.

'**Writer, Composer or Artist**' means a migrant granted leave under paragraphs 232 to 237 of the Rules in force before 30th June 2008.

In paragraph 320(7B) and paragraph 320(11) of these Rules:

'Deception' means making false representations or submitting false documents (whether or not material to the application), or failing to disclose material facts.

'Illegal Entrant' has the same definition as in section 33(1) of the Immigration Act 1971.

'Overstayed' or 'Overstaying' means the applicant has stayed in the UK beyond the time limit attached to his leave, or beyond the period that his leave was extended under sections 3C or 3D of the Immigration Act 1971.

In paragraph 320(22) and 322(12) of these Rules:

'relevant NHS body' means

(a) in relation to England–

(i) a National Health Service Trust established under section 25 of the National Health Service Act 2006,

(ii) a NHS foundation trust.

(b) in relation to Wales–

(i) a Local Health Board established under section 11 of the National Health Service (Wales) Act 2006,

(ii) a National Health Service Trust established under section 18 of the National Health Service (Wales) Act 2006,

(iii) a Special Health Authority established under 22 of the National Health Service (Wales) Act 2006.

(c) in relation to Scotland–

(i) a Health Board or Special Health Board established under section 2 of the National Health Service (Scotland) Act 1978,

(ii) the Common Services Agency for the Scottish Health Service established under section 10 of that Act,

(iii) Healthcare Improvement Scotland established under section 10A of that Act.

(d) in relation to Northern Ireland–

(i) the Regional Health and Social Care Board established under the Health and Social Care (Reform) Act (Northern Ireland) 2009,

(ii) a Health and Social Care trust established under the Health and Personal Social Services (Northern Ireland) Order 1991 and renamed under the Health and Social Care (Reform) Act (Northern Ireland) 2009.

'relevant NHS regulations' means

(i) The National Health Service (Charges to Overseas Visitors) (Amendment) (Wales) Regulations 2004;

(ii) The National Health Service (Charges to Overseas Visitors) (Scotland) Regulations 1989 as amended;

(iii) The Health and Personal Social Services (Provision of Health Services to Persons not Ordinarily Resident) Regulations (Northern Ireland) 2005; or

(iv) The National Health Service (Charges to Overseas Visitors) Regulations 2011.

6A. For the purpose of these Rules, a person (P) is not to be regarded as having (or potentially having) recourse to public funds merely because P is (or will be) reliant in whole or in part on public funds provided to P's sponsor unless, as a result of P's presence in the United Kingdom, the sponsor is (or would be) entitled to increased or additional public funds (save where such entitlement to increased or additional public funds is by virtue of P and the sponsor's joint entitlement to benefits under the regulations referred to in paragraph 6B).

6B. Subject to paragraph 6C, a person (P) shall not be regarded as having recourse to public funds if P is entitled to benefits specified under section 115 of the Immigration and Asylum Act 1999 by virtue of regulations made under sub-sections (3) and (4) of that section or section 42 of the Tax Credits Act 2002.

6C. A person (P) making an application from outside the United Kingdom will be regarded as having recourse to public funds where P relies upon the future entitlement to any public funds that would be payable to P or to P's sponsor as a result of P's presence in the United Kingdom, (including those benefits to which P or the sponsor would be entitled as a result of P's presence in the United Kingdom under the regulations referred to in to paragraph 6B)'.

Part 1 – General provisions regarding leave to enter or remain in the United Kingdom

Leave to enter the United Kingdom

7. A person who is neither a British citizen nor a Commonwealth citizen with the right of abode nor a person who is entitled to enter or remain in the United Kingdom by virtue of the provisions of the 2006 EEA Regulations requires leave to enter the United Kingdom.

8. Under Sections 3 and 4 of the Immigration Act 1971 an Immigration Officer when admitting to the United Kingdom a person subject to immigration control under that Act may give leave to enter for a limited period and, if he does, may impose all or any of the following conditions:

(i) a condition restricting employment or occupation in the United Kingdom;

(ii) a condition requiring the person to maintain and accommodate himself, and any dependants of his, without recourse to public funds; and

(iii) a condition requiring the person to register with the police.

He may also require him to report to the appropriate Medical Officer of Environmental Health. Under Section 24 of the 1971 Act it is an offence knowingly to remain beyond the time limit or fail to comply with such a condition or requirement.

9. The time limit and any conditions attached will be made known to the person concerned either:

(i) by written notice given to him or endorsed by the Immigration Officer in his passport or travel document; or

(ii) in any other manner permitted by the Immigration (Leave to Enter and Remain) Order 2000.

Exercise of the power to refuse leave to enter the United Kingdom or to cancel leave to enter or remain which is in force

10. The power to refuse leave to enter the United Kingdom or to cancel leave to enter or remain which is already in force is not to be exercised by an Immigration Officer acting on his own. The authority of a Chief Immigration Officer or of an Immigration Inspector must always be obtained.

Suspension of leave to enter or remain in the United Kingdom

10A. Where a person has arrived in the United Kingdom with leave to enter or remain which is in force but which was given to him before his arrival he may be examined by an Immigration Officer under paragraph 2A of Schedule 2 to the Immigration Act 1971. An Immigration Officer examining a person under paragraph 2A may suspend that person's leave to enter or remain in the United Kingdom until the examination is completed.

Cancellation of leave to enter or remain in the United Kingdom

10B. Where a person arrives in the United Kingdom with leave to enter or remain in the United Kingdom which is already in force, an Immigration Officer may cancel that leave.

Requirement for persons arriving in the United Kingdom or seeking entry through the Channel Tunnel to produce evidence of identity and nationality

11. A person must, on arrival in the United Kingdom or when seeking entry through the Channel Tunnel, produce on request by the Immigration Officer:

(i) a valid national passport or other document satisfactorily establishing his identity and nationality; and

(ii) such information as may be required to establish whether he requires leave to enter the United Kingdom and, if so, whether and on what terms leave to enter should be given.

Requirement for a person not requiring leave to enter the United Kingdom to prove that he has the right of abode

12. A person claiming to be a British citizen must prove that he has the right of abode in the United Kingdom by producing either:

(i) a United Kingdom passport describing him as a British citizen or as a citizen of the United Kingdom and Colonies having the right of abode in the United Kingdom; or

(ii) a certificate of entitlement duly issued by or on behalf of the Government of the United Kingdom certifying that he has the right of abode.

13. A person claiming to be a Commonwealth citizen with the right of abode in the United Kingdom must prove that he has the right of abode by producing a certificate of entitlement duly issued to him by or on behalf of the Government of the United Kingdom certifying that he has the right of abode.

14. A Commonwealth citizen who has been given limited leave to enter the United Kingdom may later claim to have the right of abode. The time limit on his stay may be removed if he is able to establish a claim to the right of abode, for example by showing that:

(i) immediately before the commencement of the British Nationality Act 1981 he was a Commonwealth citizen born to or legally adopted by a parent who at the time of the birth had citizenship of the United Kingdom and Colonies by his birth in the United Kingdom or any of the Islands; and

(ii) he has not ceased to be a Commonwealth citizen in the meanwhile.

Common Travel Area

15. The United Kingdom, the Channel Islands, the Isle of Man and the Republic of Ireland collectively form a common travel area. A person who has been examined for the purpose of immigration control at the point at which he entered the area does not normally require leave to enter any other part of it. However certain persons subject to the Immigration (Control of Entry through the Republic of Ireland) Order 1972 (as amended) who enter the United Kingdom through the Republic of Ireland do require leave to enter. This includes:

(i) those who merely passed through the Republic of Ireland;

(ii) persons requiring visas;

(iii) persons who entered the Republic of Ireland unlawfully;

(iv) persons who are subject to directions given by the Secretary of State for their exclusion from the United Kingdom on the ground that their exclusion is conducive to the public good;

(v) persons who entered the Republic from the United Kingdom and Islands after entering there unlawfully or overstaying their leave.

Admission of certain British passport holders

16. A person in any of the following categories may be admitted freely to the United Kingdom on production of a United Kingdom passport issued in the United Kingdom and Islands or the Republic of Ireland prior to 1 January 1973, unless his passport has been endorsed to show that he was subject to immigration control:

(i) a British Dependent Territories citizen;

(ii) a British National (Overseas);

(iii) a British Overseas citizen;

(iv) a British protected person;

(v) a British subject by virtue of Section 30(a) of the British Nationality Act 1981, (who, immediately before the commencement of the 1981 Act would have been a British subject not possessing citizenship of the United Kingdom and Colonies or the citizenship of any other Commonwealth country or territory).

17. British Overseas citizens who hold United Kingdom passports wherever issued and who satisfy the Immigration Officer that they have, since 1 March 1968, been given indefinite leave to enter or remain in the United Kingdom may be given indefinite leave to enter.

Persons outside the United Kingdom

17A. Where a person is outside the United Kingdom but wishes to travel to the United Kingdom an Immigration Officer may give or refuse him leave to enter. An Immigration Officer may exercise these powers whether or not he is, himself, in the United Kingdom. However, an Immigration Officer is not obliged to consider an application for leave to enter from a person outside the United Kingdom.

17B. Where a person having left the common travel area, has leave to enter the United Kingdom which remains in force under article 13 of the Immigration (Leave to Enter and Remain) Order 2000, an Immigration Officer may cancel that leave. An Immigration Officer may exercise these powers whether or not he is, himself, in the United Kingdom. If a person outside the United Kingdom has leave to remain in the United Kingdom which is in force in this way, the Secretary of State may cancel that leave.

Returning Residents

18. A person seeking leave to enter the United Kingdom as a returning resident may be admitted for settlement provided the Immigration Officer is satisfied that the person concerned:

(i) had indefinite leave to enter or remain in the United Kingdom when he last left; and

(ii) has not been away from the United Kingdom for more than 2 years; and

(iii) did not receive assistance from public funds towards the cost of leaving the United Kingdom; and

(iv) now seeks admission for the purpose of settlement.

19. A person who does not benefit from the preceding paragraph by reason only of having been away from the United Kingdom too long may nevertheless be admitted as a returning resident if, for example, he has lived here for most of his life.

19A. Where a person who has indefinite leave to enter or remain in the United Kingdom accompanies, on a tour of duty abroad, a spouse, civil partner, unmarried partner or same-sex partner who is a member of HM Forces serving overseas, or a permanent member of HM Diplomatic Service, or a comparable United Kingdom-based staff member of the British Council, or a staff member of the Department for International Development who is a British Citizen or is settled in the United Kingdom, sub-paragraphs (ii) and (iii) of paragraph 18 shall not apply.

20. The leave of a person whose stay in the United Kingdom is subject to a time limit lapses on his going to a country or territory outside the common travel area if the leave was given for a period of six months or less or conferred by a visit visa. In other cases, leave lapses on the holder remaining outside the United Kingdom for a continuous period of more than two years. A person whose leave has lapsed and who returns after a temporary absence abroad within the period of this earlier leave has no claim to admission as a returning resident. His application to re-enter the United Kingdom should be considered in the light of all the relevant circumstances. The same time limit and any conditions attached will normally be reimposed if he meets the requirements of these Rules, unless he is seeking admission in a different capacity from the one in which he was last given leave to enter or remain.

Non-lapsing leave

20A. Leave to enter or remain in the United Kingdom will usually lapse on the holder going to a country or territory outside the common travel area. However, under article 13 of the Immigration (Leave to Enter and Remain) Order 2000 such leave will not lapse where it was given for a period exceeding six months or where it was conferred by means of an entry clearance (other than a visit visa).

Holders of restricted travel documents and passports

21. The leave to enter or remain in the United Kingdom of the holder of a passport or travel document whose permission to enter another country has to be exercised before a given date may be restricted so as to terminate at least 2 months before that date.

22. If his passport or travel document is endorsed with a restriction on the period for which he may remain outside his country of normal residence, his leave to enter or remain in the United Kingdom may be limited so as not to extend beyond the period of authorised absence.

23. The holder of a travel document issued by the Home Office should not be given leave to enter or remain for a period extending beyond the validity of that document. This paragraph and paragraphs 21–22 do not apply to a person who is eligible for admission for settlement or to a spouse or civil partner who is eligible for admission under paragraph 282 or to a person who qualifies for the removal of the time limit on his stay.

Leave to enter granted on arrival in the United Kingdom

23A. A person who is not a visa national and who is seeking leave to enter on arrival in the United Kingdom for a period not exceeding 6 months for a purpose for which prior entry clearance is not required under these Rules may be granted such leave, for a period not exceeding 6 months. This paragraph does not apply where the person is a British National (Overseas), a British overseas territories citizen, a British Overseas citizen, a British protected person, or a person who under the British Nationality Act 1981 is a British subject.

23B. A person who is a British National (Overseas), a British overseas territories citizen, a British Overseas citizen, a British protected person, or a person who under the British Nationality Act 1981 is a British subject, and who is seeking leave to enter on arrival in the United Kingdom for a purpose for which prior entry clearance is not required under these Rules may be granted such leave, irrespective of the period of time for which he seeks entry, for a period not exceeding 6 months.

Entry clearance

24. The following must produce to the Immigration Officer a valid passport or other identity document endorsed with a United Kingdom entry clearance issued to him for the purpose for which he seeks entry:

(i) a visa national;

(ii) any other person (other than British Nationals (Overseas), a British overseas territories citizen, a British Overseas citizen, a British protected person or a person who under the British Nationality Act 1981 is a British subject) who is seeking entry for a period exceeding six months or is seeking entry for a purpose for which prior entry clearance is required under these Rules.

Such a person will be refused leave to enter if he has no such current entry clearance. Any other person who wishes to ascertain in advance whether he is eligible for admission to the United Kingdom may apply for the issue of an entry clearance.

25. Entry clearance takes the form of a visa (for visa nationals) or an entry certificate (for non visa nationals). These documents are to be taken as evidence of the holder's eligibility for entry into the United Kingdom, and accordingly accepted as 'entry clearances' within the meaning of the Immigration Act 1971.

25A. An entry clearance which satisfies the requirements set out in article 3 of the Immigration (Leave to Enter and Remain) Order 2000 will have effect as leave to enter the United Kingdom. The requirements are that the entry clearance must specify the purpose for which the holder wishes to enter the United Kingdom and should be endorsed with the conditions to which it is subject or wish a statement that it has effect as indefinite leave to enter the United Kingdom. The holder of such an entry clearance will not require leave to enter on arrival in the United Kingdom and, for the purposes of these Rules, will be treated as a person who has arrived in the United Kingdom with leave to enter the United Kingdom which is in force but which was given to him before his arrival.

26. An application for entry clearance will be considered in accordance with the provisions in these Rules governing the grant or refusal of leave to enter. Where appropriate, the term 'Entry Clearance Officer' should be substituted for 'Immigration Officer'.

27. An application for entry clearance is to be decided in the light of the circumstances existing at the time of the decision, except that an applicant will not be refused an entry clearance where entry is sought in one of the categories contained in paragraphs 296–316 solely on account of his attaining the age of 18 years between receipt of his application and the date of the decision on it.

28. An applicant for an entry clearance must be outside the United Kingdom and Islands at the time of the application. An applicant for an entry clearance who is seeking entry as a visitor must apply to a post designated by the Secretary of State to accept applications for entry clearance for that purpose and from that category of applicant. Subject to paragrapgh 28A, any other application must be made to the post in the country or territory where the applicant is living which has been designated by the Secretary of State to accept applications for entry clearance for that purpose and from that category of applicant. Where there is no such post the applicant must apply to the appropriate designated post outside the country or territory where he is living.

28A. (a) An application for entry clearance as a Tier 5 (Temporary Worker) Migrant in the creative and sporting sub-category of Tier 5 may also be made at the post in the country or territory where the applicant is situated at the time of the application, provided that:

(i) the post has been designated by the Secretary of State to accept applications for entry clearance for that purpose and from that category of applicant,

(ii) the applicant is in that country or territory for a similar purpose to the activity he proposes to undertake in the UK, and

(iii) the applicant is able to demonstrate to the Entry Clearance Officer that he has authority to be living in that country or territory in accordance with its immigration laws. Those applicants who are known to the authorities of that country or territory but who have not been given permission to live in that country or territory will not be eligible to make an application.

(b) An application for entry clearance as a Tier 5 (Youth Mobility Scheme) Temporary Migrant may also be made at the post in the country or territory where the applicant is situated at the time of the application, provided that:

(i) the post has been designated by the Secretary of State to accept applications for entry clearance for that purpose and from that category of applicant, and

(ii) the applicant is able to demonstrate to the Entry Clearance Officer that he has authority to be living in that country or territory in accordance with its immigration laws and that when he was given authority to live in that country or territory he was given authority to live in that country or territory for a period of more than 6 months. Those applicants who are known to the authorities of that country or territory but who have not been given permission to live in that country or territory will not be eligible to make an application.

29. For the purposes of paragraph 28 'post' means a British Diplomatic Mission, British Consular post or the office of any person outside the United Kingdom and Islands who has been authorised by the Secretary of State to accept applications for entry clearance. A list of designated posts is published by the Foreign and Commonwealth Office.

30. An application for an entry clearance is not made until any fee required to be paid under the Consular Fees Act 1980 (including any Regulations or Orders made under that Act) has been paid.

30A. An entry clearance may be revoked if the Entry Clearance Officer is satisfied that:

(i) whether or not to the holder's knowledge, false representations were employed or material facts were not disclosed, either in writing or orally, for the purpose of obtaining the entry clearance; or

(ii) a change of circumstances since the entry clearance was issued has removed the basis of the holder's claim to be admitted to the United Kingdom, except where the change of circumstances amounts solely to his exceeding the age for entry in one of the categories contained in paragraphs 296–316 of these Rules since the issue of the entry clearance; or

(iii) the holder's exclusion from the United Kingdom would be conducive to the public good.

30B. An entry clearance shall cease to have effect where the entry clearance has effect as leave to enter and an Immigration Officer cancels that leave in accordance with paragraph 2A(8) of Schedule 2 to the Immigration Act 1971.

30C. An Immigration Officer may cancel an entry clearance which is capable of having effect as leave to enter if the holder arrives in the United Kingdom before the day on which the entry clearance becomes effective or if the holder seeks to enter the United Kingdom for a purpose other than the purpose specified in the entry clearance.

Variation of leave to enter or remain in the United Kingdom

31. Under Section 3(3) of the 1971 Act a limited leave to enter or remain in the United Kingdom may be varied by extending or restricting its duration, by adding, varying or revoking conditions or by removing the time limit (where upon any condition attached to the leave ceases to apply). When leave to enter or remain is varied an entry is to be made in the applicant's passport or travel document (and his registration certificate where appropriate) or the decision may be made known in writing in some other appropriate way.

31A. Where a person has arrived in the United Kingdom with leave to enter or remain in the United Kingdom which is in force but was given to him before his arrival, he may apply, on arrival at the port of entry in the United Kingdom, for variation of that leave. An Immigration Officer acting on behalf of the Secretary of State may vary the leave at the port of entry but is not obliged to consider an application for variation made at the port of entry. If an Immigration Officer acting on behalf of the Secretary of State has declined to consider an application for variation of leave at a port of entry but the leave has not been cancelled under paragraph 2A(8) of Schedule 2 to the Immigration Act 1971, the person seeking variation should apply to the Home office under paragraph 32.

32. DELETED

33. DELETED

33A. Where a person having left the common travel area, has leave to enter or remain in the United Kingdom which remains in force under article 13 of the Immigration (Leave to Enter and Remain) Order 2000., his leave may be varied (including any condition to which it is subject in such form and manner as permitted for the giving of leave to enter. However, the Secretary of State is not obliged to consider an application for variation of leave to enter or remain from a person outside the United Kingdom.

Knowledge of language and life in the United Kingdom

33B. A person has sufficient knowledge of the English language and sufficient knowledge about life in the United Kingdom for the purpose of an application for indefinite leave to remain under these rules (unless paragraph 33BA applies) if–

(a) (i) he has attended an ESOL course at an accredited college;

(ii) the course used teaching materials derived from the document entitled 'Citizenship Materials for ESOL Learners' (ISBN 1-84478-5424);

(iii) he has demonstrated relevant progress in accordance with paragraph 33F; and

(iv) he has attained a relevant qualification; or

(b) he has passed the test known as the 'Life in the UK Test' administered by an educational institution or other person approved for this purpose by the Secretary of State; or

(c) in the case of a person who is the spouse or civil partner or unmarried or same sex partner of:

(i) a permanent member of HM Diplomatic Service; or

(ii) a comparable UK-based staff member of the British Council on a tour of duty abroad; or

(iii) a staff member of the Department for International Development who is a British citizen or is settled in the UK, a person designated by the Secretary of State certifies in writing that he has sufficient knowledge of the English language and sufficient knowledge about life in the United Kingdom for this purpose.

33BA. (a) subject to sub-paragraph (b), for the purposes of an application for indefinite leave to remain under these Rules, where a person is making an application for indefinite leave to remain as:

(i) a work permit holder under paragraph 134;

(ii) a Highly Skilled Migrant under paragraph 135G;

(iii) a representative of an overseas newspaper, news agency or broadcasting organisation under paragraph 142;

(iv) a representative of an overseas business under paragraph 150;

(v) an overseas government employee under paragraph 167;

(vi) a Minister of religion, religious missionary, or member of a religious order under paragraph 176;

(vii) an airport based operational ground staff of an overseas-owned airline under paragraph 184;

(viii) a person established in business under paragraph 209;

(ix) an innovator under paragraph 210G;

(x) a person established in business under the provisions of EC Association Agreements under paragraph 222;

(xi) an investor under paragraph 230;

(xii) a writer, composer or artist under paragraph 238;

(xiii) a Tier 1 (Exceptional Talent) Migrant under paragraph 245BF;

(xiv) a Tier 1 (General) Migrant under paragraph 245CD;

(xv) a Tier 1 (Entrepreneur) Migrant under paragraph 245DF;

(xvi) a Tier 1 (Investor) Migrant under paragraph 245EF;

(xvii) a Tier 2 (Intra-Company Transfer) under paragraph 245GF;

(xviii) a Tier 2 (General), Tier 2 (Minister of religion) and Tier 2 (Sportsperson) Migrant under paragraph 245HF.

that person has sufficient knowledge of the English language and sufficient knowledge about life in the United Kingdom, only if they have passed the test known as the 'Life in the UK Test' administered by an educational institution or other person approved for this purpose by the Secretary of State.

(b) This sub-paragraph makes provision for transitional arrangements with regards to the requirement to pass the life in the UK Test for those people applying for indefinite leave to remain in one of the categories listed in 33BA(i)–(xviii):

(i) Where an applicant enrolled on an ESOL course or gained an ESOL qualification prior to 23rd November 2010, that applicant will be able to rely on an ESOL qualification to meet the requirement to demonstrate sufficient knowledge of the English language and sufficient knowledge about life in the United Kingdom for any future application for indefinite leave to remain under one of the categories listed in 33BA.

(ii) An applicant who enrolled on an ESOL course after 23rd November 2010 and applies for indefinite leave to remain in one of the categories listed in 33BA after 6th April 2011 will have to pass the life in the UK Test.

(iii) An applicant who enrolled on an ESOL course after 23rd November 2010 and who gains an ESOL qualification can continue to use that qualification in an application for indefinite leave to remain in one of the categories listed in 33BA if that application was made before 6th April 2011.

33C. In these Rules, an 'accredited college' is:

(a) a publicly funded college that is subject to inspection by the Office for Standards in Education, Children's Services and Skills (if situated in England), the Education and Training Inspectorate (if situated in Northern Ireland), Education Scotland (if situated in Scotland), Estyn (if situated in Wales); or an inspection programme that has been approved by the Island's Government (if situated in the Channel Islands or Isle of Man); or

(b) a private college that has been accredited by Accreditation UK, The British Accreditation Council (BAC), the Accreditation Body for Language Services (ABLS), the Accreditation Service for International Colleges (ASIC).

33D. In these Rules, a 'relevant qualification' is:

(a) an ESOL qualification in speaking and listening which is awarded or authenticated by a body which is recognised by the Office of Qualifications and Examinations Regulation (Ofqual) under section 132 of the Apprenticeships, Skills, Children and Learning Act 2009 and is determined by Ofqual as being at Entry Level; or

(b) one National Qualifications Unit in ESOL at Access 2, Access 3 or Intermediate 1 Level approved by the Scottish Qualifications Authority.

33E. In these Rules, a 'suitably qualified person' is a person who is deemed suitably qualified by the institution in which the assessment is undertaken.

33F. An applicant has 'demonstrated relevant progress' if he meets the requirements of paragraphs 33F (a) or (b).

(a) The requirements in respect of a relevant qualification awarded or authenticated by a body which is recognised by Ofqual under section 132 of the Apprenticeships, Skills, Children and Learning Act 2009, are that the applicant provides evidence to the Secretary of State that:

(i) prior to his commencing a course of study leading to a relevant qualification an ESOL assessment was undertaken by a suitably qualified person to assess his level of English language ability; and

(ii) he has successfully completed a course of study leading to a relevant qualification; and

(iii) having been assessed in accordance with paragraph (i) as being below Entry 1, he has attained a relevant qualification at Entry 1, 2 or 3; or

(iv) having been assessed in accordance with paragraph (i) as being at Entry 1, he has attained a relevant qualification at Entry 2 or 3; or

(v) having been assessed in accordance with paragraph (i) as being at Entry 2, he has attained a relevant qualification at Entry 3.

(b) The requirements in respect of a relevant qualification approved by the Scottish Qualifications Authority are that the applicant provides evidence to the Secretary of State that–

(i) prior to his commencing a course of study leading to a relevant qualification an ESOL assessment was undertaken by a suitably qualified person to assess his level of English language ability; and

(ii) he has successfully completed a course of study leading to a relevant qualification; and

(iii) having been assessed in accordance with paragraph (i) as being below Access 2, he has attained a relevant qualification at Access 2 or 3 or at Intermediate 1 level; or

(iv) having been assessed in accordance with paragraph (i) at Access 2, he has attained a relevant qualification at Access 3 or Intermediate 1 level; or

(v) having been assessed in accordance with paragraph (i) at Access 3, he has attained a relevant qualification at Intermediate 1 level.

33G. If in the special circumstances of any particular case the Secretary of State thinks fit, he may waive the need to fulfil the requirement to have sufficient knowledge of the English language and sufficient knowledge about life in the United Kingdom if he considers that, because of the applicant's physical or mental condition, it would be unreasonable to expect him to fulfil that requirement.

Specified forms and procedures for applications or claims in connection with immigration

34. An application form is specified when:

(i) it is posted on the website of the United Kingdom Border Agency of the Home Office,

(ii) it is marked on the form that it is a specified form for the purpose of the immigration rules,

(iii) it comes into force on the date specified on the form and/or in any accompanying announcement.

34A. Where an application form is specified, the application or claim must also comply with the following requirements:

(i) the application or claim must be made using the specified form,

(ii) any specified fee in connection with the application or claim must be paid in accordance with the method specified in the application form, separate payment form and/or related guidance notes, as applicable,

(iii) any section of the form which is designated as mandatory in the application form and/or related guidance notes must be completed as specified,

(iv) if the application form and/or related guidance notes require the applicant to provide biographical information, such information must be provided as specified,

(v) an appointment for the purposes stated in subparagraph (iv) must be made and must take place by the dates specified in any subsequent notification by the Secretary of State following receipt of the application, or as agreed by the Secretary of State,

(vi) where the application or claim is made by post or courier, or submitted in person:

(a) the application or claim must be accompanied by the photographs and documents specified as mandatory in the application form and/or related guidance notes,

(ab) those photographs must be in the same format specified as mandatory in the application form and/or related guidance notes, and

(b) the form must be signed by the applicant, and where applicable, the applicant's spouse, civil partner, same-sex partner or unmarried partner, save that where the applicant is under the age of eighteen, the form may be signed by the parent or legal guardian of the applicant on his behalf,

(vii) where the application or claim is made online:

(a) the photographs and documents specified as mandatory must be submitted in the manner directed in the application form and/or related online guidance notes and by such date as is specified in the acknowledgement of the online application,

(ab) those photographs must be in the same format specified as mandatory in the application form and/or related guidance notes, and

(b) the confirmation box (which states that the information contained in the application form is true and complete) must be completed by the applicant or, if the form is completed by an immigration adviser on the applicant's behalf, by the immigration adviser on specific instructions from the applicant that the information given is true and complete, and

(viii) the application or claim must be delivered in accordance with paragraph 34B.

34B. Where an application form is specified, it must be sent by prepaid post to the United Kingdom Border Agency of the Home Office, or submitted in person at a public enquiry office of the United Kingdom Border Agency of the Home Office, save for the following exceptions:

(i) an application may not be submitted at a public enquiry office of the United Kingdom Border Agency of the Home Office if it is an application for:

(a) limited or indefinite leave to remain as a sole representative or retired person of independent means (ba) limited or indefinite leave to remain as a Tier 1 (Investor) Migrant or Tier 1 (Entrepreneur) Migrant,

(b) indefinite leave to remain as a victim of domestic violence,

(c) a certificate of approval for a marriage or civil partnership,

(d) a Tier 4 or Tier 5 (Temporary Worker) sponsorship licence;

(e) Indefinite leave to remain as a businessperson, investor or innovator, or

(f) an extension of stay or indefinite leave to remain on the basis of long residence in the United Kingdom.

(ii) an application may be sent by courier to the United Kingdom Border Agency of the Home Office if it is an application for:

(a) limited or indefinite leave to remain as a sole representative, retired person of independent means or as a Tier 1 Migrant or Tier 2 Migrant;

(b) limited leave to remain for work permit employment, as a seasonal agricultural worker, for the purpose of employment under the Sectors-Based Scheme.

(c) Indefinite leave to remain as a businessperson, investor or innovator, or

(d) limited leave to remain as a Tier 5 (Temporary Worker) Migrant.

(iv) an applicant may submit an application online where this option is available on the United Kingdom Border Agency's website

34C. Where an application or claim in connection with immigration for which an application form is specified does not comply with the requirements in paragraph 34A, such application or claim will be invalid and will not be considered.

34D. Where the main applicant wishes to include applications or claims by any members of his family as his dependants on his own application form, the applications or claims of the dependants must meet the following requirements or they will be invalid and will not be considered:

(i) the application form must expressly permit the applications or claims of dependants to be included, and

(ii) such dependants must be the spouse, civil partner, unmarried or same-sex partner and/or children under the age of 18 of the main applicant.

Variation of Applications or Claims for Leave to Remain

34E. If a person wishes to vary the purpose of an application or claim for leave to remain in the United Kingdom and an application form is specified for such new purpose, the variation must comply with the requirements of paragraph 34A (as they apply at the date the variation is made) as if the variation were a new application or claim, or the variation will be invalid and will not be considered.

34F. Any valid variation of a leave to remain application will be decided in accordance with the immigration rules in force at the date such variation is made.

Determination of the date of an application or claim (or variation of an application or claim) in connection with immigration

34G. For the purposes of these rules, the date on which an application or claim (or a variation in accordance with paragraph 34E) is made is as follows:

(i) where the application form is sent by post, the date of posting,

(ii) where the application form is submitted in person, the date on which it is accepted by a public enquiry office of the United Kingdom Border Agency of the Home Office,

(iii) where the application form is sent by courier, the date on which it is delivered to the United Kingdom Border Agency of the Home Office, or

(iv) where the application form is submitted online, the date on which it is so submitted.

34H. Applications or claims for leave to remain made before 29 February 2008 for which a form was prescribed prior to 29 February 2008 shall be subject to the forms and procedures as in force on the date on which the application or claim was made.

34I. Where an application or claim is made no more than 21 days after the date on which a form is specified under the immigration rules and on a form that was permitted for such application or claim immediately prior to the date of such specification, the application or claim shall be deemed to have been made on the specified form.

Withdrawn applications or claims for leave to remain in the United Kingdom

34J. Where a person whose application or claim for leave to remain is being considered requests the return of his passport for the purpose of travel outside the common travel area, the application for leave shall, provided it has not already been determined, be treated as withdrawn as soon as the passport is returned in response to that request.

Undertakings

35. A sponsor of a person seeking leave to enter or variation of leave to enter or remain in the United Kingdom may be asked to give an undertaking in writing to be responsible for that person's maintenance and accommodation for the period of any leave granted, including any further variation. Under the Social Security Administration Act 1992 and the Social Security Administration (Northern Ireland) Act 1992, the Department of Social Security or, as the case may be, the Department of Health and Social Services in Northern Ireland, may seek to recover from the person giving such an undertaking any income support paid to meet the needs of the person in respect of whom the undertaking has been given. Under the Immigration and Asylum Act 1999 the Home Office may seek to recover from the person giving such an undertaking amounts attributable to any support provided under section 95 of the Immigration and Asylum Act 1999 (support for asylum seekers) to, or in respect of, the person in respect of whom the undertaking has been given. Failure by the sponsor to maintain that person in accordance with the undertaking, may also be an offence under section 105 of the Social Security Administration Act 1992 and/or under section 108 of the Immigration and Asylum Act 1999 if, as a consequence, asylum support and/or income support is provided to, or in respect of, that person.

Medical

36. A person who intends to remain in the United Kingdom for more than 6 months should normally be referred to the Medical Inspector for examination. If he produces a medical certificate he should be advised to hand it to the Medical Inspector. Any person seeking entry who mentions health or medical treatment as a reason for his visit, or who appears not to be in good mental or physical health, should also be referred to the Medical Inspector; and the Immigration Officer has discretion, which should be exercised sparingly, to refer for examination in any other case.

37. Where the Medical Inspector advises that a person seeking entry is suffering from a specified disease or condition which may interfere with his ability to support himself or his dependants, the Immigration Officer should take account of this, in conjunction with other factors, in deciding whether to admit that person. The Immigration Officer should also take account of the Medical Inspector's assessment of the likely course of treatment in deciding whether a person seeking entry for private medical treatment has sufficient means at his disposal.

38. A returning resident should not be refused leave to enter or have existing leave to enter or remain cancelled on medical grounds. But where a person would be refused leave to enter or have existing leave to enter or remain cancelled on medical grounds if he were not a returning resident or in any case where it is decided on compassionate grounds not to exercise the power to refuse leave to enter or to cancel existing leave to enter or remain, or in any other case where the Medical Inspector so recommends, the Immigration Officer should give the person concerned a notice requiring him to report to the Medical Officer of Environmental Health designated by the Medical Inspector with a view to further examination and any necessary treatment.

39. The Entry Clearance Officer has the same discretion as an Immigration Officer to refer applicants for entry clearance for medical examination and the same principles will apply to the decision whether or not to issue an entry clearance.

Students

39A. An application for a variation of leave to enter or remain made by a student who is sponsored by a government or international sponsorship agency may be refused if the sponsor has not given written consent to the proposed variation.

Part 2 – Persons seeking to enter or remain in the United Kingdom for visits

Visitors

Requirements for leave to enter as a general visitor

40. For the purposes of paragraphs 41–46 a general visitor includes a person living and working outside the United Kingdom who comes to the United Kingdom as a tourist. A person seeking leave to enter the United Kingdom as a Business Visitor, which includes Academic Visitors, must meet the requirements of paragraph 46G. A person seeking entry as a Sports Visitor must meet the requirements of paragraph 46M. A person seeking entry as an Entertainer Visitor must meet the requirements of paragraph 46S. A visitor seeking leave to enter for the purposes of marriage or to enter into a civil partnership must meet the requirements of paragraph 56D.

41. The requirements to be met by a person seeking leave to enter the United Kingdom as a general visitor are that he:

(i) is genuinely seeking entry as a general visitor for a limited period as stated by him, not exceeding 6 months or not exceeding 12 months in the case of a person seeking entry to accompany an academic visitor, provided in the latter case the visitor accompanying the academic visitor has entry clearance; and

(ii) intends to leave the United Kingdom at the end of the period of the visit as stated by him; and

(iii) does not intend to take employment in the United Kingdom; and

(iv) does not intend to produce goods or provide services within the United Kingdom, including the selling of goods or services direct to members of the public; and

(v) does not intend to undertake a course of study; and

(vi) will maintain and accommodate himself and any dependants adequately out of resources available to him without recourse to public funds or taking employment; or will, with any dependants, be maintained and accommodated adequately by relatives or friends; and

(vii) can meet the cost of the return or onward journey.; and

(viii) is not a child under the age of 18.

(ix) does not intend to do any of the activities provided for in paragraphs 46G(iii), 46M(iii) or 46S(iii); and

(x) does not, during his visit, intend to marry or form a civil partnership, or to give notice of marriage or civil partnership; and

(xi) does not intend to receive private medical treatment during his visit; and

(xii) is not in transit to a country outside the common travel area.

Leave to enter as a general visitor

42. A person seeking leave to enter to the United Kingdom as a general visitor may be admitted for a period not exceeding 6 months, or not exceeding 12 months in the case of a person accompanying an academic visitor, subject to a condition prohibiting employment, provided the Immigration Officer is satisfied that each of the requirements of paragraph 41 is met.

Refusal of leave to enter as a general visitor

43. Leave to enter as a general visitor is to be refused if the Immigration Officer is not satisfied that each of the requirements of paragraph 41 is met.

Requirements for an extension of stay as a general visitor

44. Six months is the maximum permitted leave which may be granted to a general visitor. The requirements for an extension of stay as a general visitor are that the applicant:

(i) meets the requirements of paragraph 41(ii)–(vii) and (ix)–(xii); and

(ii) has not already spent, or would not as a result of an extension of stay spend, more than 6 months in total in the United Kingdom or not more than 12 months in the case of a person accompanying an academic visitor as a general visitor. Any periods spent as a child visitor are to be counted as a period spent as a general visitor; and

(iii) has, or was last granted, entry clearance, leave to enter or leave to remain as a general visitor or as a child visitor.

Extension of stay as a general visitor

45. An extension of stay as a general visitor may be granted, subject to a condition prohibiting employment, provided the Secretary of State is satisfied that each of the requirements of paragraph 44 is met.

Refusal of extension of stay as a general visitor

46. An extension of stay as a general visitor is to be refused if the Secretary of State is not satisfied that each of the requirements of paragraph 44 is met.

Child visitors

Requirements for leave to enter as a child visitor

46A. The requirements to be met by a person seeking leave to enter the United Kingdom as a child visitor are that the applicant:

(i) is genuinely seeking entry as a child visitor for a limited period as stated, not exceeding 6 months or not exceeding 12 months to accompany an academic visitor, provided in the latter case the applicant has entry clearance; and

(ii) meets the requirements of paragraph 41(ii)–(iv), (vi)–(vii) and (x)–(xii); and

(iii) is under the age of 18; and

(iv) can demonstrate that suitable arrangements have been made for their travel to, and reception and care in the United Kingdom. If a foster carer or relative (not a parent or guardian) will be responsible for the care of the applicant, the arrangements must meet the requirements laid down in guidance published by the UK Border Agency; and

(v) has a parent or guardian in their home country or country of habitual residence who is responsible for their care and who confirms that they consent to the arrangements for the applicant's travel, reception and care in the United Kingdom; and

(vi) if a visa national:

(a) the applicant holds a valid United Kingdom entry clearance for entry as an accompanied child visitor and is travelling in the company of the adult identified on the entry clearance, who is on the same occasion being admitted to the United Kingdom; or

(b) the applicant holds a valid United Kingdom entry clearance for entry as an unaccompanied child visitor; and

(vii) if the applicant has been accepted for a course of study, this is to be provided by an institution which is outside the maintained sector and is:

(a) the holder of a Sponsor Licence for Tier 4 of the Points Based System, or

(b) the holder of valid accreditation from a UK Border Agency approved accreditation body, or

(c) inspected by one of the bodies set out in guidance published by the UK Border Agency, and

(viii) if the applicant is undertaking an exchange or educational visit only, this is to be provided by a school in the maintained sector, a non-maintained special school, an independent non fee-paying or an independent fee-paying school, as described in guidance published by the UK Border Agency.

Leave to enter as a child visitor

46B. An applicant seeking leave to enter the United Kingdom as a child visitor may be admitted for a period not exceeding 6 months, or not exceeding 12 months in the case of a child visitor accompanying an academic visitor subject to a condition prohibiting employment, providing that the Immigration Officer is satisfied that each of the requirements of paragraph 46A is met.

Refusal of leave to enter as a child visitor

46C. Leave to enter as a child visitor is to be refused if the Immigration Officer is not satisfied that each of the requirements of paragraph 46A is met.

Requirements for an extension of stay as a child visitor

46D. Six months is the maximum permitted leave which may be granted to a child visitor. The requirements for an extension of stay as a child visitor are that the applicant:

(i) meets the requirements of paragraph 41(ii)–(vii) and (x)–(xii); and

(ii) is under the age of 18; and

(iii) can demonstrate that there are suitable arrangements for his care in the United Kingdom. If a foster carer or relative (not a parent or guardian) will be responsible for the care of the applicant, the arrangements must meet the requirements laid down in guidance published by the UK Border Agency; and

(iv) has a parent or guardian in his home country or country of habitual residence who is responsible for his care, and who confirms that they consent to the arrangements for the applicant's travel, reception and care in the United Kingdom; and

(v) has not already spent, or would not as a result of an extension of stay spend, more than 6 months in total in the United Kingdom, or not more than 12 months in the case of a child visitor accompanying an academic visitor, as a child visitor; and

(vi) has, or was last granted, entry clearance, leave to enter or leave to remain as a child visitor

Extension of stay as a child visitor

46E. An extension of stay as a child visitor may be granted, subject to a condition prohibiting employment, provided the Secretary of State is satisfied that each of the requirements of paragraph 46D is met.

Refusal of extension of stay as a child visitor

46F. An extension of stay as a child visitor is to be refused if the Secretary of State is not satisfied that each of the requirements of paragraph 46D is met.

Business Visitors

Requirements for leave to enter as a Business Visitor

46G. The requirements to be met by a person seeking leave to enter the United Kingdom as a business visitor are that he:

(i) is genuinely seeking entry as a Business Visitor for a limited period as stated by him:

(a) not exceeding 6 months; or

(b) not exceeding 12 months if seeking entry as an Academic Visitor

(ii) meets the requirements of paragraphs 41(ii)–(viii) and (x)–(xii)

(iii) intends to do one or more of the following during his visit:

(a) to carry out a 'Permissible Activity' as defined in paragraph 6;

(b) to take part in a location shoot as a member of a film crew;

(c) to represent overseas news media including as a journalist, correspondent, producer or cameraman provided he is employed or paid by an overseas company and is gathering information for an overseas publication;

(d) to act as an Academic Visitor but only if he has been working as an academic in an institution of higher education overseas, or in the field of their academic expertise immediately prior to seeking entry;

(e) to act as a Visiting Professor;

(f) to be a secondee to a UK company which is directly contracted with the visitor's overseas company, with which it has no corporate relationship, to provide goods or services, provided the secondee remains employed and paid by the overseas company throughout the secondee's visit;

(g) to undertake some preaching or pastoral work as a religious worker, provided his base is abroad and he is not taking up an office, post or appointment;

(h) To act as an adviser, consultant, trainer or trouble shooter, to the UK branch of the same group of companies as the visitor's overseas company, provided the visitor remains employed and paid by the overseas company and does not undertake work, paid or unpaid with the UK company's clients;

(i) specific, one-off training on techniques and work practices used in the UK where:

(a) the training is to be delivered by the UK branch of the same group of companies to which the individual's employer belongs; or

(b) the training is to be provided by a UK company contracted to provide goods or services to the overseas company; or

(c) a UK company is contracted to provide training facilities only, to an overseas company.

Leave to enter as a Business Visitor

46H. A person seeking leave to enter to the United Kingdom as a Business Visitor may be admitted for a period not exceeding 6 months, subject to a condition prohibiting employment, provided the Immigration Officer is satisfied that each of the requirements of paragraph 46G is met. A person seeking leave to enter the United Kingdom as an Academic Visitor who does not have entry clearance may, if otherwise eligible, be admitted for a period not exceeding 6 months, subject to a condition prohibiting employment, provided the Immigration Officer is satisfied that each of the requirements of paragraph 46G are met. An Academic Visitor who has entry clearance may be admitted for up to 12 months subject to a condition prohibiting employment.

Refusal of leave to enter as a Business Visitor

46I. Leave to enter as a Business Visitor is to be refused if the Immigration Officer is not satisfied that each of the requirements of paragraph 46G are met.

Requirements for an extension of stay as a Business Visitor

46J. Twelve months is the maximum permitted leave which may be granted to an Academic Visitor and six months is the maximum that may be granted to any other form of Business Visitor. The requirements for an extension of stay as a Business Visitor are that the applicant:

(i) meets the requirements of paragraph 46G(ii)–(iii); and

(ii) if he is a Business Visitor other than an Academic Visitor, has not already spent, or would not as a result of an extension of stay spend, more than 6 months in total in the United Kingdom as a Business Visitor; and

(iii) if he is an Academic Visitor, has not already spent, or would not as a result of an extension of stay spend, more than 12 months in total in the United Kingdom as a Business Visitor; and

(iv) has, or was last granted, entry clearance, leave to enter or leave to remain as a Business Visitor.

Extension of stay as a Business Visitor

46K. An extension of stay as a Business Visitor may be granted, subject to a condition prohibiting employment, provided the Secretary of State is satisfied that each of the requirements of paragraph 46J is met.

Refusal of extension of stay as a Business Visitor

46L. An extension of stay as a Business Visitor is to be refused if the Secretary of State is not satisfied that each of the requirements of paragraph 46J is met.

Sports Visitors

Requirements for leave to enter as a Sports Visitor

46M. The requirements to be met by a person seeking leave to enter the United Kingdom as a Sports Visitor are that he:

(i) is genuinely seeking entry as a Sports Visitor for a limited period as stated by him, not exceeding six months; and

(ii) meets the requirements of paragraphs 41(ii)–(viii) and (x)–(xii); and

(iii) intends to do one or more of the following during his visit:

a. To take part in a particular sporting event as defined in guidance published by the United Kingdom Border Agency, tournament or series of events;

b. To take part in a specific one off charity sporting event, provided no payment is received other than for travelling and other expenses;

c. To join, as an Amateur, a wholly or predominantly amateur team provided no payment is received other than for board and lodging and reasonable expenses;

d. To serve as a member of the technical or personal staff, or as an official, attending the same event as a visiting sportsperson coming for one or more of the purposes listed in (a), (b) or (c).

Leave to enter as a Sports Visitor

46N. A person seeking leave to enter to the United Kingdom as a Sports Visitor may be admitted for a period not exceeding 6 months, subject to a condition prohibiting employment, provided the Immigration Officer is satisfied that each of the requirements of paragraph 46M is met.

Refusal of leave to enter as a Sports Visitor

46O. Leave to enter as a Sports Visitor is to be refused if the Immigration Officer is not satisfied that each of the requirements of paragraph 46M is met.

Requirements for an extension of stay as a Sports Visitor

46P. Six months is the maximum permitted leave which may be granted to a Sports Visitor. The requirements for an extension of stay as a sports visitor are that the applicant:

(i) meets the requirements of paragraph 46M(ii)–(iii); and

(ii) has not already spent, or would not as a result of an extension of stay spend, more than 6 months in total in the United Kingdom as a Sports Visitor; and

(iii) has, or was last granted, entry clearance, leave to enter or leave to remain as a Sports Visitor.

Extension of stay as a Sports Visitor

46Q. An extension of stay as a Sports Visitor may be granted, subject to a condition prohibiting employment, provided the Secretary of State is satisfied that each of the requirements of paragraph 46P is met.

Refusal of extension of stay as a Sports Visitor

46R. An extension of stay as a Sports Visitor is to be refused if the Secretary of State is not satisfied that each of the requirements of paragraph 46P is met.

Entertainer Visitors

Requirements for leave to enter as an Entertainer Visitor

46S. The requirements to be met by a person seeking leave to enter the United Kingdom as an Entertainer Visitor are that he:

(i) is genuinely seeking entry as an Entertainer Visitor for a limited period as stated by him, not exceeding six months and

(ii) meets the requirements of paragraphs 41(ii)–(viii) and (x)–(xii) and

(iii) intends to do one or more of the following during his visit:

a. to take part as a professional entertainer in one or more music competitions; and/or

b. to fulfil one or more specific engagements as either an individual Amateur entertainer or as an Amateur group; and/or

c. to take part, as an Amateur or professional entertainer, in a cultural event (or one or more of such events) that appears in the list of events to which this provision applies that is published in guidance issued by the United Kingdom Border Agency; and/or

d. serve as a member of the technical or personal staff, or of the production team, of an entertainer coming for one or more of the purposes listed in (a), (b), or (c).

Leave to enter as an Entertainer Visitor

46T. A person seeking leave to enter to the United Kingdom as an Entertainer Visitor may be admitted for a period not exceeding 6 months, subject to a condition prohibiting employment, provided the Immigration Officer is satisfied that each of the requirements of paragraph 46S is met.

Refusal of leave to enter as an Entertainer Visitor

46U. Leave to enter as an Entertainer Visitor is to be refused if the Immigration Officer is not satisfied that each of the requirements of paragraph 46S is met.

Requirements for an extension of stay as an Entertainer Visitor

46V. Six months is the maximum permitted leave which may be granted to an Entertainer Visitor. The requirements for an extension of stay as an Entertainer Visitor are that the applicant:

(i) meets the requirements of paragraph 46S(ii)–(iii); and

(ii) has not already spent, or would not as a result of an extension of stay spend, more than 6 months in total in the United Kingdom as an Entertainer Visitor; and

(iii) has, or was last granted, entry clearance, leave to enter or leave to remain as an Entertainer Visitor.

Extension of stay as an Entertainer Visitor

46W. An extension of stay as an Entertainer Visitor may be granted, subject to a condition prohibiting employment, provided the Secretary of State is satisfied that each of the requirements of paragraph 46V is met.

Refusal of extension of stay as an Entertainer Visitor

46X. An extension of stay as an Entertainer Visitor is to be refused if the Secretary of State is not satisfied that each of the requirements of paragraph 46V is met.

Visitors in transit

Requirements for admission as a visitor in transit to another country

47. The requirements to be met by a person (not being a member of the crew of a ship, aircraft, hovercraft, hydrofoil or train) seeking leave to enter the United Kingdom as a visitor in transit to another country are that he:

(i) is in transit to a country outside the common travel area; and

(ii) has both the means and the intention of proceeding at once to another country; and

(iii) is assured of entry there; and

(iv) intends and is able to leave the United Kingdom within 48 hours.

Leave to enter as a visitor in transit

48. A person seeking leave to enter the United Kingdom as a visitor in transit may be admitted for a period not exceeding 48 hours with a prohibition on employment provided the Immigration Officer is satisfied that each of the requirements of paragraph 47 is met.

Refusal of leave to enter as a visitor in transit

49. Leave to enter as a visitor in transit is to be refused if the Immigration Officer is not satisfied that each of the requirements of paragraph 47 is met.

Extension of stay as a visitor in transit

50. The maximum permitted leave which may be granted to a visitor in transit is 48 hours. An application for an extension of stay beyond 48 hours from a person admitted in this category is to be refused.

Visitors seeking to enter or remain for private medical treatment

Requirements for leave to enter as a visitor for private medical treatment

51. The requirements to be met by a person seeking leave to enter the United Kingdom as a visitor for private medical treatment are that he:

(i) meets the requirements set out in paragraph 41(iii)–(vii), (ix)–(x) and (xii) for entry as a general visitor; and

(ii) in the case of a person suffering from a communicable disease, has satisfied the Medical Inspector that there is no danger to public health; and

(iii) can show, if required to do so, that any proposed course of treatment is of finite duration; and

(iv) intends to leave the United Kingdom at the end of his treatment; and

(v) can produce satisfactory evidence, if required to do so, of:

(a) the medical condition requiring consultation or treatment; and

(b) satisfactory arrangements for the necessary consultation or treatment at his own expense; and

(c) the estimated costs of such consultation or treatment; and

(d) the likely duration of his visit; and

(e) sufficient funds available to him in the United Kingdom to meet the estimated costs and his undertaking to do so.

Leave to enter as a visitor for private medical treatment

52. A person seeking leave to enter the United Kingdom as a visitor for private medical treatment may be admitted for a period not exceeding 6 months, subject to a condition prohibiting employment, provided the Immigration Officer is satisfied that each of the requirements of paragraph 51 is met.

Refusal of leave to enter as a visitor for private medical treatment

53. Leave to enter as a visitor for private medical treatment is to be refused if the Immigration Officer is not satisfied that each of the requirements of paragraph 51 is met.

Requirements for an extension of stay as a visitor for private medical treatment

54. The requirements for an extension of stay as a visitor to undergo or continue private medical treatment are that the applicant:

(i) meets the requirements set out in paragraph 41(iii)–(vii), (ix)–(x) and (xii) and paragraph 51(ii)–(v); and

(ii) has produced evidence from a registered medical practitioner who holds an NHS consultant post or who appears in the Specialist Register of the General Medical Council of satisfactory arrangements for private medical consultation or treatment and its likely duration; and, where treatment has already begun, evidence as to its progress; and

(iii) can show that he has met, out of the resources available to him, any costs and expenses incurred in relation to his treatment in the United Kingdom; and

(iv) has sufficient funds available to him in the United Kingdom to meet the likely costs of his treatment and intends to meet those costs; and

(v) was not last admitted to the United Kingdom under the Approved Destination Status Agreement with China.

Extension of stay as a visitor for private medical treatment

55. An extension of stay to undergo or continue private medical treatment may be granted, with a prohibition on employment, provided the Secretary of State is satisfied that each of the requirements of paragraph 54 is met.

Refusal of extension of stay as a visitor for private medical treatment

56. An extension of stay as a visitor to undergo or continue private medical treatment is to be refused if the Secretary of State is not satisfied that each of the requirements of paragraph 54 is met.

Parent of a child at school

Requirements for leave to enter or remain as the parent of a child at school

56A. The requirements to be met by a person seeking leave to enter or remain in the United Kingdom as the parent of a child at school are that:

(i) the parent meets the requirements set out in paragraph 41(ii)–(xii); and

(ii) (1) if the child has leave under paragraphs 57 to 62 of these Rules, the child is attending an independent fee paying day school and meets the requirements set out in paragraph 57(i) to (ix), or

(2) if the child is a Tier 4 (Child) Student, the child is attending an independent fee paying day school and meets the requirements set out in paragraph 245ZZA (if seeking leave to enter) or 245ZZC (if seeking leave to remain); and

(iii) the child is under 12 years of age; and

(iv) the parent can provide satisfactory evidence of adequate and reliable funds for maintaining a second home in the United Kingdom; and

(v) the parent is not seeking to make the United Kingdom his main home; and

(vi) the parent was not last admitted to the United Kingdom under the Approved Destination Status Agreement with China.

Leave to enter or remain as the parent of a child at school

56B. A person seeking leave to enter or remain in the United Kingdom as the parent of a child at school may be admitted or allowed to remain for a period not exceeding 12 months, subject to a condition prohibiting employment, provided the Immigration Officer or, in the case of an application for limited leave to remain, the Secretary of State is satisfied that each of the requirements of paragraph 56A is met.

Refusal of leave to enter or remain as the parent of a child at school

56C. Leave to enter or remain in the United Kingdom as the parent of a child at school is to be refused if the Immigration Officer or, in the case of an application for limited leave to remain, the Secretary of State is not satisfied that each of the requirements of paragraph 56A is met.

Visitors seeking to enter for the purposes of marriage or to enter a civil partnership

Requirements for leave to enter as a visitor for marriage or to enter a civil partnership

56D. The requirements to be met by a person seeking leave to enter the United Kingdom as a visitor for marriage or civil partnership are that he:

(i) meets the requirements set out in paragraph 41(i)–(ix) and (xi)–(xii); and

(ii) can show that he intends to give notice of marriage or civil partnership, or marry or form a civil partnership, in the United Kingdom within the period for which entry is sought; and

(iii) can produce satisfactory evidence, if required to do so, of the arrangements for giving notice of marriage or civil partnership, or for his wedding or civil partnership to take place, in the United Kingdom during the period for which entry is sought; and

(iv) holds a valid United Kingdom entry clearance for entry in this capacity.

Leave to enter as a visitor for marriage or civil partnership

56E. A person seeking leave to enter the United Kingdom as a visitor for marriage or civil partnership may be admitted for a period not exceeding 6 months, subject to a condition prohibiting employment, provided the Immigration Officer is satisfied that each of the requirements of paragraph 56D is met.

Refusal of leave to enter as a visitor for marriage or civil partnership

56F. Leave to enter as a visitor for marriage or civil partnership is to be refused if the Immigration Officer is not satisfied that each of the requirements of paragraph 56D is met.

Visitors seeking leave to enter under the Approved Destinations Status (ADS) agreement with China

Requirements for leave to enter as a visitor under the Approved Destination Status Agreement with China ('ADS Agreement')

56G. The requirements to be met by a person seeking leave to enter the United Kingdom as a visitor under the ADS agreement with China are that he:

(i) meets the requirements set out in paragraph 41(ii)–(xii); and

(ii) is a national of the People's Republic of China; and

(iii) is genuinely seeking entry as a visitor for a limited period as stated by him, not exceeding 30 days; and

(iv) intends to enter, leave and travel within the territory of the United Kingdom as a member of a tourist group under the ADS agreement; and

(v) holds a valid ADS agreement visit visa.

Leave to enter as a visitor under the ADS agreement with China

56H. A person seeking leave to enter the United Kingdom as a visitor under the ADS Agreement may be admitted for a period not exceeding 30 days, subject to a condition prohibiting employment, provided they hold an ADS Agreement visit visa.

Refusal of leave to enter as a visitor under the ADS agreement with China

56I. Leave to enter as a visitor under the ADS agreement with China is to be refused if the person does not hold an ADS Agreement visit visa.

Extension of stay as a visitor under the ADS agreement with China

56J. Any application for an extension of stay as a visitor under the ADS Agreement with China is to be refused.

Student visitors

Requirements for leave to enter as a student visitor

56K. The requirements to be met by a person seeking leave to enter the United Kingdom as a student visitor are that he:

(i) is genuinely seeking entry as a student visitor for a limited period as stated by him, not exceeding six months; and

(ii) has been accepted on a course of study which is to be provided by an institution which is:

(a) the holder of a Sponsor licence for Tier 4 of the Points Based System, or

(b) the holder of valid accreditation from a UK Border Agency approved accreditation body, or

(c) inspected or audited by one of the bodies set out in guidance published by the UK Border Agency, or

(d) an overseas Higher Education Institution offering only part of their programmes in the United Kingdom, holding its own national accreditation and offering programmes that are an equivalent level to a United Kingdom degree, and

(iii) intends to leave the United Kingdom at the end of his visit as stated by him; and

(iv) does not intend to take employment in the United Kingdom; and

(v) does not intend to engage in business, to produce goods or provide services within the United Kingdom, including the selling of goods or services direct to members of the public; and

(vi) does not intend to study at a maintained school; and

(vii) will maintain and accommodate himself and any dependants adequately out of resources available to him without recourse to public funds or taking employment; or will, with any dependants, be maintained and accommodated adequately by relatives or friends; and

(viii) can meet the cost of the return or onward journey; and

(ix) is not a child under the age of 18; and

(x) meets the requirements set out in paragraph 41(ix)–(xii).

Leave to enter as a student visitor

56L. A person seeking leave to enter to the United Kingdom as a student visitor may be admitted for a period not exceeding 6 months, subject to a condition prohibiting employment, provided the Immigration Officer is satisfied that each of the requirements of paragraph 56K is met.

Refusal of leave to enter as a student visitor

56M. Leave to enter as a student visitor is to be refused if the Immigration Officer is not satisfied that each of the requirements of paragraph 56K is met.

Prospective Entrepreneurs

Purpose

56N. This Special Visitor route is to enable individuals who are at the time of applying for leave under this route in discussions with:

(i) one or more registered venture capitalist firms regulated by the Financial Services Authority, and/or

(ii) one or more UK entrepreneurial seed funding competitions which is listed as endorsed on the UK Trade & Investment website, and/or

(iii) one or more UK Government Departments,

to secure funding in order to join, set up or take over, and be actively involved in the running of, a business in the UK.

Requirements for leave to enter as a Prospective Entrepreneur

56O. The requirements to be met by a person seeking leave to enter the United Kingdom as a Prospective Entrepreneur are that:

(a) The applicant must provide an original, signed letter on headed paper supporting the application from:

(i) one or more registered venture capitalist firms regulated by the financial services authority,

(ii) one or more UK entrepreneurial seed funding competitions which is listed as endorsed on the UK Trade & Investment website, or

(iii) one or more UK Government Departments;

(b) The letter referred to in (a) must be dated no earlier than three months before the date of the application, be signed by an authorised official, and contain:

(i) a description of the nature of the individual(s) and/or organisation(s) supporting the application;

(ii) a description of the background and nature of the proposed business;

(iii) a description of the applicant's suitability to be involved with the proposed business;

(iv) a commitment by the individual(s) and/or organisation(s) supporting the applicant to make a decision whether to make a decision whether to provide a minimum of £50,000 funding for the proposed business within 6 months of the applicant entering the UK. (if more than one individual and/or organisation is supporting the applicant, each amount proposed may be less than £50k, provided that the total amount is a minimum of £50k);

(v) a commitment by the individual(s) or organisation(s) supporting the applicant that the proposed business will be set up and run from the UK;

(vi) details of a contact name, telephone number and e-mail address for the individual(s) and/or organisation(s) supporting the applicant; and

(vii) confirmation that the individual(s) and/or organisation(s) supporting the applicant is content to be contacted about the applicant;

(c) The applicant's primary intention in applying as a Prospective Entrepreneur is to secure funding in order to join, set up or take over, and be actively involved in the running of a business in the UK;

(d) The applicant intends to carry out one of the activities as listed in guidance published by the UK Border Agency, specifying the activities that a Prospective Entrepreneur may undertake during a visit to the UK;

(e) The applicant intends to leave the United Kingdom at the end of the period of the visit as stated by him, unless he makes a successful application for leave to remain as a Tier 1 (Entrepreneur) Migrant before the end of the period of the visit;

(f) The applicant will maintain and accommodate himself and any dependants adequately out of resources available to him without recourse to public funds or taking employment; or will, with any dependants, be maintained and accommodated adequately by relatives or friends;

(g) The applicant does not intend during his visit to:

(i) take employment in the United Kingdom;

(ii) produce goods or provide services within the United Kingdom, including the selling of goods or services direct to members of the public;

(iii) undertake a course of study;

(iv) marry or form a civil partnership, or to give notice of marriage or civil partnership; or

(v) receive private medical treatment.

(h) The applicant is not under the age of 18;

(i) The applicant is not in transit to a country outside the common travel area; and

(j) The applicant holds a valid United Kingdom entry clearance for entry in this capacity.

Leave to enter as a Prospective Entrepreneur

56P. a person seeking leave to enter to the United Kingdom as a Prospective Entrepreneur may be admitted for a period not exceeding 6 months, subject to a condition prohibiting employment, provided the secretary of state is satisfied that each of the requirements of paragraph 56O is met.

Refusal of leave to enter as a Prospective Entrepreneur

56Q. Leave to enter as a Prospective Entrepreneur is to be refused if the secretary of state is not satisfied that each of the requirements of paragraph 56O is met.

Olympic or Paralympic Games Family Member Visitor

Requirements for leave to enter or remain as an Olympic or Paralympic Games Family Member Visitor

56R. The requirements to be met by a person seeking leave to enter or remain as an Olympic or Paralympic Games Family Member Visitor are that the applicant:

(i) is genuinely seeking leave to enter or remain as an Olympic or Paralympic Games Family Member Visitor; and

(ii) is accredited by the London Organising Committee of the Olympic Games and Paralympic Games Limited for the 2012 London Olympic and Paralympic Games and that accreditation has not been revoked by the International Olympic Committee or the International Paralympic Committee; and

(iii) is not accredited for the 2012 London Olympic and Paralympic Games in accreditation category codes OCOG, S or X; and

(iv) when seeking leave to enter or remain presents an Olympic Identity and Accreditation Card or a Paralympic Identity and Accreditation Card issued by the London Organising Committee of the Olympic Games and Paralympic Games Limited; and

(v) is seeking leave to enter or remain during the period commencing on 30 March 2012 and ending on 8 November 2012; and

(vi) if seeking leave to enter or remain during the period commencing on 30 March 2012 and ending on 8 May 2012 is seeking leave for a period not exceeding 6 months; or if seeking leave to enter or remain during the period commencing on 9 May 2012 and ending on 8 November 2012 is not seeking leave beyond 8November 2012; and

(vii) if seeking leave to enter or remain on or after 13 August 2012 and presents an Olympic Identity and Accreditation Card must have held leave to enter, leave to remain or entry clearance at any time during the period commencing on 30 March 2012 and ending on 12 August 2012; or if seeking leave enter or remain on or after 10 September 2012 and presents a Paralympic Identity and Accreditation Card must have held leave to enter, leave to remain or entry clearance at any time during the period commencing on 30 March 2012 and ending on 9 September 2012; and

(viii) if intending to take employment, takes employment only related to the Olympic and Paralympic Games; and

(ix) will maintain and accommodate himself and any dependents adequately out of resources available to him without recourse to public funds; or will, with any dependents, be maintained and accommodated adequately by relatives, friends, or associates; and

(x) does not intend to undertake a course of study; and

(xi) does not, during his visit, intend to marry or form a civil partnership, or to give notice of marriage or civil partnership; and

(xii) can meet the cost of the return or onward journey; and

(xiii) intends to leave the United Kingdom by or on 8 November 2012; and

(xiv) is not a child under the age of 18.

Leave to enter or remain as an Olympic or Paralympic Games Family Member Visitor

56S. A person seeking leave to enter or remain in the United Kingdom as an Olympic or Paralympic Games Family Member Visitor during the period commencing on 30 March 2012 and ending on 8 May 2012 may be admitted or allowed to stay in the United Kingdom for upto 6 months subject to a condition prohibiting recourse to public funds and restricting employment to employment only related to the Olympic or Paralympic Games, provided the Immigration Officer is satisfied that each of the requirements of paragraph 56R is met. A person seeking leave to enter or remain in the United Kingdom as an Olympic or Paralympic Games Family Member Visitor during the period commencing on 9 May 2012 and ending on 8 November 2012 may be admitted or allowed to stay in the United Kingdom until 8 November 2012 subject to a condition prohibiting recourse to public funds and restricting employment to employment only related to the Olympic and Paralympic Games provided the Immigration Officer is satisfied that each of the requirements of paragraph 56R is met.

Refusal of leave to enter or remain as an Olympic or Paralympic Games Family Member Visitor

56T. Leave to enter or remain as an Olympic or Paralympic Games Family Member Visitor is to be refused if the Immigration Officer is not satisfied that each of the requirements of paragraph 56R is met.

Olympic or Paralympic Games Family Member Child Visitor

Requirements for leave to enter or remain as an Olympic or Paralympic Games Family Member Child Visitor

56U. The requirements to be met by a person seeking leave to enter or remain as an Olympic or Paralympic Games Family Member Child Visitor are that the applicant:

(i) is genuinely seeking leave to enter or remain as an Olympic or Paralympic Games Family Member Child Visitor; and

(ii) meets the requirements of paragraph 56R (ii) to (xiii); and

(iii) is under the age of 18; and

(iv) can demonstrate that suitable arrangements have been made for their travel to, and reception and care in the United Kingdom; and

(v) can demonstrate that their parent or guardian in their home country or country of habitual residence who is responsible for their care consents to arrangements for applicant's travel, reception and care in the United Kingdom.

Leave to enter or remain as an Olympic or Paralympic Games Family Member Child Visitor

56V. A person seeking leave to enter or remain in the United Kingdom as an Olympic or Paralympic Games Family Member Child Visitor during the period commencing on 30 March 2012 and ending on 8 May 2012 may be admitted or allowed to stay in the United Kingdom for up to 6 months subject to a condition prohibiting recourse to public funds and restricting employment to employment only related to the Olympic or Paralympic Games, provided the Immigration Officer is satisfied that each of the requirements of paragraph 56U is met. A person seeking leave to enter or remain in the United Kingdom as an Olympic or Paralympic Games Family Member Child Visitor during the period commencing on 9 May 2012 and ending on 8 November 2012 may be admitted or allowed to stay in the United Kingdom until 8 November 2012 subject to a condition prohibiting recourse to public funds and restricting employment to employment only related to the Olympic and Paralympic Games providing the Immigration Officer is satisfied that each of the requirements of paragraph 56U is met.

Refusal of leave to enter or remain as an Olympic or Paralympic Games Family

Member Child Visitor

56W. Leave to enter or remain as an Olympic or Paralympic Games Family Member Child Visitor is to be refused if the Immigration Officer is not satisfied that each of the requirements of paragraph 56U is met.

Part 3 – Persons seeking to enter or remain in the United Kingdom for studies

Students

Requirements for leave to enter as a student

57. DELETED.

Leave to enter as a student

58. DELETED.

Refusal of leave to enter as a student

59. DELETED.

Requirements for an extension of stay as a student

60. DELETED.

Extension of stay as a student

61. DELETED.

Refusal of extension of stay as a student

62. DELETED.

Student nurses

Definition of a student nurse

63. DELETED.

Requirements for leave to enter as a student nurse

64. DELETED.

Leave to enter the United Kingdom as a student nurse

65. DELETED.

Refusal of leave to enter as a student nurse

66. DELETED.

Requirements for an extension of stay as a student nurse

67. DELETED.

Extension of stay as a student nurse

68. DELETED.

Refusal of extension of stay as a student nurse

69. DELETED.

Re-sits of examinations

Requirements for leave to enter to re-sit an examination

69A. DELETED.

Leave to enter to re-sit an examination

69B. DELETED.

Refusal of leave to enter to re-sit an examination

69C. DELETED.

Requirements for an extension of stay to re-sit an examination

69D. DELETED.

Extension of stay to re-sit an examination

69E. DELETED.

Refusal of extension of stay to re-sit an examination

69F. DELETED.

Writing up a thesis

Requirements for leave to enter to write up a thesis

69G. DELETED.

Leave to enter to write up a thesis

69H. DELETED.

Refusal of leave to enter to write up a thesis

69I. DELETED.

Requirements for an extension of stay to write up a thesis

69J. DELETED.

Extension of stay to write up a thesis

69K. DELETED.

Refusal of extension of stay to write up a thesis

69L. DELETED.

Overseas qualified nurse or midwife

Requirements for leave to enter as an overseas qualified nurse or midwife

69M. Deleted on 27 November 2008 by paragraph 39 of Statement of Changes HC 1113 except insofar as relevant to paragraph 69P.

Leave to enter the United Kingdom as an overseas qualified nurse or midwife

69N. DELETED.

Refusal of leave to enter as an overseas qualified nurse or midwife

69O. DELETED.

Requirements for an extension of stay as an overseas qualified nurse or midwife

69P. The requirements to be met by a person seeking an extension of stay as an overseas qualified nurse or midwife are that the applicant:

(i)–(iii) Deleted by HC 1113

(iv) has leave to enter or remain as an overseas qualified nurse or midwife in accordance with paragraphs 69M–69R of these Rules; and

(v) meets the requirements set out in paragraph 69M(i)–(vi); and

(vi) can provide satisfactory evidence of regular attendance during any previous period of supervised practice or midwife adaptation course; and

(vii) if he has previously been granted leave:

(a) as an overseas qualified nurse or midwife under paragraphs 69M–69R of these Rules, or

(b) to undertake an adaptation course as a student nurse under paragraphs 63–69 of these Rules; is not seeking an extension of stay in this category which, when amalgamated with those previous periods of leave, would total more than 18 months; and

(viii) if his previous studies, supervised practice placement or midwife adaptation programme placement were sponsored by a government or international scholarship agency, he has the written consent of his official sponsor to remain in the United Kingdom as an overseas qualified nurse or midwife.

Extension of stay as an overseas qualified nurse or midwife

69Q. An extension of stay as an overseas qualified nurse or midwife may be granted for a period not exceeding 18 months, provided that the Secretary of State is satisfied that each of the requirements of paragraph 69P is met.

Refusal of extension of stay as an overseas qualified nurse or midwife

69R. An extension of stay as an overseas qualified nurse or midwife is to be refused if the Secretary of State is not satisfied that each of the requirements of paragraph 69P is met.

Postgraduate doctors, dentists and trainee general practitioners

Requirements for leave to enter the United Kingdom as a postgraduate doctor or dentist

70. DELETED.

Leave to enter as a postgraduate doctor or dentist

71. DELETED.

Refusal of leave to enter as a postgraduate doctor or dentist

72. DELETED.

Requirements for an extension of stay as a postgraduate doctor or dentist

73. DELETED.

Extension of stay as a postgraduate doctor or dentist

74. DELETED.

Refusal of an extension of stay as a postgraduate doctor or dentist

75. DELETED.

Requirements for leave to enter the United Kingdom to take the PLAB Test

75A. The requirements to be met by a person seeking leave to enter in order to take the PLAB Test are that the applicant:

(i) is a graduate from a medical school and intends to take the PLAB Test in the United Kingdom; and

(ii) can provide documentary evidence of a confirmed test date or of his eligibility to take the PLAB Test; and

(iii) meets the requirements of paragraph 41(iii)–(vii) for entry as a visitor; and

(iv) intends to leave the United Kingdom at the end of the leave granted under this paragraph unless he is successful in the PLAB Test and granted leave to remain to undertake a clinical attachment in accordance with paragraphs 75G to 75M of these Rules.

Leave to enter to take the PLAB Test

75B. A person seeking leave to enter the United Kingdom to take the PLAB Test may be admitted for a period not exceeding 6 months, provided the Immigration Officer is satisfied that each of the requirements of paragraph 75A is met.

Refusal of leave to enter to take the PLAB Test

75C. Leave to enter the United Kingdom to take the PLAB Test is to be refused if the Immigration Officer is not satisfied that each of the requirements of paragraph 75A is met.

Requirements for an extension of stay in order to take the PLAB Test

75D. The requirements for an extension of stay in the United Kingdom in order to take the PLAB Test are that the applicant:

(i) was given leave to enter the United Kingdom for the purposes of taking the PLAB Test in accordance with paragraph 75B of these Rules; and

(ii) intends to take the PLAB Test and can provide documentary evidence of a confirmed test date; and

(iii) meets the requirements set out in paragraph 41(iii)–(vii); and

(iv) intends to leave the United Kingdom at the end of the leave granted under this paragraph unless he is successful in the PLAB Test and granted leave to remain to undertake a clinical attachment in accordance with paragraphs 75G to 75M of these Rules; and

(v) would not as a result of an extension of stay spend more than 18 months in the United Kingdom for the purpose of taking the PLAB Test.

Extension of stay to take the PLAB Test

75E. A person seeking leave to remain in the United Kingdom to take the PLAB Test may be granted an extension of stay for a period not exceeding 6 months, provided the Secretary of State is satisfied that each of the requirements of paragraph 75D is met.

Refusal of extension of stay to take the PLAB Test

75F. Leave to remain in the United Kingdom to take the PLAB Test is to be refused if the Secretary of State is not satisfied that each of the requirements of paragraph 75D is met.

Requirements for leave to enter to undertake a clinical attachment or dental observer post

75G. The requirements to be met by a person seeking leave to enter to undertake a clinical attachment or dental observer post are that the applicant:

(i) is a graduate from a medical or dental school and intends to undertake a clinical attachment or dental observer post in the United Kingdom; and

(ii) can provide documentary evidence of the clinical attachment or dental observer post which will:

(a) be unpaid; and

(b) only involve observation, not treatment, of patients; and

(iii) meets the requirements of paragraph 41(iii)–(vii) of these Rules; and

(iv) intends to leave the United Kingdom at the end of the leave granted under this paragraph;

(v) if he has previously been granted leave in this category, is not seeking leave to enter which, when amalgamated with those previous periods of leave, would total more than 6 months.

Leave to enter to undertake a clinical attachment or dental observer post

75H. A person seeking leave to enter the United Kingdom to undertake a clinical attachment or dental observer post may be admitted for the period of the clinical attachment or dental observer post, up to a maximum of 6 weeks at a time or 6 months in total in this category, provided the Immigration Officer is satisfied that each of the requirements of paragraph 75G is met.

Refusal of leave to enter to undertake a clinical attachment or dental observer post

75J. Leave to enter the United Kingdom to undertake a clinical attachment or dental observer post is to be refused if the Immigration Officer is not satisfied that each of the requirements of paragraph 75G is met.

Requirements for an extension of stay in order to undertake a clinical attachment or dental observer post

75K. The requirements to be met by a person seeking an extension of stay to undertake a clinical attachment or dental observer post are that the applicant:

(i) was given leave to enter or remain in the United Kingdom to undertake a clinical attachment or dental observer post or:

(a) for the purposes of taking the PLAB Test in accordance with paragraphs 75A to 75F and has passed both parts of the PLAB Test;

(b) as a postgraduate doctor, dentist or trainee general practitioner in accordance with paragraphs 70 to 75; or

(c) as a work permit holder for employment in the UK as a doctor or dentist in accordance with paragraphs 128 to 135; and

(ii) is a graduate from a medical or dental school and intends to undertake a clinical attachment or dental observer post in the United Kingdom; and

(iii) can provide documentary evidence of the clinical attachment or dental observer post which will:

(a) be unpaid; and

(b) only involve observation, not treatment, of patients; and

(iv) intends to leave the United Kingdom at the end of the leave granted under this paragraph; and

(v) meets the requirements of paragraph 41(iii)–(vii) of these Rules; and

(vi) if he has previously been granted leave in this category, is not seeking an extension of stay which, when amalgamated with those previous periods of leave, would total more than 6 months.

Extension of stay to undertake a clinical attachment or dental observer post

75L. A person seeking leave to remain in the United Kingdom to undertake a clinical attachment or dental observer post up to a maximum of 6 weeks at a time or 6 months in total in this category, may be granted an extension of stay for the period of their clinical attachment or dental observer post, provided that the Secretary of State is satisfied that each of the requirements of paragraph 75K is met.

Refusal of extension of stay to undertake a clinical attachment or dental observer post

75M. Leave to remain in the United Kingdom to undertake a clinical attachment or dental observer post is to be refused if the Secretary of State is not satisfied that each of the requirements of paragraph 75K is met.

Spouses or civil partners of students or prospective students granted leave under this part of the Rules

Requirements for leave to enter or remain as the spouse or civil partner of a student or prospective student

76. The requirements to be met by a person seeking leave to enter or remain in the United Kingdom as the spouse or civil partner of a student or a prospective student are that:

(i) the applicant is married to or the civil partner of a person admitted to or allowed to remain in the United Kingdom under paragraphs 57–75 or 82–87F; and

(ii) each of the parties intends to live with the other as his or her spouse or civil partner during the applicant's stay and the marriage or the civil partner of is subsisting; and

(iii) there will be adequate accommodation for the parties and any dependants without recourse to public funds; and

(iv) the parties will be able to maintain themselves and any dependants adequately without recourse to public funds; and

(v) the applicant does not intend to take employment except as permitted under paragraph 77 below; and

(vi) the applicant intends to leave the United Kingdom at the end of any period of leave granted to him.

Leave to enter or remain as the spouse or civil partner of a student or prospective student

77. A person seeking leave to enter or remain in the United Kingdom as the spouse or civil partner of a student or a prospective student may be admitted or allowed to remain for a period not in excess of that granted to the student or prospective student provided the Immigration Officer or, in the case of an application for limited leave to remain, the Secretary of State is satisfied that each of the requirements of paragraph 76 is met. Employment may be permitted where the period of leave granted to the student or prospective student is, or was, 12 months or more.

Refusal of leave to enter or remain as the spouse or civil partner of a student or prospective student

78. Leave to enter or remain as the spouse or civil partner of a student or prospective student is to be refused if the Immigration Officer or, in the case of an application for limited leave to remain, the Secretary of State is not satisfied that each of the requirements of paragraph 76 is met.

Children of students or prospective students granted leave under this part of the Rules

Requirements for leave to enter or remain as the child of a student or prospective student

79. The requirements to be met by a person seeking leave to enter or remain in the United Kingdom as the child of a student or prospective student are that he:

(i) is the child of a parent admitted to or allowed to remain in the United Kingdom as a student or prospective student under paragraphs 57–75 or 82–87F; and

(ii) is under the age of 18 or has current leave to enter or remain in this capacity; and

(iii) is unmarried, has not formed an independent family unit and is not leading an independent life; and

(iv) can, and will, be maintained and accommodated adequately without recourse to public funds; and

(v) will not stay in the United Kingdom beyond any period of leave granted to his parent; and

(vi) meets the requirements of paragraph 79A.

79A. Both of the applicant's parents must either be lawfully present in the UK, or being granted entry clearance or leave to remain at the same time as the applicant, unless:

(i) The student or prospective student is the applicant's sole surviving parent, or

(ii) The student or prospective student parent has and has had sole responsibility for the applicant's upbringing, or

(iii) there are serious or compelling family or other considerations which would make it desirable not to refuse the application and suitable arrangements have been made in the UK for the applicant's care.

Leave to enter or remain as the child of a student or prospective student

80. A person seeking leave to enter or remain in the United Kingdom as the child of a student or prospective student may be admitted or allowed to remain for a period not in excess of that granted to the student or prospective student provided the Immigration Officer or, in the case of an application for limited leave to remain, the Secretary of State is satisfied that each of the requirements of paragraph 79 is met. Employment may be permitted where the period of leave granted to the student or prospective student is, or was, 12 months or more.

Refusal of leave to enter or remain as the child of a student or prospective student

81. Leave to enter or remain in the United Kingdom as the child of a student or prospective student is to be refused if the Immigration Officer or, in the case of an application for limited leave to remain, the Secretary of State, is not satisfied that each of the requirements of paragraph 79 is met.

Prospective students

Requirements for leave to enter as a prospective student

82. The requirements to be met by a person seeking leave to enter the United Kingdom as a prospective student are that he:

(i) can demonstrate a genuine and realistic intention of undertaking, within 6 months of his date of entry:

  (a) a course of study which would meet the requirements for an extension of stay as a student under paragraph 245ZX or paragraph 245ZZC; and

  (b) DELETED

(ii) intends to leave the United Kingdom on completion of his studies or on the expiry of his leave to enter if he is not able to meet the requirements for an extension of stay:

(a) as a student in accordance with paragraph 245ZX or paragraph 245ZZC; and

(b) DELETED

(iii) is able without working or recourse to public funds to meet the costs of his intended course and accommodation and the maintenance of himself and any dependants while making arrangements to study and during the course of his studies; and

(iv) holds a valid United Kingdom entry clearance for entry in this capacity.

Leave to enter as a prospective student

83. A person seeking leave to enter the United Kingdom as a prospective student may be admitted for a period not exceeding 6 months with a condition prohibiting employment, provided he is able to produce to the Immigration Officer on arrival a valid United Kingdom entry clearance for entry in this capacity.

Refusal of leave to enter as a prospective student

84. Leave to enter as a prospective student is to be refused if the Immigration Officer is not satisfied that each of the requirements of paragraph 82 is met.

Requirements for extension of stay as a prospective student

85. Six months is the maximum permitted leave which may be granted to a prospective student. The requirements for an extension of stay as a prospective student are that the applicant:

(i) was admitted to the United Kingdom with a valid prospective student entry clearance; and

(ii) meets the requirements of paragraph 82; and

(iii) would not, as a result of an extension of stay, spend more than 6 months in the United Kingdom.

Extension of stay as a prospective student

86. An extension of stay as a prospective student may be granted, with a prohibition on employment, provided the Secretary of State is satisfied that each of the requirements of paragraph 85 is met.

Refusal of extension of stay as a prospective student

87. An extension of stay as a prospective student is to be refused if the Secretary of State is not satisfied that each of the requirements of paragraph 85 is met.

Students' unions sabbatical officers

Requirements for leave to enter as a sabbatical officer

87A. DELETED.

Leave to enter the United Kingdom as a sabbatical officer

87B. DELETED.

Refusal of leave to enter the United Kingdom as a sabbatical officer

87C. DELETED.

Requirements for an extension of stay as a sabbatical officer

87D. DELETED.

Extension of stay as a sabbatical officer

87E. DELETED.

Refusal of extension of stay as a sabbatical officer

87F. DELETED.

Part 4 – Persons seeking to enter or remain in the United Kingdom in an 'au pair' placement, as a working holidaymaker or for training or work experience

'Au pair' placements

DELETED

Working holidaymakers

DELETED

Requirements for an extension of stay as a working holidaymaker

98. DELETED

Extension of stay as a working holidaymaker

99. DELETED

Refusal of extension of stay as a working holidaymaker

100. DELETED

Children of working holidaymakers

DELETED

Seasonal agricultural workers

Requirements for leave to enter as a seasonal agricultural worker

104. The requirements to be met by a person seeking leave to enter the United Kingdom as a seasonal agricultural worker are that he:

(i) is a student in full time education aged 18 or over; and

(ii) holds an immigration employment document in the form of a valid Home Office work card issued by the operator of a scheme approved by the Secretary of State; and

(iii) intends to leave the United Kingdom at the end of his period of leave as a seasonal worker; and

(iv) does not intend to take employment except as permitted by his work card and within the terms of this paragraph; and

(v) is not seeking leave to enter on a date less than 3 months from the date on which an earlier period of leave to enter or remain granted to him in this capacity expired; and

(vi) is able to maintain and accommodate himself without recourse to public funds.

Leave to enter as a seasonal agricultural worker

105. A person seeking leave to enter the United Kingdom as a seasonal agricultural worker may be admitted with a condition restricting his freedom to take employment for a period not exceeding 6 months providing the Immigration Officer is satisfied that each of the requirements of paragraph 104 is met.

Refusal of leave to enter as a seasonal agricultural worker

106. Leave to enter the United Kingdom as a seasonal agricultural worker is to be refused if the Immigration Officer is not satisfied that each of the requirements of paragraph 104 is met.

Requirements for extension of stay as a seasonal agricultural worker

107. The requirements for an extension of stay as a seasonal agricultural worker are that the applicant:

(i) entered the United Kingdom as a seasonal agricultural worker under paragraph 105; and

(ii) meets the requirements of paragraph 104(iii)–(vi); and

(iii) would not, as a result of an extension of stay sought, remain in the United Kingdom as a seasonal agricultural worker beyond 6 months from the date on which he was given leave to enter the United Kingdom on this occasion in this capacity.

Extension of stay as a seasonal agricultural worker

108. An extension of stay as a seasonal agricultural worker may be granted with a condition restricting his freedom to take employment for a period which does not extend beyond 6 months from the date on which he was given leave to enter the United Kingdom on this occasion in this capacity, provided the Secretary of State is satisfied that the applicant meets each of the requirements of paragraph 107.

Refusal of extension of stay as a seasonal worker

109. An extension of stay as a seasonal worker is to be refused if the Secretary of State is not satisfied that each of the requirements of paragraph 107 is met.

Requirements for leave to enter as a teacher or language assistant under an approved exchange scheme

DELETED

Home Office approved training or work experience

Requirements for leave to enter for Home Office approved training or work experience

Spouses of persons with limited leave to enter or remain under paragraphs 110–121

DELETED

Requirements for leave to enter or remain as the spouse or civil partners of a person with limited leave to enter or remain in the United Kingdom under paragraphs 110–121

122. The requirements to be met by a person seeking leave to enter or remain in the United Kingdom as the spouse or civil partners of a person with limited leave to enter or remain in the United Kingdom under paragraphs 110–121 are that:

(i) the applicant is married or the civil partner of to a person with limited leave to enter or remain in the United Kingdom under paragraphs 110–121; and

(ii) each of the parties intends to live with the other as his or her spouse or civil partners during the applicant's stay and the marriage or civil partnership is subsisting; and

(iii) there will be adequate accommodation for the parties and any dependants without recourse to public funds in accommodation which they own or occupy exclusively; and

(iv) the parties will be able to maintain themselves and any dependants adequately without recourse to public funds; and

(v) the applicant does not intend to stay in the United Kingdom beyond any period of leave granted to his spouse; and

(vi) if seeking leave to enter, the applicant holds a valid United Kingdom entry clearance for entry in this capacity or, if seeking leave to remain, was admitted with a valid United Kingdom entry clearance for entry in this capacity.

Leave to enter or remain as the spouse of a person with limited leave to enter or remain in the United Kingdom under paragraphs 110–121

123. A person seeking leave to enter or remain in the United Kingdom as the spouse of a person with limited leave to enter or remain in the United Kingdom under paragraphs 110–121 may be given leave to enter or remain in the United Kingdom for a period of leave not in excess of that granted to the person with limited leave to enter or remain under paragraphs 110–121 provided that, in relation to an application for leave to enter, he is able, on arrival, to produce to the Immigration Officer a valid United Kingdom entry clearance for entry in this capacity or, in the case of an application for limited leave to remain, was admitted with a valid United Kingdom entry clearance for entry in this capacity and he is able to satisfy the Secretary of State that each of the requirements of paragraph 122(i)–(v) is met.

Refusal of leave to enter or remain as the spouse of a person with limited leave to enter or remain in the United Kingdom under paragraphs 110–121

124. Leave to enter or remain in the United Kingdom as the spouse of a person with limited leave to enter or remain in the United Kingdom under paragraphs 110–121 is to be refused if, in relation to an application

for leave to enter, a valid United Kingdom entry clearance for entry in this capacity is not produced to the Immigration Officer on arrival or, in the case of an application for limited leave to remain, if the applicant was not admitted with a valid United Kingdom entry clearance for entry in this capacity or is unable to satisfy the Secretary of State that each of the requirements of paragraph 122(i)–(v) is met.

Children of persons admitted or allowed to remain under paragraphs 110 121

Requirements for leave to enter or remain as the child of a person with limited leave to enter or remain in the United Kingdom under paragraphs 110–121

125. The requirements to be met by a person seeking leave to enter or remain in the United Kingdom as the child of a person with limited leave to enter or remain in the United Kingdom under paragraphs 110–121 are that:

(i) he is the child of a parent who has limited leave to enter or remain in the United Kingdom under paragraphs 110–121; and

(ii) he is under the age of 18 or has current leave to enter or remain in this capacity; and

(iii) he is unmarried and is not a civil partner, has not formed an independent family unit and is not leading an independent life; and

(iv) he can, and will, be maintained and accommodated adequately without recourse to public funds in accommodation which his parent(s) own or occupy exclusively; and

(v) he will not stay in the United Kingdom beyond any period of leave granted to his parent(s); and

(vi) both parents are being or have been admitted to or allowed to remain in the United Kingdom save where:

(a) the parent he is accompanying or joining is his sole surviving parent; or

(b) the parent he is accompanying or joining has had sole responsibility for his upbringing; or

(c) there are serious and compelling family or other considerations which make exclusion from the United Kingdom undesirable and suitable arrangements have been made for his care; and

(vii) if seeking leave to enter, he holds a valid United Kingdom entry clearance for entry in this capacity or, if seeking leave to remain, was admitted with a valid United Kingdom entry clearance for entry in this capacity.

Leave to enter or remain as the child of a person with limited leave to enter or remain in the United Kingdom under paragraphs 110–121

126. A person seeking leave to enter or remain in the United Kingdom as the child of a person with limited leave to enter or remain in the United Kingdom under paragraphs 110–121 may be given leave to enter or remain in the United Kingdom for a period of leave not in excess of that granted to the person with limited leave to enter or remain under paragraphs 110–121 provided that, in relation to an application for leave to enter, he is able, on arrival, to produce to the Immigration Officer a valid United Kingdom entry clearance for entry in this capacity or, in the case of an application for limited leave to remain, he was admitted with a valid United Kingdom entry clearance for entry in this capacity and is able to satisfy the Secretary of State that each of the requirements of paragraph 125(i)–(vi) is met.

Refusal of leave to enter or remain as the child of a person with limited leave to enter or remain in the United Kingdom under paragraphs 110–121

127. Leave to enter or remain in the United Kingdom as the child of a person with limited leave to enter or remain in the United Kingdom under paragraphs 110–121 is to be refused if, in relation to an application for leave to enter, a valid United Kingdom entry clearance for entry in this capacity is not produced to the Immigration Officer on arrival, or, in the case of an application for limited leave to remain, if the applicant was not admitted with a valid United Kingdom entry clearance for entry in this capacity or is unable to satisfy the Secretary of State that each of the requirements of paragraph 125(i)–(vi) is met.

Part 5 – Persons seeking to enter or remain in the United Kingdom for employment

Work permit employment

Requirements for leave to enter the United Kingdom for work permit employment

128. The requirements to be met by a person coming to the United Kingdom to seek or take employment (unless he is otherwise eligible for admission for employment under these Rules or is eligible for admission as a seaman under contract to join a ship due to leave British waters) are that he:

(i) holds a valid Home Office work permit; and

(ii) is not of an age which puts him outside the limits for employment; and

(iii) is capable of undertaking the employment specified in the work permit; and

(iv) does not intend to take employment except as specified in his work permit; and

(v) is able to maintain and accommodate himself and any dependants adequately without recourse to public funds; and

(vi) in the case of a person in possession of a work permit which is valid for a period of 12 months or less, intends to leave the United Kingdom at the end of his approved employment; and

(vii) holds a valid United Kingdom entry clearance for entry in this capacity except where he holds a work permit valid for 6 months or less or he is a British National (Overseas), a British overseas territories citizen, a British Overseas citizen, a British protected person or a person who under the British Nationality Act 1981 is a British subject.

Leave to enter for work permit employment

129. A person seeking leave to enter the United Kingdom for the purpose of work permit employment may be admitted for a period not exceeding the period of employment approved by the Home Office (as specified in his work permit), subject to a condition restricting him to that approved employment, provided he is able to produce to the Immigration Officer, on arrival, a valid United Kingdom entry clearance for entry in this capacity or, where entry clearance is not required, provided the Immigration Officer is satisfied that each of the requirements of paragraph 128(i)–(vi) is met.

Refusal of leave to enter for employment

130. Leave to enter for the purpose of work permit employment is to be refused if a valid United Kingdom entry clearance for entry in this capacity is not produced to the Immigration Officer on arrival or, where entry clearance is not required, if the Immigration Officer is not satisfied that each of the requirements of paragraph 128(i)–(vi) is met.

Requirements for an extension of stay for work permit employment

131. The requirements for an extension of stay to seek or take employment (unless the applicant is otherwise eligible for an extension of stay for employment under these Rules) are that the applicant:

(i) entered the United Kingdom with a valid work permit under paragraph 129; and

(ii) has written approval from the Home Office for the continuation of his employment; and

(iii) meets the requirements of paragraph 128(ii)–(v).

131A. The requirements for an extension of stay to take employment (unless the applicant is otherwise eligible for an extension of stay for employment under these Rules) for a student are that the applicant:

(i) entered the United Kingdom or was given leave to remain as a student in accordance with paragraphs 57 to 62 of these Rules; and

(ii) has obtained a degree qualification on a recognised degree course at either a United Kingdom publicly funded further or higher education institution or a bona fide United Kingdom private education institution which maintains satisfactory records of enrolment and attendance; and

(iii) holds a valid Home Office immigration employment document for employment; and

(iv) has the written consent of his official sponsor to such employment if he is a member of a government or international scholarship agency sponsorship and that sponsorship is either ongoing or has recently come to an end at the time of the requested extension; and

(v) meets each of the requirements of paragraph 128(ii) to (vi).

131B. The requirements for an extension of stay to take employment (unless the applicant is otherwise eligible for an extension of stay for employment under these Rules) for a student nurse overseas qualified nurse or midwife, postgraduate doctor or postgraduate dentist are that the applicant:

(i) entered the United Kingdom or was given leave to remain as a student nurse in accordance with paragraphs 63 to 69 of these Rules; or

(ia) entered the United Kingdom or was given leave to remain as an overseas qualified nurse or midwife in accordance with paragraphs 69M to 69R of these Rules; and

(ii) entered the United Kingdom or was given leave to remain as a postgraduate doctor or a postgraduate dentist in accordance with paragraphs 70 to 75 of these Rules; and

(iii) holds a valid Home Office immigration employment document for employment as a nurse, doctor or dentist; and

(iv) has the written consent of his official sponsor to such employment if he is a member of a government or international scholarship agency sponsorship and that sponsorship is either ongoing or has recently come to an end at the time of the requested extension; and

(v) meets each of the requirements of paragraph 128(ii) to (vi).

131C. The requirements for an extension of stay to take employment for a Science and Engineering Graduate Scheme or International Graduates Scheme participant are that the applicant:

(i) entered the United Kingdom or was given leave to remain as a Science and Engineering Graduate Scheme or International Graduates Scheme participant in accordance with paragraphs 135O to 135T of these Rules; and

(ii) holds a valid Home Office immigration employment document for employment; and

(iii) meets each of the requirements of paragraph 128(ii) to (vi).

131D. The requirements for an extension of stay to take employment (unless the applicant is otherwise eligible for an extension of stay for employment under these Rules) for a working holidaymaker are that the applicant:

(i) entered the United Kingdom as a working holidaymaker in accordance with paragraphs 95 to 96 of these Rules; and

(ii) he has spent more than 12 months in total in the UK in this capacity; and

(iii) holds a valid Home Office immigration employment document for employment in an occupation listed on the Work Permits (UK) shortage occupations list; and

(iv) meets each of the requirements of paragraph 128(ii) to (vi).

131E. The requirements for an extension of stay to take employment for a highly skilled migrant are that the applicant:

(i) entered the United Kingdom or was given leave to remain as a highly skilled migrant in accordance with paragraphs 135A to 135E of these Rules; and

(ii) holds a valid work permit; and

(iii) meets each of the requirements of paragraph 128(ii) to (vi).

131F. The requirements for an extension of stay to take employment (unless the applicant is otherwise eligible for an extension of stay for employment under these Rules) for an Innovator are that the applicant:

(i) entered the United Kingdom or was given leave to remain as an Innovator in accordance with paragraphs 210A to 210E of these Rules; and

(ii) holds a valid Home Office immigration employment document for employment; and

(iii) meets each of the requirements of paragraph 128(ii) to (vi).

131G. The requirements for an extension of stay to take employment (unless the applicant is otherwise eligible for an extension of stay for employment under these Rules) for an individual who has leave to enter or leave to remain in the United Kingdom to take the PLAB Test or to undertake a clinical attachment or dental observer post are that the applicant:

(i) entered the United Kingdom or was given leave to remain for the purposes of taking the PLAB Test in accordance with paragraphs 75A to 75F of these Rules; or

(ii) entered the United Kingdom or was given leave to remain to undertake a clinical attachment or dental observer post in accordance with paragraphs 75G to 75M of these Rules; and

(iii) holds a valid Home Office immigration employment document for employment as a doctor or dentist; and

(iv) meets each of the requirements of paragraph 128(ii) to (vi).

131H. The requirements for an extension of stay to take employment (unless the applicant is otherwise eligible for an extension of stay for employment under these Rules) in the case of a person who has leave to enter or remain as a Fresh Talent: Working in Scotland scheme participant are that the applicant:

(i) entered the United Kingdom or was given leave to remain as a Fresh Talent: Working in Scotland scheme participant in accordance with paragraphs 143A to 143F of these Rules; and

(ii) holds a valid Home Office immigration employment document for employment in Scotland; and

(iii) has the written consent of his official sponsor to such employment if the studies which led to him being granted leave under the Fresh Talent: Working in Scotland scheme in accordance with paragraphs 143A to 143F of these Rules, or any studies he has subsequently undertaken, were sponsored by a government or international scholarship agency; and

(iv) meets each of the requirements of paragraph 128(ii) to (vi).

131I. The requirements for an extension of stay to take employment for a Tier 1 Migrant are that the applicant:

(i) entered the UK or was given leave to remain as a Tier 1 Migrant, and

(ii) holds a valid work permit; and

(iii) meets each of the requirements of paragraph 128(ii) to (vi).

Extension of stay for work permit employment

132. An extension of stay for work permit employment may be granted for a period not exceeding the period of approved employment recommended by the Home Office provided the Secretary of State is satisfied that each of the requirements of paragraphs 131, 131A, 131B, 131C, 131D, 131E, 131F, 131G, 131H or 131I is met. An extension of stay is to be subject to a condition restricting the applicant to employment approved by the Home Office.

133. An extension of stay for employment is to be refused if the Secretary of State is not satisfied that each of the requirements of paragraphs 131, 131A, 131B, 131C, 131D, 131E, 131F, 131G, 131H or 131I is met (unless the applicant is otherwise eligible for an extension of stay for employment under these Rules).

Indefinite leave to remain for a work permit holder

134. Indefinite leave to remain may be granted on application to a person provided:

(i) he has spent a continuous period of 5 years lawfully in the UK, of which the most recent period must have been spent with leave as a work permit holder (under paragraphs 128 to 133 of these rules), and the remainder must be any combination of leave as a work permit holder or leave as a highly skilled migrant (under paragraphs 135A to 135F of these rules) or leave as a self-employed lawyer (under the concession that appeared in Chapter 6, Section 1 Annex D of the Immigration Directorate Instructions), or leave as a writer, composer or artist (under paragraphs 232 to 237 of these rules);

(ii) he has met the requirements of paragraph 128(i) to (v) throughout his leave as a work permit holder, and has met the requirements of paragraph 135G(ii) throughout any leave as a highly skilled migrant;

(iii) he is still required for the employment in question, as certified by his employer; and

(iv) his employer certifies that he is paid at or above the appropriate rate for the job as stated in the codes of practice for Tier 2 Sponsors published by the UK Border Agency, and

(v) the applicant provides the specified documents as set out in the application form for settlement and accompanying guidance to evidence the employer's certification in sub-section (iv), and

(vi) he has sufficient knowledge of the English language and sufficient knowledge about life in the United Kingdom, in accordance with paragraph 33BA of these Rules, unless he is under the age of 18 or aged 65 or over at the date of his application;

(vii) he does not have one or more unspent convictions within the meaning of the Rehabilitation of Offenders act 1974

Refusal of indefinite leave to remain for a work permit holder

135. Indefinite leave to remain in the United Kingdom for a work permit holder is to be refused if the Secretary of State is not satisfied that each of the requirements of paragraph 134 is met.

Highly skilled migrants

Requirements for leave to enter the United Kingdom as a highly skilled migrant

135A. DELETED

Leave to enter as a highly skilled migrant

135B. DELETED

Refusal of leave to enter as a highly skilled migrant

135C. DELETED.

Requirements for an extension of stay as a highly skilled migrant

135D. DELETED

135DA. DELETED

135DB. DELETED

135DC. DELETED

135DD. DELETED

135DE. DELETED

135DF. DELETED

135DG. DELETED

135DH. DELETED

Extension of stay as a highly skilled migrant

135E. DELETED

Refusal of extension of stay as a highly skilled migrant

135F. DELETED

Requirements for indefinite leave to remain as a highly skilled migrant

135G. The requirements for indefinite leave to remain for a person who has been granted leave as a highly skilled migrant are that the applicant:

(i) has spent a continuous period of 5 years (or four years where the applicant is applying under the terms of the HSMP ILR Judicial Review Policy Document) lawfully in the United Kingdom, of which the most recent period must have been spent with leave as a highly skilled migrant (in accordance with paragraphs 135A to 135F of these Rules), and the remainder must be made up of leave as a highly skilled migrant, leave as a work permit holder (under paragraphs 128 to 133 of these Rules), or leave as an Innovator (under paragraphs 210A to 210F of these Rules); and

(ii) throughout the five years (or four years where the applicant is applying under the terms of the HSMP ILR Judicial Review Policy Document) spent in the United Kingdom has been able to maintain and accommodate himself and any dependants adequately without recourse to public funds; and

(iii) is lawfully economically active in the United Kingdom in employment, self-employment or a combination of both; and

(iv) has sufficient knowledge of the English language and sufficient knowledge about life in the United Kingdom, in accordance with paragraph 33BA of these Rules unless he is under the age of 18 or aged 65 or over at the time he makes his application or the applicant is applying under the terms of the HSMP ILR Judicial Review Policy Document, and

(v) unless the applicant is applying under the terms of the HSMP ILR Judical Review Policy Document, does not have one or more unspent convictions within the meaning of the Rehabilitation of Offenders Act 1974.

Indefinite leave to remain as a highly skilled migrant

135GA. Indefinite leave to remain may be granted provided that the Secretary of State is satisfied that each of the requirements of paragraph 135G is met and that the application does not fall for refusal under paragraph 135HA.

Refusal of indefinite leave to remain as a highly skilled migrant

135H. Indefinite leave to remain in the United Kingdom is to be refused if the Secretary of State is not satisfied that each of the requirements of paragraph 135G is met or if the application falls for refusal under paragraph 135HA.

Additional grounds for refusal for highly skilled migrants

135HA. An application under paragraphs 135A–135C or 135G–135H of these Rules is to be refused, even if the applicant meets all the requirements of those paragraphs, if the Immigration Officer or Secretary of State has cause to doubt the genuineness of any document submitted by the applicant and, having taken reasonable steps to verify the document, has been unable to verify that it is genuine.

Sectors-Based Scheme

Requirements for leave to enter the United Kingdom for the purpose of employment under the Sectors-Based Scheme

135I. DELETED.

Leave to enter for the purpose of employment under the Sectors-Based Scheme

135J. DELETED.

Refusal of leave to enter for the purpose of employment under the Sectors-Based Scheme

135K. DELETED.

Requirements for an extension of stay for Sector-Based employment

135L. DELETED.

Extension of stay for Sectors-Based Scheme employment

135M. DELETED.

Refusal of extension of stay for Sectors-Based Scheme employment

135N. DELETED.

International Graduates Scheme

Requirements for leave to enter as a participant in the International Graduates Scheme

135O. DELETED

Leave to enter as a participant in the International Graduates Scheme

135P. DELETED

Refusal of leave to enter as a participant in the International Graduates Scheme

135Q. DELETED

Requirements for leave to remain as a participant in the International Graduates Scheme

135R. DELETED

Leave to remain as a participant in the International Graduates Scheme

135S. DELETED

Refusal of leave to remain as a participant in the International Graduates Scheme

135T. DELETED

Representatives of overseas newspapers, news agencies and broadcasting organisations

Requirements for leave to enter as a representative of an overseas newspaper, news agency or broadcasting organisation

136. Deleted on 27 November 2008 by paragraph 39 of Statement of Changes HC 1113 except insofar as relevant to paragraph 142 and 143.

Indefinite leave to remain for a representative of an overseas newspaper, news agency or broadcasting organisation

142. Indefinite leave to remain may be granted, on application, to a representative of an overseas newspaper, news agency or broadcasting organisation provided:

(i) he has spent a continuous period of 5 years in the United Kingdom in this capacity; and

(ii) he has met the requirements of paragraph 139 throughout the 5 year period; and

(iii) he is still required for the employment in question, as certified by his employer; and

(iv) he has sufficient knowledge of the English language and sufficient knowledge about life in the United Kingdom in accordance with paragraph 33BA of these Rules, unless he is under the age of 18 or aged 65 or over at the time he makes his application; and

(v) he does not have one or more unspent convictions within the meaning of the Rehabilitation of Offenders Act 1974.

Refusal of indefinite leave to remain for a representative of an overseas newspaper, news agency or broadcasting organisation.

143. Indefinite leave to remain in the United Kingdom for a representative of an overseas newspaper, news agency or broadcasting organisation is to be refused if the Secretary of State is not satisfied that each of the requirements of paragraph 142 is met.

143A. DELETED

Leave to enter as a Fresh Talent: Working in Scotland scheme participant

143B. DELETED

Refusal of leave to enter as a Fresh Talent: Working in Scotland scheme participant

143C. DELETED

Requirements for an extension of stay as a Fresh Talent: Working in Scotland scheme participant

143D. DELETED

Extension of stay as a Fresh Talent: Working in Scotland scheme participant

143E. DELETED

Refusal of an extension of stay as a Fresh Talent: Working in Scotland scheme participant

143F. DELETED

Representatives of overseas businesses

Requirements for leave to enter as a representative of an overseas business

144. The requirements to be met by a person seeking leave to enter the United Kingdom as a representative of an overseas business are that he:

(i) has been recruited and taken on as an employee outside the United Kingdom of a business which has its headquarters and principal place of business outside the United Kingdom; and

(ii) is seeking entry to the United Kingdom:

(a) as a senior employee of an overseas business which has no branch, subsidiary or other representative in the United Kingdom with full authority to take operational decisions on behalf of the overseas business for the purpose of representing it in the United Kingdom by establishing and operating a registered branch or wholly owned subsidiary of that overseas business, the branch or subsidiary of which will be concerned with same type of business activity as the overseas business; or

(b) as an employee of an overseas newspaper, news agency or broadcasting organisation being posted on a long-term assignment as a representative of their overseas employer.

(iii) where entry is sought under (ii)(a), the person:

(a) will be the sole representative of the employer present in the United Kingdom under the terms of this paragraph;

(b) intends to be employed full time as a representative of that overseas business; and

(c) is not a majority shareholder in that overseas business.

(iv) where entry is sought under (ii)(b), the person intends to work full-time as a representative of their overseas employer.

(v) does not intend to take employment except within the terms of this paragraph; and

(vi) has competence in the English language to the required standard on the basis that

(a) paragraphs 2(b) or (c) of Appendix B of these Rules applies to the person, or

(b) the person is competent in the English language to a basic user standard, including the ability to understand and use familiar everyday expressions, to introduce himself and others and to ask and answer questions about basic personal details, and

(1) provides an original English language test certificate from an English language test provider approved by the Secretary of State for these purposes, which clearly shows the applicant's name, the qualification obtained (which must meet or exceed the level that the Secretary of State specifies in the guidance as being required to meet the standard described above) and the date of the award, or

(2) has obtained an academic qualification (not a professional or vocational qualification) which is deemed by UK NARIC to meet the recognised standard of a Bachelor's degree in the UK, and

(i) provides the specified evidence to show he has the qualification, and

(ii) UK NARIC has confirmed that the qualification was taught or researched in English to level C1 of the Council of Europe's Common European Framework for Language learning or above, or

(3) has obtained an academic qualification (not a professional or vocational qualification) which is deemed by UK NARIC to meet or exceed the recognised standard of a Bachelor's or Master's degree in the UK, and provides the specified evidence to show that:

(i) he has the qualification, and

(ii) the qualification was taught or researched in English,

(vii) can maintain and accommodate himself and any dependants adequately without recourse to public funds; and

(viii) holds a valid United Kingdom entry clearance for entry in this capacity.

Leave to enter as a representative of an overseas business

145. A person seeking leave to enter the United Kingdom as a representative of an overseas business may be admitted for a period not exceeding 3 years provided he is able to produce to the Immigration Officer, on arrival, a valid United Kingdom entry clearance for entry in this capacity, and his leave may be subject to the following conditions:

(i) no recourse to public funds,

(ii) registration with the police, if this is required by paragraph 326 of these Rules, and

(iii) no employment other than working for the business which the applicant has been admitted to represent.

Refusal of leave to enter as a representative of an overseas business

146. Leave to enter as a representative of an overseas business is to be refused if a valid United Kingdom entry clearance for entry in this capacity is not produced to the Immigration Officer on arrival.

Requirements for an extension of stay as a representative of an overseas business

147. The requirements for an extension of stay as a representative of an overseas business are that the applicant:

(i) entered the United Kingdom with a valid United Kingdom entry clearance as:

(a) a sole representative of an overseas business, including entry under the rules providing for the admission of sole representatives in force prior to 1 October 2009; or

(b) a representative of an overseas newspaper, news agency or broadcasting organisation;

(ii) the person was admitted in accordance with paragraph 144(ii)(a) and can show that:

(a) the overseas business still has its headquarters and principal place of business outside the United Kingdom; and

(b) he is employed full time as a representative of that overseas business and has established and is in charge of its registered branch or wholly owned subsidiary; and

(c) he is still required for the employment in question, as certified by his employer;

(iii) the person was admitted in accordance with paragraph 144(ii)(b) and can show that:

(a) he is still engaged in the employment for which the entry clearance was granted; and

(b) he is still required for the employment in question, as certified by his employer.

(iv) does not intend to take employment except within the terms of this paragraph; and

(v) can maintain and accommodate himself and any dependants adequately without recourse to public funds.

Extension of stay as a representative of an overseas business

148. An extension of stay as a representative of an overseas business may be granted provided the Secretary of State is satisfied that each of the requirements of paragraph 147 is met. The extension of stay will be granted for:

(i) a period not exceeding 2 years, unless paragraph (ii) applies.

(ii) a period not exceeding 3 years, if the applicant was last granted leave prior to 1 October 2009, and will be subject to the following conditions:

(i) no recourse to public funds,

(ii) registration with the police, if this is required by paragraph 326 of these Rules, and

(iii) no employment other than working for the business which the applicant has been admitted to represent.

Refusal of extension of stay as a representative of an overseas business

149. An extension of stay as a representative of an overseas business is to be refused if the Secretary of State is not satisfied that each of the requirements of paragraph 147 is met.

Indefinite leave to remain for a representative of an overseas business

150. Indefinite leave to remain may be granted, on application, to a representative of an overseas business provided:

(i) he has spent a continuous period of 5 years in the United Kingdom in this capacity; and

(ii) he has met the requirements of paragraph 147 throughout the 5 year period; and

(iii) he is still required for the employment in question, as certified by his employer; and

(iv) he has sufficient knowledge of the English language and sufficient knowledge about life in the United Kingdom in accordance with paragraph 33BA of these Rules, unless he is under the age of 18 or aged 65 or over at the time he makes his application, and

(v) he does not have one or more unspent convictions within the meaning of the Rehabilitation of Offenders Act 1974.

Refusal of indefinite leave to remain for a sole representative of an overseas business

151. Indefinite leave to remain in the United Kingdom for a representative of an overseas business is to be refused if the Secretary of State is not satisfied that each of the requirements of paragraph 150 is met.

Private servants in diplomatic households

Requirements for leave to enter as a private servant in a diplomatic household

152. Deleted on 27 November 2008 by paragraph 39 of Statement of Changes HC 1113 except insofar as relevant to paragraph 158 and 159.

Indefinite leave to remain for a servant in a diplomatic household

158. Indefinite leave to remain may be granted, on application, to a private servant in a diplomatic household provided:

(i) he has spent a continuous period of 5 years in the United Kingdom in this capacity; and

(ii) he has met the requirements of paragraph 155 throughout the 5 year period; and

(iii) he is still required for the employment in question, as certified by his employer; and

(iv) he has sufficient knowledge of the English language and sufficient knowledge about life in the United Kingdom, unless he is under the age of 18 or aged 65 or over at the time he makes his application.

(v) he does not have one or more unspent convictions within the meaning of the Rehabilitation of Offenders Act 1974.

Refusal of indefinite leave to remain for a servant in a diplomatic household

159. Indefinite leave to remain in the United Kingdom for a private servant in a diplomatic household is to be refused if the Secretary of State is not satisfied that each of the requirements of paragraph 158 is met.

Domestic workers in private households

Requirements for leave to enter as a domestic worker in a private household

159A. The requirements to be met by a person seeking leave to enter the United Kingdom as a domestic worker in a private household are that he:

(i) is aged 18–65 inclusive;

(ii) has been employed as a domestic worker for one year or more immediately prior to application for entry clearance under the same roof as his employer or in a household that the employer uses for himself on a regular basis and where there is evidence that there is a connection between employer and employee;

(iii) that he intends to travel to the United Kingdom in the company of his employer, his employer's spouse or civil partner or his employer's minor child;

(iv) intends to work full time as a domestic worker under the same roof as his employer or in a household that the employer uses for himself on a regular basis and where there is evidence that there is a connection between employer and employee;

(v) does not intend to take employment except within the terms of this paragraph; and

(vi) can maintain and accommodate himself adequately without recourse to public funds; and

(vii) holds a valid United Kingdom entry clearance for entry in this capacity.

Leave to enter as a domestic worker in a private household

159B. A person seeking leave to enter the United Kingdom as a domestic worker in a private household may be given leave to enter for that purpose for a period not exceeding 12 months provided he is able to produce to the Immigration Officer, on arrival, a valid United Kingdom entry clearance for entry in this capacity.

Refusal of leave to enter as a domestic worker in a private household

159C. Leave to enter as a domestic worker in a private household is to be refused if a valid United Kingdom entry clearance for entry in this capacity is not produced to the Immigration Officer on arrival.

Requirements for extension of stay as a domestic worker in a private household

159D. The requirements for an extension of stay as a domestic worker in a private household are that the applicant:

(i) entered the United Kingdom with a valid United Kingdom entry clearance as a domestic worker in a private household; and

(ii) has continued to be employed for the duration of his leave as a domestic worker in a private household; and

(iii) continues to be required for employment for the period of the extension sought as a domestic worker in a private household within the terms of paragraph 159A as certified by his current employer; and

(iv) meets each of the requirements of paragraph 159A(i) to (vi).

Extension of stay as a domestic worker in a private household

159E. An extension of stay as a domestic worker in a private household may be granted for a period not exceeding 12 months at a time provided the Secretary of State is satisfied that each of the requirements of paragraph 159D is met.

Refusal of extension of stay as a domestic worker in a private household

159F. An extension of stay as a domestic worker may be refused if the Secretary of State is not satisfied that each of the requirements of paragraph 159D is met.

Indefinite leave to remain for a domestic worker in a private household

159G. Indefinite leave to remain may be granted, on application, to a domestic worker in a private household provided that:

(i) he has spent a continuous period of 5 years in the United Kingdom employed in this capacity; and

(ii) he has met the requirements of paragraph 159A throughout the 5 year period; and

(iii) he is still required for employment as a domestic worker in a private household, as certified by the current employer; and

(iv) he has sufficient knowledge of the English language and sufficient knowledge about life in the United Kingdom, unless he is under the age of 18 or aged 65 or over at the time he makes his application, and

(v) he does not have one or more unspent convictions within the meaning of the Rehabilitation of Offenders Act 1974.

Refusal of indefinite leave to remain for a domestic worker in a private household

159H. Indefinite leave to remain in the United Kingdom for a domestic worker in a private household is to be refused if the Secretary of State is not satisfied that each of the requirements of paragraph 159G is met.

Overseas government employees

Requirements for leave to enter as an overseas government employee

160. Deleted on 27 November 2008 by paragraph 39 of Statement of Changes HC 1113 except insofar as relevant to paragraph 167 and 168.

Indefinite leave to remain for an overseas government employee

167. Indefinite leave to remain may be granted, on application, to an overseas government employee provided:

(i) he has spent a continuous period of 5 years in the United Kingdom in this capacity; and

(ii) he has met the requirements of paragraph 164 throughout the 5 year period; and

(iii) he is still required for the employment in question, as certified by his employer; and

(iv) he has sufficient knowledge of the English language and sufficient knowledge about life in the United Kingdom, in accordance with paragraph 33BA of these Rules, unless he is under the age of 18 or aged 65 or over at the time he makes his application; and

(v) he does not have one or more unspent convictions within the meaning of the Rehabilitation of Offenders Act 1974

Refusal of indefinite leave to remain for an overseas government employee

168. Indefinite leave to remain in the United Kingdom for an overseas government employee is to be refused if the Secretary of State is not satisfied that each of the requirements of paragraph 167 is met.

169. For the purposes of these Rules:

(i) a minister of religion means a religious functionary whose main regular duties comprise the leading of a congregation in performing the rites and rituals of the faith and in preaching the essentials of the creed;

(ii) a missionary means a person who is directly engaged in spreading a religious doctrine and whose work is not in essence administrative or clerical;

(iii) a member of a religious order means a person who is coming to live in a community run by that order.

Requirements for leave to enter as a minister of religion, missionary, or member of a religious order

170. Deleted on 27 November 2008 by paragraph 39 of Statement of Changes HC 1113 except insofar as relevant to paragraph 176 AND 177.

Refusal of extension of stay as a minister of religion, missionary or member of a religious order

175. An extension of stay as a minister of religion, missionary or member of a religious order is to be refused if the Secretary of State is not satisfied that each of the requirements of paragraph 173 or 174A is met.

Indefinite leave to remain for a minister of religion, missionary or member of a religious order

176. Indefinite leave to remain may be granted, on application, to a person admitted as a minister of religion, missionary or member of a religious order provided:

(i) he has spent a continuous period of 5 years in the United Kingdom in this capacity; and

(ii) he has met the requirements of paragraph 173 or 174A throughout the 5 year period; and

(iii) he is still required for the employment in question as certified by the leadership of his congregation, his employer or the head of the religious order to which he belongs; and

(iv) he has sufficient knowledge of the English language and sufficient knowledge about life in the United Kingdom in accordance with paragraph 33BA of these Rules, unless he is under the age of 18 or aged 65 or over at the time he makes his application; and

(v) he does not have one or more unspent convictions within the meaning of the Rehabilitation of Offenders Act 1974.

Refusal of indefinite leave to remain for a minister of religion, missionary or member of a religious order

177. Indefinite leave to remain in the United Kingdom for a minister of religion, missionary or member of a religious order is to be refused if the Secretary of State is not satisfied that each of the requirements of paragraph 176 is met.

177A. DELETED

Requirements for leave to enter the United Kingdom as a visiting religious worker or a religious worker in a non-pastoral role

DELETED

Leave to enter as a visiting religious worker or a religious worker in a non-pastoral role

177C. DELETED

177D. DELETED

Requirements for an extension of stay as a visiting religious worker or a religious worker in a non pastoral role

177E. DELETED

Extension of stay as a visiting religious worker or a religious worker in a non-pastoral role

177F. DELETED

Refusal of an extension of stay as a visiting religious worker or a religious worker in a non pastoral role

177G. DELETED

Airport based operational ground staff of overseas-owned airlines

Requirements for leave to enter the United Kingdom as a member of the operational ground staff of an overseas-owned airline

178. Deleted on 27 November 2008 by paragraph 39 of Statement of Changes HC 1113 except insofar as relevant to paragraph 184 and 185.

Indefinite leave to remain for a member of the operational ground staff of an overseas owned airline

184. Indefinite leave to remain may be granted, on application, to a member of the operational ground staff of an overseas-owned airline provided:

(i) he has spent a continuous period of 5 years in the United Kingdom in this capacity; and

(ii) he has met the requirements of paragraph 181 throughout the 5 year period; and

(iii) he is still required for the employment in question as certified by the employer; and

(iv) he has sufficient knowledge of the English language and sufficient knowledge about life in the United Kingdom in accordance with paragraph 33BA of these Rules, unless he is under the age of 18 or aged 65 or over at the time he makes his application; and

(v) he does not have one or more unspent convictions within the meaning of the Rehabilitation of Offenders Act 1974.

Refusal of indefinite leave to remain for a member of the operational ground staff of an overseas owned airline

185. Indefinite leave to remain in the United Kingdom for a member of the operational ground staff of an overseas owned airline is to be refused if the Secretary of State is not satisfied that each of the requirements of paragraph 184 is met.

Persons with United Kingdom ancestry

Requirements for leave to enter on the grounds of United Kingdom ancestry

186. The requirements to be met by a person seeking leave to enter the United Kingdom on the grounds of his United Kingdom ancestry are that he:

(i) is a Commonwealth citizen; and

(ii) is aged 17 or over; and

(iii) is able to provide proof that one of his grandparents was born in the United Kingdom and Islands and that any such grandparent is the applicant's blood grandparent or grandparent by reason of an adoption recognised by the laws of the United Kingdom relating to adoption; and

(iv) is able to work and intends to take or seek employment in the United Kingdom; and

(v) will be able to maintain and accommodate himself and any dependants adequately without recourse to public funds; and

(vi) holds a valid United Kingdom entry clearance for entry in this capacity.

Leave to enter the United Kingdom on the grounds of United Kingdom ancestry

187. A person seeking leave to enter the United Kingdom on the grounds of his United Kingdom ancestry may be given leave to enter for a period not exceeding 5 years provided he is able to produce to the Immigration Officer, on arrival, a valid United Kingdom entry clearance for entry in this capacity.

Refusal of leave to enter on the grounds of United Kingdom ancestry

188. Leave to enter the United Kingdom on the grounds of United Kingdom ancestry is to be refused if a valid United Kingdom entry clearance for entry in this capacity is not produced to the Immigration Officer on arrival.

Requirements for an extension of stay on the grounds of United Kingdom ancestry

189. The requirements to be met by a person seeking an extension of stay on the grounds of United Kingdom ancestry are that:

(i) he is able to meet each of the requirements of paragraph 186(i)–(v); and

(ii) he was admitted to the United Kingdom on the grounds of United Kingdom ancestry in accordance with paragraphs 186 to 188 or has been granted an extension of stay in this capacity.

Extension of stay on the grounds of United Kingdom ancestry

190. An extension of stay on the grounds of United Kingdom ancestry may be granted for a period not exceeding 5 years provided the Secretary of State is satisfied that each of the requirements of paragraph 189 is met.

Refusal of extension of stay on the grounds of United Kingdom ancestry

191. An extension of stay on the grounds of United Kingdom ancestry is to be refused if the Secretary of State is not satisfied that each of the requirements of paragraph 189 is met.

Indefinite leave to remain on the grounds of United Kingdom ancestry

192. Indefinite leave to remain may be granted, on application, to a Commonwealth citizen with a United Kingdom born grandparent provided:

(i) he meets the requirements of paragraph 186(i)–(v); and

(ii) he has spent a continuous period of 5 years in the United Kingdom in this capacity; and

(iii) he has sufficient knowledge of the English language and sufficient knowledge about life in the United Kingdom, unless he is under the age of 18 or aged 65 or over at the time he makes his application; and

(iv) he does not have one or more unspent convictions within the meaning of the Rehabilitation of Offenders Act 1974.

Refusal of indefinite leave to remain on the grounds of United Kingdom ancestry

193. Indefinite leave to remain in the United Kingdom on the grounds of a United Kingdom born grandparent is to be refused if the Secretary of State is not satisfied that each of the requirements of paragraph 192 is met.

Spouses or civil partners of persons who have or have had leave to enter or remain under paragraphs 128–193 (but not paragraphs 135I–135K)

Requirements for leave to enter as the spouse or civil partner of a person with limited leave to enter or remain in the United Kingdom under paragraphs 128–193 (but not paragraphs 135I–135K)

194. The requirements to be met by a person seeking leave to enter the United Kingdom as the spouse or civil partner of a person with limited leave to enter or remain in the United Kingdom under paragraphs 128–193 (but not paragraphs 135I–135K) are that:

(i) the applicant is married to or a civil partner of a person with limited leave to enter in the United Kingdom under paragraphs 128–193 (but not paragraphs 135I–135K); and

(ii) each of the parties intends to live with the other as his or her spouse or civil partner during the applicant's stay and the marriage or civil partnership is subsisting; and

(iii) there will be adequate accommodation for the parties and any dependants without recourse to public funds in accommodation which they own or occupy exclusively; and

(iv) the parties will be able to maintain themselves and any dependants adequately without recourse to public funds; and

(v) the applicant does not intend to stay in the United Kingdom beyond any period of leave granted to his spouse; and

(vi) the applicant holds a valid United Kingdom entry clearance for entry in this capacity.

Leave to enter as the spouse or civil partner of a person with limited leave to enter or remain in the United Kingdom under paragraphs 128–193 (but not paragraphs 135I–135K)

195. A person seeking leave to enter the United Kingdom as the spouse or civil partner of a person with limited leave to enter or remain in the United Kingdom under paragraphs 128–193 (but not paragraphs 135I–135K) may be given leave to enter for a period not in excess of that granted to the person with limited leave to enter or remain under paragraphs 128–193 (but not paragraphs 135I–135K) provided the Immigration Officer is satisfied that each of the requirements of paragraph 194 is met. If the person is seeking leave to enter as the spouse or civil partner of a Highly Skilled Migrant, leave which is granted will be subject to a condition prohibiting Employment as a Doctor or Dentist in Training, unless the applicant has obtained a degree in medicine or dentistry at bachelor's level or above from a UK institution that is a UK recognised or listed body, or which holds a sponsor licence under Tier 4 of the Points Based System.

Refusal of leave to enter as the spouse or civil partners of a person with limited leave to enter or remain in the United Kingdom under paragraphs 128–193 (but not paragraphs 135I–135K)

196. Leave to enter the United Kingdom as the spouse or civil partner of a person with limited leave to enter or remain in the United Kingdom under paragraphs 128–193 (but not paragraphs 135I–135K) is to be refused if the Immigration Officer is not satisfied that each of the requirements of paragraph 194 is met.

Requirements for extension of stay as the spouse or civil partner of a person who has or has had leave to enter or remain in the United Kingdom under paragraphs 128–193 (but not paragraphs 135I–135K)

196A. The requirements to be met by a person seeking an extension of stay in the United Kingdom as the spouse or civil partner of a person who has or has had leave to enter or remain in the United Kingdom under paragraphs 128–193 (but not paragraphs 135I–135K) are that the applicant:

(i) is married to or civil partner of a person with limited leave to enter or remain in the United Kingdom under paragraphs 128–193 (but not paragraphs 135I–135K); or

(ii) is married to or civil partner of a person who has limited leave to enter or remain in the United Kingdom under paragraphs 128–193 (but not paragraphs 135I–135K) and who is being granted indefinite leave to remain at the same time; or

(iii) is married to or a civil partner of a person who has indefinite leave to remain in the United Kingdom and who had limited leave to enter or remain in the United Kingdom under paragraphs 128–193 (but not paragraphs 135I–135K) immediately before being granted indefinite leave to remain; and

(iv) meets the requirements of paragraph 194(ii)–(v); and

(v) was admitted with a valid United Kingdom entry clearance for entry in this capacity.

Extension of stay as the spouse or civil partner of a person who has or has had leave to enter or remain in the United Kingdom under paragraphs 128–193 (but not paragraphs 135I–135K)

196B. An extension of stay in the United Kingdom as:

(i) the spouse or civil partner of a person who has limited leave to enter or remain under paragraphs 128–193 (but not paragraphs 135I–135K) may be granted for a period not in excess of that granted to the person with limited leave to enter or remain; or

(ii) the spouse or civil partner of a person who is being admitted at the same time for settlement, or the spouse or civil partner of a person who has indefinite leave to remain, may be granted for a period not exceeding 2 years, in both instances, provided the Secretary of State is satisfied that each of the requirements of paragraph 196A is met.

If the person is seeking an extension of stay as the spouse or civil partner, of a Highly Skilled Migrant, leave which is granted will be subject to a condition prohibiting Employment as a Doctor or Dentist in Training, unless the applicant:

(1) has obtained a primary degree in medicine or dentistry at bachelor's level or above from a UK institution that is a UK recognised or listed body, or which holds a sponsor licence under Tier 4 of the Points Based System; or

(2) has, or has last been granted, entry clearance, leave to enter or leave to remain that was not subject to any condition restricting him from taking employment as a Doctor in Training, and has been employed during that leave as a Doctor in Training; or

(3) has, or has last been granted, entry clearance, leave to enter or leave to remain that was not subject to any condition restricting him from taking employment as a Dentist in Training, and has been employed during that leave as a Dentist in Training.

Refusal of extension of stay as the spouse or civil partner of a person who has or has had leave to enter or remain in the United Kingdom under paragraphs 128–193 (but not paragraphs 135I–135K)

196C. An extension of stay in the United Kingdom as the spouse or civil partner of a person who has or has had leave to enter or remain in the United Kingdom under paragraphs 128–193 (but not paragraphs 135I–135K) is to be refused if the Secretary of State is not satisfied that each of the requirements of paragraph 196A is met.

Requirements for indefinite leave to remain for the spouse or civil partner of a person who has or has had leave to enter or remain in the United Kingdom under paragraphs 128–193 (but not paragraphs 135I–135K)

196D. The requirements to be met by a person seeking indefinite leave to remain in the United Kingdom as the spouse or civil partner of a person who has or has had leave to enter or remain in the United Kingdom under paragraphs 128–193 (but not paragraphs 135I–135K) are that the applicant:

(i) is married to or civil partner of a person who has limited leave to enter or remain in the United Kingdom under paragraphs 128–193 (but not paragraphs 135I–135K) and who is being granted indefinite leave to remain at the same time; or

(ii) is married to or a civil partner of a person who has indefinite leave to remain in the United Kingdom and who had limited leave to enter or remain in the United Kingdom under paragraphs 128–193 (but not paragraphs 135I–135K) immediately before being granted indefinite leave to remain; and

(iii) meets the requirements of paragraph 194(ii)–(v); and

(iv) has sufficient knowledge of the English language and sufficient knowledge about life in the United Kingdom, unless he is under the age of 18 or aged 65 or over at the time he makes his application; and

(v) was admitted with a valid United Kingdom entry clearance for entry in this capacity; and

(vi) does not have one or more unspent convictions within the meaning of the Rehabilitation of Offenders Act 1974.

Indefinite leave to remain as the spouse or civil partner of a person who has or has had leave to enter or remain in the United Kingdom under paragraphs 128–193 (but not paragraphs 135I–135K)

196E. Indefinite leave to remain in the United Kingdom for the spouse or civil partner of a person who has or has had leave to enter or remain in the United Kingdom under paragraphs 128–193 (but not paragraphs 135I–135K) may be granted provided the Secretary of State is satisfied that each of the requirements of paragraph 196D is met.

Refusal of indefinite leave to remain as the spouse or civil partner of a person who has or has had leave to enter or remain in the United Kingdom under paragraphs 128–193 (but not paragraphs 135I–135K)

196F. Indefinite leave to remain in the United Kingdom for the spouse or civil partner of a person who has or has had limited leave to enter or remain in the United Kingdom under paragraphs 128–193 (but not paragraphs 135I–135K) is to be refused if the Secretary of State is not satisfied that each of the requirements of paragraph 196D is met.

Children of persons with limited leave to enter or remain in the United Kingdom under paragraphs 128–193 (but not paragraphs 135i–135k)

Requirements for leave to enter or remain as the child of a person with limited leave to enter or remain in the United Kingdom under paragraphs 128–193 (but not paragraphs 135I–135K)

197. The requirements to be met by a person seeking leave to enter or remain in the United Kingdom as a child of a person with limited leave to enter or remain in the United Kingdom under paragraphs 128–193 (but not paragraphs 135I–135K) are that:

(i) he is the child of a parent with limited leave to enter or remain in the United Kingdom under paragraphs 128–193(but not paragraphs 135I–135K); and

(ii) he is under the age of 18 or has current leave to enter or remain in this capacity; and

(iii) he is unmarried and is not a civil partner, has not formed an independent family unit and is not leading an independent life; and

(iv) he can and will be maintained and accommodated adequately without recourse to public funds in accommodation which his parent(s) own or occupy exclusively; and

(v) he will not stay in the United Kingdom beyond any period of leave granted to his parent(s); and

(vi) both parents are being or have been admitted to or allowed to remain in the United Kingdom save where:

(a) the parent he is accompanying or joining is his sole surviving parent; or

(b) the parent he is accompanying or joining has had sole responsibility for his upbringing; or

(c) there are serious and compelling family or other considerations which make exclusion from the United Kingdom undesirable and suitable arrangements have been made for his care; and

(vii) if seeking leave to enter, he holds a valid United Kingdom entry clearance for entry in this capacity or, if seeking leave to remain, was admitted with a valid United Kingdom entry clearance for entry in this capacity.

Leave to enter or remain as the child of a person with limited leave to enter or remain in the United Kingdom under paragraphs 128–193 (but not paragraphs 135I–135K)

198. A person seeking leave to enter or remain in the United Kingdom as the child of a person with limited leave to enter or remain in the United Kingdom under paragraphs 128–193 (but not paragraphs 135I–135K) may be given leave to enter or remain in the United Kingdom for a period of leave not in excess of that granted to the person with limited leave to enter or remain under paragraphs 128–193 (but not paragraphs 135I–135K) provided that, in relation to an application for leave to enter, he is able to produce to the Immigration Officer, on arrival, a valid United Kingdom entry clearance for entry in this capacity or, in the case of an application for limited leave to remain, he was admitted with a valid United Kingdom entry clearance for entry in this capacity and is able to satisfy the Secretary of State that each of the requirements of paragraph 197(i)–(vi) is met. An application for indefinite leave to remain in this category may be granted provided the applicant was admitted with a valid United Kingdom entry clearance for entry in this capacity and is able to satisfy the Secretary of State that each of the requirements of paragraph 197(i)–(vi) is met and provided indefinite leave to remain is, at the same time, being granted to the person with limited leave to enter or remain under paragraphs 128–193 (but not paragraphs 135I–135K) .

Refusal of leave to enter or remain as the child of a person with limited leave to enter or remain in the United Kingdom under paragraphs 128–193 (but not paragraphs 135I–135K)

199. Leave to enter or remain in the United Kingdom as the child of a person with limited leave to enter or remain in the United Kingdom under paragraphs 128–193 (but not paragraphs 135I–135K) is to be refused if, in relation to an application for leave to enter, a valid United Kingdom entry clearance for entry in this capacity is not produced to the Immigration Officer on arrival or, in the case of an application for limited leave to remain, if the applicant was not admitted with a valid United Kingdom entry clearance for entry in this capacity or is unable to satisfy the Secretary of State that each of the requirements of paragraph 197(i)–(vi) is met. An application for indefinite leave to remain in this category is to be refused if the applicant was not admitted with a valid United Kingdom entry clearance for entry in this capacity or is unable to satisfy the Secretary of State that each of the requirements of

paragraph 197(i)–(vi) is met or if indefinite leave to remain is not, at the same time, being granted to the person with limited leave to enter or remain under paragraphs 128–193 (but not paragraphs 135I–135K).

Multiple entry work permit employment

Requirements for leave to enter for Multiple Entry work permit employment

199A. The requirements to be met by a person coming to the United Kingdom to seek or take Multiple Entry work permit employment are that he:

(i) holds a valid work permit;

(ii) is not of an age which puts him outside the limits for employment;

(iii) is capable of undertaking the employment specified in the work permit;

(iv) does not intend to take employment except as specified in his work permit;

(v) is able to maintain and accommodate himself adequately without recourse to public funds; and

(vi) intends to leave the United Kingdom at the end of the employment covered by the Multiple Entry work permit and holds a valid United Kingdom Entry clearance for entry into this capacity excepts where he holds a work permit valid for 6 months or less or he is a British National (Overseas), a British overseas territories citizen, a British Overseas citizen, a British protected person or a person who under the British Nationality Act 1981 ia a British subject.

Leave to enter for Multiple Entry work permit employment

199B. A person seeking leave to enter the United Kingdom for the purpose of Multiple Entry work permit employment may be admitted for a period not exceeding 2 years provided that the Immigration Officer is satisfied that each of the requirements of paragraph 199A are met.

Refusal of leave to enter for Multiple Entry work permit employment

199C. Leave to enter for the purpose of Multiple Entry work permit employment is to be refused if the Immigration Officer is not satisfied that each of the requirements of paragraph 199A is met.

Part 6 – Persons seeking to enter or remain in the United Kingdom as a businessman, self-employed person, investor, writer, composer or artist

Persons intending to establish themselves in business

Requirements for leave to enter the United Kingdom as a person intending to establish himself in business

200. Deleted on 30 June 2008 by paragraph 17 of Statement of Changes HC 607 except insofar as relevant to paragraph 209. Please see Appendix F for the wording of these Rules in a case in which they are relevant.

201. Deleted on 30 June 2008 by paragraph 17 of Statement of Changes HC 607 except insofar as relevant to paragraph 209. Please see Appendix F for the wording of these Rules in a case in which they are relevant.

202. Deleted on 30 June 2008 by paragraph 17 of Statement of Changes HC 607 except insofar as relevant to paragraph 209. Please see Appendix F for the wording of these Rules in a case in which they are relevant.

203. Deleted on 30 June 2008 by paragraph 17 of Statement of Changes HC 607 except insofar as relevant to paragraph 209. Please see Appendix F for the wording of these Rules in a case in which they are relevant.

Leave to enter the United Kingdom as a person seeking to establish himself in business

204. Deleted on 30 June 2008 by paragraph 17 of Statement of Changes HC 607 except insofar as relevant to paragraph 209. Please see Appendix F for the wording of these Rules in a case in which they are relevant.

Refusal of leave to enter the United Kingdom as a person seeking to establish himself in business

205. Deleted on 30 June 2008 by paragraph 17 of Statement of Changes HC 607 except insofar as relevant to paragraph 209. Please see Appendix F for the wording of these Rules in a case in which they are relevant.

Requirements for an extension of stay in order to remain in business

206. Deleted on 30 June 2008 by paragraph 17 of Statement of Changes HC 607 except insofar as relevant to paragraph 209. Please see Appendix F for the wording of these Rules in a case in which they are relevant.

206A. Deleted on 30 June 2008 by paragraph 17 of Statement of Changes HC 607 except insofar as relevant to paragraph 209. Please see Appendix F for the wording of these Rules in a case in which they are relevant.

206B. Deleted on 30 June 2008 by paragraph 17 of Statement of Changes HC 607 except insofar as relevant to paragraph 209. Please see Appendix F for the wording of these Rules in a case in which they are relevant.

206C. Deleted on 30 June 2008 by paragraph 17 of Statement of Changes HC 607 except insofar as relevant to paragraph 209. Please see Appendix F for the wording of these Rules in a case in which they are relevant.

206D. Deleted on 30 June 2008 by paragraph 17 of Statement of Changes HC 607 except insofar as relevant to paragraph 209. Please see Appendix F for the wording of these Rules in a case in which they are relevant.

206E. Deleted on 30 June 2008 by paragraph 17 of Statement of Changes HC 607 except insofar as relevant to paragraph 209. Please see Appendix F for the wording of these Rules in a case in which they are relevant.

206F. Deleted on 30 June 2008 by paragraph 17 of Statement of Changes HC 607 except insofar as relevant to paragraph 209. Please see Appendix F for the wording of these Rules in a case in which they are relevant.

206G. Deleted on 30 June 2008 by paragraph 17 of Statement of Changes HC 607 except insofar as relevant to paragraph 209. Please see Appendix F for the wording of these Rules in a case in which they are relevant.

206H. Deleted on 30 June 2008 by paragraph 17 of Statement of Changes HC 607 except insofar as relevant to paragraph 209. Please see Appendix F for the wording of these Rules in a case in which they are relevant.

206I. Deleted on 30 June 2008 by paragraph 17 of Statement of Changes HC 607 except insofar as relevant to paragraph 209. Please see Appendix F for the wording of these Rules in a case in which they are relevant.

Extension of stay in order to remain in business

207. Deleted on 30 June 2008 by paragraph 17 of Statement of Changes HC 607 except insofar as relevant to paragraph 209. Please see Appendix F for the wording of these Rules in a case in which they are relevant.

Refusal of extension of stay in order to remain in business

208. Deleted on 30 June 2008 by paragraph 17 of Statement of Changes HC 607 except insofar as relevant to paragraph 209. Please see Appendix F for the wording of these Rules in a case in which they are relevant.

Indefinite leave to remain for a person established in business

209. Indefinite leave to remain may be granted, on application, to a person established in business provided he:

(i) has spent a continuous period of 5 years in the United Kingdom in this capacity and is still engaged in the business in question; and

(ii) has met the requirements of paragraph 206 throughout the 5 year period; and

(iii) submits audited accounts for the first 4 years of trading and management accounts for the 5th year.; and

(iv) has sufficient knowledge of the English language and sufficient knowledge about life in the United Kingdom, in accordance with paragraph 33BA of these Rules, unless he is under the age of 18 or aged 65 or over at the time he makes his application; and

(v) does not have one or more unspent convictions within the meaning of the Rehabilitation of Offenders Act 1974.

Refusal of indefinite leave to remain for a person established in business

210. Indefinite leave to remain in the United Kingdom for a person established in business is to be refused if the Secretary of State is not satisfied that each of the requirements of paragraph 209 is met.

Innovators

Requirements for leave to enter the United Kingdom as an innovator

210A. Deleted on 30 June 2008 by paragraph 17 of Statement of Changes HC 607 except insofar as relevant to paragraph 210G. Please see Appendix F for the wording of these Rules in a case in which they are relevant.

Leave to enter as an innovator

210B. Deleted on 30 June 2008 by paragraph 17 of Statement of Changes HC 607 except insofar as relevant to paragraph 210G. Please see Appendix F for the wording of these Rules in a case in which they are relevant.

Refusal of leave to enter as an innovator

210C. Deleted on 30 June 2008 by paragraph 17 of Statement of Changes HC 607 except insofar as relevant to paragraph 210G. Please see Appendix F for the wording of these Rules in a case in which they are relevant.

Requirements for an extension of stay as an innovator

210D. Deleted on 30 June 2008 by paragraph 17 of Statement of Changes HC 607 except insofar as relevant to paragraph 210G. Please see Appendix F for the wording of these Rules in a case in which they are relevant.

210DA. Deleted on 30 June 2008 by paragraph 17 of Statement of Changes HC 607 except insofar as relevant to paragraph 210G. Please see Appendix F for the wording of these Rules in a case in which they are relevant.

210DB. Deleted on 30 June 2008 by paragraph 17 of Statement of Changes HC 607 except insofar as relevant to paragraph 210G. Please see Appendix F for the wording of these Rules in a case in which they are relevant.

210DC. Deleted on 30 June 2008 by paragraph 17 of Statement of Changes HC 607 except insofar as relevant to paragraph 210G. Please see Appendix F for the wording of these Rules in a case in which they are relevant.

210DD. Deleted on 30 June 2008 by paragraph 17 of Statement of Changes HC 607 except insofar as relevant to paragraph 210G. Please see Appendix F for the wording of these Rules in a case in which they are relevant.

210DE. Deleted on 30 June 2008 by paragraph 17 of Statement of Changes HC 607 except insofar as relevant to paragraph 210G. Please see Appendix F for the wording of these Rules in a case in which they are relevant.

210DF. Deleted on 30 June 2008 by paragraph 17 of Statement of Changes HC 607 except insofar as relevant to paragraph 210G. Please see Appendix F for the wording of these Rules in a case in which they are relevant.

210DG. Deleted on 30 June 2008 by paragraph 17 of Statement of Changes HC 607 except insofar as relevant to paragraph 210G. Please see Appendix F for the wording of these Rules in a case in which they are relevant.

210DH. Deleted on 30 June 2008 by paragraph 17 of Statement of Changes HC 607 except insofar as relevant to paragraph 210G. Please see Appendix F for the wording of these Rules in a case in which they are relevant.

210DI. Deleted on 30 June 2008 by paragraph 17 of Statement of Changes HC 607 except insofar as relevant to paragraph 210G. Please see Appendix F for the wording of these Rules in a case in which they are relevant.

Extension of stay as an innovator

210E. Deleted on 30 June 2008 by paragraph 17 of Statement of Changes HC 607 except insofar as relevant to paragraph 210G. Please see Appendix F for the wording of these Rules in a case in which they are relevant.

Refusal of extension of stay as an innovator

210F. Deleted on 30 June 2008 by paragraph 17 of Statement of Changes HC 607 except insofar as relevant to paragraph 210G. Please see Appendix F for the wording of these Rules in a case in which they are relevant.

Indefinite leave to remain for an innovator

210G. Indefinite leave to remain may be granted, on application, to a person currently with leave as an innovator provided that he:

(i) has spent a continuous period of at least 5 years leave in the United Kingdom in this capacity; and

(ii) has met the requirements of paragraph 210D throughout the 5 year period; and

(iii) he has sufficient knowledge of the English language and sufficient knowledge about life in the United Kingdom, *in accordance with paragraph 33BA of these Rules*, unless he is under the age of 18 or aged 65 or over at the time he makes his application; *and*

(iv) *he does not have one or more unspent convictions within the meaning of the Rehabilitation of Offenders Act 1974.*

Refusal of indefinite leave to remain as an innovator

210H. Indefinite leave to remain in the United Kingdom as a person currently with leave as a innovator is to be refused if the Secretary of State is not satisfied that each of the requirements of paragraph 210G is met.

Persons intending to establish themselves in business under provisions of EC Association Agreements

Requirements for leave to enter the United Kingdom as a person intending to establish himself in business under the provisions of an EC Association Agreement

211–221. DELETED

Indefinite leave to remain for a person established in business under the provisions of an EC Association Agreement

222. Indefinite leave to remain may be granted, on application, to a person established in business provided he–

(i) is a national of Bulgaria or Romania; and

(ii) entered the United Kingdom with a valid United Kingdom entry clearance as a person intending to establish himself in business under the provisions of an EC Association Agreement; and

(iii) was granted an extension of stay before 1st January 2007 in order to remain in business under the provisions of the Agreement; and

(iv) established himself in business in the United Kingdom, spent a continuous period of 5 years in the United Kingdom in this capacity and is still so engaged; and

(v) met the requirements of paragraph 222A throughout the period of 5 years; and

(vi) submits audited accounts for the first 4 years of trading and management accounts for the 5th year; and

(vii) he has sufficient knowledge of the English language and sufficient knowledge about life in the United Kingdom in accordance with paragraph 33BA of these Rules, unless he is under the age of 18 or aged 65 or over at the time he makes his application; and

(viii) does not have one or more unspent convictions within the meaning of the Rehabilitation of Offenders Act 1974.

222A. The requirements mentioned in paragraph 222(v) are that throughout the period of 5 years–

(i) the applicant's share of the profits of the business has been sufficient to maintain and accommodate himself and any dependants without recourse to employment (other than his work for the business) or to public funds; and

(ii) he has not supplemented his business activities by taking or seeking employment in the United Kingdom (other than his work for the business); and

(iii) he has satisfied the requirements in paragraph 222B or 222C.

222B. Where the applicant has established himself in a company in the United Kingdom which he effectively controls, the requirements for the purpose of paragraph 222A(iii) are that–

(i) the applicant has been actively involved in the promotion and management of the company; and

(ii) he has had a controlling interest in the company; and

(iii) the company was registered in the United Kingdom and has been trading or providing services in the United Kingdom; and

(iv) the company owned the assets of the business.

222C. Where the applicant has established himself as a sole trader or in a partnership in the United Kingdom, the requirements for the purpose of paragraph 222A(iii) are that–

(i) the applicant has been actively involved in trading or providing services on his own account or in a partnership in the United Kingdom; and

(ii) the applicant owned, or together with his partners owned, the assets of the business; and

(iii) in the case of a partnership, the applicant's part in the business did not amount to disguised employment.

Refusal of indefinite leave to remain for a person established in business under the provisions of an EC Association Agreement

223. Indefinite leave to remain in the United Kingdom for a person established in business is to be refused if the Secretary of State is not satisfied that each of the requirements of paragraph 222 is met.

223A. Notwithstanding paragraph 5, paragraphs 222 to 223 shall apply to a person who is entitled to remain in the United Kingdom by virtue of the provisions of the 2006 EEA Regulations.

Requirements for leave to enter the United Kingdom as an investor

224. Deleted on 30 June 2008 by paragraph 17 of Statement of Changes HC 607 except insofar as relevant to paragraph 230. Please see Appendix F for the wording of these Rules in a case in which they are relevant.

Leave to enter as an investor

225. Deleted on 30 June 2008 by paragraph 17 of Statement of Changes HC 607 except insofar as relevant to paragraph 230. Please see Appendix F for the wording of these Rules in a case in which they are relevant.

Refusal of leave to enter as an investor

226. Deleted on 30 June 2008 by paragraph 17 of Statement of Changes HC 607 except insofar as relevant to paragraph 230. Please see Appendix F for the wording of these Rules in a case in which they are relevant.

Requirements for an extension of stay as an investor

Extension of stay as an investor

227. Deleted on 30 June 2008 by paragraph 17 of Statement of Changes HC 607 except insofar as relevant to paragraph 230. Please see Appendix F for the wording of these Rules in a case in which they are relevant.

227A. Deleted on 30 June 2008 by paragraph 17 of Statement of Changes HC 607 except insofar as relevant to paragraph 230. Please see Appendix F for the wording of these Rules in a case in which they are relevant.

227B. Deleted on 30 June 2008 by paragraph 17 of Statement of Changes HC 607 except insofar as relevant to paragraph 230. Please see Appendix F for the wording of these Rules in a case in which they are relevant.

227C. Deleted on 30 June 2008 by paragraph 17 of Statement of Changes HC 607 except insofar as relevant to paragraph 230. Please see Appendix F for the wording of these Rules in a case in which they are relevant.

227D. Deleted on 30 June 2008 by paragraph 17 of Statement of Changes HC 607 except insofar as relevant to paragraph 230. Please see Appendix F for the wording of these Rules in a case in which they are relevant.

227E. Deleted on 30 June 2008 by paragraph 17 of Statement of Changes HC 607 except insofar as relevant to paragraph 230. Please see Appendix F for the wording of these Rules in a case in which they are relevant.

228. Deleted on 30 June 2008 by paragraph 17 of Statement of Changes HC 607 except insofar as relevant to paragraph 230. Please see Appendix F for the wording of these Rules in a case in which they are relevant.

Refusal of extension of stay as an investor

229. Deleted on 30 June 2008 by paragraph 17 of Statement of Changes HC 607 except insofar as relevant to paragraph 230. Please see Appendix F for the wording of these Rules in a case in which they are relevant.

Indefinite leave to remain for an investor

230. Indefinite leave to remain may be granted, on application, to a person admitted as an investor provided he:

(i) has spent a continuous period of 5 years in the United Kingdom in this capacity; and

(ii) has met the requirements of paragraph 227 throughout the 5 year period including the requirement as to the investment of £750,000 and continues to do so; and

(iii) has sufficient knowledge of the English language and sufficient knowledge about life in the United Kingdom in accordance with paragraph 33BA of these Rules, unless he is under the age of 18 or aged 65 or over at the time he makes his application.

(iv) does not have one or more unspent convictions within the meaning of the Rehabilitation of Offenders Act 1974.

Refusal of indefinite leave to remain for an investor

231. Indefinite leave to remain in the United Kingdom for an investor is to be refused if the Secretary of State is not satisfied that each of the requirements of paragraph 230 is met.

Writers, composers and artists

Requirements for leave to enter the United Kingdom as a writer, composer or artist

232. Deleted on 30 June 2008 by paragraph 17 of Statement of Changes HC 607 except insofar as relevant to paragraph 238. Please see Appendix F for the wording of these Rules in a case in which they are relevant.

Leave to enter as a writer, composer or artist

233. Deleted on 30 June 2008 by paragraph 17 of Statement of Changes HC 607 except insofar as relevant to paragraph 238. Please see Appendix F for the wording of these Rules in a case in which they are relevant.

Refusal of leave to enter as a writer, composer or artist

234. Deleted on 30 June 2008 by paragraph 17 of Statement of Changes HC 607 except insofar as relevant to paragraph 238. Please see Appendix F for the wording of these Rules in a case in which they are relevant.

Requirements for an extension of stay as a writer, composer or artist

235. Deleted on 30 June 2008 by paragraph 17 of Statement of Changes HC 607 except insofar as relevant to paragraph 238. Please see Appendix F for the wording of these Rules in a case in which they are relevant.

Extension of stay as a writer, composer or artist

236. Deleted on 30 June 2008 by paragraph 17 of Statement of Changes HC 607 except insofar as relevant to paragraph 238. Please see Appendix F for the wording of these Rules in a case in which they are relevant.

Refusal of extension of stay as a writer, composer or artist

237. Deleted on 30 June 2008 by paragraph 17 of Statement of Changes HC 607 except insofar as relevant to paragraph 238. Please see Appendix F for the wording of these Rules in a case in which they are relevant.

Indefinite leave to remain for a writer, composer or artist

238. Indefinite leave to remain may be granted, on application, to a person admitted as a writer, composer or artist provided he:

(i) has spent a continuous period of 5 years in the United Kingdom in this capacity; and

(ii) has met the requirement of paragraph 235 throughout the 5 year period; and

(iii) he has sufficient knowledge of the English language and sufficient knowledge about life in the United Kingdom in accordance with paragraph 33BA of these Rules, unless he is under the age of 18 or aged 65 or over at the time he makes his application; and

(iv) does not have one or more unspent convictions within the meaning of the Rehabilitation of Offenders Act 1974.

Refusal of indefinite leave to remain for a writer, composer or artist

239. Indefinite leave to remain for a writer, composer or artist is to be refused if the Secretary of State is not satisfied that each of the requirements of paragraph 238 is met.

Spouses of persons with limited leave to enter or remain under paragraphs 200–239

Requirements for leave to enter or remain as the spouse or civil partners of a person with limited leave to enter or remain under paragraphs 200–239

240. The requirements to be met by a person seeking leave to enter the United Kingdom as the spouse or civil partner of a person with limited leave to enter or remain in the United Kingdom under paragraphs 200–239 are that:

(i) the applicant is married to or the civil partner of a person with limited leave to enter or remain in the United Kingdom under paragraphs 200–239; and

(ii) each of the parties intends to live with the other as his or her spouse or civil partner during the applicant's stay and the marriage or civil partnership is subsisting; and

(iii) there will be adequate accommodation for the parties and any dependants without recourse to public funds in accommodation which they own or occupy exclusively; and

(iv) the parties will be able to maintain themselves and any dependants adequately without recourse to public funds; and

(v) the applicant does not intend to stay in the United Kingdom beyond any period of leave granted to his spouse or civil partner; and

(vi) the applicant holds a valid United Kingdom entry clearance for entry in this capacity.

Leave to enter as the spouse or civil partner of a person with limited leave to enter or remain in the United Kingdom under paragraphs 200–239

241. A person seeking limited leave to enter the United Kingdom as the spouse or civil partner of a person with limited leave to enter or remain in the United Kingdom under paragraphs 200–239 may be given leave to enter for a period not in excess of that granted to the person with limited leave to enter or remain under paragraphs 200–239 provided the Immigration Officer is satisfied that each of the requirements of paragraph 240 is met.

Refusal of leave to enter as the spouse or civil partner of a person with limited leave to enter or remain in the United Kingdom under paragraphs 200–239

242. Leave to enter the United Kingdom as the spouse or civil partner of a person with limited leave to enter or remain in the United Kingdom under paragraphs 200–239 is to be refused if the Immigration Officer is not satisfied that each of the requirements of paragraph 240 is met.

Requirements for extension of stay as the spouse or civil partner of a person who has or has had leave to enter or remain in the United Kingdom under paragraphs 200–239

242A. The requirements to be met by a person seeking an extension of stay in the United Kingdom as the spouse or civil partner of a person who has or has had leave to enter or remain under paragraphs 200–239 are that the applicant:

(i) is married to or the civil partner of a person with limited leave to enter or remain in the United Kingdom under paragraphs 200–239; or

(ii) is married to or civil partner of a person who has limited leave to enter or remain in the United Kingdom under paragraphs 200–239 and who is being granted indefinite leave to remain at the same time; or

(iii) is married to or civil partner of a person who has indefinite leave to remain in the United Kingdom and who had limited leave to enter or remain in the United Kingdom under paragraphs 200–239 immediately before being granted indefinite leave to remain; and

(iv) meets the requirements of paragraph 240(ii)–(v); and

(v) was admitted with a valid United Kingdom entry clearance for entry in this capacity.

Extension of stay as the spouse or civil partner of a person who has or has had leave to enter or remain in the United Kingdom under paragraphs 200–239

242B. An extension of stay in the United Kingdom as:

(i) the spouse or civil partner of a person who has limited leave to enter or remain under paragraphs 200–239 may be granted for a period not in excess of that granted to the person with limited to enter or remain; or

(ii) the spouse or civil partner of a person who is being admitted at the same time for settlement or the spouse or civil partner of a person who has indefinite leave to remain may be granted for a period not exceeding 2 years, in both instances, provided the Secretary of State is satisfied that each of the requirements of paragraph 242A is met.

Refusal of extension of stay as the spouse or civil partner of a person who has or has had leave to enter or remain in the United Kingdom under paragraphs 200–239

242C. An extension of stay in the United Kingdom as the spouse or civil partner of a person who has or has had leave to enter or remain under paragraphs 200–239 is to be refused if the Secretary of State is not satisfied that each of the requirements of paragraph 242A is met.

Requirements for indefinite leave to remain as the spouse or civil partner of a person who has or has had leave to enter or remain in the United Kingdom under paragraphs 200–239

242D. The requirements to be met by a person seeking indefinite leave to remain in the United Kingdom as the spouse or civil partner of a person who has or has had leave to enter or remain in the United Kingdom under paragraphs 200–239 are that the applicant:

(i) is married to or civil partner of a person who has limited leave to enter or remain in the United Kingdom under paragraphs 200–239 and who is being granted indefinite leave to remain at the same time; or

(ii) is married to or civil partner of a person who has indefinite leave to remain in the United Kingdom and who had limited leave to enter or remain under paragraphs 200–239 immediately before being granted indefinite leave to remain; and

(iii) meets the requirements of paragraph 240(II) to (v);

(iv) has sufficient knowledge of the English language and sufficient knowledge about life in the United Kingdom, unless the applicant is under the age of 18 or aged 65 or over at the time he makes his application; and

(v) was admitted with a valid United Kingdom entry clearance for entry in this capacity; and

(vi) does not have one or more unspent convictions within the meaning of the Rehabilitation of Offenders Act 1974.

Indefinite leave to remain as the spouse or civil partner of a person who has or has had leave to enter or remain in the United Kingdom under paragraphs 200–239

242E. Indefinite leave to remain in the United Kingdom as the spouse or civil partner of a person who has or has had limited leave to enter or remain in the United Kingdom under paragraphs 200–239 may be granted provided the Secretary of State is satisfied that each of the requirements of paragraph 242D is met.

Refusal of indefinite leave to remain as the spouse or civil partner of a person who has or has had leave to enter or remain in the United Kingdom under paragraphs 200–239

242F. Indefinite leave to remain in the United Kingdom as the spouse or civil partner of a person who has or has had limited leave to enter or remain in the United Kingdom under paragraphs 200–239 is to be refused if the Secretary of State is not satisfied that each of the requirements of paragraph 242D is met.

Children of persons with limited leave to enter or remain under paragraphs 200–239

Requirements for leave to enter or remain as the child of a person with limited leave to enter or remain in the United Kingdom under paragraphs 200–239

243. The requirements to be met by a person seeking leave to enter or remain in the United Kingdom as a child of a person with limited leave to enter or remain in the United Kingdom under paragraphs 200–239 are that:

(i) he is the child of a parent who has leave to enter or remain in the United Kingdom under paragraphs 200–239; and

(ii) he is under the age of 18 or has current leave to enter or remain in this capacity; and

(iii) he is unmarried and is not a civil partner, has not formed an independent family unit and is not leading an independent life; and

(iv) he can and will be maintained and accommodated adequately without recourse to public funds in accommodation which his parent(s) own or occupy exclusively; and

(v) he will not stay in the United Kingdom beyond any period of leave granted to his parent(s); and

(vi) both parents are being or have been admitted to or allowed to remain in the United Kingdom save where:

(a) the parent he is accompanying or joining is his sole surviving parent; or

(b) the parent he is accompanying or joining has had sole responsibility for his upbringing; or

(c) there are serious and compelling family or other considerations which make exclusion from the United Kingdom undesirable and suitable arrangements have been made for his care; and

(vii) if seeking leave to enter, he holds a valid United Kingdom entry clearance for entry in this capacity or, if seeking leave to remain, was admitted with a valid United Kingdom entry clearance for entry in this capacity.

Leave to enter or remain as the child of a person with limited leave to enter or remain in the United Kingdom under paragraphs 200–239

244. A person seeking leave to enter or remain in the United Kingdom as the child of a person with limited leave to enter or remain in the United Kingdom under paragraphs under paragraphs 200–239 may be admitted to or allowed to remain in the United Kingdom for the same period of leave as that granted to the person given limited leave to enter or remain under paragraphs 200–239 provided that, in relation to an application for leave to enter, he is able to produce to the Immigration Officer, on arrival, a valid United Kingdom entry clearance for entry in this capacity or, in the case of an application for limited leave to remain, he was admitted with a valid United Kingdom entry clearance for entry in this capacity and is able to satisfy the Secretary of State that each of the requirements of paragraph 243(i)–(vi) is met. An application for indefinite leave to remain in this category may be granted provided the applicant was admitted with a valid United Kingdom entry clearance for entry in this capacity and is able to satisfy the Secretary of State that each of the requirements of paragraph 243(i)–(vi) is met and provided indefinite leave to remain is, at the same time, being granted to the person with limited leave to remain under paragraphs 200–239.

Refusal of leave to enter or remain as the child of a person with limited leave to enter or remain in the United Kingdom under paragraphs 200–239

245. Leave to enter or remain in the United Kingdom as the child of a person with limited leave to enter or remain in the United Kingdom under paragraphs 200–239 is to be refused if, in relation to an application for leave to enter, a valid United Kingdom entry clearance for entry in this capacity is not produced to the Immigration Officer on arrival or, in the case of an application for limited leave to remain, if the applicant was not admitted with a valid United Kingdom entry clearance for entry in this capacity or is unable to satisfy the Secretary of State that each of the requirements of paragraph 243(i)–(vi) is met. An application for indefinite leave to remain in this capacity is to be refused if the applicant was not admitted with a valid United Kingdom entry clearance for entry in this capacity or is unable to satisfy the Secretary of State that each of the requirements of paragraph 243(i)–(vi) is met or if indefinite leave to remain is not, at the same time, being granted to the person with limited leave to remain under paragraphs 200–239.

Part 6A – Points-based system

Documentary evidence

245A. (a) Where Part 6A or Appendices A to C, or E of these Rules state that specified documents must be provided, that means documents specified by the Secretary of State in either the Points Based System Policy Guidance, or for applications for settlement the application form or accompanying guidance, as being specified documents for the route under which the applicant is applying. If the specified documents are not provided, the applicant will not meet the requirement for which the specified documents are required as evidence.

(b) If the Entry Clearance Officer or Secretary of State has reasonable cause to doubt the genuineness of any document submitted by an applicant which is, or which purports to be, a specified document under Part 6A or Appendices A to C, or E of these Rules and having taken reasonable steps to verify the document, is unable to verify that it is genuine, the document will be discounted for the purposes of this application.

(c) Where Part 6A or Appendices A to C, or E of these Rules refer to the United Kingdom Border Agency guidance, this means guidance published by the United Kingdom Border Agency for use by Sponsors or migrants to ensure compliance with these Rules. If the Sponsor or applicant does not satisfy the requirements set out in guidance and referred to in these Rules, the applicant will not meet the related requirement in these Rules.

Tier 1 (Exceptional Talent) Migrants

Purpose

245B. This route is for exceptionally talented individuals in the fields of science, humanities, engineering and the arts, who wish to work in the UK. These individuals are those who are already internationally recognised at the highest level as world leaders in their particular field, or who have already demonstrated exceptional promise and are likely to become world leaders in their particular area.

Entry to the UK

245BA. All migrants arriving in the UK and wishing to enter as a Tier 1 (Exceptional Talent) Migrant must have a valid entry clearance for entry under this route. If they do not have a valid entry clearance, entry will be refused.

Requirements for entry clearance

245BB. To qualify for entry clearance as a Tier 1 (Exceptional Talent) Migrant, an applicant must meet the requirements listed below. If the applicant meets these requirements, entry clearance will be granted. If the applicant does not meet these requirements, the application will be refused.

Requirements:

(a) The applicant must not fall for refusal under the general grounds for refusal.

(b) The applicant must have a Tier 1 (Exceptional Talent) Unique Reference Number, which:

- (i) was assigned by the UK Border Agency to the applicant no more than 10 working days before the date of application;
- (ii) relates to the Designated Competent Body the applicant states he is seeking endorsement from in his application; and
- (iii) has not been used in support of a previous application.

(c) The applicant must have a minimum of 75 points under paragraphs 1 to 6 of Appendix A.

(d) an applicant who has, or was last granted, leave as a student or a Postgraduate Doctor or Dentist, a Student Nurse, a Student Writing-Up a Thesis, a Student Re-Sitting an Examination or as a Tier 4 Migrant and:

- (i) is currently being sponsored by a government or international scholarship agency, or
- (ii) was being sponsored by a government or international scholarship agency, and that sponsorship came to an end 12 months ago or less,

must provide the unconditional written consent of the sponsoring Government or agency to the application and must provide the specified documents as set out in the Tier 1 (Exceptional Talent) guidance published on the UK Border Agency website, to show that this requirement has been met.

Period and conditions of grant

245BC. Entry clearance will be granted for a period of 3 years and 4 months and will be subject to the following conditions:

(i) no recourse to public funds,

(ii) registration with the police, if this is required by paragraph 326,

(iii) no employment as a Doctor or Dentist in Training, and

(iv) no employment as a professional sportsperson (including as a sports coach).

Requirements for leave to remain

245BD. To qualify for leave to remain as a Tier 1 (Exceptional Talent) Migrant, an applicant must meet the requirements listed below. If the applicant meets these requirements, leave to remain will be granted. If the applicant does not meet these requirements, the application will be refused.

Requirements:

(a) The applicant must not fall for refusal under the general grounds for refusal, and must not be an illegal entrant.

(b) The applicant must have a minimum of 75 points under paragraphs 1 to 6 of Appendix A.

(c) The applicant must have a minimum of 10 points under paragraphs 1 to 9 of Appendix B.

(d) The applicant must have, or have last been granted, entry clearance, leave to enter or remain as a Tier 1 (Exceptional Talent) Migrant.

Period and conditions of grant

245BE. Leave to remain will be granted for a period of 2 years and will be subject to the following conditions:

(i) no recourse to public funds,

(ii) registration with the police, if this is required by paragraph 326,

(iii) no employment as a Doctor or Dentist in Training, and

(iv) no employment as a professional sportsperson (including as a sports coach).

Requirements for indefinite leave to remain

245BF. To qualify for indefinite leave to remain, a Tier 1 (Exceptional Talent) Migrant must meet the requirements listed below. If the applicant meets these requirements, indefinite leave to remain will be granted. If the applicant does not meet these requirements, the application will be refused.

Requirements:

(a) The applicant must not have one or more unspent convictions within the meaning of the Rehabilitation of Offenders Act 1974.

(b) The applicant must not fall for refusal under the general grounds for refusal, and must not be an illegal entrant.

(c) The applicant must have spent a continuous period of 5 years lawfully in the UK with leave as a Tier 1 (Exceptional Talent) Migrant.

(d) The applicant must have a minimum of 75 points under paragraphs 1 to 6 of Appendix A.

(e) The applicant must have sufficient knowledge of the English language and sufficient knowledge about life in the United Kingdom, in accordance with paragraph 33BA of these Rules, unless the applicant is under the age of 18 or aged 65 or over at the date the application is made.

Tier 1 (General) Migrants

Purpose

245C. This route is for highly skilled migrants who wish to work, or become self-employed, to extend their stay in the UK.

Requirements for leave to remain

245CA. To qualify for leave to remain as a Tier 1 (General) Migrant, an applicant must meet the requirements listed below. If the applicant meets these requirements, leave to remain will be granted. If the applicant does not meet these requirements, the application will be refused.

Requirements:

(a) The applicant must not fall for refusal under the general grounds for refusal, and must not be an illegal entrant.

(b) if the applicant has, or has had, leave as a Highly Skilled Migrant, as a Writer, Composer or Artist, Self-Employed Lawyer, or as a Tier 1 (General) Migrant under the Rules in place before 19 July 2010, and has not been granted leave in any categories other than these under the Rules in place since 19 July 2010, the applicant must have 75 points under paragraphs 7 to 34 of Appendix A.

(c) in all cases other than those referred to in (b) above, the applicant must have 80 points under paragraphs 7 to 34 of Appendix A.

(d) The applicant must have 10 points under paragraphs 1 to 2 of Appendix B.

(e) The applicant must have 10 points under paragraphs 1 to 3 of appendix C.

(f) The applicant must have, or have last been granted, entry clearance, leave to enter or remain:

(i) as a Tier 1 (General) Migrant,

(ii) as a Highly Skilled Migrant,

(iii) as a Writer, Composer or Artist, or

(iv) as a self-employed lawyer.

Period and conditions of grant

245CB. (a) Leave to remain will be granted for a period of 2 years, to an applicant who has, or was last granted, leave as a Tier 1 (General) Migrant under the Rules in place before 6 April 2010.

(b) in all other cases, leave to remain will be granted for a period of 3 years.

(c) leave to remain under this route will be subject to the following conditions:

(i) no recourse to public funds,

(ii) registration with the police, if this is required by paragraph 326, and

(iii) no employment as a Doctor or Dentist in Training, unless the applicant:

(1) has obtained a primary degree in medicine or dentistry at bachelor's level or above from a UK institution that is a UK recognised or listed body, or which holds a sponsor licence under Tier 4 of the Points Based system;

(2) has, or has last been granted, entry clearance, leave to enter or leave to remain that was not subject to any condition restricting him from taking employment as a Doctor in Training, and has been employed during that leave as a Doctor in Training; or

(3) has, or has last been granted, entry clearance, leave to enter or leave to remain that was not subject to any condition restricting him from taking employment as a dentist in Training, and has been employed during that leave as a Dentist in Training,

(iv) no employment as a professional sportsperson (including as a sports coach).

Requirements for indefinite leave to remain

245CD. To qualify for indefinite leave to remain, a Tier 1 (General) Migrant must meet the requirements listed below. If the applicant meets these requirements, indefinite leave to remain will be granted. If the applicant does not meet these requirements, the application will be refused.

Requirements:

(a) The applicant must not have one or more unspent convictions within the meaning of the Rehabilitation of Offenders Act 1974 unless the applicant is applying under the terms of the HSMP ILR Judicial Review Policy Document.

(b) The applicant must not fall for refusal under the general grounds for refusal, and must not be an illegal entrant.

(c) Unless the application is being made under the terms of the HSMP ILR Judicial Review Policy Document, the applicant must have spent a continuous period of 5 years lawfully in the UK, of which the most recent period must have been spent with leave as a Tier 1 (General) Migrant, in any combination of the following categories:

(i) as a Tier 1 (General) Migrant,

(ii) as a Highly Skilled Migrant,

(iii) as a Work Permit Holder,

(iv) as an innovator,

(v) as a Self-Employed Lawyer,

(vi) as a Writer, Composer or Artist,

(vii) as a Tier 2 (General) Migrant, a Tier 2 (Minister of Religion) Migrant or a Tier 2 (Sportsperson) Migrant, or

(viii) as a Tier 2 (Intra-Company Transfer) Migrant, provided the continuous period of 5 years spent lawfully in the UK includes a period of leave as a Tier 2 (Intra-Company Transfer) Migrant granted under the Rules in place before 6 April 2010.

(d) if the applicant has or has had leave as a Highly skilled Migrant, a Writer, Composer or artist, a self-employed lawyer or as a Tier 1 (General) Migrant under the Rules in place before 19 July 2010, and has not been granted leave in any categories other than these under the Rules in place since 19 July 2010, the applicant must have 75 points under paragraphs 7 to 34 of Appendix A.

(e) Where the application is being made under the terms of the HSMP ILR Judicial Review Policy document, the applicant must have a continuous period of 4 years lawful leave in the UK, or 5 years lawful leave in the UK if the applicant applied to the HSMP between 3 April 2006 and 7

November 2006, received an approval letter and came to or stayed in the United Kingdom on the basis of that letter, of which the most recent must have been spent with leave as a Tier 1 (General) Migrant, in any combination of the following categories:

(i) as a Tier 1 (General) Migrant;

(ii) as a Highly Skilled Migrant;

(iii) as a Work Permit Holder; or

(iv) as an innovator.

(f) Where the application is being made under the terms of the HSMP ILR Judicial Review Policy Document, the applicant must be economically active in the UK, in employment or self-employment or both.

(g) in all other cases than those referred to in (d) or (e) above, the applicant must have 80 points under paragraphs 7 to 34 of Appendix A.

(h) The applicant must have sufficient knowledge of the English language and sufficient knowledge about life in the United Kingdom, in accordance with paragraph 33BA, unless the applicant is under the age of 18 or aged 65 or over at the time the application is made or the applicant is applying under the terms of the HSMP ILR Judicial Review Policy Document.

Transitional arrangements

245CE. This paragraph makes special provision for applicants who on 29 February 2008 are in the UK, or on 1 April 2008 are in India, and who are in the process of applying to become a Highly Skilled Migrant. It will also be relevant to applicants who have, or have last been granted, leave to remain as a Highly Skilled Migrant, who are Self-Employed, and who fall within subparagraph (c) below.

(a) If an applicant has made an application for entry clearance in India as a Highly Skilled Migrant before 1 April 2008, and the application has not been decided before that date, it will be decided in accordance with the Rules in force on 31 March 2008 as set out in Appendix D.

(b) If an applicant has made an application for limited leave to remain as a Highly Skilled Migrant before 29 February 2008, and the application has not been decided before that date, it will be decided in accordance with these Rules in force on 28 February 2008 as set out in Appendix D.

(c) If an applicant has made an application in India for entry clearance on or after 1 April 2008, or has made an application in the UK for limited leave to remain on or after 29 February 2008, and has submitted with that application a valid Highly Skilled Migrant Programme Approval Letter, the applicant will be automatically awarded 75 points under Appendix A and 10 points under Appendix B.

(ca) If an applicant has made an application other than in India for entry clearance on or after 30th June 2008, and has submitted with that application a valid Highly Skilled Migrant Programme Approval Letter, the applicant will be automatically awarded 75 points under Appendix A and 10 points under Appendix B.

Requirements:

(i) The applicant must not fall for refusal under the general grounds for refusal, and must not be an illegal entrant.

(ii) The applicant must have, or have last been granted, entry clearance, leave to enter or remain as a Highly Skilled Migrant which was granted in accordance with these Rules in force on or before 8 November 2006.

(iii) The applicant must have become Self-Employed in the UK whilst having leave as a Highly Skilled Migrant, and must provide the specified documents.

(iv) The applicant must have been Self-Employed for at least 4 months prior to the date the current application for leave to remain was made, and the specified documents must be provided.

(v) The applicant must have ongoing business commitments for at least 6 months after the date the current application for leave to remain was made, and the specified documents must be provided.

(vi) The applicant must have 10 points under Appendix B.

(vii) The applicant must have 10 points under Appendix C.

If the requirements above are met, leave to remain as a Tier 1 (General) Migrant will be granted for a period of 3 years, subject to the conditions in paragraph 245D(c) above.

Tier 1 (Entrepreneur) Migrants

Purpose of this route and meaning of business

245D. (a) This route is for migrants who wish to establish, join or take over one or more businesses in the UK.

(b) For the purpose of paragraphs 245D to 245DF and paragraphs 35 to 53 of Appendix A 'business' means an enterprise as:

(i) a sole trader,

(ii) a partnership, or

(iii) a company registered in the UK.

Entry to the UK

245DA. All migrants arriving in the UK and wishing to enter as a Tier 1 (Entrepreneur) Migrant must have a valid entry clearance for entry under this route. If they do not have a valid entry clearance, entry will be refused.

Requirements for entry clearance

245DB. To qualify for entry clearance as a Tier 1 (Entrepreneur) Migrant, an applicant must meet the requirements listed below. If the applicant meets those requirements, entry clearance will be granted. If the applicant does not meet these requirements, the application will be refused.

Requirements:

(a) The applicant must not fall for refusal under the general grounds for refusal.

(b) The applicant must have a minimum of 75 points under paragraphs 35 to 53 of Appendix A.

(c) The applicant must have a minimum of 10 points under paragraph 1 to 3 of Appendix B.

(d) The applicant must have a minimum of 10 points under **paragraph 1 to 2 of** Appendix C.

(e) An applicant who has, or was last granted, leave as a Student or a Postgraduate Doctor or Dentist, a Student Nurse, a Student Writing-Up a Thesis, a Student Re-Sitting an Examination or as a Tier 4 Migrant and:

(i) is currently being sponsored by a government or international scholarship agency, or

(ii) was being sponsored by a government or international scholarship agency, and that sponsorship came to an end 12 months ago or less,

must provide the unconditional written consent of the sponsoring Government or agency to the application and must provide the specified documents to show that this requirement has been met.

Period and conditions of grant

245DC. (a) Entry clearance will be granted for a period of 3 years and four months and will be subject to the following conditions:

(i) no recourse to public funds,

(ii) registration with the police, if this is required by paragraph 326 of these Rules, and

(iii) no employment other than working for the business(es) the applicant has established, joined or taken over, and

(iv) no employment as a professional sportsperson (including as a sports coach).

Requirements for leave to remain

245DD. To qualify for leave to remain as a Tier 1 (Entrepreneur) Migrant under this rule, an applicant must meet the requirements listed below. If the applicant meets these requirements, leave to remain will be granted. If the applicant does not meet these requirements, the application will be refused.

Requirements:

(a) The applicant must not fall for refusal under the general grounds for refusal, and must not be an illegal entrant.

(b) The applicant must have a minimum of 75 points under paragraphs 35 to 53 of Appendix A.

(c) The applicant must have a minimum of 10 points under paragraphs 1 to 3 of Appendix B.

(d) The applicant must have a minimum of 10 points under paragraphs 1 to 2 of Appendix C.

(e) The applicant who is applying for leave to remain must have, or have last been granted, entry clearance, leave to enter or remain:

(i) as a Highly Skilled Migrant,

(ii) as a Tier 1 (General) Migrant,

(iii) as a Tier 1 (Entrepreneur) Migrant,

(iv) as a Tier 1 (Investor) Migrant,

(v) as a Tier 1 (Post-Study Work) Migrant,

(vi) as a Businessperson,

(vii) as an Innovator,

(viii) as an Investor,

(ix) as a Participant in the Fresh Talent: Working in Scotland Scheme,

(x) as a Participant in the International Graduates Scheme (or its predecessor, the Science and Engineering Graduates Scheme),

(xi) as a Postgraduate Doctor or Dentist,

(xii) as a Self-employed Lawyer,

(xiii) as a Student,

(xiv) as a Student Nurse,

(xv) as a Student Re-sitting an Examination,

(xvi) as a Student Writing Up a Thesis,

(xvii) as a Work Permit Holder,

(xviii) as a Writer, Composer or Artist,

(xix) as a Tier 2 Migrant

(xx) as a Tier 4 Migrant, or

(xxi) as a Prospective Entrepreneur

(f) An applicant who has, or was last granted, leave as a Student or a Postgraduate Doctor or Dentist, Student Nurse, Student Re-Sitting an Examination, a Student Writing-Up a Thesis or as a Tier 4 Migrant and:

(i) is currently being sponsored by a government or international scholarship agency, or

(ii) was being sponsored by a government or international scholarship agency, and that sponsorship came to an end 12 months ago or less,

must provide the unconditional written consent of the sponsoring Government or agency to the application and must provide the specified documents to show that this requirement has been met.

Period, conditions and curtailment of grant

245DE. (a) Leave to remain will be granted:

(i) for a period of 2 years, to an applicant who has, or was last granted, leave as a Tier 1 (Entrepreneur) Migrant,

(ii) for a period of 3 years, to any other applicant.

(b) Leave to remain under this route will be subject to the following conditions:

(i) no recourse to public funds,

(ii) registration with the police, if this is required by paragraph 326 of these Rules, and

(iii) no employment, other than working for the business or businesses which he has established, joined or taken over, and

(iv) no employment as a professional sportsperson (including as a sports coach).

(c) Without prejudice to the grounds for curtailment in paragraph 323 of these Rules, leave to enter or remain granted to a Tier 1 (Entrepreneur) Migrant may be curtailed if, within 6 months of the date specified in paragraph (d), the applicant has not done one or more of the following things:

(i) registered with HM Revenue and Customs as self-employed,

(ii) registered a new business in which he is a director, or

(iii) registered as a director of an existing business.

(d) The date referred to in paragraph (c) is:

(i) the date of the applicant's entry to the UK, in the case of an applicant granted entry clearance as a Tier 1 (Entrepreneur) Migrant where there is evidence to establish the applicant's date of entry to the UK,

(ii) the date of the grant of entry clearance to the applicant, in the case of an applicant granted entry clearance as a Tier 1 (Entrepreneur) Migrant where there is no evidence to establish the applicant's date of entry to the UK, or

(iii) the date of the grant of leave to remain to the applicant, in any other case.

(e) Paragraph 245DE(c) does not apply where the applicant's last grant of leave prior to the grant of the leave that he currently has was as a Tier 1 (Entrepreneur) Migrant, a Businessperson or an Innovator.

Requirements for indefinite leave to remain

245DF. To qualify for indefinite leave to remain as a Tier 1 (Entrepreneur) Migrant, an applicant must meet the requirements listed below. If the applicant meets these requirements, indefinite leave to remain will be granted. If the applicant does not meet these requirements, the application will be refused.

Requirements:

(a) The applicant must not have one or more unspent convictions within the meaning of the Rehabilitation of Offenders Act 1974.

(b) The applicant must not fall for refusal under the general grounds for refusal, and must not be an illegal entrant.

(c) The applicant must have a minimum of 75 points under paragraphs 35 to 53 of Appendix A.

(d) The applicant must have sufficient knowledge of the English language and sufficient knowledge about life in the United Kingdom, in accordance with paragraph 33BA, unless the applicant is under the age of 18 or aged 65 or over at the date the application is made.

Tier 1 (Investor) Migrants

Purpose

245E. This route is for high net worth individuals making a substantial financial investment to the UK.

Entry to the UK

245EA. All migrants arriving in the UK and wishing to enter as a Tier 1 (Investor) Migrant must have a valid entry clearance for entry under this route. If they do not have a valid entry clearance, entry will be refused.

Requirements for entry clearance

245EB. To qualify for entry clearance or leave to remain as a Tier 1 (Investor) Migrant, an applicant must meet the requirements listed below. If the applicant meets these requirements, entry clearance will be granted. If the applicant does not meet these requirements, the application will be refused.

Requirements:

(a) The applicant must not fall for refusal under the general grounds for refusal.

(b) The applicant must have a minimum of 75 points under paragraphs 54 to 65 of Appendix A.

(c) An applicant who has, or was last granted, leave as a Student or a Postgraduate Doctor or Dentist, a Student Nurse, a Student Re-Sitting an Examination, a Student Writing-Up a Thesis or as a Tier 4 Migrant and:

(i) is currently being sponsored by a government or international scholarship agency, or

(ii) was being sponsored by a government or international scholarship agency, and that sponsorship came to an end 12 months ago or less must provide the unconditional written consent of the sponsoring Government or agency to the application and must provide the specified documents to show that this requirement has been met.

Period and conditions of grant

245EC. (a) Entry clearance will be granted for a period of 3 years and four months and will be subject to the following conditions:

(i) no recourse to public funds,

(ii) registration with the police, if this is required by paragraph 326 of these Rules, and

(iii) no Employment as a Doctor or Dentist in Training, unless the applicant has obtained a primary degree in medicine or dentistry at bachelor's level or above from a UK institution that is a UK recognised or listed body, or which holds a sponsor licence under Tier 4 of the Points Based System.

Requirements for leave to remain

245ED. To qualify for leave to remain as a Tier 1 (Investor) Migrant, an applicant must meet the requirements listed below. If the applicant meets these requirements, leave to remain will be granted. If the applicant does not meet these requirements, the application will be refused.

Requirements:

(a) The applicant must not fall for refusal under the general grounds for refusal, and must not be an illegal entrant.

(b) The applicant must have a minimum of 75 points under paragraphs 54 to 65 of Appendix A.

(c) The applicant must have, or have last been granted, entry clearance, leave to enter or remain:

(i) as a Highly Skilled Migrant,

(ii) as a Tier 1 (General) Migrant,

(iii) as a Tier 1 (Entrepreneur) Migrant,

(iv) as a Tier 1 (Investor) Migrant,

(v) as a Tier 1 (Post-Study Work) Migrant,

(vi) as a Businessperson,

(vii) as an Innovator,

(viii) as an Investor,

(ix) as a Student,

(x) as a Student Nurse,

(xi) as a Student Re-Sitting an Examination,

(xii) as a Student Writing Up a Thesis,

(xiii) as a Work Permit Holder,

(xiv) as a Writer, Composer or Artist,

(xv) as a Tier 2 Migrant, or

(xiv) as a Tier 4 Migrant.

(d) An applicant who has, or was last granted, leave as a Student Nurse, Student Re-Sitting an Examination, Student Writing-Up a Thesis or as a Tier 4 Migrant and:

(i) is currently being sponsored by a government or international scholarship agency, or

(ii) was being sponsored by a government or international scholarship agency, and that sponsorship came to an end 12 months ago or less,

must provide the unconditional written consent of the sponsoring Government or agency to the application and must provide the specified documents to show that this requirement has been met.

Period, conditions and curtailment of grant

245EE. (a) Leave to remain will be granted:

(i) for a period of 2 years, to an applicant who has, or was last granted, leave as a Tier 1 (Investor) Migrant,

(ii) for a period of 3 years, to any other applicant.

(b) Leave to remain under this route will be subject to the following conditions:

(i) no recourse to public funds,

(ii) registration with the police, if this is required by paragraph 326 of these Rules, and

(iii) no Employment as a Doctor or Dentist in Training, unless the applicant:

(1) has obtained a degree in medicine or dentistry at bachelor's level or above from a UK institution that is a UK recognised or listed body, or which holds a sponsor licence under Tier 4 of the Points Based System; or

(2) has, or has last been granted, entry clearance, leave to enter or leave to remain that was not subject to any condition restricting him from taking employment as a Doctor in Training, and has been employed during that leave as a Doctor in Training; or

(3) has, or has last been granted, entry clearance, leave to enter or leave to remain that was not subject to any condition restricting him from taking employment as a Dentist in Training, and has been employed during that leave as a Dentist in Training.

(c) Without prejudice to the grounds for curtailment in paragraph 323 of these Rules, leave to enter or remain as a Tier 1 (Investor) Migrant may be curtailed if within 3 months of the date specified in paragraph (d), the applicant has not invested, or had invested on his behalf, at least £750,000 of his capital in the UK by way of UK Government bonds, share capital or loan capital in active and trading UK registered companies other than those principally engaged in property investment.

(d) The date referred to in paragraph (c) is:

(i) the date of the applicant's entry to the UK, in the case of an applicant granted entry clearance as a Tier 1 (Investor) Migrant where there is evidence to establish the applicant's date of entry to the UK,

(ii) the date of the grant of entry clearance to the applicant, in the case of an applicant granted entry clearance as a Tier 1 (Investor) Migrant where there is no evidence to establish the applicant's date of entry to the UK, or

(iii) the date of the grant of leave to remain to the applicant, in any other case.

(e) Paragraph 245EE(c) does not apply where the applicant's last grant of leave prior to the grant of the leave that he currently has was as a Tier 1 (Investor) Migrant or as an Investor.

Requirements for indefinite leave to remain

245EF. To qualify for indefinite leave to remain, a Tier 1 (Investor) Migrant must meet the requirements listed below. if the applicant meets these requirements, indefinite leave to remain will be granted. if the applicant does not meet these requirements, the application will be refused.

Requirements:

(a) The applicant must not have one or more unspent convictions within the meaning of the Rehabilitation of Offenders Act 1974.

(b) The applicant must not fall for refusal under the general grounds for refusal, and must not be an illegal entrant.

(c) The applicant must have a minimum of 75 points under paragraphs 54 to 65 of Appendix A

(d) The applicant must have sufficient knowledge of the English language and sufficient knowledge about life in the United Kingdom, in accordance with paragraph 33BA, unless the applicant is under the age of 18 or aged 65 or over at the date the application is made.

Tier 1 (Post-Study Work) Migrants

Purpose

245F. The purpose of this route is to encourage international graduates who have studied in the UK to stay on and do skilled or highly skilled work.

Entry to the UK

245FA. All migrants arriving in the UK and wishing to enter as a Tier 1 (Post-Study Work) Migrant must have a valid entry clearance for entry under this route. If they do not have a valid entry clearance, entry will be refused.

Requirements for entry clearance

245FB. To qualify for entry clearance as a Tier 1 (Post-Study Work) Migrant, an applicant must meet the requirements listed below. If the applicant meets these requirements, entry clearance will be granted. If the applicant does not meet these requirements, the application will be refused.

Requirements:

(a) The applicant must not fall for refusal under the general grounds for refusal.

(b) The applicant must not previously have been granted entry clearance or leave to remain as a Tier 1 (Post-Study Work) Migrant as a Participant in the International Graduates Scheme (or its predecessor, the Science and Engineering Graduates Scheme), or as a Participant in the Fresh Talent: Working in Scotland Scheme.

(c) The applicant must have a minimum of 75 points under paragraphs 66 to 72 of Appendix A.

(d) The applicant must have a minimum of 10 points under paragraphs 1 to 3 of Appendix B.

(e) The applicant must have a minimum of 10 points under paragraphs 1 to 2 of Appendix C.

(f) If:

(i) the studies that led to the qualification for which the applicant obtains points under paragraphs 66 to 72 of Appendix A were sponsored by a Government or international scholarship agency, and

(ii) those studies came to an end 12 months ago or less the applicant must provide the unconditional written consent of the sponsoring Government or agency to the application and must provide the specified documents to show that this requirement has been met.

Period and conditions of grant

245FC. Entry clearance will be granted for a period of 2 years and will be subject to the following conditions:

(a) no recourse to public funds,

(b) registration with the police, if this is required by paragraph 326 of these Rules, and

(c) no Employment as a Doctor or Dentist in Training, unless the applicant has obtained a degree in medicine or dentistry at bachelor's level or above from a UK institution that is a UK recognised or listed body, or which holds a sponsor licence under Tier 4 of the Points Based System.

Requirements for leave to remain

245FD. To qualify for leave to remain as a Tier 1 (Post-Study Work) Migrant, an applicant must meet the requirements listed below. Subject to paragraph 245FE(a)(i), if the applicant meets these requirements, leave to remain will be granted. If the applicant does not meet these requirements, the application will be refused.

Requirements:

(a) The applicant must not fall for refusal under the general grounds for refusal, and must not be an illegal entrant.

(b) The applicant must not previously have been granted entry clearance or leave to remain as a Tier 1 (Post-Study Work) migrant.

(c) The applicant must have a minimum of 75 points under paragraphs 66 to 72 of Appendix A.

(d) The applicant must have a minimum of 10 points under paragraphs 1 to 3 of Appendix B.

(e) The applicant must have a minimum of 10 points under paragraphs 1 to 2 of Appendix C.

(f) The applicant must have, or have last been granted, entry clearance, leave to enter or leave to remain:

(i) as a Participant in the Fresh Talent: Working in Scotland Scheme,

(ii) as a Participant in the International Graduates Scheme (or its predecessor, the Science and Engineering Graduates Scheme),

(iii) as a Student, provided the applicant has not previously been granted leave in any of the categories referred to in paragraphs (i) and (ii) above,

(iv) as a Student Nurse, provided the applicant has not previously been granted leave in any of the categories referred to in paragraphs (i) and (ii) above,

(v) as a Student Re-Sitting an Examination, provided the applicant has not previously been granted leave in any of the categories referred to in paragraphs (i) and (ii) above,

(vi) as a Student Writing Up a Thesis, provided the applicant has not previously been granted leave as a Tier 1 Migrant or in any of the categories referred to in paragraphs (i) and (ii) above,

(vii) as a Tier 4 Migrant, provided the applicant has not previously been granted leave as a Tier 1 (Post-Study Work) Migrant or in any of the categories referred to in paragraphs (i) and (ii) above, or

(viii) as a Postgraduate Doctor or Dentist, provided the applicant has not previously been granted leave as a Tier 1 (Post-Study Work) Migrant or in any of the categories referred to in paragraphs (i) and (ii) above.

(g) An applicant who has, or was last granted leave as a Participant in the Fresh Talent: Working in Scotland Scheme must be a British National (Overseas), British overseas territories citizen, British Overseas citizen, British protected person or a British subject as defined in the British Nationality Act 1981.

(h) If:

(i) the studies that led to the qualification for which the applicant obtains points under paragraphs 66 to 72 of Appendix A were sponsored by a Government or international scholarship agency, and

(ii) those studies came to an end 12 months ago or less the applicant must provide the unconditional written consent of the sponsoring Government or agency to the application and must provide the specified documents to show that this requirement has been met.

Period and conditions of grant

245FE. (a) Leave to remain will be granted:

(i) for a period of the difference between 2 years and the period of the last grant of entry clearance, leave to enter or remain , to an applicant who has or was last granted leave as a Participant in the Fresh Talent: Working in Scotland Scheme, as a Participant in the International Graduates Scheme (or its predecessor the Science and Engineering Graduates Scheme). If this calculation results in no grant of leave then leave to remain is to be refused;

(ii) for a period of 2 years, to any other applicant.

(b) Leave to remain under this route will be subject to the following conditions:

(i) no access to public funds,

(ii) registration with the police, if this is required by paragraph 326 of these Rules, and

(iii) no Employment as a Doctor or Dentist in Training, unless the applicant:

(1) has obtained a primary degree in medicine or dentistry at bachelor's level or above from a UK institution that is a UK recognised or listed body, or which holds a sponsor licence under Tier 4 of the Points Based System; or

(2) has, or has last been granted, entry clearance, leave to enter or leave to remain that was not subject to any condition restricting him from taking employment as a Doctor in Training, and has been employed during that leave as a Doctor in Training; or

(3) has, or has last been granted, entry clearance, leave to enter or leave to remain that was not subject to any condition restricting him from taking employment as a Dentist in Training, and has been employed during that leave as a Dentist in Training.

Tier 2 Migrants

Tier 2 (Intra-Company Transfer) Migrants

Purpose of this route and definitions

245G. This route enables multinational employers to transfer their existing employees from outside the EEA to their UK branch for training purposes or to fill a specific vacancy that cannot be filled by a British or EEA worker. There are four sub-categories in this route:

(i) Short Term staff: for established employees of multi-national companies who are being transferred to a skilled job in the UK for 12 months or less that could not be carried out by a new recruit from the resident workforce;

(ii) Long Term staff: for established employees of multi-national companies who are being transferred to a skilled job in the UK which will, or may, last for more than 12 months and could not be carried out by a new recruit from the resident workforce;

(iii) Graduate Trainee: for recent graduate recruits of multi-national companies who are being transferred to the UK branch of the same organisation as part of a structured graduate training programme, which clearly defines progression towards a managerial or specialist role;

(iv) Skills Transfer: for overseas employees of multi-national companies who are being transferred to the UK branch of the same organisation in a graduate occupation to learn the skills and knowledge they will need to perform their jobs overseas, or to impart their specialist skills to the UK workforce.

Entry clearance

245GA. All migrants arriving in the UK and wishing to enter as a Tier 2 (Intra-Company Transfer) Migrant must have a valid entry clearance for entry under this route. If they do not have a valid entry clearance, entry will be refused.

Requirements for entry clearance

245GB. To qualify for entry clearance as a Tier 2 (Intra-Company Transfer) Migrant, an applicant must meet the requirements listed below. If the applicant meets these requirements, entry clearance will be granted. if the applicant does not meet these requirements, the application will be refused.

Requirements:

(a) The applicant must not fall for refusal under the general grounds for refusal.

(b) The applicant must have a minimum of 50 points under paragraphs 73 to 75E of Appendix A.

(c) The applicant must have a minimum of 10 points under paragraphs 4 to 5 of Appendix C.

(d) The applicant must not have had entry clearance or leave to remain as a Tier 2 (Intra-Company Transfer) Migrant at any time during the 12 months immediately before the date of the application, regardless of whether he was in the UK during that time, unless paragraph (e) below applies.

(e) Paragraph (d) above does not apply to an applicant who is applying under the Long Term Staff sub-category and who has, or last had entry clearance or leave to remain as a Tier 2 (Intra-Company Transfer) Migrant in the Short Term staff, Graduate Trainee or Skills Transfer sub-categories, or under the Rules in place before 6 April 2011.

(f) an applicant who has, or was last granted, leave as a Student, a Student Nurse, a Student Re-Sitting an Examination, a Student Writing-Up a Thesis, a Postgraduate Doctor or Dentist or a Tier 4 Migrant and:

(i) is currently being sponsored by a government or international scholarship agency, or

(ii) was being sponsored by a government or international scholarship agency, and that sponsorship came to an end 12 months ago or less,

must provide the unconditional written consent of the sponsoring Government or agency to the application and must provide the specified documents to show that this requirement has been met.

(g) The applicant must be at least 16 years old.

(h) Where the applicant is under 18 years of age, the application must be supported by the applicant's parents or legal guardian, or by one parent if that parent has sole legal responsibility for the child.

(i) Where the applicant is under 18 years of age, the applicant's parents or legal guardian, or just one parent if that parent has sole responsibility for the child, must confirm that they consent to the arrangements for the applicant's travel to, and reception and care in, the UK.

Period and conditions of grant

245GC. (a) if the applicant is applying as a Tier 2 (Intra-Company Transfer) Migrant in either of the short Term staff or Graduate Trainee sub-categories, entry clearance will be granted for:

(i) a period equal to the length of the period of engagement plus 1 month, or

(ii) a period of 1 year, whichever is the shorter.

(b) if the applicant is applying as a Tier 2 (Intra-Company Transfer) Migrant in the Skills Transfer sub-category, entry clearance will be granted for:

(i) a period equal to the length of the period of engagement plus 1 month, or

(ii) a period of 6 months, whichever is the shorter.

(c) if the applicant is applying as a Tier 2 (Intra-Company Transfer) Migrant in the Long Term Staff sub-category, entry clearance will be granted for:

(i) a period equal to the length of the period of engagement plus 1 month, or

(ii) a period of 3 years and 1 month, whichever is the shorter.

(d) entry clearance will be granted with effect from 14 days before the date that the Certificate of Sponsorship Checking Service records as the start date for the applicant's employment in the UK, unless entry clearance is being granted less than 14 days before that date, in which case it will be granted with immediate effect.

(e) Entry clearance will be subject to the following conditions:

(i) no recourse to public funds,

(ii) registration with the police, if this is required by paragraph 326, and

(iii) no employment except:

(1) working for the sponsor in the employment that the Certificate of Sponsorship Checking Service records that the migrant is being sponsored to do, subject to any notification of a permissible change to the details of that employment as defined in UK Border Agency guidance published on the UK Border Agency website,

(2) supplementary employment, and

(3) voluntary work.

Requirements for leave to remain

245GD. To qualify for leave to remain as a Tier 2 (Intra-Company Transfer) Migrant under this rule, an applicant must meet the requirements listed below. If the applicant meets these requirements, leave to remain will be granted. If the applicant does not meet these requirements, the application will be refused.

Requirements:

(a) The applicant must not fall for refusal under the general grounds for refusal, and must not be an illegal entrant.

(b) if the applicant is applying for leave to remain as a Tier 2 (Intra-Company Transfer) Migrant in the Long Term Staff sub-category:

(i) the applicant must have, or have last been granted, entry clearance, leave to enter or leave to remain as either:

(1) a Tier 2 (Intra-Company Transfer) Migrant in the Long Term Staff sub-category, or

(2) a Tier 2 (Intra-Company Transfer) Migrant in the established Staff sub-category under the Rules in place before 6 April 2011, or

(3) a Tier 2 (Intra-Company Transfer) Migrant granted under the Rules in place before 6 April 2010, or

(4) a Qualifying Work Permit Holder, provided that the work permit was granted because the applicant was the subject of an Intra-Company Transfer, or

(5) as a representative of an overseas Business, and

(ii) the applicant must still be working for the same employer as he was at the time of that earlier grant of leave.

(c) if the applicant is applying for leave to remain as a Tier 2 (Intra-Company Transfer) Migrant in the Short Term Staff sub-category:

(i) the applicant must have, or have last been granted, entry clearance, leave to enter or leave to remain as a Tier 2 (Intra-Company Transfer) Migrant in the Short Term Staff sub-category, and

(ii) the applicant must still be working for the same employer as he was at the time of that earlier grant of leave.

(d) if the applicant is applying for leave to remain as a Tier 2 (Intra-Company Transfer) Migrant in the Graduate Trainee sub-category:

(i) the applicant must have, or have last been granted, entry clearance, leave to enter or leave to remain as a Tier 2 (Intra-Company Transfer) Migrant in the Graduate Trainee sub-category, and

(ii) the applicant must still be working for the same employer as he was at the time of that earlier grant of leave.

(e) if the applicant is applying for leave to remain as a Tier 2 (Intra-Company Transfer) Migrant in the Skills Transfer sub-category:

(i) the applicant must have, or have last been granted, entry clearance, leave to enter or leave to remain as a Tier 2 (Intra-Company Transfer) Migrant in the skills Transfer sub-category, and

(ii) the applicant must still be working for the same employer as he was at the time of that earlier grant of leave.

(f) in all cases the applicant must have a minimum of 50 points under paragraphs 73 to 75E of Appendix A.

(g) if the applicant is seeking a grant of leave to remain that would extend his total stay as a Tier 2 (Intra-Company Transfer) Migrant beyond 3 years, the applicant must have a minimum of 10 points under paragraphs 5 to 10 of Appendix B.

(h) The applicant must have a minimum of 10 points under paragraphs 4 to 5 of Appendix C.

(i) The applicant must be at least 16 years old.

(j) Where the applicant is under 18 years of age, the application must be supported by the applicant's parents or legal guardian or by one parent if that parent has sole legal responsibility for the child.

(k) Where the applicant is under 18 years of age, the applicant's parents or legal guardian, or one parent if that parent has sole legal responsibility for the child, must confirm that they consent to the arrangements for the applicant's care in the UK.

Period and conditions of grant

245GE. (a) if the applicant is applying for leave to remain as a Tier 2 (Intra-Company Transfer) Migrant in either the Short Term Staff or Graduate Trainee sub-categories, leave to remain will be granted for:

(i) the length of the period of engagement plus 14 days, or

(ii) the difference between the period of leave that the applicant has already been granted, beginning with his last grant of entry clearance as a Tier 2 (Intra-Company Transfer) Migrant, and 12 months,

whichever is the shorter. If the calculation of period of leave comes to zero or a negative number, leave to remain will be refused.

(b) if the applicant is applying for leave to remain as a Tier 2 (Intra-Company Transfer) Migrant in the Skills Transfer sub-category, leave to remain will be granted for:

(i) the length of the period of engagement plus 14 days, or

(ii) the difference between the period of leave that the applicant has already been granted, beginning with his last grant of entry clearance as a Tier 2 (Intra-Company Transfer) Migrant, and 6 months,

whichever is the shorter. If the calculation of period of leave comes to zero or a negative number, leave to remain will be refused.

(c) in the cases set out in paragraph (d) below, leave to remain will be granted for:

(i) subject to paragraph (ii) below, a period equal to 5 years less X, where X is the continuous period of time that the applicant has already spent in the UK with entry clearance, leave to enter or remain in any combination of the categories set out in paragraph 245GD(b), and where X commences on the date on which the applicant was granted entry clearance, leave to enter or leave to remain at the start of the continuous period;

(ii) where the calculation in paragraph (1) would lead to a period of leave of less than 2 years or a period of leave longer than the length of the period of engagement plus 14 days, a period equal to:

(1) the length of the period of engagement plus 14 days, or

(2) 2 years,

whichever is the shorter.

(d) The cases referred to in paragraph (c) are those where the applicant is applying for leave to remain as a Tier 2 (Intra-Company Transfer) Migrant in the Long Term Staff sub-category, and was last granted:

(i) entry clearance, leave to enter or leave to remain as a Qualifying Work Permit Holder, or

(ii) leave to remain as a Tier 2 (Intra-Company Transfer) Migrant, provided:

(1) he previously had leave as a Qualifying Work Permit Holder,

(2) at some time during that period of leave as a Qualifying Work Permit Holder he was granted leave to remain as a Tier 2 (Intra-Company Transfer) Migrant,

(3) he has not been granted entry clearance in this or any other route since his last grant of leave as a Qualifying Work Permit Holder, and

(4) he is still working for the same employer named on the Work Permit document which led to his last grant of leave as a Qualifying Work Permit Holder.

(e) in the cases set out in paragraph (f) below, leave to remain will be granted for:

(i) a period equal to the length of the period of engagement plus 14 days, or

(ii) a period of 2 years,

whichever is the shorter.

(f) The cases referred to in paragraph (e) are those where:

(i) the applicant is applying for leave to remain as a Tier 2 (Intra-Company Transfer) Migrant in the Long Term Staff sub-category, and

(ii) the applicant previously had leave as a Tier 2 (Intra-Company Transfer)Migrant under the Rules in place before 6 April 2011; and

(iii) the applicant has not been granted entry clearance in this or any other route since the grant of leave referred to in (ii) above; and

(iv) paragraphs (c) to (d) do not apply.

(g) if the applicant is applying for leave to remain as a Tier 2 (Intra-Company Transfer) Migrant in the Long Term Staff sub-category and paragraphs (c) to (f) do not apply, leave to remain will be granted for:

(i) a period equal to the length of the period of engagement plus 14 days, or

(ii) a period of 2 years,(iii) the difference between the period that the applicant has already spent in the UK since his last grant of entry clearance as a Tier 2 (Intra-Company Transfer) Migrant and 5 years,

whichever is the shorter. if the calculation of period of leave comes to zero or a negative number, leave to remain will be refused.

(h) in addition to the periods in paragraphs (a) to (g), leave to remain will be granted for the period between the date that the application is decided and the date that the Certificate of Sponsorship Checking Service records as the start date of employment in the UK, provided this is not a negative value.

(i) leave to remain will be granted subject to the following conditions:(i) no recourse to public funds,

(ii) registration with the police, if this is required by paragraph 326, and

(iii) no employment except:

(1) working for the sponsor in the employment that the Certificate of Sponsorship Checking Service records that the migrant is being sponsored to do, subject to any notification of a permissible change to the details of that employment as defined in UK Border Agency guidance,

(2) supplementary employment, and

(3) voluntary work.

Requirements for indefinite leave to remain

245GF. To qualify for indefinite leave to remain as a Tier 2 (Intra-Company Transfer) Migrant, an applicant must meet the requirements listed below. If the applicant meets these requirements, indefinite leave to remain will be granted. if the applicant does not meet these requirements, the application will be refused.

Requirements:

(a) The applicant must not have one or more unspent convictions within the meaning of the Rehabilitation of Offenders Act 1974.

(b) The applicant must not fall for refusal under the general grounds for refusal, and must not be an illegal entrant.

(c) The applicant must have spent a continuous period of 5 years lawfully in the UK, of which the most recent period must have been spent with leave as a Tier 2 (Intra-Company Transfer) Migrant, in any combination of the following categories:

(i) as a Tier 2 (Intra-Company Transfer) Migrant,

(ii) as a Qualifying Work Permit Holder, or

(iii) as a representative of an overseas Business.

(d) The continuous period of 5 years referred to in paragraph (b) must include a period of leave as:

(i) a Tier 2 (Intra-Company Transfer) Migrant granted under the Rules in place before 6 April 2010, or

(ii) a Qualifying Work Permit Holder, provided that the work permit was granted because the applicant was the subject of an Intra-Company Transfer.

(e) The sponsor that issued the Certificate of Sponsorship that led to the applicant's last grant of leave must certify in writing that:

(i) he still requires the applicant for the employment in question, and

(ii) he is paid at or above the appropriate rate for the job as stated in the codes of practice for Tier 2 sponsors published by the UK Border Agency.

(f) The applicant provides the specified documents as set out in the application form for settlement and accompanying guidance to evidence the sponsor's certification in subsection (e)(ii).

(g) The applicant must have sufficient knowledge of the English language and sufficient knowledge about life in the United Kingdom, in accordance with paragraph 33BA of these Rules, unless the applicant is under the age of 18 or aged 65 or over at the date the application is made.

Tier 2 (General) Migrants, Tier 2 (Minister of Religion) Migrants and Tier 2 (Sportsperson) Migrants

Purpose of these routes and definitions

245H. These routes enable UK employers to recruit workers from outside the EEA to fill a particular vacancy that cannot be filled by a British or EEA worker.

Entry clearance

245HA. All Migrants arriving in the UK and wishing to enter as a Tier 2 (General) Migrant, Tier 2 (Minister of Religion) Migrant or Tier 2 (Sportsperson) Migrant must have a valid entry clearance for entry under the relevant one of these routes. If they do not have a valid entry clearance, entry will be refused.

Requirements for entry clearance

245HB. To qualify for entry clearance as a Tier 2 (General) Migrant, Tier 2 (Minister of Religion) Migrant or Tier 2 (Sportsperson) Migrant, an applicant must meet the requirements listed below. If the applicant meets these requirements, entry clearance will be granted. if the applicant does not meet these requirements, the application will be refused.

Requirements:

(a) The applicant must not fall for refusal under the general grounds for refusal.

(b) If applying as a Tier 2 (General) Migrant, the applicant must have a minimum of 50 points under paragraphs 76 to 84A of Appendix A.

(c) If applying as a Tier 2 (Minister of religion) Migrant, the applicant must have a minimum of 50 points under paragraphs 85 to 92 of Appendix A.

(d) If applying as a Tier 2 (sportsperson) Migrant, the applicant must have a minimum of 50 points under paragraphs 93 to 100 of Appendix A.

(e) The applicant must have a minimum of 10 points under paragraphs 5 to 10 of Appendix B.

(f) The applicant must have a minimum of 10 points under paragraphs 4 to 5 of Appendix C.

(g) An applicant who has, or was last granted, leave as a Student, a Student Nurse, a Student Re-Sitting an Examination, a Student Writing-Up a Thesis, a Postgraduate Doctor or Dentist or a Tier 4 Migrant and:

(i) is currently being sponsored by a government or international scholarship agency, or

(ii) was being sponsored by a government or international scholarship agency, and that sponsorship came to an end 12 months ago or less

must provide the unconditional written consent of the sponsoring Government or agency to the application and must provide the specified documents to show that this requirement has been met.

(h) The applicant must be at least 16 years old.

(i) Where the applicant is under 18 years of age, the application must be supported by the applicant's parents or legal guardian, or by one parent if that parent has sole legal responsibility for the child.

(j) Where the applicant is under 18 years of age, the applicant's parents or legal guardian, or one parent if that parent has sole responsibility for the child, must confirm that they consent to the arrangements for the applicant's travel to, and reception and care in, the UK.

(k) If the Sponsor is a limited company, the applicant must not own more than 10% of its shares.

Period and conditions of grant

245HC. (a) Entry clearance will be granted for:

(i) a period equal to the length of the period of engagement plus 1 month, or

(ii) a period of 3 years and 1 month,

whichever is the shorter.

(d) Entry clearance will be granted with effect from 14 days before the date that the Certificate of Sponsorship Checking Service records as the start date for the applicant's employment in the UK, unless entry clearance is being granted less than 14 days before that date, in which case it will be granted with immediate effect.

(e) Entry clearance will be subject to the following conditions:

(i) no recourse to public funds,

(ii) registration with the police, if this is required by paragraph 326 of these Rules, and

(iii) no employment except:

(1) working for the sponsor in the employment that the Certificate of Sponsorship Checking Service records that the migrant is being sponsored to do, subject to any notification of a permissible change to the details of that employment as defined in UK Border Agency guidance,

(2) supplementary employment,

(3) voluntary work, and

(4) if the applicant is applying as a Tier 2 (Sportsperson) Migrant, employment as a sportsperson for his national team while his national team is in the UK.

(f) (i) Applicants who meet the requirements for entry clearance and who obtain points under paragraphs 76 to 79D of Appendix A shall be granted entry clearance as a Tier 2 (General) Migrant.

(ii) Applicants who meet the requirements for entry clearance and who obtain points under paragraphs 85 to 92 of Appendix A shall be granted entry clearance as a Tier 2 (Minister of Religion) Migrant.

(iii) Applicants who meet the requirements for entry clearance and who obtain points under paragraphs 93 to 100 of Appendix A shall be granted entry clearance as a Tier 2 (Sportsperson) Migrant.

Requirements for leave to remain

245HD. To qualify for leave to remain as a Tier 2 (General) Migrant, Tier 2 (Minister of Religion Migrant or Tier 2 (Sportsperson) Migrant under this rule, an applicant must meet the requirements listed below. if the applicant meets these requirements, leave to remain will be granted. if the applicant does not meet these requirements, the application will be refused.

Requirements:

(a) The applicant must not fall for refusal under the general grounds for refusal, and must not be an illegal entrant.

(b) The applicant must have, or have last been granted, entry clearance, leave to enter or leave to remain:

(i) as a Tier 1 Migrant,

(ii) as a Tier 2 (General) Migrant,

(iii) as a Tier 2 (Minister of Religion) Migrant,

(iv) as a Tier 2 (Sportsperson) Migrant,

(v) as a Highly Skilled Migrant,

(vi) as an Innovator,

(vii) as a Jewish Agency Employee,

(viii) as a Member of the Operational Ground Staff of an Overseas-owned Airline,

(ix) as a Minister of Religion, Missionary or Member of a Religious Order,

(x) as an Overseas Qualified Nurse or Midwife,

(xi) as a Participant in the Fresh Talent: Working in Scotland Scheme,

(xii) as a Participant in the International Graduates Scheme (or its predecessor, the Science and Engineering Graduates Scheme),

(xiii) as a Person Writing Up a Thesis,

(xiv) as a Postgraduate Doctor or Dentist,

(xv) as a Qualifying Work Permit Holder,

(xvi) as a Representative of an Overseas Business

(xvii) as a Representative of an Overseas Newspaper, News Agency or Broadcasting Organisation,

(xviii) as a student,

(xix) as a Student Re-Sitting an Examination,

(xx) as a Student Nurse,

(xxi) as a Student Union Sabbatical Officer,

(xxii) as a Tier 4 Migrant,

(xxiii) as a Tier 5 (Temporary Worker) Migrant, or

(xxiv) as the partner of a Relevant Points Based System Migrant if the relevant Points Based System Migrant is a Tier 4 Migrant.

(f) an applicant who has, or was last granted, leave as a Person Writing up a Thesis or a Postgraduate Doctor or Dentist and:

(i) is currently being sponsored by a government or international scholarship agency, or

(ii) was being sponsored by a government or international scholarship agency, and that sponsorship came to an end 12 months ago or less,

must provide the unconditional written consent of the sponsoring Government or agency to the application and must provide the specified documents to show that this requirement has been met.

(g) an applicant who was last granted leave as a Student, a Student Re-Sitting an Examination, a Student Nurse, a Student Union Sabbatical Officer, or a Tier 4 Migrant must have completed studying a course of study of at least one academic year in duration during that period of leave.

(h) an applicant who was last granted leave as a Tier 5 (Temporary Worker) Migrant must have been granted such leave in the Creative and Sporting sub-category of Tier 5 in order to allow the applicant to work as a professional footballer, and the applicant must provide the specified documents to show that this requirement has been met.

(i) If applying as a Tier 2 (General) Migrant, the applicant must have a minimum of 50 points under paragraphs 76 to 79D of Appendix A.

(j) If applying as a Tier 2 (Minister of Religion) Migrant, the applicant must have a minimum of 50 points under paragraphs 85 to 92 of Appendix A.

(k) If applying as a Tier 2 (Sportsperson) Migrant, the applicant must have a minimum of 50 points under paragraphs 93 to 100 of Appendix A.

(l) The applicant must have a minimum of 10 points under paragraphs 5 to 10 of Appendix B.

(m) The applicant must have a minimum of 10 points under paragraphs 4 to 5 of Appendix C.

(n) The applicant must be at least 16 years old.

(o) Where the applicant is under 18 years of age, the application must be supported by the applicant's parents or legal guardian, or by just one parent if that parent has sole legal responsibility for the child.

(p) Where the applicant is under 18 years of age, the applicant's parents or legal guardian, or just one parent if that parent has sole legal responsibility for the child, must confirm that they consent to the arrangements for the applicant's care in the UK.

(q) if the sponsor is a limited company, the applicant must not own more than 10% of its shares.

Period and conditions of grant

245HE. (a) In the cases set out in paragraphs (b) and (c) below, leave to remain will be granted for:

(i) subject to paragraph (ii), a period equal to 5 years less X, where X is the period of time that the applicant has already spent in the UK with entry clearance, leave to enter or remain in any combination of the categories set out in paragraph (b), and where X commences on the date on which the applicant was granted entry clearance, leave to enter or leave to remain at the start of the continuous period;

(ii) where the calculation in paragraph (i) would lead to a period of leave of less than 2 years or a period of leave longer than the length of the period of engagement plus 14 days, a period equal to:

(1) the length of the period of engagement plus 14 days, or

(2) 2 years,

whichever is the shorter.

(b) The cases referred to in paragraph (a) are those where the applicant was last granted:

(i) entry clearance, leave to enter or leave to remain as a Jewish Agency Employee,

(ii) entry clearance, leave to enter or leave to remain as a Member of the Operational Ground Staff of an Overseas-owned Airline,

(iii) entry clearance, leave to enter or leave to remain as a Minister of Religion, Missionary or Member of a religious Order,

(iv) entry clearance, leave to enter or leave to remain as a Qualifying Work Permit Holder,

(v) entry clearance, leave to enter or leave to remain as a Representative of an Overseas Newspaper, News Agency or Broadcasting Organisation,

(vi) leave to remain as a Tier 2 (Minister of religion) Migrant, provided:

(1) he previously had leave as a Minister of Religion, Missionary or Member of a Religious Order, and received his last grant of entry clearance or leave in one of those categories,

(2) at some time during that period of leave as a Minister of religion, Missionary or Member of a religious order he was granted leave to remain as a Tier 2 (Minister of Religion) Migrant, and

(3) he has not been granted entry clearance in these or any other route since his last grant of leave in one of the categories in (1) above,

(vii) leave to remain as a Tier 2 (Sportsperson) Migrant, provided:

(1) he previously had leave as a Work Permit Holder,

(2) at some time during that period of leave as a Work Permit Holder he was granted leave to remain as a Tier 2 (sportsperson) Migrant,

(3) he has not been granted entry clearance in these or any other route since his last grant of leave as a Work Permit Holder, or

(viii) leave to remain as a Tier 2 (General) Migrant, provided:

(1) he previously had leave in one of the categories in (i) to (v) above,

(2) at some point during the period of leave referred to in (1) he was granted leave to remain as a Tier 2 (General) Migrant, and

(3) he has not been granted entry clearance in these or any other route since his last grant of leave in one of the categories in (i) to (v) above.

and paragraph (c) below applies.

(c) In order for paragraph (a) to apply, in respect of all criteria in paragraph (b) the sponsor must be the same employer:

(i) as the sponsor on the previous application that was granted, in the case of an applicant whose last grant of leave was as a Tier 2 (General) Migrant,

(ii) that the work permit was issued to, in the case of an applicant whose last grant of leave was as a Qualifying Work Permit Holder,

(iii) for whom the applicant was working or stated he was intending to work when last granted leave, in the case of an applicant whose last grant of leave was as a Representative of an Overseas Newspaper, News Agency or Broadcasting Organisation, a Member of the Operational Ground Staff of an Overseas-owned Airline, or a Jewish Agency Employee.

(d) Where:

(i) paragraphs (a) to (c) do not apply,

(ii) the applicant has, or was last granted, entry clearance, leave to enter or leave to remain as a Tier 2 Migrant, and

(iii) the applicant is working for the same employer doing the same job as he was at the time of that earlier grant,

leave to remain will be granted for a period equal to the length of the period of engagement plus 14 days, or for a period of 2 years, whichever is the shorter.

(e) in all other cases, leave to remain will be granted for:

(i) a period equal to the length of the period of engagement plus 14 days, or

(ii) 3 years

whichever is the shorter.

(f) in addition to the periods in paragraphs (a), (d) and (e), leave to remain will be granted for the period between the date that the application is decided and the date that the Certificate of Sponsorship Checking Service records as the start date of employment in the UK, provided this is not a negative value.

(g) leave to remain will be granted subject to the following conditions:

(i) no recourse to public funds,

(ii) registration with the police, if this is required by paragraph 326 of these Rules, and

(iii) no employment except:

(1) working for the sponsor in the employment that the Certificate of Sponsorship Checking Service records that the migrant is being sponsored to do, subject to any notification of a permissible change to the details of that employment as defined in UK Border Agency guidance,

(2) supplementary employment,

(3) voluntary work, and

(4) if the applicant is applying as a Tier 2 (Sportsperson) Migrant, employment as a sportsperson for his national team while his national team is in the UK.

(h) (i) Applicants who meet the requirements for leave to remain and who obtain points under paragraphs 76 to 79D of Appendix A shall be granted leave to remain as a Tier 2 (General) Migrant.

(ii) Applicants who meet the requirements for leave to remain and who obtain points under paragraphs 85 to 92 of Appendix A shall be granted leave to remain as a Tier 2 (Minister of Religion) Migrant.

(iii) Applicants who meet the requirements for leave to remain and who obtain points under paragraphs 93 to 100 of Appendix A shall be granted leave to remain as a Tier 2 (Sportsperson) Migrant.

Requirements for indefinite leave to remain

245HF. To qualify for indefinite leave to remain as a Tier 2 (General) Migrant, Tier 2 (Minister of Religion) Migrant or Tier 2 (Sportsperson) Migrant, an applicant must meet the requirements listed below. If the applicant meets these requirements, indefinite leave to remain will be granted. If the applicant does not meet these requirements, the application will be refused.

Requirements:

(a) The applicant must not have one or more unspent convictions within the meaning of the Rehabilitation of Offenders Act 1974.

(b) The applicant must not fall for refusal under the general grounds for refusal, and must not be an illegal entrant.

(c) The applicant must have spent a continuous period of 5 years lawfully in the UK, of which the most recent period must have been spent with leave as a Tier 2 Migrant, in any combination of the following categories:

(i) as a Member of the Operational Ground Staff of an Overseas-owned Airline,

(ii) as a Minister of Religion, Missionary or Member of a Religious Order,

(iii) as a Qualifying Work Permit Holder,

(iv) as a Representative of an Overseas Business,

(v) as a Representative of an Overseas Newspaper, News Agency or Broadcasting Organisation,

(vi) as a Tier 1 Migrant, other than a Tier 1 (Post Study Work) Migrant,

(vii) as a Highly Skilled Migrant,

(viii) as an innovator,

(ix) as a Tier 2 (General) Migrant, a Tier 2 (Minister of Religion) Migrant or a Tier 2 (Sportsperson) Migrant, or

(x) as a Tier 2 (Intra-Company Transfer) Migrant, provided the continuous period of 5 years spent lawfully in the UK includes a period of leave as:

(1) a Tier 2 (Intra-Company Transfer) Migrant granted under the Rules in place before 6 April 2010, or

(2) a Qualifying Work Permit Holder, provided that the work permit was granted because the applicant was the subject of an Intra-Company Transfer.

(d) The Sponsor that issued the Certificate of Sponsorship that led to the applicant's last grant of leave must certify in writing that:

(i) he still requires the applicant for the employment in question, and

(ii) in the case of a Tier 2 (General) Migrant applying for settlement, that they are paid at or above the appropriate rate for the job as stated in the codes of practice for Tier 2 Sponsors published by the United Kingdom Border Agency.

(e) The applicant provides the specified documents as set out in the application form for settlement and accompanying guidance to evidence the sponsor's certification in subsection (d)(ii).

(f) The applicant must have sufficient knowledge of the English language and sufficient knowledge about life in the United Kingdom, in accordance with paragraph 33BA of these Rules, unless the applicant is under the age of 18 or aged 65 or over at the time the application is made.

Tier 5 (Youth Mobility Scheme) Temporary Migrants

Purpose of this route

245ZI. This route is for sponsored young people from participating countries who wish to live and work temporarily in the UK.

Entry clearance

245ZJ. All migrants arriving in the UK and wishing to enter as a Tier 5 (Youth Mobility Scheme) Temporary Migrant must have a valid entry clearance for entry under this route. If they do not have a valid entry clearance, entry will be refused.

Requirements for entry clearance

245ZK. To qualify for entry clearance as a Tier 5 (Youth Mobility Scheme) Temporary Migrant, an applicant must meet the requirements listed below. However, whether or not the requirements listed below are met, if a citizen of a country listed in Appendix G makes an application for entry clearance which, if granted, would mean that the annual allocation of places under this route for citizens of that country would be exceeded, the application will be refused. The applicant will also be refused if the requirements listed below are not met.

Requirements:

(a) The applicant must not fall for refusal under the general grounds for refusal.

(b) The applicant must be:

(i) a citizen of a country listed in Appendix G to these Rules, or

(ii) a British Overseas Citizen, British Overseas Territories Citizen or British National (Overseas), as defined by the British Nationality Act 1981 and must provide the specified documents to show that this requirement has been met.

(c) The applicant must have a minimum of 40 points under paragraphs 101 to 104 of Appendix A.

(d) The applicant must have a minimum of 10 points under paragraphs 6 to 7 of Appendix C.

(e) The applicant must have no children under the age of 18 who are either living with him or for whom he is financially responsible.

(f) The applicant must not previously have spent time in the UK as a Working Holidaymaker or a Tier 5 (Youth Mobility Scheme) Temporary Migrant.

Period and conditions of grant

245ZL. Entry clearance will be granted for a period of 2 years subject to the following conditions:

(a) no recourse to public funds,

(b) registration with the police, if this is required by paragraph 326 of these Rules,

(c) no employment as a professional sportsperson (including as a sports coach), and

(d) no employment as a Doctor or Dentist in Training, unless the applicant has obtained a degree in medicine or dentistry at bachelor's level or above from a UK institution that is a UK recognised or listed body, or which holds a sponsor licence under Tier 4 of the Points Based System, and

(e) no self employment, except where the following conditions are met:

(i) the migrant has no premises which he owns, other than his home, from which he carries out his business,

(ii) the total value of any equipment used in the business does not exceed £5,000, and

(iii) the migrant has no employees.

Tier 5 (Temporary Worker) Migrants

Purpose of this route and definitions

245ZM. (a) This route is for certain types of temporary worker whose entry helps to satisfy cultural, charitable, religious or international objectives.

(b) For the purposes of paragraphs 245ZM to 245ZS and paragraphs 105 to 112 of Appendix A:

a migrant has 'consecutive engagements' if:

(i) more than one Certificate of Sponsorship reference number has been allocated in respect of the migrant,

(ii) there is no gap of more than 14 days between any of the periods of engagement, and

(iii) all the Certificate of Sponsorship Checking Service references record that the migrant is being sponsored in the creative and sporting subcategory of the Tier 5 (Temporary Worker) Migrant route.

'Period of engagement' means a period beginning with the employment start date as recorded on the Certificate of Sponsorship Checking Service entry which relates to the Certificate of Sponsorship reference number for which the migrant was awarded points under paragraphs 105 to 111 of Appendix A, and ending on the employment end date as recorded in the same entry.

Entry clearance

245ZN. (a) Subject to paragraph (b), all migrants arriving in the UK and wishing to enter as a Tier 5 (Temporary Worker) Migrant must have a valid entry clearance for entry under this route. If they do not have a valid entry clearance, entry will be refused.

(b) A migrant arriving in the UK and wishing to enter as a Tier 5 (Temporary Worker) Migrant who does not have a valid entry clearance will not be refused entry if the following conditions are met:

(i) the migrant is not a visa national,

(ii) the Certificate of Sponsorship reference number provided by the migrant leading to points being obtained under Appendix A links to an entry in the Certificate of Sponsorship Checking Service recording that their Sponsor has sponsored them in the creative and sporting subcategory of the Tier 5 (Temporary Worker) Migrant route,

(iii) if the migrant has consecutive engagements, the total length of all the periods of engagement, together with any gap between those engagements, is 3 months or less,

(iv) if the migrant does not have consecutive engagements, the total length of the period of engagement is 3 months or less, and

(v) the migrant meets the requirements in paragraph 245ZO below.

Requirements for entry clearance or leave to enter

245ZO. To qualify for entry clearance or, as the case may be, leave to enter, as a Tier 5 (Temporary Worker) Migrant, an applicant must meet the requirements listed below. If the applicant meets these requirements, entry clearance will be granted. If the applicant does not meet these requirements, the application will be refused.

Requirements:

(a) The applicant must not fall for refusal under the general grounds for refusal.

(b) The applicant must have a minimum of 30 points under paragraphs 105 to 112 of Appendix A.

(c) The applicant must have a minimum of 10 points under paragraphs 8 to 9 of Appendix C.

(d) Where the applicant is under 18 years of age, the application must be supported by the applicant's parents or legal guardian, or by just one parent if that parent has sole legal responsibility for the child.

(e) Where the applicant is under 18 years of age, the applicant's parents or legal guardian, or just one parent if that parent has sole responsibility for the child, must confirm that they consent to the arrangements for the applicant's travel to, and reception and care in, the UK.

Period and conditions of grant

245ZP. (a) Where paragraph 245ZN(b) applies and the applicant has consecutive engagements, leave to enter will be granted for:

(i) a period commencing not more than 14 days before the beginning of the first period of engagement and ending 14 days after the end of the last period of engagement, or

(ii) 3 months

whichever is the shorter.

(b) Where paragraph 245ZN(b) applies and the applicant does not have consecutive engagements, leave to enter will be granted for:

(i) a period commencing not more than 14 days before the beginning of the period of engagement and ending 14 days after the end of that period of engagement, or

(ii) 3 months

whichever is the shorter.

(c) Where paragraph 245ZN(b) does not apply and the Certificate of Sponsorship Checking Service reference number for which the applicant was awarded points under Appendix A records that the applicant is being sponsored in the creative and sporting or charity workers sub-category of the Tier 5 (Temporary Worker) Migrant route, leave to enter will be granted for:

(i) a period commencing 14 days before the beginning of the period of engagement (or of the first period of engagement, where the applicant has consecutive engagements) and ending 14 days after the end of that period of engagement (or of the last period of engagement, where the applicant has consecutive engagements), or

(ii) 12 months

whichever of (i) or (ii) is the shorter.

(d) Where paragraph 245ZN(b) does not apply and the Certificate of Sponsorship Checking Service reference number for which the applicant was awarded points under Appendix A records that the applicant is being sponsored in the religious workers, government authorised exchange or international agreement subcategory of the Tier 5 (Temporary Worker) Migrant route, leave to enter will be granted for:

(i) a period commencing 14 days before the beginning of the period of engagement and ending 14 days after the end of that period of engagement, or

(ii) 2 years

whichever is the shorter.

(e) Leave to enter and entry clearance will be granted subject to the following conditions:

(i) no recourse to public funds,

(ii) registration with the police if this is required by paragraph 326 of these Rules, and

(iii) no employment except:

(1) unless paragraph (2) applies, working for the person who for the time being is the Sponsor in the employment that the Certificate of Sponsorship Checking Service records that the migrant is being sponsored to do for that Sponsor,

(2) in the case of a migrant whom the Certificate of Sponsorship Checking Service records as being sponsored in the government authorised exchange subcategory of Tier 5 (Temporary Workers), working for any person for whom the Sponsor directs him to work, provided that work is in the employment that the Certificate of Sponsorship Checking Service records that the migrant is being sponsored to do,

(3) supplementary employment, and

(4) in the case of a migrant whom the Certificate of Sponsorship Checking Service records as being sponsored in the creative and sporting subcategory of Tier 5 (Temporary Workers), employment as a sportsperson for his national team while his national team is in the UK.

Requirements for leave to remain

245ZQ. To qualify for leave to remain as a Tier 5 (Temporary Worker) Migrant under this rule, an applicant must meet the requirements listed below. Subject to paragraph 245ZR(a), if the applicant meets these requirements, leave to remain will be granted. If the applicant does not meet these requirements, the application will be refused.

Requirements:

(a) The applicant must not fall for refusal under the general grounds for refusal, and must not be an illegal entrant.

(b) The applicant must have, or have last been granted.

(i) entry clearance or leave to remain as a Tier 5 (Temporary Worker) Migrant, or

(ii) entry clearance, leave to enter or leave to remain as a Sports Visitor or Entertainer Visitor, provided:

(1) the Certificate of Sponsorship Checking Service reference for which he is being awarded points in this application shows that he is being sponsored in the creative and sporting subcategory; and

(2) the Certificate of Sponsorship reference number was allocated to the applicant before he entered the UK as a Sports Visitor or Entertainer Visitor, or

(iii) entry clearance, leave to enter or leave to remain as an Overseas Government Employee, provided

(a) the Certificate of Sponsorship Checking Service reference for which he is being awarded points in this application shows he is being sponsored in the international agreement sub-category, and

(b) the applicant is continuing employment with the same overseas government or international organisation for which earlier leave was granted, or

(iv) entry clearance, leave to enter or leave to remain as a Qualifying Work Permit Holder, provided

(a) the applicant was previously issued with a work permit for the purpose of employment by an overseas government, and

(b) the Certificate of Sponsorship Checking Service reference for which he is being awarded points in this application shows he is being sponsored in the international agreement sub-category, and

(c) the applicant is continuing employment with the same overseas government or international organisation for which earlier leave was granted

(v) entry clearance, leave to enter or leave to remain as a Qualifying Work Permit Holder, provided

(1) the applicant was previously issued with a work permit for the purpose of employment as a sponsored researcher, and

(2) the Certificate of Sponsorship Checking Service reference for which he is being awarded points in this application shows he is being sponsored in the government authorised exchange sub-category, and

(3) the applicant is continuing employment with the same organisation for which his most recent period of leave was granted.

(c) The applicant must have a minimum of 30 points under paragraphs 105 to 112 of Appendix A.

(d) The applicant must have a minimum of 10 points under paragraphs 8 to 9 of Appendix C.

(e) The Certificate of Sponsorship Checking Service entry to which the Certificate of Sponsorship reference number for which points under Appendix A were awarded relates must record that the applicant is being sponsored in the same subcategory of the Tier 5 (Temporary Worker) Migrant route as the one in which he was being sponsored when he was last granted entry clearance or leave to remain as a Tier 5 (Temporary Worker) Migrant.

(f) Where the applicant is under 18 years of age, the application must be supported by the applicant' parents or legal guardian, or by just one parent if that parent has sole legal responsibility for the child.

(g) Where the applicant is under 18 years of age, the applicant's parents or legal guardian, or just one parent if that parent has sole legal responsibility for the child, must confirm that they consent to the arrangements for the applicant's care in the UK.

Period and conditions of grant

245ZR. (a) If any calculation of period of leave comes to zero or a negative number, leave to remain will be refused.

(b) Subject to paragraphs (c) to (f) below, leave to remain will be granted for:

(i) the length of the period of engagement, as recorded in the Certificate of Sponsorship Checking Service entry, plus 14 days (or, where the applicant has consecutive engagements, a period beginning on the first day of the first period of engagement and ending 14 days after the last day of the last period of engagement) or

(ii) the difference between the period that the applicant has already spent in the UK since his last grant of entry clearance or leave to enter as a Tier 5 (Temporary Worker) Migrant and:

(1) 12 months, if he is being sponsored in the creative and sporting or charity worker subcategories, or

(2) 2 years, if he is being sponsored in the religious workers, government authorised exchange or international agreement subcategories,

whichever of (i) or (ii) is the shorter.

(c) Where the provisions in paragraph 245ZQ(b)(ii) apply, the migrant will be granted leave to remain for:

(i) the period of engagement plus 14 days (or, where the applicant has consecutive engagements, a period beginning on the first day of the first period of engagement and ending 14 days after the last day of the last period of engagement), or

(ii) 12 months

whichever of (i) or (ii) is the shorter.

(d) Where the Certificate of Sponsorship Checking Service reference records that the migrant is being sponsored in the international agreement subcategory of the Tier 5 (Temporary Worker) Migrant route as an overseas government employee or a private servant in a diplomatic household, leave to remain will be granted for:

(i) the period of engagement plus 14 days, or

(ii) 12 months,

whichever of (i) or (ii) is the shorter, unless at the date of the application for leave to remain the applicant has spent more than 5 years continuously in the UK with leave as a Tier 5 (Temporary Worker) Migrant, in which case leave to remain will be granted for:

(iii) the period of engagement plus 14 days, or

(iv) a period equal to 6 years less X, where X is the period of time, beginning with the date on which the applicant was last granted entry clearance or leave to enter as a Tier 5 (Temporary Worker) Migrant, that the applicant has already spent in the UK as a Tier 5 (Temporary Worker) Migrant

whichever of (iii) or (iv) is the shorter.

(e) Where:

(i) the Certificate of Sponsorship Checking Service reference number records that the applicant is being sponsored in the creative and sporting subcategory of the Tier 5 (Temporary Worker) Migrant route as a creative worker, and

(ii) the Sponsor is the Sponsor who sponsored the applicant when he received his last grant of leave

leave to remain will be granted for the period set out in paragraph (f) below.

(f) Where the conditions in paragraph (e) above are met, leave to remain will be granted for:

(i) the period of engagement plus 14 days (or, where the applicant has consecutive engagements, a period beginning on the first day of the first period of engagement and ending 14 days after the last day of the last period of engagement), or

(ii) 12 months

whichever of (i) or (ii) is the shorter, unless the applicant has spent more than 1 year continuously in the UK with leave as a Tier 5 (Temporary Worker) Migrant, in which case leave to remain will be granted for:

(iii) the period of engagement plus 14 days (or, where the applicant has consecutive engagements, a period beginning on the first day of the first period of engagement and ending 14 days after the last day of the last period of engagement), or

(iv) a period equal to 2 years less X, where X is the period of time, beginning with the date on which the applicant was last granted entry clearance or leave to enter as a Tier 5 (Temporary Worker) Migrant, that the applicant has already spent in the UK as a Tier 5 (Temporary Worker) Migrant

whichever of (iii) or (iv) is the shorter.

(g) Leave to remain will be granted subject to the following conditions:

(i) no recourse to public funds,

(ii) registration with the police if this is required by paragraph 326 of these Rules, and

(iii) no employment except:

(1) unless paragraph (2) applies, working for the person who for the time being is the Sponsor in the employment that the Certificate of Sponsorship Checking Service records that the migrant is being sponsored to do for that Sponsor,

(2) in the case of a migrant whom the Certificate of Sponsorship Checking Service records as being sponsored in the government authorised exchange subcategory of Tier 5 (Temporary Workers), working for any person for whom the Sponsor directs him to work, provided that work is in the employment that the Certificate of Sponsorship Checking Service records that the migrant is being sponsored to do,

(3) supplementary employment, and

(4) in the case of a migrant whom the Certificate of Sponsorship Checking Service records as being sponsored in the creative and sporting subcategory of Tier 5 (Temporary Workers), employment as a sportsperson for his national team while his national team is in the UK.

Requirements for indefinite leave to remain

245ZS. To qualify for indefinite leave to remain as a Tier 5 (Temporary Worker) Migrant, an applicant must meet the requirements listed below. If the applicant meets these requirements, indefinite leave to remain will be granted. If the applicant does not meet these requirements, the application will be refused.

Requirements:

(aa) The applicant must not have one or more unspent convictions within the meaning of the Rehabilitation of Offenders Act 1974.

(a) The applicant must not fall for refusal under the general grounds for refusal and must not be an illegal entrant.

(b) The applicant must have spent a continuous period of 5 years lawfully in the UK with leave in the international agreement sub-category of Tier 5 and working as a private servant in a diplomatic household.

(c) The applicant must have sufficient knowledge of the English language and sufficient knowledge about life in the United Kingdom, with reference to paragraphs 33B to 33D of these Rules, unless the applicant is under the age of 18 or aged 65 or over at the time the application is made.

Tier 4 (General) Student

Purpose of this route

245ZT. This route is for migrants aged 16 or over who wish to study in the UK.

Entry clearance

245ZU. All migrants arriving in the UK and wishing to enter as a Tier 4 (General) Student must have a valid entry clearance for entry under this route. If they do not have a valid entry clearance, entry will be refused.

Requirements for entry clearance

245ZV. To qualify for entry clearance as a Tier 4 (General) Student, an applicant must meet the requirements listed below. If the applicant meets these requirements, entry clearance will be granted. If the applicant does not meet these requirements, the application will be refused.

Requirements:

(a) The applicant must not fall for refusal under the General Grounds for Refusal.

(b) The applicant must have a minimum of 30 points under paragraphs 113 to 120 of Appendix A.

(c) The applicant must have a minimum of 10 points under paragraphs 10 to 14 of Appendix C.

(ca) Where an applicant has been issued with a Confirmation of Acceptance for Studies on or after 21 April 2011, the applicant must, if required to do so on examination or interview, be able to demonstrate without the assistance of an interpreter English language proficiency of a standard to be expected from an individual who has reached the standard specified in a Confirmation of Acceptance for Studies assigned in accordance with Appendix A paragraph 118(c) (for the avoidance of doubt, the applicant will not be subject to a test at the standard set out in Appendix A, paragraph 118(c).

(d) If the applicant wishes to undertake:

(i) postgraduate studies leading to a Doctorate or Masters degree by research in one of the disciplines listed in paragraph 1 of Appendix 6 to these Rules, or

(ii) postgraduate studies leading to a taught Masters degree in one of the disciplines listed in paragraph 2 of Appendix 6 to these Rules, or

(iii) a period of study or research in excess of 6 months in one of the disciplines listed in paragraphs 1 or 2 of Appendix 6 of these Rules at an institution of higher education where this forms part of an overseas postgraduate qualification

the applicant must hold a valid Academic Technology Approval Scheme clearance certificate from the Counter-Proliferation Department of the Foreign and Commonwealth Office which relates to the course, or area of research, that the applicant will be taking and at the institution at which the applicant wishes to undertake it and must provide the specified documents to show that these requirements have been met.

(e) If the applicant wishes to be a postgraduate doctor or dentist on a recognised Foundation Programme:

(i) the applicant must have successfully completed a recognised UK degree in medicine or dentistry from:

(1) an institution with a Tier 4 General Sponsor Licence,

(2) a UK publicly funded institution of further or higher education or

(3) a UK bona fide private education institution which maintains satisfactory records of enrolment and attendance,

(ii) the applicant must have previously been granted leave:

(1) as a Tier 4 (General) Student, or as a Student, for the final academic year of the studies referred to in paragraph (i) above, and

(2) as a Tier 4 (General) Student, or as a Student, for at least one other academic year (aside from the final year) of the studies referred to in paragraph (i) above,

(iii) if the applicant has previously been granted leave as a Postgraduate Doctor or Dentist, the applicant must not be seeking entry clearance or leave to enter or remain to a date beyond 3 years from the date on which he was first granted leave to enter or remain in that category, and

(iv) if the applicant has previously been granted leave as a Tier 4 (General) Student to undertake a course as a postgraduate doctor or dentist, the applicant must not be seeking entry clearance or leave to enter or remain to a date beyond 3 years from the date on which the applicant was first granted leave to undertake such a course.

(f) If the applicant is currently being sponsored by a Government or international scholarship agency, or within the last 12 months has come to the end of such a period of sponsorship, the applicant must provide the written consent of the sponsoring Government or agency to the application and must provide the specified documents to show that this requirement has been met.

(g) If the course is below degree level the grant of entry clearance the applicant is seeking must not lead to the applicant having spent more than 3 years in the UK as a Tier 4 Migrant since the age of 18 studying courses that did not consist of degree level study.

(h) The applicant must be at least 16 years old.

(i) Where the applicant is under 18 years of age, the application must be supported by the applicant's parents or legal guardian, or by just one parent if that parent has sole legal responsibility for the child.

(j) Where the applicant is under 18 years of age, the applicant's parents or legal guardian, or just one parent if that parent has sole responsibility for the child, must confirm that they consent to the arrangements for the applicant's travel to, and reception and care in, the UK.

Period and conditions of grant

245ZW. (a) Subject to paragraph (b), entry clearance will be granted for the duration of the course.

(b) In addition to the period of entry clearance granted in accordance with paragraph (a), entry clearance will also be granted for the periods set out in the following table. Notes to accompany the table appear below the table.

Type of course	Period of entry clearance to be granted before the course starts	Period of entry clearance to be granted after the course ends
12 months or more	1 month	4 months
6 months or more but less than 12 months	1 month	2 months
Pre-sessional course of less than 6 months	1 month	1 month
Course of less than 6 months that is not a pre-sessional course	7 days	7 days
Postgraduate doctor or dentist	1 month	1 month

Notes

(i) If the grant of entry clearance is made less than 1 month or, in the case of a course of less than 6 months that is not a pre-sessional course, less than 7 days before the start of the course, entry clearance will be granted with immediate effect.

(ii) A pre-sessional course is a course which prepares a student for the student's main course of study in the UK.

(c) Entry clearance will be granted subject to the following conditions:

(i) no recourse to public funds,

(ii) registration with the police, if this is required by paragraph 326 of these Rules,

(iii) no employment except:

(1) employment during term time of no more than 20 hours per week and employment (of any duration) during vacations, where the student is following a course of degree level study and is either:

(a) sponsored by a Sponsor that is a Recognised Body or a body in receipt of public funding as a higher education institution from the Department of Employment and Learning in Northern Ireland, the Higher Education Funding Council for England, the Higher Education Funding Council for Wales or the Scottish Funding Council; or

(b) sponsored by an overseas higher education institution to undertake a short-term Study Abroad Programme in the United Kingdom.

(2) employment during term time of no more than 10 hours per week and employment (of any duration) during vacations, where the student is following a course of below degree level study and is sponsored by a Sponsor that is a Recognised Body or a body in receipt of public funding as a higher education institution from the Department of Employment and Learning in Northern Ireland, the Higher Education Funding Council for England, the Higher Education Funding Council for Wales or the Scottish Funding Council,

(3) employment during term time of no more than 10 hours per week and employment (of any duration) during vacations, where the student is following a course of study at any academic level and is sponsored by a Sponsor that is a publicly funded further education college,

(4) employment as part of a course-related work placement which forms an assessed part of the applicant's course and provided that any period that the applicant spends on that placement does not exceed half of the total length of the course undertaken in the UK except where it is a United Kingdom statutory requirement that the placement should exceed half the total length of the course.

(5) employment as a Student Union Sabbatical Officer, for up to 2 years, provided the post is elective and is at the institution which is the applicant's Sponsor.

(6) employment as a postgraduate doctor or dentist on a recognised Foundation Programme

provided that the migrant is not self employed, or employed as a Doctor or Dentist in Training other than a vacancy on a recognised Foundation Programme, professional sportsperson (including a sports coach) or an entertainer, and provided that the migrant's employment would not fill a permanent full time vacancy other than a vacancy on a recognised Foundation Programme or as a sabbatical officer; and

(iv) no study except:

(1) study at the institution that the Confirmation of Acceptance for Studies Checking Service records as the migrant's Sponsor, or where the migrant was awarded points for a visa letter, study at the institution which issued that visa letter unless the migrant is studying at an institution which is a partner institution of the migrant's Sponsor.

(2) until such time as a decision is received from the UK Border Agency on an application which is supported by a Confirmation of Acceptance for Studies assigned by a Highly Trusted Sponsor and which is made while the applicant has extant leave, and any appeal against that decision has been determined, study at the Highly Trusted Sponsor institution which the Confirmation of Acceptance for Studies Checking Service records as having assigned a Confirmation of Acceptance for Studies to the Tier 4 migrant; and (3) supplementary study.

Requirements for leave to remain

245ZX. To qualify for leave to remain as a Tier 4 (General) Student under this rule, an applicant must meet the requirements listed below. If the applicant meets these requirements, leave to remain will be granted. If the applicant does not meet these requirements, the applicant will be refused.

Requirements:

(a) The applicant must not fall for refusal under the general grounds for refusal and must not be an illegal entrant.

(b) The applicant must have, or have last been granted, entry clearance, leave to enter or leave to remain:

(i) as a Tier 4 (General) Student,

(ii) as a Tier 4 (Child) Student,

(iii) as a Tier 1 (Post-study Work) Migrant,

(iv) as a Tier 2 Migrant,

(v) as a Participant in the International Graduates Scheme (or its predecessor, the Science and Engineering Graduates Scheme),

(vi) as a Participant in the Fresh Talent: Working in Scotland Scheme,

(vii) as a Postgraduate Doctor or Dentist,

(viii) as a Prospective Student,

(ix) as a Student,

(x) as a Student Nurse,

(xi) as a Student Re-sitting an Examination,

(xii) as a Student Writing-Up a Thesis,

(xiii) as a Student Union Sabbatical Officer, or

(xiv) as a Work Permit Holder.

(c) The applicant must have a minimum of 30 points under paragraphs 113 to 120 of Appendix A.

(d) The applicant must have a minimum of 10 points under paragraphs 10 to 14 of Appendix C.

(e) If the applicant wishes to undertake:

(i) postgraduate studies leading to a Doctorate or Masters degree by research in one of the disciplines listed in paragraph 1 of Appendix 6 to these Rules, or

(ii) postgraduate studies leading to a taught Masters degree in one of the disciplines listed in paragraph 2 of Appendix 6 to these Rules, or

(iii) a period of study or research in excess of 6 months in one of the disciplines listed in paragraphs 1 or 2 of Appendix 6 of these Rules at a publicly funded institution of higher education where this forms part of an overseas postgraduate qualification the applicant must hold a valid Academic Technology Approval Scheme clearance certificate from the Counter-Proliferation Department of the Foreign and Commonwealth Office which relates to the course, or area of research, that the applicant will be taking and at the institution at which the applicant wishes to undertake it and must provide the specified documents to show that these requirements have been met.

(f) If the applicant wishes to be a postgraduate doctor or dentist on a recognised Foundation Programme:

(i) the applicant must have successfully completed a recognised UK degree in medicine or dentistry from:

(1) an institution with a Tier 4 General Sponsor Licence,

(2) a UK publicly funded institution of further or higher education or

(3) a UK bona fide private education institution which maintains satisfactory records of enrolment and attendance,

(ii) the applicant must have previously been granted leave:

(1) as a Tier 4 (General) Student, or as a Student, for the final academic year of the studies referred to in paragraph (i) above, and

(2) as a Tier 4 (General) Student, or as a Student, for at least one other academic year (aside from the final year) of the studies referred to in paragraph (i) above,

(iii) if the applicant has previously been granted leave as a Postgraduate Doctor or Dentist the applicant must not be seeking entry clearance or leave to enter or remain to a date beyond 3 years from the date on which he was first granted leave to enter or remain in that category, and

(iv) if the applicant has previously been granted leave as a Tier 4 (General) Student to undertake a course as a postgraduate doctor or dentist, the applicant must not be seeking entry clearance or leave to enter or remain to a date beyond 3 years from the date on which he was first granted leave to undertake such a course.

(g) If the applicant is currently being sponsored by a Government or international scholarship agency, or within the last 12 months has come to the end of such a period of sponsorship, the applicant must provide the unconditional written consent of the sponsoring Government or agency to the application and must provide the specified documents to show that this requirement has been met.

(h) If the course is below degree level the grant of leave to remain the applicant is seeking must not lead to the applicant having spent more than 3 years in the UK as a Tier 4 Migrant since the age of 18 studying courses that did not consist of degree level study.

(i) The applicant must be at least 16 years old.

(j) Where the applicant is under 18 years of age, the application must be supported by the applicant's parents or legal guardian, or by just one parent if that parent has sole legal responsibility for the child.

(k) Where the applicant is under 18 years of age, the applicant's parents or legal guardian, or just one parent if that parent has sole legal responsibility for the child, must confirm that they consent to the arrangements for the applicant's care in the UK.

(l) The applicant must not be applying for leave to remain for the purpose of studies which would commence more than one month after the applicant's current entry clearance or leave to remain granted under these Rules expires.

Period and conditions of grant

245ZY. (a) Subject to paragraphs (b) and (c) below, leave to remain will be granted for the duration of the course.

(b) In addition to the period of leave to remain granted in accordance with paragraph (a), leave to remain will also be granted for the periods set out in the following table. Notes to accompany the table appear below the table.

Type of course	Period of leave to remain to be granted before the course starts	Period of leave to remain to be granted after the course ends
12 months or more	1 month	4 months
6 months or more but less than 12 months	1 month	2 months
Pre-sessional course of less than 6 months	1 month	1 month
Course of less than 6 months that is not a pre-sessional course	7 days	7 days
Postgraduate doctor or dentist	1 month	1 month

Notes

(i) If the grant of leave to remain is being made less than 1 month or, in the case of a course of less than 6 months that is not a pre-sessional course, less than 7 days before the start of the course, leave to remain will be granted with immediate effect.

(ii) A pre-sessional course is a course which prepares a student for the student's main course of study in the UK.

(c) Leave to remain will be granted subject to the following conditions:

(i) no recourse to public funds,

(ii) registration with the police, if this is required by paragraph 326 of these Rules,

(iii) no employment except:

(1) employment during term time of no more than 20 hours per week and employment (of any duration) during vacations, where the student is following a course of degree level study and is either:

(a) sponsored by a Sponsor that is a Recognised Body or a body in receipt of public funding as a higher education institution from the Department of Employment and Learning in Northern Ireland, the Higher Education Funding Council for England, the Higher Education Funding Council for Wales or the Scottish Funding Council; or

(b) sponsored by an overseas higher education institution to undertake a short-term Study Abroad Programme in the United Kingdom.

(2) employment during term time of no more than 10 hours per week and employment (of any duration) during vacations, where the student is following a course of below degree level study and is sponsored by a Sponsor that is a Recognised Body or a body in receipt of public funding as a higher education institution from the Department of Employment and Learning in Northern Ireland, the Higher Education Funding Council for England, the Higher Education Funding Council for Wales or the Scottish Funding Council,

(3) employment during term time of no more than 10 hours per week and employment (of any duration) during vacations, where the student is following a course of study at any academic level and is sponsored by a Sponsor that is a publicly funded further education college,

(4) employment as part of a course-related work placement which forms an assessed part of the applicant's course and provided that any period that the applicant spends on that placement does not exceed half of the total length of the course undertaken in the UK except where it is a United Kingdom statutory requirement that the placement should exceed half the total length of the course.

(5) employment as a Student Union Sabbatical Officer for up to 2 years provided the post is elective and is at the institution which is the applicant's Sponsor,

(6) employment as a postgraduate doctor or dentist on a recognised Foundation Programme

provided that the migrant is not self-employed, or employed as a Doctor or Dentist in Training other than a vacancy on a recognised Foundation Programme, a professional sportsperson (including a sports coach) or an entertainer, and provided that the migrant's employment would not fill a permanent full time vacancy other than a vacancy on a recognised Foundation Programme or as a sabbatical officer.

(iv) no study except:

(1) study at the institution that the Confirmation of Acceptance for Studies Checking Service records as the migrant's Sponsor, or where the migrant was awarded points for a visa letter, study at the institution which issued that visa letter unless the migrant is studying at an institution which is a partner institution of the migrant's Sponsor,

(2) until such time as a decision is received from the UK Border Agency on an application which is supported by a Confirmation of Acceptance for Studies assigned by a Highly Trusted Sponsor and which is made while the applicant has extant leave, and any appeal against that decision has been determined, study at the Highly Trusted Sponsor institution which the Confirmation of Acceptance for Studies Checking Service records as having assigned a Confirmation of Acceptance for Studies to the Tier 4 migrant; and (3) supplementary study.

Tier 4 (Child) Student

Purpose of route

245ZZ. This route is for children at least 4 years old and under the age of 18 who wish to be educated in the UK.

Entry clearance

245ZZA. All migrants arriving in the UK and wishing to enter as a Tier 4 (Child) Student must have a valid entry clearance for entry under this route. If they do not have a valid entry clearance, entry will be refused.

Requirements:

(a) The applicant must not fall for refusal under the general grounds for refusal.

(b) The applicant must have a minimum of 30 points under paragraphs 121 to 126 of Appendix A.

(c) The applicant must have a minimum of 10 points under paragraphs 15 to 22 of Appendix C.

(d) The applicant must be at least 4 years old and under the age of 18.

(e) The applicant must have no children under the age of 18 who are either living with the applicant or for whom the applicant is financially responsible.

(f) If a foster carer or a relative (not a parent or guardian) of the applicant will be responsible for the care of the applicant:

(i) the arrangements for the care of the applicant by the foster carer or relative must meet the requirements laid down in guidance published by the United Kingdom Border Agency and the applicant must provide the specified documents to show that this requirement has been met, and

(ii) the applicant must provide details of the care arrangements as specified in guidance published by the United Kingdom Border Agency.

(g) The application must be supported by the applicant's parents or legal guardian, or by just one parent if that parent has sole legal responsibility for the child.

(h) The applicant's parents or legal guardian, or just one parent if that parent has sole responsibility for the child, must confirm that they consent to the arrangements for the applicant's travel to, and reception and care in, the UK.

(i) If the applicant is currently being sponsored by a Government or international scholarship agency, or within the last 12 months has come to the end of such a period of sponsorship, the applicant must provide the written consent of the sponsoring Government or agency to the application and must provide the specified documents to show that this requirement has been met

Period and conditions of grant

245ZZB. (a) Where the applicant is under the age of 16, entry clearance will be granted for:

(i) a period of no more than 1 month before the course starts, plus

(ii) a period:

(1) requested by the applicant,

(2) equal to the length of the programme the applicant is following, or

(3) of 6 years

whichever is the shorter, plus

(iii) 4 months.

(b) Where the applicant is aged 16 or over, entry clearance will be granted for:

(i) a period of no more than 1 month before the course starts, plus

(ii) a period:

(1) requested by the applicant,

(2) equal to the length of the programme the applicant is following, or

(3) of 3 years

whichever is the shorter, plus

(iii) 4 months.

(c) Entry clearance will be granted subject to the following conditions:

(i) no recourse to public funds,

(ii) registration with the police, if this is required by paragraph 326 of these Rules,

(iii) no employment whilst the migrant is aged under 16,

(iv) no employment whilst the migrant is aged 16 or over except:

(1) employment during term time of no more than 10 hours per week,

(2) employment (of any duration) during vacations,

(3) employment as part of a course-related work placement which forms an assessed part of the applicant's course and provided that any period that the applicant spend on that placement does not exceed half of the total length of the course undertaken in the UK except where it is a United Kingdom statutory requirement that the placement should exceed half the total length of the course

(4) employment as a Student Union Sabbatical Officer for up to 2 years provided the post is elective and is at the institution which is the applicant's Sponsor

provided that the migrant is not self employed, or employed as a Doctor in Training, a professional sportsperson (including a sports coach) or an entertainer, and provided that the migrant's employment would not fill a permanent full time vacancy other than a vacancy as a sabbatical officer.

(v) no study except:

(1) study at the institution that the Confirmation of Acceptance for Studies Checking Service records as the migrant's Sponsor, or where the migrant was awarded points for a visa letter, study at the institution which issued that visa letter unless the migrant is studying at an institution which is a partner institution of the migrant's Sponsor;

(2) until such time as a decision is received from the UK Border Agency on an application which is supported by a Confirmation of Acceptance for Studies assigned by a Highly Trusted Sponsor and which is made while the applicant has extant leave, and any appeal against that decision has been determined, study at the Highly Trusted Sponsor institution which the Confirmation of Acceptance for Studies Checking Service records as having assigned a Confirmation of Acceptance for Studies to the Tier 4 migrant; and

(3) supplementary study.

Requirements for leave to remain

245ZZC. To qualify for leave to remain as a Tier 4 (Child) Student under this rule, an applicant must meet the requirements listed below. If the applicant meets these requirements, leave to remain will be granted. If the applicant does not meet these requirements, leave to remain will be refused.

Requirements:

(a) The applicant must not fall for refusal under the general grounds for refusal and must not be an illegal entrant.

(b) The applicant must have, or have last been granted, entry clearance, leave to enter or leave to remain:

(i) as a Tier 4 Migrant,

(ii) as a Student, or

(iii) as a Prospective Student.

(c) The applicant must have a minimum of 30 points under paragraphs 121 to 126 of Appendix A.

(d) The applicant must have a minimum of 10 points under paragraphs 15 to 22 of Appendix C.

(e) The applicant must be under the age of 18.

(f) The applicant must have no children under the age of 18 who are either living with the applicant or for whom the applicant is financially responsible.

(g) If a foster carer or a relative (not a parent or guardian) will be responsible for the care of the applicant:

(i) the arrangements for the care of the applicant by the foster carer or relative must meet the requirements laid down in guidance published by the United Kingdom Border Agency and the applicant must provide the specified documents to show that this requirement has been met, and

(ii) the applicant must provide details of the care arrangements as specified in guidance published by the United Kingdom Border Agency.

(h) The application must be supported by the applicant's parents or legal guardian, or by just one parent if that parent has sole legal responsibility for the child.

(i) The applicant's parents or legal guardian, or just one parent if that parent has sole legal responsibility for the child, must confirm that they consent to the arrangements for the applicant's care in the UK.

(j) The applicant must not be applying for leave to remain for the purpose of studies which would commence more than one month after the applicant's current entry clearance or leave to remain granted under these Rules expires.

(k) If the applicant is currently being sponsored by a Government or international scholarship agency, or within the last 12 months has come to the end of such a period of sponsorship, the applicant must provide the written consent of the sponsoring Government or agency to the application and must provide the specified documents to show that this requirement has been met.

Period and conditions of grant

245ZZD. (a) Where the applicant is under the age of 16, leave to remain will be granted for:

(i) a period of no more than 1 month before the course starts, plus

(ii) a period:

(1) requested by the applicant,

(2) equal to the length of the programme the applicant is following, or

(3) of 6 years

whichever is the shorter, plus

(iii) 4 months.

(b) Where the applicant is aged 16 or over, leave to remain will be granted for:

(i) a period of no more than 1 month before the course starts, plus

(ii) a period:

(1) requested by the applicant,

(2) equal to the length of the programme the applicant is following, or

(3) of 3 years

whichever is the shorter, plus

(iii) 4 months.

(c) Leave to remain will be granted subject to the following conditions:
   (i) no recourse to public funds,
   (ii) registration with the police, if this is required by paragraph 326 of these Rules,
   (iii) no employment whilst the migrant is aged under 16,
   (iv) no employment whilst the migrant is aged 16 or over except:
      (1) employment during term time of no more than 10 hours per week,
      (2) employment (of any duration) during vacations,
      (3) employment as part of a course-related work placement which forms an assessed part of the applicant's course, and provided that any period that the applicant spend on that placement does not exceed half of the total length of the course undertaken in the UK except where it is a United Kingdom statutory requirement that the placement should exceed half the total length of the course,
      (4) employment as a Student Union Sabbatical Officer for up to 2 years provided the post is elective and is at the institution which is the applicant's Sponsor,

   provided that the migrant is not self-employed, or employed as a Doctor in Training, a professional sportsperson (including a sports coach) or an entertainer, and provided that the migrant's employment would not fill a permanent full time vacancy other than a vacancy as a sabbatical officer.
   (v) no study except:
      (1) study at the institution that the Confirmation of Acceptance for Studies Checking Service records as the migrant's Sponsor, or where the migrant was awarded points for a visa letter, study at the institution which issued that visa letter *unless the migrant is studying at an institution which is a partner institution of the migrant's Sponsor;*
      (2) until such time as a decision is received from the UK Border Agency on an application which is supported by a Confirmation of Acceptance for Studies assigned by a Highly Trusted Sponsor and which is made while the applicant has extant leave, and any appeal against that decision has been determined, study at the Highly Trusted Sponsor institution which the Confirmation of Acceptance for Studies Checking Service records as having assigned a Confirmation of Acceptance for Studies to the Tier 4 migrant; and
      (3) supplementary study.

Part 7 – Other Categories

Requirements for leave to enter the United Kingdom as a person exercising rights of access to a child resident in the United Kingdom

246. The requirements to be met by a person seeking leave to enter the United Kingdom to exercise access rights to a child resident in the United Kingdom are that:
   (i) the applicant is the parent of a child who is resident in the United Kingdom; and
   (ii) the parent or carer with whom the child permanently resides is resident in the United Kingdom; and
   (iii) the applicant produces evidence that he has access rights to the child in the form of:
      (a) a Residence Order or a Contact Order granted by a Court in the United Kingdom; or
      (b) a certificate issued by a district judge confirming the applicant's intention to maintain contact with the child; and
   (iv) the applicant intends to take an active role in the child's upbringing; and
   (v) the child is under the age of 18; and
   (vi) there will be adequate accommodation for the applicant and any dependants without recourse to public funds in accommodation which the applicant owns or occupies exclusively; and
   (vii) the applicant will be able to maintain himself and any dependants adequately without recourse to public funds; and
   (viii) the applicant holds a valid United Kingdom entry clearance for entry in this capacity.

Leave to enter the United Kingdom as a person exercising rights of access to a child resident in the United Kingdom

247. Leave to enter as a person exercising access rights to a child resident in the United Kingdom may be granted for 12 months in the first instance, provided that a valid United Kingdom entry clearance for entry in this capacity is produced to the Immigration Officer on arrival.

Refusal of leave to enter the United Kingdom as a person exercising rights of access to a child resident in the United Kingdom

248. Leave to enter as a person exercising rights of access to a child resident in the United Kingdom is to be refused if a valid United Kingdom entry clearance for entry in this capacity is not produced to the Immigration Officer on arrival.

Requirements for leave to remain in the United Kingdom as a person exercising rights of access to a child resident in the United Kingdom

248A. The requirements to be met by a person seeking leave to remain in the United Kingdom to exercise access rights to a child resident in the United Kingdom are that:

(i) the applicant is the parent of a child who is resident in the United Kingdom; and

(ii) the parent or carer with whom the child permanently resides is resident in the United Kingdom; and

(iii) the applicant produces evidence that he has access rights to the child in the form of:

(a) a Residence Order or a Contact Order granted by a Court in the United Kingdom; or

(b) a certificate issued by a district judge confirming the applicant's intention to maintain contact with the child; or

(c) a statement from the child's other parent (or, if contact is supervised, from the supervisor) that the applicant is maintaining contact with the child; and

(iv) the applicant takes and intends to continue to take an active role in the child's upbringing; and

(v) the child visits or stays with the applicant on a frequent and regular basis and the applicant intends this to continue; and

(vi) the child is under the age of 18; and

(vii) the applicant has limited leave to remain in the United Kingdom as the spouse, civil partner, unmarried partner or same-sex partner of a person present and settled in the United Kingdom who is the other parent of the child; and

(viii) the applicant has not remained in breach of the immigration laws; and

(ix) there will be adequate accommodation for the applicant and any dependants without recourse to public funds in accommodation which the applicant owns or occupies exclusively; and

(x) the applicant will be able to maintain himself and any dependants adequately without recourse to public funds.

Leave to remain in the United Kingdom as a person exercising rights of access to a child resident in the United Kingdom

248B. Leave to remain as a person exercising access rights to a child resident in the United Kingdom may be granted for 12 months in the first instance, provided the Secretary of State is satisfied that each of the requirements of paragraph 248A is met.

Refusal of leave to remain in the United Kingdom as a person exercising rights of access to a child resident in the United Kingdom

248C. Leave to remain as a person exercising rights of access to a child resident in the United Kingdom is to be refused if the Secretary of State is not satisfied that each of the requirements of paragraph 248A is met.

Indefinite leave to remain in the United Kingdom as a person exercising rights of access to a child resident in the United Kingdom

248D. The requirements for indefinite leave to remain in the United Kingdom as a person exercising rights of access to a child resident in the United Kingdom are that:

(i) the applicant was admitted to the United Kingdom or granted leave to remain in the United Kingdom for a period of 12 months as a person exercising rights of access to a child and has completed a period of 12 months as a person exercising rights of access to a child; and

(ii) the applicant takes and intends to continue to take an active role in the child's upbringing; and

(iii) the child visits or stays with the applicant on a frequent and regular basis and the applicant intends this to continue; and

(iv) there will be adequate accommodation for the applicant and any dependants without recourse to public funds in accommodation which the applicant owns or occupies exclusively; and

(v) the applicant will be able to maintain himself and any dependants adequately without recourse to public funds; and

(vi) the child is under 18 years of age; and

(vi) the applicant has sufficient knowledge of the English language and sufficient knowledge about life in the United Kingdom, unless he is under the age of 18 or aged 65 or over at the time he makes his application; and

(vii) the applicant does not have one or more unspent convictions within the meaning of the Rehabilitation of Offenders Act 1974.

Indefinite leave to remain as a person exercising rights of access to a child resident in the United Kingdom

248E. Indefinite leave to remain as a person exercising rights of access to a child may be granted provided the Secretary of State is satisfied that each of the requirements of paragraph 248D is met.

Refusal of indefinite leave to remain in the United Kingdom as a person exercising rights of access to a child resident in the United Kingdom

248F. Indefinite leave to remain as a person exercising rights of access to a child is to be refused if the Secretary of State is not satisfied that each of the requirements of paragraph 248D is met.

Holders of special vouchers

Requirements for indefinite leave to enter as the holder of a special voucher

249. DELETED

Indefinite leave to enter as the holder of a special voucher

250. DELETED

Refusal of indefinite leave to enter as the holder of a special voucher

251. DELETED

Requirements for indefinite leave to enter as the spouse or child of a special voucher holder

252. DELETED

Indefinite leave to enter as the spouse or child of a special voucher holder

253. DELETED

Refusal of indefinite leave to enter as the spouse or child of a special voucher holder

254. DELETED

EEA Nationals and their families

Settlement

255. DELETED. But this is subject to the transitional provision in paragraph 5 continues to apply for the purpose of determining an application made before 30 April 2006 for an endorsement under paragraph 255.

255A. DELETED. But this is subject to the transitional provision in paragraph 5 continues to apply for the purpose of determining an application made before 30 April 2006 for an endorsement under paragraph 255.

255B. DELETED. But this is subject to the transitional provision in paragraph 5 continues to apply for the purpose of determining an application made before 30 April 2006 for an endorsement under paragraph 255.

256. DELETED

257. DELETED

257A. DELETED. But this is subject to the transitional provision in paragraph 8 continues to apply for the purpose of determining an application made before 30 April 2006 for an endorsement under paragraph 257A.

257B. DELETED. But this is subject to the transitional provision in paragraph 8 continues to apply for the purpose of determining an application made before 30 April 2006 for an endorsement under paragraph 257B.

Requirements for leave to enter or remain as the primary carer or relative of an EEA national self-sufficient child

257C. The requirements to be met by a person seeking leave to enter or remain as the primary carer or relative of an EEA national self-sufficient child are that the applicant:

(i) is:

(a) the primary carer; or

(b) the parent; or

(c) the sibling,

of an EEA national under the age of 18 who has a right of residence in the United Kingdom under the 2006 EEA Regulations as a self-sufficient person; and

(ii) is living with the EEA national or is seeking entry to the United Kingdom in order to live with the EEA national; and

(iii) in the case of a sibling of the EEA national:

(a) is under the age of 18 or has current leave to enter or remain in this capacity; and

(b) is unmarried and is not a civil partner, has not formed an independent family unit and is not leading an independent life; and

(iv) can, and will, be maintained and accommodated without taking employment or having recourse to public funds; and

(v) if seeking leave to enter, holds a valid United Kingdom entry clearance for entry in this capacity.

In this paragraph, 'sibling', includes a half-brother or half-sister and a stepbrother or stepsister.

Leave to enter or remain as the primary carer or relative of an EEA national self-sufficient child

257D. Leave to enter or remain in the United Kingdom as the primary carer or relative of an EEA national self-sufficient child may be granted for a period not exceeding five years or the remaining period of validity of any residence permit held by the EEA national under the 2006 EEA Regulations, whichever is the shorter, provided that, in the case of an application for leave to enter, the applicant is able to produce to the Immigration Officer, on arrival a valid entry clearance for entry in this capacity or, in the case of an application for leave to remain, the applicant is able to satisfy the Secretary of State that each of the requirements of paragraph 257C(i) to (iv) is met. Leave to enter or remain is to be subject to a condition prohibiting employment and recourse to public funds.

Refusal of leave to enter or remain as the primary carer or relative of an EEA national self-sufficient child

257E. Leave to enter or remain in the United Kingdom as the primary carer or relative of an EEA national self-sufficient child is to be refused if, in the case of an application for leave to enter, the applicant is unable to produce to the Immigration Officer on arrival a valid United Kingdom entry clearance for entry in this capacity or, in the case of an application for leave to remain, if the applicant is unable to satisfy the Secretary of State that each of the requirements of paragraph 257C(i) to (iv) is met.

The EEA family permit

258. DELETED

Requirements for the issue of an EEA family permit

259. DELETED

Issue of an EEA family permit

260. DELETED

Refusal of an application for an EEA family permit

261. DELETED

Registration with the police for family members of EEA nationals

262. DELETED

Retired persons of independent means

Requirements for leave to enter the United Kingdom as a retired person of independent means

263. DELETED

Leave to enter as a retired person of independent means

264. DELETED

Refusal of leave to enter as a retired person of independent means

265. DELETED

Requirements for an extension of stay as a retired person of independent means

266. The requirements for an extension of stay as a retired person of independent means are that the applicant:
   (i) entered the United Kingdom with a valid United Kingdom entry clearance as a retired person of independent means; and
   (ii) meets the following requirements:
      (a) has under his control and disposable in the United Kingdom an income of his own of not less than £25,000 per annum; and
      (b) is able and willing to maintain and accommodate himself and any dependants indefinitely in the United Kingdom from his own resources with no assistance from any other person and without taking employment or having recourse to public funds; and
      (c) can demonstrate a close connection with the United Kingdom; and
   (iii) has made the United Kingdom his main home.

Extension of stay as a retired person of independent means

266A. DELETED

266C. DELETED

266D. DELETED

266E. DELETED

267. An extension of stay as a retired person of independent means, with a prohibition on the taking of employment, may be granted so as to bring the person's stay in this category up to a maximum of 5 years in aggregate, provided the Secretary of State is satisfied that each of the requirements of paragraph 266 is met.

Refusal of extension of stay as a retired person of independent means

268. An extension of stay as a retired person of independent means is to be refused if the Secretary of State is not satisfied that each of the requirements of paragraph 266 is met.

Indefinite leave to remain for a retired person of independent means

269. Indefinite leave to remain may be granted, on application, to a person admitted as a retired person of independent means provided he:

(i) has spent a continuous period of 5 years in the United Kingdom in this capacity; and

(ii) has met the requirements of paragraph 266 throughout the 5 year period and continues to do so; and

(iii) does not have one or more unspent convictions within the meaning of the Rehabilitation of Offenders Act 1974.

Refusal of indefinite leave to remain for a retired person of independent means

270. Indefinite leave to remain in the United Kingdom for a retired person of independent means is to be refused if the Secretary of State is not satisfied that each of the requirements of paragraph 269 is met.

Spouses or civil partners of persons with limited leave to enter or remain in the United Kingdom as retired persons of independent means

Requirements for leave to enter or remain as the spouse or civil partners of a person with limited leave to enter or remain in the United Kingdom as a retired person of independent means

271. The requirements to be met by a person seeking leave to enter the United Kingdom as the spouse or civil partner of a person with limited leave to enter or remain in the United Kingdom as a retired person of independent means are that:

(i) the applicant is married to or the civil partner of a person with limited leave to enter or remain in the United Kingdom as a retired person of independent means; and

(ii) each of the parties intends to live with the other as his or her spouse or civil partners during the applicant's stay and the marriage or civil partnership is subsisting; and

(iii) there will be adequate accommodation for the parties and any dependants without recourse to public funds in accommodation which they own or occupy exclusively; and

(iv) the parties will be able to maintain themselves and any dependants adequately without recourse to public funds; and

(v) the applicant does not intend to stay in the United Kingdom beyond any period of leave granted to his spouse or civil partner; and

(vi) the applicant holds a valid United Kingdom entry clearance for entry in this capacity.

Leave to enter as the spouse or civil partner of a person with limited leave to enter or remain in the United Kingdom as a retired person of independent means

272. A person seeking leave to enter the United Kingdom as the spouse or civil partner of a person with limited leave to enter or remain in the United Kingdom as a retired person of independent means may be given leave to enter for a period not in excess of that granted to the person with limited leave to enter or remain as a retired person of independent means, provided the Immigration Officer is satisfied that each of the requirements of paragraph 271 is met.

Refusal of leave to enter as the spouse or civil partner of a person with limited leave to enter or remain in the United Kingdom as a retired person of independent means

273. Leave to enter as the spouse or civil partner of a person with limited leave to enter or remain in the United Kingdom as a retired person of independent means is to be refused if the Immigration Officer is not satisfied that each of the requirements of paragraph 271 is met.

Requirements for extension of stay as the spouse or civil partner of a person who has or has had leave to enter or remain in the United Kingdom as a retired person of independent means

273A. The requirements to be met by a person seeking an extension of stay in the United Kingdom as the spouse or civil partner of a person who has or has had leave to enter or remain in the United Kingdom as a retired person of independent means are that the applicant:

(i) is married to or the civil partner of a person with limited leave to enter or remain in the United Kingdom as a retired person of independent means; or

(ii) is married to or the civil partner of a person who has limited leave to enter or remain in the United Kingdom as a retired person of independent means and who is being granted indefinite leave to remain at the same time; or

(iii) is married to or the civil partner of a person who has indefinite leave to remain in the United Kingdom and who had limited leave to enter or remain as a retired person of independent means immediately before being granted indefinite leave to remain; and

(iv) meets the requirements of paragraph 271(ii)–(v); and

(v) was admitted with a valid United Kingdom entry clearance for entry in this capacity.

Extension of stay as the spouse or civil partner of a person who has or has had leave to enter or remain in the United Kingdom as a retired person of independent means

273B. An extension of stay in the United Kingdom as:

(i) the spouse or civil partner of a person who has limited leave to enter or remain as a retired person of independent means may be granted for a period not in excess of that granted to the person with limited leave to enter or remain; or

(ii) the spouse or civil partner of a person who is being admitted at the same time for settlement or the spouse or civil partner of a person who has indefinite leave to remain may be granted for a period not exceeding 2 years, in both instances, provided the Secretary of State is satisfied that each of the requirements of paragraph 273A is met.

Refusal of extension of stay as the spouse or civil partner of a person who has or has had leave to enter or remain in the United Kingdom as a retired person of independent means

273C. An extension of stay in the United Kingdom as the spouse or civil partner of a person who has or has had leave to enter or remain in the United Kingdom as a retired person of independent means is to be refused if the Secretary of State is not satisfied that each of the requirements of paragraph 273A is met.

Requirements for indefinite leave to remain for the spouse or civil partner of a person who has or has had leave to enter or remain in the United Kingdom as a retired person of independent means

273D. The requirements to be met by a person seeking indefinite leave to remain in the United Kingdom as the spouse or civil partner of a person who has or has had leave to enter or remain in the United Kingdom as a retired person of independent means are that the applicant:

(i) is married to or the civil partner of a person who has limited leave to enter or remain in the United Kingdom as a retired person of independent means and who is being granted indefinite leave to remain at the same time; or

(ii) is married to or the civil partner of a person who has indefinite leave to remain in the United Kingdom and who had limited leave to enter or remain as a retired person of independent means immediately before being granted indefinite leave to remain; and

(iii) meets the requirements of paragraph 271(ii)–(v); and

(iv) has sufficient knowledge of the English language and sufficient knowledge about life in the United Kingdom, unless he is under the age of 18 or aged 65 or over at the time he makes his application; and

(v) was admitted with a valid United Kingdom entry clearance for entry in this capacity, and

(vi) does not have one or more unspent convictions within the meaning of the Rehabilitation of Offenders Act 1974.

Indefinite leave to remain as the spouse or civil partner of a person who has or has had leave to enter or remain in the United Kingdom as a retired person of independent means

273E. Indefinite leave to remain in the United Kingdom for the spouse or civil partner of a person who has or has had leave to enter or remain in the United Kingdom as a retired person of independent means may be granted provided the Secretary of State is satisfied that each of the requirements of paragraph 273D is met.

Refusal of indefinite leave to remain as the spouse or civil partner of a person who has or has had leave to enter or remain in the United Kingdom as a retired person of independent means

273F. Indefinite leave to remain in the United Kingdom for the spouse or civil partner of a person who has or has had leave to enter or remain in the United Kingdom as a retired person of independent means is to be refused if the Secretary of State is not satisfied that each of the requirements of paragraph 273D is met.

Children of persons with limited leave to enter or remain in the United Kingdom as retired persons of independent means

Requirements for leave to enter or remain as the child of a person with limited leave to enter or remain in the United Kingdom as a retired person of independent means

274. The requirements to be met by a person seeking leave to enter or remain in the United Kingdom as the child of a person with limited leave to enter or remain in the United Kingdom as a retired person of independent means are that:

(i) he is the child of a parent who has been admitted to or allowed to remain in the United Kingdom as a retired person of independent means; and

(ii) he is under the age of 18 or has current leave to enter or remain in this capacity; and

(iii) he is unmarried and is not a civil partner, has not formed an independent family unit and is not leading an independent life; and

(iv) he can, and will, be maintained and accommodated adequately without recourse to public funds in accommodation which his parent(s) own or occupy exclusively; and

(v) he will not stay in the United Kingdom beyond any period of leave granted to his parent(s); and

(vi) both parents are being or have been admitted to or allowed to remain in the United Kingdom save where:

(a) the parent he is accompanying or joining is his sole surviving parent; or

(b) the parent he is accompanying or joining has had sole responsibility for his upbringing; or

(c) there are serious and compelling family or other considerations which make exclusion from the United Kingdom undesirable and suitable arrangements have been made for his care; and

(vii) if seeking leave to enter, he holds a valid United Kingdom entry clearance for entry in this capacity or, if seeking leave to remain, was admitted with a valid United Kingdom entry clearance for entry in this capacity.

Leave to enter or remain as the child of a person with limited leave to enter or remain in the United Kingdom as a retired person of independent means

275. A person seeking leave to enter or remain in the United Kingdom as the child of a person with limited leave to enter or remain in the United Kingdom as a retired person of independent means may be given leave to enter or remain in the United Kingdom for a period of leave not in excess of that granted to the person with limited leave to enter or remain as a retired person of independent means provided that, in relation to an application for leave to enter, he is able to produce to the Immigration Officer, on arrival, a valid United Kingdom entry clearance for entry in this capacity or, in the case of an application for limited leave to remain, he was admitted with a valid United Kingdom entry clearance for entry in this capacity and is able to satisfy the Secretary of State that each of the requirements of paragraph 274(i)–(vi) is met. An application for indefinite leave to remain in this category may be granted provided the applicant was admitted to the United Kingdom with a valid United Kingdom entry clearance for entry in this capacity and is able to satisfy the Secretary of State that each of the requirements of paragraph 274(i)–(vi) is met and provided indefinite leave to remain is, at the same time, being granted to the person with limited leave to enter or remain as a retired person of independent means. Leave to enter or remain is to be subject to a condition prohibiting employment except in relation to the grant of indefinite leave to remain.

Refusal of leave to enter or remain as the child of a person with limited leave to enter or remain in the United Kingdom as a retired person of independent means

276. Leave to enter or remain in the United Kingdom as the child of a person with limited leave to enter or remain in the United Kingdom as a retired person of independent means is to be refused if, in relation to

an application for leave to enter, a valid United Kingdom entry clearance for entry in this capacity is not produced to the Immigration Officer on arrival, or in the case of an application for limited leave to remain, if the applicant was not admitted with a valid United Kingdom entry clearance for entry in this capacity or is unable to satisfy the Secretary of State that each of the requirements of paragraph 274(i)–(vi) is met. An application for indefinite leave to remain in this category is to be refused if the applicant was not admitted with a valid United Kingdom entry clearance for entry in this capacity or is unable to satisfy the Secretary of State that each of the requirements of paragraph 274(i)–(vi) is met or if indefinite leave to remain is not, at the same time, being granted to the person with limited leave to enter or remain as a retired person of independent means.

Long residence

Long residence in the United Kingdom

276A. For the purposes of paragraphs 276B to 276D:

(a) 'continuous residence' means residence in the United Kingdom for an unbroken period, and for these purposes a period shall not be considered to have been broken where an applicant is absent from the United Kingdom for a period of 6 months or less at any one time, provided that the applicant in question has existing limited leave to enter or remain upon their departure and return, but shall be considered to have been broken if the applicant:

(i) has been removed under Schedule 2 of the 1971 Act, section 10 of the 1999 Act, has been deported or has left the United Kingdom having been refused leave to enter or remain here; or

(ii) has left the United Kingdom and, on doing so, evidenced a clear intention not to return; or

(iii) left the United Kingdom in circumstances in which he could have had no reasonable expectation at the time of leaving that he would lawfully be able to return; or

(iv) has been convicted of an offence and was sentenced to a period of imprisonment or was directed to be detained in an institution other than a prison (including, in particular, a hospital or an institution for young offenders), provided that the sentence in question was not a suspended sentence; or

(v) has spent a total of more than 18 months absent from the United Kingdom during the period in question.

(b) 'lawful residence' means residence which is continuous residence pursuant to:

(i) existing leave to enter or remain; or

(ii) temporary admission within section 11 of the 1971 Act where leave to enter or remain is subsequently granted; or

(iii) an exemption from immigration control, including where an exemption ceases to apply if it is immediately followed by a grant of leave to enter or remain.

Requirements for an extension of stay on the ground of long residence in the United Kingdom

276A1. The requirement to be met by a person seeking an extension of stay on the ground of long residence in the United Kingdom is that the applicant meets all the requirements in paragraph 276B of these rules, except the requirement to have sufficient knowledge of the English language and sufficient knowledge about life in the United Kingdom contained in paragraph 276B(iii).

Extension of stay on the ground of long residence in the United Kingdom

276A2. An extension of stay on the ground of long residence in the United Kingdom may be granted for a period not exceeding 2 years provided that the Secretary of State is satisfied that the requirement in paragraph 276A1 is met.

Conditions to be attached to extension of stay on the ground of long residence in the United Kingdom

276A3. Where an extension of stay is granted under paragraph 276A2:

(i) if the applicant has spent less than 14 years in the UK , the grant of leave should be subject to the same conditions attached to his last period of lawful leave, or

(ii) if the applicant has spent 14 years or more in the UK, the grant of leave should not contain any restriction on employment.

Refusal of extension of stay on the ground of long residence in the United Kingdom

276A4. An extension of stay on the ground of long residence in the United Kingdom is to be refused if the Secretary of State is not satisfied that the requirement in paragraph 276A1 is met.

Requirements for indefinite leave to remain on the ground of long residence in the United Kingdom

276B. The requirements to be met by an applicant for indefinite leave to remain on the ground of long residence in the United Kingdom are that:

(i) (a) he has had at least 10 years continuous lawful residence in the United Kingdom; or

(b) he has had at least 14 years continuous residence in the United Kingdom, excluding any period spent in the United Kingdom following service of notice of liability to removal or notice of a decision to remove by way of directions under paragraphs 8 to 10A, or 12 to 14, of Schedule 2 to the Immigration Act 1971 or section 10 of the Immigration and Asylum Act 1999 Act, or of a notice of intention to deport him from the United Kingdom; and

(ii) having regard to the public interest there are no reasons why it would be undesirable for him to be given indefinite leave to remain on the ground of long residence, taking into account his:

(a) age; and

(b) strength of connections in the United Kingdom; and

(c) personal history, including character, conduct, associations and employment record; and

(d) domestic circumstances; and

(e) compassionate circumstances; and

(f) any representations received on the person's behalf; and

(iii) the applicant does not have one or more unspent convictions within the meaning of the Rehabilitation of Offenders Act 1974.

(iv) the applicant has sufficient knowledge of the English language and sufficient knowledge about life in the United Kingdom, unless he is under the age of 18 or aged 65 or over at the time he makes his application.

Indefinite leave to remain on the ground of long residence in the United Kingdom

276C. Indefinite leave to remain on the ground of long residence in the United Kingdom may be granted provided that the Secretary of State is satisfied that each of the requirements of paragraph 276B is met.

Refusal of indefinite leave to remain on the ground of long residence in the United Kingdom

276D. Indefinite leave to remain on the ground of long residence in the United Kingdom is to be refused if the Secretary of State is not satisfied that each of the requirements of paragraph 276B is met.

HM Forces

Definition of Gurkha

276E. For the purposes of these Rules the term 'Gurkha' means a citizen or national of Nepal who has served in the Brigade of Gurkhas of the British Army under the Brigade of Gurkhas' terms and conditions of service.

Leave to enter or remain in the United Kingdom as a Gurkha discharged from the British Army

Requirements for indefinite leave to enter the United Kingdom as a Gurkha discharged from the British Army

276F. The requirements for indefinite leave to enter the United Kingdom as a Gurkha discharged from the British Army are that:

(i) the applicant has completed at least four years' service as a Gurkha with the British Army; and

(ii) was discharged from the British Army in Nepal on completion of engagement on or after 1 July 1997; and

(iii) was not discharged from the British Army more than 2 years prior to the date on which the application is made; and

(iv) holds a valid United Kingdom entry clearance for entry in this capacity; and

(v) does not have one or more unspent convictions within the meaning of the Rehabilitation of Offenders Act 1974.

Indefinite leave to enter the United Kingdom as a Gurkha discharged from the British Army

276G. A person seeking indefinite leave to enter the United Kingdom as a Gurkha discharged from the British Army may be granted indefinite leave to enter provided a valid United Kingdom entry clearance for entry in this capacity is produced to the Immigration Officer on arrival.

Refusal of indefinite leave to enter the United Kingdom as a Gurkha discharged from the British Army

276H. Indefinite leave to enter the United Kingdom as a Gurkha discharged from the British Army is to be refused if a valid United Kingdom entry clearance for entry in this capacity is not produced to the Immigration Officer on arrival.

Requirements for indefinite leave to remain in the United Kingdom as a Gurkha discharged from the British Army

276I. The requirements for indefinite leave to remain in the United Kingdom as a Gurkha discharged from the British Army are that:

(i) the applicant has completed at least four years' service as a Gurkha with the British Army; and

(ii) was discharged from the British Army in Nepal on completion of engagement on or after 1 July 1997; and

(iii) was not discharged from the British Army more than 2 years prior to the date on which the application is made; and

(iv) on the date of application has leave to enter or remain in the United Kingdom; and

(v) does not have one or more unspent convictions within the meaning of the Rehabilitation of Offenders Act 1974.

Indefinite leave to remain in the United Kingdom as a Gurkha discharged from the British Army

276J. A person seeking indefinite leave to remain in the United Kingdom as a Gurkha discharged from the British Army may be granted indefinite leave to remain provided the Secretary of State is satisfied that each of the requirements of paragraph 276I is met.

Refusal of indefinite leave to remain in the United Kingdom as a Gurkha discharged from the British Army

276K. Indefinite leave to remain in the United Kingdom as a Gurkha discharged from the British Army is to be refused if the Secretary of State is not satisfied that each of the requirements of paragraph 276I is met.

Leave to enter or remain in the United Kingdom as a foreign or Commonwealth citizen di scharged from HM Forces

Requirements for indefinite leave to enter the United Kingdom as a foreign or Commonwealth citizen discharged from HM Forces

276L. The requirements for indefinite leave to enter the United Kingdom as a foreign or Commonwealth citizen discharged from HM Forces are that:

(i) the applicant has completed at least four years' service with HM Forces; and

(ii) was discharged from HM Forces on completion of engagement; and

(iii) was not discharged from HM Forces more than 2 years prior to the date on which the application is made; and

(iv) holds a valid United Kingdom entry clearance for entry in this capacity; and

(v) does not have one or more unspent convictions within the meaning of the Rehabilitation of Offenders Act 1974.

Indefinite leave to enter the United Kingdom as a foreign or Commonwealth citizen discharged from HM Forces

276M. A person seeking indefinite leave to enter the United Kingdom as a foreign or Commonwealth citizen discharged from HM Forces may be granted indefinite leave to enter provided a valid United Kingdom entry clearance for entry in this capacity is produced to the Immigration Officer on arrival.

Refusal of indefinite leave to enter the United Kingdom as a foreign or Commonwealth citizen discharged from HM Forces

276N. Indefinite leave to enter the United Kingdom as a foreign or Commonwealth citizen discharged from HM Forces is to be refused if a valid United Kingdom entry clearance for entry in this capacity is not produced to the Immigration Officer on arrival.

Requirements for indefinite leave to remain in the United Kingdom as a foreign or Commonwealth citizen discharged from HM Forces

276O. The requirements for indefinite leave to remain in the United Kingdom as a foreign or Commonwealth citizen discharged from HM Forces are that:

(i) the applicant has completed at least four years' service with HM Forces; and

(ii) was discharged from HM Forces on completion of engagement; and

(iii) was not discharged from HM Forces more than 2 years prior to the date on which the application is made; and

(iv) on the date of application has leave to enter or remain in the United Kingdom; and

(v) does not have one or more unspent convictions within the meaning of the Rehabilitation of Offenders Act 1974.

Indefinite leave to remain in the United Kingdom as a foreign or Commonwealth citizen discharged from HM Forces

276P. A person seeking indefinite leave to remain in the United Kingdom as a foreign or Commonwealth citizen discharged from HM Forces may be granted indefinite leave to remain provided the Secretary of State is satisfied that each of the requirements of paragraph 276O is met.

Refusal of indefinite leave to remain in the United Kingdom as a foreign or Commonwealth citizen discharged from HM Forces

276Q. Indefinite leave to remain in the United Kingdom as a foreign or Commonwealth citizen discharged from HM Forces is to be refused if the Secretary of State is not satisfied that each of the requirements of paragraph 276O is met.

Spouses, civil partners, unmarried or same-sex partners of persons settled or seeking settlement in the United Kingdom in accordance with paragraphs 276E to 276Q (HM Forces rules) or of members of HM Forces who are exempt from immigration control under section 8(4)(a) of the Immigration Act 1971 and have at least 5 years' continuous service

Leave to enter or remain in the UK as the spouse, civil partner, unmarried or same-sex partner of a person present and settled in the United Kingdom or being granted settlement on the same occasion in accordance with paragraphs 276E to 276Q or of a member of HM Forces who is exempt from immigration control under section 8(4)(a) of the Immigration Act 1971 and has at least 5 years' continuous service.

Requirements for indefinite leave to enter the United Kingdom as the spouse, civil partner, unmarried or same-sex partner of a person present and settled in the United Kingdom or being admitted on the same occasion for settlement under paragraphs 276E to 276Q or of a member of HM Forces who is exempt from immigration control under section 8(4)(a) of the Immigration Act 1971 and has at least 5 years' continuous service

276R. The requirements to be met by a person seeking indefinite leave to enter the United Kingdom as the spouse, civil partner, unmarried or same-sex partner of a person present and settled in the United

Kingdom or being admitted on the same occasion for settlement in accordance with paragraphs 276E to 276Q or of a member of HM Forces who is exempt from immigration control under section 8(4)(a) of the Immigration Act 1971 and has at least 5 years' continuous service are that:

(i) the applicant is married to, or the civil partner, unmarried or same-sex partner of, a person present and settled in the United Kingdom or who is being admitted on the same occasion for settlement in accordance with paragraphs 276E to 276Q or of a member of HM Forces who is exempt from immigration control under section 8(4)(a) of the Immigration Act 1971 and has at least 5 years' continuous service; and

(ii) the parties to the marriage, or civil partnership or relationship akin to marriage or civil partnership have met; and

(iii) the parties were married or formed a civil partnership or a relationship akin to marriage or civil partnership at least 2 years ago; and

(iv) each of the parties intends to live permanently with the other as his or her spouse, civil partner, unmarried or same-sex partner; and

(v) the marriage, civil partnership or relationship akin to marriage or civil partnership is subsisting; and

(vi) the applicant holds a valid United Kingdom entry clearance for entry in this capacity; and

(vii) the applicant does not have one or more unspent convictions within the meaning of the Rehabilitation of Offenders Act 1974.

Indefinite leave to enter the United Kingdom as the spouse, civil partner, unmarried or same-sex partner of a person present and settled in the United Kingdom or being admitted on the same occasion for settlement in accordance with paragraphs 276E to 276Q or of a member of HM Forces who is exempt from immigration control under section 8(4)(a) of the Immigration Act 1971 and has at least 5 years' continuous service

276S. A person seeking leave to enter the United Kingdom as the spouse, civil partner, unmarried or same-sex partner of a person present and settled in the United Kingdom or being admitted on the same occasion for settlement in accordance with paragraphs 276E to 276Q or of a member of HM Forces who is exempt from immigration control under section 8(4)(a) of the Immigration Act 1971 and has at least 5 years' continuous service may be granted indefinite leave to enter provided a valid United Kingdom entry clearance for entry in this capacity is produced to the Immigration Officer on arrival.

Refusal of indefinite leave to enter the United Kingdom as the spouse, civil partner, unmarried or same-sex partner of a person present and settled in the UK or being admitted on the same occasion for settlement in accordance with paragraphs 276E to 276Q or of a member of HM Forces who is exempt from immigration control under section 8(4)(a) of the Immigration Act 1971 and has at least 5 years' continuous service

276T. Leave to enter the United Kingdom as the spouse, civil partner, unmarried or same-sex partner of a person present and settled in the United Kingdom or being admitted on the same occasion for settlement in accordance with paragraphs 276E to 276Q or of a member of HM Forces who is exempt from immigration control under section 8(4)(a) of the Immigration Act 1971 and has at least 5 years' continuous service is to be refused if a valid United Kingdom entry clearance for entry in this capacity is not produced to the Immigration Officer on arrival.

Requirement for indefinite leave to remain in the United Kingdom as the spouse, civil partner, unmarried or same-sex partner of a person present and settled in the United Kingdom under paragraphs 276E to 276Q or being granted settlement on the same occasion in accordance with paragraphs 276E to 276Q or of a member of HM Forces who is exempt from immigration control under section 8(4)(a) of the Immigration Act 1971 and has at least 5 years' continuous service

276U. The requirements to be met by a person seeking indefinite leave to remain in the United Kingdom as the spouse, civil partner, unmarried or same-sex partner of a person present and settled in the United Kingdom or being granted settlement on the same occasion in accordance with paragraphs 276E to 276Q or of a member of HM Forces who is exempt from immigration control under section 8(4)(a) of the Immigration Act 1971 and has at least 5 years' continuous service are that:

(i) the applicant is married to or the civil partner or unmarried or same-sex partner of a person present and settled in the United Kingdom or being granted settlement on the same occasion in accordance with paragraphs 276E to 276Q or of a member of HM Forces who is exempt from immigration control under section 8(4)(a) of the Immigration Act 1971 and has at least 5 years' continuous service; and

(ii) the parties to the marriage, civil partnership or relationship akin to marriage or civil partnership have met; and

(iii) the parties were married or formed a civil partnership or relationship akin to marriage or civil partnership at least 2 years ago; and

(iv) each of the parties intends to live permanently with the other as his or her spouse, civil partner, unmarried or same-sex partner; and

(v) the marriage, civil partnership or relationship akin to marriage or civil partnership is subsisting; and

(vi) has, or has last been granted, leave to enter or remain in the United Kingdom as the spouse, civil partner, unmarried or same-sex partner; and

(vi) the applicant does not have one or more unspent convictions within the meaning of the Rehabilitation of Offenders Act 1974.

Indefinite leave to remain in the United Kingdom as the spouse, civil partner, unmarried or same-sex partner of a person present and settled in the United Kingdom or being granted settlement on the same occasion in accordance with paragraphs 276E to 276Q or of a member of HM Forces who is exempt from immigration control under section 8(4)(a) of the Immigration Act 1971 and has at least 5 years' continuous service

276V. Indefinite leave to remain in the United Kingdom as the spouse, civil partner, unmarried or same-sex partner of a person present and settled in the United Kingdom or being granted settlement on the same occasion in accordance with paragraphs 276E to 276Q or of a member of HM Forces who is exempt from immigration control under section 8(4)(a) of the Immigration Act 1971 and has at least 5 years' continuous service may be granted provided the Secretary of State is satisfied that each of the requirements of paragraph 276U is met.

Refusal of indefinite leave to remain in the United Kingdom as the spouse, civil partner, unmarried or same-sex partner of a person present and settled in the United Kingdom or being granted settlement on the same occasion in accordance with paragraphs 276E to 276Q or of a member of HM Forces who is exempt from immigration control under section 8(4)(a) of the Immigration Act 1971 and has at least 5 years' continuous service

276W. Indefinite leave to remain in the United Kingdom as the spouse, civil partner, unmarried or same-sex partner of a person present and settled in the United Kingdom or being granted settlement on the same occasion in accordance with paragraphs 276E to 276Q or of a member of HM Forces who is exempt from immigration control under section 8(4)(a) of the Immigration Act 1971 and has at least 5 years' continuous service is to be refused if the Secretary of State is not satisfied that each of the requirements of paragraph 276U is met.

Children of a parent, parents or a relative settled or seeking settlement in the United Kingdom under paragraphs 276E to 276Q (HM Forces rules) or of members of HM Forces who are exempt from immigration control under section 8(4)(a) of the Immigration Act 1971 and have at least 5 years' continuous service

Leave to enter or remain in the United Kingdom as the child of a parent, parents or a relative present and settled in the United Kingdom or being granted settlement on the same occasion in accordance with paragraphs 276E to 276Q or of a member of HM Forces who is exempt from immigration control under section 8(4)(a) of the Immigration Act 1971 and has at least 5 years' continuous service

Requirements for indefinite leave to enter the United Kingdom as the child of a parent, parents or a relative present and settled in the United Kingdom or being admitted for settlement on the same occasion in accordance with paragraphs 276E to 276Q or of a

member of HM Forces who is exempt from immigration control under section 8(4)(a) of the Immigration Act 1971 and has at least 5 years' continuous service

276X. The requirements to be met by a person seeking indefinite leave to enter the United Kingdom as the child of a parent, parents or a relative present and settled in the United Kingdom or being admitted for settlement on the same occasion in accordance with paragraphs 276E to 276Q or of a member of HM Forces who is exempt from immigration control under section 8(4)(a) of the Immigration Act 1971 and has at least 5 years' continuous service are that:

(i) the applicant is seeking indefinite leave to enter to accompany or join a parent, parents or a relative in one of the following circumstances:

- (a) both parents are present and settled in the United Kingdom; or
- (b) both parents are being admitted on the same occasion for settlement; or
- (c) one parent is present and settled in the United Kingdom or is a member of HM Forces who is exempt from immigration control under section 8(4)(a) of the Immigration Act 1971 and has at least 5 years' continuous service and the other is being admitted on the same occasion for settlement or is a member of HM Forces who is exempt from immigration control under section 8(4)(a) of the Immigration Act 1971 and has at least 5 years' continuous service; or
- (d) one parent is present and settled in the United Kingdom or being admitted on the same occasion for settlement or is a member of HM Forces who is exempt from immigration control under section 8(4)(a) of the Immigration Act 1971 and has at least 5 years' continuous service and the other parent is dead; or
- (e) one parent is present and settled in the United Kingdom or being admitted on the same occasion for settlement or is a member of HM Forces who is exempt from immigration control under section 8(4)(a) of the Immigration Act 1971 and has at least 5 years' continuous service and has had sole responsibility for the child's upbringing; or
- (f) one parent or a relative is present and settled in the United Kingdom or being admitted on the same occasion for settlement or is a member of HM Forces who is exempt from immigration control under section 8(4)(a) of the Immigration Act 1971 and has at least 5 years' continuous service and there are serious and compelling family or other considerations which make exclusion of the child undesirable and suitable arrangements have been made for the child's care; and

(ii) is under the age of 18; and

(iii) is not leading an independent life, is unmarried and is not a civil partner, and has not formed an independent family unit; and

(iv) holds a valid United Kingdom entry clearance for entry in this capacity; and

(v) the applicant does not have one or more unspent convictions within the meaning of the Rehabilitation of Offenders Act 1974.

Indefinite leave to enter the United Kingdom as the child of a parent, parents or a relative present and settled in the United Kingdom or being admitted for settlement on the same occasion in accordance with paragraphs 276E to 276Q or of a member of HM Forces who is exempt from immigration control under section 8(4)(a) of the Immigration Act 1971 and has at least 5 years' continuous service

276Y. Indefinite leave to enter the United Kingdom as the child of a parent, parents or a relative present and settled in the United Kingdom or being admitted for settlement on the same occasion in accordance with paragraphs 276E to 276Q or of a member of HM Forces who is exempt from immigration control under section 8(4)(a) of the Immigration Act 1971 and has at least 5 years' continuous service may be granted provided a valid United Kingdom entry clearance for entry in this capacity is produced to the Immigration Officer on arrival.

Refusal of indefinite leave to enter the United Kingdom as the child of a parent, parents or a relative present and settled in the United Kingdom or being admitted for settlement on the same occasion in accordance with paragraphs 276E to 276Q or of a member of HM Forces who is exempt from immigration control under section 8(4)(a) of the Immigration Act 1971 and has at least 5 years' continuous service

276Z. Indefinite leave to enter the United Kingdom as the child of a parent, parents, or a relative present and settled in the United Kingdom or being admitted for settlement on the same occasion in accordance with paragraphs 276E to 276Q or of a member of HM Forces who is exempt from immigration control under section 8(4)(a) of the Immigration Act 1971 and has at least 5 years' continuous service is to be refused if a valid United Kingdom entry clearance for entry in this capacity is not produced to the Immigration Officer on arrival.

Requirements for indefinite leave to remain in the United Kingdom as the child of a parent, parents or a relative present and settled in the United Kingdom or being granted settlement on the same occasion in accordance with paragraphs 276E to 276Q or of a member of HM Forces who is exempt from immigration control under section 8(4)(a) of the Immigration Act 1971 and has at least 5 years' continuous service

276AA. The requirements to be met by a person seeking indefinite leave to remain in the United Kingdom as the child of a parent, parents or a relative present and settled in the United Kingdom or being granted settlement on the same occasion in accordance with paragraphs 276E to 276Q or of a member of HM Forces who is exempt from immigration control under section 8(4)(a) of the Immigration Act 1971 and has at least 5 years' continuous service are that:

(i) the applicant is seeking indefinite leave to remain with a parent, parents or a relative in one of the following circumstances:

(a) both parents are present and settled in the United Kingdom or being granted settlement on the same occasion; or

(ab) one parent is present and settled in the United Kingdom or is a member of HM Forces who is exempt from immigration control under section 8(4)(a) of the Immigration Act 1971 and has at least 5 years' continuous service and the other is being granted settlement on the same occasion or is a member of HM Forces who is exempt from immigration control under section 8(4)(a) of the Immigration Act 1971 and has at least 5 years' continuous service; or

(b) one parent is present and settled in the United Kingdom or being granted settlement on the same occasion or is a member of HM Forces who is exempt from immigration control under section 8(4)(a) of the Immigration Act 1971 and has at least 5 years' continuous service and the other parent is dead; or

(c) one parent is present and settled in the United Kingdom or being granted settlement on the same occasion or is a member of HM Forces who is exempt from immigration control under section 8(4)(a) of the Immigration Act 1971 and has at least 5 years' continuous service and has had sole responsibility for the child's upbringing; or

(d) one parent or a relative is present and settled in the United Kingdom or being granted settlement on the same occasion or is a member of HM Forces who is exempt from immigration control under section 8(4)(a) of the Immigration Act 1971 and has at least 5 years' continuous service and there are serious and compelling family or other considerations which make exclusion of the child undesirable and suitable arrangements have been made for the child's care; and

(ii) is under the age of 18; and

(iii) is not leading an independent life, is unmarried and is not a civil partner, and has not formed an independent family unit; and

(iv) has leave to enter or remain in the United Kingdom; and

(v) the applicant does not have one or more unspent convictions within the meaning of the Rehabilitation of Offenders Act 1974.

Indefinite leave to remain in the United Kingdom as the child of a parent, parents or a relative present and settled in the United Kingdom or being granted settlement on the same occasion in accordance with paragraphs 276E to 276Q or of a member of HM Forces who is exempt from immigration control under section 8(4)(a) of the Immigration Act 1971 and has at least 5 years' continuous service

276AB. Indefinite leave to remain in the United Kingdom as the child of a parent, parents or a relative present and settled in the United Kingdom or being granted settlement on the same occasion in accordance with paragraphs 276E to 276Q or of a member of HM Forces who is exempt from immigration control under section 8(4)(a) of the Immigration Act 1971 and has at least 5 years' continuous service may be granted if the Secretary of State is satisfied that each of the requirements of paragraph 276AA is met.

Refusal of indefinite leave to remain in the United Kingdom as the child of a parent, parents or a relative present and settled in the United Kingdom or being granted settlement on the same occasion in accordance with paragraphs 276E to 276Q or of a member of HM Forces who is exempt from immigration control under section 8(4)(a) of the Immigration Act 1971 and has at least 5 years' continuous service

276AC. Indefinite leave to remain in the United Kingdom as the child of a parent, parents or a relative present and settled in the United Kingdom or being granted settlement on the same occasion in accordance with paragraphs 276E to 276Q or of a member of HM Forces who is exempt from immigration control under section 8(4)(a) of the Immigration Act 1971 and has at least 5 years' continuous service is to be refused if the Secretary of State is not satisfied that each of the requirements of paragraph 276AA is met.

Spouses, civil partners, unmarried or same-sex partners of armed forces members who are exempt from immigration control under section 8(4) of the Immigration Act 1971

Requirements for leave to enter or remain as the spouse, civil partner, unmarried or same-sex partner of an armed forces member who is exempt from immigration control under section 8(4) of the Immigration Act 1971

276AD. The requirements to be met by a person seeking leave to enter or remain in the United Kingdom as the spouse, civil partner, unmarried or same-sex partner of an armed forces member who is exempt from immigration control under section 8(4) of the Immigration Act 1971 are that:

(i) the applicant is married to or the civil partner, unmarried or same-sex partner of an armed forces member who is exempt from immigration control under section 8(4) of the Immigration Act 1971; and

(ii) each of the parties intends to live with the other as his or her spouse or civil partner, unmarried or same-sex partner during the applicant's stay and the marriage, civil partnership, or relationship akin to a marriage or civil partnership is subsisting; and

(iii) there will be adequate accommodation for the parties and any dependants without recourse to public funds in accommodation which they own or occupy exclusively; and

(iv) the parties will be able to maintain themselves and any dependants adequately without recourse to public funds;

(v) the applicant does not intend to stay in the United Kingdom beyond his or her spouse's, civil partner's, unmarried or same-sex partner's enlistment in the home forces, or period of posting or training in the United Kingdom; and

(vi) where the applicant is the unmarried or same-sex partner of an armed forces member who is exempt from immigration control under section 8(4) of the Immigration Act 1971, the following requirements are also met:

(a) any previous marriage or civil partnership or relationship akin to a marriage by the applicant or the exempt armed forces member must have permanently broken down,

(b) the applicant and the exempt armed forces member must not be so closely related that they would be prohibited from marrying each other in the UK, and

(c) the applicant and the exempt armed forces member must have been living together in a relationship akin to marriage or civil partnership for a period of at least 2 years.

Leave to enter or remain as the spouse, civil partner, unmarried or same-sex partner of an armed forces member who is exempt from immigration control under section 8(4) of the Immigration Act 1971

276AE. A person seeking leave to enter or remain in the United Kingdom as the spouse, civil partner, unmarried or same-sex partner of an armed forces member who is exempt from immigration control under section 8(4) of the Immigration Act 1971 may be given leave to enter or remain in the United Kingdom for a period not exceeding 4 years or the expected duration of the enlistment, posting or training of his or her spouse, civil partner, unmarried or same-sex partner, whichever is shorter, provided that the Immigration Officer, or in the case of an application for leave to remain, the Secretary of State, is satisfied that each of the requirements of paragraph 276AD(i)–(vi) is met.

Refusal of leave to enter or remain as the spouse, civil partner, unmarried or same-sex partner of an armed forces member who is exempt from immigration control under section 8(4) of the Immigration Act 1971

276AF. Leave to enter or remain in the United Kingdom as the spouse, civil partner, unmarried or same-sex partner of an armed forces member who is exempt from immigration control under section 8(4) of the Immigration Act 1971 is to be refused if the Immigration Officer, or in the case of an application for leave to remain, the Secretary of State, is not satisfied that each of the requirements of paragraph 276AD(i)–(vi) is met.

Children of armed forces members who are exempt from immigration control under section 8(4) of the Immigration Act 1971

Requirements for leave to enter or remain as the child of an armed forces member exempt from immigration control under section 8(4) of the Immigration Act 1971

276AG. The requirements to be met by a person seeking leave to enter or remain in the United Kingdom as the child of an armed forces member exempt from immigration control under section 8(4) of the Immigration Act 1971 are that:

(i) he is the child of a parent who is an armed forces member exempt from immigration control under section 8(4) of the Immigration Act 1971; and

(ii) he is under the age of 18 or has current leave to enter or remain in this capacity; and

(iii) he is unmarried and is not a civil partner , has not formed an independent family unit and is not leading an independent life; and(iv) he can and will be maintained and accommodated adequately without recourse to public funds in accommodation which his parent(s) own or occupy exclusively; and

(v) he will not stay in the United Kingdom beyond the period of his parent's enlistment in the home forces, or posting or training in the United Kingdom; and

(vi) his other parent is being or has been admitted to or allowed to remain in the United Kingdom save where:

(a) the parent he is accompanying or joining is his sole surviving parent; or

(b) the parent he is accompanying or joining has had sole responsibility for his upbringing; or

(c) there are serious and compelling family or other considerations which make exclusion from the United Kingdom undesirable and suitable arrangements have been made for his care.

Leave to enter or remain as the child of an armed forces member exempt from immigration control under section 8(4) of the Immigration Act 1971

276AH. A person seeking leave to enter or remain in the United Kingdom as the child of an armed forces member exempt from immigration control under section 8(4) of the Immigration Act 1971 may be given leave to enter or remain in the United Kingdom for a period not exceeding 4 years or the duration of the enlistment, posting or training of his parent, whichever is the shorter, provided that the Immigration Officer, or in the case of an application for leave to remain, the Secretary of State, is satisfied that each of the requirements of 276AG(i)–(vi) is met.

Refusal of leave to enter or remain as the child of an armed forces member exempt from immigration control under section 8(4) of the Immigration Act 1971

276AI. Leave to enter or remain in the United Kingdom as the child of an armed forces member exempt from immigration control under section 8(4) of the Immigration Act 1971 is to be refused if the Immigration Officer, or in the case of an application for leave to remain, the Secretary of State, is not satisfied that each of the requirements of paragraph 276AG(i)–(vi) is met.

Part 8 – Family members

Spouses and civil partners

277. Nothing in these Rules shall be construed as permitting a person to be granted entry clearance, leave to enter, leave to remain or variation of leave as a spouse or civil partner of another if either the applicant or

the sponsor will be aged under 18 on the date of arrival in the United Kingdom or (as the case may be) on the date on which the leave to remain or variation of leave would be granted.

278. Nothing in these Rules shall be construed as allowing a person to be granted entry clearance, leave to enter, leave to remain or variation of leave as the spouse and civil partner of a man or woman (the sponsor) if:

(i) his or her marriage or civil partnership to the sponsor is polygamous; and

(ii) there is another person living who is the husband or wife of the sponsor and who:

(a) is, or at any time since his or her marriage or civil partnership to the sponsor has been, in the United Kingdom; or

(b) has been granted a certificate of entitlement in respect of the right of abode mentioned in Section 2(1)(a) of the Immigration Act 1988 or an entry clearance to enter the United Kingdom as the husband or wife of the sponsor.

For the purpose of this paragraph a marriage or civil partnership may be polygamous although at its inception neither party had any other spouse or civil partner.

279. Paragraph 278 does not apply to any person who seeks entry clearance, leave to enter, leave to remain or variation of leave where:

(i) he or she has been in the United Kingdom before 1 August 1988 having been admitted for the purpose of settlement as the husband or wife of the sponsor; or

(ii) he or she has, since their marriage or civil partnership to the sponsor, been in the United Kingdom at any time when there was no such other spouse or civil partner living as is mentioned in paragraph 278(ii).

But where a person claims that paragraph 278 does not apply to them because they have been in the United Kingdom in circumstances which cause them to fall within sub paragraphs (i) or (ii) of that paragraph it shall be for them to prove that fact.

280. For the purposes of paragraphs 278 and 279 the presence of any wife or husband in the United Kingdom in any of the following circumstances shall be disregarded:

(i) as a visitor; or

(ii) an illegal entrant; or

(iii) in circumstances whereby a person is deemed by Section 11(1) of the Immigration Act 1971 not to have entered the United Kingdom.

Spouses or civil partners of persons present and settled in the United Kingdom or being admitted on the same occasion for settlement

Requirements for leave to enter the United Kingdom with a view to settlement as the spouse or civil partner of a person present and settled in the United Kingdom or being admitted on the same occasion for settlement

281. The requirements to be met by a person seeking leave to enter the United Kingdom with a view to settlement as the spouse or civil partner of a person present and settled in the United Kingdom or who is on the same occasion being admitted for settlement are that:

(i) (a) (i) the applicant is married to or the civil partner of a person present and settled in the United Kingdom or who is on the same occasion being admitted for settlement; and

(ii) the applicant provides an original English language test certificate in speaking and listening from an English language test provider approved by the Secretary of State for these purposes, which clearly shows the applicant's name and the qualification obtained (which must meet or exceed level A1 of the Common European Framework of Reference) unless:

(a) the applicant is aged 65 or over at the time he makes his application; or

(b) the applicant has a physical or mental condition that would prevent him from meeting the requirement; or;

(c) there are exceptional compassionate circumstances that would prevent the applicant from meeting the requirement; or

(iii) the applicant is a national of one of the following countries: Antigua and Barbuda; Australia; the Bahamas; Barbados; Belize; Canada; Dominica; Grenada; Guyana;

Jamaica; New Zealand; St Kitts and Nevis; St Lucia; St Vincent and the Grenadines; Trinidad and Tobago; United States of America; or

(iv) the applicant has obtained an academic qualification(not a professional or vocational qualification), which is deemed by UK NARIC to meet the recognised standard of a Bachelor's or Master's degree or PhD in the UK, from an educational establishment in one of the following countries: Antigua and Barbuda; Australia; The Bahamas; Barbados; Belize; Dominica; Grenada; Guyana; Ireland; Jamaica; New Zealand; St Kitts and Nevis; St Lucia; St Vincent and The Grenadines; Trinidad and Tobago; the UK; the USA; and provides the specified documents; or

(v) the applicant has obtained an academic qualification (not a professional or vocational qualification) which is deemed by UK NARIC to meet the recognised standard of a Bachelor's or Master's degree or PhD in the UK, and

(1) provides the specified evidence to show he has the qualification, and

(2) UK NARIC has confirmed that the qualification was taught or researched in English, or

(vi) has obtained an academic qualification (not a professional or vocational qualification) which is deemed by UK NARIC to meet the recognised standard of a Bachelor's or Master's degree or PhD in the UK, and provides the specified evidence to show:

(1) he has the qualification, and

(2) that the qualification was taught or researched in English.

or

(b) (i) the applicant is married to or the civil partner of a person who has a right of abode in the United Kingdom or indefinite leave to enter or remain in the United Kingdom and is on the same occasion seeking admission to the United Kingdom for the purposes of settlement and the parties were married or formed a civil partnership at least 4 years ago, since which time they have been living together outside the United Kingdom; and

(ii) the applicant has sufficient knowledge of the English language and sufficient knowledge about life in the United Kingdom, unless he is under the age of 18 or aged 65 or over at the time he makes his application; and

(iii) the applicant does not have one or more unspent convictions within the meaning of the Rehabilitation of Offenders Act 1974; and

(ii) the parties to the marriage or civil partnership have met; and

(iii) each of the parties intends to live permanently with the other as his or her spouse or civil partner and the marriage or civil partnership is subsisting; and

(iv) there will be adequate accommodation for the parties and any dependants without recourse to public funds in accommodation which they own or occupy exclusively; and

(v) the parties will be able to maintain themselves and any dependants adequately without recourse to public funds; and

(vi) the applicant holds a valid United Kingdom entry clearance for entry in this capacity

For the purposes of this paragraph and paragraphs 282–289 a member of HM Forces serving overseas, or a permanent member of HM Diplomatic Service or a comparable UK-based staff member of the British Council on a tour of duty abroad, or a staff member of the Department for International Development who is a British Citizen or is settled in the United Kingdom, is to be regarded as present and settled in the United Kingdom.

Leave to enter as the spouse or civil partner of a person present and settled in the United Kingdom or being admitted for settlement on the same occasion

282. A person seeking leave to enter the United Kingdom as the spouse or civil partner of a person present and settled in the United Kingdom or who is on the same occasion being admitted for settlement may:

(a) in the case of a person who meets the requirements of paragraph 281(i)(a)(i) and one of the requirements of paragraph 281(i)(a)(ii)–(vi) be admitted for an initial period not exceeding 27 months, or

(b) in the case of a person who meets *all* of the requirements in paragraph 281(i)(b), be granted indefinite leave to enter, or

(c) in the case of a person who meets the requirement in paragraph 281(i)(b)(i), but not the requirement in paragraph 281(i)(b)(ii) to have sufficient knowledge of the English language and about life in the United Kingdom, be admitted for an initial period not exceeding 27 months, in all cases provided the Immigration Officer is satisfied that each of the relevant requirements of paragraph 281 is met.

Refusal of leave to enter as the spouse or civil partner of a person present and settled in the United Kingdom or being admitted on the same occasion for settlement

283. Leave to enter the United Kingdom as the spouse or civil partner of a person present and settled in the United Kingdom or who is on the same occasion being admitted for settlement is to be refused if the Immigration Officer is not satisfied that each of the requirements of paragraph 281 is met.

Requirements for an extension of stay as the spouse or civil partner of a person present and settled in the United Kingdom

284. The requirements for an extension of stay as the spouse or civil partner of a person present and settled in the United Kingdom are that:

(i) the applicant has limited leave to enter or remain in the United Kingdom which was given in accordance with any of the provisions of these Rules, other than where as a result of that leave he would not have been in the United Kingdom beyond 6 months from the date on which he was admitted to the United Kingdom on this occasion in accordance with these Rules, unless:

(a) the leave in question is limited leave to enter as a fiancé or proposed civil partner; or

(b) the leave in question was granted to the applicant as the spouse, civil partner, unmarried or same-sex partner of a Relevant Points Based System Migrant and that spouse or partner is the same person in relation to whom the applicant is applying for an extension of stay under this rule; and

(ii) is married to or the civil partner of a person present and settled in the United Kingdom; and

(iii) the parties to the marriage or civil partnership have met; and

(iv) the applicant has not remained in breach of the immigration laws; and

(v) the marriage or civil partnership has not taken place after a decision has been made to deport the applicant or he has been recommended for deportation or been given notice under Section 6(2) of the Immigration Act 1971 or been given directions for his removal under section 10 of the Immigration and Asylum Act 1999; and

(vi) each of the parties intends to live permanently with the other as his or her spouse or civil partner and the marriage or civil partnership is subsisting; and

(vii) there will be adequate accommodation for the parties and any dependants without recourse to public funds in accommodation which they own or occupy exclusively; and

(viii) the parties will be able to maintain themselves and any dependants adequately without recourse to public funds; and

(ix) (a) the applicant provides an original English language test certificate in speaking and listening from an English language test provider approved by the Secretary of State for these purposes, which clearly shows the applicant's name and the qualification obtained (which must meet or exceed level A1 of the Common European Framework of Reference) unless:

(i) the applicant is aged 65 or over at the time he makes his application; or

(ii) the applicant has a physical or mental condition that would prevent him from meeting the requirement; or;

(iii) there are exceptional compassionate circumstances that would prevent the applicant from meeting the requirement; or

(ix) (b) the applicant is a national of one of the following countries: Antigua and Barbuda; Australia; the Bahamas; Barbados; Belize; Canada; Dominica; Grenada; Guyana; Jamaica; New Zealand; St Kitts and Nevis; St Lucia; St Vincent and the Grenadines; Trinidad and Tobago; United States of America; or

(c) the applicant has obtained an academic qualification (not a professional or vocational qualification), which is deemed by UK NARIC to meet the recognised standard of a Bachelor's or Master's degree or PhD in the UK, from an educational establishment in one of the following countries: Antigua and Barbuda; Australia; The Bahamas; Barbados; Belize; Dominica; Grenada; Guyana; Ireland; Jamaica; New Zealand; St Kitts and Nevis; St Lucia; St Vincent and The Grenadines; Trinidad and Tobago; the UK; the USA; and provides the specified documents; or

(d) the applicant has obtained an academic qualification (not a professional or vocational qualification) which is deemed by UK NARIC to meet the recognised standard of a Bachelor's or Master's degree or PhD in the UK, and

(1) provides the specified evidence to show he has the qualification, and

(2) UK NARIC has confirmed that the qualification was taught or researched in English, or

(e) has obtained an academic qualification (not a professional or vocational qualification) which is deemed by UK NARIC to meet the recognised standard of a Bachelor's or Master's degree or PhD in the UK, and provides the specified evidence to show:

(1) he has the qualification, and

(2) that the qualification was taught or researched in English.

Extension of stay as the spouse or civil partner of a person present and settled in the United Kingdom

285. An extension of stay as the spouse or civil partner of a person present and settled in the United Kingdom may be granted for a period of 2 years in the first instance, provided the Secretary of State is satisfied that each of the requirements of paragraph 284 is met.

Refusal of extension of stay as the spouse or civil partner of a person present and settled in the United Kingdom

286. An extension of stay as the spouse or civil partner of a person present and settled in the United Kingdom is to be refused if the Secretary of State is not satisfied that each of the requirements of paragraph 284 is met.

Requirements for indefinite leave to remain for the spouse or civil partner of a person present and settled in the United Kingdom

287. (a) The requirements for indefinite leave to remain for the spouse or civil partner of a person present and settled in the United Kingdom are that:

(i) (a) the applicant was admitted to the United Kingdom for a period not exceeding 27 months or given an extension of stay for a period of 2 years in accordance with paragraphs 281 to 286 of these Rules and has completed a period of 2 years as the spouse or civil partner of a person present and settled in the United Kingdom; or

(b) the applicant was admitted to the United Kingdom for a period not exceeding 27 months or given an extension of stay for a period of 2 years in accordance with paragraphs 295AA to 295F of these Rules and during that period married or formed a civil partnership with the person whom he or she was admitted or granted an extension of stay to join and has completed a period of 2 years as the unmarried or same-sex partner and then the spouse or civil partner of a person present and settled in the United Kingdom; or

(c) was admitted to the United Kingdom in accordance with leave granted under paragraph 282(c) of these rules; *and*

(d) the applicant was admitted to the UK or given an extension of stay as the spouse or civil partner of a *Relevant Points Based System Migrant*, and then obtained an extension of stay under paragraphs 281 to 286 of these Rules and has completed a period of 2 years as the spouse or civil partner of the person who is now present and settled here; or

(e) the applicant was admitted to the UK or given an extension of stay as the unmarried or same-sex partner of a Relevant Points Based System Migrant and during that period married or formed a civil partnership with the person whom he or she was admitted or granted an extension of stay to join and has completed a period of 2 years as the unmarried or same-sex partner and then the spouse or civil partner of the person who is now present and settled in the UK; or

(f) the applicant was admitted into the UK in accordance with paragraph 319L and has completed a period of 2 years limited leave as the spouse or civil partner of a refugee or beneficiary of humanitarian protection who is now present and settled in the UK or as the spouse or civil partner of a former refugee or beneficiary of humanitarian protection who is now a British Citizen.

(ii) the applicant is still the spouse or civil partner of the person he or she was admitted or granted an extension of stay to join and the marriage or civil partnership is subsisting; and

(iii) each of the parties intends to live permanently with the other as his or her spouse or civil partner; and

(iv) there will be adequate accommodation for the parties and any dependants without recourse to public funds in accommodation which they own or occupy exclusively; and

(v) the parties will be able to maintain themselves and any dependants adequately without recourse to public funds; and

(vi) the applicant has sufficient knowledge of the English language and sufficient knowledge about life in the United Kingdom, unless he is under the age of 18 or aged 65 or over at the time he makes his application; and

(vii) the applicant does not have one or more unspent convictions within the meaning of the Rehabilitation of Offenders Act 1974.

(b) The requirements for indefinite leave to remain for the bereaved spouse or civil partner of a person who was present and settled in the United Kingdom are that:

(i) (a) the applicant was admitted to the United Kingdom for a period not exceeding 27 months or given an extension of stay for a period of 2 years as the spouse or civil partner of a person present and settled in the United Kingdom in accordance with paragraphs 281 to 286 of these Rules; or;

(b) the applicant was admitted to the United Kingdom for a period not exceeding 27 months or given an extension of stay for a period of 2 years as the unmarried or same-sex partner of a person present and settled in the United Kingdom in accordance with paragraphs 295AA to 295F of these Rules and during that period married or formed a civil partnership with the person whom he or she was admitted or granted an extension of stay to join; and

(ii) the person whom the applicant was admitted or granted an extension of stay to join died during that period; and

(iii) the applicant was still the spouse or civil partner of the person he or she was admitted or granted an extension of stay to join at the time of the death; and

(iv) each of the parties intended to live permanently with the other as his or her spouse or civil partner and the marriage or civil partnership was subsisting at the time of the death*; and*

(v) the applicant does not have one or more unspent convictions within the meaning of the Rehabilitation of Offenders Act 1974.

Indefinite leave to remain for the spouse or civil partner of a person present and settled in the United Kingdom

288. Indefinite leave to remain for the spouse or civil partner of a person present and settled in the United Kingdom may be granted provided the Secretary of State is satisfied that each of the requirements of paragraph 287 is met.

Refusal of indefinite leave to remain for the spouse or civil partner of a person present and settled in the United Kingdom

289. Indefinite leave to remain for the spouse or civil partner of a person present and settled in the United Kingdom is to be refused if the Secretary of State is not satisfied that each of the requirements of paragraph 287 is met.

Victims of domestic violence

Requirements for indefinite leave to remain in the United Kingdom as the victim of domestic violence

289A. The requirements to be met by a person who is the victim of domestic violence and who is seeking indefinite leave to remain in the United Kingdom are that the applicant:

(i) was admitted to the United Kingdom for a period not exceeding 27 months or given an extension of stay for a period of 2 years as the spouse or civil partner of a person present and settled here; or;

(ii) was admitted to the United Kingdom for a period not exceeding 27 months or given an extension of stay for a period of 2 years as the unmarried or same-sex partner of a person present and settled here; and

(iii) the relationship with their spouse or civil partner or unmarried partner or same-sex partner , as appropriate, was subsisting at the beginning of the relevant period of leave or extension of stay referred to in (i) or (ii) above; and

(iv) is able to produce such evidence as may be required by the Secretary of State to establish that the relationship was caused to permanently break down before the end of that period as a result of domestic violence*; and*

(v) the applicant does not have one or more unspent convictions within the meaning of the Rehabilitation of Offenders Act 1974.

Indefinite leave to remain as the victim of domestic violence

289B. Indefinite leave to remain as the victim of domestic violence may be granted provided the Secretary of State is satisfied that each of the requirements of paragraph 289A is met.

Refusal of indefinite leave to remain as the victim of domestic violence

289C. Indefinite leave to remain as the victim of domestic violence is to be refused if the Secretary of State is not satisfied that each of the requirements of paragraph 289A is met.

Fiance(e)s and proposed civil partners

289AA. Nothing in these Rules shall be construed as permitting a person to be granted entry clearance, leave to enter or variation of leave as a fiance(e) or proposed civil partner if either the applicant or the sponsor will be aged under 18 on the date of arrival of the applicant in the United Kingdom or (as the case may be) on the date on which the leave to enter or variation of leave would be granted.

Requirements for leave to enter the United Kingdom as a fiance(e) or proposed civil partner (i.e. with a view to marriage or civil partnership and permanent settlement in the United Kingdom)

290. The requirements to be met by a person seeking leave to enter the United Kingdom as a fiance(e) or proposed civil partner are that:

(i) the applicant is seeking leave to enter the United Kingdom for marriage or civil partnership to a person present and settled in the United Kingdom or who is on the same occasion being admitted for settlement; and

(ii) the parties to the proposed marriage or civil partnership have met; and

(iii) each of the parties intends to live permanently with the other as his or her spouse or civil partner after the marriage or civil partnership ; and

(iv) adequate maintenance and accommodation without recourse to public funds will be available for the applicant until the date of the marriage or civil partnership; and

(v) there will, after the marriage or civil partnership, be adequate accommodation for the parties and any dependants without recourse to public funds in accommodation which they own or occupy exclusively; and

(vi) the parties will be able after the marriage or civil partnership to maintain themselves and any dependants adequately without recourse to public funds; and

(vii) (a) the applicant provides an original English language test certificate in speaking and listening from an English language test provider approved by the Secretary of State for these purposes, which clearly shows the applicant's name and the qualification obtained (which must meet or exceed level A1 of the Common European Framework of Reference) unless:

(i) the applicant is aged 65 or over at the time he makes his application; or

(ii) the applicant has a physical or mental condition that would prevent him from meeting the requirement; or;

(iii) there are exceptional compassionate circumstances that would prevent the applicant from meeting the requirement; or

(b) the applicant is a national of one of the following countries: Antigua and Barbuda; Australia; the Bahamas; Barbados; Belize; Canada; Dominica; Grenada; Guyana; Jamaica; New Zealand; St Kitts and Nevis; St Lucia; St Vincent and the Grenadines; Trinidad and Tobago; United States of America; or

(c) the applicant has obtained an academic qualification (not a professional or vocational qualification), which is deemed by UK NARIC to meet the recognised standard of a Bachelor's or Master's degree or PhD in the UK, from an educational establishment in one of the following countries: Antigua and Barbuda; Australia; The Bahamas; Barbados; Belize; Dominica; Grenada; Guyana; Ireland; Jamaica; New Zealand; St Kitts and Nevis; St Lucia; St Vincent and The Grenadines; Trinidad and Tobago; the UK; the USA; and provides the specified documents; or

(d) the applicant has obtained an academic qualification (not a professional or vocational qualification) which is deemed by UK NARIC to meet the recognised standard of a Bachelor's or Master's degree or PhD in the UK, and

(1) provides the specified evidence to show he has the qualification, and

(2) UK NARIC has confirmed that the qualification was taught or researched in English, or

(e) has obtained an academic qualification (not a professional or vocational qualification) which is deemed by UK NARIC to meet the recognised standard of a Bachelor's or Master's degree or PhD in the UK, and provides the specified evidence to show:

(1) he has the qualification, and

(2) that the qualification was taught or researched in English.

and

(viii) the applicant holds a valid United Kingdom entry clearance for entry in this capacity.

290A. For the purposes of paragraph 290 and paragraphs 291–295, an EEA national who holds a registration certificate or a document certifying permanent residence issued under the 2006 EEA Regulations (including an EEA national who holds a residence permit issued under the Immigration (European Economic Area) Regulations 2000 which is treated as if it were such a certificate or document by virtue of Schedule 4 to the 2006 EEA Regulations) is to be regarded as present and settled in the United Kingdom.

Leave to enter as a fiance(e) or proposed civil partner

291. A person seeking leave to enter the United Kingdom as a fiance(e) or proposed civil partner may be admitted, with a prohibition on employment, for a period not exceeding 6 months to enable the marriage or civil partnership to take place provided a valid United Kingdom entry clearance for entry in this capacity is produced to the Immigration Officer on arrival.

Refusal of leave to enter as a fiance(e) or proposed civil partner

292. Leave to enter the United Kingdom as a fiance(e) or proposed civil partner is to be refused if a valid United Kingdom entry clearance for entry in this capacity is not produced to the Immigration Officer on arrival.

Requirements for an extension of stay as a fiance(e) or proposed civil partner

293. The requirements for an extension of stay as a fiance(e) or proposed civil partner are that:

(i) the applicant was admitted to the United Kingdom with a valid United Kingdom entry clearance as a fiance(e) or proposed civil partner; and

(ii) good cause is shown why the marriage or civil partnership did not take place within the initial period of leave granted under paragraph 291; and

(iii) there is satisfactory evidence that the marriage or civil partnership will take place at an early date; and

(iv) the requirements of paragraph 290(ii)–(vii) are met.

Extension of stay as a fiance(e) or proposed civil partner

294. An extension of stay as a fiance(e) or proposed civil partner may be granted for an appropriate period with a prohibition on employment to enable the marriage or civil partnership to take place provided the Secretary of State is satisfied that each of the requirements of paragraph 293 is met.

Refusal of extension of stay as a fiance(e) or proposed civil partner

295. An extension of stay is to be refused if the Secretary of State is not satisfied that each of the requirements of paragraph 293 is met.

Unmarried and same-sex partners

Leave to enter as the unmarried or same-sex partner of a person present and settled in the United Kingdom or being admitted on the same occasion for settlement

295AA. Nothing in these Rules shall be construed as permitting a person to be granted entry clearance, leave to enter or variation of leave as an unmarried or same-sex partner if either the applicant or the sponsor will be aged under 18 on the date of arrival of the applicant in the United Kingdom or (as the case may be) on the date on which the leave to enter or variation of leave would be granted.

Requirements for leave to enter the United Kingdom with a view to settlement as the unmarried or same-sex partner of a person present and settled in the United Kingdom or being admitted on the same occasion for settlement

295A. The requirements to be met by a person seeking leave to enter the United Kingdom with a view to settlement as the unmarried or same-sex partner of a person present and settled in the United Kingdom or being admitted on the same occasion for settlement, are that:

(i) (a) (i) the applicant is the unmarried or same-sex partner of a person present and settled in the United Kingdom or who is on the same occasion being admitted for settlement and the parties have been living together in a relationship akin to marriage or civil partnership which has subsisted for two years or more; and

(ii) the applicant provides an original English language test certificate in speaking and listening from an English language test provider approved by the Secretary of State for these purposes, which clearly shows the applicant's name and the qualification obtained (which must meet or exceed level A1 of the Common European Framework of Reference) unless:

(a) the applicant is aged 65 or over at the time he makes his application; or

(b) the applicant has a physical or mental condition that would prevent him from meeting the requirement; or

(c) there are exceptional compassionate circumstances that would prevent the applicant from meeting the requirement; or

(iii) the applicant is a national of one of the following countries: Antigua and Barbuda; Australia; the Bahamas; Barbados; Belize; Canada; Dominica; Grenada; Guyana; Jamaica; New Zealand; St Kitts and Nevis; St Lucia; St Vincent and the Grenadines; Trinidad and Tobago; United States of America; or

(iv) the applicant has obtained an academic qualification (not a professional or vocational qualification), which is deemed by UK NARIC to meet the recognised standard of a Bachelor's or Master's degree or PhD in the UK, from an educational establishment in one of the following countries: Antigua and Barbuda; Australia; The Bahamas; Barbados; Belize; Dominica; Grenada; Guyana; Ireland; Jamaica; New Zealand; St Kitts and Nevis; St Lucia; St Vincent and The Grenadines; Trinidad and Tobago; the UK; the USA; and provides the specified documents; or

(v) the applicant has obtained an academic qualification (not a professional or vocational qualification) which is deemed by UK NARIC to meet the recognised standard of a Bachelor's or Master's degree or PhD in the UK, and

(1) provides the specified evidence to show he has the qualification, and

(2) UK NARIC has confirmed that the qualification was taught or researched in English, or

(vi) has obtained an academic qualification (not a professional or vocational qualification) which is deemed by UK NARIC to meet the recognised standard of a Bachelor's or Master's degree or PhD in the UK, and provides the specified evidence to show:

(1) he has the qualification, and

(2) that the qualification was taught or researched in English.

or

(b) (i) the applicant is the unmarried or same-sex partner of a person who has a right of abode in the United Kingdom or indefinite leave to enter or remain in the United Kingdom and is on the same occasion seeking admission to the United Kingdom for the purposes of settlement and the parties have been living together outside the United Kingdom in a relationship akin to marriage or civil partnership which has subsisted for 4 years or more; and

(ii) the applicant has sufficient knowledge of the English language and sufficient knowledge about life in the United Kingdom, unless he is under the age of 18 or aged 65 or over at the time he makes his application; and

(iii) the applicant does not have one or more unspent convictions within the meaning of the Rehabilitation of Offenders Act 1974; and

(ii) any previous marriage or civil partnership (or similar relationship) by either partner has permanently broken down; and

(iii) the parties are not involved in a consanguineous relationship with one another; and

(iv) DELETED

(v) there will be adequate accommodation for the parties and any dependants without recourse to public funds in accommodation which they own or occupy exclusively; and

(vi) the parties will be able to maintain themselves and any dependants adequately without recourse to public funds; and

(vii) the parties intend to live together permanently; and

(viii) the applicant holds a valid United Kingdom entry clearance for entry in this capacity

For the purposes of this paragraph and paragraphs 295B–295I, a member of HM Forces serving overseas, or a permanent member of HM Diplomatic Service or a comparable UK-based staff member of the British Council on a tour of duty abroad, or a staff member of the Department for International Development who is a British Citizen or is settled in the United Kingdom, is to be regarded as present and settled in the United Kingdom.

Leave to enter the United Kingdom with a view to settlement as the unmarried or same-sex partner of a person present and settled in the United Kingdom or being admitted on the same occasion for settlement

295B. A person seeking leave to enter the United Kingdom as the unmarried or same-sex partner of a person present and settled in the United Kingdom or who is on the same occasion being admitted for settlement may:

(a) in the case of a person who meets the requirements of paragraph 295A(i)(a)(i), and one of the requirements of paragraph 295A(i)(a)(ii)–(vi) be admitted for an initial period not exceeding 27 months, or

(b) in the case of a person who meets all of the requirements in paragraph 295A(i)(b), be granted indefinite leave to enter, or

(c) in the case of a person who meets the requirement in paragraph 295A(i)(b)(i), but not the requirement in paragraph 295A(i)(b)(ii) to have sufficient knowledge of the English language and about life in the United Kingdom, be admitted for an initial period not exceeding 27 months, in all cases provided the Immigration Officer is satisfied that each of the relevant requirements of paragraph 295A is met.

Refusal of leave to enter the United Kingdom with a view to settlement as the unmarried or same-sex partner of a person present and settled in the United Kingdom or being admitted on the same occasion for settlement

295C. Leave to enter the United Kingdom with a view to settlement as the unmarried or same-sex partner of a person present and settled in the United Kingdom or being admitted on the same occasion for settlement, is to be refused if the Immigration Officer is not satisfied that each of the requirements of paragraph 295A is met.

Leave to remain as the unmarried or same-sex partner of a person present and settled in the United Kingdom

Requirements for leave to remain as the unmarried or same-sex partner of a person present and settled in the United Kingdom

295D. The requirements to be met by a person seeking leave to remain as the unmarried or same-sex partner of a person present and settled in the United Kingdom are that:

(i) the applicant has limited leave to enter or remain in the United Kingdom which was given in accordance with any of the provisions of these Rules, other than where as a result of that leave he would not have been in the United Kingdom beyond 6 months from the date on which he was admitted to the United Kingdom on this occasion in accordance with these rules; and

(ii) any previous marriage or civil partnership (or similar relationship) by either partner has permanently broken down; and

(iii) the applicant is the unmarried or same-sex partner of a person who is present and settled in the United Kingdom; and

(iv) the applicant has not remained in breach of the immigration laws; and

(v) the parties are not involved in a consanguineous relationship with one another; and

(vi) the parties have been living together in a relationship akin to marriage or civil partnership which has subsisted for two years or more; and

(vii) the parties' relationship pre-dates any decision to deport the applicant, recommend him for deportation, give him notice under Section 6(2) of the Immigration Act 1971, or give directions for his removal under section 10 of the Immigration and Asylum Act 1999; and

(viii) there will be adequate accommodation for the parties and any dependants without recourse to public funds in accommodation which they own or occupy exclusively; and

(ix) the parties will be able to maintain themselves and any dependants adequately without recourse to public funds; and

(x) the parties intend to live together permanently; and

(xi) (a) the applicant provides an original English language test certificate in speaking and listening from an English language test provider approved by the Secretary of State for these purposes, which clearly shows the applicant's name and the qualification obtained (which must meet or exceed level A1 of the Common European Framework of Reference) unless:

(i) the applicant is aged 65 or over at the time he makes his application; or

(ii) the applicant has a physical or mental condition that would prevent him from meeting the requirement; or;

(iii) there are exceptional compassionate circumstances that would prevent the applicant from meeting the requirement; or

(b) the applicant is a national of one of the following countries: Antigua and Barbuda; Australia; the Bahamas; Barbados; Belize; Canada; Dominica; Grenada; Guyana; Jamaica; New Zealand; St Kitts and Nevis; St Lucia; St Vincent and the Grenadines; Trinidad and Tobago; United States of America; or

(c) the applicant has obtained an academic qualification (not a professional or vocational qualification), which is deemed by UK NARIC to meet the recognised standard of a Bachelor's or Master's degree or PhD in the UK, from an educational establishment in one of the following countries: Antigua and Barbuda; Australia; The Bahamas; Barbados; Belize; Dominica; Grenada; Guyana; Ireland; Jamaica; New Zealand; St Kitts and Nevis; St Lucia; St Vincent and The Grenadines; Trinidad and Tobago; the UK; the USA; and provides the specified documents; or

(d) the applicant has obtained an academic qualification (not a professional or vocational qualification) which is deemed by UK NARIC to meet the recognised standard of a Bachelor's or Master's degree or PhD in the UK, and

(1) provides the specified evidence to show he has the qualification, and

(2) UK NARIC has confirmed that the qualification was taught or researched in English, or

(e) has obtained an academic qualification (not a professional or vocational qualification) which is deemed by UK NARIC to meet the recognised standard of a Bachelor's or Master's degree or PhD in the UK, and provides the specified evidence to show:

(1) he has the qualification, and

(2) that the qualification was taught or researched in English.

Leave to remain as the unmarried or same-sex partner of a person present and settled in the United Kingdom

295E. Leave to remain as the unmarried or same-sex partner of a person present and settled in the United Kingdom may be granted for a period of 2 years in the first instance provided that the Secretary of State is satisfied that each of the requirements of paragraph 295D are met.

Refusal of leave to remain as the unmarried or same-sex partner of a person present and settled in the United Kingdom

295F. Leave to remain as the unmarried or same-sex partner of a person present and settled in the United Kingdom is to be refused if the Secretary of State is not satisfied that each of the requirements of paragraph 295D is met.

Indefinite leave to remain as the unmarried or same-sex partner of a person present and settled in the United Kingdom

Requirements for indefinite leave to remain as the unmarried or same-sex partner of a person present and settled in the United Kingdom

295G. The requirements to be met by a person seeking indefinite leave to remain as the unmarried partner of a person present and settled in the United Kingdom are that:

(i) (a) the applicant was admitted to the United Kingdom for a period not exceeding 27 months or given an extension of stay for a period of 2 years in accordance with paragraphs 295AA to 295F of these Rules and has completed a period of 2 years as the unmarried or same-sex partner of a person present and settled here; or

(b) the applicant was admitted to the UK or given an extension of stay as the unmarried or same-sex partner of a Relevant Points Based System Migrant, and then obtained an extension of stay under paragraphs 295AA to 295F of these Rules and has completed a period of 2 years as the unmarried or same-sex partners of the person who is now present and settled here; or

(c) the applicant was admitted to the United Kingdom in accordance with leave granted under paragraph 295B(c) of these rules; or

(d) the applicant was admitted into the UK in accordance with paragraph 319O and has completed a period of 2 years limited leave as the unmarried or same-sex partner of a refugee or beneficiary of humanitarian protection who is now present and settled in the UK or as the unmarried or same-sex partner of a former refugee or beneficiary of humanitarian protection who is now a British Citizen.

(ii) the applicant is still the unmarried or same-sex partner of the person he was admitted or granted an extension of stay to join and the relationship is still subsisting; and

(iii) each of the parties intends to live permanently with the other as his partner; and

(iv) there will be adequate accommodation for the parties and any dependants without recourse to public funds in accommodation which they own or occupy exclusively; and

(v) the parties will be able to maintain themselves and any dependants adequately without recourse to public funds; and

(vi) the applicant has sufficient knowledge of the English language and sufficient knowledge about life in the United Kingdom, unless he is under the age of 18 or aged 65 or over at the time he makes his application; and

(vii) the applicant does not have one or more unspent convictions within the meaning of the Rehabilitation of Offenders Act 1974.

Indefinite leave to remain as the unmarried or same-sex partner of a person present and settled in the United Kingdom

295H. Indefinite leave to remain as the unmarried or same-sex partner of a person present and settled in the United Kingdom may be granted provided that the Secretary of State is satisfied that each of the requirements of paragraph 295G is met.

Refusal of indefinite leave to remain as the unmarried or same-sex partner of a person present and settled in the United Kingdom

295I. Indefinite leave to remain as the unmarried or same-sex partner of a person present and settled in the United Kingdom is to be refused if the Secretary of State is not satisfied that each of the requirements of paragraph 295G is met.

Leave to enter or remain as the unmarried or same-sex partner of a person with limited leave to enter or remain in the United Kingdom under paragraphs 128–193; 200–239; or 263–270

Requirements for leave to enter or remain as the unmarried or same-sex partner of a person with limited leave to enter or remain in the United Kingdom under paragraphs 128–193; 200–239; or 263–270

295J. The requirements to be met by a person seeking leave to enter or remain as the unmarried partner of a person with limited leave to enter or remain in the United Kingdom under paragraphs 128–193; 200–239; or 263–270; are that:

(i) the applicant is the unmarried or same-sex partner of a person who has limited leave to enter or remain in the United Kingdom under paragraphs 128–193; 200–239; or 263–270; and

(ii) any previous marriage or civil partnership (or similar relationship) by either partner has permanently broken down; and

(iii) the parties are not involved in a consanguineous relationship with one another; and

(iv) the parties have been living together in a relationship akin to marriage or civil partnership which has subsisted for 2 years or more; and

(v) each of the parties intends to live with the other as his partner during the applicant's stay; and

(vi) there will be adequate accommodation for the parties and any dependants without recourse to public funds in accommodation which they own or occupy exclusively; and

(vii) the parties will be able to maintain themselves and any dependants adequately without recourse to public funds; and

(viii) the applicant does not intend to stay in the United Kingdom beyond any period of leave granted to his partner; and

(ix) if seeking leave to enter, the applicant holds a valid United Kingdom entry clearance for entry in this capacity or, if seeking leave to remain, was admitted with a valid United Kingdom entry clearance for entry in this capacity.

Leave to enter or remain as the unmarried or same-sex partner of a person with limited leave to enter or remain in the United Kingdom under paragraphs 128–193; 200–239; or 263–270

295K. Leave to enter as the unmarried or same-sex partner of a person with limited leave to enter or remain in the United Kingdom under paragraphs 128–193; 200–239; or 263–270; may be granted provided that a valid United Kingdom entry clearance for entry in this capacity is produced to the Immigration Officer on arrival. Leave to remain as the unmarried partner or same-sex of a person with limited leave to enter or remain in the United Kingdom under paragraphs 128–193; 200–239; or 263–270; may be granted provided that the Secretary of State is satisfied that each of the requirements of paragraph 295J is met. If the applicant is seeking leave to enter or remain as the unmarried or same-sex partner of a Highly Skilled Migrant, any leave which is granted will be subject to a condition prohibiting Employment as a Doctor or Dentist in Training, unless the applicant:

(1) has obtained a primary degree in medicine or dentistry at bachelor's level or above from a UK institution that is a UK recognised or listed body, or which holds a sponsor licence under Tier 4 of the Points Based System; or

(2) is applying for leave to remain and has, or has last been granted, entry clearance, leave to enter or leave to remain that was not subject to any condition restricting him from taking employment as a Doctor in Training, and has been employed during that leave as a Doctor in Training; or

(3) is applying for leave to remain and has, or has last been granted, entry clearance, leave to enter or leave to remain that was not subject to any condition restricting him from taking employment as a Dentist in Training, and has been employed during that leave as a Dentist in Training.

Refusal of leave to enter or remain as the unmarried or same-sex partner of a person with limited leave to enter or remain in the United Kingdom under paragraphs 128–193; 200–239; or 263–270

295L. Leave to enter as the unmarried or same-sex partner of a person with limited leave to enter or remain in the United Kingdom under paragraphs 128–193; 200–239; or 263–270; is to be refused if a valid United Kingdom entry clearance for entry in this capacity is not produced to the Immigration Officer on arrival. Leave to remain as the unmarried or same-sex partner of a person with limited leave to enter or remain in the United Kingdom under paragraphs 128–193; 200–239; or 263–270; is to be refused if the Secretary of State is not satisfied that each of the requirements of paragraph 295J is met.

Indefinite leave to remain for the bereaved unmarried or same-sex partner of a person present and settled in the United Kingdom

Requirements for indefinite leave to remain for the bereaved unmarried or same-sex partner of a person present and settled in the United Kingdom

295M. The requirements to be met by a person seeking indefinite leave to remain as the bereaved unmarried or same-sex partner of a person present and settled in the United Kingdom, are that:

(i) the applicant was admitted to the United Kingdom admitted to the United Kingdom for a period not exceeding 27 months; or given an extension of stay for a period of 2 years in accordance with paragraphs 295AA to 295F of these Rules as the unmarried partner of a person present and settled in the United Kingdom; and

(ii) the person whom the applicant was admitted or granted an extension of stay to join died during that period of leave; and

(iii) the applicant was still the unmarried or same-sex partner of the person he was admitted or granted an extension of stay to join at the time of the death; and

(iv) each of the parties intended to live permanently with the other as his partner and the relationship was subsisting at the time of the death; and

(v) the applicant does not have one or more unspent convictions within the meaning of the Rehabilitation of Offenders Act 1974.

Indefinite leave to remain for the bereaved unmarried or same-sex partner of a person present and settled in the United Kingdom

295N. Indefinite leave to remain for the bereaved unmarried partner of a person present and settled in the United Kingdom, may be granted provided that the Secretary of State is satisfied that each of the requirements of paragraph 295M is met.

Refusal of indefinite leave to remain for the bereaved unmarried or same-sex partner of a person present and settled in the United Kingdom

295O. Indefinite leave to remain for the bereaved unmarried or same-sex partner of a person present and settled in the United Kingdom, is to be refused if the Secretary of State is not satisfied that each of the requirements of paragraph 295M is met.

Children

296. Nothing in these Rules shall be construed as permitting a child to be granted entry clearance, leave to enter or remain, or variation of leave where his parent is party to a polygamous marriage or civil partnership and any application by that parent for admission or leave to remain for settlement or with a view to settlement would be refused pursuant to paragraphs 278 or 278A.

Leave to enter or remain in the United Kingdom as the child of a parent, parents or a relative present and settled or being admitted for settlement in the United Kingdom

Requirements for indefinite leave to enter the United Kingdom as the child of a parent, parents or a relative present and settled or being admitted for settlement in the United Kingdom

297. The requirements to be met by a person seeking indefinite leave to enter the United Kingdom as the child of a parent, parents or a relative present and settled or being admitted for settlement in the United Kingdom are that he:

(i) is seeking leave to enter to accompany or join a parent, parents or a relative in one of the following circumstances:

(a) both parents are present and settled in the United Kingdom; or

(b) both parents are being admitted on the same occasion for settlement; or

(c) one parent is present and settled in the United Kingdom and the other is being admitted on the same occasion for settlement; or

(d) one parent is present and settled in the United Kingdom or being admitted on the same occasion for settlement and the other parent is dead; or

(e) one parent is present and settled in the United Kingdom or being admitted on the same occasion for settlement and has had sole responsibility for the child's upbringing; or

(f) one parent or a relative is present and settled in the United Kingdom or being admitted on the same occasion for settlement and there are serious and compelling family or other considerations which make exclusion of the child undesirable and suitable arrangements have been made for the child's care; and

(ii) is under the age of 18; and

(iii) is not leading an independent life, is unmarried and is not a civil partner, and has not formed an independent family unit; and

(iv) can, and will, be accommodated adequately by the parent, parents or relative the child is seeking to join without recourse to public funds in accommodation which the parent, parents or relative the child is seeking to join, own or occupy exclusively; and

(v) can, and will, be maintained adequately by the parent, parents, or relative the child is seeking to join, without recourse to public funds; and

(vi) holds a valid United Kingdom entry clearance for entry in this capacity; and

(vii) does not have one or more unspent convictions within the meaning of the Rehabilitation of Offenders Act 1974.

Requirements for indefinite leave to remain in the United Kingdom as the child of a parent, parents or a relative present and settled or being admitted for settlement in the United Kingdom

298. The requirements to be met by a person seeking indefinite leave to remain in the United Kingdom as the child of a parent, parents or a relative present and settled in the United Kingdom are that he:

(i) is seeking to remain with a parent, parents or a relative in one of the following circumstances:

(a) both parents are present and settled in the United Kingdom; or

(b) one parent is present and settled in the United Kingdom and the other parent is dead; or

(c) one parent is present and settled in the United Kingdom and has had sole responsibility for the child's upbringing; or

(d) one parent or a relative is present and settled in the United Kingdom and there are serious and compelling family or other considerations which make exclusion of the child undesirable and suitable arrangements have been made for the child's care; and

(ii) has limited leave to enter or remain in the United Kingdom, and

(a) is under the age of 18; or

(b) was given leave to enter or remain with a view to settlement under paragraph 302; or

(c) was admitted into the UK in accordance with paragraph 319R and has completed a period of 2 years limited leave as the child of a refugee or beneficiary of humanitarian protection who is now present and settled in the UK or as the child of a former refugee or beneficiary of humanitarian protection who is now a British Citizen, or

(d) the applicant has limited leave to enter or remain in the United Kingdom in accordance with paragraph 319X, as the child of a relative with limited leave to remain as a refugee or beneficiary of humanitarian protection in the United Kingdom and who is now present and settled here.

(iii) is not leading an independent life, is unmarried, and has not formed an independent family unit; and

(iv) can, and will, be accommodated adequately by the parent, parents or relative the child was admitted to join, without recourse to public funds in accommodation which the parent, parents or relative the child was admitted to join, own or occupy exclusively; and

(v) can, and will, be maintained adequately by the parent, parents or relative the child was admitted to join, without recourse to public funds; and

(vi) does not have one or more unspent convictions within the meaning of the Rehabilitation of Offenders Act 1974.

Indefinite leave to enter or remain in the United Kingdom as the child of a parent, parents or a relative present and settled or being admitted for settlement in the United Kingdom

299. Indefinite leave to enter the United Kingdom as the child of a parent, parents or a relative present and settled or being admitted for settlement in the United Kingdom may be granted provided a valid United Kingdom entry clearance for entry in this capacity is produced to the Immigration Officer on arrival. Indefinite leave to remain in the United Kingdom as the child of a parent, parents or a relative present and settled in the United Kingdom may be granted provided the Secretary of State is satisfied that each of the requirements of paragraph 298 is met.

Refusal of indefinite leave to enter or remain in the United Kingdom as the child of a parent, parents or a relative present and settled or being admitted for settlement in the United Kingdom

300. Indefinite leave to enter the United Kingdom as the child of a parent, parents or a relative present and settled or being admitted for settlement in the United Kingdom is to be refused if a valid United Kingdom entry clearance for entry in this capacity is not produced to the Immigration Officer on arrival. Indefinite leave to remain in the United Kingdom as the child of a parent, parents or a relative present and settled in the United Kingdom is to be refused if the Secretary of State is not satisfied that each of the requirements of paragraph 298 is met.

Requirements for limited leave to enter or remain in the United Kingdom with a view to settlement as the child of a parent or parents given limited leave to enter or remain in the United Kingdom with a view to settlement

301. The requirements to be met by a person seeking limited leave to enter or remain in the United Kingdom with a view to settlement as the child of a parent or parents given limited leave to enter or remain in the United Kingdom with a view to settlement are that he:

(i) is seeking leave to enter to accompany or join or remain with a parent or parents in one of the following circumstances:

(a) one parent is present and settled in the United Kingdom or being admitted on the same occasion for settlement and the other parent is being or has been given limited leave to enter or remain in the United Kingdom with a view to settlement; or

(b) one parent is being or has been given limited leave to enter or remain in the United Kingdom with a view to settlement and has had sole responsibility for the child's upbringing; or

(c) one parent is being or has been given limited leave to enter or remain in the United Kingdom with a view to settlement and there are serious and compelling family or other considerations which make exclusion of the child undesirable and suitable arrangements have been made for the child's care; and

(ii) is under the age of 18; and

(iii) is not leading an independent life, is unmarried and is not a civil partner, and has not formed an independent family unit; and

(iv) can, and will, be accommodated adequately without recourse to public funds, in accommodation which the parent or parents own or occupy exclusively; and

(iva) can, and will, be maintained adequately by the parent or parents without recourse to public funds; and

(ivb) does not qualify for limited leave to enter as a child of a parent or parents given limited leave to enter or remain as a refugee or beneficiary of humanitarian protection under paragraph 319R; and

(v) (where an application is made for limited leave to remain with a view to settlement) has limited leave to enter or remain in the United Kingdom; and

(vi) if seeking leave to enter, holds a valid United Kingdom entry clearance for entry in this capacity or, if seeking leave to remain, was admitted with a valid United Kingdom entry clearance for entry in this capacity.

Limited leave to enter or remain in the United Kingdom with a view to settlement as the child of a parent or parents given limited leave to enter or remain in the United Kingdom with a view to settlement

302. A person seeking limited leave to enter the United Kingdom with a view to settlement as the child of a parent or parents given limited leave to enter or remain in the United Kingdom with a view to settlement may be admitted for a period not exceeding 27 months provided he is able, on arrival, to produce to the Immigration Officer a valid United Kingdom entry clearance for entry in this capacity. A person seeking limited leave to remain in the United Kingdom with a view to settlement as the child of a parent or parents given limited leave to enter or remain in the United Kingdom with a view to settlement may be given limited leave to remain for a period not exceeding 27 months provided the Secretary of State is satisfied that each of the requirements of paragraph 301(i)–(v) is met.

Refusal of limited leave to enter or remain in the United Kingdom with a view to settlement as the child of a parent or parents given limited leave to enter or remain in the United Kingdom with a view to settlement

303. Limited leave to enter the United Kingdom with a view to settlement as the child of a parent or parents given limited leave to enter or remain in the United Kingdom with a view to settlement is to be refused if a valid United Kingdom entry clearance for entry in this capacity is not produced to the Immigration Officer on arrival. Limited leave to remain in the United Kingdom with a view to settlement as the child of a parent or parents given limited leave to enter or remain in the United Kingdom with a view to settlement is to be refused if the Secretary of State is not satisfied that each of the requirements of paragraph 301(i)–(v) is met.

Leave to enter and extension of stay in the United Kingdom as the child of a parent who is being, or has been admitted to the united kingdom as a fiance(e) or proposed civil partner

Requirements for limited leave to enter the United Kingdom as the child of a fiance(e) or proposed civil partner

303A. The requirements to be met by a person seeking limited leave to enter the United Kingdom as the child of a fiance(e) or proposed civil partner, are that:

(i) he is seeking to accompany or join a parent who is, on the same occasion that the child seeks admission, being admitted as a fiance(e) or proposed civil partner , or who has been admitted as a fiance(e) or proposed civil partner; and

(ii) he is under the age of 18; and

(iii) he is not leading an independent life, is unmarried and is not a civil partner, and has not formed an independent family unit; and

(iv) he can and will be maintained and accommodated adequately without recourse to public funds with the parent admitted or being admitted as a fiance(e) or proposed civil partner; and

(v) there are serious and compelling family or other considerations which make the child's exclusion undesirable, that suitable arrangements have been made for his care in the United Kingdom, and there is no other person outside the United Kingdom who could reasonably be expected to care for him; and

(vi) he holds a valid United Kingdom entry clearance for entry in this capacity.

Limited leave to enter the United Kingdom as the child of a parent who is being, or has been admitted to the United Kingdom as a fiance(e) or proposed civil partner

303B. A person seeking limited leave to enter the United Kingdom as the child of a fiance(e) or proposed civil partner, may be granted limited leave to enter the United Kingdom for a period not in excess of that granted to the fiance(e) or proposed civil partner, provided that a valid United Kingdom entry clearance for entry in this capacity is produced to the Immigration Officer on arrival. Where the period of limited leave granted to a fiance(e) will expire in more than 6 months, a person seeking limited leave to enter as the child of the fiance(e) or proposed civil partner should be granted leave for a period not exceeding six months.

Refusal of limited leave to enter the United Kingdom as the child of a parent who is being, or has been admitted to the United Kingdom as a fiance(e) or proposed civil partner

303C. Limited leave to enter the United Kingdom as the child of a fiance(e) or proposed civil partner, is to be refused if a valid United Kingdom entry clearance for entry in this capacity is not produced to the Immigration Officer on arrival.

Requirements for an extension of stay in the United Kingdom as the child of a fiance(e) or proposed civil partner

303D. The requirements to be met by a person seeking an extension of stay in the United Kingdom as the child of a fiance(e) or proposed civil partner are that:

(i) the applicant was admitted with a valid United Kingdom entry clearance as the child of a fiance(e) or proposed civil partner; and

(ii) the applicant is the child of a parent who has been granted limited leave to enter, or an extension of stay, as a fiance(e) or proposed civil partner; and

(iii) the requirements of paragraph 303A(ii)–(v) are met.

Extension of stay in the United Kingdom as the child of a fiance(e) or proposed civil partner

303E. An extension of stay as the child of a fiance(e) or proposed civil partner may be granted provided that the Secretary of State is satisfied that each of the requirements of paragraph 303D is met.

Refusal of an extension of stay in the United Kingdom as the child of a fiance(e) or proposed civil partner

303F. An extension of stay as the child of a fiance(e) or proposed civil partner is to be refused if the Secretary of State is not satisfied that each of the requirements of paragraph 303D is met.

Children born in the United Kingdom who are not British citizens

304. This paragraph and paragraphs 305–309 apply only to dependent children under 18 years of age who are unmarried and are not civil partners and who were born in the United Kingdom on or after 1 January 1983 (when the British Nationality Act 1981 came into force) but who, because neither of their parents was a British Citizen or settled in the United Kingdom at the time of their birth, are not British Citizens and are therefore subject to immigration control. Such a child requires leave to enter where admission to

the United Kingdom is sought, and leave to remain where permission is sought for the child to be allowed to stay in the United Kingdom. If he qualifies for entry clearance, leave to enter or leave to remain under any other part of these Rules, a child who was born in the United Kingdom but is not a British Citizen may be granted entry clearance, leave to enter or leave to remain in accordance with the provisions of that other part.

Requirements for leave to enter or remain in the United Kingdom as the child of a parent or parents given leave to enter or remain in the United Kingdom

305. The requirements to be met by a child born in the United Kingdom who is not a British Citizen who seeks leave to enter or remain in the United Kingdom as the child of a parent or parents given leave to enter or remain in the United Kingdom are that he:

(i) (a) is accompanying or seeking to join or remain with a parent or parents who have, or are given, leave to enter or remain in the United Kingdom; or

(b) is accompanying or seeking to join or remain with a parent or parents one of whom is a British Citizen or has the right of abode in the United Kingdom; or

(c) is a child in respect of whom the parental rights and duties are vested solely in a local authority; and

(ii) is under the age of 18; and

(iii) was born in the United Kingdom; and

(iv) is not leading an independent life, is unmarried and is not a civil partner, and has not formed an independent family unit; and

(v) (where an application is made for leave to enter) has not been away from the United Kingdom for more than 2 years.

Leave to enter or remain in the United Kingdom

306. A child born in the United Kingdom who is not a British Citizen and who requires leave to enter or remain in the circumstances set out in paragraph 304 may be given leave to enter for the same period as his parent or parents where paragraph 305(i)(a) applies, provided the Immigration Officer is satisfied that each of the requirements of paragraph 305(ii)–(v) is met. Where leave to remain is sought, the child may be granted leave to remain for the same period as his parent or parents where paragraph 305(i)(a) applies, provided the Secretary of State is satisfied that each of the requirements of paragraph 305(ii)–(iv) is met. Where the parent or parents have or are given periods of leave of different duration, the child may be given leave to whichever period is longer except that if the parents are living apart the child should be given leave for the same period as the parent who has day to day responsibility for him.

307. If a child does not qualify for leave to enter or remain because neither of his parents has a current leave, (and neither of them is a British Citizen or has the right of abode), he will normally be refused leave to enter or remain, even if each of the requirements of paragraph 305(ii)–(v) has been satisfied. However, he may be granted leave to enter or remain for a period not exceeding 3 months if both of his parents are in the United Kingdom and it appears unlikely that they will be removed in the immediate future, and there is no other person outside the United Kingdom who could reasonably be expected to care for him.

308. A child born in the United Kingdom who is not a British Citizen and who requires leave to enter or remain in the United Kingdom in the circumstances set out in paragraph 304 may be given indefinite leave to enter where paragraph 305(i)(b) or (i)(c) applies provided the Immigration Officer is satisfied that each of the requirements of paragraph 305(ii)–(v) is met. Where an application is for leave to remain, such a child may be granted indefinite leave to remain where paragraph 305(i)(b) or (i)(c) applies, provided the Secretary of State is satisfied that each of the requirements of paragraph 305(ii)–(iv) is met.

Refusal of leave to enter or remain in the United Kingdom

309. Leave to enter the United Kingdom where the circumstances set out in paragraph 304 apply is to be refused if the Immigration Officer is not satisfied that each of the requirements of paragraph 305 is met. Leave to remain for such a child is to be refused if the Secretary of State is not satisfied that each of the requirements of paragraph 305(i)–(iv) is met.

Adopted children

309A. For the purposes of adoption under paragraphs 310–316C a de facto adoption shall be regarded as having taken place if:

(a) at the time immediately preceding the making of the application for entry clearance under these Rules the adoptive parent or parents have been living abroad (in applications involving two parents both must have lived abroad together) for at least a period of time equal to the first period mentioned in sub-paragraph (b)(i) and must have cared for the child for at least a period of time equal to the second period material in that sub-paragraph; and

(b) during their time abroad, the adoptive parent or parents have:

(i) lived together for a minimum period of 18 months, of which the 12 months immediately preceding the application for entry clearance must have been spent living together with the child; and

(ii) have assumed the role of the child's parents, since the beginning of the 18 month period, so that there has been a genuine transfer of parental responsibility.

Requirements for indefinite leave to enter the United Kingdom as the adopted child of a parent or parents present and settled or being admitted for settlement in the United Kingdom

310. The requirements to be met in the case of a child seeking indefinite leave to enter the United Kingdom as the adopted child of a parent or parents present and settled or being admitted for settlement in the United Kingdom are that he:

(i) is seeking leave to enter to accompany or join an adoptive parent or parents in one of the following circumstances;

(a) both parents are present and settled in the United Kingdom; or

(b) both parents are being admitted on the same occasion for settlement; or

(c) one parent is present and settled in the United Kingdom and the other is being admitted on the same occasion for settlement; or

(d) one parent is present and settled in the United Kingdom or being admitted on the same occasion for settlement and the other parent is dead; or

(e) one parent is present and settled in the United Kingdom or being admitted on the same occasion for settlement and has had sole responsibility for the child's upbringing; or

(f) one parent is present and settled in the United Kingdom or being admitted on the same occasion for settlement and there are serious and compelling family or other considerations which make exclusion of the child undesirable and suitable arrangements have been made for the child's care; or

(g) in the case of a de facto adoption one parent has a right of abode in the United Kingdom or indefinite leave to enter or remain in the United Kingdom and is seeking admission to the United Kingdom on the same occasion for the purposes of settlement; and

(ii) is under the age of 18; and

(iii) is not leading an independent life, is unmarried and is not a civil partner, and has not formed an independent family unit; and

(iv) can, and will, be accommodated and maintained adequately without recourse to public funds in accommodation which the adoptive parent or parents own or occupy exclusively; and

(v) DELETED

(vi) (a) was adopted in accordance with a decision taken by the competent administrative authority or court in his country of origin or the country in which he is resident, being a country whose adoption orders are recognised by the United Kingdom; or

(b) is the subject of a de facto adoption; and

(vii) was adopted at a time when:

(a) both adoptive parents were resident together abroad; or

(b) either or both adoptive parents were settled in the United Kingdom; and

(viii) has the same rights and obligations as any other child of the adoptive parent's or parents' family; and

(ix) was adopted due to the inability of the original parent(s) or current carer(s) to care for him and there has been a genuine transfer of parental responsibility to the adoptive parents; and

(x) has lost or broken his ties with his family of origin; and

(xi) was adopted, but the adoption is not one of convenience arranged to facilitate his admission to or remaining in the United Kingdom; and

(xii) holds a valid United Kingdom entry clearance for entry in this capacity; and

(xiii) does not have one or more unspent convictions within the meaning of the Rehabilitation of Offenders Act 1974.

Requirements for indefinite leave to remain in the United Kingdom as the adopted child of a parent or parents present and settled in the United Kingdom

311. The requirements to be met in the case of a child seeking indefinite leave to remain in the United Kingdom as the adopted child of a parent or parents present and settled in the United Kingdom are that he:

(i) is seeking to remain with an adoptive parent or parents in one of the following circumstances:

(a) both parents are present and settled in the United Kingdom; or

(b) one parent is present and settled in the United Kingdom and the other parent is dead; or

(c) one parent is present and settled in the United Kingdom and has had sole responsibility for the child's upbringing; or

(d) one parent is present and settled in the United Kingdom and there are serious and compelling family or other considerations which make exclusion of the child undesirable and suitable arrangements have been made for the child's care; or

(e) in the case of a de facto adoption one parent has a right of abode in the United Kingdom or indefinite leave to enter or remain in the United Kingdom and is seeking admission to the United Kingdom on the same occasion for the purpose of settlement; and

(ii) has limited leave to enter or remain in the United Kingdom, and

(a) is under the age of 18; or

(b) was given leave to enter or remain with a view to settlement under paragraph 315 or paragraph 316B; and

(iii) is not leading an independent life, is unmarried and is not a civil partner, and has not formed an independent family unit; and

(iv) can, and will, be accommodated and maintained adequately without recourse to public funds in accommodation which the adoptive parent or parents own or occupy exclusively; and

(v) DELETED

(vi) (a) was adopted in accordance with a decision taken by the competent administrative authority or court in his country of origin or the country in which he is resident, being a country whose adoption orders are recognised by the United Kingdom; or

(b) is the subject of a de facto adoption; and

(vii) was adopted at a time when:

(a) both adoptive parents were resident together abroad; or

(b) either or both adoptive parents were settled in the United Kingdom; and

(viii) has the same rights and obligations as any other child of the adoptive parent's or parents' family; and

(ix) was adopted due to the inability of the original parent(s) or current carer(s) to care for him and there has been a genuine transfer of parental responsibility to the adoptive parents; and

(x) has lost or broken his ties with his family of origin; and

(xi) was adopted, but the adoption is not one of convenience arranged to facilitate his admission to or remaining in the United Kingdom; and

(xii) does not have one or more unspent convictions within the meaning of the Rehabilitation of Offenders Act 1974.

Indefinite leave to enter or remain in the United Kingdom as the adopted child of a parent or parents present and settled or being admitted for settlement in the United Kingdom

312. Indefinite leave to enter the United Kingdom as the adopted child of a parent or parents present and settled or being admitted for settlement in the United Kingdom may be granted provided a valid United Kingdom entry clearance for entry in this capacity is produced to the Immigration Officer on arrival. Indefinite leave to remain in the United Kingdom as the adopted child of a parent or parents present and settled in the United Kingdom may be granted provided the Secretary of State is satisfied that each of the requirements of paragraph 311 is met.

Refusal of indefinite leave to enter or remain in the United Kingdom as the adopted child of a parent or parents present and settled or being admitted for settlement in the United Kingdom

313. Indefinite leave to enter the United Kingdom as the adopted child of a parent or parents present and settled or being admitted for settlement in the United Kingdom is to be refused if a valid United Kingdom entry clearance for entry in this capacity is not produced to the Immigration Officer on arrival. Indefinite leave to remain in the United Kingdom as the adopted child of a parent or parents present and settled in the United Kingdom is to be refused if the Secretary of State is not satisfied that each of the requirements of paragraph 311 is met.

Requirements for limited leave to enter or remain in the United Kingdom with a view to settlement as the adopted child of a parent or parents given limited leave to enter or remain in the United Kingdom with a view to settlement

314. The requirements to be met in the case of a child seeking limited leave to enter or remain in the United Kingdom with a view to settlement as the adopted child of a parent or parents given limited leave to enter or remain in the United Kingdom with a view to settlement are that he:

(i) is seeking leave to enter to accompany or join or remain with a parent or parents in one of the following circumstances:

  (a) one parent is present and settled in the United Kingdom or being admitted on the same occasion for settlement and the other parent is being or has been given limited leave to enter or remain in the United Kingdom with a view to settlement; or

  (b) one parent is being or has been given limited leave to enter or remain in the United Kingdom with a view to settlement and has had sole responsibility for the child's upbringing; or

  (c) one parent is being or has been given limited leave to enter or remain in the United Kingdom with a view to settlement and there are serious and compelling family or other considerations which make exclusion of the child undesirable and suitable arrangements have been made for the child's care; or

  (d) in the case of a de facto adoption one parent has a right of abode in the United Kingdom or indefinite leave to enter or remain in the United Kingdom and is seeking admission to the United Kingdom on the same occasion for the purpose of settlement; and

(ii) is under the age of 18; and

(iii) is not leading an independent life, is unmarried and is not a civil partner, and has not formed an independent family unit; and

(iv) can, and will, be accommodated and maintained adequately without recourse to public funds in accommodation which the adoptive parent or parents own or occupy exclusively; and

(v) (a) was adopted in accordance with a decision taken by the competent administrative authority or court in his country of origin or the country in which he is resident, being a country whose adoption orders are recognised by the United Kingdom; or

  (b) is the subject of a de facto adoption; and

(vi) was adopted at a time when:

  (a) both adoptive parents were resident together abroad; or

  (b) either or both adoptive parents were settled in the United Kingdom; and

(vii) has the same rights and obligations as any other child of the adoptive parent's or parents' family; and

(viii) was adopted due to the inability of the original parent(s) or current carer(s) to care for him and there has been a genuine transfer of parental responsibility to the adoptive parents; and

(ix) has lost or broken his ties with his family of origin; and

(x) was adopted, but the adoption is not one of convenience arranged to facilitate his admission to the United Kingdom; and

(xi) (where an application is made for limited leave to remain with a view to settlement) has limited leave to enter or remain in the United Kingdom; and

(xii) if seeking leave to enter, holds a valid United Kingdom entry clearance for entry in this capacity.

Limited leave to enter or remain in the United Kingdom with a view to settlement as the adopted child of a parent or parents given limited leave to enter or remain in the United Kingdom with a view to settlement

315. A person seeking limited leave to enter the United Kingdom with a view to settlement as the adopted child of a parent or parents given limited leave to enter or remain in the United Kingdom with a view to settlement may be admitted for a period not exceeding 12 months provided he is able, on arrival, to produce to the Immigration Officer a valid United Kingdom entry clearance for entry in this capacity. A person seeking limited leave to remain in the United Kingdom with a view to settlement as the adopted child of a parent or parents given limited leave to enter or remain in the United Kingdom with a view to settlement may be granted limited leave for a period not exceeding 12 months provided the Secretary of State is satisfied that each of the requirements of paragraph 314(i)–(xi) is met.

Refusal of limited leave to enter or remain in the United Kingdom with a view to settlement as the adopted child of a parent or parents given limited leave to enter or remain in the United Kingdom with a view to settlement

316. Limited leave to enter the United Kingdom with a view to settlement as the adopted child of a parent or parents given limited leave to enter or remain in the United Kingdom with a view to settlement is to be refused if a valid United Kingdom entry clearance for entry in this capacity is not produced to the Immigration Officer on arrival. Limited leave to remain in the United Kingdom with a view to settlement as the adopted child of a parent or parents given limited leave to enter or remain in the United Kingdom with a view to settlement is to be refused if the Secretary of State is not satisfied that each of the requirements of paragraph 314(i)–(xi) is met.

Requirements for limited leave to enter the United Kingdom with a view to settlement as a child for adoption

316A. The requirements to be satisfied in the case of a child seeking limited leave to enter the United Kingdom for the purpose of being adopted (which, for the avoidance of doubt, does not include a de facto adoption) in the United Kingdom are that he:

(i) is seeking limited leave to enter to accompany or join a person or persons who wish to adopt him in the United Kingdom (the 'prospective parent(s)'), in one of the following circumstances:

(a) both prospective parents are present and settled in the United Kingdom; or

(b) both prospective parents are being admitted for settlement on the same occasion that the child is seeking admission; or

(c) one prospective parent is present and settled in the United Kingdom and the other is being admitted for settlement on the same occasion that the child is seeking admission; or

(d) one prospective parent is present and settled in the United Kingdom and the other is being given limited leave to enter or remain in the United Kingdom with a view to settlement on the same occasion that the child is seeking admission, or has previously been given such leave; or

(e) one prospective parent is being admitted for settlement on the same occasion that the other is being granted limited leave to enter with a view to settlement, which is also on the same occasion that the child is seeking admission; or

(f) one prospective parent is present and settled in the United Kingdom or is being admitted for settlement on the same occasion that the child is seeking admission, and has had sole responsibility for the child's upbringing; or

(g) one prospective parent is present and settled in the United Kingdom or is being admitted for settlement on the same occasion that the child is seeking admission, and there are serious and compelling family or other considerations which would make the child's exclusion undesirable, and suitable arrangements have been made for the child's care; and

(ii) is under the age of 18; and

(iii) is not leading an independent life, is unmarried and is not a civil partner, and has not formed an independent family unit; and

(iv) can, and will, be maintained and accommodated adequately without recourse to public funds in accommodation which the prospective parent or parents own or occupy exclusively; and

(v) will have the same rights and obligations as any other child of the marriage or civil partnership; and

(vi) is being adopted due to the inability of the original parent(s) or current carer(s) (or those looking after him immediately prior to him being physically transferred to his prospective parent or parents) to care for him, and there has been a genuine transfer of parental responsibility to the prospective parent or parents; and

(vii) has lost or broken or intends to lose or break his ties with his family of origin; and

(viii) will be adopted in the United Kingdom by his prospective parent or parents in accordance with the law relating to adoption in the United Kingdom, but the proposed adoption is not one of convenience arranged to facilitate his admission to the United Kingdom.

Limited leave to enter the United Kingdom with a view to settlement as a child for adoption

316B. A person seeking limited leave to enter the United Kingdom with a view to settlement as a child for adoption may be admitted for a period not exceeding 24 months provided he is able, on arrival, to produce to the Immigration Officer a valid United Kingdom entry clearance for entry in this capacity.

Refusal of limited leave to enter the United Kingdom with a view to settlement as a child for adoption

316C. Limited leave to enter the United Kingdom with a view to settlement as a child for adoption is to be refused if a valid United Kingdom entry clearance for entry in this capacity is not produced to the Immigration Officer on arrival.

Requirements for limited leave to enter the United Kingdom with a view to settlement as a child for adoption under the Hague Convention

316D. The requirements to be satisfied in the case of a child seeking limited leave to enter the United Kingdom for the purpose of being adopted in the United Kingdom under the Hague Convention are that he:

(i) is seeking limited leave to enter to accompany one or two people each of whom are habitually resident in the United Kingdom and who wish to adopt him under the Hague Convention ('the prospective parents');

(ii) is the subject of an agreement made under Article 17(c) of the Hague Convention; and

(iii) has been entrusted to the prospective parents by the competent administrative authority of the country from which he is coming to the United Kingdom for adoption under the Hague Convention; and

(iv) is under the age of 18; and

(v)* can, and will, be maintained and accommodated adequately without recourse to public funds in accommodation which the prospective parent or parents own or occupy exclusively; and

(vi)* holds a valid United Kingdom entry clearance for entry in this capacity.

Limited leave to enter the United Kingdom with a view to settlement as a child for adoption under the Hague Convention

316E. A person seeking limited leave to enter the United Kingdom with a view to settlement as a child for adoption under the Hague Convention may be admitted for a period not exceeding 24 months provided he is able, on arrival, to produce to the Immigration Officer a valid United Kingdom entry clearance for entry in this capacity.

Refusal of limited leave to enter the United Kingdom with a view to settlement as a child for adoption under the Hague Convention

316F. Limited leave to enter the United Kingdom with a view to settlement as a child for adoption under the Hague Convention is to be refused if a valid United Kingdom entry clearance for entry in this capacity is not produced to the Immigration Officer on arrival.

Parents, grandparents and other dependent relatives of persons present and settled in the United Kingdom

Requirements for indefinite leave to enter or remain in the United Kingdom as the parent, grandparent or other dependent relative of a person present and settled in the United Kingdom

317. The requirements to be met by a person seeking indefinite leave to enter or remain in the United Kingdom as the parent, grandparent or other dependent relative of a person present and settled in the United Kingdom are that the person:

(i) is related to a person present and settled in the United Kingdom in one of the following ways:

(a) parent or grandparent who is divorced, widowed, single or separated aged 65 years or over; or

(b) parents or grandparents travelling together of whom at least one is aged 65 or over; or

(c) a parent or grandparent aged 65 or over who has entered into a second relationship of marriage or civil partnership but cannot look to the spouse, civil partner or children of that second relationship for financial support; and where the person settled in the United Kingdom is able and willing to maintain the parent or grandparent and any spouse or civil partner or child of the second relationship who would be admissible as a dependant; or

(d) parent or grandparent under the age of 65 if living alone outside the United Kingdom in the most exceptional compassionate circumstances; or

(e) parents or grandparents travelling together who are both under the age of 65 if living in the most exceptional compassionate circumstances; or

(f) the son, daughter, sister, brother, uncle or aunt over the age of 18 if living alone outside the United Kingdom in the most exceptional compassionate circumstances; and

(ii) is joining or accompanying a person who is present and settled in the United Kingdom or who is on the same occasion being admitted for settlement; and

(iii) is financially wholly or mainly dependent on the relative present and settled in the United Kingdom; and

(iv) can, and will, be accommodated adequately, together with any dependants, without recourse to public funds, in accommodation which the sponsor owns or occupies exclusively; and

(iva) can, and will, be maintained adequately, together with any dependants, without recourse to public funds; and

(v) has no other close relatives in his own country to whom he could turn for financial support; and

(vi) if seeking leave to enter, holds a valid United Kingdom entry clearance for entry in this capacity; *and*

(vii) does not have one or more unspent convictions within the meaning of the Rehabilitation of Offenders Act 1974.

Indefinite leave to enter or remain as the parent, grandparent or other dependent relative of a person present and settled in the United Kingdom

318. Indefinite leave to enter the United Kingdom as the parent, grandparent or other dependent relative of a person present and settled in the United Kingdom may be granted provided a valid United Kingdom entry clearance for entry in this capacity is produced to the Immigration Officer on arrival. Indefinite leave to remain in the United Kingdom as the parent, grandparent or other dependent relative of a person present and settled in the United Kingdom may be granted provided the Secretary of State is satisfied that each of the requirements of paragraph 317(i)–(v) is met.

Refusal of indefinite leave to enter or remain in the United Kingdom as the parent, grandparent or other dependent relative of a person present and settled in the United Kingdom

319. Indefinite leave to enter the United Kingdom as the parent, grandparent or other dependent relative of a person settled in the United Kingdom is to be refused if a valid United Kingdom entry clearance for entry in this capacity is not produced to the Immigration Officer on arrival. Indefinite leave to remain in the United Kingdom as the parent, grandparent or other dependent relative of a person present and settled in the United Kingdom is to be refused if the Secretary of State is not satisfied that each of the requirements of paragraph 317(i)–(v) is met.

Family members of relevant points-based system migrants

Partners of relevant points-based system migrants

319AA. In paragraphs 319A to 319K and Appendix E, 'Relevant Points Based System Migrant' means a migrant granted to leave as a Tier 1 Migrant, a Tier 2 Migrant, a Tier 4 (General) Student or a Tier 5 (Temporary Worker) Migrant.

Purpose

319A. This route is for the spouse, civil partner, unmarried or same-sex partner of a Relevant Points Based System Migrant (Partner of a Relevant Points Based System Migrant). Paragraphs 277 to 280 of these Rules apply to spouses or civil partners of Relevant Points Based System Migrant; paragraph 277 of these Rules applies to civil partners of Relevant Points Based System Migrant; and paragraph 295AA of these Rules applies to unmarried and same-sex partners of Relevant Points Based System Migrant

Entry to the UK

319B. (a) Subject to paragraph (b), all migrants wishing to enter as the Partner of a relevant Points Based System Migrant must have a valid entry clearance for entry under this route. If they do not have a valid entry clearance, entry will be refused.

(b) A Migrant arriving in the UK and wishing to enter as a partner of a Tier 5 (Temporary Worker) Migrant, who does not have a valid entry clearance will not be refused entry if the following conditions are met:

(i) the migrant wishing to enter as partner is not a visa national,

(ii) the migrant wishing to enter as a Partner is accompanying an applicant who at the same time is being granted leave to enter under paragraph 245ZN(b), and

(iii) the migrant wishing to enter as a Partner meets the requirements of entry clearance in paragraph 319C.

Requirements for entry clearance or leave to remain

319C. To qualify for entry clearance or leave to remain as the Partner of a Relevant Points Based System Migrant, an applicant must meet the requirements listed below. If the applicant meets these requirements, entry clearance or leave to remain will be granted. If the applicant does not meet these requirements, the application will be refused.

Requirements:

(a) The applicant must not fall for refusal under the general grounds for refusal, and if applying for leave to remain, must not be an illegal entrant.

(b) The applicant must be the spouse or civil partner, unmarried or same-sex partner of a person who:

(i) has valid leave to enter or remain as a Relevant Points Based System Migrant, or

(ii) is, at the same time, being granted entry clearance or leave to remain as a Relevant Points Based System Migrant.

(c) An applicant who is the unmarried or same-sex partner of a Relevant Points Based System Migrant must also meet the following requirements:

(i) any previous marriage or civil partnership or similar relationship by the applicant or the Relevant Points Based System Migrant with another person must have permanently broken down,

(ii) the applicant and the Relevant Points Based System Migrant must not be so closely related that they would be prohibited from marrying each other in the UK, and

(iii) the applicant and the Relevant Points Based System Migrant must have been living together in a relationship similar to marriage or civil partnership for a period of at least 2 years.

(d) The marriage or civil partnership, or relationship similar to marriage or civil partnership, must be subsisting at the time the application is made.

(e) The applicant and the Relevant Points Based System Migrant must intend to live with the other as their spouse or civil partner, unmarried or same-sex partner throughout the applicants stay in the UK.

(f) The applicant must not intend to stay in the UK beyond any period of leave granted to the Relevant Points Based System Migrant .

(g) Unless the Relevant Points Based System Migrant is a Tier 1 (Investor) Migrant, there must be a sufficient level of funds available to the applicant, as set out in Appendix E.

(h) An applicant who is applying for leave to remain, must have, or have last been granted, leave:

(i) as the Partner of a Relevant Points Based System Migrant,

(ii) as the spouse or civil partner, unmarried or same-sex partner of a person with leave under another category of these Rules who has since been granted, or is, at the same time, being granted leave to remain as a Relevant Points Based System Migrant, or

(iii) in any other category of these Rules, provided the Relevant Points Based System Migrant has, or is being granted, leave to remain as a Tier 5 (Temporary Worker) Migrant in the creative and sporting subcategory on the basis of having met the requirement at paragraph 245ZQ(b)(ii).

(i) If the Relevant Points Based System Migrant is a Tier 4 (General) Student,

(1) the Relevant Points Based System Migrant must be applying for a course of study of more than six months duration and must have or have last had entry clearance, leave to enter or leave to remain as a Tier 4 (General) Student or Student for a course of more than six months duration within the three months immediately preceding the date of the application; and

(2) the Partner must have or have last had entry clearance, leave to enter or leave to remain as the Partner of a Tier 4 (General) Student or Student with leave for a course of more than six months duration within the three months immediately preceding the date of the application; and

(3) the Relevant Points Based System Migrant and Partner must be applying at the same time; or

(4) the Relevant Points Based System Migrant must be a Government Sponsored student who is applying for or has entry clearance or leave to remain for a course of study that is longer than six months; or

(5) the Relevant Points Based System Migrant must be undertaking a course which is 12 months or longer in duration, and is of post-graduate level study, sponsored by a Sponsor which is a Recognised Body or a body in receipt of funding as a higher education institution from the Department for Employment and Learning in Northern Ireland, the Higher Education Funding Council for England, the Higher Education Funding Council for Wales or the Scottish Funding Council.

Period and conditions of grant

319D. (a) Entry clearance and leave to remain will be granted for a period which expires on the same day as the leave granted to the Relevant Points Based System Migrant.

(b) Entry clearance and leave to remain under this route will be subject to the following conditions:

(i) no recourse to public funds,

(ii) registration with the police, if this is required under paragraph 326 of these Rules,

(iii) no Employment as a Doctor or Dentist in Training, unless the applicant:

(1) has obtained a primary degree in medicine or dentistry at bachelor's level or above from a UK institution that is a UK recognised or listed body, or which holds a sponsor licence under Tier 4 of the Points Based System; or

(2) is applying for leave to remain and has, or has last been granted, entry clearance, leave to enter or leave to remain that was not subject to any condition restricting him from taking employment as a Doctor in Training, and has been employed during that leave as a Doctor in Training; or

(3) is applying for leave to remain and has, or has last been granted, entry clearance, leave to enter or leave to remain that was not subject to any condition restricting him from taking employment as a Dentist in Training, and has been employed during that leave as a Dentist in Training.

(iv) if the Relevant Points Based System Migrant is a Tier 4 (General) Student and the Partner meets the requirements of paragraphs 319C(i)(1),(2) and (3) and:

(1) the Relevant Points Based System Migrant is a Tier 4 (General) Student applying for leave for less than 12 months, no employment, or

(2) the Relevant Points Based System Migrant is a Tier 4 (General) Student who is following a course of below degree level study, no employment.

Requirements for indefinite leave to remain

319E. To qualify for indefinite leave to remain as the Partner of a Relevant Points Based System Migrant, an applicant must meet the requirements listed below. If the applicant meets these requirements, indefinite leave to remain will be granted. If the applicant does not meet these requirements, the application will be refused.

Requirements:

(a) The applicant must not fall for refusal under the general grounds for refusal, and must not be an illegal entrant.

(b) The applicant must be the spouse or civil partner, unmarried or same-sex partner of a person who is, at the same time, being granted indefinite leave to remain as a Relevant Points Based System Migrant .

(c) The applicant must have, or have last been granted, leave as the Partner of the Relevant Points Based System Migrant who is being granted indefinite leave to remain.

(d) The applicant and the Relevant Points Based System Migrant must have been living together in the UK in marriage or civil partnership, or in a relationship similar to marriage or civil partnership, for a period of at least 2 years.

(e) The marriage or civil partnership, or relationship similar to marriage or civil partnership, must be subsisting at the time the application is made.

(f) The applicant and the Relevant Points Based System Migrant must intend to live permanently with the other as their spouse or civil partner, unmarried or same-sex partner.

(g) The applicant must have sufficient knowledge of the English language and sufficient knowledge about life in the United Kingdom, with reference to paragraphs 33B to 33F of these Rules, unless the applicant is aged 65 or over at the time this application is made; and

(h) The applicant does not have one or more unspent convictions within the meaning of the Rehabilitation of Offenders Act 1974.

Children of relevant points-based system migrants

Purpose

319F. This route is for the children of Relevant Points Based System Migrant who are under the age of 18 when they apply to enter under this route. Paragraph 296 of these Rules applies to children of Relevant Points Based System Migrants.

Entry to the UK

319G. (a) Subject to paragraph (b), all migrants wishing to enter as the Child of a relevant Points Based System Migrant must have a valid entry clearance for entry under this route. If they do not have a valid entry clearance, entry will be refused.

(b) A Migrant arriving in the UK and wishing to enter as a child of a Tier 5 (Temporary Worker) Migrant, who does not have a valid entry clearance will not be refused entry if the following conditions are met:

(i) the migrant wishing to enter as child is not a visa national,

(ii) the migrant wishing to enter as a child is accompanying an applicant who at the same time is being granted leave to enter under paragraph 245ZN(b), and

(iii) the migrant wishing to enter as a Child meets the requirements of entry clearance in paragraph 319H.

Requirements for entry clearance or leave to remain

319H. To qualify for entry clearance or leave to remain under this route, an applicant must meet the requirements listed below. If the applicant meets these requirements, entry clearance or leave to remain will be granted. If the applicant does not meet these requirements, the application will be refused.

Requirements:

(a) The applicant must not fall for refusal under the general grounds for refusal, and if applying for leave to remain, must not be an illegal entrant.

(b) The applicant must be the child of a parent who:

(i) has valid leave to enter or remain as a Relevant Points Based System Migrant, or

(ii) is, at the same time, being granted entry clearance or leave to remain as a Relevant Points Based System Migrant.

(c) The applicant must be under the age of 18 on the date the application is made, or if over 18 and applying for leave to remain, must have, or have last been granted, leave as the child of a **Relevant Points Based System Migrant** or as the child of the parent who had leave under another category of these Rules and who has since been granted, or, is at the same time being granted, leave to remain as a Relevant Points Based System Migrant.

(d) The applicant must not be married or in a civil partnership, must not have formed an independent family unit, and must not be leading an independent life.

(e) The applicant must not intend to stay in the UK beyond any period of leave granted to the Relevant Points Based System Migrant parent.

(f) Both of the applicant's parents must either be lawfully present in the UK, or being granted entry clearance or leave to remain at the same time as the applicant, unless:

(i) The Relevant Points Based System Migrantis the applicant's sole surviving parent, or

(ii) The Relevant Points Based System Migrant parent has and has had sole responsibility for the applicant's upbringing, or

(iii) there are serious or compelling family or other considerations which would make it desirable not to refuse the application and suitable arrangements have been made in the UK for the applicant's care.

(g) Unless the Relevant Points Based System Migrant is a Relevant Points Based System (Investor) Migrant, there must be a sufficient level of funds available to the applicant, as set out in Appendix E.

(h) an applicant who is applying for leave to remain must have, or have last been granted leave as the child of a parent who had leave under any category of these Rules.

(i) If the Relevant Points Based System Migrant is a Tier 4 (General) Student,

(1) the Relevant Points Based System Migrant must be applying for a course of study of more than six months duration and must have or have last had entry clearance, leave to enter or leave to remain as a Tier 4 (General) Student or Student for a course of more than six months duration within the three months immediately preceding the date of the application; and

(2) the Child must have or last have had entry clearance, leave to enter or leave to remain as the Child of a Tier 4 (General) Student or Student with leave for a course of more than six months duration within the three months immediately preceding the date of the application; and

(3) the Relevant Points Based System Migrant and Child must be applying at the same time; or

(4) the Relevant Points Based System Migrant must be a Government Sponsored student who is applying for or has entry clearance or leave to remain for a course of study that is longer than six months; or

(5) the Relevant Points Based System Migrant must be undertaking a course which is 12 months or longer in duration, and is of post-graduate level study, sponsored by a Sponsor which is a Recognised Body or a body in receipt of funding as a higher education institution from the Department for Employment and Learning in Northern Ireland, the Higher Education Funding Council for England, the Higher Education Funding Council for Wales or the Scottish Funding Council.

(j) A Child whose parent is a Relevant Points Based System Migrant, who is a Tier 4 (General) Student or Student, and who does not otherwise meet the requirements of paragraph 319H(i):

(1) must have been born during the Relevant Points Based System Migrant's most recent grant of entry clearance, leave to enter or leave to remain as a Tier 4 (General) Student or Student with leave for a course of more than six months duration; or

(2) where the Relevant Points Based System Migrant's most recent grant of entry clearance, leave to enter or leave to remain was to re-sit examinations or repeat a module of a course, must either have been born during a period of leave granted for the purposes of re-sitting examinations or repeating a module of a course or during the Relevant Points Based System Migrant's grant of leave for a course of more than six months, where that course is the same as the one for which the most recent grant of leave was to re-sit examinations or repeat a module; or

(3) must have been born no more than three months after the expiry of that most recent grant of leave; and

(4) must be applying for entry clearance.

Period and conditions of grant

319I. (a) Entry clearance and leave to remain will be granted for a period which expires on the same day as the leave granted to the Relevant Points Based System Migrant parent.

(b) Entry clearance and leave to remain under this route will be subject to the following conditions:

(i) no recourse to public funds,

(ii) registration with the police, if this is required under paragraph 326 of these Rules, and

(iii) if the Relevant Points Based System Migrant is a Tier 4 (General) Student and the Child meets the requirements of paragraphs 319H(i)(1), (2) and (3) or 319H(j) and:

(1) the Relevant Points Based System Migrant is a Tier 4 (General) Student applying for leave for less than 12 months, no employment, or

(2) the Relevant Points Based System Migrant is a Tier 4 (General) Student who is following a course of below degree level study, no employment.

Requirements for indefinite leave to remain

319J. To qualify for indefinite leave to remain under this route, an applicant must meet the requirements listed below. If the applicant meets these requirements, indefinite leave to remain will be granted. If the applicant does not meet these requirements, the application will be refused.

Requirements:

(a) The applicant must not fall for refusal under the general grounds for refusal, and must not be an illegal entrant.

(b) The applicant must be the child of a parent who is, at the same time, being granted indefinite leave to remain as a Points Based System Migrant .

(c) The applicant must have, or have last been granted, leave as the child of the Points Based System Migrant who is being granted indefinite leave to remain.

(d) The applicant must not be married or in a civil partnership, must not have formed an independent family unit, and must not be leading an independent life.

(e) Both of an applicant's parents must either be lawfully present in the UK, or being granted entry clearance, limited leave to remain, or indefinite leave to remain at the same time as the applicant, unless:

(i) The Points Based System Migrant is the applicant's sole surviving parent, or

(ii) The Points Based System Migrant parent has and has had sole responsibility for the applicant's upbringing, or

(iii) there are serious or compelling family or other considerations which would make it desirable not to refuse the application and suitable arrangements have been made for the applicant's care.

(f) The applicant must have sufficient knowledge of the English language and sufficient knowledge about life in the United Kingdom, with reference to paragraphs 33B to 33F of these Rules, unless the applicant is under the age of 18 at the time this application is made; and

(g) The applicant does not have one or more unspent convictions within the meaning of the Rehabilitation of Offenders Act 1974.

Documentary evidence

319K. (a) Where Appendix E of these Rules states that specified documents must be provided, that means documents specified by the Secretary of State in the Points Based system (dependants) Policy Guidance. If the specified documents are not provided, the applicant will not meet the requirement for which the specified documents are required as evidence.

(b) If the Entry Clearance Officer or Secretary of State has reasonable cause to doubt the genuineness of any document submitted by an applicant which is, or which purports to be a specified document under Appendix E of these Rules and, having taken reasonable steps to verify the document, is unable to verify that it is genuine, the document will be discounted for the purposes of this application.

Please note in the printed version of CM5829 these points appear in error numbered as an alternative version of 316D(iii) and (iv).

Other family members of persons with limited leave to enter or remain in the United Kingdom as a refugee or beneficiary of humanitarian protection.

Requirements for leave to enter the United Kingdom as the spouse or civil partner of a person with limited leave to enter or remain in the United Kingdom as a refugee or beneficiary of humanitarian protection.

319L. The requirements to be met by a person seeking leave to enter the United Kingdom as the spouse or civil partner of a person with limited leave to enter or remain in the United Kingdom as a refugee or beneficiary of humanitarian protection, are that:

(i) (a) the applicant is married to or the civil partner of a person who has limited leave to enter or remain in the United Kingdom as a refugee or beneficiary of humanitarian protection granted such status under the immigration rules and the parties are married or have formed a civil partnership after the person granted asylum or humanitarian protection left the country of his former habitual residence in order to seek asylum or humanitarian protection; and

(b) the applicant provides an original English language test certificate in speaking and listening from an English language test provider approved by the Secretary of State for these purposes, which clearly shows the applicant's name and the qualification obtained (which must meet or exceed level A1 of the Common European Framework of Reference) unless:

(i) the applicant is aged 65 or over at the date he makes his application; or

(ii) the Secretary of State or Entry Clearance Officer considers that the applicant has a physical or mental condition that would prevent him from meeting the requirement; or

(iii) the Secretary of State or entry Clearance officer considers there are exceptional compassionate circumstances that would prevent the applicant from meeting the requirement; or

(iv) the applicant is a national of one of the following countries: Antigua and Barbuda; Australia; the Bahamas; Barbados; Belize; Canada; Dominica; Grenada; Guyana; Jamaica; New Zealand; St Kitts and Nevis; St Lucia; St Vincent and the Grenadines; Trinidad and Tobago; USA; or

(v) the applicant has obtained an academic qualification(not a professional or vocational qualification), which is deemed by UK NARIC to meet the recognised standard of a Bachelor's or Masters degree or PhD in the UK, from an educational establishment in one of the following countries: Antigua and Barbuda; Australia; The Bahamas; Barbados; Belize; Dominica; Grenada; Guyana; Ireland; Jamaica; New Zealand; St Kitts and Nevis; St Lucia; St Vincent and The Grenadines; Trinidad and Tobago; the UK; the USA; and provides the specified documents; or

(vi) the applicant has obtained an academic qualification (not a professional or vocational qualification) which is deemed by UK NARIC to meet the recognised standard of a Bachelor's or Masters degree or PhD in the UK, and

(1) provides the specified evidence to show he has the qualification, and

(2) UK NARIC has confirmed that the degree was taught or researched in English, or

(vii) has obtained an academic qualification (not a professional or vocational qualification) which is deemed by UK NARIC to meet the recognised standard of a Bachelor's or Masters degree or PhD in the UK, and provides the specified evidence to show:

(1) he has the qualification, and

(2) that the qualification was taught or researched in English; and

(ii) the parties to the marriage or civil partnership have met; and

(iii) each of the parties intends to live permanently with the other as his or her spouse or civil partner and the marriage or civil partnership is subsisting; and

(iv) there will be adequate accommodation for the parties and any dependants without recourse to public funds in accommodation which they own or occupy exclusively; and

(v) the parties will be able to maintain themselves and any dependants adequately without recourse to public funds; and

(vi) the applicant holds a valid United Kingdom entry clearance for entry in this capacity.

319M. Leave to enter the United Kingdom as the spouse or civil partner of a refugee or beneficiary of humanitarian protection may be granted for 63 months provided the Immigration Officer is satisfied that each of the requirements of paragraph 319l(i)–(vi) are met.

319N. Leave to enter the United Kingdom as the spouse or civil partner of a refugee or beneficiary of humanitarian protection is to be refused if the Immigration Officer is not satisfied that each of the requirements of paragraph 319L(i)–(vi) are met.

Requirements for leave to enter the United Kingdom as the unmarried or same-sex partner of a person with limited leave to enter or remain in the United Kingdom as a refugee or beneficiary of humanitarian protection.

319O. The requirements to be met by a person seeking leave to enter the United Kingdom as the unmarried or same-sex partner of a person with limited leave to enter or remain in the United Kingdom as a refugee or beneficiary of humanitarian protection, are that:

(i) (a) the applicant is the unmarried or same-sex partner of a person who has limited leave to enter or remain in the United Kingdom as a refugee or beneficiary of humanitarian protection granted such status under the immigration rules, and the parties have been living together in a relationship akin to either a marriage or civil partnership subsisting for two years or more after the person granted asylum or humanitarian protection left the country of his former habitual residence in order to seek asylum or humanitarian protection; and

(b) the applicant provides an original English language test certificate in speaking and listening from an English language test provider approved by the Secretary of State for these purposes, which clearly shows the applicant's name and the qualification obtained (which must meet or exceed level A1 of the Common European Framework of Reference) unless:

(i) the applicant is aged 65 or over at the time he makes his application;

(ii) the Secretary of State or entry Clearance officer considers that the applicant has a physical or mental condition that would prevent him from meeting the requirement;

(iii) the Secretary of State or Entry Clearance Officer considers there are exceptional compassionate circumstances that would prevent the applicant from meeting the requirement;

(iv) the applicant is a national of one of the following countries: Antigua and Barbuda; Australia; the Bahamas; Barbados; Belize; Canada; Dominica; Grenada; Guyana; Jamaica; New Zealand; St Kitts and Nevis; St Lucia; St Vincent and the Grenadines; Trinidad and Tobago; USA;

(v) the applicant has obtained an academic qualification(not a professional or vocational qualification), which is deemed by UK NARIC to meet the recognised standard of a Bachelor's or Masters degree or PhD in the UK, from an educational establishment in one of the following countries: Antigua and Barbuda; Australia; The Bahamas; Barbados; Belize; Dominica; Grenada; Guyana; Ireland; Jamaica; New Zealand; St Kitts and Nevis; St Lucia; St Vincent and The Grenadines; Trinidad and Tobago; the UK; the USA; and provides the specified documents; or

(vi) the applicant has obtained an academic qualification (not a professional or vocational qualification) which is deemed by UK NARIC to meet the recognised standard of a Bachelor's or Masters degree or PhD in the UK, and

(1) provides the specified evidence to show he has the qualification, and

(2) UK NARIC has confirmed that the degree was taught or researched in English, or

(vii) has obtained an academic qualification (not a professional or vocational qualification) which is deemed by UK NARIC to meet the recognised standard of a Bachelor's or Masters degree or PhD in the UK, and provides the specified evidence to show:

(1) he has the qualification, and

(2) that the qualification was taught or researched in English; and

(ii) any previous marriage or civil partnership (or similar relationship) by either partner has permanently broken down; and

(iii) the parties are not involved in a consanguineous relationship with one another; and

(iv) there will be adequate accommodation for the parties and any dependants without recourse to public funds in accommodation which they own or occupy exclusively; and

(v) the parties will be able to maintain themselves and any dependants adequately without recourse to public funds; and

(vi) the parties intend to live together permanently; and

(vii) the applicant holds a valid United Kingdom entry clearance for entry in this capacity.

319P. Leave to enter the United Kingdom as the unmarried or same-sex partner of a refugee or beneficiary of humanitarian protection may be granted for 63 months provided the Immigration Officer is satisfied that each of the requirements of paragraph 319O(i)–(vii) are met.

319Q. Leave to enter the United Kingdom as the unmarried or same-sex partner of a refugee or beneficiary of humanitatrian protection is to be refused if the Immigration Officer is not satisfied that each of the requirements of paragraph 319O(i)–(vii) are met.

Requirements for leave to enter the United Kingdom as the child of a parent or parents given limited leave to enter or remain in the United Kingdom as a refugee or beneficiary of humanitarian protection

319R. The requirements to be met by a person seeking leave to enter the United Kingdom as the child of a parent or parents given limited leave to enter or remain in the United Kingdom as a refugee or beneficiary of humanitarian protection, are that the applicant:

(i) is the child of a parent or parents granted limited leave to enter or remain as a refugee or beneficiary of humanitarian protection granted as such under the immigration rules; and

(ii) is under the age of 18, and

(iii) is not leading an independent life, is unmarried, is not in a civil partnership, and has not formed an independent family unit; and

(iv) was conceived after the person granted asylum or humanitarian protection left the country of his habitual residence in order to seek asylum in the UK; and

(v) can, and will, be accommodated adequately by the parent or parents the child is seeking to join without recourse to public funds in accommodation which the parent or parents the child is seeking to join, own or occupy exclusively; and

(vi) can, and will, be maintained adequately by the parent or parents the child is seeking to join, without recourse to public funds; and

(vii) if seeking leave to enter, holds a valid United Kingdom entry clearance for entry in this capacity.

319S. Limited leave to enter the United Kingdom as the child of a refugee or beneficiary of humanitarian protection may be granted for 63 months provided the Immigration Officer is satisfied that each of the requirements in paragraph 319R(i)–(vii) are met.

319T. Limited leave to enter the United Kingdom as the child of a refugee or beneficiary humanitarian protection is to be refused if the Immigration Officer is not satisfied that each of the requirements in paragraph 319R(i)–(vii) are met.

Requirements for indefinite leave to remain in the United Kingdom as the spouse or civil partner, unmarried or same-sex partner or child of a refugee or beneficiary of humanitatrian protection present and settled in the United Kingdom

319U. To qualify for indefinite leave to remain in the UK, an applicant must meet the requirements set out in paragraph 287 if the applicant is a spouse or civil partner, paragraph 295G if they are an unmarried or same-sex partner, or 298 if the applicant is a child and the sponsor must be present and settled in the United Kingdom at the time the application is made. if an applicant meets the requirements as set out in the relevant paragraphs, indefinite leave to remain will be granted. if the applicant does not meet these requirements, the application will be refused.

Parents, grandparents and other dependent relatives of persons with limited leave to enter or remain in the United Kingdom as a refugee or beneficiary of humanitarian protection

Requirements for leave to enter or remain in the United Kingdom as the parent, grandparent or other dependent relative of a person with limited leave to enter or remain in the United Kingdom as a refugee or beneficiary of humanitarian protection

319V. The requirements to be met by a person seeking leave to enter or remain in the United Kingdom as the parent, grandparent or other dependent relative of a person with limited leave to enter or remain in the United Kingdom as a refugee or beneficiary of humanitarian protection are that the person:

(i) is related to a refugee or beneficiary of humanitarian protection with limited leave to enter or remain in the United Kingdom in one of the following ways:

(a) parent or grandparent who is divorced, widowed, single or separated aged 65 years or over; or

(b) parents or grandparents travelling together of whom at least one is aged 65 or over; or

(c) a parent or grandparent aged 65 or over who has entered into a second relationship of marriage or civil partnership but cannot look to the spouse, civil partner or children of that second relationship for financial support; and where the person with limited leave to enter or remain in the United Kingdom is able and willing to maintain the parent or grandparent and any spouse or civil partner or child of the second relationship who would be admissible as a dependant; or

(d) a parent or grandparent under the age of 65 if living alone outside the United Kingdom in the most exceptional compassionate circumstances; or

(e) parents or grandparents travelling together who are both under the age of 65 if living in the most exceptional compassionate circumstances; or

(f) the son, daughter, sister, brother, uncle or aunt over the age of 18 if living alone outside the United Kingdom in the most exceptional compassionate circumstances; and

(ii) is joining a refugee or beneficiary of humanitarian protection with limited leave to enter or remain in the United Kingdom; and

(iii) is financially wholly or mainly dependent on the relative who has limited leave to enter or remain as a refugee or beneficiary of humanitarian protection in the United Kingdom; and

(iv) can, and will, be accommodated adequately, together with any dependants, without recourse to public funds, in accommodation which the sponsor owns or occupies exclusively; and

(v) can, and will, be maintained adequately, together with any dependants, without recourse to public funds; and

(vi) has no other close relatives in his own country to whom he could turn for financial support; and

(vii) if seeking leave to enter, holds a valid United Kingdom entry clearance for entry in this capacity or, if seeking leave to remain, holds valid leave to remain in another capacity.

319VA. Limited leave to enter the United Kingdom as the parent, grandparent or other dependent relative of a refugee or beneficiary of humanitarian protection with limited leave to enter or remain in the United Kingdom may be granted for 5 years provided a valid United Kingdom entry clearance for entry in this capacity is produced to the Immigration Officer on arrival. Limited leave to remain in the United Kingdom as the parent, grandparent or other dependent relative of a refugee or beneficiary of humanitarian protection with limited leave to enter or remain in the United Kingdom may be granted provided the Secretary of State is satisfied that each of the requirements of paragraph 319V(i)–(vii) is met.

319VB. Limited leave to enter the United Kingdom as the parent, grandparent or other dependent relative of a refugee or beneficiary of humanitarian protection with limited leave to enter or remain in the United Kingdom is to be refused if a valid United Kingdom entry clearance for entry in this capacity is not produced to the Immigration Officer on arrival. Limited leave to remain in the United Kingdom as the parent, grandparent or other dependent relative of a refugee or beneficiary of humanitarian protection with limited leave to enter or remain in the United Kingdom is to be refused if the Secretary of State is not satisfied that each of the requirements of paragraph 319V(i)–(vii) is met.

Requirements for indefinite leave to remain in the United Kingdom as the parent, grandparent or other dependent relative of a refugee or beneficiary of humanitarian protection who is present and settled in the United Kingdom or of a former refugee or beneficiary humanitarian protection, who is now a British Citizen.

319W. The requirements for indefinite leave to remain in the United Kingdom as the parent, grandparent or other dependent relative of a refugee or beneficiary of humanitarian protection who is now present and settled in the United Kingdom or who is now a British Citizen are that:

(i) the applicant has limited leave to enter or remain in the United Kingdom in accordance with paragraph 319V as a dependent relative of a refugee or beneficiary of humanitarian protection with limited leave to enter or remain in the United Kingdom; and

(ii) the sponsor the applicant was admitted to join is now present and settled in the United Kingdom, or is now a British Citizen; and

(iii) the applicant is financially wholly or mainly dependent on the relative who is present and settled in the United Kingdom; and

(iv) the applicant can, and will, be accommodated adequately, together with any dependants, without recourse to public funds, in accommodation which the sponsor owns or occupies exclusively; and

(v) the applicant can, and will, be maintained adequately, together with any dependants, without recourse to public funds; and

(vi) the applicant has no other close relatives in their country of former habitual residence to whom he could turn for financial support; and

(vii) does not have one or more unspent convictions within the meaning of the Rehabilitation of Offenders Act 1974.

319WA. Indefinite leave to remain in the United Kingdom as the parent, grandparent or other dependent relative of a refugee or beneficiary of humanitarian protection who is present and settled in the United Kingdom, or who is now a British Citizen may be granted provided the Secretary of State is satisfied that each of the requirements of paragraph 319W(i)–(vii) is met.

319WB. Indefinite leave to remain in the United Kingdom as the parent, grandparent or other dependent relative of a person present and settled in the United Kingdom is to be refused if the Secretary of State is not satisfied that each of the requirements of paragraph 319W(i)–(vii) is met.

Requirements for leave to enter or remain in the United Kingdom as the child of a relative with limited leave to enter or remain in the United Kingdom as a refugee or beneficiary of humanitarian protection.

319X. The requirements to be met by a person seeking leave to enter or remain in the United Kingdom as the child of a relative with limited leave to remain as a refugee or beneficiary of humanitarian protection in the United Kingdom are that:

(i) the applicant is seeking leave to enter or remain to join a relative with limited leave to enter or remain as a refugee or person with humanitarian protection; and:

(ii) the relative has limited leave in the United Kingdom as a refugee or beneficiary of humanitarian protection and there are serious and compelling family or other considerations which make exclusion of the child undesirable and suitable arrangements have been made for the child's care; and

(iii) the relative is not the parent of the child who is seeking leave to enter or remain in the United Kingdom; and

(iv) the applicant is under the age of 18; and

(v) the applicant is not leading an independent life, is unmarried and is not a civil partner, and has not formed an independent family unit; and

(vi) the applicant can, and will, be accommodated adequately by the relative the child is seeking to join without recourse to public funds in accommodation which the relative in the United Kingdom owns or occupies exclusively; and

(vii) the applicant can, and will, be maintained adequately by the relative in the United Kingdom without recourse to public funds; and

(viii) if seeking leave to enter, the applicant holds a valid United Kingdom entry clearance for entry in this capacity or, if seeking leave to remain, holds valid leave to remain in another capacity.

319XA. Limited leave to enter the United Kingdom as the child of a relative with limited leave to enter or remain as a refugee or beneficiary of humanitarian protection in the United Kingdom may be granted for 5 years provided a valid United Kingdom entry clearance for entry in this capacity is produced to the Immigration Officer on arrival. Limited leave to remain in the United Kingdom as the child of a relative with limited leave to enter or remain as a refugee or beneficiary of humanitarian protection in the United Kingdom may be granted provided the Secretary of State is satisfied that each of the requirements of paragraph 319X(i)–(viii) is met.

319XB. Limited leave to enter the United Kingdom as the child of a relative with limited leave to enter or remain as a refugee or beneficiary of humanitarian protection in the United Kingdom is to be refused if a valid United Kingdom entry clearance for entry in this capacity is not produced to the Immigration Officer on arrival. Limited leave to remain in the United Kingdom as the child of a relative with limited leave to enter or remain as a refugee or beneficiary of humanitarian protection in the United Kingdom is to be refused if the Secretary of State is not satisfied that each of the requirements of paragraph 319X(i)–(viii) is met.

Requirements for indefinite leave to remain in the United Kingdom as the child of a relative who is present and settled in the United Kingdom or as a former refugee or beneficiary of humanitarian protection who is now a British Citizen

319Y. To qualify for indefinite leave to remain as the child of a relative who is present and settled in the United Kingdom, an applicant must meet the requirements set out in paragraph 298.

Part 9 – General grounds for the refusal of entry clearance, leave to enter or variation of leave to enter or remain in the United Kingdom

Refusal of entry clearance or leave to enter the United Kingdom

320. In addition to the grounds of refusal of entry clearance or leave to enter set out in Parts 2–8 of these Rules, and subject to paragraph 321 below, the following grounds for the refusal of entry clearance or leave to enter apply:

Grounds on which entry clearance or leave to enter the United Kingdom is to be refused

(1) the fact that entry is being sought for a purpose not covered by these Rules;

(2) the fact that the person seeking entry to the United Kingdom is currently the subject of a deportation order;

(3) failure by the person seeking entry to the United Kingdom to produce to the Immigration Officer a valid national passport or other document satisfactorily establishing his identity and nationality;

(4) failure to satisfy the Immigration Officer, in the case of a person arriving in the United Kingdom or seeking entry through the Channel Tunnel with the intention of entering any other part of the common travel area, that he is acceptable to the immigration authorities there;

(5) failure, in the case of a visa national, to produce to the Immigration Officer a passport or other identity document endorsed with a valid and current United Kingdom entry clearance issued for the purpose for which entry is sought;

(6) where the Secretary of State has personally directed that the exclusion of a person from the United Kingdom is conducive to the public good;

(7) save in relation to a person settled in the United Kingdom or where the Immigration Officer is satisfied that there are strong compassionate reasons justifying admission, confirmation from the Medical Inspector that, for medical reasons, it is undesirable to admit a person seeking leave to enter the United Kingdom.

(7A) where false representations have been made or false documents or information have been submitted (whether or not material to the application, and whether or not to the applicant's knowledge), or material facts have not been disclosed, in relation to the application.

(7B) subject to paragraph 320(7C), where the applicant has previously breached the UK's immigration laws by:

- (a) Overstaying;
- (b) breaching a condition attached to his leave;
- (c) being an Illegal Entrant;
- (d) using Deception in an application for entry clearance, leave to enter or remain (whether successful or not);

  unless the applicant:

  - (i) Overstayed for 28 days or less and left the UK voluntarily, not at the expense (directly or indirectly) of the Secretary of State;
  - (ii) used Deception in an application for entry clearance more than 10 years ago;
  - (iii) left the UK voluntarily, not at the expense (directly or indirectly) of the Secretary of State, more than 12 months ago;
  - (iv) left the UK voluntarily, at the expense (directly or indirectly) of the Secretary of State, more than 2 years ago; and the date the person left the UK was no more than 6 months after the date on which the person was given notice of the removal decision, or no more than 6 months after the date on which the person no longer had a pending appeal; whichever is the later;
  - (v) left the UK voluntarily, at the expense (directly or indirectly) of the Secretary of State, more than 5 years ago; or
  - (vi) was removed or deported from the UK more than 10 years ago.

  Where more than one breach of the UK's immigration laws has occurred, only the breach which leads to the longest period of absence from the UK will be relevant under this paragraph.

(7C) Paragraph 320(7B) shall not apply in the following circumstances:

- (a) where the applicant is applying as:
  - (i) a spouse, civil partner or unmarried or same-sex partner under paragraphs 281 or 295A,
  - (ii) a fiancé(e) or proposed civil partner under paragraph 290,
  - (iii) a parent, grandparent or other dependent relative under paragraph 317,
  - (iv) a person exercising rights of access to a child under paragraph 246, or

(v) a spouse, civil partner, unmarried or same-sex partner of a refugee or person with Humanitarian Protection under paragraphs 352A, 352AA, 352FA or 352FD; or

(b) where the individual was under the age of 18 at the time of his most recent breach of the UK's immigration laws.

Grounds on which entry clearance or leave to enter the United Kingdom should normally be refused

(8) failure by a person arriving in the United Kingdom to furnish the Immigration Officer with such information as may be required for the purpose of deciding whether he requires leave to enter and, if so, whether and on what terms leave should be given;

(8A) where the person seeking leave is outside the United Kingdom, failure by him to supply any information, documents, copy documents or medical report requested by an Immigration Officer;

(9) failure by a person seeking leave to enter as a returning resident to satisfy the Immigration Officer that he meets the requirements of paragraph 18 of these Rules, or that he seeks leave to enter for the same purpose as that for which his earlier leave was granted;

(10) production by the person seeking leave to enter the United Kingdom of a national passport or travel document issued by a territorial entity or authority which is not recognised by Her Majesty's Government as a state or is not dealt with as a government by them, or which does not accept valid United Kingdom passports for the purpose of its own immigration control; or a passport or travel document which does not comply with international passport practice;

(11) where the applicant has previously contrived in a significant way to frustrate the intentions of these Rules. Guidance will be published giving examples of circumstances in which an applicant who has previously overstayed, breached a condition attached to his leave, been an Illegal Entrant or used Deception in an application for entry clearance, leave to enter or remain (whether successful or not) is likely to be considered as having contrived in a significant way to frustrate the intentions of these Rules.

(11) DELETED

(12) DELETED

(13) failure, except by a person eligible for admission to the United Kingdom for settlement or a spouse or civil partner eligible for admission under paragraph 282, to satisfy the Immigration Officer that he will be admitted to another country after a stay in the United Kingdom;

(14) refusal by a sponsor of a person seeking leave to enter the United Kingdom to give, if requested to do so, an undertaking in writing to be responsible for that person's maintenance and accommodation for the period of any leave granted;

(15) whether or not to the holder's knowledge, the making of false representations or the failure to disclose any material fact for the purpose of obtaining an immigration employment document;

(16) failure, in the case of a child under the age of 18 years seeking leave to enter the United Kingdom otherwise than in conjunction with an application made by his parent(s) or legal guardian to provide the Immigration Officer, if required to do so, with written consent to the application from his parent(s) or legal guardian; save that the requirement as to written consent does not apply in the case of a child seeking admission to the United Kingdom as an asylum seeker;

(17) save in relation to a person settled in the United Kingdom, refusal to undergo a medical examination when required to do so by the Immigration Officer;

(18) save where the Immigration Officer is satisfied that admission would be justified for strong compassionate reasons, conviction in any country including the United Kingdom of an offence which, if committed in the United Kingdom, is punishable with imprisonment for a term of 12 months or any greater punishment or, if committed outside the United Kingdom, would be so punishable if the conduct constituting the offence had occurred in the United Kingdom;

(19) where, from information available to the Immigration Officer, it seems right to refuse leave to enter on the ground that exclusion from the United Kingdom is conducive to the public good; if, for example, in the light of the character, conduct or associations of the person seeking leave to enter it is undesirable to give him leave to enter.

(20) failure by a person seeking entry into the United Kingdom to comply with a requirement relating to the provision of physical data to which he is subject by regulations made under section 126 of the Nationality, Immigration and Asylum Act 2002.

(21) DELETED

(22) Where one or more relevant NHS body has notified the Secretary of State that the person seeking entry or leave to enter has failed to pay a charge or charges with a total value of at least £1000 in accordance with the relevant NHS regulations on charges to overseas visitors.

Refusal of leave to enter in relation to a person in possession of an entry clearance

321. A person seeking leave to enter the United Kingdom who holds an entry clearance which was duly issued to him and is still current may be refused leave to enter only where the Immigration Officer is satisfied that:

(i) False representations were made or false documents or information were submitted (whether or not material to the application, and whether or not to the holder's knowledge), or material facts were not disclosed, in relation to the application for entry clearance; or

(ii) a change of circumstances since it was issued has removed the basis of the holder's claim to admission, except where the change of circumstances amounts solely to the person becoming over age for entry in one of the categories contained in paragraphs 296–316 of these Rules since the issue of the entry clearance; or

(iii) refusal is justified on grounds of restricted return ability; on medical grounds; on grounds of criminal record; because the person seeking leave to enter is the subject of a deportation order or because exclusion would be conducive to the public good.

Grounds on which leave to enter or remain which is in force is to be cancelled at port or while the holder is outside the United Kingdom

321A. The following grounds for the cancellation of a person's leave to enter or remain which is in force on his arrival in, or whilst he is outside, the United Kingdom apply;

(1) there has been such a change in the circumstances of that person's case since the leave was given, that it should be cancelled; or

(2) false representations were made or false documents were submitted (whether or not material to the application, and whether or not to the holder's knowledge), or material facts were not disclosed, in relation to the application for leave; or

(3) save in relation to a person settled in the United Kingdom or where the Immigration Officer or the Secretary of State is satisfied that there are strong compassionate reasons justifying admission, where it is apparent that, for medical reasons, it is undesirable to admit that person to the United Kingdom; or

(4) where the Secretary of State has personally directed that the exclusion of that person from the United Kingdom is conducive to the public good; or

(5) where from information available to the Immigration Officer or the Secretary of State, it seems right to cancel leave on the ground that exclusion from the United Kingdom is conductive to the public good; if, for example, in the light of the character, conduct or associations of that person it is undesirable for him to have leave to enter the United Kingdom; or

(6) where that person is outside the United Kingdom, failure by that person to supply any information, documents, copy documents or medical report requested by an Immigration Officer or the Secretary of State.

Refusal of leave to remain, variation of leave to enter or remain or curtailment of leave

322. In addition to the grounds for refusal of extension of stay set out in Parts 2–8 of these Rules, the following provisions apply in relation to the refusal of an application for leave to remain, variation of leave to enter or remain or, where appropriate, the curtailment of leave:

Grounds on which leave to remain and variation of leave to enter or remain in the United Kingdom are to be refused

(1) the fact that variation of leave to enter or remain is being sought for a purpose not covered by these Rules.

(1A) where false representations have been made or false documents or information have been submitted (whether or not material to the application, and whether or not to the applicant's knowledge), or material facts have not been disclosed, in relation to the application.

Grounds on which leave to remain and variation of leave to enter or remain in the United Kingdom should normally be refused

(2) the making of false representations or the failure to disclose any material fact for the purpose of obtaining leave to enter or a previous variation of leave;

(3) failure to comply with any conditions attached to the grant of leave to enter or remain;

(4) failure by the person concerned to maintain or accommodate himself and any dependants without recourse to public funds;

(5) the undesirability of permitting the person concerned to remain in the United Kingdom in the light of his character, conduct or associations or the fact that he represents a threat to national security;

(6) refusal by a sponsor of the person concerned to give, if requested to do so, an undertaking in writing to be responsible for his maintenance and accommodation in the United Kingdom or failure to honour such an undertaking once given;

(7) failure by the person concerned to honour any declaration or undertaking given orally or in writing as to the intended duration and/or purpose of his stay;

(8) failure, except by a person who qualifies for settlement in the United Kingdom or by the spouse or civil partner of a person settled in the United Kingdom, to satisfy the Secretary of State that he will be returnable to another country if allowed to remain in the United Kingdom for a further period;

(9) failure by an applicant to produce within a reasonable time information, documents or other evidence required by the Secretary of State to establish his claim to remain under these Rules;

(10) failure, without providing a reasonable explanation, to comply with a request made on behalf of the Secretary of State to attend for interview;

(11) failure, in the case of a child under the age of 18 years seeking a variation of his leave to enter or remain in the United Kingdom otherwise than in conjunction with an application by his parent(s) or legal guardian, to provide the Secretary of State, if required to do so, with written consent to the application from his parent(s) or legal guardian; save that the requirement as to written consent does not apply in the case of a child who has been admitted to the United Kingdom as an asylum seeker.

(12) Where one or more relevant NHS body has notified the Secretary of State that the person seeking leave to remain or a variation of leave to enter or remain has failed to pay a charge or charges with a total value of at least £1000 in accordance with the relevant NHS regulations on charges to overseas visitors.

Grounds on which leave to enter or remain may be curtailed

323. A person's leave to enter or remain may be curtailed:

(i) on any of the grounds set out in paragraph 322(2)–(5) above; or

(ii) if he ceases to meet the requirements of the Rules under which his leave to enter or remain was granted; or

(iii) if he is the dependant, or is seeking leave to remain as the dependant, of an asylum applicant whose claim has been refused and whose leave has been curtailed under section 7 of the1993 Act, and he does not qualify for leave to remain in his own right.

(iv) on any of the grounds set out in paragraph 339A(i)–(vi) and paragraph 339G(i)–(vi).

Curtailment of leave or alteration of duration of leave in relation to a Tier 2 Migrant, a Tier 5 Migrant or a Tier 4 Migrant

323A. In addition to the grounds specified in paragraph 323, the leave to enter or remain of a Tier 2 Migrant, a Tier 4 Migrant or a Tier 5 (Temporary Worker) Migrant may be curtailed, or its duration altered, if:

(a) the migrant's Sponsor ceases to have a sponsor licence (for whatever reason)

(b) the migrant's Sponsor transfers the business for which the migrant works or at which the migrant is studying to another person, that person does not have a sponsor licence and that person:

(i) fails to apply for a sponsor licence within 28 days of the date of the transfer of the business,

(ii) applies for a sponsor licence but is refused, or

(iii) applies for a sponsor licence and is granted one, but not in a category that would allow it to issue a Certificate of Sponsorship to the migrant,

(c) the migrant fails to commence, or ceases, working for the Sponsor, or

(d) in the case of a Tier 4 Migrant:

(i) the migrant fails to commence studying with the Sponsor, or

(ii) the migrant studies at an institution other than that which issued the visa letter on the basis of which the migrant's current entry clearance, leave to enter or leave to remain was granted unless the Sponsor is a Highly Trusted Sponsor, the UK Border Agency has granted written permission for the migrant to change to another Sponsor, or the migrant is studying at an institution which is a partner institution of the migrant's sponsor, or

(iii) the migrant ceases studying with the Sponsor.

Curtailment of leave in relation to a Tier 1 (Exceptional Talent) Migrant

323B. In addition to the grounds specified in paragraph 323, the leave to enter or remain of a Tier 1 (Exceptional Talent) Migrant may be curtailed if the Designated Competent Body that endorsed the application which led to the migrant's current grant of leave withdraws its endorsement of the migrant.

Crew members

324. A person who has been given leave to enter to join a ship, aircraft, hovercraft, hydrofoil or international train service as a member of its crew, or a crew member who has been given leave to enter for hospital treatment, repatriation or transfer to another ship, aircraft, hovercraft, hydrofoil or international train service in the United Kingdom, is to be refused leave to remain unless an extension of stay is necessary to fulfil the purpose for which he was given leave to enter or unless he meets the requirements for an extension of stay as a spouse or civil partner in paragraph 284.

Part 10 – Registration with the police

325. For the purposes of paragraph 326, a 'relevant foreign national' is a person aged 16 or over who is:

(i) a national or citizen of a country or territory listed in Appendix 2 to these Rules;

(ii) a stateless person; or

(iii) a person holding a non-national travel document.

326. (1) Subject to sub-paragraph (2) below, a condition requiring registration with the police should normally be imposed on any relevant foreign national who is:

(i) given limited leave to enter the United Kingdom for longer than six months; or

(ii) given limited leave to remain which has the effect of allowing him to remain in the United Kingdom for longer than six months, reckoned from the date of his arrival (whether or not such a condition was imposed when he arrived).

(2) Such a condition should not normally be imposed where the leave is given:

(i) as a seasonal agricultural worker;

(ii) as a Tier 5 (Temporary Worker) Migrant, provided the Certificate of Sponsership Checking System refrence for which points were awarded records that the applicant is being sponsored as an overseas goverment employee or a private servant is a diplomatic household;

(iii) as a Tier 2 (Minister of Religion) Migrant;

(iv) on the basis of marriage to or civil partnership with a person settled in the United Kingdom or as the unmarried or same-sex partner of a person settled in the United Kingdom

(v) as a person exercising access rights to a child resident in the United Kingdom;

(vi) as the parent of a child at school; or

(vii) following the grant of asylum.

(3) Such a condition should also be imposed on any foreign national given limited leave to enter the United Kingdom where, exceptionally, the Immigration Officer considers it necessary to ensure that he complies with the terms of the leave.

Part 11 – Asylum

Procedure

326A. The procedures set out in these Rules shall apply to the consideration of asylum and humanitarian protection.

Definition of asylum applicant

327. Under the Rules an asylum applicant is a person who either;

(a) makes a request to be recognised as a refugee under the Geneva Convention on the basis that it would be contrary to the United Kingdom's obligations under the Geneva Convention for him to be removed from or required to leave the United Kingdom, or

(b) otherwise makes a request for international protection. 'Application for asylum' shall be construed accordingly.

327A. Every person has the right to make an application for asylum on his own behalf.

Applications for asylum

328. All asylum applications will be determined by the Secretary of State in accordance with the Geneva Convention. Every asylum application made by a person at a port or airport in the United Kingdom will be referred by the Immigration Officer for determination by the Secretary of State in accordance with these Rules.

328A. The Secretary of State shall ensure that authorities which are likely to be addressed by someone who wishes to make an application for asylum are able to advise that person how and where such an application may be made.

329. Until an asylum application has been determined by the Secretary of State or the Secretary of State has issued a certificate under Part 2, 3, 4 or 5 of Schedule 3 to the Asylum and Immigration (Treatment of Claimants, etc.) Act 2004 no action will be taken to require the departure of the asylum applicant or his dependants from the United Kingdom.

330. If the Secretary of State decides to grant asylum and the person has not yet been given leave to enter, the Immigration Officer will grant limited leave to enter.

331. If a person seeking leave to enter is refused asylum or their application for asylum is withdrawn or treated as withdrawn under paragraph 333C of these Rules, the Immigration Officer will consider whether or not he is in a position to decide to give or refuse leave to enter without interviewing the person further. If the Immigration Officer decides that a further interview is not required he may serve the notice giving or refusing leave to enter by post. If the Immigration Officer decides that a further interview is required, he will then resume his examination to determine whether or not to grant the person leave to enter under any other provision of these Rules. If the person fails at any time to comply with a requirement to report to an Immigration Officer for examination, the Immigration Officer may direct that the person's examination shall be treated as concluded at that time. The Immigration Officer will then consider any outstanding applications for entry on the basis of any evidence before him.

332. If a person who has been refused leave to enter applies for asylum and that application is refused or withdrawn or treated as withdrawn under paragraph 333C of these Rules, leave to enter will again be refused unless the applicant qualifies for admission under any other provision of these Rules.

333. Written notice of decisions on applications for asylum shall be given in reasonable time. Where the applicant is legally represented, notice may instead be given to the representative. Where the applicant has no legal representative and free legal assistance is not available, he shall be informed of the decision on the application for asylum and, if the application is rejected, how to challenge the decision, in a language that he may reasonably be supposed to understand.

333A. The Secretary of State shall ensure that a decision is taken by him on each application for asylum as soon as possible, without prejudice to an adequate and complete examination.

Where a decision on an application for asylum cannot be taken within six months of the date it was recorded, the Secretary of State shall either:

(a) inform the applicant of the delay; or

(b) if the applicant has made a specific written request for it, provide information on the timeframe within which the decision on his application is to be expected. The provision of such information shall not oblige the Secretary of State to take a decision within the stipulated time-frame.

333B. Applicants for asylum shall be allowed an effective opportunity to consult, at their own expense or at public expense in accordance with provision made for this by the Legal Services Commission or otherwise, a person who is authorised under Part V of the Immigration and Asylum Act 1999 to give immigration advice. This paragraph shall also apply where the Secretary of State is considering revoking a person's refugee status in accordance with these Rules.

Withdrawal of applications

333C. If an application for asylum is withdrawn either explicitly or implicitly, consideration of it may be discontinued. An application will be treated as explicitly withdrawn if the applicant signs the relevant form provided by the Secretary of State. An application may be treated as impliedly withdrawn if an applicant fails to attend the personal interview as provided in paragraph 339NA of these Rules unless the applicant demonstrates within a reasonable time that that failure was due to circumstances beyond his or her control. The Secretary of State will indicate on the applicant's asylum file that the application for asylum has been withdrawn and consideration of it has been discontinued.

Grant of asylum

334. An asylum applicant will be granted asylum in the United Kingdom if the Secretary of State is satisfied that:

(i) he is in the United Kingdom or has arrived at a port of entry in the United Kingdom;

(ii) he is a refugee, as defined in regulation 2 of The Refugee or Person in Need of International Protection (Qualification) Regulations 2006;

(iii) there are no reasonable grounds for regarding him as a danger to the security of the United Kingdom;

(iv) he does not, having been convicted by a final judgment of a particularly serious crime, he does not constitute danger to the community of the United Kingdom; and

(v) refusing his application would result in him being required to go (whether immediately or after the time limited by any existing leave to enter or remain) in breach of the Geneva Convention, to a country in which his life or freedom would threatened on account of his race, religion, nationality, political opinion or membership of a particular social group.

335. If the Secretary of State decides to grant asylum to a person who has been given leave to enter (whether or not the leave has expired) or to a person who has entered without leave, the Secretary of State will vary the existing leave or grant limited leave to remain.

Refusal of asylum

336. An application which does not meet the criteria set out in paragraph 334 will be refused. Where an application for asylum is refused, the reasons in fact and law shall be stated in the decision and information provided in writing on how to challenge the decision.

337. DELETED

338. When a person in the United Kingdom is notified that asylum has been refused he may, if he is liable to removal as an illegal entrant , removal under section 10 of the Immigration and Asylum Act 1999 or to deportation, at the same time be notified of removal directions, served with a notice of intention to make a deportation order, or served with a deportation order, as appropriate.

339. DELETED

Revocation or refusal to renew a grant of asylum

339A. A person's grant of asylum under paragraph 334 will be revoked or not renewed if the Secretary of State is satisfied that:

(i) he has voluntarily re-availed himself of the protection of the country of nationality;

(ii) having lost his nationality, he has voluntarily re-acquired it; or

(iii) he has acquired a new nationality, and enjoys the protection of the country of his new nationality;

(iv) he has voluntarily re-established himself in the country which he left or outside which he remained owing to a fear of persecution;

(v) he can no longer, because the circumstances in connection with which he has been recognised as a refugee have ceased to exist, continue to refuse to avail himself of the protection of the country of nationality;

(vi) being a stateless person with no nationality, he is able, because the circumstances in connection with which he has been recognised a refugee have ceased to exist, to return to the country of former habitual residence;

(vii) he should have been or is excluded from being a refugee in accordance with regulation 7 of The Refugee or Person in Need of International Protection (Qualification) Regulations 2006;

(viii) his misrepresentation or omission or facts, including the use of false documents, were decisive for the grant of asylum;

(ix) there are reasonable grounds for regarding him as a danger to the security of the United Kingdom; or

(x) having been convicted by a final judgment of a particularly serious crime he constitutes danger to the community of the United Kingdom.

In considering (v) and (vi), the Secretary of State shall have regard to whether the change of circumstances is of such a significant and non-temporary nature that the refugee's fear of persecution can no longer be regarded as well-founded.

Where an application for asylum was made on or after the 21st October 2004, the Secretary of State will revoke or refuse to renew a person's grant of asylum where he is satisfied that at least one of the provisions in sub-paragraph(i)–(vi) apply.

339B. When a person's grant of asylum is revoked or not renewed any limited leave which they have may be curtailed.

339BA. Where the Secretary of State is considering revoking refugee status in accordance with these Rules, the person concerned shall be informed in writing that the Secretary of State is reconsidering his qualification for refugee status and the reasons for the reconsideration. That person shall be given the opportunity to submit, in a personal interview or in a written statement, reasons as to why his refugee status should not be revoked. If there is a personal interview, it shall be subject to the safeguards set out in these Rules. However, where a person acquires British citizenship status, his refugee status is automatically revoked in accordance with paragraph 339A(iii) upon acquisition of that status without the need to follow the procedure set out above.

Grant of humanitarian protection

339C. A person will be granted humanitarian protection in the United Kingdom if the Secretary of State is satisfied that:

(i) he is in the United Kingdom or has arrived at a port of entry in the United Kingdom;

(ii) he does not qualify as a refugee as defined in regulation 2 of The Refugee or Person in Need of International Protection (Qualification) Regulations 2006;

(iii) substantial grounds have been shown for believing that the person concerned, if he returned to the country of return, would face a real risk of suffering serious harm and is unable, or, owing to such risk, unwilling to avail himself of the protection of that country; and

(iv) he is not excluded from a grant of humanitarian protection.

Serious harm consists of:

- (i) the death penalty or execution;
- (ii) unlawful killing;
- (iii) torture or inhuman or degrading treatment or punishment of a person in the country of return; or
- (iv) serious and individual threat to a civilian's life or person by reason of indiscriminate violence in situations of international or internal armed conflict.

Exclusion from humanitarian protection

339D. A person is excluded from a grant of humanitarian protection under paragraph 339C(iv) where the Secretary of State is satisfied that:

(i) there are serious reasons for considering that he has committed a crime against peace, a war crime, a crime against humanity, or any other serious crime or instigated or otherwise participated in such crimes;

(ii) there are serious reasons for considering that he is guilty of acts contrary to the purposes and principles of the United Nations or has committed, prepared or instigated such acts or encouraged or induced others to commit, prepare or instigate instigated such acts;

(iii) there are serious reasons for considering that he constitutes a danger to the community or to the security of the United Kingdom; or

(iv) prior to his admission to the United Kingdom the person committed a crime outside the scope of (i) and (ii) that would be punishable by imprisonment were it committed in the United Kingdom and the person left his country of origin solely in order to avoid sanctions resulting from the crime.

339E. If the Secretary of State decides to grant humanitarian protection and the person has not yet been given leave to enter, the Secretary of State or an Immigration Officer will grant limited leave to enter. If the Secretary of State decides to grant humanitarian protection to a person who has been given limited leave to enter (whether or not that leave has expired) or a person who has entered without leave, the Secretary of State will vary the existing leave or grant limited leave to remain.

Refusal of humanitarian protection

339F. Where the criteria set out in paragraph 339C is not met humanitarian protection will be refused.

Revocation of humanitarian protection

339G. A person's humanitarian protection granted under paragraph 339C will be revoked or not renewed if the Secretary of State is satisfied that at least one of the following applies:

(i) the circumstances which led to the grant of humanitarian protection have ceased to exist or have changed to such a degree that such protection is no longer required;

(ii) the person granted humanitarian protection should have been or is excluded from humanitarian protection because there are serious reasons for considering that he has committed a crime against peace, a war crime, a crime against humanity, or any other serious crime or instigated or otherwise participated in such crimes;

(iii) the person granted humanitarian protection should have been or is excluded from humanitarian protection because there are serious reasons for considering that he is guilty of acts contrary to the purposes and principles of the United Nations or has committed, prepared or instigated such acts or encouraged or induced others to commit, prepare or instigate such acts;

(iv) the person granted humanitarian protection should have been or is excluded from humanitarian protection because there are serious reasons for considering that he constitutes a danger to the community or to the security of the United Kingdom;

(v) the person granted humanitarian protection misrepresented or omitted facts, including the use of false documents, which were decisive to the grant of humanitarian protection; or

(vi) the person granted humanitarian protection should have been or is excluded from humanitarian protection because prior to his admission to the United Kingdom the person committed a crime outside the scope of (ii) and (iii) that would be punishable by imprisonment had it been committed in the United Kingdom and the person left his country of origin solely in order to avoid sanctions resulting from the crime.

In applying (i) the Secretary of State shall have regard to whether the change of circumstances is of such a significant and non-temporary nature that the person no longer faces a real risk of serious harm;

339H. When a person's humanitarian protection is revoked or not renewed any limited leave which they have may be curtailed.

Consideration of applications

339HA. The Secretary of State shall ensure that the personnel examining applications for asylum and taking decisions on his behalf have the knowledge with respect to relevant standards applicable in the field of asylum and refugee law.

339I. When the Secretary of State considers a person's asylum claim, eligibility for a grant of humanitarian protection or human rights claim it is the duty of the person to submit to the Secretary of State as soon as possible all material factors needed to substantiate the asylum claim or establish that he is a person eligible for humanitarian protection or substantiate the human rights claim, which the Secretary of State shall assess in cooperation with the person.

The material factors include:

(i) the person's statement on the reasons for making an asylum claim or on eligibility for a grant of humanitarian protection or for making a human rights claim;

(ii) all documentation at the person's disposal regarding the person's age, background (including background details of relevant relatives), identity, nationality(ies), country(ies) and place(s) of previous residence, previous asylum applications, travel routes; and

(iii) identity and travel documents.

339IA. For the purposes of examining individual applications for asylum

(i) information provided in support of an application and the fact that an application has been made shall not be disclosed to the alleged actor(s) of persecution of the applicant, and

(ii) information shall not be obtained from the alleged actor(s) of persecution that would result in their being directly informed that an application for asylum has been made by the applicant in question and would jeopardise the physical integrity of the applicant and his dependants, or the liberty and security of his family members still living in the country of origin.

This paragraph shall also apply where the Secretary of State is considering revoking a person's refugee status in accordance with these Rules.

339J. The assessment by the Secretary of State of an asylum claim, eligibility for a grant of humanitarian protection or a human rights claim will be carried out on an individual, objective and impartial basis. This will include taking into account in particular:

(i) all relevant facts as they relate to the country of origin or country of return at the time of taking a decision on the grant; including laws and regulations of the country of origin or country of return and the manner in which they are applied;

(ii) relevant statements and documentation presented by the person including information on whether the person has been or may be subject to persecution or serious harm;

(iii) the individual position and personal circumstances of the person, including factors such as background, gender and age, so as to assess whether, on the basis of the person's personal circumstances, the acts to which the person has been or could be exposed would amount to persecution or serious harm;

(iv) whether the person's activities since leaving the country of origin or country of return were engaged in for the sole or main purpose of creating the necessary conditions for making an asylum claim or establishing that he is a person eligible for humanitarian protection or a human rights claim, so as to assess whether these activities will expose the person to persecution or serious harm if he returned to that country; and

(v) whether the person could reasonably be expected to avail himself of the protection of another country where he could assert citizenship.

339JA. Reliable and up-to-date information shall be obtained from various sources as to the general situation prevailing in the countries of origin of applicants for asylum and, where necessary, in countries through which they have transited. Such information shall be made available to the personnel responsible for examining applications and taking decisions and may be provided to them in the form of a consolidated country information report.

This paragraph shall also apply where the Secretary of State is considering revoking a person's refugee status in accordance with these Rules.

339K. The fact that a person has already been subject to persecution or serious harm, or to direct threats of such persecution or such harm, will be regarded as a serious indication of the person's well-founded fear of persecution or real risk of suffering serious harm, unless there are good reasons to consider that such persecution or serious harm will not be repeated.

339L. It is the duty of the person to substantiate the asylum claim or establish that he is a person eligible humanitarian protection or substantiate his human rights claim. Where aspects of the person's statements are not supported by documentary or other evidence, those aspects will not need confirmation when all of the following conditions are met:

(i) the person has made a genuine effort to substantiate his asylum claim or establish that he is a person eligible humanitarian protection or substantiate his human rights claim;

(ii) all material factors at the person's disposal have been submitted, and a satisfactory explanation regarding any lack of other relevant material has been given;

(iii) the person's statements are found to be coherent and plausible and do not run counter to available specific and general information relevant to the person's case;

(iv) the person has made an asylum claim or sought to establish that he is a person eligible for humanitarian protection or made a human rights claim at the earliest possible time, unless the person can demonstrate good reason for not having done so; and

(v) the general credibility of the person has been established.

339M. The Secretary of State may consider that a person has not substantiated his asylum claim or established that he is a person eligible for humanitarian protection or substantiated his human rights claim, and thereby reject his application for asylum, determine that he is not eligible for humanitarian protection or reject his human rights claim, if he fails, without reasonable explanation, to make a prompt and full disclosure of material facts, either orally or in writing, or otherwise to assist the Secretary of State in establishing the facts of the case; this includes, for example, failure to report to a designated place to be fingerprinted, failure to complete an asylum questionnaire or failure to comply with a requirement to report to an immigration officer for examination.

339MA. Applications for asylum shall be neither rejected nor excluded from examination on the sole ground that they have not been made as soon as possible.

339N. In determining whether the general credibility of the person has been established the Secretary of State will apply the provisions in s.8 of the Asylum and Immigration (Treatment of Claimants, etc.) Act 2004.

Personal interview

339NA. Before a decision is taken on the application for asylum, the applicant shall be given the opportunity of a personal interview on his application for asylum with a representative of the Secretary of State who is legally competent to conduct such an interview.

The personal interview may be omitted where:

(i) the Secretary of State is able to take a positive decision on the basis of evidence available;

(ii) the Secretary of State has already had a meeting with the applicant for the purpose of assisting him with completing his application and submitting the essential information regarding the application;

(iii) the applicant, in submitting his application and presenting the facts, has only raised issues that are not relevant or of minimal relevance to the examination of whether he is a refugee, as defined in regulation 2 of the Refugee or Person in Need of International Protection (Qualification) Regulations 2006;

(iv) the applicant has made inconsistent, contradictory, improbable or insufficient representations which make his claim clearly unconvincing in relation to his having been the object of persecution;

(v) the applicant has submitted a subsequent application which does not raise any relevant new elements with respect to his particular circumstances or to the situation in his country of origin;

(vi) the applicant is making an application merely in order to delay or frustrate the enforcement of an earlier or imminent decision which would result in his removal; and

(vii) it is not reasonably practicable, in particular where the Secretary of State is of the opinion that the applicant is unfit or unable to be interviewed owing to enduring circumstances beyond his control.

The omission of a personal interview shall not prevent the Secretary of State from taking a decision on the application.

Where the personal interview is omitted, the applicant and dependants shall be given a reasonable opportunity to submit further information.

339NB. (i) The personal interview mentioned in paragraph 339NA above shall normally take place without the presence of the applicant's family members unless the Secretary of State considers it necessary for an appropriate examination to have other family members present.

(ii) The personal interview shall take place under conditions which ensure appropriate confidentiality.

339NC. (i) A written report shall be made of every personal interview containing at least the essential information regarding the asylum application as presented by the applicant in accordance with paragraph 339I of these Rules.

(ii) The Secretary of State shall ensure that the applicant has timely access to the report of the personal interview and that access is possible as soon as necessary for allowing an appeal to be prepared and lodged in due time.

339ND. The Secretary of State shall provide at public expense an interpreter for the purpose of allowing the applicant to submit his case, wherever necessary. The Secretary of State shall select an interpreter who can ensure appropriate communication between the applicant and the representative of the Secretary of State who conducts the interview.

Internal relocation

339O. (i) The Secretary of State will not make:

(a) a grant of asylum if in part of the country of origin a person would not have a well founded fear of being persecuted, and the person can reasonably be expected to stay in that part of the country;

or

(b) a grant of humanitarian protection if in part of the country of return a person would not face a real risk of suffering serious harm, and the person can reasonably be expected to stay in that part of the country.

(ii) In examining whether a part of the country of origin or country of return meets the requirements in (i) the Secretary of State, when making his decision on whether to grant asylum or humanitarian protection, will have regard to the general circumstances prevailing in that part of the country and to the personal circumstances of the person.

(iii) (i) applies notwithstanding technical obstacles to return to the country of origin or country of return

Sur place claims

339P. A person may have a well-founded fear of being persecuted or a real risk of suffering serious harm based on events which have taken place since the person left the country of origin or country of return and/or activates which have been engaged in by a person since he left he country of origin or country of return, in particular where it is established that the activities relied upon constitute the expression and continuation of convictions or orientations held in the country of origin or country of return.

Residence Permits

339Q. (i) The Secretary of State will issue to a person granted asylum in the United Kingdom a United Kingdom Residence Permit (UKRP) as soon as possible after the grant of asylum. The UKRP will be valid for five years and renewable, unless compelling reasons of national security or public order otherwise require or where there are reasonable grounds for considering that the applicant is a danger to the security of the UK or having been convicted by a final judgment of a particularly serious crime, the applicant constitutes a danger to the community of the UK.

(ii) The Secretary of State will issue to a person granted humanitarian protection in the United Kingdom a UKRP as soon as possible after the grant of humanitarian protection. The UKRP will be valid for five years and renewable, unless compelling reasons of national security or public order otherwise require or where there are reasonable grounds for considering that the person granted humanitarian protection is a danger to the security of the UK or having been convicted by a final judgment of a serious crime, this person constitutes a danger to the community of the UK.

(iii) The Secretary of State will issue a UKRP to a family member of a person granted asylum or humanitarian protection where the family member does not qualify for such status. A UKRP will be granted for a period of five years. The UKRP is renewable on the terms set out in (i) and (ii) respectively. 'Family member' for the purposes of this sub-paragraph refers only to those who are treated as dependants for the purposes of paragraph 349.

(iv) The Secretary of State may revoke or refuse to renew a person's UKRP where their grant of asylum or humanitarian protection is revoked under the provisions in the immigration rules.

Consideration of asylum applications and human rights claims

340. DELETED

341. DELETED

342. The actions of anyone acting as an agent of the asylum applicant or human rights claimant may also be taken into account in regard to the matters set out in paragraphs 340 and 341.

343. DELETED

344. DELETED

Travel documents

344A. (i) After having received a complete application for a travel document, the Secretary of State will issue to a person granted asylum in the United Kingdom and their family members travel documents, in the form set out in the Schedule to the Geneva Convention, for the purpose of travel outside the United Kingdom, unless compelling reasons of national security or public order otherwise require.

(ii) After having received a complete application for a travel document, the Secretary of State will issue travel documents to a person granted humanitarian protection in the United Kingdom where that person is unable to obtain a national passport or other identity documents which enable him to travel, unless compelling reasons of national security or public order otherwise require.

(iii) Where the person referred to in (ii) can obtain a national passport or identity documents but has not done so, the Secretary of State will issue that person with a travel document where he can show that he has made reasonable attempts to obtain a national passport or identity document and there are serious humanitarian reasons for travel.

Access to Employment

344B. The Secretary of State will not impose conditions restricting the employment or occupation in the United Kingdom of a person granted asylum or humanitarian protection.

Information

344C. A person who is granted asylum or humanitarian protection will be provided with access to information in a language that they may reasonably be supposed to understand which sets out the rights and obligations relating to that status. The Secretary of State will provide the information as soon as possible after the grant of asylum or humanitarian protection.

Third country cases

345. (1) In a case where the Secretary of State is satisfied that the conditions set out in Paragraphs 4 and 5(1), 9 and 10(1), 14 and 15(1) or 17 of Schedule 3 to the Asylum and Immigration (Treatment of Claimants, etc.) Act 2004 are fulfilled, he will normally decline to examine the asylum application substantively and issue a certificate under Part 2, 3, 4 or 5 of Schedule 3 to the Asylum and Immigration (Treatment of Claimants, etc.) Act 2004 as appropriate.

(2) The Secretary of State shall not issue a certificate under Part 2, 3, 4 or 5 of Schedule 3 to the Asylum and Immigration (Treatment of Claimants, etc.) Act 2004 unless:

(i) the asylum applicant has not arrived in the United Kingdom directly from the country in which he claims to fear persecution and has had an opportunity at the border or within the third country or territory to make contact with the authorities of that third country or territory in order to seek their protection; or

(ii) there is other clear evidence of his admissibility to a third country or territory.

Provided that he is satisfied that a case meets these criteria, the Secretary of State is under no obligation to consult the authorities of the third country or territory before the removal of an asylum applicant to that country or territory.

(2A) Where a certificate is issued under Part 2, 3, 4 or 5 of Schedule 3 to the Asylum and Immigration (Treatment of Claimants, etc.) Act 2004 the asylum applicant shall:

(i) be informed in a language that he may reasonably be expected to understand regarding his removal to a safe third country;

(ii) be provided with a document informing the authorities of the safe third country, in the language of that country, that the asylum application has not been examined in substance by the authorities in the United Kingdom;

(iii) sub-paragraph 345(2A)(ii) shall not apply if removal takes place with reference to the arrangements set out in Regulation (EC) No. 343/2003 (the Dublin Regulation); and

(iv) if an asylum applicant removed under this paragraph is not admitted to the safe third country (not being a country to which the Dublin Regulation applies as specified in paragraph 345(2A)(iii)), subject to determining and resolving the reasons for his nonadmission, the asylum applicant shall be admitted to the asylum procedure in the United Kingdom.

(3) Where a certificate is issued under Part 2, 3, 4 or 5 of Schedule 3 to the Asylum and Immigration (Treatment of Claimants, etc.) Act 2004 in relation to the asylum claim and the person is seeking leave to enter the Immigration Officer will consider whether or not he is in a position to decide to give or refuse leave to enter without interviewing the person further. If the Immigration Officer decides that a further interview is not required he may serve the notice giving or refusing leave to enter by post. If the Immigration Officer decides that a further interview is required, he will then resume his examination to determine whether or not to grant the person leave to enter under any other provision of these Rules. If the person fails at any time to comply with a requirement to report to an Immigration Officer for examination, the Immigration Officer may direct that the person's examination shall be treated as concluded at that time. The Immigration Officer will then consider any outstanding applications for entry on the basis of any evidence before him.

(4) Where a certificate is issued under Part 2, 3, 4 or 5 of Schedule 3 to the Asylum and Immigration (Treatment of Claimants, etc.) Act 2004 the person may, if liable to removal as an illegal entrant, or removal under section 10 of the Immigration and Asylum Act 1999 or to deportation, at the same time be notified of removal directions, served with a notice of intention to make a deportation order, or served with a deportation order, as appropriate.

Previously rejected applications

346. DELETED

347. DELETED

Rights of appeal

348. DELETED

Dependants

349. A spouse, civil partner, unmarried or same-sex partner, or minor child accompanying a principal applicant may be included in his application for asylum as his dependant, provided, in the case of an adult dependant with legal capacity, the dependant consents to being treated as such at the time the application is lodged. A spouse, civil partner, unmarried or same-sex partner or minor child may also claim asylum in his own right. If the principal applicant is granted asylum or humanitarian protection and leave to enter or remain any spouse, civil partner, unmarried or same-sex partner or minor child will be granted leave to enter or remain for the same duration. The case of any dependant who claims asylum in his own right will be also considered individually in accordance with paragraph 334 above. An applicant under this paragraph, including an accompanied child, may be interviewed where he makes a claim as a dependant or in his own right.

If the spouse, civil partner, unmarried or same-sex partner, or minor child in question has a claim in his own right, that claim should be made at the earliest opportunity. Any failure to do so will be taken into account and may damage credibility if no reasonable explanation for it is given. Where an asylum or humanitarian protection application is unsuccessful, at the same time that asylum or humanitarian protection is refused the applicant may be notified of removal directions or served with a notice of the Secretary of State's intention to deport him, as appropriate. In this paragraph and paragraphs 350–352 a child means a person who is under 18 years of age or who, in the absence of documentary evidence establishing age, appears to be under that age. An unmarried or same sex partner for the purposes of this paragraph, is a person who has been living together with the principal applicant in a subsisting relationship akin to marriage or a civil partnership for two years or more.

Unaccompanied children

350. Unaccompanied children may also apply for asylum and, in view of their potential vulnerability, particular priority and care is to be given to the handling of their cases.

351. A person of any age may qualify for refugee status under the Convention and the criteria in paragraph 334 apply to all cases. However, account should be taken of the applicant's maturity and in assessing the claim of a child more weight should be given to objective indications of risk than to the child's state of mind and understanding of his situation. An asylum application made on behalf of a child should not be refused solely because the child is too young to understand his situation or to have formed a well founded fear of persecution. Close attention should be given to the welfare of the child at all times.

352. Any child over the age of 12 who has claimed asylum in his own right shall be interviewed about the substance of his claim unless the child is unfit or unable to be interviewed. When an interview takes place

it shall be conducted in the presence of a parent, guardian, representative or another adult independent of the Secretary of State who has responsibility for the child. The interviewer shall have specialist training in the interviewing of children and have particular regard to the possibility that a child will feel inhibited or alarmed. The child shall be allowed to express himself in his own way and at his own speed. If he appears tired or distressed, the interview will be suspended. The interviewer should then consider whether it would be appropriate for the interview to be resumed the same day or on another day.

352ZA. The Secretary of State shall as soon as possible after an unaccompanied child makes an application for asylum take measures to ensure that a representative represents and/or assists the unaccompanied child with respect to the examination of the application and ensure that the representative is given the opportunity to inform the unaccompanied child about the meaning and possible consequences of the interview and, where appropriate, how to prepare himself for the interview. The representative shall have the right to be present at the interview and ask questions and make comments in the interview, within the framework set by the interviewer.

352ZB. The decision on the application for asylum shall be taken by a person who is trained to deal with asylum claims from children.

352A. The requirements to be met by a person seeking leave to enter or remain in the United Kingdom as the spouse civil partner of a refugee are that:

(i) the applicant is married to or the civil partner of a person who is currently a refugee granted status as such under the immigration rules in the United Kingdom ; and

(ii) the marriage or civil partnership did not take place after the person granted asylum left the country of his former habitual residence in order to seek asylum; an

(iii) the applicant would not be excluded from protection by virtue of article 1F of the United Nations Convention and Protocol relating to the Status of Refugees if he were to seek asylum in his own right; and

(iv) each of the parties intends to live permanently with the other as his or her spouse civil partner and the marriage is subsisting; and

(v) if seeking leave to enter, the applicant holds a valid United Kingdom entry clearance for entry in this capacity.

352AA. The requirements to be met by a person seeking leave to enter or remain in the United Kingdom as the unmarried or the same-sex partner of a refugee are that:

(i) the applicant is the unmarried or same-sex partner of a person who is currently a refugee granted status as such under the immigration rules in the United Kingdom and was granted that status in the UK on or after 9th October 2006; and

(ii) the parties have been living together in a relationship akin to either a marriage or a civil partnership which has subsisted for two years or more; and

(iii) the relationship existed before the person granted asylum left the country of his former habitual residence in order to seek asylum; and

(iv) the applicant would not be excluded from protection by virtue of paragraph 334(iii) or

(v) of these Rules or article 1F of the Geneva Convention if he were to seek asylum in his own right; and

(vi) each of the parties intends to live permanently with the other as his or her unmarried or same-sex partner and the relationship is subsisting; and

(vii) if seeking leave to enter, the applicant holds a valid United Kingdom entry clearance for entry in this capacity.

(viii) the parties are not involved in a consanguineous relationship with one another; and

352B. Limited leave to enter the United Kingdom as the spouse civil partner of a refugee may be granted provided a valid United Kingdom entry clearance for entry in this capacity is produced to the Immigration Officer on arrival. Limited leave to remain in the United Kingdom as the spouse of a refugee may be granted provided the Secretary of State is satisfied that each of the requirements of paragraph 352A(i)–(v) are met.

352BA. Limited leave to enter the United Kingdom as the unmarried or same-sex partner of a refugee may be granted provided a valid United Kingdom entry clearance for entry in this capacity is produced to the Immigration Officer on arrival. Limited leave to remain in the United Kingdom as the unmarried or same sex partner of a refugee may be granted provided the Secretary of State is satisfied that each of the requirements of paragraph 352AA(i)–(vii) are met.

352C. Limited leave to enter the United Kingdom as the spouse civil partner of a refugee is to be refused if a valid United Kingdom entry clearance for entry in this capacity is not produced to the Immigration Officer on arrival. Limited leave to remain as the spouse civil partner of a refugee is to be refused if the Secretary of State is not satisfied that each of the requirements of paragraph 352A(i)–(v) are met.

352CA. Limited leave to enter the United Kingdom as the unmarried or same-sex partner of a refugee is to be refused if a valid United Kingdom entry clearance for entry in this capacity is not produced to the Immigration Officer on arrival. Limited leave to remain as the unmarried or same sex partner of a refugee is to be refused if the Secretary of State is not satisfied that each of the requirements of paragraph 352AA(i)–(vi) are met.

352D. The requirements to be met by a person seeking leave to enter or remain in the United Kingdom in order to join or remain with the parent who is currently a refugee granted status as such under the immigration rules in the United Kingdom are that the applicant:

(i) is the child of a parent who is currently a refugee granted status as such under the immigration rules in the United Kingdom; and

(ii) is under the age of 18, and

(iii) is not leading an independent life, is unmarried and is not a civil partner, and has not formed an independent family unit; and

(iv) was part of the family unit of the person granted asylum at the time that the person granted asylum left the country of his habitual residence in order to seek asylum; and

(v) would not be excluded from protection by virtue of article 1F of the United Nations Convention and Protocol relating to the Status of Refugees if he were to seek asylum in his own right; and

(vi) if seeking leave to enter, holds a valid United Kingdom entry clearance for entry in this capacity.

352E. Limited leave to enter the United Kingdom as the child of a refugee may be granted provided a valid United Kingdom entry clearance for entry in this capacity is produced to the Immigration Officer on arrival. Limited leave to remain in the United Kingdom as the child of a refugee may be granted provided the Secretary of State is satisfied that each of the requirements of paragraph 352D(i)–(v) are met.

352F. Limited leave to enter the United Kingdom as the child of a refugee is to be refused if a valid United Kingdom entry clearance for entry in this capacity is not produced to the Immigration Officer on arrival. Limited leave to remain as the child of a refugee is to be refused if the Secretary of State is not satisfied that each of the requirements of paragraph 352D(i)–(v) are met.

352FA. The requirements to be met by a person seeking leave to enter or remain in the United Kingdom as the spouse or civil partner of a person who is currently a beneficiary of humanitarian protection granted under the immigration rules in the United Kingdom and was granted that status on or after 30 August 2005 are that:

(i) the applicant is married to or the civil partner of a person who is currently a beneficiary of humanitarian protection granted under the immigration rules and was granted that status on or after 30 August 2005; and

(ii) the marriage or civil partnership did not take place after the person granted humanitarian protection left the country of his former habitual residence in order to seek asylum in the UK; and

(iii) the applicant would not be excluded from a grant of humanitarian protection for any of the reasons in paragraph 339D; and

(iv) each of the parties intend to live permanently with the other as his or her spouse or civil partner and the marriage or civil partnership is subsisting; and

(v) if seeking leave to enter, the applicant holds a valid United Kingdom entry clearance for entry in this capacity.

352FB. Limited leave to enter the United Kingdom as the spouse or civil partner of a person granted humanitarian protection may be granted provided a valid United Kingdom entry clearance for entry in this capacity is produced to the Immigration Officer on arrival. Limited leave to remain in the United Kingdom as the spouse or civil partner of a person granted humanitarian protection may be granted provided the Secretary of State is satisfied that each of the requirements in sub paragraphs 352FA(i)–(iv) are met.

352FC. Limited leave to enter the United Kingdom as the spouse or civil partner of a person granted humanitarian protection is to be refused if a valid United Kingdom entry clearance for entry in this capacity is not produced to the Immigration Officer on arrival. Limited leave to remain as the spouse or civil partner of a person granted humanitarian protection is to be refused if the Secretary of State is not satisfied that each of the requirements in sub paragraphs 352FA(i)–(iv) are met.

352FD. The requirements to be met by a person seeking leave to enter or remain in the United Kingdom as the unmarried or same-sex partner of a person who is currently a beneficiary of humanitarian protection granted under the immigration rules in the United Kingdom are that:

(i) the applicant is the unmarried or same-sex partner of a person who is currently a beneficiary of humanitarian protection granted under the immigration rules and was granted that status on or after 9th October 2006; and

(ii) the parties have been living together in a relationship akin to either a marriage or a civil partnership which has subsisted for two years or more; and

(iii) the relationship existed before the person granted humanitarian protection left the country of his former habitual residence in order to seek asylum; and

(iv) the applicant would not be excluded from a grant of humanitarian protection for any of the reasons in paragraph 339D; and

(v) each of the parties intends to live permanently with the other as his or her unmarried or same-sex partner and the relationship is subsisting; and

(vi) the parties are not involved in a consanguineous relationship with one another; and

(vii) if seeking leave to enter, the applicant holds a valid United Kingdom entry clearance for entry in this capacity.

352FE. Limited leave to enter the United Kingdom as the unmarried or same-sex partner of a person granted humanitarian protection may be granted provided a valid United Kingdom entry clearance for entry in this capacity is produced to the Immigration Officer on arrival. Limited leave to remain in the United Kingdom as the unmarried or same sex partner of a person granted humanitarian protection may be granted provided the Secretary of State is satisfied that each of the requirements in subparagraphs 352FD(i)–(vi) are met.

352FF. Limited leave to enter the United Kingdom as the unmarried or same-sex partner of a person granted humanitarian protection is to be refused if a valid United Kingdom entry clearance for entry in this capacity is not produced to the Immigration Officer on arrival. Limited leave to remain as the unmarried or same sex partner of a person granted humanitarian protection is to be refused if the Secretary of State is not satisfied that each of the requirements in sub paragraphs 352FD(i)–(vi) are met.

352FG. The requirements to be met by a person seeking leave to enter or remain in the United Kingdom in order to join or remain with their parent who is currently a beneficiary of humanitarian protection granted under the immigration rules in the United Kingdom and was granted that status on or after 30 August 2005 are that the applicant:

(i) is the child of a parent who is currently a beneficiary of humanitarian protection granted under the immigration rules in the United Kingdom and was granted that status on or after 30 August 2005; and

(ii) is under the age of 18, and

(iii) is not leading an independent life, is unmarried or is not in a civil partnership, and has not formed an independent family unit; and

(iv) was part of the family unit of the person granted humanitarian protection at the time that the person granted humanitarian protection left the country of his habitual residence in order to seek asylum in the UK; and

(v) would not be excluded from a grant of humanitarian protection for any of the reasons in paragraph 339D; and

(vi) if seeking leave to enter, holds a valid United Kingdom entry clearance for entry in this capacity.

352FH. Limited leave to enter the United Kingdom as the child of a person granted humanitarian protection may be granted provided a valid United Kingdom entry clearance for entry in this capacity is produced to the Immigration Officer on arrival. Limited leave to remain in the United Kingdom as the child of a person granted humanitarian protection may be granted provided the Secretary of State is satisfied that each of the requirements in sub paragraphs 352FG(i)–(v) are met.

352FI. Limited leave to enter the United Kingdom as the child of a person granted humanitarian protection is to be refused if a valid United Kingdom entry clearance for entry in this capacity is not produced to the Immigration Officer on arrival. Limited leave to remain as the child of a person granted humanitarian protection is to be refused if the Secretary of State is not satisfied that each of the requirements in sub paragraphs 352FG(i)–(v) are met.

352FJ. Nothing in paragraphs 352A–352FI shall allow a person to be granted leave to enter or remain in the United Kingdom as the spouse or civil partner, unmarried or same sex partner or child of a refugee, or of a person granted humanitarian protection under the immigration rules in the United Kingdom on or after 30 August 2005, if the refugee or, as the case may be, person granted humanitarian protection, is a British Citizen.

Interpretation

352G. For the purposes of this Part:

(a) 'Geneva Convention' means the United Nations Convention and Protocol relating to the Status of Refugees;

(b) 'Country of return' means a country or territory listed in paragraph 8(c) of Schedule 2 of the Immigration Act 1971;

(c) 'Country of origin' means the country or countries of nationality or, for a stateless person, or former habitual residence.

Part 11A – Temporary Protection

Definition of Temporary Protection Directive

354. For the purposes of paragraphs 355 to 356B, 'Temporary Protection Directive' means Council Directive 2001/55/EC of 20 July 2001 regarding the giving of temporary protection by Member States in the event of a mass influx of displaced persons.

Grant of temporary protection

355. An applicant for temporary protection will be granted temporary protection if the Secretary of State is satisfied that:

(i) the applicant is in the United Kingdom or has arrived at a port of entry in the United Kingdom; and

(ii) the applicant is a person entitled to temporary protection as defined by, and in accordance with, the Temporary Protection Directive; and

(iii) the applicant does not hold an extant grant of temporary protection entitling him to reside in another Member State of the European Union. This requirement is subject to the provisions relating to dependants set out in paragraphs 356 to 356B and to any agreement to the contrary with the Member State in question; and

(iv) the applicant is not excluded from temporary protection under the provisions in paragraph 355A.

355A. An applicant or a dependant may be excluded from temporary protection if:

(i) there are serious reasons for considering that:

(a) he has committed a crime against peace, a war crime, or a crime against humanity, as defined in the international instruments drawn up to make provision in respect of such crimes; or

(b) he has committed a serious non-political crime outside the United Kingdom prior to his application for temporary protection; or

(c) he has committed acts contrary to the purposes and principles of the United Nations, or

(ii) there are reasonable grounds for regarding the applicant as a danger to the security of the United Kingdom or, having been convicted by a final judgment of a particularly serious crime, to be a danger to the community of the United Kingdom.

Consideration under this paragraph shall be based solely on the personal conduct of the applicant concerned. Exclusion decisions or measures shall be based on the principle of proportionality.

355B. If temporary protection is granted to a person who has been given leave to enter or remain (whether or not the leave has expired) or to a person who has entered without leave, the Secretary of State will vary the existing leave or grant limited leave to remain.

355C. A person to whom temporary protection is granted will be granted limited leave to enter or remain, which is not to be subject to a condition prohibiting employment, for a period not exceeding 12 months.

On the expiry of this period, he will be entitled to apply for an extension of this limited leave for successive periods of 6 months thereafter.

355D. A person to whom temporary protection is granted will be permitted to return to the United Kingdom from another Member State of the European Union during the period of a mass influx of displaced persons as established by the Council of the European Union pursuant to Article 5 of the Temporary Protection Directive.

355E. A person to whom temporary protection is granted will be provided with a document in a language likely to be understood by him in which the provisions relating to temporary protection and which are relevant to him are set out. A person with temporary protection will also be provided with a document setting out his temporary protection status.

355F. The Secretary of State will establish and maintain a register of those granted temporary protection. The register will record the name, nationality, date and place of birth and marital status of those granted temporary protection and their family relationship to any other person who has been granted temporary protection.

355G. If a person who makes an asylum application is also eligible for temporary protection, the Secretary of State may decide not to consider the asylum application until the applicant ceases to be entitled to temporary protection.

Dependants

356. In this part:

'dependant' means a family member or a close relative.

'family member' means:

(i) the spouse or civil partner of an applicant for, or a person who has been granted, temporary protection; or

(ii) the unmarried or same-sex partner of an applicant for, or a person who has been granted, temporary protection where the parties have been living together in a relationship akin to marriage which has subsisted for 2 years or more; or

(iii) the minor child (who is unmarried and not a civil partner); of an applicant for, or a person who has been granted, temporary protection or his spouse,

who lived with the principal applicant as part of the family unit in the country of origin immediately prior to the mass influx.

'close relative' means:

(i) the adult child (who is unmarried and not a civil partner), parent or grandparent of an applicant for, or person who has been granted, temporary protection; or

(ii) sibling (who is unmarried and not a civil partner or the uncle or aunt of an applicant for, or person who has been granted, temporary protection, who lived with the principal applicant as part of the family unit in the country of origin immediately prior to the mass influx and was wholly or mainly dependent upon the principal applicant at that time, and would face extreme hardship if reunification with the principal applicant did not take place.

356A. A dependant may apply for temporary protection. Where the dependant falls within paragraph 356 and does not fall to be excluded under paragraph 355A, he will be granted temporary protection for the same duration and under the same conditions as the principal applicant.

356B. When considering any application by a dependant child, the Secretary of State shall take into consideration the best interests of that child.

Part 11B – Asylum

Reception Conditions for non-EU asylum applicants

357. Part 11B only applies to asylum applicants (within the meaning of these Rules) who are not nationals of a member State.

Information to be provided to asylum applicants

357A. The Secretary of State shall inform asylum applicants in a language they may reasonably be supposed to understand and within a reasonable time after their claim for asylum has been recorded of the procedure to be followed, their rights and obligations during the procedure, and the possible consequences of non-compliance and non-co-operation. They shall be informed of the likely timeframe for consideration of the application and the means at their disposal for submitting all relevant information.

358. The Secretary of State shall inform asylum applicants within a reasonable time not exceeding fifteen days after their claim for asylum has been recorded of the benefits and services that they may be eligible to receive and of the rules and procedures with which they must comply relating to them. The Secretary of State shall also provide information on non-governmental organisations and persons that provide legal assistance to asylum applicants and which may be able to help asylum applicants or provide information on available benefits and services.

358A. The Secretary of State shall ensure that the information referred to in paragraph 358 is available in writing and, to the extent possible, will provide the information in a language that asylum applicants may reasonably be supposed to understand. Where appropriate, the Secretary of State may also arrange for this information to be supplied orally.

Information to be provided by asylum applicants

358B. An asylum applicant must notify the Secretary of State of his current address and of any change to his address or residential status. If not notified beforehand, any change must be notified to the Secretary of State without delay after it occurs.

The United Nations High Commissioner for Refugees

358C. A representative of the United Nations High Commissioner for Refugees (UNHCR) or an organisation working in the United Kingdom on behalf of the UNHCR pursuant to an agreement with the government shall:

(a) have access to applicants for asylum, including those in detention;

(b) have access to information on individual applications for asylum, on the course of the procedure and on the decisions taken on applications for asylum, provided that the applicant for asylum agrees thereto;

(c) be entitled to present his views, in the exercise of his supervisory responsibilities under Article 35 of the Geneva Convention, to the Secretary of State regarding individual applications for asylum at any stage of the procedure.

This paragraph shall also apply where the Secretary of State is considering revoking a person's refugee status in accordance with these Rules.

Documentation

359. The Secretary of State shall ensure that, within three working days of recording an asylum application, a document is made available to that asylum applicant, issued in his own name, certifying his status as an asylum applicant or testifying that he is allowed to remain in the United Kingdom while his asylum application is pending. For the avoidance of doubt, in cases where the Secretary of State declines to examine an application it will no longer be pending for the purposes of this rule.

359A. The obligation in paragraph 359 above shall not apply where the asylum applicant is detained under the Immigration Acts, the Immigration and Asylum Act 1999 or the Nationality, Immigration and Asylum Act 2002.

359B. A document issued to an asylum applicant under paragraph 359 does not constitute evidence of the asylum applicant's identity.

359C. In specific cases the Secretary of State or an Immigration Officer may provide an asylum applicant with evidence equivalent to that provided under rule 359. This might be, for example, in circumstances in which it is only possible or desirable to issue a time-limited document.

Right to request permission to take up employment

360. An asylum applicant may apply to the Secretary of State for permission to take up employment if a decision at first instance has not been taken on the applicant's asylum application within one year of the date on which it was recorded. The Secretary of State shall only consider such an application if, in the Secretary of State's opinion, any delay in reaching a decision at first instance cannot be attributed to the applicant.

360A. If permission to take up employment is granted under paragraph 360, that permission will be subject to the following restrictions:

(i) employment may only be taken up in a post which is, at the time an offer of employment is accepted, included on the list of shortage occupations published by the United Kingdom Border Agency (as that list is amended from time to time);

(ii) no work in a self-employed capacity; and

(iii) no engagement in setting up a business.

360B. If an asylum applicant is granted permission to take up employment under paragraph 360 this shall only be until such time as his asylum application has been finally determined.

360C. Where an individual makes further submissions which raise asylum grounds and which fall to be considered under paragraph 353 of these Rules, that individual may apply to the Secretary of State for permission to take up employment if a decision pursuant to paragaph 353 of these Rules has not been taken on the further submissions within one year of the date on which they were recorded. The Secretary of State shall only consider such an application if, in the Secretary of State's opinion, any delay in reaching a decision pursuant to paragraph 353 of these Rules cannot be attributed to the individual.

360D. If permission to take up employment is granted under paragraph 360C, that permission will be subject to the following restrictions:

(i) employment may only be taken up in a post which is, at the time an offer of employment is accepted, included on the list of shortage occupations published by the United Kingdom Border Agency (as that list is amended from time to time);

(ii) no work in a self-employed capacity; and

(iii) no engagement in setting up a business.

360E. Where permission to take up employment is granted pursuant to paragraph 360C, this shall only be until such time as:

(i) a decision has been taken pursuant to paragraph 353 that the further submissions do not amount to a fresh claim; or

(ii) where the further submissions are considered to amount to a fresh claim for asylum pursuant to paragraph 353, all rights of appeal from the immigration decision made in consequence of the rejection of the further submissions have been exhausted.

Interpretation

361. For the purposes of this Part–

(a) 'working day' means any day other than a Saturday or Sunday, a bank holiday, Christmas day or Good Friday;

(b) 'member State' has the same meaning as in Schedule 1 to the European Communities Act 1972.

Part 12 – Procedure and rights of appeal

Fresh Claims

353. When a human rights or asylum claim has been refused or withdrawn or treated as withdrawn under paragraph 333C of these Rules and any appeal relating to that claim is no longer pending, the decision maker will consider any further submissions and, if rejected, will then determine whether they amount to a fresh claim. The submissions will amount to a fresh claim if they are significantly different from the material that has previously been considered. The submissions will only be significantly different if the content:

(i) had not already been considered; and

(ii) taken together with the previously considered material, created a realistic prospect of success, notwithstanding its rejection.

This paragraph does not apply to claims made overseas.

353A. Consideration of further submissions shall be subject to the procedures set out in these Rules. An applicant who has made further submissions shall not be removed before the Secretary of State has considered the submissions under paragraph 353 or otherwise.

This paragraph does not apply to submissions made overseas.

Part 13 – Deportation

A deportation order

362. A deportation order requires the subject to leave the United Kingdom and authorises his detention until he is removed. It also prohibits him from re-entering the country for as long as it is in force and invalidates any leave to enter or remain in the United Kingdom given him before the Order is made or while it is in force.

363. The circumstances in which a person is liable to deportation include:

(i) where the Secretary of State deems the person's deportation to be conducive to the public good;

(ii) where the person is the spouse or civil partner or child under 18 of a person ordered to be deported; and

(iii) where a court recommends deportation in the case of a person over the age of 17 who has been convicted of an offence punishable with imprisonment.

363A. Prior to 2 October 2000, a person would have been liable to deportation in certain circumstances in which he is now liable to administrative removal. These circumstances are listed in paragraph 394B below. However, such a person remains liable to deportation, rather than administrative removal where:

(i) a decision to make a deportation order against him was taken before 2 October 2000; or

(ii) the person has made a valid application under the Immigration (Regularisation Period for Overstayers) Regulations 2000.

364. Subject to paragraph 380, while each case will be considered on its merits, where a person is liable to deportation the presumption shall be that the public interest requires deportation. The Secretary of State will consider all relevant factors in considering whether the presumption is outweighed in any particular case, although it will only be in exceptional circumstances that the public interest in deportation will be outweighed in a case where it would not be contrary to the Human Rights Convention and the Convention and Protocol relating to the Status of Refugees to deport. The aim is an exercise of the power of deportation which is consistent and fair as between one person and another, although one case will rarely be identical with another in all material respects. In the cases detailed in paragraph 363A deportation will normally be the proper course where a person has failed to comply with or has contravened a condition or has remained without authority.

364A. Paragraph 364 does not apply where the Secretary of State must make a deportation order in respect of a foreign criminal under section 32(5) of the UK Borders Act 2007.

Deportation of family members

365. Section 5 of the Immigration Act 1971 gives the Secretary of State power in certain circumstances to make a deportation order against the spouse, civil partner or child of a person against whom a deportation order has been made. The Secretary of State will not normally decide to deport the spouse or civil partner of a deportee where:

(i) he has qualified for settlement in his own right; or

(ii) he has been living apart from the deportee.

366. The Secretary of State will not normally decide to deport the child of a deportee where:

(i) he and his mother or father are living apart from the deportee; or

(ii) he has left home and established himself on an independent basis; or

(iii) he married or formed a civil partnership before deportation came into prospect.

367. In considering whether to require a spouse or child to leave with the deportee the Secretary of State will take account of all relevant factors, including, as well as the following:

(i) the ability of the spouse or civil partner to maintain himself and any children in the United Kingdom, or to be maintained by relatives or friends without charge to public funds, not merely for a short period but for the foreseeable future; and

(ii) in the case of a child of school age, the effect of removal on his education; and

(iii) the practicality of any plans for a child's care and maintenance in this country if one or both of his parents were deported; and

(iv) any representations made on behalf of the spouse or child.

368. Where the Secretary of State decides that it would be appropriate to deport a member of a family as such, the decision, and the right of appeal, will be notified and it will at the same time be explained that it is

open to the member of the family to leave the country voluntarily if he does not wish to appeal or if he appeals and his appeal is dismissed.

Right of appeal against destination

369. DELETED

Restricted right of appeal against deportation in cases of breach of limited leave

370. DELETED

Exemption to the restricted right of appeal

371. DELETED

372. DELETED

A deportation order made on the recommendation of a Court

373. DELETED

Where deportation is deemed to be conducive to the public good

374. DELETED

375. DELETED

Hearing of appeals

376. DELETED

377. DELETED

378. A deportation order may not be made while it is still open to the person to appeal against the Secretary of State's decision, or while an appeal is pending except where the Secretary of State is required to make the deportation order in respect of a foreign criminal under section 32(5) of the UK Borders Act 2007. There is no appeal within the immigration appeal system against the making of a deportation order on the recommendation of a court; but there is a right of appeal to a higher court against the recommendation itself. A deportation order may not be made while it is still open to the person to appeal against the relevant conviction, sentence or recommendation, or while such an appeal is pending.

Persons who have claimed asylum

379. DELETED

379A. DELETED

380. A deportation order will not be made against any person if his removal in pursuance of the order would be contrary to the United Kingdom's obligations under the Convention and Protocol relating to the Status of Refugees or the Human Rights Convention.

Procedure

381. When a decision to make a deportation order has been taken (otherwise than on the recommendation of a court) a notice will be given to the person concerned informing him of the decision and of his right of appeal.

382. Following the issue of such a notice the Secretary of State may authorise detention or make an order restricting a person as to residence, employment or occupation and requiring him to report to the police, pending the making of a deportation order.

383. DELETED

384. If a notice of appeal is given within the period allowed, a summary of the facts of the case on the basis of which the decision was taken will be sent to the appropriate appellate authorities, who will notify the appellant of the arrangements for the appeal to be heard.

Arrangements for removal

385. A person against whom a deportation order has been made will normally be removed from the United Kingdom. The power is to be exercised so as to secure the person's return to the country of which he is a national, or which has most recently provided him with a travel document, unless he can show that another country will receive him. In considering any departure from the normal arrangements, regard will be had to the public interest generally, and to any additional expense that may fall on public funds.

386. The person will not be removed as the subject of a deportation order while an appeal may be brought against the removal directions or such an appeal is pending.

Supervised departure

387. DELETED

Returned deportees

388. Where a person returns to this country when a deportation order is in force against him, he may be deported under the original order. The Secretary of State will consider every such case in the light of all the relevant circumstances before deciding whether to enforce the order.

Returned family members

389. Persons deported in the circumstances set out in paragraphs 365–368 above (deportation of family members) may be able to seek re-admission to the United Kingdom under the Immigration Rules where:

(i) a child reaches 18 (when he ceases to be subject to the deportation order); or

(ii) in the case of a spouse or civil partner, the marriage or civil partnership comes to an end.

Revocation of deportation order

390. An application for revocation of a deportation order will be considered in the light of all the circumstances including the following:

(i) the grounds on which the order was made;

(ii) any representations made in support of revocation;

(iii) the interests of the community, including the maintenance of an effective immigration control;

(iv) the interests of the applicant, including any compassionate circumstances.

391. In the case of an applicant who has been deported following conviction for a criminal offence continued exclusion

(i) in the case of a conviction which is capable of being spent under the Rehabilitation of Offenders Act 1974, unless the conviction is spent within the meaning of that Act or, if the conviction is spent in less than 10 years, 10 years have elapsed since the making of the deportation order; or

(ii) in the case of a conviction not capable of being spent under that Act, at any time, unless refusal to revoke the deportation order would be contrary to the Human Rights Convention or the Convention and Protocol Relating to the Status of Refugees.

will normally be the proper course. In other cases revocation of the order will not normally be authorised unless the situation has been materially altered, either by a change of circumstances since the order was made, or by fresh information coming to light which was not before, or the appellate authorities or the Secretary of State. The passage of time since the person was deported may also in itself amount to such a change of circumstances as to warrant revocation of the order.

392. Revocation of a deportation order does not entitle the person concerned to re-enter the United Kingdom; it renders him eligible to apply for admission under the Immigration Rules. Application for revocation of the order may be made to the Entry Clearance Officer or direct to the Home Office.

Rights of appeal in relation to a decision not to revoke a deportation order

393. DELETED

394. DELETED

395. There may be a right of appeal against refusal to revoke a deportation order. Where an appeal does lie the right of appeal will be notified at the same time as the decision to refuse to revoke the order.

Administrative Removal

395A. A person is now liable to administrative removal in certain circumstances in which he would, prior to 2 October 2000, have been liable to deportation.

395B. These circumstances are set out in section 10 of the 1999 Act. They are:

(i) failure to comply with a condition attached to his leave to enter or remain, or remaining beyond the time limited by the leave;

(ii) where the person has obtained leave to remain by deception; and

(iii) where the person is the spouse civil partner, or child under 18 of someone in respect of whom directions for removal have been given under section 10.

395C. Before a decision to remove under section 10 of the Immigration and Asylum Act 1999 or section 47 of the Immigration, Asylum and Nationality Act 2006 is given, regard will be had to all the relevant factors known to the Secretary of State including:

(i) age;

(ii) length of residence in the United Kingdom;

(iii) strength of connections with the United Kingdom;

(iv) personal history, including character, conduct and employment record;

(v) domestic circumstances;

(vi) previous criminal record and the nature of any offence of which the person has been convicted;

(vii) compassionate circumstances;

(viii) any representations received on the person's behalf.

In the case of family members, the factors listed in paragraphs 365–368 must also be taken into account.

395D. No one shall be removed under section 10 if his removal would be contrary to the United Kingdom's obligations under the Convention and Protocol relating to the Status of Refugees or under the Human Rights Convention.

Procedure

395E. When a decision that a person is to be removed under section 10 has been given, a notice will be given to the person concerned informing him of the decision and of any right of appeal.

395F. Following the issue of such a notice an Immigration Officer may authorise detention or make an order restricting a person as to residence, employment or occupation and requiring him to report to the police, pending the removal.

Appendix 1 – Visa requirements for the United Kingdom

1. Subject to paragraph 2 below, the following persons need a visa for the United Kingdom:

(a) Nationals or citizens of the following countries or territorial entities:

Afghanistan
Albania
Algeria
Angola
Armenia
Azerbaijan
Bahrain
Bangladesh
Belarus
Benin
Bhutan
Bolivia
Bosnia Herzegovina
Burkina Faso
Burma
Burundi
Cambodia
Cameroon
Cape Verde
Central African Republic
Chad
People's Republic of China (except those referred to in sub-paragraphs 2(d) and (e) of this Appendix)
Colombia
Comoros
Congo

Cuba
Democratic Republic of the Congo
Djibouti
Dominican Republic
Ecuador
Egypt
Equatorial Guinea
Eritrea
Ethiopia
Fiji
Gabon
Gambia
Georgia
Ghana
Guinea
Guinea Bissau
Guyana
Haiti
India
Indonesia
Iran
Iraq
Ivory Coast
Jamaica
Jordan
Kazakhstan
Kenya
Korea (North)
Kuwait
Kyrgyzstan
Laos
Lebanon
Lesotho
Liberia
Libya
Macau
Macedonia
Madagascar
Malawi
Mali
Mauritania
Moldova
Mongolia
Montenegro
Morocco
Mozambique
Nepal
Niger
Nigeria
Oman (except those referred to in sub-paragraph 2(j) of this Appendix)
Pakistan
Palestinian Territories
Peru
Philippines
Qatar (except those referred to in sub-paragraph 2(k) of this Appendix)
Russia
Rwanda
Sao Tome e Principe

Saudi Arabia
Senegal
Serbia
Sierra Leone
Somalia
South Africa
Sri Lanka
Sudan
Surinam
Swaziland
Syria
Taiwan (except those referred to in sub-paragraph 2(h) of this Appendix)
Tajikistan
Tanzania
Thailand
Togo
Tunisia
Turkey
Turkmenistan
Uganda
Ukraine
United Arab Emirates (except those referred to in sub-paragraph 2(l) of this Appendix)
Uzbekistan
Vatican City
Venezuela (except those referred to in sub-paragraph 2(i) of this Appendix)
Vietnam
Yemen
Zambia
Zimbabwe
The territories formerly comprising the socialist Federal Republic of Yugoslavia

(b) Persons who hold passports or travel documents issued by the former Soviet Union or by the former Socialist Federal Republic of Yugoslavia.

(c) Stateless persons.

(d) Persons who hold non-national documents.

2. The following persons do not need a visa for the United Kingdom:

(a) those who qualify for admission to the United Kingdom as returning residents in accordance with paragraph 18;

(b) those who seek leave to enter the United Kingdom within the period of their earlier leave and for the same purpose as that for which that leave was granted, unless it

(i) was for a period of six months or less; or

(ii) was extended by statutory instrument or by section 3C of the Immigration Act 1971 (inserted by section 3 of the Immigration and Asylum Act 1999);

(c) DELETED

(d) those nationals or citizens of the People's Republic of China holding passports issued by Hong Kong Special Administrative Region;

(e) those nationals or citizens of the People's Republic of China holding passports issued by Macao Special Administrative Region;

(f) those who arrive in the United Kingdom with leave to enter which is in force but which was given before arrival, so long as those in question arrive within the period of their earlier leave and for the same purpose as that for which leave was granted, unless that leave–

(i) was for a period of six months or less, or

(ii) was extended by statutory instrument or by section 3C of the Immigration Act 1971 (inserted by section 3 of the Immigration and Asylum Act 1999);

(g) DELETED

(h) those nationals or citizens of Taiwan who hold a passport by Taiwan that includes the number of the identification card issued by the competent authority in Taiwan in it.

(i) those nationals or citizens of Venezuela who hold a passport issued by the Republic of Venezuela that contains biometric information held in an electronic chip.

(j) those nationals or citizens of Oman, who hold diplomatic and special passports issued by oman when travelling to the UK for the purpose of a general visit in accordance with paragraph 41,

(k) those nationals or citizens of Qatar who hold diplomatic and special passports issued by Qatar when travelling to the UK for the purpose of a general visit in accordance with paragraph 41,

(l) those nationals or citizens of the United arab emirates who hold diplomatic and special passports issued by the United arab emirates when travelling to the UK for the purpose of a general visit in accordance with paragraph 41.

(m) During the period commencing on 30 March 2012 up to and including 12 August 2012 those nationals or citizens of all the countries or territorial entities listed in paragraph 1 of Appendix 1 who hold an Olympic Identity and Accreditation Card issued by the London Organising Committee of the Olympic Games and Paralympic Games Limited unless that card has the accreditation category code OCOG, S or X;

(n) During the period commencing on 13 August 2012 up to and including 8 November 2012 those nationals or citizens of all the countries or territorial entities listed in paragraph 1 of Appendix 1 who hold an Olympic Identity and Accreditation Card issued by the London Organising Committee of the Olympic Games and Paralympic Games Limited unless (i) that card has the accreditation category code OCOG, S or X; or (ii) the holder had not held leave to enter, leave to remain or entry clearance at any time during the period commencing on 30 March 2012 and ending on 12 August 2012;

(o) During the period commencing on 30 March 2012 up to and including 9 September 2012 those nationals or citizens of all the countries or territorial entities listed in paragraph 1 of Appendix 1 who hold an Paralympic Identity and Accreditation Card issued by the London Organising Committee of the Olympic Games and Paralympic Games Limited unless that card has the accreditation category code OCOG, S or X;

(p) During the period commencing on 10 September 2012 up to and including the 8 November 2012 those nationals or citizens of all the countries or territorial entities listed in paragraph 1 of Appendix 1 who hold the Paralympic Identity and Accreditation Card issued by the London Organising Committee of the Olympic Games and Paralympic Games Limited unless (i) that card has the accreditation category code OCOG, S or X; or (ii) the holder had not held leave to enter, leave to remain or entry clearance at any time during the period commencing on 30 March 2012 and ending on 9 September 2012.

Appendix 2 – Countries or territories whose nationals or citizens are relevant foreign nationals for the purposes of Part 10 of these Rules

Registration with the police

Afghanistan
Algeria
Argentina
Armenia
Azerbaijan
Bahrain
Belarus
Bolivia
Brazil
China
Colombia
Cuba
Egypt
Georgia
Iran
Iraq

Israel
Jordan
Kazakhstan
Kuwait
Kyrgyzstan
Lebanon
Libya
Moldova
Morocco
North Korea
Oman
Palestine
Peru
Qatar
Russia
Saudi Arabia
Sudan
Syria
Tajikistan
Tunisia
Turkey
Turkmenistan
United Arab Emirates
Ukraine
Uzbekistan
Yemen

Appendix 3 – List of Countries participating in the Working Holidaymaker Scheme

Antigua and Barbuda
Australia
The Bahamas
Bangladesh
Barbados
Belize
Botswana
Brunei Darussalam
Canada
Cameroon
Dominica
Fiji Islands
The Gambia
Ghana
Grenada
Guyana
India
Jamaica
Kenya
Kiribati
Malawi
Malaysia
Maldives
Mauritius
Mozambique
Namibia
Nauru

New Zealand
Nigeria
Pakistan
Papua New Guinea
Saint Christopher and Nevis
Saint Lucia
Saint Vincent and the Grenadines
Seychelles
Sierra Leone
Singapore
Solomon Islands
South Africa
Sri Lanka
Swaziland
Tanzania, United Republic of
Tonga
Trinidad and Tobago
Tuvalu
Uganda
Vanuatu
Western Samoa
Zambia
Zimbabwe

Appendix 6 – Disciplines for which an Academic Technology Approval Scheme certificate from the Counter-Proliferation Department of the Foreign and Commonwealth Office is required for the purposes of paragraph 57(v) of these Rules

Doctorate or Masters by research:

Subjects allied to Medicine:

1. JACs codes beginning

B1 – Anatomy, Physiology and Pathology
B2 – Pharmacology, Toxicology and Pharmacy
B9 – Others in subjects allied to Medicine

Biological Sciences:

JACs codes beginning

C1 – Biology
C2 – Botany
C4 – Genetics
C5 – Microbiology
C7 – Molecular Biology, Biophysics and Biochemistry
C9 – Others in Biological Sciences

Veterinary Sciences, Agriculture and related subjects:

JACs codes beginning

D3 – Animal Science
D9 – Others in Veterinary Sciences, Agriculture and related subjects

Physical Sciences:

JACs codes beginning

F1 – Chemistry
F2 – Materials Science
F3 – Physics

F5 – Astronomy
F8 – Physical and Terrestrial Geographical and Environmental Sciences
F9 – Others in Physical Sciences

Mathematical and Computer Sciences:

JACs codes beginning
G1 – Mathematics
G2 – Operational Research
G4 – Computer Science
G7 – Artificial Intelligence
G9 – Others in Mathematical and Computing Sciences

Engineering:

JACs codes beginning
H1 – General Engineering
H2 – Civil Engineering
H3 – Mechanical Engineering
H4 – Aerospace Engineering
H5 – Naval Architecture
H6 – Electronic and Electrical Engineering
H7 – Production and Manufacturing Engineering
H8 – Chemical, Process and Energy Engineering
H9 – Others in Engineering

Technologies:

JACs codes beginning
J2 – Metallurgy
J4 – Polymers and Textiles
J5 – Materials Technology not otherwise specified
J7 – Industrial Biotechnology
J9 – Others in Technology

Taught Masters:

2. F2 – Materials Science
F3 – Physics (including Nuclear Physics)
H3 – Mechanical Engineering
H4 – Aerospace Engineering
J5 – Materials Technology/Materials Science not otherwise specified

Appendix A – Attributes

Attributes for Tier 1 (Exceptional Talent) Migrants

1. An applicant applying for entry clearance, leave to remain or indefinite leave to remain as a Tier 1 (Exceptional Talent) Migrant must score 75 points for attributes.
2. Available points are shown in Table 1.
3. Notes to accompany the table are shown below the table.

Table 1

Applications for entry clearance

Criterion	Points
Endorsed by Designated Competent Body according to that Body's criteria as published on the UK Border Agency website	75

Applications for leave to remain and indefinite leave to remain

Criterion	Points
The applicant is economically active in his expert field as previously endorsed by a Designated Competent Body, in employment or self-employment or both; and that Designated Competent Body has not withdrawn its endorsement of the applicant.	75

Notes

Tier 1 (Exceptional Talent) Limit

4. (a) The Secretary of State shall be entitled to limit the total number of Tier 1 (Exceptional Talent) endorsements Designated Competent Bodies may make in support of successful applications in a particular period, to be referred to as the Tier 1 (Exceptional Talent) Limit.

(b) The Tier 1 (Exceptional Talent) Limit for the period 9 August 2011 to 5 April 2012 is 1,000 endorsements in total, which will be allocated to the Designated Competent Bodies as follows:

(i) 300 endorsements to The Arts Council for the purpose of endorsing applicants with exceptional talent in the fields of arts and culture;

(ii) 300 endorsements to The Royal Society for the purpose of endorsing applicants with exceptional talent in the fields of natural sciences and medical science research;

(iii) 200 endorsements to The Royal Academy of Engineering for the purpose of endorsing applicants with exceptional talent in the field of engineering; and

(iv) 200 endorsements to The British Academy for the purpose of endorsing applicants with exceptional talent in the fields of humanities and social sciences.

(c) The Tier 1 (Exceptional Talent) Limit will be operated by assigning Tier 1 (Exceptional Talent) Unique Reference Numbers to prospective applicants according to the practice set out in paragraph 5 below.

(d) If a Designated Competent Body chooses to transfer part of its unused allocation of endorsements to another Designated Competent Body by mutual agreement of both bodies and the Secretary of State, the allocations of both bodies will be adjusted accordingly and the adjusted allocations will be published on the UK Border Agency website.

Tier 1 (Exceptional Talent) Unique Reference Numbers

5. (a) Before making his application, the prospective applicant must request a Tier 1 (Exceptional Talent) Unique Reference Number from the UK Border Agency, stating which Designated Competent Body he wishes to endorse his application.

(b) A number of places will be made available for each Designated Competent Body, under which Tier 1 (Exceptional Talent) Unique Reference Numbers can be assigned, as follows:

(i) From 9 August 2011 to 30 November 2011, a number of places equal to half that body's allocated endorsements under paragraph 4 above.

(ii) From 1 December 2011 to 5 April 2012, a number of places equal to that body's remaining unused allocated endorsements under paragraph 4 above.

(c) If:

(i) An applicant does not make a valid application within 10 working days of being assigned a Tier 1 (Exceptional Talent) Unique Reference Number, or

(ii) An application is refused, and that refusal is not subsequently overturned, the Tier 1 (Exceptional Talent) Unique Reference Number assigned to that applicant will be cancelled and the used place will be returned to the number of places available for the relevant Designated Competent Body.

(d) A request to be assigned a Tier 1 (Exceptional Talent) Unique Reference Number will be granted if:

(i) The applicant has not previously been granted three Tier 1 (Exceptional Talent) Unique Reference Numbers during the period 9 August 2011 to 5 April 2012, and

(ii) Places are available for the relevant Designated Competent Body on the date the applicant makes his request.

(e) A request to be assigned a Tier 1 (Exceptional Talent) Unique Reference Number will be refused if:

(i) The applicant has previously been granted three Tier 1 (Exceptional Talent) Unique Reference Numbers during the period 9 August 2011 to 5 April 2012, or

(ii) (1) No places are available for the relevant Designated Competent Body on the date the applicant makes his request, and

(2) No places have been used which could potentially be returned to the number of places available under paragraph (c) above.

(f) In all other cases, no decision will be made regarding the request until the conditions of either (d) or (e) are met.

Endorsement by the relevant Designated Competent Body

6. Points will only be awarded for an endorsement from the relevant Designated Competent Body if the endorsement has not been withdrawn by the relevant Designated Competent Body at the time the application for Entry Clearance is considered by the UK Border Agency.

Attributes for Tier 1 (General) Migrants

7. An applicant applying for leave to remain or indefinite leave to remain as a Tier 1 (General) Migrant must score 75 points for attributes, if the applicant has, or has had, leave as a Highly Skilled Migrant, as a Writer, Composer or Artist, Self-employed Lawyer, or as a Tier 1 (General) Migrant under the rules in place before 19 July 2010, and has not been granted leave in any categories other than these under the rules in place since 19 July 2010.

8. An applicant applying for leave to remain or indefinite leave to remain as a Tier 1 (General) Migrant who does not fall within the scope of paragraph 7 above or paragraph 9 below must score 80 points for attributes.

9. An applicant applying for indefinite leave to remain as a Tier 1 (General) Migrant whose application is being made under terms of the HSMP ILR Judicial Review Policy Document is not required to score points for attributes.

10. Available points are shown in Table 2 and Table 3 below. only one set of points will be awarded per column in each table. For example, points will only be awarded for one qualification.

11. Notes to accompany Table 2 and Table 3 appear below Table 3.

Table 2 – Applications for leave to remain and indefinite leave to remain where the applicant has, or has had, leave as a Highly Skilled Migrant, as a Writer, Composer or Artist, Self-employed Lawyer, or as a Tier 1 (General) Migrant under the rules in place before 6 April 2010, and has not been granted leave in any categories other than these since 6 April 2010

Qualification	Points	Previous earnings	Points	UK Experience	Points	Age (at date of application for first grant)	Points
Bachelor's degree (see paragraph 13 below)	30	£16,000–£17,999.99 (see paragraph 18 below)	5	If £16,000 or more of the previous earnings for which points are claimed were earned in the UK	5	Under 28 years of age	20
Master's degree	35	£18,000–£19,999.99 (see paragraph 18 below)	10	If £16,000 or more of the previous earnings for which points are claimed were earned in the UK		28 or 29 years of age	10
PhD	50	£20,000–£22,999.99	15			30 or 31 years of age	5
		£23,000–£25,999.99	20				
		£26,000–£28,999.99	25				

Qualification	Points	Previous earnings	Points	UK Experience	Points	Age (at date of application for first grant)	Points
		£29,000–£31,999.99	30				
		£32,000–£34,999.99	35				
		£35,000–£39,999.99	40				
		£40,000 or more	45				

Table 3 – All other applications for leave to remain and indefinite

Qualification	Points	Previous earnings	Points	UK Experience	Points	Age (at date of application for first grant)	Points
Bachelor's degree	30	£25,000–£29,999.99	5	If £25,000 or more of the previous earnings for which points are claimed were earned in the UK	5	Under 30 years of age	20
Master's degree	35	£30,000–£34,999.99	15			30 to 34 years of age	10
PhD	45	£35,000–£39,999.99	20			35 to 39 years of age	5
		£40,000–£49,999.99	25				
		£50,000–£54,999.99	30				
		£55,000–£64,999.99	35				
		£65,000–£74,999.99	40				
		£75,000–£149,999.99	45				
		£150,000 or more	80				

Notes

12. Qualifications and/or earnings will not be taken into account if the applicant was in breach of the UK's immigration laws at the time those qualifications were studied for or those earnings were made.

Qualifications: notes

13. An applicant will be awarded no points for a Bachelor's degree if:
    - (a) his last grant of entry clearance was as a Tier 1 (General) Migrant under the rules in place between 31 March 2009 and 5 April 2010, or
    - (b) (i) he has had leave to remain as a Tier 1 (General) Migrant under the rules in place between 31 March 2009 and 5 April 2010, and
      - (ii) his previous entry clearance, leave to enter or leave to remain before that leave was not as a Highly skilled Migrant, as a Writer, Composer or artist, as a self-employed lawyer, or as a Tier 1 (General) Migrant.

14. Specified documents must be provided as evidence of the qualification, unless the applicant has, or was last granted, leave as a Highly skilled Migrant or a Tier 1 (General) Migrant and previously scored points for the same qualification in respect of which points are being claimed in this application.

15. Points will only be awarded for an academic qualification if an applicant's qualification is deemed by the national academic recognition information Centre for the United Kingdom (UK NARIC) to meet or exceed the recognised standard of a Bachelor's or Master's degree or a PhD, as appropriate, in the UK.

16. Points will also be awarded for vocational and professional qualifications that are deemed by UK NARIC or the appropriate UK professional body to be equivalent to a Bachelor's or Master's degree or a PhD in the UK.

17. If the applicant has, or was last granted, leave as a Tier 1 (General) Migrant or a Highly skilled Migrant and the qualification for which points are now claimed was, in the applicant's last successful application for leave or for a Highly Skilled Migrant Programme approval letter, assessed to be of a higher level than now indicated by UK NARIC, the higher score of points will be awarded in this application too.

Previous earnings: notes

18. An applicant will be awarded no points for previous earnings of less than £20,000 if:

    (a) his last grant of entry clearance was as a Tier 1 (General) Migrant under the rules in place between 31 March 2009 and 5 April 2010, or

    (b) (i) he has had leave to remain as a Tier 1 (General) Migrant under the rules in place between 31 March 2009 and 5 April 2010, and

    (ii) his previous entry clearance, leave to enter or leave to remain before that leave was not as a Highly Skilled Migrant, as a Writer, Composer or artist, as a self-employed lawyer, or as a Tier 1 (General) Migrant.

19. Specified documents from two or more sources must be provided as evidence for each source of previous earnings.

Period for assessment

20. Applicants should indicate in the application form for which 12-month period their earnings should be assessed.

21. (a) for all applicants the period for assessment of earnings must:

    (i) consist of no more than 12 months which must run consecutively, and

    (ii) fall within the 15 months immediately preceding the application.

    (b) if the applicant:

    (i) has been on maternity or adoption leave at some point within the 12 months preceding the application, and

    (ii) has provided the specified documents, or where due to exceptional circumstances the specified documents are not available, has provided alternative documents which show that the circumstances provided for in (i) apply,

    the applicant may choose for a period of no more than 12 months spent on maternity or adoption leave to be disregarded when calculating both the 12-month and 15-month period.

22. If the applicant has not indicated a period for assessment of earnings, or has indicated a period which does not meet the conditions in paragraph 24 above, their earnings will be assessed against the 12-month period immediately preceding their application, assuming the specified documents have been provided. Where the specified documents have not been provided, points will not be awarded for previous earnings.

Earnings

23. Earnings include, but are not limited to:

    (a) salaries (includes full-time, part-time and bonuses),

    (b) earnings derived through self-employment,

    (c) earnings derived through business activities,

    (d) statutory and contractual maternity pay, statutory and contractual adoption pay,

    (e) allowances (such as accommodation, schooling or car allowances) which form part of an applicant's remuneration package and are specified in the applicant's payslips,

(f) dividends paid by a company in which the applicant is active in the day-to-day management, or where the applicant receives the dividend as part or all of their remuneration package,

(g) property rental income, where this constitutes part of the applicant's business, and

(h) payments in lieu of notice.

24. Where the earnings take the form of a salary or wages, they will be assessed before tax (i.e. gross salary).

25. Where the earnings are the profits of a business derived through self-employment or other business activities:

(a) the earnings that will be assessed are the profits of the business before tax. Where the applicant only has a share of the business, the earnings that will be assessed are the profits of the business before tax to which the applicant is entitled, and

(b) the applicant must be registered as self-employed in the UK, and must provide the specified evidence.

26. Earnings do not include unearned sources of income, such as:

(a) allowances (such as accommodation, schooling or car allowances) which are paid as reimbursement for monies the applicant has previously paid,

(b) any other allowances, unless part of the applicant's remuneration package and specified in the applicant's payslips,

(c) dividends, unless paid by a company in which the applicant is active in the day-to-day management, or unless the applicant receives the dividend as part or all of their remuneration package,

(d) property rental income, unless this constitutes part of the applicant's business,

(e) interest on savings and investments,

(f) funds received through inheritance,

(g) monies paid to the applicant as a pension,

(h) expenses where the payment constitutes a reimbursement for monies the applicant has previously outlaid,

(i) redundancy payment,

(j) sponsorship for periods of study,

(k) state benefits, or

(l) prize money or competition winnings, other than where they are directly related to the applicant's main profession or occupation.

Converting foreign currencies

27. Earnings in a foreign currency will be converted to pound sterling (£) using the closing spot exchange rate for the last day of the period for which the applicant has claimed earnings in that currency.

28. If the applicant's earnings fall either side of a period of maternity or adoption leave, earnings in a foreign currency will be converted to pounds sterling (£) using the closing spot exchange rate which exists:

(a) for the earnings earned before maternity or adoption leave, on the last day of the period before maternity leave, and

(b) for the earnings earned after maternity or adoption leave, on the last day of the period after maternity leave.

29. The spot exchange rate which will be used is that which appears on www.oanda.com*

30. Where the previous earnings claimed are in different currencies, any foreign currencies will be converted before being added together, and then added to any UK earnings, to give a total amount.

UK experience: notes

31. Previous earnings will not be taken into account for the purpose of awarding points for UK experience if the applicant was not physically present in the UK at the time those earnings were made.

32. Previous earnings will not be taken into account for the purpose of awarding points for UK experience if the applicant was physically present in the Isle of Man or the Channel Islands at the time those earnings were made.

Age: notes

33. If the applicant was first granted leave in the categories of Highly Skilled Migrant, Writer, Composer or Artist, Self-employed Lawyer or Tier 1 (General) Migrant and has not been granted leave in any category other than those listed here since the first grant of leave, points will be awarded based on the applicant's age at the date of the application for that first grant of leave. if the applicant has been granted leave since his first grant of leave in a category not listed in this paragraph, points will be awarded based on his age at the date of application for a grant of leave in a category listed in this paragraph where leave has not been granted in any category not listed in this paragraph between that grant of leave and the current application.

34. Specified documents must be provided as evidence of age.

Attributes for Tier 1 (Entrepreneur) Migrants

35. An applicant applying for entry clearance, leave to remain or indefinite leave to remain as a Tier 1 (Entrepreneur) Migrant must score 75 points for attributes.

36. Subject to paragraph 37, available points for applications for entry clearance or leave to remain are shown in Table 4.

37. Available points for an applicant applying for leave to remain who has, or has last been granted entry clearance, leave to enter or remain as:

(i) a Tier 1 (Entrepreneur),

(ii) a Businessperson,

(iii) an Innovator

are shown in Table 5.

38. Available points for applications for indefinite leave to remain are shown in Table 6.

39. (a) Notes to accompany Table 4 appear below Table 4.

(b) Notes to accompany Table 5 and Table 6 appear below Table 6.

(c) Notes on entrepreneurial teams appear below Table 6 and apply to Tables 4, 5 and 6.

Table 4: Applications for entry clearance or leave to remain referred to in paragraph 36

Investment	Points
(a) The applicant has access to not less than £200,000, or	25
(b) The applicant has access to not less than £50,000 from: (i) one or more registered venture capitalist firms regulated by the Financial Services Authority, (ii) one or more UK Entrepreneurial seed funding competitions which is listed as endorsed on the UK Trade & Investment website, or (iii) one or more UK Government Departments, and made available by the Department(s) for the specific purpose of establishing or expanding a UK business.	
The money is held in one or more regulated financial institutions	25
The money is disposable in the UK	25

Investment: notes

40. Specified documents as set out in the Tier 1 (Entrepreneur) Guidance, published on the UK Border Agency website, must be provided as evidence of any investment.

41. An applicant will only be considered to have access to funds if:

(a) The specified documents are provided to show cash money to the amount required (this must not be in the form of assets);

(b) The specified documents are provided to show that the applicant has permission to use the money to invest in a business in the UK; and

(c) The money is either held in a UK regulated financial institution or is transferable to the UK.

42. Points will only be awarded to an applicant to whom Table 4, paragraph (b) applies if the total sum of those funds derives from one or more of the sources listed in (b)(i) to (iii) in Table 4.

43. A regulated financial institution is one, which is regulated by the appropriate regulatory body for the country in which the financial institution operates.

44. Money is disposable in the UK if all of the money is held in a UK based financial institution or if the money is freely transferable to the UK and convertible to sterling. Funds in a foreign currency will be converted to pounds sterling (£) using the spot exchange rate which appeared on www.oanda.com* on the date on which the application was made.

45. If the applicant has invested the money referred to in Table 4 in the UK before the date of the application, points will be awarded for funds available as if the applicant had not yet invested the funds, providing the investment was made no more than 12 months before the date of the application.

Table 5: Applications for leave to remain referred to in paragraph 37

Investment and business activity	Points
The applicant has invested, or had invested on his behalf, not less than £200,000 (or £50,000 if, in his last grant of leave, he was awarded points for funds of £50,000 from one of the sources listed in Table 4 paragraph (b) above) in cash directly into one or more businesses in the UK.	20
The applicant has: (a) registered with HM revenue and Customs as self-employed, or (b) registered a new business in which he is a director, or (c) registered as a director of an existing business. Where the applicant's last grant of entry clearance, leave to enter or leave to remain was as a Tier 1 (Entrepreneur) Migrant, the above condition must have been met within 6 months of his entry to the UK (if he was granted entry clearance as a Tier 1 (Entrepreneur) Migrant and there is evidence to establish his date of arrival to the UK), or, in any other case, the date of the grant of leave to remain.	20
On a date no earlier than three months prior to the date of application, the applicant was: (a) registered with HM revenue and Customs as self-employed, or (b) registered a new business in which he is a director, or (c) registered as a director of an existing business.	15
The applicant has: (a) established a new business or businesses that has or have created the equivalent of at least two new full time jobs for persons settled in the UK, or (b) taken over or invested in an existing business or businesses and his services or investment have resulted in a net increase in the employment provided by the business or businesses for persons settled in the UK by creating the equivalent of at least two new full time jobs. Where the applicant's last grant of entry clearance or leave to enter or remain was as a Tier 1 (Entrepreneur) Migrant, the jobs must have existed for at least 12 months of the period for which the previous leave was granted.	20

Table 6: Applications for indefinite leave to remain as referred to in paragraph 38

Row	Investment and business activity	Points
1.	On a date no earlier than three months prior to the date of application, the applicant was: (a) registered with HM Revenue and Customs as self-employed, or (b) registered a new business in which he is a director, or (c) registered as a director of an existing business.	20
2.	The applicant has: (a) established a new UK business or businesses that has or have created the equivalent of X new full time jobs for persons settled in the UK, or (b) taken over or invested in an existing UK business or businesses and his services or investment have resulted in a net increase in the employment provided by the business or businesses for persons settled in the UK by creating the equivalent of X new full time jobs where X is at least 2. Where the applicant's last grant of entry clearance or leave to enter or remain was as a Tier 1 (Entrepreneur) Migrant, the jobs must have existed for at least 12 months of the period for which the previous leave was granted.	20

Row	Investment and business activity	Points
3.	The applicant has spent the specified continuous period lawfully in the UK, with absences from the UK of no more than 180 days in any 12 calendar months during that period. The specified period must have been spent with leave as a Tier 1 (Entrepreneur) Migrant, as a Businessperson and/or as an Innovator, of which the most recent period must have been spent with leave as a Tier (1) (Entrepreneur) Migrant. The specified continuous period is: (a) 3 years if the number of new full time jobs, X, referred to in row 2 above is at least 10, (b) 3 years if the applicant has: (i) established a new UK business that has had an income from business activity of at least £5 million during a 3 year period in which the applicant has had leave as a Tier 1 (Entrepreneur) Migrant, or (ii) taken over or invested in an existing UK business and his services or investment have resulted in a net increase in income from business activity to that business of £5 million during a 3 year period in which the applicant has had leave as a Tier 1 (Entrepreneur) Migrant, when compared to the immediately preceding 3 year period, or (c) 5 years in all other cases.	35

Investment and business activity: notes

46. Documentary evidence must be provided in all cases. Specified documents as set out in the Tier 1 (Entrepreneur) Guidance, published on the UK Border Agency website, must be provided as evidence of any investment and business activity that took place when the applicant had leave as a Tier 1 (Entrepreneur) Migrant.

47. For the purposes of tables 4, 5 and 6, 'investment' does not include the value of any residential accommodation, property development or property management and must not be in the form of a director's loan, unless it is unsecured and subordinated in favour of the business.

48. Points will only be awarded in respect of a UK business or businesses. a business will be considered to be in the UK if:
    (i) it is trading within the UK economy, and
    (ii) it has a registered office in the UK, except where the applicant is registered with HM revenue & Customs as self-employed and does not have a business office, and
    (iii) it has a UK bank account, and
    (iv) it is subject to UK taxation.

    Multinational companies that are registered as UK companies with either a registered office or head office in the UK are considered to be UK businesses for the purposes of tables 4, 5 and 6.

49. A full time job is one involving at least 30 hours' of work a week. Two or more part time jobs that add up to 30 hours a week will count as one full time job but one full time job of more than 30 hours work a week will not count as more than one full time job.

50. Where the applicant's last grant of entry clearance or leave was as a Tier (Entrepreneur) Migrant, the jobs must have existed for a total of at least 12 months during the period in which the migrant had leave in that category. This need not consist of 12 consecutive months and the jobs need not exist at the date of application, provided they existed for at least 12 months during the period in which the migrant had leave as a Tier 1 (Entrepreneur) Migrant.

51. The jobs must comply with all relevant UK legislation including, but not limited to, the national Minimum Wage and the Working Time Directive.

Entrepreneurial teams: Notes

52. Two applicants may claim points for the same investment and business activity in Tables 4, 5 or 6 providing the following requirements are met.

Requirements:

(a) The applicants have equal level of control over the funds and/or the business or businesses in question;

(b) The applicants are both shown by name in each other's applications and in the specified evidence required in the relevant table; and

(c) Neither applicant has previously been granted leave as a Tier 1 (Entrepreneur) Migrant on the basis of investment and/or business activity linked in this way with any applicant other than each other if the same funds are being relied on as in a previous application.

53. If the two applicants referred to in paragraph 52 above make their applications on different dates, or are granted leave on different dates, where the dates referred to in Table 4, Table 5 and the associated notes relate to investment and/or business activity, the relevant date will be taken as the date of the earlier application or grant of leave of the two, for both applications. The dates referred to in Table 6 will be the date of each individual application.

Attributes for Tier 1 (Investor) Migrants

54. An applicant applying for entry clearance, leave to remain or indefinite leave to remain as a Tier 1 (Investor) Migrant must score 75 points for attributes.

55. Subject to paragraph 56, available points for applications for entry clearance or leave to remain are shown in Table 7.

56. Available points for an applicant applying for leave to remain who has, or has last been granted, entry clearance, leave to enter or remain as:

(i) a Tier 1 (Investor) Migrant, or

(ii) an Investor

are shown in Table 8.

57. Available points for applications for indefinite leave to remain are shown in Table 9.

58. Notes to accompany Table 7, Table 8 and Table 9 appear below Table 9.

Table 7: applications for entry clearance or leave to remain referred to in paragraph 60

Assets	**Points**
The applicant: (a) has money of his own under his control held in a regulated financial institution and disposable in the UK amounting to not less than £1 million; or (b) (i) owns personal assets which, taking into account any liabilities to which they are subject, have a value exceeding £2 million, and (ii) has money under his control held in a regulated financial institution and disposable in the UK amounting to not less than £1 million which has been loaned to him by a UK regulated financial institution.	75

Table 8: Applications for leave to remain referred to in paragraph 61

Assests and investment	**Points**
The applicant: (a) has money of his own under his control in the UK amounting to not less than £1 million, or (b) (i) owns personal assets which, taking into account any liabilities to which they are subject, have a value of not less than £2 million, and (ii) has money under his control and disposable in the UK amounting to not less than £1 million which has been loaned to him by a UK regulated financial institution.	30
The applicant has invested not less than £750,000 of his capital in the UK by way of UK Government bonds, share capital or loan capital in active and trading UK registered companies, subject to the restrictions set out in paragraph 65 below and has invested the remaining balance of £1,000,000 in the UK by the purchase of assets or by maintaining the money on deposit in a UK regulated financial institution.	30

Assests and investment	Points
The investment referred to above was made within 3 months of his entry to the UK (if he was granted entry clearance as a as a Tier 1 (Investor) Migrant and there is evidence to establish his date of arrival to the UK), or the date of the grant of entry clearance as a Tier 1 (Investor) Migrant (if there is no evidence to establish his date of arrival to the UK), or, in any other case, the date of the grant of leave to remain as a Tier 1 (Investor) Migrant and in each case the investment has been maintained for the whole of the remaining period of that leave; or The migrant has, or was last granted, entry clearance, leave to enter or leave to remain as an Investor.	15

Table 9: applications for indefinite leave to remain

Row	Assests and investment	Points
1	The applicant: (a) (i) has money of his own under his control in the UK amounting to not less than £10 million, or (ii) (1) owns personal assets which, taking into account any liabilities to which they are subject, have a value of not less than £20 million, and (2) has money under his control and disposable in the UK amounting to not less than £10 million which has been loaned to him by a UK regulated financial institution, or (b) (i) has money of his own under his control in the UK amounting to not less than £5 million, or (ii) (1) owns personal assets which, taking into account any liabilities to which they are subject, have a value of not less than £10 million, and (2) has money under his control and disposable in the UK amounting to not less than £5 million which has been loaned to him by a UK regulated financial institution, or (c) (i) has money of his own under his control in the UK amounting to not less than £1 million, or (ii) (1) owns personal assets which, taking into account any liabilities to which they are subject, have a value of not less than £2 million, and (2) has money under his control and disposable in the UK amounting to not less than £1 million which has been loaned to him by a UK regulated financial institution,	20
2.	The applicant has invested not less than 75% of the specified invested amount of his capital in the UK by way of UK Government bonds, share capital or loan capital in active and trading UK registered companies, subject to the restrictions set out in paragraph 65 below, and has invested the remaining balance of the specified invested amount in the UK by the purchase of assets or by maintaining the money on deposit in a UK regulated financial institution. The specified invested amount is: (a) £10,000,000 if the applicant scores points from row 1(a) above, (b) £5,000,000 if the applicant scores points from row 1(b) above, or (c) £1,000,000 if the applicant scores points from row 1(c) above.	20

Row	Assests and investment	Points
3.	The applicant has spent the specified continuous period lawfully in the UK, with absences from the UK of no more than 180 days in any 12 calendar months during that period. The specified continuous period must have been spent with leave as a Tier 1 (Investor) Migrant and/or as an Investor, of which the most recent period must have been spent with leave as a Tier 1 (Investor) Migrant. The specified continuous period is: (a) 2 years if the applicant scores points from row 1(a) above, (b) 3 years if the applicant scores points from row 1(b) above, or (c) 5 years if the applicant scores points from row 1(c) above.	20
4.	The applicant has maintained the full specified invested amount referred to in the relevant part of row 2 throughout the relevant specified continuous period referred to in row 3, other than in the first 3 months of that period and, in relation to time spent with leave as a Tier 1 (Investor) Migrant, has provided specified documents to show that this requirement has been met. When calculating the specified continuous period, the first day of that period will be taken to be the day 3 months before the full specified amount is invested.	15

Assets and investment: notes

59. Specified documents as set out in the Tier 1 (Investor) Guidance, published on the UK Border Agency website, must be provided as evidence of investment.

60. Money is disposable in the UK if all of the money is held in a UK based financial institution or if the money is freely transferable to the UK and convertible to sterling. funds in a foreign currency will be converted to pounds sterling (£) using the spot exchange rate which appeared on www.oanda.com* on the date on which the application was made.

61. 'Money of his own', 'personal assets' and 'his capital' include money or assets belonging to the applicant's spouse, civil partner or unmarried or same-sex partner, provided that:
  (a) the applicant's spouse, civil partner or unmarried or same-sex partner meets the requirements of paragraphs 319(c) and (d) of these rules, and
  (b) specified documents are provided to show that the money or assets are under the applicant's control and that he is free to invest them

62. 'Regulated financial institution' is defined in paragraph 43, Appendix A.

63. In the case of an application where Table 7 applies, where the money or assets referred to in Table 7 have already been invested in the UK before the date of application, points will only be awarded if they were invested in the UK no more than 12 months before the date of application.

64. In the case of an application where Table 7 applies, points will only be awarded if the applicant:
  (a) has had the money or assets referred to in Table 7 for a consecutive 90-day period of time, ending no earlier than one calendar month before the date of application, and provides the specified evidence; or
  (b) provides additional specified evidence of the source of the money or assets.

65. Investment excludes investment by the applicant by way of:
  (a) an offshore company or trust,
  (b) Open-ended investment companies, investment trust companies or pooled investment vehicles,
  (c) Companies mainly engaged in property investment, property management or property development,
  (d) Deposits with a bank, building society or other enterprise whose normal course of business includes the acceptance of deposits,
  (e) ISAs, premium bonds and saving certificates issued by the National Savings and Investment Agency (NS&I), for an applicant who has, or last had leave as a Tier 1 (Investor) Migrant, or
  (f) Leveraged investment funds.

Attributes for Tier 1 (Post-Study Work) Migrants

66. An applicant applying for entry clearance or leave to remain as a Tier 1 (Post-Study Work) Migrant must score 75 points for attributes.

67. Available points are shown in Table 10.

68. Notes to accompany the table appear below the table.

Table 10

Qualifications	**Points**
The applicant has been awarded: (a) a UK recognised bachelor or postgraduate degree, or (b) a UK postgraduate certificate in education or Professional Graduate Diploma of Education, or (c) a Higher National Diploma ('HND') from a Scottish institution.	20
(a) The applicant studied for his award at a UK institution that is a UK recognised or listed body, or which holds a sponsor licence under Tier 4 of the Points Based System, or (b) If the applicant is claiming points for having been awarded a Higher National Diploma from a Scottish Institution, he studied for that diploma at a Scottish publicly funded institution of further or higher education, or a Scottish bona fide private education institution which maintains satisfactory records of enrolment and attendance. The Scottish institution must: (i) be on the list of Education and Training Providers list on the Department of Business, Innovation and Skills website, or (ii) hold a Sponsor licence under Tier 4 of the Points Based System.	20
The applicant's periods of UK study and/or research towards his eligible award were undertaken whilst he had entry clearance, leave to enter or leave to remain in the UK that was not subject to a restriction preventing him from undertaking a course of study and/or research.	20
The applicant made the application for entry clearance or leave to remain as a Tier 1 (Post-Study Work) Migrant within 12 months of obtaining the relevant qualification or within 12 months of completing a United Kingdom Foundation Programme Office affiliated Foundation Programme as a postgraduate doctor or dentist.	15
The applicant is applying for leave to remain and has, or was last granted, leave as a Participant in the International Graduates Scheme (or its predecessor, the Science and Engineering Graduates Scheme) or as a Participant in the Fresh Talent: Working in Scotland Scheme.	75

Qualification: notes

69. Specified documents must be provided as evidence of the qualification and, where relevant, completion of the United Kingdom Foundation Programme Office affiliated Foundation Programme as a postgraduate doctor or dentist.

70. A qualification will have been deemed to have been 'obtained' on the date on which the applicant was first notified in writing, by the awarding institution, that the qualification had been awarded.

71. If the institution studied at is removed from one of the relevant lists referred to in Table 10, or from the Tier 4 Sponsor Register, no points will be awarded for a qualification obtained on or after the date the institution was removed from the relevant list or from the Tier 4 Sponsor Register.

72. To qualify as an HND from a Scottish institution, a qualification must be at level 8 on the Scottish Credit and Qualifications Framework.

Attributes for Tier 2 (Intra-Company Transfer) Migrants

73. An applicant applying for entry or leave to remain as a Tier 2 (Intra-Company Transfer) Migrant must score 50 points for attributes.

73A. Available points for entry clearance or leave to remain are shown in Table 11.

73B. Notes to accompany Table 11 appear below the table.

Table 11

Criterion	**Points**
Certificate of Sponsorship	30
Appropriate salary	20

Notes

Certificate of Sponsorship

74. In order to obtain points for a Certificate of Sponsorship, the applicant must provide a valid Certificate of Sponsorship reference number.

74A. A Certificate of Sponsorship reference number will only be considered to be valid if:

(a) the number supplied links to a Certificate of Sponsorship Checking Service entry that names the applicant as the migrant and confirms that the Sponsor is Sponsoring him as a Tier 2 (Intra-Company Transfer) Migrant and specifies the sub-category of Tier 2 (Intra-Company Transfer) under which he is applying,

(b) the Sponsor assigned the Certificate of Sponsorship reference number to the migrant no more than 3 months before the application for entry clearance or leave to remain is made,

(c) the application for entry clearance or leave to remain is made no more than 3 months before the start of the employment as stated on the Certificate of Sponsorship,

(d) The migrant must not previously have applied for entry clearance, leave to enter or leave to remain using the same Certificate of Sponsorship reference number, if that application was either approved or refused (not rejected as an invalid application or withdrawn),

(e) that reference number must not have been withdrawn or cancelled by the Sponsor or by the UK Border Agency since it was assigned, including where it has been cancelled by the UK Border Agency due to having been used in a previous application, and

(f) the Sponsor is an A-rated Sponsor, unless the application is for leave to remain and the applicant has, or was last granted, leave as a Tier 2 (Intra-Company) Migrant or a Qualifying Work Permit Holder.

74B. (a) Except in the cases referred to in paragraph (b) below, no points will be awarded for a Certificate of Sponsorship unless the job that the Certificate of Sponsorship Checking Service entry records that the person is being Sponsored to do appears on the list of graduate level occupations as stated in the codes of practice for Tier 2 Sponsors published by the UK Border Agency.

(b) Paragraph (a) does not apply where the applicant is applying for leave to remain as a Tier 2 (Intra-Company Transfer) Migrant in the Long Term Staff sub-category, and was last granted entry clearance, leave to enter or leave to remain as:

(i) a Qualifying Work Permit Holder, or

(ii) a Tier 2 (Intra-Company Transfer) Migrant under the rules in place before 6 April 2011.

(c) In the cases referred to in paragraph (b) above, no points will be awarded for a Certificate of Sponsorship unless:

(i) the job that the Certificate of Sponsorship Checking Service entry records that the person is being Sponsored to do appears on the list of occupations skilled to national Qualifications framework level 3 as stated in the codes of practice for Tier 2 Sponsors published by the UK Border Agency, or

(ii) the applicant is a Senior Care Worker or an Established Entertainer as defined in paragraph 6 of these Rules.

74C. (a) if the applicant is applying as a Tier 2 (Intra-Company Transfer) Migrant in either the Short Term Staff or Long Term Staff sub-categories, no points will be awarded for a Certificate of Sponsorship unless:

(i) the applicant has been working for the Sponsor for the specified period in paragraph (b) below,

(ii) the applicant has been working for the Sponsor outside the UK and/or in the UK, provided he had leave to work for the Sponsor as:

(1) a Tier 2 (Intra-Company Transfer) Migrant in either of the Short Term Staff or Long Term Staff sub-categories,

(2) a Tier 2 (Intra-Company Transfer) Migrant in the established staff sub-category under the rules in place before 6 April 2011,

(3) a Tier 2 (Intra-Company Transfer) Migrant under the rules in place before 6 April 2010,

(4) a Qualifying Work Permit Holder (provided that the work permit was granted because the holder was the subject of an Intra-Company Transfer), and/or

(5) as a representative of an Overseas Business, and

(iii) the applicant provides the specified documents as set out in the Tier 2 (Intra-Company Transfer) Guidance published on the UK Border Agency website.

(b) The specified period referred to in paragraph (a)(i) above is:

(i) a continuous period of 12 months immediately prior to the date of application, or

(ii) if at some point within the 12 months preceding the date of application, the applicant has been:

(1) on maternity, paternity or adoption leave,

(2) on long-term sick leave lasting one month or longer, or

(3) working for the Sponsor in the UK as a Tier 2 (Intra-Company Transfer) Migrant in either of the Graduate Trainee or Skills Transfer sub-categories,

and provides the specified evidence as set out in the Tier 2 (Intra-Company Transfer) Guidance published on the UK Border Agency website, an aggregated period of at least 12 months within the 24 month period immediately prior to the date of application.

74D. If the applicant is applying as a Tier 2 (Intra-Company Transfer) Migrant in the Graduate Trainee sub-category, no points will be awarded for a Certificate of Sponsorship unless:

(a) the job that the Certificate of Sponsorship Checking Service entry records that the person is being Sponsored to do is part of a structured graduate training programme as defined in Tier 2 (Intra-Company Transfer) Guidance published on the UK Border Agency website,

(b) the Sponsor has assigned Certificates of Sponsorship to 5 applicants or fewer, including the applicant in question, under the Graduate Trainee sub-category in the current year, beginning 6 April 2011 and ending 5 April 2012, and

(c) the applicant has been working for the Sponsor outside the UK for a continuous period of 3 months immediately prior to the date of application, and must provide the specified documents to prove this,

74E. If the applicant is applying as a Tier 2 (Intra-Company Transfer) Migrant in the Skills Transfer subcategory, no points will be awarded for a Certificate of Sponsorship unless the job that the Certificate of Sponsorship Checking Service entry records that the person is being Sponsored to do is for the sole purpose of transferring skills to or from the Sponsor's UK work environment. The appointment must be additional to staffing requirements that is the role in the UK would not exist but for the need for skills transfer.

74F. An applicant cannot score points for a Certificate of Sponsorship from Table 11 if the job that the Certificate of Sponsorship Checking Service entry records that he is being Sponsored to do is as a sports person or a Minister of Religion.

Appropriate salary

75. The points awarded for appropriate salary will be based on the applicant's gross annual salary to be paid by the Sponsor, as recorded in the Certificate of Sponsorship Checking Service entry to which the applicant's Certificate of Sponsorship reference number relates, subject to the following conditions:

(i) Points will be awarded based on basic pay (excluding overtime);

(ii) Allowances will be included in the salary for the awarding of points where they are part of the guaranteed salary package and:

(1) would be paid to a local settled worker in similar circumstances, or

(2) are paid to cover the additional cost of living in the UK;

(iii) Where allowances are made available solely for the purpose of accommodation, they will only be included up to a value of:

(1) 40% of the total salary package for which points are being awarded, if the applicant is applying in either the Short Term Staff, Graduate Trainee or Skills Transfer sub-categories, or

(2) 30% of the total salary package for which points are being awarded, if the applicant is applying in the Long Term Staff sub-category;

(iv) Allowances to cover business expenses, including (but not limited to) travel to and from the sending country, will not be included.

75A. No points will be awarded if the salary referred to in paragraph 75 above is less than £40,000 per year where the applicant is applying in the Long Term Staff sub-category, unless the applicant is applying for leave to remain and has, or last had entry clearance, leave to enter or leave to remain as:

(i) a Qualifying Work Permit Holder, or

(ii) a Tier 2 (Intra-Company Transfer) Migrant under the rules in place before 6 April 2011.

75B. No points will be awarded if the salary referred to in paragraph 75 above is less than £24,000 per year where the applicant is applying in the Short Term Staff, Graduate Trainee or Skills Transfer sub-categories, unless the applicant is applying for leave to remain and has, or last had entry clearance, leave to enter or leave to remain as a Tier 2 (Intra-Company Transfer) Migrant under the rules in place before 6 April 2011.

75C. No points will be awarded if the salary referred to in paragraph 75 above is less than the appropriate rate for the job as stated in the codes of practice for Tier 2 Sponsors published by the UK Border Agency, unless the applicant is an established entertainer as defined in paragraph 6 of these Rules.

75D. Where the applicant is paid hourly, the appropriate salary consideration will be based on earnings up to a maximum of 48 hours a week, even if the applicant works for longer than this. For example, an applicant who works 60 hours a week for £8 per hour be considered to have a salary of £19,968 (8x48x52) and not £25,960 (8x60x52), and will therefore not be awarded points for appropriate salary.

75E. No points will be awarded for appropriate salary if the applicant does not provide a valid Certificate of Sponsorship reference number with his application.

Attributes for Tier 2 (General) Migrants

76. An applicant applying for entry or leave to remain as a Tier 2 (General) Migrant must score 50 points for attributes.

76A. Available points for entry clearance or leave to remain are shown in Table 11A.

76B. Notes to accompany Table 11A appear below the table.

Table 11A

Certificate of Sponsorship	Points	Appropriate salary	Points
Shortage occupation	30	Appropriate salary	20
Job offer with a salary of £150,000 or more	30		
Job offer passes resident labour Market Test	30		
Post-Study Work	30		
Continuing to work in the same job for the same Sponsor	30		

Notes

Certificate of Sponsorship

77. Points may only be scored for one entry in the Certificate of Sponsorship column.

77A. In order to obtain points for a Certificate of Sponsorship, the applicant must provide a valid Certificate of Sponsorship reference number.

77B. The only Certificates of Sponsorship to be allocated to Sponsors for applicants to be Sponsored as Tier 2 (General) Migrants during the period 6 April 2011 to 5 April 2012 are:

(a) Certificates of Sponsorship to be assigned to applicants for entry clearance as a Tier 2 (General) Migrant, as allocated to Sponsors under the Tier 2 (General) limit, which is set out in paragraphs 80 to 84A below.

(b) Certificates of Sponsorship to be assigned to applicants for leave to remain as a Tier 2 (General) Migrant,

(c) Certificates of Sponsorship to be assigned to an applicant to do a job for which the gross annual salary (including such allowances as are specified as acceptable for this purpose in guidance issued by the UK Border Agency) is £150,000 or higher,

and

77C. A Certificate of Sponsorship reference number will only be considered to be valid if:

(a) the number supplied links to a Certificate of Sponsorship Checking Service entry that names the applicant as the migrant and confirms that the Sponsor is Sponsoring him as a Tier 2 (General) Migrant,

(b) the Sponsor assigned that reference number to the migrant no more than 3 months after the Sponsor was allocated the Certificate of Sponsorship, if the Certificate of Sponsorship was allocated to the Sponsor under the Tier 2 (General) limit,

(c) the Sponsor assigned that reference number to the migrant no more than 3 months before the application for entry clearance or leave to remain is made,

(d) the application for entry clearance or leave to remain is made no more than 3 months before the start of the employment as stated on the Certificate of Sponsorship,

(e) the migrant must not previously have applied for entry clearance, leave to enter or leave to remain using the same Certificate of Sponsorship reference number, regardless of whether that previous application was successful,

(f) that reference number must not have been withdrawn or cancelled by the Sponsor or by the UK Border Agency since it was assigned, including where it has been cancelled by the UK Border Agency due to having been used in a previous application, and

(g) the Sponsor is an A-rated Sponsor, unless:

(1) the application is for leave to remain, and

(2) the applicant has, or was last granted, leave as a Tier 2 (General) Migrant, a Jewish Agency Employee, a Member of the Operational Ground Staff of an Overseas-owned Airline, a Representative of an Overseas Newspaper, News Agency or Broadcasting Organisation, or a Qualifying Work Permit Holder, and

(3) the applicant is applying to work for the same employer named on the Certificate of Sponsorship or Work Permit document which led to his last grant of leave or, in the case of an applicant whose last grant of leave was as a Jewish Agency Employee, a Member of the Operational Ground Staff of an Overseas-owned Airline, a Representative of an Overseas Newspaper, News Agency or Broadcasting Organisation, the same employer for whom the applicant was working or stated he was intending to work when last granted leave.

77D. No points will be awarded for a Certificate of Sponsorship unless:

(a) in the case of a Certificate of Sponsorship which was allocated to the Sponsor under the Tier 2 (General) limit, the number supplied links to a Certificate of Sponsorship Checking Service entry which contains the same job and at least the same salary details as stated in the Sponsor's application for that Certificate of Sponsorship,

(b) in the case of a Certificate of Sponsorship which was not allocated to the Sponsor under the Tier 2 (General) limit:

(i) the applicant is applying for leave to remain, or

(ii) the number supplied links to a Certificate of Sponsorship Checking Service entry which shows that the applicant's gross annual salary (including such allowances as are specified as acceptable for this purpose in paragraph 79 of this appendix) to be paid by the Sponsor is £150,000 or higher.

77E. (a) Except in the cases referred to in paragraphs (b) and (c) below, no points will be awarded for a Certificate of Sponsorship unless the job that the Certificate of Sponsorship Checking Service entry records that the person is being sponsored to do appears on the list of graduate level occupations as stated in the codes of practice for Tier 2 Sponsors published by the UK Border Agency, or on the list of shortage occupations published by the UK Border Agency.

(b) Paragraph (a) above does not apply to cases where the applicant:

(i) is applying for leave to remain as a Tier 2 (General) Migrant,

(ii) has previously had entry clearance, leave to enter or leave to remain as:

(1) a Qualifying Work Permit Holder,

(2) a Representative of an Overseas Newspaper, News Agency or Broadcasting Organisation,

(3) a Member of the Operational Ground Staff of an Overseas-owned Airline

(4) a Jewish Agency Employee, or

(5) a Tier 2 (General) Migrant under the rules in place before 6 April 2011,

less than 5 years before the date that the applicant's last grant of entry clearance, leave to enter or leave to remain expires, and

(iii) has not been granted entry clearance as a Tier 2 (General) Migrant or in any other category since his last grant of leave in one of the categories in (ii) above.

(c) Paragraph (a) above also does not apply to cases where:

(i) the applicant is applying for leave to remain,

(ii) the applicant has, or last had, entry clearance, leave to enter or leave to remain as a Tier 2 (General) Migrant or a Qualifying Work Permit Holder,

(iii) at the time the Certificate of Sponsorship or Work Permit which led to the grant of leave in (ii) was issued, the job referred to in that Certificate of Sponsorship or Work Permit appeared on the list of shortage occupations published by the UK Border Agency, and

(iv) the job that the Certificate of Sponsorship Checking service entry records that the person is being sponsored to do in his current application is the same as the job referred to in (iii), for either the same or a different employer.

(d) in the cases referred to in paragraphs (b) and (c) above, no points will be awarded for a Certificate of Sponsorship unless:

(i) the job that the Certificate of Sponsorship Checking Service entry records that the person is being Sponsored to do appears on the list of occupations skilled to National Qualifications Framework level 3 as stated in the codes of practice for Tier 2 Sponsors published by the UK Border Agency, or

(ii) the applicant is a senior Care Worker or an Established Entertainer as defined in paragraph 6 of these Rules.

77F. An applicant cannot score points for a Certificate of Sponsorship from Table 11A if the job that the Certificate of Sponsorship Checking Service entry records that he is being sponsored to do is as a sports person or a Minister of Religion.

Shortage occupation

78. In order for the applicant to be awarded points for a job offer in a shortage occupation:

(a) the job must, at the time the Certificate of Sponsorship was assigned to the applicant, have appeared on the list of shortage occupations published by the UK Border Agency,

(b) in all cases, contracted working hours must be for at least 30 hours a week, and

(c) in all cases, if the UK Border Agency list of shortage occupations indicates that the job appears on the 'Scotland only' shortage occupation list, the job offer must be for employment in which the applicant will be working at a location in Scotland.

Job offer with a salary of £150,000 or more

78A. In order for the applicant to be awarded points for a job offer with a salary of £150,000 or more, the Certificate of Sponsorship Checking Service entry must show that the applicant's gross annual salary (including such allowances as are specified as acceptable for this purpose in paragraph 79 of this appendix) to be paid by the Sponsor is £150,000 or higher.

Job offer passes Resident Labour Market Test

78B. In order for the applicant to be awarded points for a job offer that passes the resident labour market test:

(a) the Certificate of Sponsorship Checking Service entry must indicate that the Sponsor has met the requirements of that test, as defined in guidance published by the UK Border Agency, in respect of the job, and

(b) if the guidance referred to in (a) specifies that the job must have been advertised in Jobcentre Plus or JobCentre online, the Certificate of Sponsorship Checking Service entry must also contain the Jobcentre Plus or JobCentre online vacancy reference number.

Post-Study Work

78C. In order for the applicant to be awarded points for post-study work:

(a) the applicant must be applying for leave to remain,

(b) the applicant must have entry clearance or leave to remain as a Tier 1 (Post study Work) Migrant, or as a Participant in the International Graduates' Scheme (or its predecessor, the Science and Engineering Graduates Scheme) or as a Participant in the Fresh Talent: Working in Scotland Scheme,

(c) the applicant must have been working for the Sponsor for the specified period, and must provide the specified documents to prove this. The specified period is:

(i) a continuous period of 6 months immediately prior to the date of application, or

(ii) if at some point within the 6 months preceding the date of application the applicant has been:

(1) on maternity, paternity or adoption leave, or

(2) on long-term sick leave lasting one month or longer

and provides the specified evidence as set out in the Tier 2 (General) Guidance published on the UK Border Agency website, an aggregated period of at least 6 months within the 18 month period immediately prior to the date of application, and

(d) the job the applicant is being sponsored to do must be the same as the one he is doing at the time of his application.

Continuing to work in the same job for the same Sponsor

78D. In order for the applicant to be awarded points for continuing to work in the same job for the same Sponsor:

(a) the applicant must be applying for leave to remain,

(b) the applicant must have entry clearance or leave to remain as:

(i) a Tier 2 (General) Migrant,

(ii) a Qualifying Work Permit Holder,

(iii) a Representative of an Overseas Newspaper, News Agency or Broadcasting Organisation,

(iv) a Member of the Operational Ground Staff of an Overseas-owned Airline or

(v) a Jewish Agency Employee,

(b) the Sponsor must be the same employer:

(i) as the Sponsor on the previous application that was granted, in the case of an applicant whose last grant of leave was as a Tier 2 (General) Migrant,

(ii) that the work permit was issued to, in the case of an applicant whose last grant of leave was as a Qualifying Work Permit Holder,

(iii) for whom the applicant was working or stated he was intending to work when last granted leave, in the case of an applicant whose last grant of leave was a Representative of an Overseas Newspaper, News Agency or Broadcasting Organisation, a Member of the Operational Ground Staff of an Overseas-owned Airline, or a Jewish Agency Employee.

(c) the job that the Certificate of Sponsorship Checking Service entry records the applicant as having been engaged to do must be the same job:

(i) in respect of which the Certificate of Sponsorship that led to the previous grant was issued, in the case of an applicant whose last grant of leave was as a Tier 2 (General) Migrant,

(ii) in respect of which the previous work permit was issued, in the case of an applicant whose last grant of leave was as a Qualifying Permit Holder, or

(iii) that the applicant was doing, or intended to do, when he received his last grant of leave, in the case of an applicant whose last grant of leave was a Representative of an Overseas Newspaper, News Agency or Broadcasting Organisation, a Member of the Operational Ground Staff of an Overseas-owned Airline, or a Jewish Agency Employee.

Appropriate salary

79. The points awarded for appropriate salary will be based on the applicant's gross annual salary to be paid by the Sponsor, as recorded in the Certificate of Sponsorship Checking Service entry to which the applicant's Certificate of Sponsorship reference number relates, subject to the following conditions:
    (i) Points will be awarded based on basic pay (excluding overtime);
    (ii) Allowances, such as London weighting, will be included in the salary for the awarding of points where they are part of the guaranteed salary package and would be paid to a local settled worker in similar circumstances;
    (iii) Other allowances and benefits, such as bonus or incentive pay, travel and subsistence (including travel to and from the applicant's home country), will not be included.

79A. No points will be awarded if the salary referred to in paragraph 79 above is less than £20,000 per year, unless the applicant is applying for leave to remain and has, or last had entry clearance, leave to enter or leave to remain as:
    (i) a Qualifying Work Permit Holder,
    (ii) a Representative of an Overseas Newspaper, News Agency or Broadcasting Organisation,
    (iii) a Member of the operational Ground Staff of an Overseas-owned Airline
    (iv) a Jewish Agency Employee, or
    (v) a Tier 2 (General) Migrant under the Rules in place before 6 April 2011.

79B. No points will be awarded for appropriate salary if the salary referred to in paragraph 79 above is less than the appropriate rate for the job as stated in the codes of practice for Tier 2 Sponsors published by the UK Border Agency, unless the applicant is an established entertainer as defined in paragraph 6 of these Rules.

79C. Where the applicant is paid hourly, the appropriate salary consideration will be based on earnings up to a maximum of 48 hours a week, even if the applicant works for longer than this. for example, an applicant who works 60 hours a week for £8 per hour be considered to have a salary of £19,968 (8x48x52) and not £25,960 (8x60x52), and will therefore not be awarded points for appropriate salary.

79D. No points will be awarded for appropriate salary if the applicant does not provide a valid Certificate of Sponsorship reference number with his application.

Tier 2 (General) limit

Overview

80. The Secretary of State shall be entitled to limit the number of Certificates of Sponsorship available to be allocated to Sponsors in any specific period under the Tier 2 (General) limit referred to in paragraph 77B(a) above;

80A. The Tier 2 (General) limit for the specific period 6 April 2011 to 5 April 2012 is 20,700 Certificates of Sponsorship.

80B. The process by which Certificates of Sponsorship shall be allocated to Sponsors under the Tier 2 (General) limit is set out in paragraphs 80C to 84a and Tables 11B and 11C below.

80C. A Sponsor must apply to the Secretary of State for a Certificate of Sponsorship.

80D. Available points for an application for a Certificate of Sponsorship are shown in Table 11B. No application will be granted unless it scores a minimum of 30 points under the heading 'Type of Job' and a minimum of 2 points under the heading 'Salary on Offer'.

80E. Notes to accompany Table 11B appear below the table.

Table 11B Applications for Certificates of Sponsorship under the Tier 2 (General) limit

Type of job	Points	Salary on offer	Points
Shortage Occupation	75	£20,000–£20,999.99	2
PhD-level occupation code and job passes resident labour Market Test	50	£21,000–£21,999.99	3
Job passes resident labour Market Test	30	£22,000–£22,999.99	4
		£23,000–£23,999.99	5
		£24,000–£24,999.99	6
		£25,000–£25,999.99	7

Type of job	Points	Salary on offer	Points
		£26,000–£26,999.99	8
		£27,000–£27,999.99	9
		£28,000–£31,999.99	10
		£32,000–£45,999.99	15
		£46,000–£74,999.99	20
		£75,000–£99,999.99	25
		£100,000–£149,999.99	30

Notes

81. Points may only be scored for one entry in each column.

81A. No points will be awarded under the heading 'Type of Job' unless the job described in the Sponsor's application for a Certificate of Sponsorship appears on the list of graduate level occupations as stated in the codes of practice for Tier 2 Sponsors published by the UK Border Agency.

81B. In order for the Sponsor's application to be awarded points for a job in a shortage occupation, the job must, at the time the application for a Certificate of Sponsorship is decided, appear on the list of shortage occupations published by the UK Border Agency, and contracted working hours must be for at least 30 hours a week. Furthermore, if the UK Border Agency list of shortage occupations indicates that the job appears on the 'Scotland only' shortage occupation list, the job must be for employment in Scotland.

81C. In order for the Sponsor's application to be awarded points for a job in a PhD-level occupation code, the job must be in an occupation code which appears on the list of PhD-level occupation codes as stated in the Sponsor Guidance published by the UK Border Agency. The Sponsor's application must also meet the requirements of paragraph 81D.

81D. In order for the Sponsor's application to be awarded points for a job that passes the resident labour market test, the Sponsor must certify that it has met the requirements of that test, as defined in guidance published by the UK Border Agency, in respect of the job.

81E. The points awarded under the heading 'Salary on Offer' will be based on the gross annual salary on offer to be paid by the Sponsor, as stated in the Sponsor's application, subject to the following conditions:

(i) Points will be awarded based on basic pay (excluding overtime);

(ii) Allowances, such as London weighting, will be included in the salary for the awarding of points where they are part of the guaranteed salary package and would be paid to a local settled worker in similar circumstances;

(iii) Other allowances and benefits, such as bonus or incentive pay, travel and subsistence (including travel to and from the applicant's home country), will not be included.

81F. No points will be awarded for the salary on offer if the salary referred to in paragraph 81e above is less than the appropriate rate for the job as stated in the codes of practice for Tier 2 Sponsors published by the UK Border Agency.

81G. Where the salary on offer will be paid hourly, the salary on offer will be calculated on the basis of earnings up to a maximum of 48 hours a week, even if the jobholder works for longer than this.

Monthly allocations

82. The Tier 2 (General) limit will be divided into monthly allocations.

82A. There will be a monthly allocation specifying the number of Certificates of Sponsorship available to be allocated in respect of applications for Certificates of Sponsorship received during each application period. The provisional monthly allocation, subject to the processes set out in paragraphs 83 to 84a below, in respect of each application period is set out in table 11C below.

82B. Applications by Sponsors for Certificates of Sponsorship will be accepted for consideration against each monthly allocation in the relevant application period as set out in table 11C below.

82C. An application that would fall to be considered as having been received in a particular application period may be deferred for consideration as if it had been received in the following application period if the Secretary of State considers that the information stated in the application requires verification checks, and may be refused if the information cannot be verified or is confirmed as false. If the verification checks are prolonged due to the failure of the Sponsor to co-operate with the verification process such that the application cannot be considered as if it had been received in the next monthly allocation period, the application will be refused.

82D. These provisional monthly allocations may be adjusted according to the processes set out in paragraphs 83 to 84a in the notes below the table.

Table 11C Certificates of Sponsorship under the Tier 2 (General) limit available to be allocated each month (subject to the processes set out at paragraphs 83 to 84A)

Application Period	Provisional monthly allocation
Up to 6 April 2011	4,200
7 April–5 May 2011	1,500
6 May 2011–5 June 2011	1,500
6 June 2011–5 July 2011	1,500
6 July 2011–5 August 2011	1,500
6 August 2011–5 September 2011	1,500
6 September 2011–5 October 2011	1,500
6 October 2011–5 November 2011	1,500
6 November 2011–5 December 2012	1,500
6 December 2012–5 January 2012	1,500
6 January 2012–5 February 2012	1,500
6 February 2012–5 March 2012	1,500

Notes

83. In paragraphs 83A to 84a below:

(a) 'number of applications' means the number of applications by Sponsors for a Certificate of Sponsorship under the Tier 2 (General) limit in one of the monthly periods set out in Table 11C above.

(b) 'monthly allocation' means the monthly allocation for that period as set out in Table 11C above, including if applicable any adjustment according to the processes set out in these paragraphs following the assigning of Certificates of Sponsorship under the Tier 2 (General) limit in the previous monthly period.

83A. Subject to paragraph 83e below, if the number of applications is equal to or less than the monthly allocation:

(a) All applications by Sponsors which score 32 points or more from the points available in Table 11B above will be granted, and

(b) If the number of applications granted under (a) above is less than the monthly allocation, the next monthly allocation will be increased by a number equivalent to the Certificates of Sponsorship remaining for allocation in the undersubscribed current month.

83B. Subject to paragraph 83e below, if the number of applications is greater than the monthly allocation:

(a) The minimum points level at which applications for Certificates of Sponsorship will be granted will be calculated as follows:

(i) if the number of applications scoring 32 points or more is no more than 100 greater than the monthly allocation, all applications which score 32 points or more will be granted.

(ii) if the number of applications scoring 32 points or more is more than 100 greater than the monthly allocation, X (being both the number of points scored in Table 11B above and the minimum number of points required for an application to be granted) will be increased by 1 point incrementally until the number of applications scoring X points is:

(1) less than or equal to the monthly allocation; or

(2) no more than 100 greater than the monthly allocation;

whichever results in the higher value of X, at which stage all applications which score X points or more will be granted.

(b) if the number of applications granted under (a) above is less than the monthly allocation, the number remaining under the monthly allocation will be added to the next monthly allocation.

(c) if the number of applications granted under (a) above is more than the monthly allocation, the number by which the monthly allocation is exceeded will be subtracted from the next monthly allocation.

83C. If a Sponsor is allocated one or more Certificates of Sponsorship under the Tier 2 (General) limit which it then elects not to assign to a migrant it may return them to the Secretary of State and the Secretary of State will subsequently add such Certificates of Sponsorship to the following monthly allocation.

83D. If:

(i) a Sponsor is allocated one or more Certificates of Sponsorship under the Tier 2 (General) limit; and

(ii) the application(s) by the Sponsor scored points from Table 11C for a job in a shortage occupation; and

(iii) the Sponsor has not assigned the Certificate(s) of Sponsorship to a migrant(s); and

(iv) the job(s) in question no longer appear on the list of shortage occupations published by the UK Border Agency,

the Certificate(s) of Sponsorship in question will be cancelled and the Secretary of State will subsequently add such Certificates of Sponsorship to the following monthly allocation.

83E.

With regard to the final monthly allocation under the Tier 2 (General) limit for 6 April 2011 to 5 April 2012 to which the application period of 6 February 2012 to 5 March 2012 relates:

(i) Paragraphs 83a(b), 83B(b) and 83B(c) do not apply to this monthly allocation, such that no adjustments will be made to the next monthly allocation, and

(ii) References to 'more than 100 greater than the monthly allocation' in paragraphs 83B(a)(ii) to (iii) are amended to 'greater than the monthly allocation', such that the total Tier 2 (General) limit of 20,700 Certificates of Sponsorship in the period 6 April 2011 to 5 April 2012 will not be exceeded.

84. The Secretary of State is entitled (but not required) to grant an application for a Certificate of Sponsorship under the Tier 2 (General) limit exceptionally outside of the processes set out in paragraphs 82a to 83B above if:

(a) the application is considered by the Secretary of State to require urgent treatment when considered in line with the Tier 2 (Sponsor) guidance published on the UK Border Agency website, and

(b) the application scores enough points from Table 11B above that it would have met the requirements to be granted under the previous monthly allocation.

84A. For each Certificate of Sponsorship application granted under the urgent treatment process set out in paragraph 84 above:

(i) the current monthly allocation for granting Certificates of Sponsorship further to requests for urgent treatment will be reduced by one, if the current monthly allocation has not yet been reached; or

(ii) In all other cases, the subsequent monthly allocation for granting Certificates of Sponsorship further to requests for urgent treatment will be reduced by one.

Attributes for Tier 2 (Ministers of Religion) Migrants

85. An applicant applying for entry clearance or leave to remain as a Tier 2(Ministers of Religion) Migrant must score 50 points for attributes.

86. Available points are shown in Table 12 below.

87. Notes to accompany Table 12 appear below that table.

Table 12

Criterion	**Points**
Certificate of Sponsorship	50

Notes

88. In order to obtain points for sponsorship. the applicant will need to provide a valid Certificate of Sponsorship reference number in this category.

89. A Certificate of Sponsorship reference number will only be considered to be valid for the purposes of this sub-category if:

(a) the number supplied links to a Certificate of Sponsorship Checking Service entry that names the applicant as the Migrant and confirms that the sponsor is sponsoring him as a Tier 2 (Minister of Religion) Migrant, and

(b) the Sponsor is an A-rated Sponsor, unless:

(1) the application is for leave to remain, and

(2) the applicant has, or was last granted, leave as a Tier 2 (Minister of Religion) Migrant, a Minister of Religion, Missionary or Member of a Religious Order, and

(3) the applicant is applying to work for the same employer named on the Certificate of Sponsorship which led to his last grant of leave or, in the case of an applicant whose last grant of leave was as a Minister of Religion, Missionary or Member of a Religious Order, the same employer for whom the applicant was working or stated he was intending to work when last granted leave.

90. The sponsor must have assigned the Certificate of Sponsorship reference number to the migrant no more than 3 months before the application is made and the reference number must not have been cancelled by the Sponsor or by the United Kingdom Border Agency since then.

91. The migrant must not previously have been granted entry clearance, leave to enter or leave to remain relying on the same Certificate of Sponsorship reference number.

92. In addition, the Certificate of Sponsorship Checking Service entry must confirm that:

(a) the resident labour market test, as defined in guidance published by the United Kingdom Border Agency, in respect of the job, has been complied with, unless the applicant has, or was last granted, entry clearance, leave to enter or leave to remain as a Tier 2 (Minister of Religion) Migrant or Minister of Religion and the Sponsor is the same person as he was working for, or intending to work for, when last granted leave,

(b) the migrant:

(i) is qualified to do the job in respect of which he is seeking leave as a Tier 2 (Minister of Religion) Migrant,

(ii) intends to base himself in the UK, and,

(iii) will complay with the conditions of his leave, if his application is successful, and

(c) the Sponsor will maintain or accommodate the migrant.

Attributes for Tier 2 (Sportsperson) Migrants

93. An applicant applying for entry clearance or leave to remain as a Tier 2 (Sportsperson) Migrant must score 50 points for attributes.

94. Available points are shown in Table 13 below

95. Notes to accompany Table 13 appear below that table.

Table 13

Criterion	**Points**
Certificate of Sponsorship	50

Notes

96. In order to obtain points for sponsorship, the applicant will need to provide a valid Certificate of Sponsorship reference number for sponsorship in this subcategory.

97. A Certificate of Sponsorship reference number will only be considered to be valid for the purposes of this sub-category if:

(a) the number supplied links to a Certificate of Sponsorship Checking Service entry that names the applicant as the Migrant and confirms that the sponsor is sponsoring him as a Tier 2 (Sportsperson) Migrant, and

(b) the Sponsor is an A-rated Sponsor, unless:

(1) the application is for leave to remain, and

(2) the applicant has, or was last granted, leave as a Tier 2 (Sportsperson) Migrant or a Qualifying Work Permit Holder, and

(3) the applicant is applying to work for the same employer named on the Certificate of Sponsorship or Work Permit document which led to his last grant of leave.

98. The Sponsor must have assigned the Certificate of Sponsorship reference number to the migrant no more than 3 months before the application is made and the reference number must not have been cancelled by the Sponsor or by the United Kingdom Border Agency since then.

99. The migrant must not previously have been granted entry clearance. leave to enter or leave to remain relying on the same Certificate of Sponsorship reference number.

100. In addition the Certificate of Sponsorship Checking Service entry must confirm that the migrant:

(a) is qualified to do the job in question

(b) has been endorsed by the Governing Body for his Sport (that is, the organisation which is specified in the United Kingdom Border Agency published guidance as being the Governing Body for the sport in question),

(c) The endorsement referred to in (b) above must confirm that the player or coach is internationally established at the highest level whose employment will make a significant contribution to the development of his sport at the highest level in the UK, and that the post could not be filled by a suitable settled worker,

(d) intends to base himself in the UK, and

(e) will comply with the conditions of his leave, if his application is successful.

Attributes for Tier 5 (Youth Mobility Scheme) Temporary Migrants

101. An applicant applying for entry clearance as a Tier 5 (Youth Mobility Scheme) Temporary Migrant must score 40 points for attributes

102. Available points are shown in Table 14 below.

103. Notes to accompany Table 14 below.

Table 14

Criterion	**Points**
Citizen of a country in Appendix G or Is a British Overseas Citizen, British Territories Overseas Citizen or British National (Overseas.)	30
Will be 18 or over when his entry clearance becomes valid for use and was under the age of 31 on the date his application was made.	10

Notes

104. Specified documents must be provided as evidence of all of the above.

Attributes for Tier 5 (Temporary Worker) Migrants

105. An applicant applying for entry clearance or leave enter or remain as a Tier 5 (Temporary Worker) Migrant must score 30 points for attributes.

106. Available points are shown in Table 15 below.

107. Notes to accompany Table 15 appear below in that table.

Table 15

Criterion	**Points Awarded**
Holds a Tier 5 (Temporary Worker) Certificate of Sponsorship	30

Notes

108. In order to meet the 'holds a Certificate of Sponsorship' requirement, the applicant will provide a valid Certificate of Sponsorship reference number for sponsorship in this category.

109. A Certificate of Sponsorship reference number will only be considered to be valid if the number supplied links to a Certificate of Sponsorship Checking Service reference that names the applicant as the migrant and confirms that the Sponsor is sponsoring him as a Tier 5 (Temporary Worker) Migrant in the subcategory indicated by the migrant in his application for entry clearance or leave.

109A. A Certificate of Sponsorship reference number will only be considered to be valid if:

(a) the Sponsor assigned the reference number to the migrant no more than 3 months before the application for entry clearance or leave to remain is made, unless the migrant is applying for leave to enter and has previously been granted leave to enter using the same Certificate of Sponsorship reference number,

(b) the application for entry clearance or leave to remain is made no more than 3 months before the start date of the employment as stated on the Certificate of Sponsorship,

(c) that reference number must not have been cancelled by the Sponsor or by the United Kingdom Border Agency since it was assigned, and

(d) the Sponsor is an A-rated sponsor, unless the application is for leave to remain and the applicant has, or was last granted, leave as a Tier 5 Migrant, an Overseas Government Employee or a Qualifying Work Permit Holder.

110. The migrant must not previously have applied for entry clearance or leave to remain using the same Certificate of Sponsorship reference number, regardless of whether that previous application was successful.

111. In addition, where the Certificate of Sponsorship Checking Service entry shows that the Certificate of Sponsorship has been issued in creative and sporting subcategory of a Tier 5 (Temporary Worker) route to enable the applicant to work as a sportsperson:

(a) The Certificate of Sponsorship Checking Service entry must show that the applicant has been endorsed by the Governing Body for his sport (that is, the organisation which is specified in the UK Border Agency's published guidelines as being the Governing Body for the sport in question), and

(b) The endorsement referred to in (a) above must confirm that the player or coach is internationally established at the highest level and/or will make a significant contribution to the development of his sport at the highest level in the UK, and that the post could not be filled by a suitable settled worker.

112. Points will not be awarded for a Tier 5 (Temporary Worker) Certificate of Sponsorship where the claimed basis for its issuance are the provisions under Mode 4 of the General Agreement on Trade in Services relating to intra-corporate transfers.

Attributes for Tier 4 (General) Students

113. An applicant applying for entry clearance or leave to remain as a Tier 4 (General) Student must score 30 points for attributes.

114. Available points are shown in Table 16 below.

115. Notes to accompany Table 16 appear below that table.

Table 16

Criterion	**Points Awarded**
Confirmation of Acceptance for Studies	30

Notes

115A. In order to obtain points for a Confirmation of Acceptance for Studies, the applicant must provide a valid Confirmation of Acceptance for Studies reference number.

Tier 4 Interim Limit

115B. The Secretary of State shall be entitled to limit the number of Confirmations of Acceptance for Studies allocated to any specific Sponsor in any one period.

115C. The limit on the number of Confirmations of Acceptance for Studies allocated to specific Sponsors shall be known as the Tier 4 Interim Limit.

115D. The Tier 4 Interim Limit will apply from 21 April 2011 to 5 April 2012 (inclusive) (the 'Tier 4 Interim Limit Period').

115E. The Tier 4 Interim Limit will be applied to any Tier 4 Sponsor that does not satisfy both of the following criteria throughout the Tier 4 Interim Limit Period:

(i) has Highly Trusted Sponsor status; and

(ii) is subject to and holds a valid and satisfactory full institutional inspection, review or audit by one of the following bodies:

(a) the Bridge Schools Inspectorate; or

(b) the Education and Training Inspectorate; or

(c) Estyn; or

(d) Education Scotland; or

(e) the Independent Schools Inspectorate; or

(f) Ofsted; or

(g) the Quality Assurance Agency for Higher Education; or

(h) The Schools Inspection Service;

or is not:

(iii) an independent school;

(iv) the Foundation Programme Office;

(v) the Yorkshire and Humber Strategic Health Authority

(vi) a Tier 4 Sponsor that applied for a Tier 4 Sponsor licence on or after 21 April 2011 and meets the requirements of (ii) (but not (i)) above; or

(vii) an overseas higher education institution which has Highly Trusted Sponsor Status.

115F. A Tier 4 Sponsor who does not satisfy the requirements of paragraph 115E and is therefore subject to the Tier 4 Interim Limit is known as a Limited Sponsor.

115G. All Confirmations of Acceptance for Studies allocated by the Secretary of State to Limited Sponsors prior to 21 April 2011 and which have not been assigned to an applicant for entry clearance, leave to enter or leave to remain under Tier 4 prior to 21 April 2011 are withdrawn and the only Confirmations of Acceptance for Studies allocated to a Limited Sponsor are the Confirmations of Acceptance for Studies allocated in acccordance with paragraph 115H below.

115H. The Tier 4 Interim Limit will be calculated as follows:

(i) A Limited Sponsor who has that status as at 21 April 2011 will be allocated:

(a) where the Limited Sponsor had a Tier 4 Sponsor Licence for the entirety of the period 1 March 2010 to 28 February 2011, a number of Confirmations of Acceptance for Studies equal to the number assigned by that Limited Sponsor to Tier 4 Migrants which were used for an application which resulted in a grant of entry clearance, leave to enter or leave to remain, where both the assignment and grant of leave were between 1 March 2010 and 28 February 2011;

(b) where the Limited Sponsor had a Tier 4 Sponsor Licence for only part of the period 1 March 2010 to 28 February 2011, a number of Confirmations of Acceptance for Studies equal to:

(i) the number of Confirmations of Acceptance for Studies assigned by the Limited Sponsor to Tier 4 Migrants which were used for an application which resulted in a grant of entry clearance, leave to enter or leave to remain, where both the assignment and grant of leave were between 1 March 2010 and 28 February 2011;

(ii) multiplied by the appropriate factor to increase the figure in (i) until it is equal to the number of Confirmations of Acceptance for Studies that would have been assigned and granted in a period of 12 months;

(c) where the Limited Sponsor did not have a Tier 4 Sponsor licence during the period 1 March 2010 to 28 February 2011, a number of Confirmations of Acceptance for Studies equal to:

(i) the annual allocation the Limited Sponsor received when it was granted its Tier 4 Sponsor licence;

(ii) less 26% which is the average percentage of Confirmations of Acceptance for Studies assigned by Limited Sponsors which did not result in a grant of entry clearance, leave to enter or leave to remain, where both the assignment and refusal of leave were between 1 March 2010 and 28 February 2011;

(d) where the calculation in paragraphs (a) to (c) above results in 0 or a negative number, the Limited Sponsor will be allocated 0 Confirmations of Acceptance for Studies under the Tier 4 Interim Limit.

(ii) A Limited Sponsor who acquires that status after 21 April 2011 will be allocated a number of Confirmations of Acceptance for Studies:

(a) equal to the result of the calculation appropriate for the Limited Sponsor's circumstances as set out in 115H(i) above; and

(b) subject to a reduction equal to the number of Confirmations of Acceptance for Studies assigned by the Limited Sponsor to Tier 4 Migrants since 21 April 2011 which were used for an application which resulted in a grant of entry clearance, leave to enter or leave to remain since 21 April 2011.

115I. A Limited Sponsor will, on provision to the UK Border Agency of evidence that it meets the criteria set out in paragraph 115E above, be exempt from the Tier 4 Interim Limit from the date the UK Border Agency provides written confirmation that it is so exempt.

116. A Confirmation of Acceptance for Studies will only be considered to be valid if:

(a) it was issued no more than 6 months before the application is made,

(b) the application for entry clearance or leave to remain is made no more than 3 months before the start date of the course of study as stated on the Confirmation of Acceptance for Studies,

(c) the Sponsor has not withdrawn the offer since the Confirmation of Acceptance for Studies was issued,

(d) it was issued by an institution with a Tier 4 (General) Student Sponsor Licence,

(da) where the application for entry clearance or leave to remain is for the applicant to commence a new course of study, not for completion of a course already commenced by way of re-sitting examinations or repeating a module of a course, the Sponsor must hold an A-rated or Highly Trusted Sponsor Licence,

(e) the institution must still hold such a licence at the time the application for entry clearance or leave to remain is determined

(ea) the migrant must not previously have applied for entry clearance, leave to enter or leave to remain using the same Confirmation of Acceptance for Studies reference number where that application was either approved or refused (not rejected as an invalid application or withdrawn),

(f) it contains such information as is specified as mandatory in guidance published by the United Kingdom Border Agency, and

(g) if it was not issued for a course of studies, it was issued for a full-time, salaried, elected executive position as a student union sabbatical officer to an applicant who is part-way through their studies or who is being sponsored to fill the position in the academic year immediately after their graduation.

117. A Confirmation of Acceptance for Studies reference number will only be considered to be valid if:

(a) the number supplied links to a Confirmation of Acceptance for Studies Checking Service entry that names the applicant as the migrant and confirms that the Sponsor is sponsoring him in the Tier 4 category indicated by the migrant in his application for leave to remain (that is, as a Tier 4 (General) Student or a Tier 4 (Child) Student), and

(b) that reference number must not have been withdrawn or cancelled by the Sponsor or the UK Border Agency since it was assigned.

118. No points will be awarded for a Confirmation of Acceptance for Studies unless:

(a) the applicant supplies, as evidence of previous qualifications, specified documents that the applicant used to obtain the offer of a place on a course from the Sponsor unless the applicant is sponsored by a Highly Trusted Sponsor, is a national of one of the countries or the rightful holder of a qualifying passport issued by one of the relevant competent authorities, as appropriate, listed in Appendix H, and is applying for entry clearance in his country of nationality or in the territory related to the passport he holds, as appropriate, or leave to remain in the UK. The UK Border Agency reserves the right to request the specified documents from these applicants. The application will be refused if the specified documents are not provided in accordance with the request made; and

(b) for Confirmation of Acceptance for Studies assigned on or before 20 April 2011, one of the requirements in (i) to (vii) below is met:

(i) the Confirmation of Acceptance for Studies was assigned before 3 March 2010, or

(ii) the course is degree level study, or

(iii) the course is a foundation degree course, or

(iv) the course is a pre-sessional course before a degree-level course, or

(v) the applicant is a Government Sponsored student and the course is an English language course, or

(vi) the applicant is a national of one of the following countries:

Antigua and Barbuda
Australia
The Bahamas
Barbados
Belize
Canada
Dominica

Grenada
Guyana
Jamaica
New Zealand
St Kitts and Nevis
St Lucia
St Vincent and the Grenadines
Trinidad and Tobago
United States of America, and provides the specified documents, or

(vii) the Confirmation of Acceptance for Studies Checking Service entry confirms that the applicant has a knowledge of English equivalent to level B1 of the Council of Europe's Common European Framework for Language Learning or above and:

(1) if the Confirmation of Acceptance for Studies was assigned before 12 August 2010, the applicant provides documents to support the Sponsor's assessment of his knowledge of English, or

(2) if the course of study stated on the Confirmation of Acceptance for Studies is an English language course, the applicant provides documents to support the Sponsor's assessment of his knowledge of English, or

(3) the applicant provides an original English language test certificate from an English language test provider approved by the Secretary of State for these purposes, which is within its validity date, and clearly shows:

i. the applicant's name,

ii. that the applicant has achieved or exceeded level B1 of the Council of Europe's Common European Framework for Language Learning in all four components (reading, writing, speaking and listening), unless exempted from sitting a component on the basis of the applicant's disability, and

iii. the date of the award, or

(4) the applicant has successfully completed a course as a Tier 4 (Child) student (or under the student rules that were in force before 31 March 2009, where the student was granted permission stay whilst he was under 18 years old) which:

i. was at least six months in length, and

ii. ended within two years of the date the sponsor assigned the Confirmation of Acceptance for Studies.

(c) For Confirmation of Acceptance for Studies assigned on or after 21 April 2011, one of the requirements in (i) to (iii) below is met:

(i) the course is degree level study and the Confirmation of Acceptance for Studies has been assigned by a Sponsor which is a Recognised Body or a body in receipt of funding as a higher education institution from the Department for Employment and Learning in Northern Ireland, the Higher Education Funding Council for England, the Higher Education Funding Council for Wales, or the Scottish Funding Council, and:

(1) the applicant is a national of one of the following countries: Antigua and Barbuda; Australia; The Bahamas; Barbados; Belize; Canada; Dominica; Grenada; Guyana; Jamaica; New Zealand; St Kitts and Nevis; St Lucia; St Vincent and the Grenadines; Trinidad and Tobago; United States of America, and provides the specified documents; or

(2) has obtained an academic qualification (not a professional or vocational qualification), which is deemed by UK NARIC to meet or exceed the recognised standard of a Bachelor's or Master's degree or a PhD in the UK, from an educational establishment in one of the following countries: Antigua and Barbuda; Australia; The Bahamas; Barbados; Belize; Dominica; Grenada; Guyana; Ireland; Jamaica; New Zealand; St Kitts and Nevis; St Lucia; St Vincent and The Grenadines; Trinidad and Tobago; the UK; the USA, and provides the specified documents; or

(3) the applicant has successfully completed a course as a Tier 4 (Child) Student (or under the student rules that were in force before 31 March 2009, where the student was granted permission stay whilst he was under 18 years old) which:

i. was at least six months in length, and

ii. ended within two years of the date the sponsor assigned the Confirmation of Acceptance for Studies; or

(4) the Confirmation of Acceptance for Studies Checking Service entry confirms that the applicant has a knowledge of English equivalent to level B2 of the Council of Europe's Common European Framework for Language Learning in all four components (reading, writing, speaking and listening), or above.

Or

(ii) the course is degree level study and the Confirmation of Acceptance for Studies has been assigned by a Sponsor which is not a Recognised Body or is not a body in receipt of funding as a higher education institution from the Department for Employment and Learning in Northern Ireland, the Higher Education Funding Council for England, the Higher Education Funding Council for Wales, or the Scottish Funding Council, and:

(1) the applicant is a national of one of the following countries: Antigua and Barbuda; Australia; The Bahamas; Barbados; Belize; Canada; Dominica; Grenada; Guyana; Jamaica; New Zealand; St Kitts and Nevis; St Lucia; St Vincent and the Grenadines; Trinidad and Tobago; United States of America, and provides the specified documents; or

(2) has obtained an academic qualification (not a professional or vocational qualification), which is deemed by UK NARIC to meet or exceed the recognised standard of a Bachelor's or Master's degree or a PhD in the UK, from an educational establishment in one of the following countries: Antigua and Barbuda; Australia; The Bahamas; Barbados; Belize; Dominica; Grenada; Guyana; Ireland; Jamaica; New Zealand; St Kitts and Nevis; St Lucia; St Vincent and The Grenadines; Trinidad and Tobago; the UK; the USA, and provides the specified documents; or

(3) the applicant has successfully completed a course as a Tier 4 (Child) Student (or under the student rules that were in force before 31 March 2009, where the student was granted permission stay whilst he was under 18 years old) which:

i. was at least six months in length, and

ii. ended within two years of the date the sponsor assigned the Confirmation of Acceptance for Studies; or

(4) the applicant provides an original English language test certificate from an English language test provider approved by the Secretary of State for these purposes, which is within its validity date, and clearly shows:

i. the applicant's name,

ii. that the applicant has achieved or exceeded level B2 of the Council of Europe's Common European Framework for Language Learning in all four components (reading, writing, speaking and listening), unless exempted from sitting a component on the basis of the applicant's disability, and

iii. the date of the award.

Or

(iii) the course is for below degree level study and:

(1) the applicant is a national of one of the following countries: Antigua and Barbuda; Australia; The Bahamas; Barbados; Belize; Canada; Dominica; Grenada; Guyana; Jamaica; New Zealand; St Kitts and Nevis; St Lucia; St Vincent and the Grenadines; Trinidad and Tobago; United States of America, and provides the specified documents; or

(2) has obtained an academic qualification (not a professional or vocational qualification), which is deemed by UK NARIC to meet or exceed the recognised standard of a Bachelor's or Master's degree or a PhD in the UK, from an educational establishment in one of the following countries: Antigua and Barbuda; Australia; The Bahamas; Barbados; Belize; Dominica; Grenada; Guyana; Ireland; Jamaica; New Zealand; St Kitts and Nevis; St Lucia; St Vincent and The Grenadines; Trinidad and Tobago; the UK; the USA, and provides the specified documents; or

(3) the applicant has successfully completed a course as a Tier 4 (Child) student (or under the student rules that were in force before 31 March 2009, where the student was granted permission stay whilst he was under 18 years old) which:

i. was at least six months in length, and

ii. ended within two years of the date the sponsor assigned the Confirmation of Acceptance for Studies; or

(4) the applicant provides an original English language test certificate from an English language test provider approved by the Secretary of State for these purposes, which is within its validity date, and clearly shows:

i. the applicant's name,

ii. that the applicant has achieved or exceeded level B1 of the Council of Europe's Common European Framework for Language Learning in all four components (reading, writing, speaking and listening), unless exempted from sitting a component on the basis of the applicant's disability, and

iii. the date of the award.

119. If the applicant is re-sitting examinations or repeating a module of a course, the applicant must not previously have re-sat the same examination or repeated the same module more than once, unless the Sponsor is a Highly Trusted Sponsor. If this requirement is not met then no points will be awarded for the Confirmation of Acceptance for Studies, unless the Sponsor is a Highly Trusted Sponsor.

120. Points will only be awarded for a Confirmation of Acceptance for Studies assigned on or before 20 April 2011 (even if all the above requirements are met) if the course in respect of which it is issued meets each of the following requirements:

(a) The course must meet the following minimum academic requirements:

i. for applicants applying to study in England, Wales or Northern Ireland, the course must be at National Qualifications Framework (NQF) Level 3 or above if the Sponsor is:

(aa) a Highly Trusted Sponsor; or

(bb) an A-rated Sponsor and the Confirmation of Acceptance for Studies was assigned on or before
30 April 2010; or

(cc) an A-rated Sponsor with an application for Highly Trusted Sponsor status pending determination by the UK Border Agency and the Confirmation of Acceptance for Studies assigned on or before 20 April 2011 was assigned between 1 May 2010 and 30 June 2010; or

(dd) a B-rated Sponsor and the Confirmation of Acceptance for Studies was assigned on or before 5 April 2010; or

ii. for applicants applying to study in England, Wales or Northern Ireland, the course must be at National Qualifications Framework (NQF) Level 4 or above if the requirements at 120(a)(i)(aa) to (dd) are not met;
or

iii. for applicants applying to study in Scotland, the course must be accredited at Level 6 or above in the Scottish Credit and Qualifications Framework (SCQF) by the Scottish Qualifications Authority if the Sponsor is:

(aa) a Highly Trusted Sponsor; or

(bb) an A rated Sponsor and the Confirmation of Acceptance for Studies was assigned on or before 30 April 2010; or

(cc) an A rated Sponsor with an application for Highly Trusted Sponsor status pending determination by the UK Border Agency and the Confirmation of Acceptance for Studies was assigned between 1 May 2010 and 30 June 2010; or

(dd) a B rated Sponsor and the Confirmation of Acceptance for Studies was assigned on or before 5 April 2010; or

iv. for applicants applying to study in Scotland, the course must be accredited at Level 7 or above in the Scottish Credit and Qualifications Framework (SCQF) by the Scottish Qualifications Authority if the requirements at 120(a)(iii)(aa) to (dd) are not met; or

v. the course must be a short-term Study Abroad Programme in the United Kingdom as part of the applicant's qualification at an overseas higher education institution, and that qualification must be confirmed as the same as a United Kingdom degree level by the National Recognition Information Centre for the United Kingdom (UK NARI C); or

vi. the course must be an English language course at level B2 or above of the Common European Framework of Reference for Languages; or

vii. the course may be an English language course at any level, where the applicant is a Government Sponsored student or the course is a pre-sessional course before a degree course; or

viii. the course may be an English language course at level A2 or above on the Common European Framework of Reference for Languages where the Confirmation of Acceptance for Studies was assigned before 23 July 2010; or

ix. the course must be a recognised Foundation Programme for postgraduate doctors or dentists.

(b) The course must, except in the case of a pre-sessional course, lead to an approved qualification as defined in sponsor guidance published by the United Kingdom Border Agency.

(c) Other than when the applicant is actually on a work placement, all study that forms part of the course must take place on the premises of the sponsoring educational institution.

(d) The course must meet one of the following requirements:

i. be a full time course of degree level study that leads to an approved qualification as defined in UKBA guidance;

ii. be an overseas course of degree level study that is recognised as being equivalent to a UK Higher Education course and is being provided by an overseas Higher Education Institution,

iii. be a full time course of study involving a minimum of 15 hours per week organised daytime study and, except in the case of a pre-sessional course, lead to an approved qualification, below bachelor degree level as defined in paragraph 120(a).

(e) If the course contains a course-related work placement, any period that the applicant will be spending on that placement must not exceed half of the total length of the course spent in the United Kingdom except where it is a United Kingdom statutory requirement that the placement should exceed half the total length of the course. Where the student is following a course of study below degree level study (excluding a foundation degree course), the course can only be offered if the Sponsor is:

(aa) a Highly Trusted Sponsor; or

(bb) an A-rated Sponsor and the Confirmation of Acceptance for Studies was assigned on or before 30 April 2010; or

(cc) an A-rated Sponsor with an application for Highly Trusted Sponsor status pending determination by the UK Border Agency and the Confirmation of Acceptance for Studies was assigned between 1 May 2010 and 30 June 2010; or

(dd) a B-rated Sponsor and the Confirmation of Acceptance for Studies was assigned on or before 5 April 2010.

120A. Points will only be awarded for a Confirmation of Acceptance for Studies assigned on or after 21 April 2011 (even if all the requirements in paragraphs 116 to 119 above are met) if the course in respect of which it is issued meets each of the following requirements:

(a) The course must meet the following minimum academic requirements:

i. for applicants applying to study in England, Wales or Northern Ireland, the course must be at National Qualifications Framework (NQF) / Qualifications and Credit Framework (QCF) Level 3 or above if the Sponsor is a Highly Trusted Sponsor; or

ii. for applicants applying to study in England, Wales or Northern Ireland, the course must be at National Qualifications Framework (NQF) / Qualifications and Credit Framework (QCF) Level 4 or above if the Sponsor is an A-Rated Sponsor or a B-Rated Sponsor; or

iii. for applicants applying to study in Scotland, the course must be accredited at Level 6 or above in the Scottish Credit and Qualifications Framework (SCQF) by the Scottish Qualifications Authority and the Sponsor must be a Highly Trusted Sponsor; or

iv. for applicants applying to study in Scotland, the course must be accredited at Level 7 or above in the Scottish Credit and Qualifications Framework (SCQF) by the Scottish Qualifications Authority if the Sponsor is an A-Rated Sponsor or B-Rated Sponsor; or

v. the course must be a short-term Study Abroad Programme in the United Kingdom as part of the applicant's qualification at an overseas higher education institution, and that qualification must be confirmed as the same as a United Kingdom degree level by the National Recognition Information Centre for the United Kingdom (UK NARIC); or

vi. the course must be an English language course at level B2 or above of the Common European Framework of Reference for Languages; or

vii. the course must be a recognised Foundation Programme for postgraduate doctors or dentists.

(b) The Confirmation of Acceptance for Studies must be for a single course of study except where the Confirmation of Acceptance for Studies is:

(i) issued by a Sponsor which is a Recognised Body or a body in receipt of funding as a higher education institution from the Department for Employment and Learning in Northern Ireland, the Higher Education Funding Council for England, the Higher Education Funding Council for Wales, or the Scottish Funding Council to cover both a pre-sessional course of no longer than three months' duration and a course of degree level study at that Sponsor; and

(ii) the applicant has an unconditional offer of a place on a course of degree level study at that Sponsor; and

(iii) the course of degree level study commences no later than one month after the end date of the pre-sessional course.

(c) The course must, except in the case of a pre-sessional course, lead to an approved qualification as defined in the Tier 4 (Sponsor) guidance published by the UK Border Agency on the UK Border Agency website.

(ca) A course leading to an approved qualification must be offered by a Sponsor that, if approval at a specified level is required from a relevant awarding organisation, has that approval at the specified level, as set out in the UK Border Agency sponsor guidance published on the UK Border Agency website.

(d) Other than when the applicant is on a course-related work placement or a pre-sessional course, all study that forms part of the course must take place on the premises of the sponsoring educational institution or an institution which is a partner institution of the migrant's Sponsor.

(e) The course must meet one of the following requirements:

i. be a full time course of degree level study that leads to an approved qualification as defined in UKBA guidance;

ii. be an overseas course of degree level study that is recognised as being equivalent to a UK Higher Education course and is being provided by an overseas Higher Education Institution; or

iii. be a full time course of study involving a minimum of 15 hours per week organised daytime study and, except in the case of a pre-sessional course, lead to an approved qualification, below bachelor degree level as defined in the Tier 4 (Sponsor) guidance published by the UK Border Agency on the UK Border Agency website.

(f) If the course contains a course-related work placement, any period that the applicant will be spending on that placement must not exceed half of the total length of the course spent in the United Kingdom except where it is a United Kingdom statutory requirement that the placement should exceed half the total length of the course. Where the student is following a course of study below degree level study including a course-related work placement, the course can only be offered if the Sponsor is a Highly Trusted Sponsor.

120B. Points will only be awarded for a valid Confirmation of Acceptance for Studies assigned on or after 4 July 2011 (even if all the requirements in paragraphs 116 to 120A above are met) if the Sponsor has confirmed that the course for which the Confirmation of Acceptance for Studies has been assigned represents academic progress from previous study undertaken during the last period of leave as a Tier 4 (General) Student or as a Student, except where:

(i) the applicant is re-sitting examinations or repeating modules in accordance with paragraph 119 above, or

(ii) the applicant is making a first application to move to a new institution to complete a course commenced elsewhere.

Attributes for Tier 4 (Child) Students

121. An applicant applying for entry clearance or leave to remain as a Tier 4 (Child) Student must score 30 points for attributes.

122. Available points are show in Table 17 below.

123. Notes to accompany Table 17 appear below that table.

Table 17

Criterion	**Points Awarded**
Confirmation of Acceptance for Studies	30

Notes

124. A Confirmation of Acceptance for Studies will be considered to be valid only if:

(a) where the applicant is under 16, it was issued by an independent, fee paying school,

(b) it was issued no more than 6 months before the application is made,

(c) the application for entry clearance or leave to remain is made no more than 3 months before the start date of the course of study as stated on the Confirmation of Acceptance for Studies,

(d) the Sponsor has not withdrawn the offer since the Confirmation of Acceptance for Studies was issued,

(e) it was issued by an institution with a Tier 4 (Child) Student Sponsor Licence,

(f) the institution must still hold such a licence at the time the application for entry clearance or leave to remain is determined, and

(fa) the migrant must not previously have applied for entry clearance, leave to enter or leave to remain using the same Confirmation of Acceptance for Studies reference number, if that application was either approved or refused (not rejected as an invalid application or withdrawn), and

(g) it contains such information as is specified as mandatory in guidance published by the United Kingdom Border Agency.

125. A Confirmation of Acceptance for Studies reference number will only be considered to be valid if:

(a) the number supplied links to a Confirmation of Acceptance for Studies Checking Service entry that names the applicant as the migrant and confirms that the Sponsor is sponsoring him in the Tier 4 category indicated by the migrant in his application for leave to remain (that is, as a Tier 4 (General) Student or a Tier 4 (Child) Student), and

(b) that reference number must not have been withdrawn or cancelled by the Sponsor or the UK Border Agency since it was assigned.

125A. Points will only be awarded for a Confirmation of Acceptance for Studies if the applicant:

(a) supplies, as evidence of previous qualifications, specified documents that the applicant used to obtain the offer of a place on a course from the Sponsor, or

(b) is sponsored by a Highly Trusted Sponsor, is a national of one of the countries or the rightful holder of a qualifying passport issued by one of the relevant competent authorities, as appropriate, listed in Appendix H and is applying for entry clearance in his country of nationality or in the territory related to the passport he holds, as appropriate, or leave to remain in the UK. The UK Border Agency reserves the right to request the specified documents from these applicants. The application will be refused if the specified documents are not provided in accordance with the request made.

126. Points will not be awarded under Table 17 unless the course that the student will be pursuing meets one of the following requirements:

(a) be taught in accordance with the National Curriculum,

(b) be taught in accordance with the National Qualification Framework (NQF),

(c) be accepted as being of equivalent academic status to (a) or (b) above by Ofsted (England), the Education and Training Inspectorate (Northern Ireland), Her Majesty's Inspectorate of Education (Scotland) or Estyn (Wales),

(d) be provided as required by prevailing independent school education inspection standards.

(e) is a single course of study, except where the Confirmation of Acceptance for Studies is:

(i) issued by an independent school to cover both a pre-sessional course and a course at an independent school; and

(ii) the applicant has an unconditional offer of a place at the independent school; and

(iii) the duration of the pre-sessional course and period of study at the independent school does not exceed the maximum period of entry clearance or leave to remain that can be granted under paragraphs 245ZZB and 245ZZD of the Immigration Rules.

Appendix B – English language

Tier 1 Migrants

1. An applicant applying for entry clearance or leave to remain as a Tier 1 Migrant (other than a Tier 1 (Exceptional Talent) Migrant who is applying for entry clearance or a Tier 1 (Investor) Migrant) must have 10 points for English language.

2. 10 points will only be awarded to an applicant in Tier 1 (General) or Tier 1 (Entrepreneur) if the applicant:

(a) has the level of English language shown in the table below and:

(i) provides an original English language test certificate from an English language test provider approved by the Secretary of State for these purposes, which is within its validity date and clearly shows:

(1) the applicant's name,

(2) the qualification obtained, which must meet or exceed the level shown in the table below in all four components (reading, writing, speaking and listening), unless the applicant was exempted from sitting a component on the basis of his disability, and

(3) the date of the award, or

(ii) has obtained an academic qualification (not a professional or vocational qualification) which is deemed by UK NARIC to meet the recognised standard of a Bachelor's degree in the UK, and:

(1) provides the specified evidence as set out in the appropriate Tier 1 guidance, published on the UK Border Agency website, to show he has the qualification, and

(2) UK NARIC has confirmed that the degree was taught or researched in English to level C1 of the Council of Europe's Common European Framework for Language learning or above, or

Level of English language	Points
A knowledge of English equivalent to level C1 of the Council of Europe's Common European Framework for Language Learning or above	10

(b) is a national of one of the following countries:

Antigua and Barbuda
Australia
The Bahamas
Barbados
Belize
Canada
Dominica
Grenada
Guyana
Jamaica
New Zealand
St Kitts and Nevis
St Lucia
St Vincent and the Grenadines
Trinidad and Tobago
USA,

and provides the specified documents, or

(c) has obtained an academic qualification (not a professional or vocational qualification), which is deemed by UK NARIC to meet or exceed the recognised standard of a Bachelor's or Master's degree or a PhD in the UK, from an educational establishment
in one of the following countries:

Antigua and Barbuda
Australia
The Bahamas
Barbados
Belize
Dominica
Grenada
Guyana
Ireland
Jamaica
New Zealand
St Kitts and Nevis
St Lucia
St Vincent and The Grenadines
Trinidad and Tobago
the UK
the USA,

and provides the specified documents, or

(d) has ever been granted leave as a Tier 1 (General) Migrant or a Tier 1 (Entrepreneur) Migrant or Business person, or

(e) has ever been granted leave as a Highly Skilled Migrant, if that leave was granted under these Rules at a time when they included the changes which came into force on 5 December 2006.

3. 10 points will only be awarded to an applicant in Tier 1 (Post Study Work) if the applicant has achieved 75 points under Appendix A.

4. 10 points will only be awarded to an applicant who is applying for leave to remain as a Tier 1 (Exceptional Talent) Migrant if the applicant meets the requirements of paragraphs 6 to 9 below.

Tier 2 Migrants and Tier 1 (Exceptional Talent) Migrants

5. An applicant applying for entry clearance or leave to remain as a Tier 2 Migrant must have 10 points for English language unless:

(a) the applicant is applying for entry clearance as a Tier 2 (Intra-Company Transfer) Migrant, or

(b) the applicant is:

(i) applying for leave to remain as a Tier 2 (Intra-Company Transfer) Migrant, and

(ii) is not seeking a grant of leave to remain that would extend his total stay in this category beyond 3 years.

6. 10 points will only be awarded to an applicant if:

(a) The applicant has the level of English shown in the table below and:

(i) provides an original English language test certificate from an English language test provider approved by the Secretary of State for these purposes, which is within its validity period and clearly shows:

(1) the applicant's name,

(2) the qualification obtained, which must meet or exceed the level that the Secretary of State specifies in the guidance as being required to meet the standard laid down in the table below in all four components (reading, writing, speaking and listening), and:

(3) the date of the award, or

(ii) has obtained an academic qualification (not a professional or vocational qualification) which is deemed by UK NARIC to meet the recognised standard of a Bachelor's degree in the UK, and

(1) provides the specified evidence to show he has the qualification, and

(2) UK NARIC has confirmed that the degree was taught or researched in English to level C1 of the Council of Europe's Common European Framework for Language learning or above, or

(iii) in the cases referred to in row 1 of the table below, the applicant has obtained an academic qualification (not a professional or vocational qualification) which is deemed by UK NARIC to meet or exceed the recognised standard of a Bachelor's or Master's degree in the UK, and provides the specified evidence to show that:

(1) he has the qualification, and

(2) the qualification was taught or researched in English,

and

(b) one or more of paragraph 2(b)–2(e), 7 or 8 applies to the applicant.

Row	Route	Level of English language	Points
1.	Applications for leave to remain as a Tier 2 (Intra-Company Transfer) Migrant, other than the cases referred to in paragraph 5(b) above Applications for leave to remain as a Tier 2 (General) Migrant where the applicant has, or was last granted, entry clearance, leave to enter or leave to remain as: (i) a Tier 2 (General) Migrant under the rules in place before 6 April 2011, (ii) a Qualifying Work Permit Holder, (iii) a representative of an overseas newspaper, news agency or Broadcasting organisation, (iv) a Member of the Operational Ground Staff of an Overseas-owned Airline, or (v) a Jewish Agency Employee, and All applications for entry clearance or leave to remain as a Tier 2 (Sportsperson) Migrant	Competence of English to a basic user standard, including the ability to understand and use familiar everyday expressions, to introduce himself and others and to ask and answer questions about basic personal details.	10
2.	Applications for entry clearance and all other applications for leave to remain as a Tier 2 (General) Migrant Applications for leave to remain as a Tier 1 (Exceptional Talent) Migrant	A level of English equivalent to level B1 of the Council of Europe's Common European Framework for Language learning or above.	10
3.	All applications for entry clearance or leave to remain as a Tier 2 (Minister of Religion) Migrant	A level of English equivalent to level B2 of the Council of Europe's Common European Framework for Language learning or above.	10

7. 10 points will be awarded in the cases referred to in row 1 of the table above if the applicant has ever been granted:

(a) entry clearance, leave to enter or leave to remain as a Minister of Religion, provided that leave was granted on or after 23 august 2004, or

(b) entry clearance, leave to enter or leave to remain as a Tier 2 (General), Tier 2 (Intra-Company Transfer) or Tier 2 (Sportsperson) Migrant, provided that when he was granted that leave he obtained points for English language from paragraph 6(a), 6(b), or

(c) entry clearance, leave to enter or leave to remain as a Tier 2 (Minister of religion) migrant, provided that when he was granted that leave he obtained points for English language from paragraph 6(a) or (b) above, or paragraph 10 below.

8. 10 points will be awarded if the applicant:

(a) is applying for leave to remain as a Tier 2 (General) or a Tier 2 (Intra-Company Transfer) Migrant,

(b) has, or was granted entry clearance, leave to enter or leave to remain as:

(i) a Jewish Agency Employee,

(ii) a Member of the Operational Ground Staff of an Overseas-owned Airline,

(iii) a Minister of Religion, Missionary or Member of a Religious Order,

(iv) a Qualifying Work Permit Holder,

(v) a Representative of an Overseas Newspaper, News Agency or Broadcasting Organisation

less than 5 years before the date that his last grant of entry clearance, leave to enter or leave to remain expires, and

(c) has not been granted leave in any categories other than those listed in (b) above under the rules in place since 28 November 2008.

9. 10 points will be awarded in the cases referred to in row 2 of the table above if the applicant has ever been granted:

(i) leave as a Tier 2 (General) Migrant under the rules in place on or after 6 April 2011, provided that when he was granted

that leave he obtained points for the level of English language in row 2 of the table above,

(ii) leave to remain as a Tier 1 (Exceptional Talent) Migrant, or

(iii) leave as a Tier 2 (Minister of religion) Migrant, provided that when he was granted that leave he obtained points for English language from this paragraph, paragraph 6(a) or 6(b) above, or paragraph 10 below.

10. 10 points will be awarded in the cases referred to in row 3 of the table above if the applicant has ever been granted

leave as:

(i) a Minister of Religion, provided the leave was granted on or after 19 April 2007, or

(ii) a Tier 2 (Minister of Religion) Migrant, provided that when he was granted that leave he obtained points for English language from paragraph 6(a), 6(b) or 10(a) above.

11. 10 points will be awarded if the applicant:

(a) is applying for leave to remain as a Tier 2 (Minister of Religion) Migrant,

(b) has been granted entry clearance, leave to enter and/or leave to remain as a Minister of religion, Missionary or Member of a religious order less than 5 years before the date that his last grant of entry clearance, leave to enter or leave to remain expires, and

(c) has not been granted leave in any categories other than those listed in (b) above under the rules in place since 28 November 2008.

Appendix C – Maintenance (funds)

1A. In all cases where an applicant is required to obtain points under Appendix C, the applicant must meet the requirements listed below:

(a) The applicant must have the funds specified in the relevant part of Appendix C at the date of the application;

(b) If the applicant is applying as a Tier 1 Migrant, a Tier 2 Migrant or a Tier 5 (Temporary Worker) Migrant, the applicant must have had the funds referred to in (a) above for a consecutive 90-day period of time, unless applying as a Tier 1 (Exceptional Talent) Migrant or a Tier 1 (Investor) Migrant;

(c) If the applicant is applying as a Tier 4 Migrant, the applicant must have had the funds referred to in (a) above for a consecutive 28-day period of time;

(ca) If the applicant is applying for entry clearance or leave to remain as a Tier 4 Migrant, he must confirm that the funds referred to in (a) above are:

(i) available in the manner specified in paragraph 13 below for his use in studying and living in the UK; and

(ii) that the funds will remain available in the manner specified in paragraph 13 below unless used to pay for course fees and living costs;

(d) If the funds were obtained when the applicant was in the UK, the funds must have been obtained while the applicant had valid leave and was not acting in breach of any conditions attached to that leave;

(e) The applicant must provide the specified documents.

(f) Where the funds are in one or more foreign currencies, the applicant must have the specified level of funds when converted to pound sterling (£) using the spot exchange rate which appears on www.oanda.com* for the date of the application;

(g) Where the applicant is applying as a Tier 1 Migrant, a Tier 2 Migrant or a Tier 5 Migrant, the funds must have been under his own control on the date of the application and for the period specified in (b) above; and

(h) Where the application is made at the same time as applications by the partner or child of the applicant (such that the applicant is a Relevant Points Based System Migrant for the purposes of paragraph 319AA), each applicant must have the total requisite funds specified in the relevant parts of appendices C and E. If each applicant does not individually meet the requirements of appendices C and / or E, as appropriate, all the applications (the application by the Relevant Points Based System Migrant and applications as the partner or child of that relevant Points Based system Migrant) will be refused.

(i) the end date of the 90-day and 28-day periods referred to in (b) and (c) above will be taken as the date of the closing balance on the most recent of the specified documents, and must be no earlier than 31 days before the date of application.

Tier 1 Migrants

1. An applicant applying for entry clearance or leave to remain as a Tier 1 Migrant must score 10 points for funds, unless applying as a Tier 1 (Exceptional Talent) Migrant or a Tier 1 (Investor) Migrant.

2. 10 points will only be awarded if an applicant:

(a) applying for entry clearance, has the level of funds shown in the table below and provides the specified documents, or

Level of funds	Points
£2,800	50

(b) applying for leave to remain, has the level of funds shown in the table below and provides the specified documents.

Level of funds	Points
£800	10

Tier 2 Migrants

4. An applicant applying for entry clearance or leave to remain as a Tier 2 Migrant must score 10 points for Funds.

5. 10 points will only be awarded if:

(a) the applicant has the level of funds shown in the table below and provides the specified documents, or

Level of funds	Points awarded
£800	10

(b) the applicant has entry clearance, leave to enter or leave to remain as:

(i) a Tier 2 Migrant

(ii) a Jewish Agency Employee

(iii) A member of the Operational Ground Staff of an Overseas-owned Airline,

(iv) a Minister of Religion, Missionary or Member of a Religious Order,

(v) a Representative of an Overseas Newspaper, News Agency or Broadcasting Organisation, or

(vi) a Work Permit Holder, or

(c) he is applying for leave to remain as a Tier 2 (General) Migrant and obtains points under the post-study work provisions in Table 11A of Appendix A, or

(d) the Sponsor is an a rated Sponsor and has certified on the Certificate of Sponsorship that, should it become necessary, it will maintain and accommodate the migrant up to the end of the first month of his employment. The Sponsor may limit the amount of the undertaking but any limit must be at least £800. Points will only be awarded if the applicant provides a valid Certificate of Sponsorship reference number with his application.

Tier 5 (Youth Mobility) Temporary Migrants

6. An applicant applying for entry clearance as a Tier 5 (Youth Mobility) Temporary Migrant must score 10 points for funds.

7. **10 points will only be awarded if an applicant has the level of funds shown in the table below and provides the specified documents:**

Level of funds	Points awarded
£1,600	10

Tier 5 (Temporary Worker) Migrants

8. A migrant applying for entry clearance or leave to remian as a Tier 5 (Temporary Worker) Migrant must score 10 points for funds.

9. 10 points will only be awarded if an applicant has the level of funds shown in the table below and provides the specified documents:

Criterion	Points awarded
Meets one of the following criteria:	10
Has £800; or	
The Sponsor is an A rated Sponsor and the Certificate of Sponsorship Checking Service confirms that the Sponsor has certified that the applicant will not claim public funds during his period of leave as a Tier 5 (Temporary Worker) Migrant. Points will only be awarded if the applicant provides a valid Certificate of Sponsorship reference number with his application.	

Tier 4 (General) Students

10. A Tier 4 (General) Student must score 10 points for funds.

11. 10 points will only be awarded if the funds shown in the table below are available in the manner specified in paragraph 13 below to the applicant. The applicant must either:

(a) provide the specified documents to show that the funds are available to him, or

(b) where the applicant is sponsored by a Highly Trusted Sponsor, is a national of one of the countries or the rightful holder of a qualifying passport issued by one of the relevant competent authorities, as appropriate, listed in Appendix H, and is applying for entry clearance in his country of nationality or in the territory related to the passport he holds, as appropriate, or leave to remain in the UK, confirm that the funds are available to him in the specified manner. The UK Border Agency reserves the right to request the specified documents from these applicants to support this confirmation. The application will be refused if the specified documents are not provided in accordance with the request made.

Criterion	Points
If studying in inner London:	10
(i) Where the applicant does not have an established presence studying in the United Kingdom, the applicant must have funds amounting to the full course fees for the first academic year of the course, or for the entire course if it is less than a year long, plus £800 for each month of the course up to a maximum of nine months.	
(ii) Where the applicant has an established presence studying in the United Kingdom, the applicant must have funds amounting to the course fees required either for the remaining academic year if the applicant is applying part-way through, or for the next academic year if the applicant will continue or commence a new course at the start of the next academic year, or for the entire course if it is less than a year long, plus £800 for each month of the course up to a maximum of two months.	

If studying in outer London and elsewhere in the United Kingdom: 10

(i) Where the applicant does not have an established presence studying in the United Kingdom, the applicant must have funds amounting to the full course fees for the first academic year of the course, or for the entire course if it is less than a year long, plus £600 for each month of the course up to a maximum of nine months.

(ii) Where the applicant has an established presence studying in the United Kingdom, the applicant must have funds amounting to the course fees required either for the remaining academic year if the applicant is applying part-way through, or for the next academic year if the applicant will continue or commence a new course at the start of the next academic year, or for the entire course if it is less than a year long, plus £600 for each month of the course up to a maximum of two months.

Notes

12. An applicant will be considered to be studying in inner London if the institution, or branch of the institution, at which the applicant will be studying is situated in a inner London Borough specified in United Kingdom Border Agency guidance. If the applicant will be studying at more than one site, one or more of which is in inner London and one or more outside, then the applicant will be considered to be studying in inner London if the applicant's Confirmation of Acceptance for Studies states that the applicant will be spending the majority of time studying at a site or sites situated in inner London.

12A. If the length of the applicant's course includes a part of a month, the time will be rounded up to the next full month.

13. Funds will be available to the applicant only where the specified documents show or, where permitted by these Rules, the applicant confirms that the funds are held or provided by:

(i) the applicant (whether as a sole or joint account holder); and/or

(ii) the applicant's parent(s) or legal guardian(s), and the parent(s) or legal guardian(s) have provided written consent that their funds may be used by the applicant in order to study in the UK; and/or

(iii) an official financial sponsor which must be Her Majesty's Government, the applicant's home government, the British Council or any international organisation, international company, University or Independent school.

13A. No points will be awarded where the specified documents show that the funds are held in a financial institution with which the UK Border Agency is unable to make satisfactory verification checks. A list of financial institutions which do not satisfactorily verify financial statements is published on the UK Border Agency website.

14. An applicant will have an established presence studying in the UK if the applicant has current entry clearance, leave to enter or leave to remain as a Tier 4 migrant, Student or as a Postgraduate Doctor or Dentist and at the date of application:

(i) has finished a single course that was at least six months long within the applicant's last period of entry clearance, leave to enter or leave to remain, or

(ii) is applying for continued study on a single course where the applicant has completed at least six months of that course.

Tier 4 (Child) Students

15. A Tier 4 (Child) Student must score 10 points for funds.

16. 10 points will only be awarded if the funds shown in the table below are available in the manner specified in paragraph 21 below to the applicant. The applicant must either:

(a) provide the specified documents to show that the funds are available to him, or

(b) where the applicant is sponsored by a Highly Trusted Sponsor, is a national of one of the countries or the rightful holder of a qualifying passport issued by one of the relevant competent authorities, as appropriate, listed in Appendix H, and is applying for entry clearance in his country of nationality or in the territory related to the passport he holds, as appropriate, or leave to remain in the UK, confirm that the funds are available to him in the specified manner. The UK Border Agency reserves the right to request the specified documents from these applicants to support this confirmation. The application will be refused if the specified documents are not provided in accordance with the request made.

Criterion	Points
Where the child is (or will be) studying at a residential independent school: sufficient funds are available to the applicant to pay boarding fees (being course fees plus board/lodging fees) for an academic year.	10
Where the child is (or will be) studying at a non-residential independent school and is in a private foster care arrangement (see notes below) or staying with and cared for by a close relative (see notes below): sufficient funds are available to the applicant to pay school fees for an academic year, the foster carer or relative (who must meet such requirements as are specified in guidance published by the United Kingdom Border Agency) has undertaken to maintain and accommodate the child for the duration of the course, and that foster carer or relative has funds equivalent to at least £500 per month, for up to a maximum of nine months, to support the child while he is in the United Kingdom.	10
Where the child is (or will be) studying at a non-residential independent school, is under the age of 12 and is (or will be) accompanied by a parent, sufficient funds are available to the applicant to pay school fees for an academic year, plus: • if no other children are accompanying the applicant and the parent, £1333 per month of stay up to a maximum of nine months; or • if other children are accompanying the applicant and the parent, £1333 per month, plus £533 per month for each additional child, up to a maximum of nine months.	10
Where the child is aged 16 or 17 years old and is living independently and studying in inner London: (i) Where the applicant does not have an established presence studying in the United Kingdom, the applicant must have funds amounting to the full course fees for the first academic year of the course, or for the entire course if it is less than a year long, plus £800 for each month of the course up to a maximum of nine months. (ii) Where the applicant has an established presence studying in the United Kingdom, the applicant must have funds amounting to the course fees required either for the remaining academic year if the applicant is applying part-way through, or for the next academic year if the applicant will continue or commence a new course at the start of the next academic year, or for the entire course if it is less than a year long, plus £800 for each month of the course up to a maximum of two months.	10
Where the child is aged 16 or 17 years old, is living independently and studying in outer London or elsewhere in the United Kingdom: (iii) Where the applicant does not have an established presence studying in the United Kingdom, the applicant must have funds amounting to the full course fees for the first academic year of the course, or for the entire course if it is less than a year long, plus £600 for each month of the course up to a maximum of nine months. (iv) Where the applicant has an established presence studying in the United Kingdom, the applicant must have funds amounting to the course fees required either for the remaining academic year if the applicant is applying part-way through, or for the next academic year if the applicant will continue or commence a new course at the start of the next academic year, or for the entire course if it is less than a year long, plus £600 for each month of the course up to a maximum of two months.	10

Notes

17. Children (under 16, or under 18 if disabled) are privately fostered when they are cared for on a full-time basis by a person or persons aged 18 or over, who are not their parents or a close relative, for a period of 28 days or more.
18. A close relative is a grandparent, brother, sister, step-parent, uncle (brother or half-brother of the child's parent) or aunt (sister or half-sister of the child's parent) who is aged 18 or over.
19. The care arrangement made for the child's care in the UK must comply with the requirements specified in guidance published by the United Kingdom Border Agency.
20. If the length of the applicant's course includes a part of a month, the time will be rounded up to the next full month.

21. Funds will be available to the applicant only where the specified documents show or, where permitted by these Rules, the applicant confirms that the funds are held or provided by:
    (i) the applicant (whether as a sole or joint account holder); and/or
    (ii) the applicant's parent(s) or legal guardian(s), and the parent(s) or legal guardian(s) have provided written consent that their funds may be used by the applicant in order to study in the UK; and/or
    (iii) an official financial sponsor which must be Her Majesty's Government, the applicant's home government, the British Council or any international organisation, international company, University or Independent school.

21A. No points will be awarded where the specified documents show that the funds are held in a financial institution with which the UK Border Agency is unable to make satisfactory verification checks. A list of financial institutions which do not satisfactorily verify financial statements is published on the UK Border Agency website.

22. An applicant will have an established presence studying in the UK if the applicant has current entry clearance, leave to enter or leave to remain as a Tier 4 migrant or Student and at the date of application:
    (i) has finished a single course that was at least six months long within the applicant's last period of entry clearance, leave to enter or leave to remain, or
    (ii) is applying for continued study on a single course where the applicant has completed at least six months of that course.

Appendix E – Maintenance (funds) for the family of Relevant Points Based Systems Migrants

A sufficient level of funds must be available to an applicant applying as the Partner or Child of a Relevant Points Based System Migrant. A sufficient level of funds will only be available if the requirements below are met.

(a) Where the application is connected to a Tier 1 Migrant (other than a Tier 1 (Investor) Migrant) or a Tier 1 (Exceptional Talent) Migrant who is outside the UK or who has been in the UK for a period of less than 12 months, there must be £1600 in funds.

(b) Where:
    (i) paragraph (a) does not apply, and
    (ii) the application is connected to a Relevant Points Based System Migrant who is not a Tier 1 (Investor) Migrant a Tier 1 (Exceptional Talent) Migrant or a Tier 4 (General) Student there must be £533 in funds.

(ba) (i) Where the application is connected to a Tier 4 (General) Student:
        (1) if the Tier 4 (General) Student is studying in inner London (as defined in paragraph 12 of Appendix C), there must be £533 in funds for each month for which the applicant would, if successful, be granted leave under paragraph 319D(a), up to a maximum of £ 4,797, or
        (2) if the Tier 4 (General) Student is not studying in inner London, there must be £400 in funds for each month for which the applicant would, if successful, be granted leave under paragraph 319D(a), up to a maximum of £3,600, and in each case
        (3) the applicant must confirm that the funds referred to in (1) or (2) above are:
            (i) available in the manner specified in paragraph (f) below for use in living costs in the UK; and
            (ii) that the funds will remain available in the manner specified in paragraph (f) below unless used to pay for living costs.

(c) Where the applicant is applying as the Partner of a Relevant Points Based System Migrant the relevant amount of funds must be available to either the applicant or the Relevant Points Based System Migrant .

(d) Where the applicant is applying as the Child of a Relevant Points Based System Migrant, the relevant amount of funds must be available to the applicant, the Relevant Points Based System Migrant, or the applicant's other parent who is Lawfully present in the UK or being granted entry clearance, or leave to enter or remain, at the same time.

(e) Where the Relevant Points Based System Migrant is applying for entry clearance or leave to remain at the same time as the applicant, the amount of funds available to the applicant must be in addition to the level of funds required separately of the Relevant Points Based System Migrant.

(f) In all cases, the funds in question must be available to:

(i) the applicant, or

(ii) where he is applying as the partner of a Relevant Points Based System Migrant, either to him or to that Relevant Points Based System Migrant, or

(iii) where he is applying as the child of a Relevant Points Based System Migrant, either to him, to the Relevant Points Based System Migrant or to the child's other parent who is lawfully present in the UK or being granted entry clearance, or leave to enter or remain, at the same time;

(g) The funds in question must have been available to the person referred to in (f) above for:

(i) a consecutive 90-day period of time, ending no earlier than one calendar month before the date of application, if the applicant is applying as the Partner or Child of a Tier 1 Migrant (other than a Tier 1 (Investor) Migrant) or a Tier 1 (Exceptional Talent) Migrant, a Tier 2 Migrant or a Tier 5 (Temporary Worker) Migrant;

(ii) a consecutive 28-day period of time, ending no earlier than one calendar month before the date of application, if the applicant is applying as the Partner or Child of a Tier 4 (General) Student;

(h) If the funds in question were obtained when the person referred to in (f) above was in the UK, the funds must have been obtained while that person had valid leave and was not acting in breach of any conditions attached to that leave; and

(i) In the following cases, sufficient funds will be deemed to be available where all of the following conditions are met:

(1) the Relevant Points Based System Migrant to whom the application is connected has, or is being granted, leave as a Tier 2 Migrant,

(2) the Sponsor of that Relevant Points Based System Migrant is A-rated, and

(3) that Sponsor has certified on the Certificate of Sponsorship that, should it become necessary, it will maintain and accommodate the dependants of the relevant Points Based System Migrant up to the end of the first month of the relevant Points Based System Migrant's employment. The undertaking may be limited provided the limit is at least £533 per dependant. If the relevant Points Based System Migrant is applying at the same time as the applicant, points will only be awarded if the Relevant Points Based System Migrant provides a valid Certificate of Sponsorship reference number with his application.

(ia) Sufficient funds will not be deemed to be available to the Partner or Child if the specified documents show that the funds are held in a financial institution with which the UK Border Agency is unable to make satisfactory verification checks, and the Relevant Points Based System Migrant to whom the application is connected has, or is being granted, leave as a Tier 4 (General) Student. A list of financial institutions which do not satisfactorily verify financial statements is published on the UK Border Agency website.

(j) In all cases the applicant must provide the specified documents, unless the applicant is applying at the same time as the Relevant Points Based System Migrant who is a Tier 4 (General) Student sponsored by a Highly Trusted Sponsor, is a national of one of the countries or the rightful holder of a qualifying passport issued by one of the relevant competent authorities, as appropriate, listed in Appendix H, and is applying for entry clearance in his country of nationality or in the territory related to the passport he holds, as appropriate, or leave to remain in the UK and the applicant is also a national of the same country, and confirms these requirements are met, in which case the specified documents shall not be required. The UK Border Agency reserves the right to request the specified documents from these applicants. The application will be refused if the specified documents are not provided in accordance with the request made.

(k) Where the funds are in one or more foreign currencies, the applicant must have the specified level of funds when converted to pound sterling (£) using the spot exchange rate which appears on www.oanda.com* for the date of the application.

(l) Where the application is one of a number of applications made at the same time as a partner or child of a Relevant Points Based System Migrant (as set out in paragraphs 319A and 319F) each applicant, including the Relevant Points Based System Migrant if applying at the same time, must have the total requisite funds specified in the relevant parts of appendices C and E. if each applicant does not individually meet the requirements of appendices C and / or E, as appropriate, all the applications (the application by the Relevant Points Based System Migrant and applications as the partner or child of that Relevant Points Based System Migrant) will be refused.

Appendix G – Countries participating in the Tier 5 Youth Mobility Scheme

Australia
Canada
Japan
New Zealand
Monaco

Appendix H – Applicants who are subject to different documentary requirements under Tier 4 of the Points Based System

An applicant will be subject to different documentary requirements under Tier 4 of the Points Based System where he is a national of one of the following countries and he is applying for entry clearance in his country of nationality or leave to remain in the UK:

Argentina
Australia
Brunei
Canada
Chile
Croatia
Japan
New Zealand
Singapore
South Korea
Trinidad and Tobago
United States of America

Where an applicant is a dual national, and only one of their nationalities is listed above, he will be able to apply using the different documentary requirements that apply to these nationals, provided he is applying either for entry clearance in his country of nationality listed above or for leave to remain in the UK.

An applicant will be subject to different documentary requirements under Tier 4 of the Points Based System where he is the rightful holder of one of the following passports, which has been issued by the relevant competent authority, and where he is applying for leave to remain in the UK or for entry clearance in the territory related to the passport he holds:

- British National (Overseas)
- Hong Kong
- Taiwan (those who hold a passport issued by Taiwan that includes the number of the identification card issued by the competent authority in Taiwan)

Where an applicant is the rightful holder of a passport issued by a relevant competent authority listed above and also holds another passport or is the national of a country not listed above, he will be able to apply using the different documentary requirements that apply to rightful holders of those passports listed in this Appendix provided he is applying either for entry clearance in the territory related to the passport he holds or for leave to remain in the UK.

Appendix 2

The European Union and Associated States

Member States of the European Union (see Chapter 4)

Austria
Belgium
Bulgaria
Cyprus
Czech Republic
Denmark
Estonia
Finland
France
Germany
Greece
Hungary
Republic of Ireland
Italy
Latvia
Lithuania
Luxembourg
Malta
The Netherlands
Poland
Portugal
Romania
Slovakia
Slovenia
Spain
Sweden
United Kingdom

Other Members of the European Economic Area (see Chapter 4)

Iceland
Norway
Liechtenstein
(As to Switzerland, see **4.1**)

Appendix 3

Directive 2004/38/EC

CHAPTER I – GENERAL PROVISIONS

Article 1 – Subject

This Directive lays down:

(a) the conditions governing the exercise of the right of free movement and residence within the territory of the Member States by Union citizens and their family members;

(b) the right of permanent residence in the territory of the Member States for Union citizens and their family members;

(c) the limits placed on the rights set out in (a) and (b) on grounds of public policy, public security or public health.

Article 2 – Definitions

For the purposes of this Directive:

1. 'Union citizen' means any person having the nationality of a Member State;
2. 'family member' means:
   (a) the spouse;
   (b) the partner with whom the Union citizen has contracted a registered partnership, on the basis of the legislation of a Member State, if the legislation of the host Member State treats registered partnerships as equivalent to marriage and in accordance with the conditions laid down in the relevant legislation of the host Member State;
   (c) the direct descendants who are under the age of 21 or are dependants and those of the spouse or partner as defined in point (b);
   (d) the dependent direct relatives in the ascending line and those of the spouse or partner as defined in point (b);
3. 'host Member State' means the Member State to which a Union citizen moves in order to exercise his/her right of free movement and residence.

Article 3 – Beneficiaries

1. This Directive shall apply to all Union citizens who move to or reside in a Member State other than that of which they are a national, and to their family members as defined in point 2 of Article 2 who accompany or join them.
2. Without prejudice to any right to free movement and residence the persons concerned may have in their own right, the host Member State shall, in accordance with its national legislation, facilitate entry and residence for the following persons:
   (a) any other family members, irrespective of their nationality, not falling under the definition in point 2 of Article 2 who, in the country from which they have come, are dependants or members of the household of the Union citizen having the primary right of residence, or where serious health grounds strictly require the personal care of the family member by the Union citizen;
   (b) the partner with whom the Union citizen has a durable relationship, duly attested.

   The host Member State shall undertake an extensive examination of the personal circumstances and shall justify any denial of entry or residence to these people.

CHAPTER II – RIGHT OF EXIT AND ENTRY

Article 4 – Right of exit

1. Without prejudice to the provisions on travel documents applicable to national border controls, all Union citizens with a valid identity card or passport and their family members who are not nationals of a Member State and who hold a valid passport shall have the right to leave the territory of a Member State to travel to another Member State.
2. No exit visa or equivalent formality may be imposed on the persons to whom paragraph 1 applies.
3. Member States shall, acting in accordance with their laws, issue to their own nationals, and renew, an identity card or passport stating their nationality.
4. The passport shall be valid at least for all Member States and for countries through which the holder must pass when travelling between Member States. Where the law of a Member State does not provide for identity cards to be issued, the period of validity of any passport on being issued or renewed shall be not less than five years.

Article 5 – Right of entry

1. Without prejudice to the provisions on travel documents applicable to national border controls, Member States shall grant Union citizens leave to enter their territory with a valid identity card or passport and shall grant family members who are not nationals of a Member State leave to enter their territory with a valid passport.

   No entry visa or equivalent formality may be imposed on Union citizens.
2. Family members who are not nationals of a Member State shall only be required to have an entry visa in accordance with Regulation (EC) No 539/2001 or, where appropriate, with national law. For the purposes of this Directive, possession of the valid residence card referred to in Article 10 shall exempt such family members from the visa requirement.

   Member States shall grant such persons every facility to obtain the necessary visas. Such visas shall be issued free of charge as soon as possible and on the basis of an accelerated procedure.
3. The host Member State shall not place an entry or exit stamp in the passport of family members who are not nationals of a Member State provided that they present the residence card provided for in Article 10.
4. Where a Union citizen, or a family member who is not a national of a Member State, does not have the necessary travel documents or, if required, the necessary visas, the Member State concerned shall, before turning them back, give such persons every reasonable opportunity to obtain the necessary documents or have them brought to them within a reasonable period of time or to corroborate or prove by other means that they are covered by the right of free movement and residence.
5. The Member State may require the person concerned to report his/her presence within its territory within a reasonable and non-discriminatory period of time. Failure to comply with this requirement may make the person concerned liable to proportionate and non-discriminatory sanctions.

CHAPTER III – RIGHT OF RESIDENCE

Article 6 – Right of residence for up to three months

1. Union citizens shall have the right of residence on the territory of another Member State for a period of up to three months without any conditions or any formalities other than the requirement to hold a valid identity card or passport.
2. The provisions of paragraph 1 shall also apply to family members in possession of a valid passport who are not nationals of a Member State, accompanying or joining the Union citizen.

Article 7 – Right of residence for more than three months

1. All Union citizens shall have the right of residence on the territory of another Member State for a period of longer than three months if they:
   (a) are workers or self-employed persons in the host Member State; or
   (b) have sufficient resources for themselves and their family members not to become a burden on the social assistance system of the host Member State during their period of residence and have comprehensive sickness insurance cover in the host Member State; or
   (c) — are enrolled at a private or public establishment, accredited or financed by the host Member State on the basis of its legislation or administrative practice, for the principal purpose of following a course of study, including vocational training; and
   — have comprehensive sickness insurance cover in the host Member State and assure the relevant national authority, by means of a declaration or by such equivalent means as they may choose, that they have sufficient resources for themselves and their family members not to become a burden on the social assistance system of the host Member State during their period of residence; or
   (d) are family members accompanying or joining a Union citizen who satisfies the conditions referred to in points (a), (b) or (c).
2. The right of residence provided for in paragraph 1 shall extend to family members who are not nationals of a Member State, accompanying or joining the Union citizen in the host Member State, provided that such Union citizen satisfies the conditions referred to in paragraph 1(a), (b) or (c).
3. For the purposes of paragraph 1(a), a Union citizen who is no longer a worker or self-employed person shall retain the status of worker or self-employed person in the following circumstances:
   (a) he/she is temporarily unable to work as the result of an illness or accident;
   (b) he/she is in duly recorded involuntary unemployment after having been employed for more than one year and has registered as a job-seeker with the relevant employment office;
   (c) he/she is in duly recorded involuntary unemployment after completing a fixed-term employment contract of less than a year or after having become involuntarily unemployed during the first twelve months and has registered as a job-seeker with the relevant employment office. In this case, the status of worker shall be retained for no less than six months;
   (d) he/she embarks on vocational training. Unless he/she is involuntarily unemployed, the retention of the status of worker shall require the training to be related to the previous employment.
4. By way of derogation from paragraphs 1(d) and 2 above, only the spouse, the registered partner provided for in Article 2(2)(b) and dependent children shall have the right of residence as family members of a Union citizen meeting the conditions under 1(c) above. Article 3(2) shall apply to his/her dependent direct relatives in the ascending lines and those of his/her spouse or registered partner.

Article 8 – Administrative formalities for Union citizens

1. Without prejudice to Article 5(5), for periods of residence longer than three months, the host Member State may require Union citizens to register with the relevant authorities.
2. The deadline for registration may not be less than three months from the date of arrival. A registration certificate shall be issued immediately, stating the name and address of the person registering and the date of the registration. Failure to comply with the registration requirement may render the person concerned liable to proportionate and non-discriminatory sanctions.
3. For the registration certificate to be issued, Member States may only require that
   — Union citizens to whom point (a) of Article 7(1) applies present a valid identity card or passport, a confirmation of engagement from the employer or a certificate of employment, or proof that they are self-employed persons,
   — Union citizens to whom point (b) of Article 7(1) applies present a valid identity card or passport and provide proof that they satisfy the conditions laid down therein,

— Union citizens to whom point (c) of Article 7(1) applies present a valid identity card or passport, provide proof of enrolment at an accredited establishment and of comprehensive sickness insurance cover and the declaration or equivalent means referred to in point (c) of Article 7(1). Member States may not require this declaration to refer to any specific amount of resources.

4. Member States may not lay down a fixed amount which they regard as 'sufficient resources', but they must take into account the personal situation of the person concerned. In all cases this amount shall not be higher than the threshold below which nationals of the host Member State become eligible for social assistance, or, where this criterion is not applicable, higher than the minimum social security pension paid by the host Member State.

5. For the registration certificate to be issued to family members of Union citizens, who are themselves Union citizens, Member States may require the following documents to be presented:
   (a) a valid identity card or passport;
   (b) a document attesting to the existence of a family relationship or of a registered partnership;
   (c) where appropriate, the registration certificate of the Union citizen whom they are accompanying or joining;
   (d) in cases falling under points (c) and (d) of Article 2(2), documentary evidence that the conditions laid down therein are met;
   (e) in cases falling under Article 3(2)(a), a document issued by the relevant authority in the country of origin or country from which they are arriving certifying that they are dependants or members of the household of the Union citizen, or proof of the existence of serious health grounds which strictly require the personal care of the family member by the Union citizen;
   (f) in cases falling under Article 3(2)(b), proof of the existence of a durable relationship with the Union citizen.

Article 9 – Administrative formalities for family members who are not nationals of a Member State

1. Member States shall issue a residence card to family members of a Union citizen who are not nationals of a Member State, where the planned period of residence is for more than three months.

2. The deadline for submitting the residence card application may not be less than three months from the date of arrival.

3. Failure to comply with the requirement to apply for a residence card may make the person concerned liable to proportionate and non-discriminatory sanctions.

Article 10 – Issue of residence cards

1. The right of residence of family members of a Union citizen who are not nationals of a Member State shall be evidenced by the issuing of a document called 'Residence card of a family member of a Union citizen' no later than six months from the date on which they submit the application. A certificate of application for the residence card shall be issued immediately.

2. For the residence card to be issued, Member States shall require presentation of the following documents:
   (a) a valid passport;
   (b) a document attesting to the existence of a family relationship or of a registered partnership;
   (c) the registration certificate or, in the absence of a registration system, any other proof of residence in the host MemberState of the Union citizen whom they are accompanying or joining;
   (d) in cases falling under points (c) and (d) of Article 2(2), documentary evidence that the conditions laid down therein are met;
   (e) in cases falling under Article 3(2)(a), a document issued by the relevant authority in the country of origin or country from which they are arriving certifying that they are dependants or members of the household of the Union citizen, or proof of the existence of

serious health grounds which strictly require the personal care of the family member by the Union citizen;

(f) in cases falling under Article 3(2)(b), proof of the existence of a durable relationship with the Union citizen.

Article 11 – Validity of the residence card

1. The residence card provided for by Article 10(1) shall be valid for five years from the date of issue or for the envisaged period of residence of the Union citizen, if this period is less than five years.

2. The validity of the residence card shall not be affected by temporary absences not exceeding six months a year, or by absences of a longer duration for compulsory military service or by one absence of a maximum of 12 consecutive months for important reasons such as pregnancy and childbirth, serious illness, study or vocational training, or a posting in another Member State or a third country.

Article 12 – Retention of the right of residence by family members in the event of death or departure of the Union citizen

1. Without prejudice to the second subparagraph, the Union citizen's death or departure from the host Member State shall not affect the right of residence of his/her family members who are nationals of a Member State.

   Before acquiring the right of permanent residence, the persons concerned must meet the conditions laid down in points (a), (b), (c) or (d) of Article 7(1).

2. Without prejudice to the second subparagraph, the Union citizen's death shall not entail loss of the right of residence of his/her family members who are not nationals of a Member State and who have been residing in the host Member State as family members for at least one year before the Union citizen's death.

   Before acquiring the right of permanent residence, the right of residence of the persons concerned shall remain subject to the requirement that they are able to show that they are workers or self-employed persons or that they have sufficient resources for themselves and their family members not to become a burden on the social assistance system of the host Member State during their period of residence and have comprehensive sickness insurance cover in the host Member State, or that they are members of the family, already constituted in the host Member State, of a person satisfying these requirements. 'Sufficient resources' shall be as defined in Article 8(4).

   Such family members shall retain their right of residence exclusively on a personal basis.

3. The Union citizen's departure from the host Member State or his/her death shall not entail loss of the right of residence of his/her children or of the parent who has actual custody of the children, irrespective of nationality, if the children reside in the host Member State and are enrolled at an educational establishment, for the purpose of studying there, until the completion of their studies.

Article 13 – Retention of the right of residence by family members in the event of divorce, annulment of marriage or termination of registered partnership

1. Without prejudice to the second subparagraph, divorce, annulment of the Union citizen's marriage or termination of his/her registered partnership, as referred to in point 2(b) of Article 2 shall not affect the right of residence of his/her family members who are nationals of a Member State.

   Before acquiring the right of permanent residence, the persons concerned must meet the conditions laid down in points (a), (b), (c) or (d) of Article 7(1).

2. Without prejudice to the second subparagraph, divorce, annulment of marriage or termination of the registered partnership referred to in point 2(b) of Article 2 shall not entail loss of the right of residence of a Union citizen's family members who are not nationals of a Member State where:

(a) prior to initiation of the divorce or annulment proceedings or termination of the registered partnership referred to in point 2(b) of Article 2, the marriage or registered partnership has lasted at least three years, including one year in the host Member State; or

(b) by agreement between the spouses or the partners referred to in point 2(b) of Article 2 or by court order, the spouse or partner who is not a national of a Member State has custody of the Union citizen's children; or

(c) this is warranted by particularly difficult circumstances, such as having been a victim of domestic violence while the marriage or registered partnership was subsisting; or

(d) by agreement between the spouses or partners referred to in point 2(b) of Article 2 or by court order, the spouse or partner who is not a national of a Member State has the right of access to a minor child, provided that the court has ruled that such access must be in the host Member State, and for as long as is required.

Before acquiring the right of permanent residence, the right of residence of the persons concerned shall remain subject to the requirement that they are able to show that they are workers or self-employed persons or that they have sufficient resources for themselves and their family members not to become a burden on the social assistance system of the host Member State during their period of residence and have comprehensive sickness insurance cover in the host Member State, or that they are members of the family, already constituted in the host Member State, of a person satisfying these requirements. 'Sufficient resources' shall be as defined in Article 8(4).

Such family members shall retain their right of residence exclusively on personal basis.

Article 14 – Retention of the right of residence

1. Union citizens and their family members shall have the right of residence provided for in Article 6, as long as they do not become an unreasonable burden on the social assistance system of the host Member State.

2. Union citizens and their family members shall have the right of residence provided for in Articles 7, 12 and 13 as long as they meet the conditions set out therein.

   In specific cases where there is a reasonable doubt as to whether a Union citizen or his/her family members satisfies the conditions set out in Articles 7, 12 and 13, Member States may verify if these conditions are fulfilled. This verification shall not be carried out systematically.

3. An expulsion measure shall not be the automatic consequence of a Union citizen's or his or her family member's recourse to the social assistance system of the host Member State.

4. By way of derogation from paragraphs 1 and 2 and without prejudice to the provisions of Chapter VI, an expulsion measure may in no case be adopted against Union citizens or their family members if:

   (a) the Union citizens are workers or self-employed persons, or

   (b) the Union citizens entered the territory of the host Member State in order to seek employment. In this case, the Union citizens and their family members may not be expelled for as long as the Union citizens can provide evidence that they are continuing to seek employment and that they have a genuine chance of being engaged.

Article 15 – Procedural safeguards

1. The procedures provided for by Articles 30 and 31 shall apply by analogy to all decisions restricting free movement of Union citizens and their family members on grounds other than public policy, public security or public health.

2. Expiry of the identity card or passport on the basis of which the person concerned entered the host Member State and was issued with a registration certificate or residence card shall not constitute a ground for expulsion from the host Member State.

3. The host Member State may not impose a ban on entry in the context of an expulsion decision to which paragraph 1 applies.

CHAPTER IV – RIGHT OF PERMANENT RESIDENCE

Section I – Eligibility

Article 16 – General rule for Union citizens and their family members

1. Union citizens who have resided legally for a continuous period of five years in the host Member State shall have the right of permanent residence there. This right shall not be subject to the conditions provided for in Chapter III.
2. Paragraph 1 shall apply also to family members who are not nationals of a Member State and have legally resided with the Union citizen in the host Member State for a continuous period of five years.
3. Continuity of residence shall not be affected by temporary absences not exceeding a total of six months a year, or by absences of a longer duration for compulsory military service, or by one absence of a maximum of 12 consecutive months for important reasons such as pregnancy and childbirth, serious illness, study or vocational training, or a posting in another Member State or a third country.
4. Once acquired, the right of permanent residence shall be lost only through absence from the host Member State for a period exceeding two consecutive years.

Article 17 – Exemptions for persons no longer working in the host Member State and their family members

1. By way of derogation from Article 16, the right of permanent residence in the host Member State shall be enjoyed before completion of a continuous period of five years of residence by:

   (a) workers or self-employed persons who, at the time they stop working, have reached the age laid down by the law of that Member State for entitlement to an old age pension or workers who cease paid employment to take early retirement, provided that they have been working in that Member State for at least the preceding twelve months and have resided there continuously for more than three years.

   If the law of the host Member State does not grant the right to an old age pension to certain categories of self-employed persons, the age condition shall be deemed to have been met once the person concerned has reached the age of 60;

   (b) workers or self-employed persons who have resided continuously in the host Member State for more than two years and stop working there as a result of permanent incapacity to work.

   If such incapacity is the result of an accident at work or an occupational disease entitling the person concerned to a benefit payable in full or in part by an institution in the host Member State, no condition shall be imposed as to length of residence;

   (c) workers or self-employed persons who, after three years of continuous employment and residence in the host Member State, work in an employed or self-employed capacity in another Member State, while retaining their place of residence in the host Member State, to which they return, as a rule, each day or at least once a week.

   For the purposes of entitlement to the rights referred to in points (a) and (b), periods of employment spent in the Member State in which the person concerned is working shall be regarded as having been spent in the host Member State.

   Periods of involuntary unemployment duly recorded by the relevant employment office, periods not worked for reasons not of the person's own making and absences from work or cessation of work due to illness or accident shall be regarded as periods of employment.

2. The conditions as to length of residence and employment laid down in point (a) of paragraph 1 and the condition as to length of residence laid down in point (b) of paragraph 1 shall not apply if the worker's or the self-employed person's spouse or partner as referred to in point 2(b) of Article 2 is a national of the host Member State or has lost the nationality of that Member State by marriage to that worker or self-employed person.

3. Irrespective of nationality, the family members of a worker or a self-employed person who are residing with him in the territory of the host Member State shall have the right of permanent residence in that Member State, if the worker or self-employed person has acquired himself the right of permanent residence in that Member State on the basis of paragraph 1.
4. If, however, the worker or self-employed person dies while still working but before acquiring permanent residence status in the host Member State on the basis of paragraph 1, his family members who are residing with him in the host Member State shall acquire the right of permanent residence there, on condition that:
   (a) the worker or self-employed person had, at the time of death, resided continuously on the territory of that Member State for two years; or
   (b) the death resulted from an accident at work or an occupational disease; or
   (c) the surviving spouse lost the nationality of that Member State following marriage to the worker or self-employed person.

Article 18 – Acquisition of the right of permanent residence by certain family members who are not nationals of a Member State

Without prejudice to Article 17, the family members of a Union citizen to whom Articles 12(2) and 13(2) apply, who satisfy the conditions laid down therein, shall acquire the right of permanent residence after residing legally for a period of five consecutive years in the host Member State.

Section II – Administrative formalities

Article 19 – Document certifying permanent residence for Union citizens

1. Upon application Member States shall issue Union citizens entitled to permanent residence, after having verified duration of residence, with a document certifying permanent residence.
2. The document certifying permanent residence shall be issued as soon as possible.

Article 20 – Permanent residence card for family members who are not nationals of a Member State

1. Member States shall issue family members who are not nationals of a Member State entitled to permanent residence with a permanent residence card within six months of the submission of the application. The permanent residence card shall be renewable automatically every 10 years.
2. The application for a permanent residence card shall be submitted before the residence card expires. Failure to comply with the requirement to apply for a permanent residence card may render the person concerned liable to proportionate and non-discriminatory sanctions.
3. Interruption in residence not exceeding two consecutive years shall not affect the validity of the permanent residence card.

Article 21 – Continuity of residence

For the purposes of this Directive, continuity of residence may be attested by any means of proof in use in the host Member State. Continuity of residence is broken by any expulsion decision duly enforced against the person concerned.

CHAPTER V – PROVISIONS COMMON TO THE RIGHT OF RESIDENCE AND THE RIGHT OF PERMANENT RESIDENCE

Article 22 – Territorial scope

The right of residence and the right of permanent residence shall cover the whole territory of the host Member State. Member States may impose territorial restrictions on the right of residence and the right of permanent residence only where the same restrictions apply to their own nationals.

Article 23 – Related rights

Irrespective of nationality, the family members of a Union citizen who have the right of residence or the right of permanent residence in a Member State shall be entitled to take up employment or self-employment there.

Article 24 – Equal treatment

1. Subject to such specific provisions as are expressly provided for in the Treaty and secondary law, all Union citizens residing on the basis of this Directive in the territory of the host Member State shall enjoy equal treatment with the nationals of that Member State within the scope of the Treaty. The benefit of this right shall be extended to family members who are not nationals of a Member State and who have the right of residence or permanent residence.
2. By way of derogation from paragraph 1, the host Member State shall not be obliged to confer entitlement to social assistance during the first three months of residence or, where appropriate, the longer period provided for in Article 14(4)(b), nor shall it be obliged, prior to acquisition of the right of permanent residence, to grant maintenance aid for studies, including vocational training, consisting in student grants or student loans to persons other than workers, self-employed persons, persons who retain such status and members of their families.

Article 25 – General provisions concerning residence documents

1. Possession of a registration certificate as referred to in Article 8, of a document certifying permanent residence, of a certificate attesting submission of an application for a family member residence card, of a residence card or of a permanent residence card, may under no circumstances be made a precondition for the exercise of a right or the completion of an administrative formality, as entitlement to rights may be attested by any other means of proof.
2. All documents mentioned in paragraph 1 shall be issued free of charge or for a charge not exceeding that imposed on nationals for the issuing of similar documents.

Article 26 – Checks

Member States may carry out checks on compliance with any requirement deriving from their national legislation for non-nationals always to carry their registration certificate or residence card, provided that the same requirement applies to their own nationals as regards their identity card. In the event of failure to comply with this requirement, Member States may impose the same sanctions as those imposed on their own nationals for failure to carry their identity card.

CHAPTER VI – RESTRICTIONS ON THE RIGHT OF ENTRY AND THE RIGHT OF RESIDENCE ON GROUNDS OF PUBLIC POLICY, PUBLIC SECURITY OR PUBLIC HEALTH

Article 27 – General principles

1. Subject to the provisions of this Chapter, Member States may restrict the freedom of movement and residence of Union citizens and their family members, irrespective of nationality, on grounds of public policy, public security or public health. These grounds shall not be invoked to serve economic ends.
2. Measures taken on grounds of public policy or public security shall comply with the principle of proportionality and shall be based exclusively on the personal conduct of the individual concerned. Previous criminal convictions shall not in themselves constitute grounds for taking such measures.

   The personal conduct of the individual concerned must represent a genuine, present and sufficiently serious threat affecting one of the fundamental interests of society. Justifications that are isolated from the particulars of the case or that rely on considerations of general prevention shall not be accepted.

3. In order to ascertain whether the person concerned represents a danger for public policy or public security, when issuing the registration certificate or, in the absence of a registration system, not later than three months from the date of arrival of the person concerned on its territory or from the date of reporting his/her presence within the territory, as provided for in Article 5(5), or when issuing the residence card, the host Member State may, should it consider this essential, request the Member State of origin and, if need be, other Member States to provide information concerning any previous police record the person concerned may have. Such enquiries shall not be made as a matter of routine. The Member State consulted shall give its reply within two months.
4. The Member State which issued the passport or identity card shall allow the holder of the document who has been expelled on grounds of public policy, public security, or public health from another Member State to re-enter its territory without any formality even if the document is no longer valid or the nationality of the holder is in dispute.

Article 28 – Protection against expulsion

1. Before taking an expulsion decision on grounds of public policy or public security, the host Member State shall take account of considerations such as how long the individual concerned has resided on its territory, his/her age, state of health, family and economic situation, social and cultural integration into the host Member State and the extent of his/her links with the country of origin.
2. The host Member State may not take an expulsion decision against Union citizens or their family members, irrespective of nationality, who have the right of permanent residence on its territory, except on serious grounds of public policy or public security.
3. An expulsion decision may not be taken against Union citizens, except if the decision is based on imperative grounds of public security, as defined by Member States, if they:
   (a) have resided in the host Member State for the previous 10 years; or
   (b) are a minor, except if the expulsion is necessary for the best interests of the child, as provided for in the United Nations Convention on the Rights of the Child of 20 November 1989.

Article 29 – Public health

1. The only diseases justifying measures restricting freedom of movement shall be the diseases with epidemic potential as defined by the relevant instruments of the World Health Organisation and other infectious diseases or contagious parasitic diseases if they are the subject of protection provisions applying to nationals of the host Member State.
2. Diseases occurring after a three-month period from the date of arrival shall not constitute grounds for expulsion from the territory.
3. Where there are serious indications that it is necessary, Member States may, within three months of the date of arrival, require persons entitled to the right of residence to undergo, free of charge, a medical examination to certify that they are not suffering from any of the conditions referred to in paragraph 1. Such medical examinations may not be required as a matter of routine.

Article 30 – Notification of decisions

1. The persons concerned shall be notified in writing of any decision taken under Article 27(1), in such a way that they are able to comprehend its content and the implications for them.
2. The persons concerned shall be informed, precisely and in full, of the public policy, public security or public health grounds on which the decision taken in their case is based, unless this is contrary to the interests of State security.
3. The notification shall specify the court or administrative authority with which the person concerned may lodge an appeal, the time limit for the appeal and, where applicable, the time allowed for the person to leave the territory of the Member State. Save in duly substantiated cases of urgency, the time allowed to leave the territory shall be not less than one month from the date of notification.

Article 31 – Procedural safeguards

1. The persons concerned shall have access to judicial and, where appropriate, administrative redress procedures in the host Member State to appeal against or seek review of any decision taken against them on the grounds of public policy, public security or public health.
2. Where the application for appeal against or judicial review of the expulsion decision is accompanied by an application for an interim order to suspend enforcement of that decision, actual removal from the territory may not take place until such time as the decision on the interim order has been taken, except:
   — where the expulsion decision is based on a previous judicial decision; or
   — where the persons concerned have had previous access to judicial review; or
   — where the expulsion decision is based on imperative grounds of public security under Article 28(3).
3. The redress procedures shall allow for an examination of the legality of the decision, as well as of the facts and circumstances on which the proposed measure is based. They shall ensure that the decision is not disproportionate, particularly in view of the requirements laid down in Article 28.
4. Member States may exclude the individual concerned from their territory pending the redress procedure, but they may not prevent the individual from submitting his/her defence in person, except when his/her appearance may cause serious troubles to public policy or public security or when the appeal or judicial review concerns a denial of entry to the territory.

Article 32 – Duration of exclusion orders

1. Persons excluded on grounds of public policy or public security may submit an application for lifting of the exclusion order after a reasonable period, depending on the circumstances, and in any event after three years from enforcement of the final exclusion order which has been validly adopted in accordance with Community law, by putting forward arguments to establish that there has been a material change in the circumstances which justified the decision ordering their exclusion.

   The Member State concerned shall reach a decision on this application within six months of its submission.
2. The persons referred to in paragraph 1 shall have no right of entry to the territory of the Member State concerned while their application is being considered.

Article 33 – Expulsion as a penalty or legal consequence

1. Expulsion orders may not be issued by the host Member State as a penalty or legal consequence of a custodial penalty, unless they conform to the requirements of Articles 27, 28 and 29.
2. If an expulsion order, as provided for in paragraph 1, is enforced more than two years after it was issued, the Member State shall check that the individual concerned is currently and genuinely a threat to public policy or public security and shall assess whether there has been any material change in the circumstances since the expulsion order was issued.

CHAPTER VII – FINAL PROVISIONS

Article 34 – Publicity

Member States shall disseminate information concerning the rights and obligations of Union citizens and their family members on the subjects covered by this Directive, particularly by means of awareness-raising campaigns conducted through national and local media and other means of communication.

Article 35 – Abuse of rights

Member States may adopt the necessary measures to refuse, terminate or withdraw any right conferred by this Directive in the case of abuse of rights or fraud, such as marriages of convenience. Any such measure shall be proportionate and subject to the procedural safeguards provided for in Articles 30 and 31.

Article 36 – Sanctions

Member States shall lay down provisions on the sanctions applicable to breaches of national rules adopted for the implementation of this Directive and shall take the measures required for their application. The sanctions laid down shall be effective and proportionate. Member States shall notify the Commission of these provisions not later than 30 April 2006 and as promptly as possible in the case of any subsequent changes.

Article 37 – More favourable national provisions

The provisions of this Directive shall not affect any laws, regulations or administrative provisions laid down by a Member State which would be more favourable to the persons covered by this Directive.

Article 38 – Repeals

1. Articles 10 and 11 of Regulation (EEC) No 1612/68 shall be repealed with effect from 30 April 2006.
2. Directives 64/221/EEC, 68/360/EEC, 72/194/EEC, 73/148/EEC, 75/34/EEC, 75/35/EEC, 90/364/EEC, 90/365/EEC and 93/96/EEC shall be repealed with effect from 30 April 2006.
3. References made to the repealed provisions and Directives shall be construed as being made to this Directive.

Article 39 – Report

No later than 30 April 2006 the Commission shall submit a report on the application of this Directive to the European Parliament and the Council, together with any necessary proposals, notably on the opportunity to extend the period of time during which Union citizens and their family members may reside in the territory of the host Member State without any conditions. The Member States shall provide the Commission with the information needed to produce the report.

Article 40 – Transposition

1. Member States shall bring into force the laws, regulations and administrative provisions necessary to comply with this Directive by 30 April 2006.

   When Member States adopt those measures, they shall contain a reference to this Directive or shall be accompanied by such a reference on the occasion of their official publication. The methods of making such reference shall be laid down by the Member States.
2. Member States shall communicate to the Commission the text of the provisions of national law which they adopt in the field covered by this Directive together with a table showing how the provisions of this Directive correspond to the national provisions adopted.

Article 41 – Entry into force

This Directive shall enter into force on the day of its publication in the *Official Journal of the European Union*.

Article 42 – Addressees

This Directive is addressed to the Member States.

Done at Strasbourg, 29 April 2004.

Appendix 4

Immigration (European Economic Area) Regulations 2006

SI 2006/1003 amended by SI 2006/3317, SI 2007/3224, SI 2009/1117 and SI 2011/1247

PART I

INTERPRETATION ETC

1. Citation and commencement

These Regulations may be cited as the Immigration (European Economic Area) Regulations 2006 and shall come into force on 30th April 2006.

2. General interpretation

(1) In these Regulations—

'the 1971 Act' means the Immigration Act 1971;

'the 1999 Act' means the Immigration and Asylum Act 1999;

'the 2002 Act' means the Nationality, Immigration and Asylum Act 2002;

'civil partner' does not include a party to a civil partnership of convenience;

'decision maker' means the Secretary of State, an immigration officer or an entry clearance officer (as the case may be);

'deportation order' means an order made pursuant to regulation 24(3);

'document certifying permanent residence' means a document issued to an EEA national, in accordance with regulation 18, as proof of the holder's permanent right of residence under regulation 15 as at the date of issue;

'EEA decision' means a decision under these Regulations that concerns a person's—

(a) entitlement to be admitted to the United Kingdom;

(b) entitlement to be issued with or have renewed, or not to have revoked, a registration certificate, residence card, document certifying permanent residence or permanent residence card; or

(c) removal from the United Kingdom;

'EEA family permit' means a document issued to a person, in accordance with regulation 12, in connection with his admission to the United Kingdom;

'EEA national' means a national of an EEA State;

'EEA State' means—

(a) a member State, other than the United Kingdom;

(b) Norway, Iceland or Liechtenstein; or

(c) Switzerland;

'entry clearance' has the meaning given in section 33(1) of the 1971 Act;

'entry clearance officer' means a person responsible for the grant or refusal of entry clearance;

'exclusion order' means an order made under regulation 19(1B);

'immigration rules' has the meaning given in section 33(1) of the 1971 Act;

'military service' means service in the armed forces of an EEA State;

'permanent residence card' means a card issued to a person who is not an EEA national, in accordance with regulation 18, as proof of the holder's permanent right of residence under regulation 15 as at the date of issue;

'registration certificate' means a certificate issued to an EEA national, in accordance with regulation 16, as proof of the holder's right of residence in the United Kingdom as at the date of issue;

'relevant EEA national' in relation to an extended family member has the meaning given in regulation 8(6);

'residence card' means a card issued to a person who is not an EEA national, in accordance with regulation 17, as proof of the holder's right of residence in the United Kingdom as at the date of issue;

'spouse' does not include a party to a marriage of convenience;

'United Kingdom national' means a person who falls to be treated as a national of the United Kingdom for the purposes of the Community Treaties.

(2) Paragraph (1) is subject to paragraph 1(a) of Schedule 4 (transitional provisions).

(3) Section 11 of the 1971 Act (construction of references to entry) shall apply for the purpose of determining whether a person has entered the United Kingdom for the purpose of these Regulations as it applies for the purpose of determining whether a person has entered the United Kingdom for the purpose of that Act.

3. Continuity of residence

(1) This regulation applies for the purpose of calculating periods of continuous residence in the United Kingdom under regulation 5(1) and regulation 15.

(2) Continuity of residence is not affected by—

(a) periods of absence from the United Kingdom which do not exceed six months in total in any year;

(b) periods of absence from the United Kingdom on military service; or

(c) any one absence from the United Kingdom not exceeding twelve months for an important reason such as pregnancy and childbirth, serious illness, study or vocational training or an overseas posting.

(3) But continuity of residence is broken if a person is removed from the United Kingdom under these Regulations.

4. 'Worker', 'self-employed person', 'self-sufficient person' and 'student'

(1) In these Regulations —

(a) 'worker' means a worker within the meaning of Article 39 of the Treaty establishing the European Community;

(b) 'self-employed person' means a person who establishes himself in order to pursue activity as a self-employed person in accordance with Article 43 of the Treaty establishing the European Community;

(c) 'self-sufficient person' means a person who has—

(i) sufficient resources not to become a burden on the social assistance system of the United Kingdom during his period of residence; and

(ii) comprehensive sickness insurance cover in the United Kingdom;

(d) 'student' means a person who—

(i) is enrolled at a private or public establishment, included on the Register of Education and Training Providers maintained by the Department of Innovation, Universities and Skills or financed from public funds, for the principal purpose of following a course of study, including vocational training;

(ii) has comprehensive sickness insurance cover in the United Kingdom; and

(iii) assures the Secretary of State, by means of a declaration, or by such equivalent means as the person may choose, that he has sufficient resources not to become a burden on the social assistance system of the United Kingdom during his period of residence.

(2) For the purposes of paragraph (1)(c), where family members of the person concerned reside in the United Kingdom and their right to reside is dependent upon their being family members of that person—

(a) the requirement for that person to have sufficient resources not to become a burden on the social assistance system of the United Kingdom during his period of residence shall only be satisfied if his resources and those of the family members are sufficient to avoid him and the family members becoming such a burden;

(b) the requirement for that person to have comprehensive sickness insurance cover in the United Kingdom shall only be satisfied if he and his family members have such cover.

(3) For the purposes of paragraph (1)(d), where family members of the person concerned reside in the United Kingdom and their right to reside is dependent upon their being family members of that person, the requirement for that person to assure the Secretary of State that he has sufficient resources not to become a burden on the social assistance system of the United Kingdom during his period of residence shall only be satisfied if he assures the Secretary of State that his resources and those of the family members are sufficient to avoid him and the family members becoming such a burden.

(4) For the purposes of paragraphs (1)(c) and (d) and paragraphs (2) and (3), the resources of the person concerned and, where applicable, any family members, are to be regarded as sufficient if—

(a) they exceed the maximum level of resources which a United Kingdom national and his family members may possess if he is to become eligible for social assistance under the United Kingdom benefit system; or

(b) paragraph (a) does not apply but, taking into account the personal situation of the person concerned and, where applicable, any family members, it appears to the decision maker that the resources of the person or persons concerned should be regarded as sufficient.

5. 'Worker or self-employed person who has ceased activity'

(1) In these Regulations, 'worker or self-employed person who has ceased activity' means an EEA national who satisfies the conditions in paragraph (2), (3), (4) or (5).

(2) A person satisfies the conditions in this paragraph if he—

(a) terminates his activity as a worker or self-employed person and—

(i) has reached the age at which he is entitled to a state pension on the date on which he terminates his activity; or

(ii) in the case of a worker, ceases working to take early retirement;

(b) pursued his activity as a worker or self-employed person in the United Kingdom for at least twelve months prior to the termination; and

(c) resided in the United Kingdom continuously for more than three years prior to the termination.

(3) A person satisfies the conditions in this paragraph if—

(a) he terminates his activity in the United Kingdom as a worker or self-employed person as a result of a permanent incapacity to work; and

(b) either—

(i) he resided in the United Kingdom continuously for more than two years prior to the termination; or

(ii) the incapacity is the result of an accident at work or an occupational disease that entitles him to a pension payable in full or in part by an institution in the United Kingdom.

(4) A person satisfies the conditions in this paragraph if—

(a) he is active as a worker or self-employed person in an EEA State but retains his place of residence in the United Kingdom, to which he returns as a rule at least once a week; and

(b) prior to becoming so active in that EEA State, he had been continuously resident and continuously active as a worker or self-employed person in the United Kingdom for at least three years.

(5) A person who satisfies the condition in paragraph (4)(a) but not the condition in paragraph (4)(b) shall, for the purposes of paragraphs (2) and (3), be treated as being active and resident in the United Kingdom during any period in which he is working or self-employed in the EEA State.

(6) The conditions in paragraphs (2) and (3) as to length of residence and activity as a worker or self-employed person shall not apply in relation to a person whose spouse or civil partner is a United Kingdom national.

(7) For the purposes of this regulation—

(a) periods of inactivity for reasons not of the person's own making;

(b) periods of inactivity due to illness or accident; and

(c) in the case of a worker, periods of involuntary unemployment duly recorded by the relevant employment office,

shall be treated as periods of activity as a worker or self-employed person, as the case may be.

6. 'Qualified person'

(1) In these Regulations, 'qualified person' means a person who is an EEA national and in the United Kingdom as—

(a) a jobseeker;

(b) a worker;

(c) a self-employed person;

(d) a self-sufficient person; or

(e) a student.

(2) A person who is no longer working shall not cease to be treated as a worker for the purpose of paragraph (1)(b) if—

(a) he is temporarily unable to work as the result of an illness or accident;

(b) he is in duly recorded involuntary unemployment after having been employed in the United Kingdom, provided that he has registered as a jobseeker with the relevant employment office and—

(i) he was employed for one year or more before becoming unemployed;

(ii) he has been unemployed for no more than six months; or

(iii) he can provide evidence that he is seeking employment in the United Kingdom and has a genuine chance of being engaged;

(c) he is involuntarily unemployed and has embarked on vocational training; or

(d) he has voluntarily ceased working and embarked on vocational training that is related to his previous employment.

(3) A person who is no longer in self-employment shall not cease to be treated as a self-employed person for the purpose of paragraph (1)(c) if he is temporarily unable to pursue his activity as a self-employed person as the result of an illness or accident.

(4) For the purpose of paragraph (1)(a), 'jobseeker' means a person who enters the United Kingdom in order to seek employment and can provide evidence that he is seeking employment and has a genuine chance of being engaged.

7. Family member

(1) Subject to paragraph (2), for the purposes of these Regulations the following persons shall be treated as the family members of another person—

(a) his spouse or his civil partner;

(b) direct descendants of his, his spouse or his civil partner who are—

(i) under 21; or

(ii) dependants of his, his spouse or his civil partner;

(c) dependent direct relatives in his ascending line or that of his spouse or his civil partner;

(d) a person who is to be treated as the family member of that other person under paragraph (3).

(2) A person shall not be treated under paragraph (1)(b) or (c) as the family member of a student residing in the United Kingdom after the period of three months beginning on the date on which the student is admitted to the United Kingdom unless—

(a) in the case of paragraph (b), the person is the dependent child of the student or of his spouse or civil partner; or

(b) the student also falls within one of the other categories of qualified persons mentioned in regulation 6(1).

(3) Subject to paragraph (4), a person who is an extended family member and has been issued with an EEA family permit, a registration certificate or a residence card shall be treated as the family member of the relevant EEA national for as long as he continues to satisfy the conditions in regulation 8(2), (3), (4) or (5) in relation to that EEA national and the permit, certificate or card has not ceased to be valid or been revoked.

(4) Where the relevant EEA national is a student, the extended family member shall only be treated as the family member of that national under paragraph (3) if either the EEA family permit was issued under regulation 12(2), the registration certificate was issued under regulation 16(5) or the residence card was issued under regulation 17(4).

8. 'Extended family member'

(1) In these Regulations 'extended family member" means a person who is not a family member of an EEA national under regulation 7(1)(a), (b) or (c) and who satisfies the conditions in paragraph (2), (3), (4) or (5).

(2) A person satisfies the condition in this paragraph if the person is a relative of an EEA national, his spouse or his civil partner and—

(a) the person is residing in a country other than the United Kingdom in which the EEA national also resides and is dependent upon the EEA national or is a member of his household;

(b) the person satisfied the condition in paragraph (a) and is accompanying the EEA national to the United Kingdom or wishes to join him there; or

(c) the person satisfied the condition in paragraph (a), has joined the EEA national in the United Kingdom and continues to be dependent upon him or to be a member of his household.

(3) A person satisfies the condition in this paragraph if the person is a relative of an EEA national or his spouse or his civil partner and, on serious health grounds, strictly requires the personal care of the EEA national his spouse or his civil partner.

(4) A person satisfies the condition in this paragraph if the person is a relative of an EEA national and would meet the requirements in the immigration rules (other than those relating to entry clearance) for indefinite leave to enter or remain in the United Kingdom as a dependent relative of the EEA national were the EEA national a person present and settled in the United Kingdom.

(5) A person satisfies the condition in this paragraph if the person is the partner of an EEA national (other than a civil partner) and can prove to the decision maker that he is in a durable relationship with the EEA national.

(6) In these Regulations 'relevant EEA national' means, in relation to an extended family member, the EEA national who is or whose spouse or civil partner is the relative of the extended family member for the purpose of paragraph (2), (3) or (4) or the EEA national who is the partner of the extended family member for the purpose of paragraph (5).

9. Family members of United Kingdom nationals

(1) If the conditions in paragraph (2) are satisfied, these Regulations apply to a person who is the family member of a United Kingdom national as if the United Kingdom national were an EEA national.

(2) The conditions are that—

(a) the United Kingdom national is residing in an EEA State as a worker or self-employed person or was so residing before returning to the United Kingdom; and

(b) if the family member of the United Kingdom national is his spouse or civil partner, the parties are living together in the EEA State or had entered into the marriage or civil partnership and were living together in that State before the United Kingdom national returned to the United Kingdom.

(3) Where these Regulations apply to the family member of a United Kingdom national the United Kingdom national shall be treated as holding a valid passport issued by an EEA State for the purpose of the application of regulation 13 to that family member.

10. 'Family member who has retained the right of residence'

(1) In these Regulations, 'family member who has retained the right of residence' means, subject to paragraph (8), a person who satisfies the conditions in paragraph (2), (3), (4) or (5).

(2) A person satisfies the conditions in this paragraph if—

(a) he was a family member of a qualified person when the qualified person died;

(b) he resided in the United Kingdom in accordance with these Regulations for at least the year immediately before the death of the qualified person; and

(c) he satisfies the condition in paragraph (6).

(3) A person satisfies the conditions in this paragraph if—

(a) he is the direct descendant of—

(i) a qualified person who has died;

(ii) a person who ceased to be a qualified person on ceasing to reside in the United Kingdom; or

(iii) the person who was the spouse or civil partner of the qualified person mentioned in sub-paragraph (i) when he died or is the spouse or civil partner of the person mentioned in sub-paragraph (ii); and

(b) he was attending an educational course in the United Kingdom immediately before the qualified person died or ceased to be a qualified person and continues to attend such a course.

(4) A person satisfies the conditions in this paragraph if the person is the parent with actual custody of a child who satisfies the condition in paragraph (3).

(5) A person satisfies the conditions in this paragraph if—

(a) he ceased to be a family member of a qualified person on the termination of the marriage or civil partnership of the qualified person;

(b) he was residing in the United Kingdom in accordance with these Regulations at the date of the termination;

(c) he satisfies the condition in paragraph (6); and

(d) either—

(i) prior to the initiation of the proceedings for the termination of the marriage or the civil partnership the marriage or civil partnership had lasted for at least three years and the parties to the marriage or civil partnership had resided in the United Kingdom for at least one year during its duration;

(ii) the former spouse or civil partner of the qualified person has custody of a child of the qualified person;

(iii) the former spouse or civil partner of the qualified person has the right of access to a child of the qualified person under the age of 18 and a court has ordered that such access must take place in the United Kingdom; or

(iv) the continued right of residence in the United Kingdom of the person is warranted by particularly difficult circumstances, such as he or another family member having been a victim of domestic violence while the marriage or civil partnership was subsisting.

(6) The condition in this paragraph is that the person—

(a) is not an EEA national but would, if he were an EEA national, be a worker, a self-employed person or a self-sufficient person under regulation 6; or

(b) is the family member of a person who falls within paragraph (a).

(7) In this regulation, 'educational course' means a course within the scope of Article 12 of Council Regulation (EEC) No. 1612/68 on freedom of movement for workers.

(8) A person with a permanent right of residence under regulation 15 shall not become a family member who has retained the right of residence on the death or departure from the

United Kingdom of the qualified person or the termination of the marriage or civil partnership, as the case may be, and a family member who has retained the right of residence shall cease to have that status on acquiring a permanent right of residence under regulation 15.

PART 2
EEA RIGHTS

11. Right of admission to the United Kingdom

(1) An EEA national must be admitted to the United Kingdom if he produces on arrival a valid national identity card or passport issued by an EEA State.

(2) A person who is not an EEA national must be admitted to the United Kingdom if he is a family member of an EEA national, a family member who has retained the right of residence or a person with a permanent right of residence under regulation 15 and produces on arrival—

(a) a valid passport; and

(b) an EEA family permit, a residence card or a permanent residence card.

(3) An immigration officer may not place a stamp in the passport of a person admitted to the United Kingdom under this regulation who is not an EEA national if the person produces a residence card or permanent residence card.

(4) Before an immigration officer refuses admission to the United Kingdom to a person under this regulation because the person does not produce on arrival a document mentioned in paragraph (1) or (2), the immigration officer must give the person every reasonable opportunity to obtain the document or have it brought to him within a reasonable period of time or to prove by other means that he is—

(a) an EEA national;

(b) a family member of an EEA national with a right to accompany that national or join him in the United Kingdom; or

(c) a family member who has retained the right of residence or a person with a permanent right of residence under regulation 15.

(5) But this regulation is subject to regulations 19(1) and (2).

12. Issue of EEA family permit

(1) An entry clearance officer must issue an EEA family permit to a person who applies for one if the person is a family member of an EEA national and—

(a) the EEA national—

(i) is residing in the UK in accordance with these Regulations; or

(ii) will be travelling to the United Kingdom within six months of the date of the application and will be an EEA national residing in the United Kingdom in accordance with these Regulations on arrival in the United Kingdom; and

(b) the family member will be accompanying the EEA national to the United Kingdom or joining him there.

(2) An entry clearance officer may issue an EEA family permit to an extended family member of an EEA national who applies for one if—

(a) the relevant EEA national satisfies the condition in paragraph (1)(a);

(b) the extended family member wishes to accompany the relevant EEA national to the United Kingdom or to join him there; and

(c) in all the circumstances, it appears to the entry clearance officer appropriate to issue the EEA family permit.

(3) Where an entry clearance officer receives an application under paragraph (2) he shall undertake an extensive examination of the personal circumstances of the applicant and if he refuses the application shall give reasons justifying the refusal unless this is contrary to the interests of national security.

(4) An EEA family permit issued under this regulation shall be issued free of charge and as soon as possible.

(5) But an EEA family permit shall not be issued under this regulation if the applicant or the EEA national concerned is subject to a deportation or exclusion order or falls to be excluded from the United Kingdom on grounds of public policy, public security or public health in accordance with regulation 21.

13. Initial right of residence

(1) An EEA national is entitled to reside in the United Kingdom for a period not exceeding three months beginning on the date on which he is admitted to the United Kingdom provided that he holds a valid national identity card or passport issued by an EEA State.

(2) A family member of an EEA national residing in the United Kingdom under paragraph (1) who is not himself an EEA national is entitled to reside in the United Kingdom provided that he holds a valid passport.

(3) But—

(a) this regulation is subject to regulation 19(3)(b); and

(b) an EEA national or his family member who becomes an unreasonable burden on the social assistance system of the United Kingdom shall cease to have the right to reside under this regulation.

14. Extended right of residence

(1) A qualified person is entitled to reside in the United Kingdom for so long as he remains a qualified person.

(2) A family member of a qualified person residing in the United Kingdom under paragraph (1) or of an EEA national with a permanent right of residence under regulation 15 is entitled to reside in the United Kingdom for so long as he remains the family member of the qualified person or EEA national.

(3) A family member who has retained the right of residence is entitled to reside in the United Kingdom for so long as he remains a family member who has retained the right of residence.

(4) A right to reside under this regulation is in addition to any right a person may have to reside in the United Kingdom under regulation 13 or 15.

(5) But this regulation is subject to regulation 19(3)(b).

15. Permanent right of residence

(1) The following persons shall acquire the right to reside in the United Kingdom permanently—

(a) an EEA national who has resided in the United Kingdom in accordance with these Regulations for a continuous period of five years;

(b) a family member of an EEA national who is not himself an EEA national but who has resided in the United Kingdom with the EEA national in accordance with these Regulations for a continuous period of five years;

(c) a worker or self-employed person who has ceased activity;

(d) the family member of a worker or self-employed person who has ceased activity;

(e) a person who was the family member of a worker or self-employed person where—

(i) the worker or self-employed person has died;

(ii) the family member resided with him immediately before his death; and

(iii) the worker or self-employed person had resided continuously in the United Kingdom for at least the two years immediately before his death or the death was the result of an accident at work or an occupational disease;

(f) a person who—

(i) has resided in the United Kingdom in accordance with these Regulations for a continuous period of five years; and

(ii) was, at the end of that period, a family member who has retained the right of residence.

(2) Once acquired, the right of permanent residence under this regulation shall be lost only through absence from the United Kingdom for a period exceeding two consecutive years.

(3) But this regulation is subject to regulation 19(3)(b).

PART 3
RESIDENCE DOCUMENTATION

16. Issue of registration certificate

(1) The Secretary of State must issue a registration certificate to a qualified person immediately on application and production of—

(a) a valid identity card or passport issued by an EEA State;

(b) proof that he is a qualified person.

(2) In the case of a worker, confirmation of the worker's engagement from his employer or a certificate of employment is sufficient proof for the purposes of paragraph (1)(b).

(3) The Secretary of State must issue a registration certificate to an EEA national who is the family member of a qualified person or of an EEA national with a permanent right of residence under regulation 15 immediately on application and production of—

(a) a valid identity card or passport issued by an EEA State; and

(b) proof that the applicant is such a family member.

(4) The Secretary of State must issue a registration certificate to an EEA national who is a family member who has retained the right of residence on application and production of—

(a) a valid identity card or passport; and

(b) proof that the applicant is a family member who has retained the right of residence.

(5) The Secretary of State may issue a registration certificate to an extended family member not falling within regulation 7(3) who is an EEA national on application if—

(a) the relevant EEA national in relation to the extended family member is a qualified person or an EEA national with a permanent right of residence under regulation 15; and

(b) in all the circumstances it appears to the Secretary of State appropriate to issue the registration certificate.

(6) Where the Secretary of State receives an application under paragraph (5) he shall undertake an extensive examination of the personal circumstances of the applicant and if he refuses the application shall give reasons justifying the refusal unless this is contrary to the interests of national security.

(7) A registration certificate issued under this regulation shall state the name and address of the person registering and the date of registration and shall be issued free of charge.

(8) But this regulation is subject to regulation 20(1).

17. Issue of residence card

(1) The Secretary of State must issue a residence card to a person who is not an EEA national and is the family member of a qualified person or of an EEA national with a permanent right of residence under regulation 15 on application and production of—

(a) a valid passport; and

(b) proof that the applicant is such a family member.

(2) The Secretary of State must issue a residence card to a person who is not an EEA national but who is a family member who has retained the right of residence on application and production of—

(a) a valid passport; and

(b) proof that the applicant is a family member who has retained the right of residence.

(3) On receipt of an application under paragraph (1) or (2) and the documents that are required to accompany the application the Secretary of State shall immediately issue the applicant with a certificate of application for the residence card and the residence card shall be issued no later than six months after the date on which the application and documents are received.

(4) The Secretary of State may issue a residence card to an extended family member not falling within regulation 7(3) who is not an EEA national on application if—

(a) the relevant EEA national in relation to the extended family member is a qualified person or an EEA national with a permanent right of residence under regulation 15; and

(b) in all the circumstances it appears to the Secretary of State appropriate to issue the residence card.

(5) Where the Secretary of State receives an application under paragraph (4) he shall undertake an extensive examination of the personal circumstances of the applicant and if he refuses the application shall give reasons justifying the refusal unless this is contrary to the interests of national security.

(6) A residence card issued under this regulation may take the form of a stamp in the applicant's passport and shall be valid for—

(a) five years from the date of issue; or

(b) in the case of a residence card issued to the family member or extended family member of a qualified person, the envisaged period of residence in the United Kingdom of the qualified person,

whichever is the shorter.

(6A) A residence card issued under this regulation shall be entitled 'Residence card of a family member of an EEA national' or 'Residence card of a family member who has retained the right of residence', as the case may be.

(7) A residence card issued under this regulation shall be issued free of charge.

(8) But this regulation is subject to regulations 20(1) and (1A).

18. Issue of a document certifying permanent residence and a permanent residence card

(1) The Secretary of State must issue an EEA national with a permanent right of residence under regulation 15 with a document certifying permanent residence as soon as possible after an application for such a document and proof that the EEA national has such a right is submitted to the Secretary of State.

(2) The Secretary of State must issue a person who is not an EEA national who has a permanent right of residence under regulation 15 with a permanent residence card no later than six months after the date on which an application for a permanent residence card and proof that the person has such a right is submitted to the Secretary of State.

(3) Subject to paragraph (5), a permanent residence card shall be valid for ten years from the date of issue and must be renewed on application.

(4) A document certifying permanent residence and a permanent residence card shall be issued free of charge.

(5) A document certifying permanent residence and a permanent residence card shall cease to be valid if the holder ceases to have a right of permanent residence under regulation 15.

(6) But this regulation is subject to regulation 20.

PART 4
REFUSAL OF ADMISSION AND REMOVAL ETC

19. Exclusion and removal from the United Kingdom

(1) A person is not entitled to be admitted to the United Kingdom by virtue of regulation 11 if his exclusion is justified on grounds of public policy, public security or public health in accordance with regulation 21.

(1A) A person is not entitled to be admitted to the United Kingdom by virtue of regulation 11 if that person is subject to a deportation or exclusion order.

(1B) If the Secretary of State considers that the exclusion of an EEA national or the family member of an EEA national is justified on the grounds of public policy, public security or public health in accordance with regulation 21 the Secretary of State may make an order for the purpose of these Regulations prohibiting that person from entering the United Kingdom.

(2) A person is not entitled to be admitted to the United Kingdom as the family member of an EEA national under regulation 11(2) unless, at the time of his arrival—

(a) he is accompanying the EEA national or joining him in the United Kingdom; and

(b) the EEA national has a right to reside in the United Kingdom under these Regulations.

(3) Subject to paragraphs (4) and (5), an EEA national who has entered the United Kingdom or the family member of such a national who has entered the United Kingdom may be removed if —

(a) that person does not have or ceases to have a right to reside under these Regulations; or

(b) the Secretary of State has decided that the person's removal is justified on grounds of public policy, public security or public health in accordance with regulation 21.

(4) A person must not be removed under paragraph (3) as the automatic consequence of having recourse to the social assistance system of the United Kingdom.

(5) A person must not be removed under paragraph (3) if he has a right to remain in the United Kingdom by virtue of leave granted under the 1971 Act unless his removal is justified on the grounds of public policy, public security or public health in accordance with regulation 21.

20. Refusal to issue or renew and revocation of residence documentation

(1) The Secretary of State may refuse to issue, revoke or refuse to renew a registration certificate, a residence card, a document certifying permanent residence or a permanent residence card if the refusal or revocation is justified on grounds of public policy, public security or public health.

(1A) The removal of a person from the United Kingdom under these Regulations invalidates a registration certificate, residence card, document certifying permanent residence or permanent residence card held by that person or an application made by that person for such a certificate, card or document.

(2) The Secretary of State may revoke a registration certificate or a residence card or refuse to renew a residence card if the holder of the certificate or card has ceased to have a right to reside under these Regulations.

(3) The Secretary of State may revoke a document certifying permanent residence or a permanent residence card or refuse to renew a permanent residence card if the holder of the certificate or card has ceased to have a right of permanent residence under regulation 15.

(4) An immigration officer may, at the time of a person's arrival in the United Kingdom—

(a) revoke that person's residence card if he is not at that time the family member of a qualified person or of an EEA national who has a right of permanent residence under regulation 15, a family member who has retained the right of residence or a person with a right of permanent residence under regulation 15;

(b) revoke that person's permanent residence card if he is not at that time a person with a right of permanent residence under regulation 15.

(5) An entry clearance officer or immigration officer may at any time revoke a person's s EEA family permit if—

(a) the revocation is justified on grounds of public policy, public security or public health; or

(b) the person is not at that time the family member of an EEA national with the right to reside in the United Kingdom under these Regulations or is not accompanying that national or joining him in the United Kingdom.

(6) Any action taken under this regulation on grounds of public policy, public security or public health shall be in accordance with regulation 21.

21. Decisions taken on public policy, public security and public health grounds

(1) In this regulation a 'relevant decision' means an EEA decision taken on the grounds of public policy, public security or public health.

(2) A relevant decision may not be taken to serve economic ends.

(3) A relevant decision may not be taken in respect of a person with a permanent right of residence under regulation 15 except on serious grounds of public policy or public security.

(4) A relevant decision may not be taken except on imperative grounds of public security in respect of an EEA national who—

(a) has resided in the United Kingdom for a continuous period of at least ten years prior to the relevant decision; or

(b) is under the age of 18, unless the relevant decision is necessary in his best interests, as provided for in the Convention on the Rights of the Child adopted by the General Assembly of the United Nations on 20th November 1989.

(5) Where a relevant decision is taken on grounds of public policy or public security it shall, in addition to complying with the preceding paragraphs of this regulation, be taken in accordance with the following principles—

(a) the decision must comply with the principle of proportionality;

(b) the decision must be based exclusively on the personal conduct of the person concerned;

(c) the personal conduct of the person concerned must represent a genuine, present and sufficiently serious threat affecting one of the fundamental interests of society;

(d) matters isolated from the particulars of the case or which relate to considerations of general prevention do not justify the decision;

(e) a person's previous criminal convictions do not in themselves justify the decision.

(6) Before taking a relevant decision on the grounds of public policy or public security in relation to a person who is resident in the United Kingdom the decision maker must take account of considerations such as the age, state of health, family and economic situation of the person, the person's length of residence in the United Kingdom, the person's social and cultural integration into the United Kingdom and the extent of the person's links with his country of origin.

(7) In the case of a relevant decision taken on grounds of public health—

(a) a disease that does not have epidemic potential as defined by the relevant instruments of the World Health Organisation or is not a disease to which section 38 of the Public Health (Control of Disease) Act 1984 applies (detention in hospital of a person with a notifiable disease) shall not constitute grounds for the decision; and

(b) if the person concerned is in the United Kingdom, diseases occurring after the three month period beginning on the date on which he arrived in the United Kingdom shall not constitute grounds for the decision.

PART 5
PROCEDURE IN RELATION TO EEA DECISIONS

22. Person claiming right of admission

(1) This regulation applies to a person who claims a right of admission to the United Kingdom under regulation 11 as—

(a) a person, not being an EEA national, who is a family member of an EEA national, a family member who has retained the right of residence or a person with a permanent right of residence under regulation 15; or

(b) an EEA national, where there is reason to believe that he may fall to be excluded under regulation 19(1) or (1A).

(2) A person to whom this regulation applies is to be treated as if he were a person seeking leave to enter the United Kingdom under the 1971 Act for the purposes of paragraphs 2, 3, 4, 7, 16 to 18 and 21 to 24 of Schedule 2 to the 1971 Act (administrative provisions as to control on entry etc), except that—

(a) the reference in paragraph 2(1) to the purpose for which the immigration officer may examine any persons who have arrived in the United Kingdom is to be read as a reference to the purpose of determining whether he is a person who is to be granted admission under these Regulations;

(b) the references in paragraphs 4(2A), 7 and 16(1) to a person who is, or may be, given leave to enter are to be read as references to a person who is, or may be, granted admission under these Regulations; and

(c) a medical examination is not be carried out under paragraph 2 or paragraph 7 as a matter of routine and may only be carried out within three months of a person's arrival in the United Kingdom.

(3) For so long as a person to whom this regulation applies is detained, or temporarily admitted or released while liable to detention, under the powers conferred by Schedule 2 to the 1971 Act, he is deemed not to have been admitted to the United Kingdom.

23. Person refused admission

(1) This regulation applies to a person who is in the United Kingdom and has been refused admission to the United Kingdom—

(a) because he does not meet the requirement of regulation 11 (including where he does not meet those requirements because his EEA family permit, residence card or permanent residence card has been revoked by an immigration officer in accordance with regulation 20); or

(b) in accordance with regulation 19(1), (1A) or (2).

(2) A person to whom this regulation applies, is to be treated as if he were a person refused leave to enter under the 1971 Act for the purpose of paragraphs 8, 10, 10A, 11, 16 to 19 and 21 to 24 of Schedule 2 to the 1971 Act, except that the reference in paragraph 19 to a certificate of entitlement, entry clearance or work permit is to be read as a reference to an EEA family permit, residence card or a permanent residence card.

24. Person subject to removal

(1) If there are reasonable grounds for suspecting that a person is someone who may be removed from the United Kingdom under regulation 19(3), that person may be detained under the authority of an immigration officer pending a decision whether or not to remove the person under that regulation, and paragraphs 17 and 18 of Schedule 2 to the 1971 Act shall apply in relation to the detention of such a person as those paragraphs apply in relation to a person who may be detained under paragraph 16 of that Schedule.

(2) Where a decision is taken to remove a person under regulation 19(3)(a), the person is to be treated as if he were a person to whom section 10(1)(a) of the 1999 Act applied, and section 10 of that Act (removal of certain persons unlawfully in the United Kingdom) is to apply accordingly.

(3) Where a decision is taken to remove a person under regulation l9(3)(b), the person is to be treated as if he were a person to whom section 3(5)(a) of the 1971 Act (liability to deportation) applied, and section 5 of that Act (procedure for deportation) and Schedule 3 to that Act (supplementary provision as to deportation) are to apply accordingly.

(4) A person who enters the United Kingdom in breach of a deportation or exclusion order shall be removable as an illegal entrant under Schedule 2 to the 1971 Act and the provisions of that Schedule shall apply accordingly.

(5) Where such a deportation order is made against a person but he is not removed under the order during the two year period beginning on the date on which the order is made, the Secretary of State shall only take action to remove the person under the order after the end of that period if, having assessed whether there has been any material change in circumstances since the deportation order was made, he considers that the removal continues to be justified on the grounds of public policy, public security or public health.

(6) A person to whom this regulation applies shall be allowed one month to leave the United Kingdom, beginning on the date on which he is notified of the decision to remove him, before being removed pursuant to that decision except—

(a) in duly substantiated cases of urgency;

(b) where the person is detained pursuant to the sentence or order of any court;

(c) where a person is a person to whom regulation 24(4) applies.

24A. Revocation of deportation and exclusion orders

(1) A deportation or exclusion order shall remain in force unless it is revoked by the Secretary of State under this regulation.

(2) A person who is subject to a deportation or exclusion order may apply to the Secretary of State to have it revoked if the person considers that there has been a material change in the circumstances that justified the making of the order.

(3) An application under paragraph (2) shall set out the material change in circumstances relied upon by the applicant and may only be made whilst the applicant is outside the United Kingdom.

(4) On receipt of an application under paragraph (2), the Secretary of State shall revoke the order if the Secretary of State considers that the order can no longer be justified on grounds of public policy, public security or public health in accordance with regulation 21.

(5) The Secretary of State shall take a decision on an application under paragraph (2) no later than six months after the date on which the application is received.

PART 6

APPEALS UNDER THESE REGULATIONS

25. Interpretation of Part 6

(1) In this Part—

'Asylum and Immigration Tribunal' has the same meaning as in the 2002 Act;

'Commission' has the same meaning as in the Special Immigration Appeals Commission Act 1997;

'the Human Rights Convention' has the same meaning as 'the Convention' in the Human Rights Act 1998; and

'the Refugee Convention' means the Convention relating to the Status of Refugees done at Geneva on 28th July 1951 and the Protocol relating to the Status of Refugees done at New York on 31st January 1967.

(2) For the purposes of this Part, and subject to paragraphs (3) and (4), an appeal is to be treated as pending during the period when notice of appeal is given and ending when the appeal is finally determined, withdrawn or abandoned.

(3) An appeal is not to be treated as finally determined while a further appeal may be brought; and, if such a further appeal is brought, the original appeal is not to be treated as finally determined until the further appeal is determined, withdrawn or abandoned.

(4) A pending appeal is not to be treated as abandoned solely because the appellant leaves the United Kingdom.

26. Appeal rights

(1) Subject to the following paragraphs of this regulation, a person may appeal under these Regulations against an EEA decision.

(2) If a person claims to be an EEA national, he may not appeal under these Regulations unless he produces a valid national identity card or passport issued by an EEA State.

(3) If a person claims to be the family member or relative of an EEA national he may not appeal under these Regulations unless he produces—

(a) an EEA family permit; or

(b) other proof that he is related as claimed to an EEA national.

(4) A person may not bring an appeal under these Regulations on a ground certified under paragraph (5) or rely on such a ground in an appeal brought under these Regulations.

(5) The Secretary of State or an immigration officer may certify a ground for the purposes of paragraph (4) if it has been considered in a previous appeal brought under these Regulations or under section 82(1) of the 2002 Act.

(6) Except where an appeal lies to the Commission, an appeal under these Regulations lies to the Asylum and Immigration Tribunal.

(7) The provisions of or made under the 2002 Act referred to in Schedule 1 shall have effect for the purposes of an appeal under these Regulations to the Asylum and Immigration Tribunal in accordance with that Schedule.

27. Out of country appeals

(1) Subject to paragraphs (2) and (3), a person may not appeal under regulation 26 whilst he is in the United Kingdom against an EEA decision—

(a) to refuse to admit him to the United Kingdom;

(aa) to make an exclusion order against him;

(b) to refuse to revoke a deportation or exclusion order made against him;

(c) to refuse to issue him with an EEA family permit; or

(d) to remove him from the United Kingdom after he has entered the United Kingdom in breach of a deportation or exclusion order.

(2) Paragraphs (1)(a) and (aa) do not apply where the person is in the United Kingdom and—

(a) the person held a valid EEA family permit, registration certificate, residence card, document certifying permanent residence or permanent residence card on his arrival in the United Kingdom or can otherwise prove that he is resident in the United Kingdom;

(b) the person is deemed not to have been admitted to the United Kingdom under regulation 22(3) but at the date on which notice of the decision to refuse to admit him is given he has been in the United Kingdom for at least 3 months; or

(c) a ground of the appeal is that, in taking the decision, the decision maker acted in breach of his rights under the Human Rights Convention or the Refugee Convention, unless the Secretary of State certifies that that ground of appeal is clearly unfounded.

(3) Paragraph (1)(d) does not apply where a ground of the appeal is that, in taking the decision, the decision maker acted in breach of the appellant's rights under the Human Rights Convention or the Refugee Convention, unless the Secretary of State certifies that that ground of appeal is clearly unfounded.

28. Appeals to the Commission

(1) An appeal against an EEA decision lies to the Commission where paragraph (2) or (4) applies.

(2) This paragraph applies if the Secretary of State certifies that the EEA decision was taken—

(a) by the Secretary of State wholly or partly on a ground listed in paragraph (3); or

(b) in accordance with a direction of the Secretary of State which identifies the person to whom the decision relates and which is given wholly or partly on a ground listed in paragraph (3).

(3) The grounds mentioned in paragraph (2) are that the person's exclusion or removal from the United Kingdom is—

(a) in the interests of national security; or

(b) in the interests of the relationship between the United Kingdom and another country.

(4) This paragraph applies if the Secretary of State certifies that the EEA decision was taken wholly or partly in reliance on information which in his opinion should not be made public—

(a) in the interests of national security;

(b) in the interests of the relationship between the United Kingdom and another country; or

(c) otherwise in the public interest.

(5) In paragraphs (2) and (4) a reference to the Secretary of State is to the Secretary of State acting in person.

(6) Where a certificate is issued under paragraph (2) or (4) in respect of a pending appeal to the Asylum and Immigration Tribunal the appeal shall lapse.

(7) An appeal against an EEA decision lies to the Commission where an appeal lapses by virtue of paragraph (6).

(8) The Special Immigration Appeals Commission Act 1997 shall apply to an appeal to the Commission under these Regulations as it applies to an appeal under section 2 of that Act to which subsection (2) of that section applies (appeals against an immigration decision) but paragraph (i) of that subsection shall not apply in relation to such an appeal.

29. Effect of appeals to the Asylum and Immigration Tribunal

(1) This Regulation applies to appeals under these Regulations made to the Asylum and Immigration Tribunal.

(2) If a person in the United Kingdom appeals against an EEA decision to refuse to admit him to the United Kingdom, any directions for his removal from the United Kingdom previously given by virtue of the refusal cease to have effect, except in so far as they have already been carried out, and no directions may be so given while the appeal is pending.

(3) If a person in the United Kingdom appeals against an EEA decision to remove him from the United Kingdom, any directions given under section 10 of the 1999 Act or Schedule 3 to the 1971 Act for his removal from the United Kingdom are to have no effect, except in so far as they have already been carried out, while the appeal is pending.

(4) But the provisions of Part I of Schedule 2, or as the case may be, Schedule 3 to the 1971 Act with respect to detention and persons liable to detention apply to a person appealing against a refusal to admit him or a decision to remove him as if there were in force directions for his removal from the United Kingdom, except that he may not be detained on board a ship or aircraft so as to compel him to leave the United Kingdom while the appeal is pending.

(5) In calculating the period of two months limited by paragraph 8(2) of Schedule 2 to the 1971 Act for—

(a) the giving of directions under that paragraph for the removal of a person from the United Kingdom; and

(b) the giving of a notice of intention to give such directions,

any period during which there is pending an appeal by him under is to be disregarded.

(6) If a person in the United Kingdom appeals against an EEA decision to remove him from the United Kingdom, a deportation order is not to be made against him under section 5 of the 1971 Act while the appeal is pending.

(7) Paragraph 29 of Schedule 2 to the 1971 Act (grant of bail pending appeal) applies to a person who has an appeal pending under these Regulations as it applies to a person who has an appeal pending under section 82(1) of the 2002 Act.

PART 7

GENERAL

30. Effect on other legislation

Schedule 2 (effect on other legislation) shall have effect.

31. Revocations, transitional provisions and consequential amendments

(1) The Regulations listed in column 1 of the table in Part 1 of Schedule 3 are revoked to the extent set out in column 3 of that table, subject to Part 2 of that Schedule and to Schedule 4.

(2) Schedule 4 (transitional provisions) and Schedule 5 (consequential amendments) shall have effect.

SCHEDULE 1 Regulation 26(7)

APPEALS TO THE ASYLUM AND IMMIGRATION TRIBUNAL

The following provisions of, or made under, the 2002 Act have effect in relation to an appeal under these Regulations to the Asylum and Immigration Tribunal as if it were an appeal against an immigration decision under section 82(1) of that Act:

section 84(1), except paragraphs (a) and (f);

sections 85 to 87;

sections 103A to lO3E;

section 105 and any regulations made under that section; and
section 106 and any rules made under that section.

SCHEDULE 2 Regulation 30

EFFECT ON OTHER LEGISLATION

1. **Leave under the 1971 Act**

(1) In accordance with section 7 of the Immigration Act 1988, a person who is admitted to or acquires a right to reside in the United Kingdom under these Regulations shall not require leave to remain in the United Kingdom under the 1971 Act during any period in which he has a right to reside under these Regulations but such a person shall require leave to remain under the 1971 Act during any period in which he does not have such a right.

(2) Where a person has leave to enter or remain under the 1971 Act which is subject to conditions and that person also has a right to reside under these Regulations, those conditions shall not have effect for as long as the person has that right to reside.

(3) Where the person mentioned in sub-paragraph (2) is an accession State national subject to worker authorisation working in the United Kingdom during the accession period and the document endorsed to show that the person has leave is an accession worker authorisation document, any conditions to which that leave is subject restricting his employment shall continue to apply.

(4) In sub-paragraph (3)—

(a) 'accession period' has the meaning given in regulation 1(2)(c) of the Accession (Immigration and Worker Authorisation) Regulations 2006;

(b) 'accession State national subject to worker authorisation' has the meaning given in regulation 2 of those Regulations; and

(c) 'accession worker authorisation document' has the meaning given in regulation 9(2) of those Regulations.

2. **Persons not subject to restriction on the period for which they may remain**

(1) For the purposes of the 1971 Act and the British Nationality Act 1981, a person who has a permanent right of residence under regulation 15 shall be regarded as a person who is in the United Kingdom without being subject under the immigration laws to any restriction on the period for which he may remain.

(2) But a qualified person, the family member of a qualified person and a family member who has retained the right of residence shall not, by virtue of that status, be so regarded for those purposes.

3. **Carriers' liability under the 1999 Act**

For the purposes of satisfying a requirement to produce a visa under section 40(1)(b) of the 1999 Act (charges in respect of passenger without proper documents), 'a visa of the required kind' includes an EEA family permit, a residence card or a permanent residence card required for admission under regulation 11(2).

4. **Appeals under the 2002 Act and previous immigration Acts**

(1) The following EEA decisions shall not be treated as immigration decisions for the purpose of section 82(2) of the 2002 Act (right of appeal against an immigration decision)—

(a) a decision that a person is to be removed under regulation 19(3)(a) by way of a direction under section 10(1)(a) of the 1999 Act (as provided for by regulation 24(2));

(b) a decision to remove a person under regulation 19(3)(b) by making a deportation order under section 5(1) of the 1971 Act (as provided for by regulation 24(3));

(c) a decision to remove a person mentioned in regulation 24(4) by way of directions under paragraphs 8 to 10 of Schedule 2 to the 1971 Act.

(2) A person who has been issued with a registration certificate, residence card, a document certifying permanent residence or a permanent residence card under these Regulations or a registration certificate under the Accession (Immigration and Worker Registration) Regulations 2004, or an accession worker card under the Accession (Immigration and Worker Authorisation) Regulations 2006, or a person whose passport has been stamped

with a family member residence stamp, shall have no right of appeal under section 2 of the Special Immigration Appeals Commission Act 1997 or section 82(1) of the 2002 Act. Any existing appeal under those sections of those Acts or under the Asylum and Immigration Appeals Act 1993, the Asylum and Immigration Act 1996 or the 1999 Act shall be treated as abandoned.

(3) Subject to paragraph (4), a person may appeal to the Asylum and Immigration Tribunal under section 83(2) of the 2002 Act against the rejection of his asylum claim where—

(a) that claim has been rejected, but

(b) he has a right to reside in the United Kingdom under these Regulations.

(4) Paragraph (3) shall not apply if the person is an EEA national and the Secretary of State certifies that the asylum claim is clearly unfounded.

(5) The Secretary of State shall certify the claim under paragraph (4) unless satisfied that it is not clearly unfounded.

(6) In addition to the national of a State which is a contracting party to the Agreement referred to in section 84(2) of the 2002 Act, a Swiss national shall also be treated as an EEA national for the purposes of section 84(1)(d) of that Act.

(7) An appeal under these Regulations against an EEA decision (including an appeal made on or after 1st April 2003 which is treated as an appeal under these Regulations under Schedule 4 but not an appeal made before that date) shall be treated as an appeal under section 82(1) of the 2002 Act against an immigration decision for the purposes of section 96(1)(a) of the 2002 Act.

(8) Section 120 of the 2002 Act shall apply to a person if an EEA decision has been taken or may be taken in respect of him and, accordingly, the Secretary of State or an immigration officer may by notice require a statement from that person under subsection (2) of that section and that notice shall have effect for the purpose of section 96(2) of the 2002 Act.

(9) In sub-paragraph (1), 'family member residence stamp' means a stamp in the passport of a family member of an EEA national confirming that he is the family member of an accession State worker requiring registration or an accession State national subject to worker authorisation working in the United Kingdom and with a right of residence under these Regulations as the family member of that worker; and in this sub-paragraph 'accession State worker requiring registration' has the same meaning as in regulation 2 of the Accession (Immigration and Worker Registration) Regulations 2004 and 'accession State national subject to worker authorisation' has the meaning given in regulation 2 of the Accession (Immigration and Worker Authorisation) Regulations 2006.

SCHEDULE 3

Regulation 31(2)

REVOCATIONS AND SAVINGS

PART 1

TABLE OF REVOCATIONS

(1)	(2)	(3)
Regulations revoked	*References*	*Extent of revocation*
The Immigration (European Economic Area) Regulations 2000	SI 2000/2326	The whole Regulations
The Immigration (European Economic Area) (Amendment) Regulations 2001	SI 2001/865	The whole Regulations
The Immigration (Swiss Free Movement of Persons) (No. 3) Regulations 2002	SI 2002/1241	The whole Regulations
The Immigration (European Economic Area) (Amendment) Regulations 2003	SI 2003/549	The whole Regulations
The Immigration (European Economic Area) (Amendment No. 2) Regulations 2003	SI 2003/3188	The whole Regulations
The Accession (Immigration and Worker Registration) Regulations 2004	SI 2004/12 19	Regulations 3 and 6

(1)	(2)	(3)
Regulations revoked	*References*	*Extent of revocation*
The Immigration (European Economic Area) and Accession (Amendment) Regulations 2004	SI 2004/1236	Regulation 2
The Immigration (European Economic Area) (Amendment) Regulations 2005	SI 2005/47	The whole Regulations
The Immigration (European Economic Area) (Amendment) (No. 2) Regulations 2005	SI 2005/671	The whole Regulations

PART 2
SAVINGS

1. The—

(a) Immigration (Swiss Free Movement of Persons) (No. 3) Regulations 2002 are not revoked insofar as they apply the 2000 Regulations to posted workers; and

(b) the 2000 Regulations and the Regulations amending the 2000 Regulations are not revoked insofar as they are so applied to posted workers;

and, accordingly, the 2000 Regulations, as amended, shall continue to apply to posted workers in accordance with the Immigration (Swiss Free Movement of Persons) (No. 3) Regulations 2002.

2. In paragraph 1, 'the 2000 Regulations' means the Immigration (European Economic Area) Regulations 2000 and 'posted worker' has the meaning given in regulation 2(4)(b) of the Immigration (Swiss Free Movement of Persons) (No. 3) Regulations 2002.

SCHEDULE 4 — Regulation 31(2)
TRANSITIONAL PROVISIONS

1. Interpretation

In this Schedule—

(a) the '2000 Regulations' means the Immigration (European Economic Area) Regulations 2000 and expressions used in relation to documents issued or applied for under those Regulations shall have the meaning given in regulation 2 of those Regulations;

(b) the 'Accession Regulations' means the Accession (Immigration and Worker Registration) Regulations 2004.

2. Existing documents

(1) An EEA family permit issued under the 2000 Regulations shall, after 29th April 2006, be treated as if it were an EEA family permit issued under these Regulations.

(2) Subject to paragraph (4), a residence permit issued under the 2000 Regulations shall, after 2th April 2006, be treated as if it were a registration certificate issued under these Regulations.

(3) Subject to paragraph (5), a residence document issued under the 2000 Regulations shall, after 29th April 2006, be treated as if it were a residence card issued under these Regulations.

(4) Where a residence permit issued under the 2000 Regulations has been endorsed under the immigration rules to show permission to remain in the United Kingdom indefinitely it shall, after 29th April 2006, be treated as if it were a document certifying permanent residence issued under these Regulations and the holder of the permit shall be treated as a person with a permanent right of residence under regulation 15.

(5) Where a residence document issued under the 2000 Regulations has been endorsed under the immigration rules to show permission to remain in the United Kingdom indefinitely it shall, after 29th April 2006, be treated as if it were a permanent residence card issued under these Regulations and the holder of the permit shall be treated as a person with a permanent right of residence under regulation 15.

(6) Paragraphs (4) and (5) shall also apply to a residence permit or residence document which is endorsed under the immigration rules on or after 30th April 2006 to show permission to remain in the United Kingdom indefinitely pursuant to an application for such an endorsement made before that date.

3. **Outstanding applications**

(1) An application for an EEA family permit, a residence permit or a residence document made but not determined under the 2000 Regulations before 30 April 2006 shall be treated as an application under these Regulations for an EEA family permit, a registration certificate or a residence card, respectively.

(2) But the following provisions of these Regulations shall not apply to the determination of an application mentioned in sub-paragraph (1)—

(a) the requirement to issue a registration certificate immediately under regulation 16(1); and

(b) the requirement to issue a certificate of application for a residence card under regulation 17(3).

4. **Decisions to remove under the 2000 Regulations**

(1) A decision to remove a person under regulation 21(3)(a) of the 2000 Regulations shall, after 29th April 2006, be treated as a decision to remove that person under regulation 19(3)(a) of these Regulations.

(2) A decision to remove a person under regulation 21(3)(b) of the 2000 Regulations, including a decision which is treated as a decision to remove a person under that regulation by virtue of regulation 6(3)(a) of the Accession Regulations, shall, after 29th April 2006, be treated as a decision to remove that person under regulation 19(3)(b) of these Regulations.

(3) A deportation order made under section 5 of the 1971 Act by virtue of regulation 26(3) of the 2000 Regulations shall, after 29th April 2006, be treated as a deportation made under section 5 of the 1971 Act by virtue of regulation 24(3) of these Regulations.

5. **Appeals**

(1) Where an appeal against an EEA decision under the 2000 Regulations is pending immediately before 30th April 2006 that appeal shall be treated as a pending appeal against the corresponding EEA Decision under these Regulations.

(2) Where an appeal against an EEA decision under the 2000 Regulations has been determined, withdrawn or abandoned it shall, on and after 30th April 2006, be treated as an appeal against the corresponding EEA decision under these Regulations which has been determined, withdrawn or abandoned, respectively.

(3) For the purpose of this paragraph—

(a) a decision to refuse to admit a person under these Regulations corresponds to a decision to refuse to admit that person under the 2000 Regulations;

(b) a decision to remove a person under regulation 19(3)(a) of these Regulations corresponds to a decision to remove that person under regulation 21(3)(a) of the 2000 Regulations;

(c) a decision to remove a person under regulation 19(3)(b) of these Regulations corresponds to a decision to remove that person under regulation 21(3)(b) of the 2000 Regulations, including a decision which is treated as a decision to remove a person under regulation 21(3)(b) of the 2000 Regulations by virtue of regulation 6(3)(a) of the Accession Regulations;

(d) a decision to refuse to revoke a deportation order made against a person under these Regulations corresponds to a decision to refuse to revoke a deportation order made against that person under the 2000 Regulations, including a decision which is treated as a decision to refuse to revoke a deportation order under the 2000 Regulations by virtue of regulation 6(3)(b) of the Accession Regulations;

(e) a decision not to issue or renew or to revoke an EEA family permit, a registration certificate or a residence card under these Regulations corresponds to a decision not to issue or renew or to revoke an EEA family permit, a residence permit or a residence document under the 2000 Regulations, respectively.

6. **Periods of residence under the 2000 Regulations**

(1) Any period during which a person carried out an activity or was resident in the United Kingdom in accordance with the 2000 Regulations shall be treated as a period during which the person carried out that activity or was resident in the United Kingdom in accordance with these Regulations for the purpose of calculating periods of activity and residence under these Regulations.

SCHEDULE 5 Regulation 31(2)

CONSEQUENTIAL AMENDMENTS

Statutory Instruments

The Channel Tunnel (International Arrangements) Order 1993

1. (1) The Channel Tunnel (International Arrangements) Order 1993 is amended as follows.

(2) In Schedule 4, in paragraph 5—

(a) at the beginning of the paragraph, for 'the Immigration (European Economic Area) Regulations 2000' there is substituted 'the Immigration (European Economic Area) Regulations 2006';

(b) in sub-paragraph (a), for 'regulation 12(2)' there is substituted 'regulation 11(2)' and for 'residence document or document proving family membership' there is substituted 'residence card or permanent residence card';

(c) for sub-paragraph (b) there is substituted—

'(b) in regulations 11(4) and 19(2) after the word 'arrival' and in regulations 20(4) and (5) after the words 'United Kingdom' insert 'or the time of his production of the required documents in a control zone or a supplementary control zone'.'

The Travel Restriction Order (Prescribed Removal Powers) Order 2002

2. (1) The Travel Restriction Order (Prescribed Removal Powers) Order 2002 is amended as follows.

(2) In the Schedule, for 'Immigration (European Economic Area) Regulations 2000 (2000/2326)' in the first column of the table there is substituted 'Immigration (European Economic Area) Regulations 2006' and for 'Regulation 21(3)' in the corresponding row in the second column of the table there is substituted 'Regulation 19(3)'.

The Immigration (Notices) Regulations 2003

3. (1) The Immigration (Notices) Regulations 2003 are amended as follows.

(2) In regulation 2, in the definition of 'EEA decision'—

(a) at the end of paragraph (b), 'or' is omitted;

(b) in paragraph (c), after 'residence document;', there is inserted 'or'; and

(c) after paragraph (c), there is inserted—

'(d) on or after 30th April 2006, entitlement to be issued with or have renewed, or not to have revoked, a registration certificate, residence card, document certifying permanent residence or permanent residence card;'

The Nationality, Immigration and Asylum Act 2002 (Juxtaposed Controls) Order 2003

4. (1) The Nationality, Immigration and Asylum Act 2002 (Juxtaposed Controls) Order 2003 is amended as follows.

(2) In article 11(1), for sub-paragraph (e) there is substituted—

'(e) the Immigration (European Economic Area) Regulations 2006.'

(3) In Schedule 2, in paragraph 5—

(a) at the beginning of the paragraph, for 'the Immigration (European Economic Area) Regulations 2000' there is substituted 'the Immigration (European Economic Area) Regulations 2006';

(b) in sub-paragraph (a), for 'in regulation 2, at the beginning insert' there is substituted 'in regulation 2(1), after the definition of 'civil partner' insert';

(c) in sub-paragraph (b), for 'regulation 12(2)' there is substituted 'regulation 11(2)' and for 'residence document or document proving family membership' there is substituted 'residence card or permanent residence card';

(d) for sub-paragraph (c) there is substituted—

'(c) in regulations 11(4) and 19(2) after the word 'arrival' and in regulations 20(4) and (5) after the words 'United Kingdom' insert 'or the time of his production of the required documents in a Control Zone'.

The Immigration and Asylum Act 1999 (Part V Exemption: Relevant Employers) Order 2003

5. (1) The Immigration and Asylum Act 1999 (Part V Exemption: Relevant Employers) Order 2003 is amended as follows.

(2) In Article 2, in the definition of 'EEA national' and 'family member of an EEA national', for 'Immigration (European Economic Area) Regulations 2000' there is substituted 'Immigration (European Economic Area) Regulations 2006'.

The Immigration (Restrictions on Employment) Order 2004

6. (1) The Immigration (Restrictions on Employment) Order 2004 is amended as follows.

(2) In Part 1 of the Schedule (descriptions of documents for the purpose of article 4(2)(a) of the Order)–

(a) for paragraph 4 there is substituted—

'4. A registration certificate or document certifying permanent residence within the meaning of regulation 2 of the Immigration (European Economic Area) Regulations 2006, including a document which is treated as a registration certificate or document certifying permanent residence by virtue of Schedule 4 to those Regulations.';

(b) for paragraph 5 there is substituted—

'5. A residence card or a permanent residence card within the meaning of regulation 2 of the Immigration (European Economic Area) Regulations 2006, including a document which is treated as a residence card or a permanent residence card by virtue of Schedule 4 to those Regulations'.

The Accession (Immigration and Worker Registration) Regulations 2004

7. (1) The Accession (Immigration and Worker Registration) Regulations 2004 are amended as follows.

(2) In regulation 1(2) (interpretation)—

(a) after paragraph (b) there is inserted—

'(ba) 'the 2006 Regulations' means the Immigration (European Economic Area) Regulations 2006;';

(b) in paragraph (j), for 'regulation 3 of the 2000 Regulations' these is substituted 'regulation 4 of the 2006 Regulations'.

(3) In regulation 2 ('accession State worker requiring registration')—

(a) . . .

(b) paragraph (9)(a) is omitted;

(c) for paragraph (9)(c) there is substituted—

'(c) 'family member' has the same meaning as in regulation 7 of the 2006 Regulations.'

(4) In regulation 4 (right of residence of work seekers and workers from relevant acceding States during the accession period)—

(a) in paragraph (1), before 'Council Directive' there is inserted 'Council Directive 2004/38/EC of the European Parliament and of the Council on the right of citizens of the Union and their family members to move and reside freely within the territory of the Member States, insofar as it takes over provisions of';

(b) in paragraph (3), for '2000 Regulations' there is substituted '2006 Regulations';

(c) in paragraph (4), for 'An' there is substituted 'A national of a relevant accession State who is seeking employment and an' and for '2000 Regulations' there is substituted '2006 Regulations'.

(5) For regulation 5 (application of 2000 Regulations in relation to accession State worker requiring registration) there is substituted—

'Application of 2006 Regulations in relation to accession State worker requiring registration

5. (1) The 2006 Regulations shall apply in relation to a national of a relevant accession State subject to the modifications set out in this regulation.

(2) A national of a relevant accession State who is seeking employment in the United Kingdom shall not be treated as a jobseeker for the purpose of the definition of 'qualified person' in regulation 6(1) of the 2006 Regulations and an accession State worker requiring registration shall be treated as a worker for the purpose of that definition only during a period in which he is working in the United Kingdom for an authorised employer.

(3) Subject to paragraph (4), regulation 6(2) of the 2006 Regulations shall not apply to an accession State worker requiring registration who ceases to work.

(4) Where an accession State worker requiring registration ceases working for an authorised employer in the circumstances mentioned in regulation 6(2) of the 2006 Regulations during the one month period beginning on the date on which the work begins, that regulation shall apply to that worker during the remainder of that one month period.

(5) An accession State worker requiring registration shall not be treated as a qualified person for the purpose of regulations 16 and 17 of the 2006 Regulations (issue of registration certificates and residence cards).'

The Asylum and Immigration Tribunal (Procedure) Rules 2005

8. (1) The Asylum and Immigration Tribunal (Procedure) Rules 2005 are amended as follows.

(2) In regulation 18(1)(b), after '('the 2000 Regulations')' there is inserted 'or, on or after 30th April 2006, paragraph 4(2) of Schedule 2 to the Immigration (European Economic Area) Regulations 2006 ('the 2006 Regulations')'.

(3) In regulation 18(2), after '2000 Regulations' there is inserted 'or paragraph 4(2) of Schedule 2 to the 2006 Regulations'.

Appendix 5

Extracts from the European Convention on Human Rights

Article 2 – right to life

1. Everyone's right to life shall be protected by law. No one shall be deprived of his life intentionally save in the execution of a sentence of a court following his conviction of a crime for which this penalty is provided by law.
2. Deprivation of life shall not be regarded as inflicted in contravention of this Article when it results from the use of force which is no more than absolutely necessary:

Article 3 – prohibition of torture

No one shall be subjected to torture or to inhuman or degrading treatment or punishment.

Article 5 – right to liberty and security

1. Everyone has the right to liberty and security of person. No one shall be deprived of his liberty save in the following cases and in accordance with a procedure prescribed by law:
   (a) the lawful detention of a person after conviction by a competent court;
   (b) the lawful arrest or detention of a person for non-compliance with the lawful order of a court or in order to secure the fulfilment of any obligation prescribed by law;
   (c) the lawful arrest or detention of a person effected for the purpose of bringing him before the competent legal authority on reasonable suspicion of having committed an offence or when it is reasonably considered necessary to prevent his committing an offence or fleeing after having done so;
   (d) the detention of a minor by lawful order for the purpose of educational supervision or his lawful detention for the purpose of bringing him before the competent legal authority;
   (e) the lawful detention of persons for the prevention of the spreading of infectious diseases, of persons of unsound mind, alcoholics or drug addicts or vagrants;
   (f) the lawful arrest or detention of a person to prevent his effecting an unauthorised entry into the country or of a person against whom action is being taken with a view to deportation or extradition.
2. Everyone who is arrested shall be informed promptly, in a language which he understands, of the reasons for his arrest and of any charge against him.
3. Everyone arrested or detained in accordance with the provisions of paragraph 1(c) of this Article shall be brought promptly before a judge or other officer authorised by law to exercise judicial power and shall be entitled to trial within a reasonable time or to release pending trial. Release may be conditioned by guarantees to appear for trial.
4. Everyone who is deprived of his liberty by arrest or detention shall be entitled to take proceedings by which the lawfulness of his detention shall be decided speedily by a court and his release ordered if the detention is not lawful.
5. Everyone who has been the victim of arrest or detention in contravention of the provisions of this Article shall have an enforceable right to compensation.

Article 6 – right to a fair trial

1. In the determination of his civil rights and obligations or of any criminal charge against him, everyone is entitled to a fair and public hearing within a reasonable time by an independent and impartial tribunal established by law. Judgment shall be pronounced publicly but the press and

public may be excluded from all or part of the trial in the interest of morals, public order or national security in a democratic society, where the interests of juveniles or the protection of the private life of the parties so require, or to the extent strictly necessary in the opinion of the court in special circumstances where publicity would prejudice the interests of justice.

2. Everyone charged with a criminal offence shall be presumed innocent until proved guilty according to law.
3. Everyone charged with a criminal offence has the following minimum rights:
   (a) to be informed promptly, in a language which he understands and in detail, of the nature and cause of the accusation against him;
   (b) to have adequate time and facilities for the preparation of his defence;
   (c) to defend himself in person or through legal assistance of his own choosing or, if he has not sufficient means to pay for legal assistance, to be given it free when the interests of justice so require;
   (d) to examine or have examined witnesses against him and to obtain the attendance and examination of witnesses on his behalf under the same conditions as witnesses against him;
   (e) to have the free assistance of an interpreter if he cannot understand or speak the language used in court.

Article 8 – right to respect for private and family life

1. Everyone has the right to respect for his private and family life, his home and his correspondence.
2. There shall be no interference by a public authority with the exercise of this right except such as is in accordance with the law and is necessary in a democratic society in the interests of national security, public safety or the economic well-being of the country, for the prevention of disorder or crime, for the protection of health or morals, or for the protection of the rights and freedoms of others.

Article 9 – freedom of thought, conscience and religion

1. Everyone has the right to freedom of thought, conscience and religion; this right includes freedom to change his religion or belief and freedom, either alone or in community with others and in public or private, to manifest his religion or belief, in worship, teaching, practice and observance.
2. Freedom to manifest one's religion or beliefs shall be subject only to such limitations as are prescribed by law and are necessary in a democratic society in the interests of public safety, for the protection of public order, health or morals, or for the protection of the rights and freedoms of others.

Article 10 – freedom of expression

1. Everyone has the right to freedom of expression. This right shall include freedom to hold opinions and to receive and impart information and ideas without interference by public authority and regardless of frontiers. This Article shall not prevent States from requiring the licensing of broadcasting, television or cinema enterprises.
2. The exercise of these freedoms, since it carries with it duties and responsibilities, may be subject to such formalities, conditions, restrictions or penalties as are prescribed by law and are necessary in a democratic society, in the interests of national security, territorial integrity or public safety, for the prevention of disorder or crime, for the protection of health or morals, for the protection of the reputation or rights of others, for preventing the disclosure of information received in confidence, or for maintaining the authority and impartiality of the judiciary.

Article 11 – freedom of assembly and association

1. Everyone has the right to freedom of peaceful assembly and to freedom of association with others, including the right to form and to join trade unions for the protection of his interests.
2. No restrictions shall be placed on the exercise of these rights other than such as are prescribed by law and are necessary in a democratic society in the interests of national security or public safety,

for the prevention of disorder or crime, for the protection of health or morals or for the protection of the rights and freedoms of others. This Article shall not prevent the imposition of lawful restrictions on the exercise of these rights by members of the armed forces, of the police or of the administration of the State.

Article 12 – right to marry

Men and women of marriageable age have the right to marry and to found a family, according to the national laws governing the exercise of this right.

Article 14 – prohibition of discrimination

The enjoyment of the rights and freedoms set forth in this Convention shall be secured without discrimination on any ground such as sex, race, colour, language, religion, political or other opinion, national or social origin, association with a national minority, property, birth or other status.

The First Protocol, Article 1 – protection of property

Every natural or legal person is entitled to the peaceful enjoyment of his possessions. No one shall be deprived of his possessions except in the public interest and subject to the conditions provided for by law and by the general principles of international law.

The preceding provisions shall not, however, in any way impair the right of a State to enforce such laws as it deems necessary to control the use of property in accordance with the general interest or to secure the payment of taxes or other contributions or penalties.

Appendix 6

British Citizenship: A Summary

The BNA 1981 sets out some basic rules for determining who is a British citizen. The following series of questions can be used to work out if a person may be a British citizen. However, remember that nationality law can be complex, and you will not always be able to work out if a person is a British citizen or not without detailed research of the law and facts.

Q1. When was the person born?

(a) Before [1st January] 1983: go to Q2.

(b) After [31st December] 1982: go to Q9.

Q2. Where was the person born?

(a) In the UK: he is a British citizen otherwise than by descent (see **2.2.1**).

(b) Outside the UK: go to Q3.

Q3. Was the person's father born [or registered/naturalised before he was born] in the UK?

(a) Yes: go to Q4.

(b) No: go to Q5.

Q4. Was the person's father married to their mother? [If after the child's birth, did that marriage legitimise the child?]

(a) Yes: he is a British citizen by descent (see **2.2.2**).

(b) No: go to Q5.

Q5. Was the person's mother born [or registered/naturalised before he was born] in the UK?

(a) Yes: go to Q6.

(b) No: go to Q7.

Q6. Did the person's mother register him as a British citizen?

(a) Yes: he is a British citizen by descent (see **2.2.6.2**).

(b) No: go to Q7.

Q7. Has the person registered as a British citizen?

(a) Yes: he is a British citizen by descent (see **2.2.6.2**).

(b) No: go to Q8.

Q8. Has the person naturalised in the UK as a British citizen?

(a) Yes: he is a British citizen otherwise than by descent (see **2.2.7**).

(b) No: he is not a British citizen under these rules but a detailed analysis of law and facts is required.

Q9. Was the person born in the UK?

(a) Yes: go to Q10.

(b) No: go to Q13.

Q10. Was either of the person's parents a British citizen or settled in the UK when he was born?

(a) Yes: he is a British citizen otherwise than by descent (see **2.2.3**).

(b) No: go to Q11.

Q11. Did either of the person's parents subsequently become settled in the UK?

(a) Yes: he can apply to register as a British citizen otherwise than by descent (see **2.2.6.1**).

(b) No: go to Q12.

Q12. Has the person remained in the UK for the first 10 years of his life and not been absent for more than 90 days?

(a) Yes: he is a British citizen otherwise than by descent (see **2.2.6.1**).

(b) No: he is not a British citizen under these rules but a detailed analysis of law and facts is required.

Q13. Was one of the person's parents a British citizen otherwise than by descent, or registered/naturalised in the UK before he was born?

(a) Yes: he is a British citizen by descent (see **2.2.4**).

(b) No: he is not a British citizen under these rules but a detailed analysis of the law and facts is required.

Note 1: a parent in this context includes the father of an illegitimate child born on or after 1 July 2006 if certain conditions are met (see **2.2.3** and **2.2.4**).

Note 2: as to second generation children born outside UK, see **2.2.5**.

Appendix 7

Naturalisation: A Summary

The following series of questions can be used to work out if a person may be eligible to apply for naturalisation as a British citizen.

Q1. Is the person settled in the UK (this includes an EEA national who has permanent residence in the UK)?

(a) Yes: go to Q2.

(b) No: ineligible.

Q2. Is the person married to a British citizen or in a civil partnership with a British citizen?

(a) Yes: go to Q3.

(b) No: go to Q7.

Q3. Has the person been living in the UK legally for three years continuously before making the application?

(a) Yes: go to Q4.

(b) No: ineligible.

Q4. Has the person been absent for less than 270 days in total and not more than 90 days in the year immediately before the application?

(a) Yes: go to Q5.

(b) No: ineligible but check Home Office policy.

Q5. Can the person produce written evidence to show sufficient knowledge of English (Welsh or Scottish Gaelic) and Life in the UK?

(a) Yes: go to Q6.

(b) No: ineligible but check to see if Home Office might waive this requirement.

Q6. Can the person show good character?

(a) Yes: may be granted naturalisation as a British citizen at discretion of Home Secretary.

(b) No: application will be refused.

Q7. Has the person been settled in the UK (this includes an EEA national who has permanent residence in the UK) for at least one year before making the application?

(a) Yes: go to Q8.

(b) No: ineligible.

Q8. Has the person been living in the UK legally for five years continuously before making the application?

(a) Yes: go to Q9.

(b) No: ineligible.

Q9. Has the person been absent for less than 450 days in total and not more than 90 days in the year immediately before the application?

(a) Yes: go to Q10.

(b) No: ineligible but check home Office policy.

Q10. Can the person produce written evidence to show sufficient knowledge of English (Welsh or Scottish Gaelic) and Life in the UK?

(a) Yes: go to Q11.

(b) No: ineligible but check to see if Home Office might waive this requirement.

Q11. Can the person show good character?

(a) Yes: go to Q12.

(b) No: application will be refused.

Q12. Can the person show an intention to live in the UK?

(a) Yes: may be granted naturalisation as a British citizen at discretion of Home Secretary.

(b) No: application will be refused.

Appendix 8

Spent Convictions under the Rehabilitation of Offenders Act 1974

Sentence	Rehabilitation period
A sentence of imprisonment or corrective training for a term exceeding 30 months or preventative detention or detention during Her Majesty's pleasure or imprisonment or detention for public protection	This will not become spent
* Imprisonment or youth custody for 6 months to 30 months	10 years
* Imprisonment or youth custody up to 6 months	7 years
* Fine, community service/community punishment order or compensation order	5 years
Bind over, conditional discharge or supervision order	One year, or when the order ceases to have effect, whichever is the later
Absolute discharge	6 months
Driving disqualification	Once the disqualification has ceased

* all halved if the person is under 18 when convicted

Appendix 9

Commonwealth Citizens

Citizens of the following countries are currently Commonwealth citizens according to Sch 3 to the British Nationality Act 1981 (as amended).

Antigua and Barbuda
Australia
The Bahamas
Bangladesh
Barbados
Belize
Botswana
Brunei
Cameroon
Canada
Republic of Cyprus
Dominica
Fiji
The Gambia
Ghana
Grenada
Guyana
India
Jamaica
Kenya
Kiribati
Lesotho
Malawi
Malaysia
Maldives
Malta
Mauritius
Mozambique
Namibia
Nauru
New Zealand
Nigeria
Pakistan
Papua New Guinea
Saint Christopher and Nevis
Saint Lucia
Saint Vincent and the Grenadines
Seychelles
Sierra Leone
Singapore
Solomon Islands
South Africa
Sri Lanka
Swaziland
Tanzania
Tonga
Trinidad and Tobago
Tuvalu
Uganda
Vanuatu
Western Samoa
Zambia
Zimbabwe

Note that British citizens, and some other categories of British Nationals (including British dependent territories citizens and British overseas citizens) are Commonwealth citizens by virtue of s 37 of the 1981 Act.

It is important to note that as Cameroon, Mozambique, Namibia, Pakistan and South Africa were not members of the Commonwealth on 31 December 1982, then nationals of those countries cannot take advantage of the provisions dealt with at **2.3**.

Appendix 10

Commonwealth Citizen with Right of Abode: A Summary

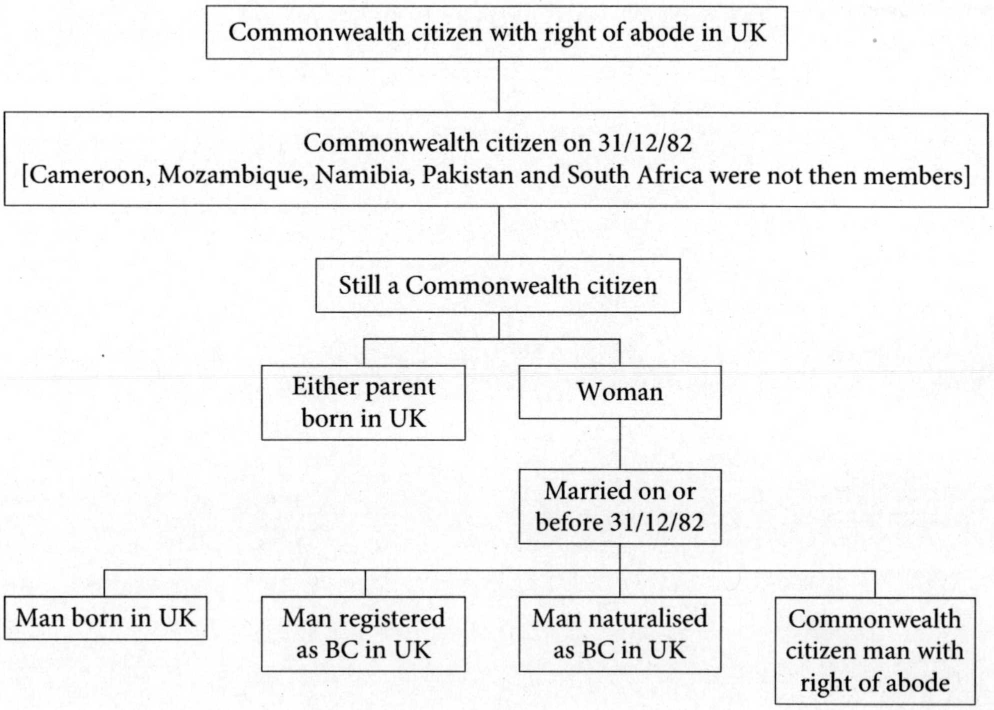

Appendix 11

British Overseas Territories

The following are currently British Overseas Territories according to Sch 6 to the British Nationality Act 1981 (as amended).

Anguilla

Bermuda

British Antarctic Territory

British Indian Ocean Territory

Cayman Islands

Gibraltar

Montserrat

Pitcairn, Henderson, Ducie and Oeno Islands

St Helena and Dependencies

South Georgia

South Sandwich Islands

The Sovereign Base Areas of Akrotiri and Dhekelia

Turks and Caicos Islands

Virgin Islands

Note that people from the Falkland Islands were made into full British citizens under the British Nationality (Falkland Islands) Act 1983.

Appendix 12

Tier 1 Entrepreneur: Overview

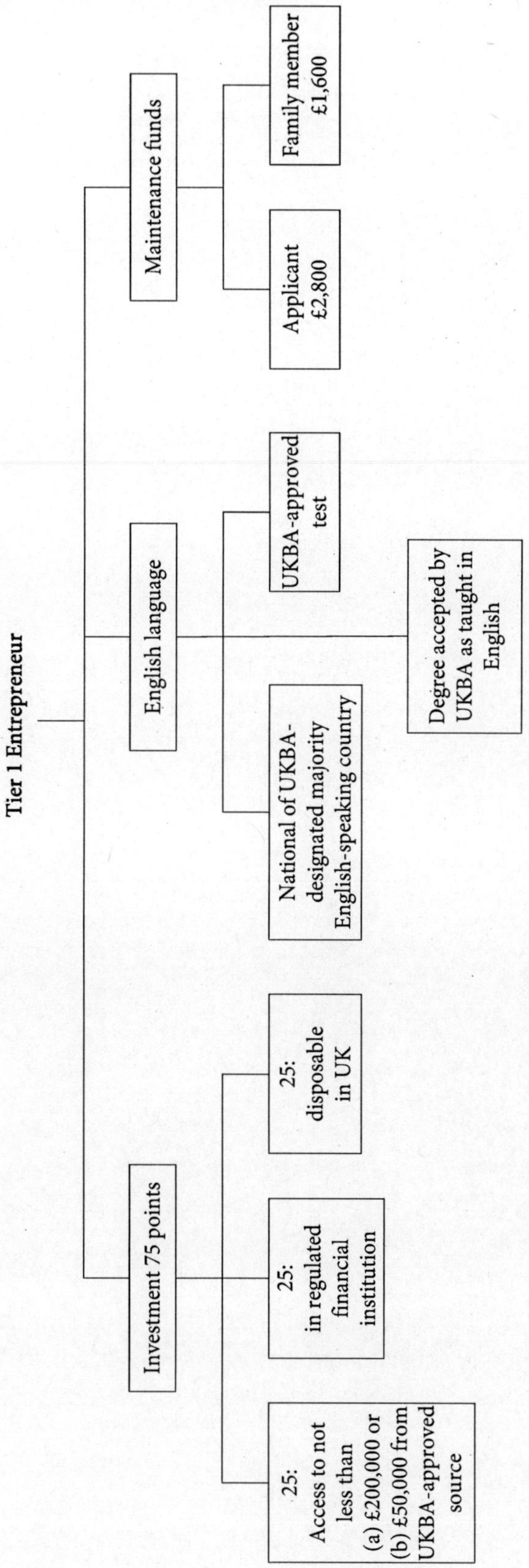

Appendix 13

Entrepreneur: Evidence of UK Business

	Type of business	Self-employed applicants	Directors of companies
1.	Business premises in the United Kingdom	Not all self-employed applicants will have a business office. For an applicant with no business premises we will use the applicant's registration with HM Revenue and Customs to show that the business is based in the UK	Printout of a Companies House document showing the address of the registered office, or head office if it has no registered office, and the name of the applicant, as it appears on the application form, as a director.
2.	Business has a United Kingdom bank account Note: Applicants whose initial grant of leave was made under the Business Person or Innovator category do not need to meet this requirement.	a) Personal bank statement showing transactions for the applicant's business b) Business bank statement c) Letter from a United Kingdom bank confirming that the applicant has a business and acts through a bank.	a) Company bank statement showing that the company has a United Kingdom bank account; or b) Letter from a United Kingdom bank confirming that the company has a bank account.
3.	Business must be subject to United Kingdom taxation Note: Applicants whose initial grant of leave was made under the Business Person or Innovator category do not need to meet this requirement.	The applicant must be registered as self-employed for National Insurance assessment. Applicants must supply one of the following: a) the welcome letter from HM Revenue & Customs; b) the Small Earnings Exception certificate; c) a copy of the quarterly National Insurance bill from HM Revenue & Customs; or d) a copy of the applicant's bank account showing that National Insurance is taken by HM Revenue & Customs by direct debit.	Business must be registered for corporation tax with HM Revenue & Customs. Applicants must supply either: a) their copy of form CT41G from HM Revenue & Customs This must be completed and show the date of registration of the company and the unique reference number; or b) a completed HM Revenue & Customs tax return document showing the tax reference number for the company. This can be either the company short return form or the company tax return form. If the reporting is done online the applicant should provide a printout of the form.

Appendix 14

UKBA's Definition of Common Ownership or Control

The UKBA states that common ownership or control may be defined as follows:

- one entity controls the composition of the other entity's board; or
- one entity is in a position to cast, or control the casting of, more than half the maximum number of votes that might be cast at a general meeting of the other entity; or
- one entity holds more than half the issued share capital of the other entity (excluding any part of that issued share capital that carries no right to participate beyond a specified amount in a distribution of either profits or capital); or
- both entities have a common parent entity that itself or through other entities meets one of the requirements of the first three bullet points above in relation to both entities that are the subject of the intra-company transfer; or
- one entity is related to the other entity as both entities are party to a joint venture agreement; or
- one entity is related to the other entity in that one entity is party to a joint venture agreement and the other entity is the entity formed by that joint venture agreement; or
- one entity is related to the other entity by agreement that would constitute a joint venture agreement other than for the fact that joint venture agreements are not permitted in the country of operation or one of the entities is not permitted to enter into joint ventures in the country of operation; or
- one entity is related to the other entity in that one entity is party to an agreement that would constitute a joint venture agreement other than for the fact that joint venture agreements are not permitted in the country of operation or that entity is not permitted to enter into joint ventures in the country of operation and the other entity is the entity formed by that agreement; or
- where both entities are either accountancy or law firms, one entity is related to the other entity by agreement which allows both entities to use a trademark which is registered or established under the laws of the United Kingdom and the jurisdiction of the other entity's country of operation; or
- where both entities are either accountancy or law firms, one entity is related to the other entity by agreement which allows both entities to operate under the same name in the United Kingdom and in the jurisdiction of the other entity's country of operation; or
- in the case of unincorporated associations, the receiving entity is a linked company if it is a registered company and its Articles of Association with the sending entity indicate a relationship of control (for example, one Member has the power to appoint the other's trustees).

Appendix 15

UK Shortage Occupations Lists: Tier 2

Tier 2 Shortage Occupation List – Government-approved version – valid from 14 November 2011

The SOC codes used in this document relate to the Standard Occupational Classification (SOC) 2000. For official job descriptions relating to SOC codes, please refer to the SOC 2000 Structure and descriptions of unit groups, published by the Office for National Statistics.

The job must be paid the minimum salary rates shown below, which are derived either from the Annual Survey of Hours and Earnings (ASHE) or, where alternative salary data is available, from an alternative code of practice. Appropriate salary rates are based on a 37½ hour working week, unless otherwise stated. Appropriate rates should be pro-rated for other working patterns, unless otherwise stated.

You cannot sponsor a migrant for a job with a salary below £20,000, unless they are applying to extend leave granted under Tier 2 (General) or the work permit arrangements under the rules in place before 6 April 2011. This includes cases where they are changing employment.

UK list:

Related occupation title and SOC code	Job titles and skill levels included on the shortage occupation list (includes additional document-keeping requirements for Sponsors where relevant)	Minimum appropriate salary rate
Directors and chief executives of major organisations (1112)	**ONLY** the following jobs in this occupation code: • the following jobs in the decommissioning and waste management areas of the nuclear industry: - managing director - programme director - site director	£38.78 per hour [Source: ASHE 2009]
Production, works and maintenance managers (1121)	**ONLY** the following job in this occupation code: • project manager in the electricity transmission and distribution industry	£13.95 per hour [Source: ASHE 2009]
Managers in mining and energy (1123)	**ONLY** the following jobs in this occupation code: • site manager in the electricity transmission and distribution industry	£18.59 per hour [Source: ASHE 2009]
Biological scientists and biochemists (2112)	**ONLY** the following jobs in this occupation code: • cardiac physiologist • clinical neurophysiologist • clinical vascular scientist • respiratory physiologist • sleep physiologist	Non NHS: £13.88 per hour NHS: • Posts at Agenda for Change band 5 or equivalent: £20,710 • Posts at Agenda for Change band 6 or equivalent: £24,831 • Posts at Agenda for Change band 7 or equivalent:

Tier 2 Shortage Occupation List – Government-approved version – valid from 14 November 2011

UK list:

Related occupation title and SOC code	Job titles and skill levels included on the shortage occupation list (includes additional document-keeping requirements for Sponsors where relevant)	Minimum appropriate salary rate
	A voluntary register for Sleep Physiologists (also known as Respiratory Physiologists) and Clinical Physiologists is held by the Registration Council for Clinical Physiologists (RCCP). If an individual is a member of the RCCP, the sponsor must retain evidence of their registration and provide it to UK Border Agency on Request. Sponsors must retain evidence of the individual's HPC registration and provide this to the UK Border Agency on request. (Registration may need to be done after the individual has entered the United Kingdom but must be done before starting work).	£29,789 • Posts at Agenda for Change band 8 or equivalent: £37,996 [Sources: NHS Agenda for Change April 2009, ASHE 2009]
Physicists, geologists and meteorologists (2113)	**ONLY** the following jobs in this occupation code: • hydro geologist • geophysicist • geoscientist • geophysical specialist • engineering geophysicist • engineering geomorphologist • geologist • geochemist • environmental scientist • technical services manager in the decommissioning and waste areas of the nuclear industry • nuclear medicine scientist • radiotherapy physicist • staff working in diagnostic radiology (including magnetic resonance imaging)	£15.33 per hour [Source: ASHE 2009]
Civil engineers (2121)	**ONLY** the following jobs in this occupation code: • geotechnical design engineer • geotechnical specialist • reservoir panel engineer	• New graduate (1st year after graduation): £20,770 • Civil engineers undertaking on the job training: £22,800 • Participate in project work: £23,000

Page 2 of 15

Tier 2 Shortage Occupation List – Government-approved version – valid from 14 November 2011

UK list:

Related occupation title and SOC code	Job titles and skill levels included on the shortage occupation list (includes additional document-keeping requirements for Sponsors where relevant)	Minimum appropriate salary rate
	• rock mechanics engineer • soil mechanics engineer • geomechanics engineer • mining geotechnical engineer • mining and coal engineer • wells engineer • tunnelling engineer • petroleum engineer • drilling engineer • completions engineer • fluids engineer • reservoir engineer • offshore and subsea engineer • control and instrument engineer • process safety engineer	• Project management: £35,000 • Senior project management: £41,042 • Civil engineering not project based: £39,000 • Manager/Director: £54,000 • Managing director/ Chief executive officer: £70,000 [Source: The Institution of Civil Engineers 2007 salary survey, based on a 40-hour week]
Mechanical engineers (2122)	**ONLY** the following job in this occupation code: • mechanical engineer in the aerospace sector	• New graduate: £23,000 [Source: Engineering UK 2009/10 Report] • Other jobs in this occupation code: £14.52 per hour [Source: ASHE 2009]
Electrical engineers (2123)	**ONLY** the following jobs in this occupation code: • all electrical engineers in the oil and gas industry • the following jobs in the electricity transmission and distribution industry: - power system engineer - control engineer - protection engineer	• New graduate: £23,000 [Source: Engineering UK 2009/10 Report] • Other jobs in this occupation code: £16.27 per hour [Source: ASHE 2009]
Chemical engineers (2125)	**ALL** jobs in this occupation code	• New Graduate: £25,400 • Non-chartered chemical engineer: £26,500

Tier 2 Shortage Occupation List – Government-approved version – valid from 14 November 2011

UK list:

Related occupation title and SOC code	Job titles and skill levels included on the shortage occupation list (includes additional document-keeping requirements for Sponsors where relevant)	Minimum appropriate salary rate
		• Chartered chemical engineer: £36,000 [Source: Institute of Chemical Engineers (IChemE)]
Design and development engineers (2126)	**ONLY** the following jobs in this occupation code: • design engineer in the electricity transmission and distribution industry • simulation development engineer	£14.40 per hour [Source: ASHE 2009]
Production and process engineers (2127)	**ONLY** the following jobs in this occupation code: • manufacturing engineer (process planning) in the aerospace sector • technical services representative in the aerospace sector	£12.78 per hour [Source: ASHE 2009]
Planning and quality control engineers (2128)	**ONLY** the following jobs in this occupation code: • the following jobs in the electricity transmission and distribution industry: - planning / development engineer - quality, health, safety and environment (QHSE) engineer	• New graduate: £23,000 [Source: Engineering UK 2009/10 Report] • Other jobs in this occupation code: £12.62 per hour [Source: ASHE 2009]
Engineering professionals not elsewhere classified (2129)	**ONLY** the following jobs in this occupation code: • geoenvironmental specialist • geoenvironmental engineer • contaminated land engineer • landfill engineer • metallurgical / mineral processing engineer • the following jobs in the aerospace sector: - aerothermal engineer - stress engineer - chief of engineering - advance tool and fixturing engineer • the following jobs in the decommissioning and waste management areas of the nuclear industry: - operations manager - decommissioning specialist manager	• New graduate: £23,000 [Source: Engineering UK 2009/10 Report] • Other jobs in this occupation code: £14.76 per hour [Source: ASHE 2009]

Tier 2 Shortage Occupation List – Government-approved version – valid from 14 November 2011

UK list:

Related occupation title and SOC code	Job titles and skill levels included on the shortage occupation list (includes additional document-keeping requirements for Sponsors where relevant)	Minimum appropriate salary rate
	- project / planning engineer - radioactive waste manager - radiological protection advisor • the following jobs in the electricity transmission and distribution industry: - project engineer - proposals engineer	
Software professionals (2132)	**ONLY** the following jobs in this occupation code: • the following jobs in visual effects and 2D / 3D computer animation for film, television or video games: - software developer - systems engineer - shader writer	• Software developer: £31,300 • Systems engineer: £41,800 • Shader Writer: £31,300 [Source: Salary Services IT Salary Survey January 2011, matched using job descriptions from Screen UK]
Medical practitioners (2211)	**ONLY** the following jobs in this occupation code: • Consultants in the following specialities: - clinical neurophysiology - emergency medicine - genito-urinary medicine - haematology - neurology - occupational medicine • Consultants in the following specialities of psychiatry: - forensic psychiatry - general psychiatry - learning disabilities psychiatry - old age psychiatry • Non-consultant, non-training, medical staff posts in the following specialities: - anaesthetics - paediatrics and general medicine specialities delivering acute	• Foundation year 1 (F1): £21,391 • Foundation year 2 (F2): £26,532 • Pre-registration house officer: £21,391 • House officer: £21,391 • Senior house officer: £26,532 • Speciality registrar (StR): £29,411 • Senior registrar: £29,364 • Staff grade practitioner: £32,547 • Associate specialist: £35,977 • Speciality Doctor: £36,443 • Senior Chief Medical officer: £44,059 • Consultant (new contract): £71,822 [Source: NHS Agenda for Change Pay circular (M&D) April 2009]

Tier 2 Shortage Occupation List – Government-approved version – valid from 14 November 2011

UK list:

Related occupation title and SOC code	Job titles and skill levels included on the shortage occupation list (includes additional document-keeping requirements for Sponsors where relevant)	Minimum appropriate salary rate
	care services (intensive care medicine, general internal medicine (acute), emergency medicine, general surgery, obstetrics and gynaecology, and trauma and orthopaedic surgery) • ST4 level trainees in paediatrics	
Secondary education teaching professionals (2314)	**ONLY** the following jobs in this occupation code: • secondary education teachers in the subjects of maths or pure sciences (physics and / or chemistry)	Inner London • Unqualified teacher: £19,007 • Qualified teacher: £25,000 • Head teacher, other school leader: £42,559 Outer London • Unqualified teacher: £17,953 • Qualified teacher: £24,000 • Head teacher, other school leader: £38,634 London fringe • Unqualified teacher: £16,106 • Qualified teacher: £21,619 • Head teacher, other school leader: £36,781 Elsewhere in England and Wales • Unqualified teacher: £15,113 • Qualified teacher: £20,627 • Head teacher, other school leader: £35,794 Scotland • Probationer: £20,427

UK list:

Tier 2 Shortage Occupation List – Government-approved version – valid from 14 November 2011

Related occupation title and SOC code	Job titles and skill levels included on the shortage occupation list (includes additional document-keeping requirements for Sponsors where relevant)	Minimum appropriate salary rate
		• Unpromoted teacher: £24,501 • Chartered teacher: £33,588 • Principal teacher: £35,523 • Head teacher, deputy head teacher: £40,290 Northern Ireland • Qualified teacher: £20,627 • Leadership Group: £35,794 These salary rates are based the following definitions of a full time teacher: • England, Wales and Northern Ireland: Full time teachers are expected to work 195 days a year (190 of these must be working with pupils). • Scotland: Full time teachers are expected to work 35 hours a week, 195 days a year over 39 weeks, with 5 days for in-service training [Source: DCSF and devolved administrations in Scotland, Wales and Northern Ireland]
Special needs education teaching professionals (2316)	**ONLY** the following jobs in this occupation code: • all teaching posts in special schools	Inner London • Unqualified teacher: £19,007 • Qualified teacher: £25,000 • Head teacher, other school leader: £42,559 Outer London • Unqualified teacher: £17,953 • Qualified teacher: £24,000 • Head teacher, other school leader: £38,634 London fringe

Tier 2 Shortage Occupation List – Government-approved version – valid from 14 November 2011

UK list:

Related occupation title and SOC code	Job titles and skill levels included on the shortage occupation list (includes additional document-keeping requirements for Sponsors where relevant)	Minimum appropriate salary rate
		• Unqualified teacher: £16,106 • Qualified teacher: £21,619 • Head teacher, other school leader: £36,781 Elsewhere in England and Wales • Unqualified teacher: £15,113 • Qualified teacher: £20,627 • Head teacher, other school leader: £35,794 Scotland • Probationer: £20,427 • Unpromoted teacher: £24,501 • Chartered teacher: £33,588 • Principal teacher: £35,523 • Head teacher, deputy head teacher: £40,290 Northern Ireland • Qualified teacher: £20,627 • Leadership Group: £35,794 These salary rates are based the following definitions of a full time teacher: • England, Wales and Northern Ireland: Full time teachers are expected to work 195 days a year (190 of these must be working with pupils). • Scotland: Full time teachers are expected to work 35 hours a week, 195 days a year over 39 weeks, with 5 days for in-service training [Source: DCSF and devolved administrations in Scotland, Wales and Northern Ireland]

Tier 2 Shortage Occupation List – Government-approved version – valid from 14 November 2011

UK list:

Related occupation title and SOC code	Job titles and skill levels included on the shortage occupation list (includes additional document-keeping requirements for Sponsors where relevant)	Minimum appropriate salary rate
Management consultants, actuaries, economists and statisticians (2423)	**ONLY** the following jobs in this occupation code: • qualified actuaries working in the life assurance, general insurance, and health and care sectors	£42,500 per year [Source: Salary survey of actuaries and actuarial students 2007: Remuneration Economics in association with The Actuarial Profession]
Social workers (2442)	**ONLY** the following job in this occupation code: • social worker in children's and family services	• Social worker entry level (band 5 or equivalent): £20,710 • Social worker (band 6 or equivalent): £24,831 • Social worker specialist or team manager (band 7 or equivalent): £29,789 [Source: NHS Agenda for Change April 2009]
Engineering Technicians (3113)	**ONLY** the following job in this occupation code: • the following jobs in the electricity transmission and distribution industry: - commissioning engineer - substation electrical engineer	£12.56 per hour [Source: ASHE 2009]
Nurses (3211)	**ONLY** the following jobs in this occupation code: • specialist nurse working in operating theatres • operating department practitioner • specialist nurse working in neonatal intensive care units Sponsors must retain evidence of the individual's provisional / full NMC registration and provide this to the UK Border Agency on request. Note: For supervised practice nurses, points will be awarded for the guaranteed annual salary that will be paid when the individual achieves NMC registration, provided he/she has a guaranteed job offer with the Sponsor on completion of the placement. If the individual has not achieved NMC registration after nine months, we may consider curtailing his/her	• Supervised practice nurse (band 3 or equivalent): £15,190 • Qualified nurse (band 5 or equivalent): £20,710 • Posts at agenda for change band 6 or equivalent: £24,831 • Posts at agenda for change band 7 or equivalent: £29,789 • Posts at agenda for change band 8 or equivalent: £39,996 [Source: NHS Agenda for Change April 2009]

Tier 2 Shortage Occupation List – Government-approved version – valid from 14 November 2011

UK list:

Related occupation title and SOC code	Job titles and skill levels included on the shortage occupation list (includes additional document-keeping requirements for Sponsors where relevant)	Minimum appropriate salary rate
	leave.	
Medical radiographers (3214)	**ONLY** the following jobs in this occupation code: • HPC-registered diagnostic radiographer • HPC-registered therapeutic radiographer • sonographer Sponsors must retain evidence of the individual's HPC registration and provide this to the UK Border Agency on request. (Registration may need to be done after the individual has entered the United Kingdom but must be done before starting work).	• Radiographer (therapeutic): £20,710 • Radiographer (diagnostic): £20,710 • Radiographer specialist (diagnostic therapeutic): £24,831 • Radiographer advanced: £29,789 • Radiographer specialist (reporting sonographer): £29,789 • Radiographer team manager: £29,789 • Radiographer principal: £37,996 • Radiographer consultant (diagnostic): £44,258 [Source: NHS Agenda for Change April 2009]
Medical and dental technicians (3218)	**ONLY** the following jobs in this occupation code: • nuclear medicine technologist • radiotherapy technologist	• Posts at agenda for change band 5 or equivalent: £20,710 • Posts at agenda for change band 6 or equivalent: £24,831 • Posts at agenda for change band 7 or equivalent: £29,789 [Source: NHS Agenda for Change April 2009]
Artists (3411)	**ONLY** the following job in this occupation code: • animator in visual effects and 2D / 3D computer animation for film, television or video games	Payment of animators should be commensurate with the relevant industry standards in the United Kingdom and at least at the level of appropriate rates as on the BECTU website.
Dancers and choreographers (3414)	**ONLY** the following jobs in this occupation code: • skilled classical ballet dancers who meet the standard required by internationally recognised United Kingdom ballet companies (e.g. Birmingham Royal Ballet, English National Ballet, Northern Ballet Theatre, The Royal Ballet and Scottish Ballet). The company must either:	Payment of migrant dancers should be commensurate with industry standards. Agreed minimum salaries are set out in Equity's collective agreements, most of which are negotiated with ITC, SOLT and TMA. The current rates of pay can

Tier 2 Shortage Occupation List – Government-approved version – valid from 14 November 2011

UK list:

Related occupation title and SOC code	Job titles and skill levels included on the shortage occupation list (includes additional document-keeping requirements for Sponsors where relevant)	Minimum appropriate salary rate
	- have performed at or been invited to perform at venues of the calibre of the Royal Opera House, Sadler's Wells or Barbican, either in the United Kingdom or overseas; or - attract dancers and/or choreographers and other artists from other countries; or - be endorsed as being internationally recognised by a United Kingdom industry body such as the Arts Councils (of England, Scotland and/or Wales) • skilled contemporary dancers who meet the standard required by internationally recognised United Kingdom contemporary dance companies (e.g. Shobana Jeyasingh Dance Company, Scottish Dance Theatre and Rambert Dance Company). The company must either: - have performed at or been invited to perform at venues of the calibre of Sadler's Wells, the Southbank Centre or The Place, either in the United Kingdom or overseas; or - attract dancers and/or choreographers and other artists from all over the world; or - be endorsed as being internationally recognised by a United Kingdom industry body such as the Arts Councils (of England, Scotland and/or Wales)	be found at: www.equity.org.uk; www.itc-arts.org; www.solt.co.uk; and www.tmauk.org.
Musicians (3415)	**ONLY** the following job in this occupation code: • skilled orchestral musicians who meet the standard required by internationally recognised United Kingdom orchestras (e.g. London Symphony Orchestra, London Philharmonic Orchestra, Philharmonia Orchestra, and Royal Philharmonic Orchestra)	Payment should be commensurate with industry standards, the salary should be at least at the level of appropriate UK rates in this sector as on the Musicians Union website. The salary must also meet National Minimum Wage regulations.

Tier 2 Shortage Occupation List – Government-approved version – valid from 14 November 2011

UK list:

Related occupation title and SOC code	Job titles and skill levels included on the shortage occupation list (includes additional document-keeping requirements for Sponsors where relevant)	Minimum appropriate salary rate
Arts officers, producers and directors (3416)	**ONLY** the following jobs in this occupation code: • the following roles within visual effects and 2D / 3D computer animation for film, television or video games: - 2D supervisor - 3D supervisor - computer graphics supervisor - producer - production manager - technical director - visual effects supervisor	Payment of Arts officers, producers and directors should be commensurate with the relevant industry standards in the United Kingdom and at least at the level of appropriate rates as on the relevant website from the following list: • Broadcasting entertainment cinematograph and theatre union (BECTU) • Equity • Producers Alliance for Cinema and Television (PACT) • Production Guild
Graphic designers (3421)	**ONLY** the following jobs in this occupation code: • the following roles within visual effects and 2D / 3D computer animation for film, television or video games: - compositing artist - matte painter - modeller - rigger - stereo artist - texture artist	£9.79 per hour [Source: ASHE] Note: Migrants cannot be sponsored for jobs with salaries below £20,000 unless they are applying to extend leave granted under Tier 2 (General) or the work permit arrangements under the rules in place before 6 April 2011.
Buyers and purchasing officers (3541)	**ONLY** the following job in this occupation code: • manufacturing engineer (purchasing) in the aerospace sector	£11.44 per hour [Source: ASHE 2009]
Welding trades (5215)	**ONLY** the following job in this occupation code: • high integrity pipe welder where the job requires three or more years relevant experience Sponsors must retain references from the individual's past employer(s) detailing three or more years' relevant experience and provide these to the UK Border Agency on request.	£11.91 per hour [Source: National Agreement for the Engineering Construction Industry 2007-2010]

UK list:

Tier 2 Shortage Occupation List – Government-approved version – valid from 14 November 2011

Related occupation title and SOC code	Job titles and skill levels included on the shortage occupation list (includes additional document-keeping requirements for Sponsors where relevant)	Minimum appropriate salary rate
	Sponsors must also retain relevant evidence to enable them to justify the following: 1) - Why does the job require someone with at least five years' previous experience in a role of at least equivalent status? What elements of the job require this experience and why? 2) - Why could the job not be carried out to the required standard by someone with less experience? 3) - How would you expect a settled worker to gain this experience before being appointed to the post?	
Metal working production and maintenance fitters (5223)	**ONLY** the following job in this occupation code: • licensed and military certifying engineer / inspector technician	£9.96 per hour [Source: ASHE 2009]
Line repairers and cable jointers (5243)	**ONLY** the following job in this occupation code: • overhead linesworker in the electricity transmission and distribution industry, working on high voltage lines that carry at least 275,000 volts	£12.33 per hour [Source: ASHE 2009]
Chefs, cooks (5434)	**ONLY** the following job in this occupation code: • skilled chef where: - the pay is at least £28,260 per year after deductions for accommodation, meals etc; **and** - the job requires five or more years relevant experience in a role of at least equivalent status to the one they are entering; **and** - the job is not in either a fast food outlet, a standard fare outlet, or an establishment which provides a take-away service; **and** - the job is in one of the following roles: o executive chef – limited to one per establishment	£28,260 per year after deductions for accommodation, meals etc. [Source: Migration Advisory Committee] Note: This salary cannot be pro-rated down for shorter working hours as it forms a key part of the shortage occupation criteria. Sponsors must retain pay records confirming that the individual is earning the appropriate skilled salary and provide these to the UK Border Agency on request.

Tier 2 Shortage Occupation List – Government-approved version – valid from 14 November 2011

UK list:

Related occupation title and SOC code	Job titles and skill levels included on the shortage occupation list (includes additional document-keeping requirements for Sponsors where relevant)	Minimum appropriate salary rate
	○ head chef – limited to one per establishment ○ sous chef – limited to one for every four kitchen staff per establishment ○ specialist chef – limited to one per speciality per establishment A fast food outlet is one where food is prepared in bulk for speed of service, rather than to individual order. A standard fare outlet is one where the menu is designed centrally for outlets in a chain / franchise, rather than by a chef or chefs in the individual restaurant. Standard fare outlets also include those where dishes and / or cooking sauces are bought in ready-made, rather than prepared from fresh / raw ingredients. Sponsors must retain references from the individual's past employer(s) detailing five or more years' relevant experience in a role of at least equivalent status and provide these to the UK Border Agency on request. Sponsors must also retain relevant evidence to enable them to justify the following: 1) - Why does the job require someone with at least five years' previous experience in a role of at least equivalent status? What elements of the job require this experience and why? 2) - Why could the job not be carried out to the required standard by someone with less experience? 3) - How would you expect a settled worker to gain this experience before being appointed to the post?	

Tier 2 Shortage Occupation List – Government-approved version – valid from 14 November 2011

Scotland list:

Related occupation title and SOC code	Job titles and skill levels included on the shortage occupation list	Minimum appropriate salary rate
N/A	**ALL** job titles and occupations on the UK shortage occupation list	See UK list for details
Medical practitioners (2211)	**ONLY** the following jobs in this occupation code: • **ALL** jobs on the UK shortage occupation list • ST3, ST5 and ST6 level trainees in paediatrics* • Staff grade and Associate Specialist (SAS) doctors in paediatrics • consultants in paediatrics * ST4 level trainees in paediatrics are included on the UK shortage occupation list	• ST3 level trainees in paediatrics: £35,596 • ST4 level trainees in paediatrics: £37,448 • ST5 level trainees in paediatrics: £39,300 • ST6 level trainees in paediatrics: £41,152 • Staff grade doctors in paediatrics: £34,100 • Associate Specialist doctors in paediatrics: £37,694 • Consultants in paediatrics: £74,504 • See UK list for other details [Source: NHS Scotland pay circular May 2010]

Appendix 16

Refugee or Person in Need of International Protection (Qualification) Regulations 2006

SI 2006/2525

1. **Citation and commencement**

(1) These Regulations may be cited as The Refugee or Person in Need of International Protection (Qualification) Regulations 2006 and shall come into force on 9th October 2006.

(2) These Regulations apply to any application for asylum which has not been decided and any immigration appeal brought under the Immigration Acts (as defined in section 64(2) of the Immigration, Asylum and Nationality Act 2006) which has not been finally determined.

2. **Interpretation**

In these Regulations—

'application for asylum' means the request of a person to be recognised as a refugee under the Geneva Convention;

'Geneva Convention' means the Convention Relating to the Status of Refugees done at Geneva on 28 July 1951 and the New York Protocol of 31 January 1967;

'immigration rules' means rules made under section 3(2) of the Immigration Act 1971;

'persecution' means an act of persecution within the meaning of Article 1(A) of the Geneva Convention;

'person eligible for humanitarian protection' means a person who is eligible for a grant of humanitarian protection under the immigration rules;

'refugee' means a person who falls within Article 1(A) of the Geneva Convention and to whom regulation 7 does not apply;

'residence permit' means a document confirming that a person has leave to enter or remain in the United Kingdom whether limited or indefinite;

'serious harm' means serious harm as defined in the immigration rules;

'person' means any person who is not a British citizen.

3. **Actors of persecution or serious harm**

In deciding whether a person is a refugee or a person eligible for humanitarian protection, persecution or serious harm can be committed by:

(a) the State;

(b) any party or organisation controlling the State or a substantial part of the territory of the State;

(c) any non-State actor if it can be demonstrated that the actors mentioned in paragraphs (a) and (b), including any international organisation, are unable or unwilling to provide protection against persecution or serious harm.

4. **Actors of protection**

(1) In deciding whether a person is a refugee or a person eligible for humanitarian protection, protection from persecution or serious harm can be provided by:

(a) the State; or

(b) any party or organisation, including any international organisation, controlling the State or a substantial part of the territory of the State.

(2) Protection shall be regarded as generally provided when the actors mentioned in paragraph (1)(a) and (b) take reasonable steps to prevent the persecution or suffering of serious harm by operating an effective legal system for the detection, prosecution and

punishment of acts constituting persecution or serious harm, and the person mentioned in paragraph (1) has access to such protection.

(3) In deciding whether a person is a refugee or a person eligible for humanitarian protection the Secretary of State may assess whether an international organisation controls a State or a substantial part of its territory and provides protection as described in paragraph (2).

5. Act of persecution

(1) In deciding whether a person is a refugee an act of persecution must be:

(a) sufficiently serious by its nature or repetition as to constitute a severe violation of a basic human right, in particular a right from which derogation cannot be made under Article 15 of the Convention for the Protection of Human Rights and Fundamental Freedoms; or

(b) an accumulation of various measures, including a violation of a human right which is sufficiently severe as to affect an individual in a similar manner as specified in (a).

(2) An act of persecution may, for example, take the form of:

(a) an act of physical or mental violence, including an act of sexual violence;

(b) a legal, administrative, police, or judicial measure which in itself is discriminatory or which is implemented in a discriminatory manner;

(c) prosecution or punishment, which is disproportionate or discriminatory;

(d) denial of judicial redress resulting in a disproportionate or discriminatory punishment;

(e) prosecution or punishment for refusal to perform military service in a conflict, where performing military service would include crimes or acts falling under regulation 7.

(3) An act of persecution must be committed for at least one of the reasons in Article 1(A) of the Geneva Convention.

6. Reasons for persecution

(1) In deciding whether a person is a refugee:

(a) the concept of race shall include consideration of, for example, colour, descent, or membership of a particular ethnic group;

(b) the concept of religion shall include, for example, the holding of theistic, non-theistic and atheistic beliefs, the participation in, or abstention from, formal worship in private or in public, either alone or in community with others, other religious acts or expressions of view, or forms of personal or communal conduct based on or mandated by any religious belief;

(c) the concept of nationality shall not be confined to citizenship or lack thereof but shall include, for example, membership of a group determined by its cultural, ethnic, or linguistic identity, common geographical or political origins or its relationship with the population of another State;

(d) a group shall be considered to form a particular social group where, for example:

(i) members of that group share an innate characteristic, or a common background that cannot be changed, or share a characteristic or belief that is so fundamental to identity or conscience that a person should not be forced to renounce it, and

(ii) that group has a distinct identity in the relevant country, because it is perceived as being different by the surrounding society;

(e) a particular social group might include a group based on a common characteristic of sexual orientation but sexual orientation cannot be understood to include acts considered to be criminal in accordance with national law of the United Kingdom;

(f) the concept of political opinion shall include the holding of an opinion, thought or belief on a matter related to the potential actors of persecution mentioned in regulation 3 and to their policies or methods, whether or not that opinion, thought or belief has been acted upon by the person.

(2) In deciding whether a person has a well-founded fear of being persecuted, it is immaterial whether he actually possesses the racial, religious, national, social or political characteristic which attracts the persecution, provided that such a characteristic is attributed to him by the actor of persecution.

7. Exclusion

(1) A person is not a refugee, if he falls within the scope of Article 1D, 1E or 1F of the Geneva Convention.

(2) In the construction and application of Article 1F(b) of the Geneva Convention:

(a) the reference to serious non-political crime includes a particularly cruel action, even if it is committed with an allegedly political objective;

(b) the reference to the crime being committed outside the country of refuge prior to his admission as a refugee shall be taken to mean the time up to and including the day on which a residence permit is issued.

(3) Article 1F(a) and (b) of the Geneva Convention shall apply to a person who instigates or otherwise participates in the commission of the crimes or acts specified in those provisions.

Appendix 17

Pre-Action Protocol for Judicial Review

INTRODUCTION

This protocol applies to proceedings *within England and Wales only.* It does not affect the time limit specified by Rule 54.5(1) of the Civil Procedure Rules which requires that any claim form in an application for judicial review must be filed promptly and in any event not later than 3 months after the grounds to make the claim first arose.[1]

1 Judicial review allows people with a sufficient interest in a decision or action by a public body to ask a judge to review the lawfulness of:

- an enactment; or
- a decision, action or failure to act in relation to the exercise of a public function.[2]

2 Judicial review may be used where there is no right of appeal or where all avenues of appeal have been exhausted.

Alternative Dispute Resolution

3.1 The parties should consider whether some form of alternative dispute resolution procedure would be more suitable than litigation, and if so, endeavour to agree which form to adopt. Both the Claimant and Defendant may be required by the Court to provide evidence that alternative means of resolving their dispute were considered. The Courts take the view that litigation should be a last resort, and that claims should not be issued prematurely when a settlement is still actively being explored. Parties are warned that if the protocol is not followed (including this paragraph) then the Court must have regard to such conduct when determining costs. However, parties should also note that a claim for judicial review 'must be filed promptly and in any event not later than 3 months after the grounds to make the claim first arose'.

3.2 It is not practicable in this protocol to address in detail how the parties might decide which method to adopt to resolve their particular dispute. However, summarised below are some of the options for resolving disputes without litigation:

- Discussion and negotiation.
- Ombudsmen – the Parliamentary and Health Service and the Local Government Ombudsmen have discretion to deal with complaints relating to maladministration. The British and Irish Ombudsman Association provide information about Ombudsman schemes and other complaint handling bodies and this is available from their website at www.bioa.org.uk . Parties may wish to note that the Ombudsmen are not able to look into a complaint once court action has been commenced.
- Early neutral evaluation by an independent third party (for example, a lawyer experienced in the field of administrative law or an individual experienced in the subject matter of the claim).
- Mediation – a form of facilitated negotiation assisted by an independent neutral party.

3.3 The Legal Services Commission has published a booklet on 'Alternatives to Court', CLS Direct Information Leaflet 23 (www.clsdirect.org.uk), which lists a number of organisations that provide alternative dispute resolution services.

3.4 *It is expressly recognised that no party can or should be forced to mediate or enter into any form of ADR.*

4 **Judicial review may not be appropriate in every instance.**

Claimants are strongly advised to seek appropriate legal advice when considering such proceedings and, in particular, before adopting this protocol or making a claim. Although the Legal Services Commission will not normally grant full representation before a letter before claim has been sent and the proposed defendant given a reasonable time to respond, initial funding may be available, for eligible claimants, to cover the work necessary to write this. (See Annex C for more information.)

5 This protocol sets out a code of good practice and contains the steps which parties should generally follow before making a claim for judicial review.

6 This protocol does not impose a greater obligation on a public body to disclose documents or give reasons for its decision than that already provided for in statute or common law. However, where the court considers that a public body should have provided relevant documents and/or information, particularly where this failure is a breach of a statutory or common law requirement, it may impose sanctions.

This protocol *will not be appropriate* where the defendant does not have the legal power to change the decision being challenged, for example decisions issued by tribunals such as the Asylum and Immigration Tribunal.

This protocol *will not be appropriate* in urgent cases, for example, when directions have been set, or are in force, for the claimant's removal from the UK, or where there is an urgent need for an interim order to compel a public body to act where it has unlawfully refused to do so (for example, the failure of a local housing authority to secure interim accomodation for a homeless claimant) a claim should be made immediately. A letter before claim will not stop the implementation of a disputed decision in all instances.

7 All claimants will need to satisfy themselves whether they should follow the protocol, depending upon the circumstances of his or her case. Where the use of the protocol is appropriate, the court will normally expect all parties to have complied with it and will take into account compliance or non-compliance when giving directions for case management of proceedings or when making orders for costs.[3] However, even in emergency cases, it is good practice to fax to the defendant the draft Claim Form which the claimant intends to issue. A claimant is also normally required to notify a defendant when an interim mandatory order is being sought.

The letter before claim

8 Before making a claim, the claimant should send a letter to the defendant. The purpose of this letter is to identify the issues in dispute and establish whether litigation can be avoided.

9 Claimants should normally use the suggested **standard format** for the letter outlined at Annex A.

10 The letter should contain **the date and details of the decision, act or omission being challenged and a clear summary of the facts** on which the claim is based. It should also contain the **details of any relevant information** that the claimant is seeking and an explanation of why this is considered relevant.

11 The letter should normally contain the **details of any interested parties**[4] known to the claimant. They should be sent a ***copy*** of the letter before claim ***for information*****. Claimants are *strongly advised to seek appropriate legal advice* when considering such proceedings and, in particular, before sending the letter before claim to other interested parties or making a claim.**

12 A claim should not normally be made until the proposed reply date given in the letter before claim has passed, unless the circumstances of the case require more immediate action to be taken.

The letter of response

13 Defendants should normally respond within 14 days using the standard format at Annex B. Failure to do so will be taken into account by the court and sanctions may be imposed unless there are good reasons.[5]

14 Where it is not possible to reply within the proposed time limit the defendant should send an interim reply and propose a reasonable extension. Where an extension is sought, reasons should be given and, where required, additional information requested. ***This will not affect the time limit for making a claim for judicial review***[6] nor will it bind the claimant where he or she considers this to be unreasonable. However, where the court considers that a subsequent claim is made prematurely it may impose sanctions.

15 If the **claim is being conceded in full**, the reply should say so in clear and unambiguous terms.

16 If the **claim is being conceded in part or not being conceded at all**, the reply should say so in clear and unambiguous terms, and:

(a) where appropriate, contain a new decision, clearly identifying what aspects of the claim are being conceded and what are not, or, give a clear timescale within which the new decision will be issued;

(b) provide a fuller explanation for the decision, if considered appropriate to do so;

(c) address any points of dispute, or explain why they cannot be addressed;

(d) enclose any **relevant** documentation requested by the claimant, or explain why the documents are not being enclosed; and

(e) where appropriate, confirm whether or not they will oppose any application for an interim remedy.

17 The response should be sent to **all interested parties**[7] identified by the claimant and contain details of any other parties who the defendant considers also have an interest.

A LETTER BEFORE CLAIM

SECTION 1. INFORMATION REQUIRED IN A LETTER BEFORE CLAIM

Proposed claim for judicial review

1 **To**

(Insert the name and address of the proposed defendant – see details in section 2)

2 **The claimant**

(Insert the title, first and last name and the address of the claimant)

3 **Reference details**

(When dealing with large organisations it is important to understand that the information relating to any particular individual's previous dealings with it may not be immediately available, therefore it is important to set out the relevant reference numbers for the matter in dispute and/or the identity of those within the public body who have been handling the particular matter in dispute – see details in section 3)

4 **The details of the matter being challenged**

(Set out clearly the matter being challenged, particularly if there has been more than one decision)

5 **The issue**

(Set out the date and details of the decision, or act or omission being challenged, a brief summary of the facts and why it is contented to be wrong)

6 **The details of the action that the defendant is expected to take**

(Set out the details of the remedy sought, including whether a review or any interim remedy are being requested)

7 **The details of the legal advisers, if any, dealing with this claim**

(Set out the name, address and reference details of any legal advisers dealing with the claim)

8 **The details of any interested parties**

(Set out the details of any interested parties and confirm that they have been sent a copy of this letter)

9 **The details of any information sought**

(Set out the details of any information that is sought. This may include a request for a fuller explanation of the reasons for the decision that is being challenged)

10 **The details of any documents that are considered relevant and necessary**

(Set out the details of any documentation or policy in respect of which the disclosure is sought and explain why these are relevant. If you rely on a statutory duty to disclose, this should be specified)

11 **The address for reply and service of court documents**

(Insert the address for the reply)

12 **Proposed reply date**

(The precise time will depend upon the circumstances of the individual case. However, although a shorter or longer time may be appropriate in a particular case, 14 days is a reasonable time to allow in most circumstances)

SECTION 2. ADDRESS FOR SENDING THE LETTER BEFORE CLAIM

Public bodies have requested that, for certain types of cases, in order to ensure a prompt response, letters before claim chould be sent to specific addresses.

- **Where the claim concerns a decision in an Immigration, Asylum or Nationality case:**
  Judicial Review Unit,
  UK Border Agency
  St Anne's House
  20-26 Wellesley Road
  Croydon CR9 2RL

- Where the claim concerns a decision by the Legal Services Commission:

  — The address on the decision letter/notification; and

  Legal Director
  Corporate Legal Team
  Legal Services Commission
  4 Abbey Orchard Street
  London SW1P 2BS

- **Where the claim concerns a decision by a local authority:**

  — The address on the decision letter/notification; and

  — Their legal department[8]

- **Where the claim concerns a decision by a department or body for whom Treasury Solicitor acts and Treasury Solicitor has already been involved in the case a copy should also be sent, quoting the Treasury Solicitor's reference, to:**

  The Treasury Solicitor,
  One Kemble Street,
  London WC2B 4TS

In all other circumstances, the letter should be sent to the address on the letter notifying the decision.

SECTION 3. SPECIFIC REFERENCE DETAILS REQUIRED

Public bodies have requested that the following information should be provided in order to ensure prompt response.

- **Where the claim concerns an Immigration, Asylum or Nationality case, dependent upon the nature of the case:**

  — The Home Office reference number

  — The Port reference number

  — The Asylum and Immigration Tribunal reference number

  — The National Asylum Support Service reference number

  Or, if these are unavailable:

  — The full name, nationality and date of birth of the claimant.

- **Where the claim concerns a decision by the Legal Services Commission:**

  — The certificate reference number.

B RESPONSE TO A LETTER BEFORE CLAIM

INFORMATION REQUIRED IN A RESPONSE TO A LETTER BEFORE CLAIM

Proposed claim for judicial review

1 **The claimant**

(Insert the title, first and last names and the address to which any reply should be sent)

2 **From**

(Insert the name and address of the defendant)

3 **Reference details**

(Set out the relevant reference numbers for the matter in dispute and the identity of those within the public body who have been handling the issue)

4 **The details of the matter being challenged**

(Set out details of the matter being challenged, providing a fuller explanation of the decision, where this is considered appropriate)

5 **Response to the proposed claim**

(Set out whether the issue in question is conceded in part, or in full, or will be contested. Where it is not proposed to disclose any information that has been requested, explain the reason for this. Where an interim reply is being sent and there is a realistic prospect of settlement, details should be included)

6 **Details of any other interested parties**

(Identify any other parties who you consider have an interest who have not already been sent a letter by the claimant)

7 **Address for further correspondence and service of court documents**

(Set out the address for any future correspondence on this matter)

C NOTES ON PUBLIC FUNDING FOR LEGAL COSTS IN JUDICIAL REVIEW

Public funding for legal costs in judicial review is available from legal professionals and advice agencies which have contracts with the Legal Services Commission as part of the Community Legal Service. Funding may be provided for:

- ***Legal Help*** to provide initial advice and assistance with any legal problem; or
- ***Legal Representation*** to allow you to be represented in court if you are taking or defending court proceedings. This is available in two forms:

  — ***Investigative Help*** is limited to funding to investigate the strength of the proposed claim. It includes the issue and conduct of proceedings only so far as is necessary to obtain disclosure of relevant information or to protect the client's position in relation to any urgent hearing or time limit for the issue of proceedings. This includes the work necessary to write a **letter before claim** to the body potentially under challenge, setting out the grounds of challenge, and giving that body a reasonable opportunity, typically 14 days, in which to respond.

  — ***Full Representation*** is provided to represent you in legal proceedings and includes litigation services, advocacy services, and all such help as is usually given by a person providing representation in proceedings, including steps preliminary or incidental to proceedings, and/or arriving at or giving effect to a compromise to avoid or bring to an end any proceedings. Except in emergency cases, a proper **letter before claim** must be sent and the other side must be given an opportunity to respond before *Full Representation* is granted.

Further information on the type(s) of help available and the criteria for receiving that help may be found in the Legal Service Manual Volume 3: "*The Funding Code*". This may be found on the Legal Services Commission website at:

www.legalservices.gov.uk

A list of contracted firms and Advice Agencies may be found on the Community Legal Services website at:

www.justask.org.uk

Footnotes

1. While the court does have the discretion under Rule 3.1(2)(a) of the Civil Procedure Rules to allow a late claim, this is only used in exceptional circumstances. **Compliance with the protocol alone is unlikely to be sufficient to persuade the court to allow a late claim.**

2. Civil Procedure Rule 54.1(2).

3. Civil Procedure Rules Costs Practice Direction.

4. See Civil Procedure Rule 54.1(2)(f).

5. See Civil Procedure Rules Pre-action Protocol Practice Direction paragraphs 2–3.

6. See Civil Procedure Rule 54.5(1).

7. See Civil Procedure Rule 54.1(2)(f).

8. The relevant address should be available from a range of sources such as the Phone Book; Business and Services Directory, Thomson's Local Directory, CAB, etc.

Index